IDEAS OF THE WORLD IN
EARLY MEDIEVAL ENGLISH LITERATURE

STUDIES IN OLD ENGLISH LITERATURE

VOLUME 1

Series Editors
Daniel Anlezark, University of Sydney
Susan Irvine, University College London
Francis Leneghan (Secretary), University of Oxford

Advisory Board
Michael D. J. Bintley, Birkbeck, University of London
Lindy Brady, University College Dublin
Marilina Cesario, Queen's University Belfast
R. D. Fulk, Indiana University
Alice Jorgensen, Trinity College Dublin
Thijs Porck, University of Leiden
Winfried Rudolf, Georg-August-Universität Göttingen

Ideas of the World in
Early Medieval English Literature

Edited by

MARK ATHERTON, KAZUTOMO KARASAWA,
and FRANCIS LENEGHAN

BREPOLS

British Library Cataloguing in Publication Data
A catalogue record for this book is available from the British Library.

© 2022, Brepols Publishers n.v., Turnhout, Belgium.

All rights reserved. No part of this publication may be reproduced, stored in a retrieval system, or transmitted, in any form or by any means, electronic, mechanical, photocopying, recording, or otherwise without the prior permission of the publisher.

ISBN: 978-2-503-59957-1
e-ISBN: 978-2-503-59958-8
DOI: 10.1484/M.SOEL-EB.5.128508

Printed in the EU on acid-free paper.

D/2022/0095/156

Table of Contents

List of Illustrations — 7

Preface and Acknowledgements — 9

Abbreviations — 10

Introduction: Foreign Contacts, Landscapes, and Empire-Building — 11
Mark ATHERTON, Kazutomo KARASAWA, and Francis LENEGHAN

Part I
HERE, THERE, AND EVERYWHERE

Alfred and the East — 43
Daniel ANLEZARK

The Wanderings of Saturn: Psychogeography, Psalms, and *Solomon and Saturn* — 69
Rachel A. BURNS

Otherwheres in the Prose Texts of the Nowell Codex: Here and Otherwhere — 103
S. C. THOMSON

Rome Away from Rome: India, Rome, and England in Ælfric's *Life of St Thomas* — 127
Luisa OSTACCHINI

Christ Embracing the World: Ælfric's Description of the Crucifixion in 'De Passione Domini' — 149
Kazutomo KARASAWA

Part II
A PLACE IN THE WORLD

Babel and Beyond: Thinking through Migration in *Genesis A*   167
Daniel THOMAS

The Sound-World of Early Medieval England:
A Case Study of the Exeter Book Storm Riddle   203
Britton Elliott BROOKS

The Place of Stillness:
Greek Patristic Thought in Cynewulf's *Juliana*   223
Eleni PONIRAKIS

St Rumwold in the Borderland   249
Hannah M. BAILEY

The World of Ealdorman Byrhtnoth: A Landscape Biography   273
Mark ATHERTON

Part III
NATION AND EMPIRE

Mapping Empire: Two World Maps
in Early Medieval England   309
Helen APPLETON

Good Neighbours? Representations of the Britons, Welsh,
Picts, and Scots in Pre-Conquest English Sources   335
Caitlin ELLIS

From (North-)East to West: Geographical Identities
and Political Communities in the Ninth- to
Eleventh-Century Anglo-Scandinavian World   365
Ryan LAVELLE

Kings, People, and Lands:
The Rhetoric of *The Battle of Brunanburh*   385
Paul CAVILL

End of Empire? Reading *The Death of Edward*
in MS Cotton Tiberius B I   403
Francis LENEGHAN

Index   435

List of Illustrations

Otherwheres in the Prose Texts of the Nowell Codex:
Here and Otherwhere — S. C. Thomson

Figure 3.1.	Cynocephali in Tiberius B V and Vitellius A XV.	107
Figure 3.2.	St Christopher Chananeus arriving at the city of Samos. Stuttgart, Württembergische Landesbibliothek, MS Cod. hist., fol. 415.	120

Christ Embracing the World: Ælfric's Description of the
Crucifixion in 'De Passione Domini' — Kazutomo Karasawa

Figure 5.1.	An eleventh-century example of a T-O Map. London, British Library, MS Royal 6 C I, fol. 108ᵛ.	151
Figure 5.2.	Diagram listing twelve winds, Trier, Stadtbibliothek, MS 2500, fol. 20. Ninth century.	152
Figure 5.3.	A reproduction of Byrhtferth's diagram, Oxford, Bodleian Library, MS Ashmole 328, p. 85.	153

St Rumwold in the Borderland — Hannah M. Bailey

Figure 9.1.	The Geography of the *Vita S. Kenelmi* and the Severn Basin.	251
Figure 9.2.	The Resting Places of St Rumwold.	258
Figure 9.3.	Kings Sutton and its Environs.	261
Figure 9.4.	Suggested Core Estate for Kings Sutton.	265

The World of Ealdorman Byrhtnoth:
A Landscape Biography — Mark Atherton

Figure 10.1.	Byrhtnoth at Cambridge.	281
Figure 10.2.	Lands of Byrhtnoth, Ealdorman.	292

Mapping Empire: Two World Maps in
Early Medieval England — Helen Appleton

Figure 11.1.	Macrobian zonal map. London, British Library, MS Cotton Tiberius B V, fol. 29ʳ.	316
Figure 11.2.	Mappa mundi. London, British Library, MS Cotton Tiberius B V, fol. 56ᵛ.	321

8 LIST OF ILLUSTRATIONS

From (North-)East to West: Geographical Identities and Political Communities in the Ninth- to Eleventh-Century Anglo-Scandinavian World — Ryan Lavelle

Figure 13.1. Map of the former Frisian kingdom, with indications of Danish influence in the late ninth century. 370

Figure 13.2. Runestone U344, from Yttergårde, Sweden, now in Orkesta churchyard. 376

End of Empire? Reading *The Death of Edward* in MS Cotton Tiberius B I — Francis Leneghan

Figure 15.1. End of Old English *Orosius* (conquest of Rome by Alaric), London, British Library, MS Cotton Tiberius B I, fol. 111^v. Early eleventh century. 410

Figure 15.2. Opening of *Menologium* (the feast of Christ the King), London, British Library, MS Cotton Tiberius B I, fol. 112^r. Mid-eleventh century. 411

Figure 15.3. End of *Maxims II*, opening of Anglo-Saxon Chronicle MS C (Julius Caesar's partial conquest of Britain), London, British Library, MS Cotton Tiberius B I, fol. 115^v. Mid-eleventh century. 415

Figure 15.4. *The Death of Edward* (ASC MS C 1065), London, British Library, MS Cotton Tiberius B I, fol. 160^v. Mid-eleventh century. 421

Figure 15.5. Details of the Bayeux Tapestry, Panels 27–31: *Hic Edwardus rex in lecto alloquitur fideles. Et hic defunctus est. Hic dederunt Haroldo corona[m] regis.* (Here Edward speaks in bed to his followers. And here he is dead. Here they gave the king's crown to Harold.) Eleventh Century, City of Bayeux. 429

Preface and Acknowledgements

This volume has its genesis in an international collaborative research project carried out by medievalists affiliated with the Department of Letters, Rikkyo University, Tokyo, and with the Faculty of English, University of Oxford. The project began in March 2019, supported by the Fund for the Promotion of Joint International Research (JSPS KAKENHI Grant Number 18KK0334) of the Japan Society for the Promotion of Science. A two-day symposium entitled 'From East to West: Ideas of the World in Anglo-Saxon England' was planned at Regent's Park College, Oxford, in March 2020, but unfortunately it had to be cancelled because of the COVID-19 pandemic. Three sessions based on the project were also scheduled at the International Medieval Congress at the University of Leeds in July 2020, but again these had to be cancelled for the same reason. As a substitute for these cancelled events, we organized a three-day online colloquium with most of the contributors to this volume and others in October and November 2020, discussing each chapter as well as the volume as a whole. A spin-off session entitled 'Interdependent Realities: Human and Non-Human Worlds in Early English Literature' was also held at the 93rd General Meeting of the English Literary Society of Japan in May 2021, with the help of Professor Richard North (University College London). The editors would like to thank all our contributors, as well as Campion Hall, Oxford, Regent's Park College, Oxford, St Cross College, Oxford, and the Faculty of English Language and Literature, Oxford, for hosting events connected with this project. Special thanks to Deborah Oosterhouse for her careful copy-editing and to Martine Maguire-Weltecke for her excellent typesetting. Thanks also to Guy Carney at Brepols for guidance throughout the editorial process.

Abbreviations

Anglia	*Anglia: Zeitschrift für Englische Philologie*
ASC	Anglo-Saxon Chronicle
ASE	*Anglo-Saxon England*
ASPR	*The Anglo-Saxon Poetic Records: A Collective Edition*, ed. by George Philip Krapp and Elliott van Kirk Dobbie, 6 vols (New York: Columbia University Press, 1931–1953)
BHL	*Bibliotheca Hagiographica Latina Antiquae et Mediae Aetatis*, ed. by the Bollandists, 2 vols (Brussels, 1898–99), with *Supplementum* (Brussels, 1911) and *Novum Supplementum* (Brussels, 1986)
CCSL	Corpus Christianorum Series Latina
DOE	*The Dictionary of Old English A to I*, ed. by Angus Cameron, Ashley Crandell Amos, Antonette diPaolo Healey, and others (Toronto: Dictionary of Old English Project, 2018), <https://www.doe.utoronto.ca>
DOE Corpus	*The Dictionary of Old English Web Corpus*, compiled by Antonette diPaolo Healey with John Price Wilkin and Xin Xiang (Toronto: Dictionary of Old English Project, 2009), <https://tapor.library.utoronto.ca/doecorpus/>
DOML	Dumbarton Oaks Medieval Library
EETS	Early English Text Society
EHD	*English Historical Documents*, I: *c. 500–1042*, ed. by Dorothy Whitelock, 2nd edn (London: Routledge, 1979; repr. 1996)
ES	*English Studies*
HE	*Historia ecclesiastica gentis Anglorum*
JEGP	*Journal of English and Germanic Philology*
MÆ	*Medium Ævum*
MGH	Monumenta Germaniae Historica
N&Q	*Notes and Queries*
OE	Old English
PL	Patrologiae cursus completus: series Latina, ed. by Jacques-Paul Migne, 221 vols (Paris: Garnier, 1844–1864)
PQ	*Philological Quarterly*
RES	*Review of English Studies*
s.a.	*sub anno/anni*
S	Sawyer number, from *The Electronic Sawyer: Online Catalogue of Anglo-Saxon Charters*, ed. by Peter H. Sawyer and others, <http://www.esawyer.org.uk>
SEM	Studies in the Early Middle Ages

MARK ATHERTON, KAZUTOMO KARASAWA,
AND FRANCIS LENEGHAN

Introduction: Foreign Contacts, Landscapes, and Empire-Building

In his *Historia ecclesiastica gentis Anglorum*, completed in 731, Bede starts his great work with a geographical survey of the island of Britain, or *Britannia* as it is called in Latin, and his opening sentence reads as follows in one of the standard modern English translations:

> Britain, formerly known as Albion, is an island in the ocean lying towards the north west at a considerable distance from the coasts of Germany, Gaul, and Spain, which together form the greater part of Europe. (*HE* I.1)

Bede proceeds to give the dimensions of the island as 800 miles long and 200 wide, while the length of the coastline is 3600 miles, and he describes the connection to Belgic Gaul and the European continent. Thereafter he goes on to record some facts about the island: its agricultural crops, its pastures, its hunting and fishing, its natural resources, the length of the day in summer and winter. Next, finding numerological parallels with the five books of the Pentateuch, Bede speaks of the five languages of Britain and its four nations (English, British, Irish, and Picts), each with their own language but all using Latin as the language of holy scripture.

Bede clearly values this common language highly. We can detect this attitude in his occasional asides on his own language, Old English, which he does not necessarily favour as highly as he does Latin, for example in the following comment on the best place to undertake a crossing of the English Channel:

> Ciuitas quae dicitur Rutubi portus, a gente Anglorum nunc corrupte Reptacaestir uocata.
>
> (from the city that is called Rutubi Portus, which the English people have corrupted to Reptacaestir.)[1]

---

1 Bede, *HE*, I.1. For text and translation, see Bede, *Ecclesiastical History of the English People*, ed. and trans. by Colgrave and Mynors. Two standard translations are Bede, *The Ecclesiastical History of the English People*, trans. by Farmer, Latham, and Sherley-Price, as cited here; and Bede, *The Ecclesiastical History of the English People*, trans. by Collins and McClure.

Ideas of the World in Early Medieval English Literature, ed. by Mark Atherton, Kazutomo Karasawa, and Francis Leneghan, SOEL 1 (Turnhout: Brepols, 2022)   pp. 11–39
BREPOLS ❧ PUBLISHERS   DOI 10.1484/M.SOEL.5.130555

As Bede sees it, the English newcomers (i.e. the Germanic settlers in the aftermath of the empire) had 'corrupted' the old Roman name, Rutubi Portus, by their careless speaking of its name. Even by Bede's time in the 730s, this place name had clearly had an eventful history. In fact the name would continue to morph and change over the centuries: in 1197 it is recorded as Ratteburg (rat's fort) which, as Watts explains in *The Cambridge Dictionary of English Place-Names*, is 'a common name for ancient ruins or defences' to be compared with the similar Ratsborough in Essex; but around 1500 it underwent 'respectable re-formation' and was changed to the phonetically similar but semantically very different *Richborowe* (the rich fort), hence the present-day name of Richborough.[2] Already we are touching on a theme of the present book, the connections between a world view and the changing language in which it is expressed.

Before Old English established itself as a written literary language, Latin naturally provided the basic paradigm for looking at the world and writing about it in literary works. Bede was a monk, educated through the medium of Latin in the study of the Bible as well as in Classical Latin grammar and literature, and Roman and European history. He naturally uses the Latin geographical term *Britannia* (Britain) to refer to the island itself, though he is aware of its older name *Albion*, and he uses *Gallia* to refer to Gaul (France), in later centuries to be superseded by *Francia*. In addition, Bede was a native speaker of the Northumbrian variety of Old English, as revealed in his spelling (and no doubt also his pronunciation) of the place name *Reptacaestir*. And when he writes about the various speakers of this language, in the various kingdoms, Bede calls them all *Angli*, or *gens Anglorum* (literally, family, or people, of the Angles), generalizing a term that originally referred only to one of these groups of peoples, since another dominant group was *Seaxi* (the Saxons), and for the speakers of Celtic languages the latter was the preferred generalizing term, hence modern Welsh *Saes* (English person). Eventually, of course, the Angles came to be regarded as the English, and the political developments that allowed the English to become the dominant power in the south of the island of Britain were mirrored in various changes that took place within the English language in the course of the long early medieval period.

To see that process of change in operation, a convenient document to which we may turn is the Anglo-Saxon Chronicle, especially to the fullest and latest version of that text, namely Manuscript E or the 'Peterborough Chronicle', as preserved in Oxford, Bodleian Library, MS Laud Misc. 636. Written towards the end of the early medieval period, but based on earlier annals and chronicles, the Peterborough Chronicle covers all the relevant details needed for investigating the changing views of the Angles/the English. For example, there is the record of the so-called *adventus* (arrival), the putative first coming of the Angles in 449 after being summoned in 443 to help the

---

2 Watts, ed., *The Cambridge Dictionary of English Place-Names*, p. 498.

British against the Pictish invasions, an event discussed critically at various points in this volume (see the essays by Daniel Thomas, Caitlin Ellis, and Paul Cavill). The Peterborough Chronicle also contains an account of the end of Norman England, the 'Anarchy' and civil war of Stephen's reign and the eventual accession of Henry II in 1154. The wide chronological coverage of this text (essentially it is an anthology of texts from different periods on a common theme) allows the student of cultural history to investigate how attitudes changed over time. Like all the versions of the Chronicle, version E begins its record in the year 60 BC, with Julius Caesar's invasion of Britain. Using information extracted from Bede and translated into Old English, the E Chronicler similarly also speaks of the dimensions of the island, its four nations, and its five languages. Significantly, the arrival of each of these nations is summarized briefly: following the model in Bede, the Britons are declared to be the original inhabitants, then came the Picts and the Scots, and later the Romans, who departed again in the fateful year 410; finally, we have the summoning of the Angles in AD 443:

> Her sendon Brytwalas ofer sæ to Rome 7 heom fultumes bædon wið Peohtas, ac hi þær nefdon nænne, forþan ðe hi feordodan wið Ætlan Huna cininge, 7 þa sendon hi to Anglum 7 Angelcynnes æðelingas þes ilcan bædon.[3]

> (Here the Britons sent messages over the sea to Rome and asked for help against the Picts, but they had none there because they were at war against Attila king of the Huns, and so they sent messages to the Angles and made the same request to the princes of the Angle-kindred.)

This passage will be discussed again in more detail below, particularly for its expression of early English attitudes to the *Brytwalas*. For now, we would offer two comments on the terminology used. First, the term *Brytwalas*, being a compound of *Bryttas* (Britons) and *Walas* (foreigners), is partly neutral-geographical and partly pejorative, for the plural noun *Bryttas* denotes the people themselves (the word is clearly derived from the noun for the country itself, i.e. *Bryten*, as in Latin *Britannia*), whereas the term *Walas* (deriving as it does from *wealh* meaning foreigner) connotes a subjective judgement, an attitude towards the Other, the Foreigner, the Speaker-of-another-tongue.[4] Secondly, where the annal for 443 speaks of messages going *to Anglum*, the fact is that at this stage it is impossible for this term to refer notionally to 'the English', for the English did not yet exist: instead, the Angles are yet another tribe or nation dwelling in the fifth century in the north of Germania. By the Alfredian period, however, it is clear that Bede's Latin term *gens Anglorum* has

---

3 All references to the ASC MS E are taken from *The Anglo-Saxon Chronicle: MS E*, ed. by Irvine; the punctuation of the text has been altered slightly, and some terms have been capitalized; translations are our own.
4 See Woolf, 'Reporting Scotland in the Anglo-Saxon Chronicle', pp. 231–32.

been rendered word-for-word as *angel-cynn* (literally Angle-family), referring essentially to the people whom we would now call 'the English', though at the time these 'English' should be understood as being various nations of similar origin and of similar language and culture living in southern Britain. Eventually the term also doubled up as the name of the English kingdom itself. And new phrases such as *angelcynnes folc* and *angelcynnes þeod* were developed to refer to the English people themselves, while *angelcynnes land* became another name for their country (or the area of land in which they lived). The related adjective, however, by the phonetic process of language change known as *Umlaut* (i-mutation), became *ænglisc* and then *englisc*; such changes would eventually lead to the replacement of *Angelcynn* and *Angelcynnes land* with a new name and, gradually also at the same time, with a new identity: at first this was *Englaland* (Land of the English), still arguably a separable compound of *Engla* (genitive plural) and *land*, whereas later still — by the end of our period — the second vowel had weakened and the term had become a single indivisible compound, that is, *Engleland* (England).

That change was, of course, gradual, but if pressed for a significant date then perhaps it might be placed in 1154, the year of the accession of 'the earl', that is, the Angevin duke Henri, to the English throne as Henry II. In this year, the last of the authors of the E version of the Chronicle finished his stint and brought a long-standing historiographical project to an end. And this particular section of the project had been started three decades beforehand in 1121, after a disastrous fire had destroyed Peterborough Abbey's only copy of the Chronicle. But a practical solution was found. Another text was duly borrowed (perhaps from Canterbury or Westminster) and copied in its entirety up to 1121, although with interpolations relating to Peterborough concerns; two continuators then followed, the first completing year by year the annals 1122–1131, the second covering piecemeal the period up to 1154, with entries for the years 1132, 1135, 1137, 1138, 1140, and 1154, and relating the intervening events in summary. Here is an extract from the famous Second Continuator's final entry, the annal for 1154:

> On þis gær wærd þe king Stephne ded 7 bebyried þer his wif 7 his sune wæron bebyried æt Fauresfeld, þæt minster hi makeden. Þa þe king was ded, þa was þe eorl beionde sæ. 7 ne durste nan man don oþer bute god for þe micel eie of him. Þa he to Engleland com, þa was he underfangen mid micel wurtscipe, 7 to king bletcæd in Lundene on þe sunnen dæi beforen Midwinter Dæi. 7 held þær micel curt.

>> (In this year King Stephen was dead and buried — where his wife and his sons were buried — at Faversham, at the minster that they themselves had built. When the king died, the earl was overseas. And none dared do anything but good for the great fear [which they had] of him. When he arrived in England he was received with great worship and consecrated as king in London on the Sunday before Christmas Day. And he held a great court there.)

In this text, the place that had by then become the chief city or capital of the kingdom is *Lunden* (dative singular *Lundene*), while the older forms *Lundenburh* (fortress London) and, even earlier, *Lundenwic* (London trading place) are no longer in use. Similarly, there is no talk here of the *Angelcynn*, for by 1154 that was an obsolete term, and even *Englaland* (land of the English), with its genitive plural *Engla*, has been reduced to the simpler name *Engleland*.

It may be stated, then, with some justification, that in this text the older view of the world is passing, and a new one has arrived. Linguistically, the language that the writer uses may be called Early Middle English, since the syntax and morphology are simpler in comparison to Old English, and there are French influences in lexis, collocation, and word order. The last sentence, for example, contains the French borrowing *curt* (court) which earlier had been *hired* (household); such a change seems slight, but the new noun is significant, symbolic of new fashions of 'court' and 'courtliness' that were to follow in the cultural world of the later Middle Ages. Syntactically, the verbal idiom of *to be* + past participle of the verb *to die* yields the expression *was ded*, which in this context is similar to French *il est mort* (he died) — used here as an announcement of the king's death. Normally, the Old English chroniclers had employed a verb denoting transition from one world to the next, such as *forðferde* (passed forth) or *gefor* (departed), as for instance in the annal on the death of Edward the Confessor in 1066.[5]

Nevertheless, not all is brave and new in the annal for 1154, for in his choice of phrase and formula, the writer echoes much earlier annals of the Chronicle. By way of illustration, here is the entry for the year 1042 in the same manuscript, the coronation of Edward:

> Her wæs Æðward gehalgod to cyng on Winceastre on Æsterdæg mid mycclum wurðscipe. 7 þa wæron Eastron on iii nonas Aprilis . Eadsige arcebiscop hine halgode. 7 toforan eallum folce hine well lærde. 7 to his agenre neode. 7 ealles folces well monude. 7 Stigand preost wæs gebletsod to biscope to East Englum.

> > (Here Edward was consecrated as king in Winchester on Easter Day with great worship. And Easter was then the third of the Nones of April. Archbishop Eadsige consecrated him and instructed him well in the presence of all the people, and for his own need and that of the people admonished him well. And Stigand the priest was blessed as bishop of East Anglia.)

One might compare the earlier time phrase 'on Æsterdæg' in 1043 with the later 'beforen Midwinter Dæi' in 1154, or the adverbial phrase 'mid mycclum wurðscipe' from 1043 with 'mid micel wurtscipe' in 1154, or the collocation *blessed* + *to* (i.e. the combination of the verb *blessed* with the preposition *to*)

---

5 For a discussion of the poem *The Death of Edward* that follows in this annal, see the chapter by Francis Leneghan in this volume.

in 'wæs gebletsod to biscope' and 'þa was he [...] to king bletcæd in Lundene'. Clearly the writer of the Second Continuation was aiming to write in the same style of discourse as his predecessors and so complete his abbey's Old English Chronicle for posterity.

If linguists are right to assert that any particular language expresses and highlights in subtly various ways a different perspective on the world, then we may argue that the Peterborough annal for 1154 marks the final expression of that 'early medieval world view' or mentality, before it changed and moved on.[6] This, then, will be our point of departure: in fifteen essays we will explore continuity and change in English ideas of the world in the early Middle Ages. Since this will not be an exhaustive treatment, three broad areas of subject matter have been selected. The first is the external world at large, the exotic world, the nature of distant lands such as Palestine and India, the geographical relation of the island of *Britannia* to the rest of the world. The second broad area of consideration is more local; here the main topic will be landscapes (real and metaphorical) and soundscapes, and this will include conceptions of space and time, how the local world was viewed and how it sounded to English men and women, attitudes of the mind at prayer, toponyms and nomenclature, the changing names that refer to the same location. Our third area of study is national and imperial, and concerns the political entities that came and went within the parts of this island that became England, and new notions of political hegemony and imperial rule that crystallized and developed over the period. Inevitably, perhaps, the three areas overlap, and the essays will not necessarily confine themselves exclusively to only one of these fields. Above all the focus will be on the expression of such ideas in writing, in the English prose and poetry of the period.

I. Here, There, and Everywhere

One strand of this book, then, explores pre-Conquest English ideas of the world outside Britain, chiefly those of remote and exotic lands that most English people could never have seen for themselves. Part I provides case studies on how the English viewed, and interacted with, the world outside Britain, and how their ideas of the world are reflected in literary works from pre-Conquest England.

As recently discussed, for instance, by Katharine Scarfe Beckett, Daniel Anlezark, Samantha Zacher, and Nicole Guenther Discenza, the *Angelcynn* developed their own ideas of far-distant lands — and the peoples that lived there — through various human, material, literary, and cultural exchanges.[7]

---

6 For a recent critique of linguistic relativity, see the discussion by Deutscher, *Through the Language Glass.*

7 See Beckett, *Anglo-Saxon Perceptions of the Islamic World;* Anlezark, 'The Anglo-Saxon World

Indeed, from this perspective, Nicole Discenza writes that 'early England was not as "insular" as we may now sometimes think'.[8] As is well known, for instance, a dish, a ladle, two spoons, and ten bowls from Byzantium, some with Greek inscriptions, as well as yellow cloaks perhaps from Syria, occur in the early seventh-century burial-site at Sutton Hoo.[9] Two coins bearing early Arabic script from the first half of the eighth century have been found on the beach at Eastbourne, Sussex, and near the end of the same century the Mercian king Offa (757–796) issued a coin with an Arabic inscription in imitation of this type of Arabic coin,[10] reflecting his interest in, or appreciation of, things from an unfamiliar remote land. Bald's *Leechbook* even mentions exotic spices and medicinal ingredients such as aloes, balsam, incense, mastic, myrtle, and wild olive from Africa, Arabia, and the Near East, and cassia, cinnamon, galbanum, and pepper from the Far East, China, Indonesia, Sri Lanka, and the Moluccas, and they seem to have been actually prescribed for various ailments.[11] At least some of these ingredients were available to the English by the latter half of the seventh century, for one of the *Enigmata* by Aldhelm (d. 709 or 710) is on the theme of 'pepper', which the author declares was used to season 'the delicacies of the kitchen: the feasts of kings and extravagant dishes and likewise sauce and stews',[12] while Cuthbert, a monk and later abbot of Monkwearmouth, reports in his 'Letter on the Death of Bede' that Bede (*c.* 673–735) on his deathbed owned some pepper and incense,[13] probably produced in India and the Middle East respectively. It is probable that most of these exotic items reached the English through trade networks linking many places rather than being imported directly from their places of origin, but these and other products obtained from afar could well have set the imaginations of the early medieval English soaring to remote and exotic lands.

While travels between England and Rome seem to have been quite common ever since the first Christian missionaries established themselves

---

View'; Zacher, *Imagining the Jew*; and Discenza, *Inhabited Spaces*. For various exchanges between England and the Continent in the early medieval period, see also Levison, *England and the Continent in the Eighth Century*; and Rollason, Leyser, and Williams, eds, *England and the Continent in the Tenth Century*.

8 Discenza, *Inhabited Spaces*, p. 63.

9 For items found in the Sutton Hoo burial-site, see Carver, *Sutton Hoo*, pp. 180–81.

10 For this coin, see Naismith, 'Islamic Coins from Early Medieval England', pp. 196–97; and Beckett, *Anglo-Saxon Perceptions of the Islamic World*, p. 55.

11 Cameron, *Anglo-Saxon Medicine*, p. 104.

12 See number 40 of *Enigmata Aldhelmi*. The words in quotations are taken from Lapidge and Rosier's translation in their Aldhelm, *The Poetic Works*, p. 78. For its original text and translation, see *The Riddles of Aldhelm*, ed. and trans. by Pitman, pp. 22–23. They are also available in *Saint Aldhelm's Riddles*, trans. by Juster, pp. 22–23; and now *The Old English and Anglo-Latin Riddle Tradition*, ed. and trans. by Orchard, pp. 32–33.

13 See 'Cuthbert's Letter on the Death of Bede', in Bede, *Ecclesiastical History of the English People*, ed. and trans. by Colgrave and Mynors, pp. 579–87 (pp. 584–85).

in Canterbury in 597,[14] travels to geographically and culturally remoter places were less usual. One intrepid traveller to exotic lands was Willibald (*c.* 700–*c.* 787), bishop of Eichstätt (741–*c.* 787). In the 720s he visited such places as Syracuse, Monemvasia in the Peloponnese, and Ephesus in Asia Minor, where he viewed the tombs of the Seven Sleepers and St John the Evangelist; like a real-life 'Widsith' (the Far-traveller), he was also in Cyprus, Jerusalem (which he visited four times), Damascus in Syria, Jericho in Palestine, Tyre in Lebanon (where he smuggled balsam), and Constantinople.[15] Since there were very few travellers from Britain to these and other far-distant lands, first-hand information about them must have been quite limited,[16] and in fact, the details of Willibald's journeys seem to have remained unknown in England, since he did not return to England after his travels were over but stayed on the Continent, where an Anglo-Saxon nun of Heidenheim named Huneberc recorded his experiences.[17]

On the other hand, many literary works of foreign origin dealing with the affairs of exotic lands were available from early days, including biblical texts,

---

14 According to Bede, the early missionaries and prelates often communicated with the pope by letters (carried by people), while the popes occasionally sent people, letters, and gifts to England. See, for instance, Bede's *HE*, I.27, I.29, I.30, I.31, I.32, II.4, II.8, II.10, II.11, II.18. There also were Anglo-Saxon clerics and kings travelling to Rome for study as in the cases of Alchfrid, Oftfor, and Wilfrid (*HE*, III.25, IV.13, IV.23, V.19), for ecclesiastical purposes as in the cases of Wighard and Willibrord (*HE*, III.29, IV.1, V.11), or in order to end one's life peacefully as in the cases of Kings Cadwalla, Coenred, and Offa (*HE*, IV.12, V.7, V.19). Benedict Biscop (d. 689) travelled to Rome as many as five times and brought back many books to build the library of the church of Monkwearmouth which nurtured and sustained the scholarship of Bede. For the life of Benedict Biscop, including his travels to Rome, see Bede's *Historia Abbatum*, Chapters 1–13, in *Venerabilis Baedae Opera Historica*, ed. by Plummer, I, pp. 364–77. See also *HE*, IV.18 and V.19. Pilgrims, traders, and other travellers from England were constantly in Rome, and an *Angelcynnes scolu*, 'an English quarter, hostel or *burh*', had been established on the Vatican Hill by the end of the eighth century, whose destruction by fire is recorded in some versions of the Anglo-Saxon Chronicle under 816. For the relationship between England and Rome in the Anglo-Saxon period, see Howe, 'Rome: Capital of Anglo-Saxon England'; Howe, *Writing the Map of Anglo-Saxon England*, pp. 101–24; and Tinti, ed., *England and Rome in the Early Middle Ages*. See also Levison, *England and the Continent in the Eighth Century*, pp. 15–44.

15 These and other details of his travels are recorded in *Vita Willibaldi* or the *Hodoeporicon*, whose standard edition is 'Vita Willibaldi Episcopi Eichstetensis', ed. by Holder-Egger. An English translation is included in Talbot, *The Anglo-Saxon Missionaries in Germany*, pp. 153–77.

16 According to Pelteret, the first reliable account of a journey from England to Jerusalem extant after Willibald's is that of Wythman, a German abbot of Ramsey, who made his pilgrimage to Jerusalem in 1019 or 1020. See Pelteret, 'Eleventh-Century Anglo-Saxon Long-Haul Travelers', p. 78. In addition, an account of a journey of a Gallic traveller, Arculf, to Jerusalem, recorded by Adomnán (d. 704), ninth abbot of Iona, was available in England. Adomnán presented the work, *De Locis Sanctis*, to Aldfrith, king of Northumbria (685–704), and Bede made an abbreviated version of it in the early eighth century. See Adomnán, 'De Locis Sanctis'. An English translation is included in Wilkinson, *Jerusalem Pilgrims before the Crusades*, pp. 93–116; also Bede, 'De Locis Sanctis', ed. by Fraipont.

17 See Beckett, *Anglo-Saxon Perceptions of the Islamic World*, p. 44.

INTRODUCTION 19

various saints' lives, and martyrologies introduced into England with the conversion, as well as classical poetry. Virgil 'seems to have been a particular favourite of Aldhelm',[18] and the *Aeneid* may well have been included in the monastic curriculum and was probably known throughout the Anglo-Saxon period.[19] Orosius's *Historiae adversus paganos* was read in the seventh century and was used by Aldhelm and Bede,[20] while the *Liber Monstrorum* was known from the late seventh century or a little later.[21] Also available were the *Epistola Alexandri ad Aristotelem* and the *Mirabilia Orientis*. Many of these works were translated or adapted into Old English, and as a result, accounts and stories of far-distant lands became accessible to a wider audience.[22] Thus Howe, for instance, points out that Old English poetic manuscripts, while often oblivious of England, display a fascination with places elsewhere,[23] many of the major poems, such as *Genesis A, Exodus, Daniel, Andreas, Elene, Juliana, Judith*, and *Beowulf*, being set in exotic lands.

Some of the aforementioned works in Latin dealing with the faraway continent of Asia, namely, Orosius's *Historiae, Mirabilia Orientis*, and *Epistola Alexandri*, were translated into Old English around 900, reflecting the interests and literary trends of the time. As Daniel Anlezark discusses in 'Alfred and the East', King Alfred (r. 871–899) shared this interest in Asia. He corresponded with Elias, the patriarch of Jerusalem (*c.* 879–907), while sending envoys, Sigehelm and Athelstan, with alms to St Thomas and St Bartholomew in India in 883. Clarifying the nature and scope of the journey of these envoys, Anlezark examines the evidence of Alfred's Asian diplomacy and interrogates the range of contexts within which it took place.

The Old English poem *Solomon and Saturn II*, which is discussed by Rachel A. Burns in 'The Wanderings of Saturn: Psychogeography, Psalms, and *Solomon and Saturn*', could be viewed as another work reflecting the interest in, and ideas of, far-distant lands around the time of King Alfred; probably composed *c.* 900, the poem presents a wisdom contest taking place between the biblical King Solomon and a wandering pagan named Saturn. Near the beginning of the poem, the description of Saturn's travels in pursuit of book learning mentions many peoples and places in the Mediterranean, eastern Europe, Central Asia, the Middle East, and North Africa, and it has been suggested that the order in which they are mentioned in this passage is not particularly meaningful but is determined chiefly by the requirements of the alliterative metre. Arguing that Saturn's apparently chaotic itinerary is

---

18 Orchard, 'Aldhelm's Library', p. 600.
19 Lapidge, 'The Anglo-Latin Background', p. 7.
20 See *The Old English History of the World*, ed. and trans. by Godden, pp. x–xi.
21 Michael Lapidge dates it as *c.* 650 x *c.* 750. See Lapidge, '*Beowulf*, Aldhelm, the *Liber Monstrorum* and Wessex', pp. 164–65.
22 See Discenza, *Inhabited Spaces*, pp. 71–101, for how numerously remote places and peoples living there are mentioned in Old English prose, verse, and glosses and glossaries.
23 Howe, *Writing the Map of Anglo-Saxon England*, p. 154.

purposefully structured and based on the poet's sense of both spiritual and spatial geography, Burns focuses on the theme of wandering and makes a case for a new reading of the poem as psychogeographic literature.

Far-distant lands were often associated with monstrous creatures and 'wonders', as typically seen in works such as *Liber Monstrorum*, *The Wonders of the East*, and *Letter of Alexander to Aristotle*.[24] The Old English versions of the last two works are recorded in the *Beowulf* manuscript (London, British Library, MS Cotton Vitellius A XV), which Howe describes as 'a book of elsewhere',[25] while *Liber Monstrorum*, which could itself be regarded as another book of elsewhere, has often been studied in relation to works in the *Beowulf* manuscript.[26] In 'Otherwheres in the Prose Texts of the Nowell Codex', S. C. Thomson, who recently published a monograph on the making of the *Beowulf* manuscript,[27] discusses 'otherwhereness' in the three prose works in this codex, namely, the *Passion of St Christopher*, *The Wonders of the East*, and *Letter of Alexander to Aristotle*. He argues that these prose works, dealing with encounters with monstrous 'others' in exotic lands, reflect the specific fantasies of otherness that were projected onto the far-distant places, and the interest in the interactions between self and other and movement between 'here' and 'there'.

Far-distant lands are not always represented by wonders and monsters alien to the Anglo-Saxons, but are also conceived of in a different way, as Luisa Ostacchini discusses in 'Rome Away from Rome: India, Rome, and England in Ælfric's "Life of St Thomas"'. Ostacchini examines descriptions of India in Ælfric's *Life of St Thomas*, and argues that Ælfric of Eynsham (*c.* 950–*c.* 1010), intending to create a believable text for tenth-century English readers, expresses the foreignness of India in a subtler manner than highlighting wonders and monsters. India is presented as a distant, esoteric, but Christian land strongly linked to Rome, and as a country that has something in common with England, another Christian land on the periphery of the inhabited world yet having a close relationship with Rome.[28] Ælfric, while depicting it as a remote and exotic land, conceives of India as a land comparable to England as part of a global Christian community.

---

24 For recent studies on monsters and exotic lands in these and other works from the Anglo-Saxon period, see, for instance, Mittman, *Maps and Monsters*; and Mittman and Kim, *Inconceivable Beasts*.

25 Howe, *Writing the Map of Anglo-Saxon England*, p. 154. For details about this manuscript and its contents, see *The Nowell Codex*, ed. by Malone. The Latin original of *The Wonders of the East*, *Mirabilia Orientis*, is recorded in BL, MS Cotton Tiberius, B V. See also note 31 below.

26 See, for instance, Orchard, *Pride and Prodigies*; and Lapidge, '*Beowulf*, Aldhelm, the *Liber Monstrorum* and Wessex'.

27 Thomson, *Communal Creativity in the Making of the 'Beowulf' Manuscript*.

28 For the idea of the location of Britain and Ireland in ancient and early medieval times, see, for instance, Lavezzo, *Angels on the Edge of the World*, pp. 1–8; Michelet, *Creation, Migration, and Conquest*, pp. 115–60; and Discenza, *Inhabited Spaces*, pp. 56–71.

The term 'global' in this case should be understood as meaning 'of the inhabited world', rather than literally 'of the whole globe'. It was known that the earth is spherical, as, for instance, Bede writes that the earth 'est enim re vera orbis idem in medio totius mundi positus' (is, in fact, a sphere set in the middle of the whole universe) in his *De Temporum Ratione* XXXII,[29] while it was also known that the inhabited world or *oikoumene*, located in the northern hemisphere, is only a part of the globe, with substantial unreachable lands lying in the southern hemisphere beyond the torrid lands and unnavigable ocean, as visualized in the Macrobian zonal map, an Anglo-Saxon example of which is found in London, British Library, MS Cotton Tiberius B V, fol. 29[r].[30] When conceiving of India and England as two Christian lands on the peripheries of the world, Ælfric must have had in mind the inhabited world, as visualized in the Anglo-Saxon *mappa mundi* preserved on folio 56[v] of the same manuscript.[31]

As Kazutomo Karasawa discusses in 'Christ Embracing the World: Ælfric's Description of the Crucifixion in "De Passione Domini"', Ælfric also had in mind the inhabited world, rather than the globe as a whole, in the description of the Crucifixion in his homily 'De Passione Domini' in the second series of his *Catholic Homilies*. Based on a Christian symbolic tradition, Ælfric writes that Christ on the cross embraced all the four corners of the world, thereby redeeming the whole world. Here Ælfric basically follows the symbolic tradition underlying his probable source text by Sedulius, yet he has modified it slightly to meet contextual requirements. Karasawa argues that the modification could have been facilitated by a peculiar Old English terminological tradition regarding the idea of the tripartite world. As schematically summarized in the T-O map, the inhabited world was supposed to consist of three major components, Asia, Africa, and Europe,[32] while the T-shape in the T-O map dividing the *oikoumene* into these three parts was represented as 'a crucifix superimposed on the spherical earth, symbolizing its salvation by Christ's sacrifice'.[33] Karasawa suggests that Ælfric could have taken advantage of the Old English terminological tradition, making it possible to read his passage on the Crucifixion in two ways based on the two slightly different symbolic traditions.

---

29 The original words are quoted from Bede, *Opera de Temporibus*, ed. by Jones, p. 239, while their translation is taken from Bede, *The Reckoning of Time*, trans. by Wallis, p. 91.

30 For the Macrobian zonal map in general, see Woodward, 'Medieval *Mappaemundi*', p. 300. For the Macrobian zonal map in BL, MS Cotton Tiberius B V, see McGurk, 'The Macrobian Zonal Map'. See also the chapter by Helen Appleton in this volume, pp. 315–18, 324–25.

31 For the Anglo-Saxon *mappa mundi*, see McGurk, 'The Mappa Mundi'. See also Appleton, 'The Northern World of the Anglo-Saxon *mappa mundi*', and her discussion in this volume. The manuscript recording this *mappa mundi* as well as the aforementioned Macrobian zonal map, namely, BL, MS Cotton Tiberius B V, is discussed by Howe as another book of elsewhere in his *Writing the Map of Anglo-Saxon England*, p. 154.

32 For the T-O map in general, see Woodward, 'Medieval *Mappaemundi*', pp. 301–03.

33 Edson, *Mapping Time and Space*, p. 5.

II. A Place in the World

In recent decades, medieval scholars have become increasingly sensitive to ideas of geography, space, and place, keeping pace with a broader 'spatial turn' in the humanities. Early medieval studies is no exception: Nicholas Howe's *Migration and Mythmaking in Anglo-Saxon England* (1989) and *Writing the Map of Anglo-Saxon England: Essays in Cultural Geography* (2008) and Fabienne Michelet's *Creation, Migration, and Conquest: Imaginary Geography and Sense of Space in Old English Literature* (2006) explored how the Anglo-Saxons, as migrant peoples, positioned themselves in relation to cultural centres such as Rome, Jerusalem, and Scandinavia, and within the narratives of salvation history and the succession of world empires. Similar studies include Catherine A. M. Clarke's *Literary Landscapes and the Idea of England, 700–1400* (2006) and Jennifer Neville's *Representations of the Natural World in Old English Poetry* (1999) investigating theories of landscape and nature. A different tack was taken by Scott T. Smith in his *Land and Book: Literature and Land Tenure in Anglo-Saxon England* (2012), focusing on the land charters and descriptions of the bounds of properties that Nicholas Howe had earlier highlighted as a valuable source of early English perceptions of land and landscape. More recently, Nicole Guenther Discenza's *Inhabited Spaces: Anglo-Saxon Constructions of Place* (2017) focuses on representations of space and place in Old English literature, while cultural memories of places within the English landscape have also been recently analysed by Michael D. J. Bintley in *Settlements and Strongholds in Early Medieval England: Texts, Landscapes, and Material Culture* (2020).

Where the chapters in Part I explore pre-Conquest English ideas of the rest of the world and the relationship that the English had with other peoples and places, the studies in Part III explore the concepts of nation and empire that developed in the island of Britain itself. In Part II, 'A Place in the World', on the other hand, the focus narrows to particular landscapes, seascapes, and soundscapes, to migrations and movements between landscapes, and to figurative uses of landscape imagery to express mental states and actions. The link is to be seen in Daniel Thomas's chapter, 'Babel and Beyond: Thinking through Migration in *Genesis A*', discussing a poem which is, of course, set in the biblical lands of the Old Testament and, at least at first sight, overlaps in its subject matter with the literary texts about exotic places covered in Part I. But Thomas's perspective is rather different, for he is concerned with the theme of movement across land and sea. In particular, Thomas engages critically with Howe's notion of 'migration and myth-making', and he addresses the question of whether and to what extent it can be applied to such themes as the journey across the Flood in Noah's Ark or dispersal of nations after the Tower of Babel.

The key term in these chapters is *landscape*, a technical term in painting that came into English from Dutch *landschap* around the year 1600 and originally meant 'a picture representing natural inland scenery' (OED, sense

1a). But recent studies by geographers and archaeologists in landscape have reinterpreted the whole notion of viewing a landscape from afar, assuming instead 'that landscapes are essentially *human* life worlds, and that people and their life worlds produce and transform each other in an ongoing dialectical movement'.[34] In other words, a landscape is not simply something that you view from a distance, for it is a place that you inhabit, where you live and work, a life world that affects you just as much as you affect it. In a similar vein, the anthropologist Tim Ingold offers the following insight:

> The landscape tells — or rather *is* — a story, a chronicle of life and dwelling. It unfolds the lives and times of predecessors who, over the generations, have moved around in it and played their part in its formation. To perceive the landscape is therefore to carry out an act of remembrance, and remembering is not so much a matter of calling up an internal image, stored in the mind, as of engaging perceptually with an environment that is itself pregnant with the past.[35]

The approach outlined here will be seen to be deeply relevant, not only to Thomas's discussion of migration theory in 'Babel and Beyond' but also to memories of the seventh-century landscape that are found to be vestigially present in an eleventh-century hagiography of St Rumwold, as explored by Hannah Bailey in 'St Rumwold in the Borderland' below, or in Mark Atherton's investigation of the 'landscape biography' of Byrhtnoth, ealdorman of Essex, the patron of Fenland monasteries and the leader and war hero celebrated and commemorated in the poem *The Battle of Maldon*.

The foundation for such approaches is a wide array of historical and philo-logical scholarship from the twentieth century that brought many advances in our empirical knowledge of the early English landscape. The classic study here came from geography and local history in the figure of W. G. Hoskins, especially his *The Making of the English Landscape* (1955).[36] Hoskins brought empirical observation and field work to his project, insisting that students should combine their scholarship with actual knowledge of the ground: the fields and woods, the waterways and roads, the hills and valleys that form the landmarks and boundaries of the estates, hundreds, and shires of the English kingdom as it developed over time. A different perspective came from the historian, botanist, and ecologist of woodland Oliver Rackham, who did much to dispel the myth that early England was one dense woodland, long abandoned by the Romano-British, which the intrepid Anglo-Saxon colonists had to level and clear when they arrived on the island in the post-Roman period. One of Rackham's points is that the landscape often reveals much continuity

---

34 Kolen and Renes, 'Landscape Biographies', p. 25.
35 Ingold, *The Perception of the Environment*, p. 189.
36 Hoskins, *The Making of the English Landscape*; Hoskins's contribution and methodology are discussed in detail in Wylie, *Landscape*, pp. 30–40.

between Romano-British and 'Anglo-Saxon' settlements, as for instance at Rivenhall in Essex.[37] A very worthy successor to these two scholars is the historian and archaeologist John Blair, especially his recent and monumental work *Building Anglo-Saxon England*, to which reference will be made in both Hannah Bailey's and Mark Atherton's chapters below.[38]

These approaches to landscape in which history is combined with a science such as local history, ecology, or archaeology have found a perhaps unlikely ally in late twentieth-century etymology and place-name studies. The place-name studies of the *early* twentieth century had many successes in establishing a sound basis for doing accurate, text-based etymology of place names, but some assumptions about the history of the period were hard to shake off: the equivalent of the 'migration to the primal woodland' theory *here* was the idea that the oldest and most significant place names were those containing interesting 'archaic' personal names, especially those ending in *-ing*, like Hastings or Reading, 'which refer to the descendants or followers of an Anglo-Saxon "chieftain"', in other words, presumably, one of the original leaders of the migration to *Britannia* in the fifth or sixth century.[39] Toponyms, that is, names referring to features of the landscape, were, by contrast, regarded as trivial in terms of historical value. The change in place-name studies came with the work of Margaret Gelling and like-minded scholars in the 1970s, and a later collaboration with a landscape geographer allowed Gelling to produce a classic study that demonstrates how early English settlers employed a rich lexicon of synonyms and descriptors for engaging with and describing the features of the landscape in which they lived and worked.[40] The maps in Mark Atherton's chapter, for example, show estates and properties held by or associated with Byrhtnoth, ealdorman of Essex. In the light of what has just been stated, it is interesting to see that among these place names are very many based either on precise landscape features (whether natural or human-made) or on directional and functional uses of the location, but hardly any are places named after legendary 'chieftains' from the migration period.[41]

Another very different aspect of the sense of place in the world is tackled by Britton Elliott Brooks for his study of Exeter Book Riddle 1 (numbered by some editors of the manuscript, for palaeographical reasons, as Riddles 1–3).

---

37 See, for example, the classic by Oliver Rackham, *The History of the Countryside*.

38 See further Baker, Brookes, and Reynolds, eds, *Landscapes of Defence in Early Medieval Europe*; Hooke, *The Anglo-Saxon Landscape*; and Jones, *Sense of Place in Anglo-Saxon England*.

39 Gelling, *Place-Names in the Landscape*, p. 2.

40 Gelling and Cole, *The Landscape of Place-Names*. See further Watts, ed., *The Cambridge Dictionary of English Place-Names*.

41 An exception to this observation is the property once owned by Byrhtnoth that is now Lawling Hall (see Mark Atherton's Figure 10.2), OE *Lelling* (Lealla's land). The name *Lealla is archaic and conjectural, though there is an Old German cognate Lallo; see Ekwall, *The Concise Oxford Dictionary of English Place-Names*, p. 290.

Brooks's interest is with the inner world of the poet, with his or her perception of the phenomena of nature. Here Brooks draws on a host of ecological and ecocritical approaches to literature in general and to Old English poetry in particular. In fact there is a long tradition going back to the 1960s for the interdisciplinary investigation of the sensorium or history of the senses (particularly sight and sound) in such thinkers and theorists as Marshall McLuhan. As well as his reflections on orality and literacy, McLuhan's one-time student Walter Ong wrote a study of the relationship between the sense of hearing and the world of sound, *The Presence of the Word: Some Prolegomena for Cultural and Religious History* (1967), with obvious relevance to the theoretical approaches taken by Brooks in his essay, which effectively demonstrates the acute sensitivity to sound effects in the world of an Old English poet, and its theological implications.

Some of the first missionaries and prelates in early medieval England were from the Greek-speaking part of the world, and the Greek influence upon England can be traced back to the seventh century. This is another kind of evidence for contacts abroad that differs from those in Part I in that we are dealing with the spread of ideas rather than political or trading contacts. Theodore of Tarsus (602–690), archbishop of Canterbury (667–690), was born in Tarsus and educated in Constantinople, while his assistant and colleague Hadrian (d. 709 or 710) was from the Greek-speaking part of North Africa. Under the influence of these and other people, as well as of various writings by Greek-speaking authors and by those under their influence, traces and echoes of Greek learning have been detected in Old English literature.[42] Eleni Ponirakis discusses in 'The Place of Stillness: Greek Patristic Thought in Cynewulf's *Juliana*' the poet Cynewulf's *Juliana* as an example of Old English poetry substantially influenced by the writings of the Greek Desert Fathers and their teachings on the way of prayer, especially by Evagrius's *Praktikos*. Based on a close reading of the poem, Ponirakis explores the Evagrian ideas of prayer, in particular the notion of *apatheia* and stillness — as expressed for instance in the landscape imagery of the house on the rock — that permeate the poem on the passion of St Juliana, whose cult became popular in England in the seventh century probably under the influence of Hadrian.

---

42 For instance, it is known that Old English medical texts depend heavily on Greek sources, and it is suggested that the Greek influence upon Anglo-Saxon medicine may well be traced back to the time of Archbishop Theodore, who may well have brought to England medical texts of Greek origin. See Stevenson, *The 'Laterculus Malalianus' and the School of Archbishop Theodore*, pp. 47–55. See also Talbot, *Medicine in Medieval England*, p. 18; and Kesling, *Medical Texts in Anglo-Saxon Literary Culture*.

III. Nation and Empire

Chapters by Helen Appleton, Caitlin Ellis, Ryan Lavelle, Paul Cavill, and Francis Leneghan in Part III demonstrate how in the centuries after the migration the various English peoples gradually came to view themselves as a single nation before their rulers assumed the status of imperial overlordship of the island in the tenth century.

The existence of a strong sense of national identity among medieval communities has long been a matter of contention. Whereas Benedict Anderson famously argued that the 'imagined communities' that we call 'nations' could only develop in a meaningful way with 'the convergence of capitalism and print technology' in the nineteenth century,[43] medievalists have traced the origins of national consciousness in western Europe back to the post-Roman era, during which a number of new polities emerged, united by common origin myths, language, and religion.[44] The tenth century was the crucial time, for, as we saw earlier, whereas in the time of Bede there were seven separate English kingdoms, each with their own ruler, by the year 1000, Ælfric of Eynsham could write in the Preface to his *Lives of Saints* that: 'gens nostra una regi subditur, et usitata est de uno rege non de duobus loqui' (our nation is subject to one king, and is accustomed to speak of one king, not of two).[45] Yet, the emergence of a single national identity among the various peoples of the *Angelcynn* was a very gradual and far from smooth process, stretching over half a millennium, the result of series of complex interactions with other peoples living in the island of Britain and outside cultural influences and pressures. And as the later chapters in this volume demonstrate, the development of the English nation in the early medieval period is as much a story of accommodation and assimilation as one of exclusion and difference.

As we have seen, Bede famously records that the first English newcomers to Britain in the mid-fifth century came 'de tribus Germaniae populis fortioribus, id est Saxonibus, Anglis, Iutis' (from three very powerful Germanic tribes, the Saxons, Angles, and Jutes), led by the warriors Hengest and Horsa, descendants of Woden, 'de cuius stirpe multarum prouinciarum regium genus originem duxit' (from whose stock the royal families of many kingdoms claimed their descent).[46] After fighting for territory, both against the Britons/Welsh, and among themselves, these Angles, Saxons, and Jutes — and doubtless other Germanic-speaking peoples such as Franks and Frisians — eventually formed a patchwork of their own small subkingdoms and regional units, many of whose names and cultures are now largely lost to us. However, an important document known as the Tribal Hidage, possibly a tribute list made at some

---

43 Anderson, *Imagined Communities*, p. 46. See also Gellner, *Nations and Nationalism*.
44 See Scales and Zimmer, 'Introduction'.
45 *Old English Lives of Saints: Ælfric*, ed. and trans. by Clayton and Mullins, I, p. 4.
46 Bede, *HE*, I.15, ed. and trans. by Colgrave and Mynors, pp. 50–51.

stage between the seventh and ninth centuries, offers a rare glimpse into the make-up of numerous smaller regional units south of the Humber in this period, listing now-obscure peoples — and perhaps kingdoms — such as the *Wocen Sættan* (7000 hides), *Herefinna* (1200 hides), and *Hwycce* (7000 hides).[47] Standing at the head of the list is the kingdom of Mercia, at 30,000 hides considerably larger than any of the other political or ethnic units. Mercia was one of the seven large and relatively stable kingdoms that emerged from this patchwork of smaller kingdoms and peoples during the seventh and eighth centuries. Each kingdom of the heptarchy had its own royal dynasty with an illustrious line of heroic ancestors, as well as its own saints, laws, and coinage. To the Midlands, north, and east were the Anglian kingdoms of Northumbria (formed from the union of Bernicia and Deira), Mercia, and East Anglia; to the south and west lay the Saxon kingdoms of Sussex, Essex, and Wessex; and in the south-east, Kent, where Hengest and Horsa had first landed in 454.[48] The principal dialectal groupings of Anglian, Saxon, and Kentish had their own distinctive features, though Bede refers to a single tongue *Anglorum* (of the English), alongside the four other languages spoken in Britain, namely British (i.e. Welsh), Pictish, Irish, and Latin.[49] From time to time, one English ruler would come to assume supremacy over multiple kingdoms. Hence Bede lists seven English kings who at one time held *imperium* south of the Humber (*HE*, II.5): Ælle of Sussex (r. 477–514); Ceawlin of Wessex (r. 560–592); Æthelberht of Kent (r. *c.* 589–616); Rædwald of East Anglia (r. *c.* 599–624); and three Northumbrian rulers, Edwin (r. 616–632/33), Oswald (r. 634–641/42), and Oswiu (r. 654–670).[50] From this list of insular overlords, Bede singles out Edwin as an especially powerful ruler who brought under his sway most of the island of Britain, and even some of its surrounding islands:

> maiore potentia cunctis qui Brittaniam incolunt, Anglorum pariter et Brettonum, populis praefuit, praeter Cantuariis tantum, necnon et Meuanias Brettonum insulas, quae inter Hiberniam et Brittaniam sitae sunt, Anglorum subiecit imperio.

> ([he] had still greater power and ruled over all the inhabitants of Britain, English and Britons alike, except for Kent only. He even brought under English rule the Mevanian Islands (Anglesey and Man) which lie between England and Ireland and belong to the Britons.)[51]

---

47 See Featherstone, 'The Tribal Hidage and the Ealdormen of Mercia'.
48 See Yorke, *Kings and Kingdoms of Early Anglo-Saxon England*; Kirby, *The Earliest English Kings*.
49 Bede, *HE*, I.1, ed. and trans. by Colgrave and Mynors, pp. 16–17.
50 Higham, *An English Empire*.
51 Bede, *HE*, II.5, ed. and trans. by Colgrave and Mynors, pp. 148–49. Bede's list of English overlords was expanded in the Anglo-Saxon Chronicle entry for 827 (= 829) to include Egbert of Wessex (r. 802–839), grandfather of Alfred, 'he wæs se eahteþa cyning se þe Bretwalda wæs' (he was the eighth king who was *Bretwalda*) (*The Anglo-Saxon Chronicle:*

Edwin was a convert king, whose evangelization by the Roman missionary Paulinus in 627 is famously recorded in detail by Bede (*HE* II.9–17). Although the kingdoms of the heptarchy were frequently at war with each other, raiding across borders for plunder and political supremacy, for Bede it was a common adherence to the Roman faith, combined with Germanic origins and a shared language, that bound together the various English peoples (*Angli*) of the heptarchy into a single *gens Anglorum* (English people).

Archaeological finds such as the Sutton Hoo ship burial and the Staffordshire Hoard, as well, perhaps, as the poem *Beowulf*, bear witness to the rich blend of pagan Scandinavian, Mediterranean Christian, and imperial Roman cultural influences and artistic styles that flourished in the age of the heptarchy.[52] Although cultural contacts with the Britons must have been extensive, and political alliances were often formed between the kings of Mercia, in particular, and Welsh rulers in wars against Northumbria, the English nevertheless cultivated a sense of separateness from their insular neighbours from an early date.[53] Indeed, as Caitlin Ellis demonstrates in her chapter in this section, scattered references to the the Britons, Welsh, Scots, and Picts in the earliest English sources betray an underlying suspicion and antipathy towards the other inhabitants of Britain. Bede concludes his *Ecclesiastical History of the English People* with an assessment of the relations between the *Angli* and the other peoples of the island, as it pertained at the time of writing, in 731:

> Pictorum quoque natio tempore hoc et foedus pacis cum gente habet Anglorum, et catholicae pacis ac ueritatis cum uniuersali ecclesia particeps existere gaudet. Scotti qui Brittaniam incolunt, suis contenti finibus, nil contra gentem Anglorum insidiarum moliuntur aut fraudium. Brettones, quamuis et maxima ex parte domestico sibi odio gentem Anglorum, et totius catholicae ecclesiae statum pascha minus recto moribusque inprobis inpugnent, tamen et diuina sibi et humana prorsus resistente uirtute in neutro cupitum possunt obtinere propositum, quippe qui, quamuis ex parte sui sint iuris, nonnulla tamen ex parte Anglorum sunt seruitio mancipati.
>
> (The Picts now have a treaty of peace with the English and rejoice to share in the catholic peace and truth of the Church universal. The Irish who live in Britain are content with their own territories and devise no plots or treachery against the English. Though, for the most part, the Britons oppose the English through their inbred hatred, and the

---

MS A, ed. by Bately). For debate over the precise meaning of the term *Bretwalda*, which could mean either 'British ruler/Ruler of Britain' or 'Wide Ruler', see Fanning, 'Bede, *Imperium*, and the Bretwaldas'; Wormald, 'Bede, the *Bretwaldas* and the Origins of the *Gens Anglorum*'.

52 See Carver, ed., *The Age of Sutton Hoo*; Fern, Dickinson, and Webster, eds, *The Staffordshire Hoard*; Leneghan, *The Dynastic Drama of 'Beowulf'*; Leneghan, 'Dishonouring the Dead'.

53 The progenitor of the West Saxon royal house, Cerdic, for example, has a suspiciously Celtic-sounding name.

whole state of the catholic Church by their incorrect Easter and their evil customs, yet being opposed by the power of God and man alike, they cannot obtain what they want in either respect. For although they are partly their own masters, yet they have also been brought partly under the rule of the English.)[54]

It is clear from Bede's account that, at least in his eyes, the *Angli* (English) are a distinct *gens* (people) who are now the dominant political force in the island of Britain.

However, with the Viking invasions, beginning with the sack of Lindisfarne in 793, the kingdoms of the heptarchy effectively ceased to exist as polities, leaving only Wessex an independent English kingdom by the time Alfred came to the throne in 871. The arrival of the Viking Great Army in 865 led to a period of sustained Scandinavian settlement in the Midlands, north, and east for much of the next century. Although English sources such as the Anglo-Saxon Chronicle typically describe the Viking armies as 'hæðene' (heathen), or simply 'here' (the army) or 'flotan' (seafarers/pirates), as Ryan Lavelle's chapter in this section demonstrates, by the mid-tenth century the Danes living in England were themselves subsumed into the *gens Anglorum*. Hence, as Francis Leneghan discusses in his chapter, a poem contained in the Anglo-Saxon Chronicle, *The Capture of the Five Boroughs*, celebrates the 'liberation' of Anglo-Scandinavian Danes from a new wave of Viking attacks in 942. This sense of kinship with the Danes may have stemmed in part from an awareness among the English of their own Scandinavian origins: for example, King Alfred's own dynasty claimed descent from the same line of Danish Scylding rulers celebrated in the opening lines of *Beowulf*, while the royal house of Mercia boasted Offa of Angeln among its ancestors.

Sarah Foot has identified Alfred's reign (871–899) as a time when Bede's idea of a *gens Anglorum* started to become a political reality. By promoting the use of the written vernacular — Old English — through a royal-sponsored programme of translation and textual production, Alfred's court circle sought to instil a sense of national cohesion among the various peoples of the *Angelcynn*.[55] A national Chronicle, now known as 'the Anglo-Saxon Chronicle', was produced, drawing together the histories of the various kingdoms into a single narrative of migration, conversion, and unification under West Saxon rule. Alfred also commissioned a single law code, the *domboc*, which incorporated elements drawn from Kentish, Mercian, and West Saxon precursors, and featured a preface tracing the history of Christian legislation back through the Acts of the Apostles and the teachings of Christ to the Ten Commandments issued to Moses by the Lord himself. West Saxon law is thereby aligned with God's

---

54 Bede, *HE*, v.24, ed. and trans. by Colgrave and Mynors, pp. 560–61.
55 Foot, 'The Making of *Angelcynn*'. For a recent overview of Alfredian literary production, see Discenza and Szarmach, eds, *A Companion to Alfred the Great*.

Law, and Alfred is presented as upholding the Christian faith 'geond Angelcyn' (throughout the English people).[56]

According to the Anglo-Saxon Chronicle, at the time of his death in 899 Alfred could lay claim to rule over all the *Angelcynn* who were not under Danish rule, that is, roughly all those living south of the Danelaw.[57] Following the annexation of the Anglian kingdom of Mercia to the Saxon Wessex, coins and charters issued by Alfred and his son Edward the Elder bore the title *Angul Saxonum rex* (King of the Anglo-Saxons), reflecting the emergence of a new polity, 'the kingdom of the Anglo-Saxons'.[58] As West Saxon power expanded into Wales, Northumbria, and even Scotland over the course of the tenth century, some — though not all — of Alfred's successors adopted ever-more impressive-sounding Roman and Byzantine imperial titles.[59] Coins proclaim Æthelstan as *Rex totius Britanniae* (King of all Britain), while in charters he is referred to variously as *basileus, imperator,* and *gubernator*.[60] While some scholars have expressed scepticism about the political import of these imperial titles, dismissing them as mere 'grecisms',[61] it seems likely that their increasing appearance in royal documents from the reign of Æthelstan onwards reflects the enhanced status of West Saxon kings, who after the treaty of Eamont in 927 and the Battle of Brunanburh in 937 — as discussed by Paul Cavill in his chapter in this volume — claimed to be not only rulers of Wessex but kings of kings and rulers of peoples within Britain.[62] Since the coronation of Charlemagne in 800, Frankish rulers had presented themselves as emperors of Rome, invested by the papacy with the revival of the *imperium romanum* as a new *imperium christianum*. The West Saxon *imperium*, by contrast, was

---

56 *King Alfred's Book of Laws*, 49.7, ed. and trans. by Preston, p. 117.

57 ASC MSS A, B, C, *s.a.* 901 (= 899). In the preface to the *Vita Alfredi*, however, Asser addresses Alfred as 'rex omnium Brittanniae insulae Christianorum rectori [...] Anglorum Saxonum regi' (ruler of all Christians of the island of Britain [...] king of the Angles and Saxons) (*Asser's Life of King Alfred*, ed. by Stevenson, p. 1; *Alfred the Great*, trans. by Keynes and Lapidge, p. 67).

58 See Keynes, 'Alfred the Great and the Kingdom of the Anglo-Saxons'; Keynes, 'Edward, King of the Anglo-Saxons'.

59 See Loyn, 'The Imperial Style of the Tenth Century Anglo-Saxon Kings'; John, '*Orbis Britanniae* and the Anglo-Saxon Kings'; Foot, *Æthelstan*, pp. 212–26.

60 For example, S 392: 'Rex Angulsexna and Norþhymbra imperator paganorum gubernator Brittanorumque propugnator' (King of the Anglo-Saxons and Emperor of the Northumbrians, Governor of the Pagans and Defender of the Britons).

61 See Molyneaux, 'Why Were Some Tenth-Century English Kings Presented as Rulers of Britain?', p. 63; Snook, *The Anglo-Saxon Chancery*, p. 76.

62 Torben Gebhardt argues that Æthelstan's adoption of imperial titles does not imply he viewed himself as emperor of Rome, but rather that it set them apart 'from ordinary kings who were his *subreguli*' (Gebhardt, 'From Bretwalda to Basileus', p. 181). Gebhardt notes that West Saxon kings were not unique in this period in adopting imperial titles to reflect the extraordinary reach of their power: Simeon of Bulgaria (r. 893–927), for example, was recognized as *basileus* after 913, while the kings of Léon used the title *imperator* from the tenth century.

limited to the island of Britain and — in some cases — its outlying islands, though some scholars have argued that for a brief period in the early tenth century, at least, West Saxon kings may even have entertained the idea that they might inherit the mantle of the Roman Empire from the Carolingians, whose own empire had collapsed in the late ninth century.[63] Certainly, these self-styled West Saxon overlords of Britain promoted a new model of sacral kingship, inspired by Carolingian models, in which the ruler was now not only a war-leader, in the mould of Hengest and Horsa, but a spiritual *rector*, shepherding his flock, and protector of the faith.[64] By the mid-tenth century, the increasing political unification of the various peoples of the *Angelcynn* was consolidated by developments in English religious life, notably the Benedictine Reform. West Saxon kings such as Edgar and Æthelred supported the efforts of reformers such as Bishops Æthelwold and Dunstan, who sought to impose the Rule of St Benedict as the sole monastic rule across England.[65]

A key literary influence on early medieval English ideas of empire was Orosius's *Historiae adversus paganos* (418), a history of the world from the Creation to the fall of Rome. Writing at the instigation of St Augustine, Orosius set out to demonstrate the miseries of life under pagan rulers when compared with the Christian era (1. Preface, 9–16). The project was intended as a corrective to those contemporaries who claimed that the sack of Rome by the Goths in 410 was a direct result of the conversion to Christianity. However, Orosius took his work into a different direction to that envisaged by Augustine, by setting out to prove that Rome's empire had never really fallen. Following the tradition of the four world empires that has its roots in Jerome's interpretation of Nebuchadnezzar's dream (Daniel 2), Orosius argued that whereas the empires of Babylon, Macedon, and Carthage met their miserable ends because of the wickedness of their pagan rulers, the cycle of the world empires came to an end with the rise of Rome, as it was during this era that Christ had come into the world.[66]

Orosius's history was known in England from the seventh century and was among a body of Latin works selected for translation into Old English during the reign of King Alfred or shortly thereafter. The Old English *Orosius*, discussed by Ryan Lavelle, Helen Appleton, and Francis Leneghan in their chapters in this section, implicitly invites its English readers to compare West Saxon kings with the Roman emperors of old, as defenders of *cristendom* and recipients of God's favour.[67] By omitting Orosius's own account of the Creation

---

63 See Wood, 'The Making of King Aethelstan's Empire'; Ortenberg, '"The King from Overseas"'; Leneghan, '*Translatio imperii*'.

64 The most comprehensive study is Pratt, *The Political Thought of King Alfred the Great*.

65 See Banton, 'Monastic Reform and the Unification of Tenth-Century England'. See also Molyneaux, *The Formation of the English Kingdom in the Tenth Century*.

66 For a recent discussion of Orosius's influential interpretation of this motif, see Breed, 'The Politics of Time'. See also Van Nuffelen, *Orosius and the Rhetoric of History*.

67 Leneghan, '*Translatio imperii*'. See further Godden, 'The Old English *Orosius* and its

from the beginning of the work, the Old English version transforms the work into a history of the institution of kingship, tracing its development from the reign of the first ruler of Babylon, the wicked pagan Ninus (OE *Orosius* I.2), through to Alaric, 'se cristena cyning and se mildesta' (the mildest Christian king) (OE *Orosius* VI.38), who oversaw the bloodless conquest of Rome and the integration of the Gothic people into the empire.[68] Likewise, the inclusion of Alfred's interview with Ohthere and Wulfstan in the geographical preface extends the narrative of kingship from Alaric to the West-Saxon present.

As the *Orosius* relates, throughout history the fall of one empire coincides with the rise of another in a different part of the world, a process of *translatio imperii* moving from East to West (II.1.5).[69] The Orosian account of imperial history would prove particularly useful for early medieval kings who styled themselves as latter-day Roman emperors. With the collapse of the Carolingian Empire in the late ninth century, in the views of at least some contemporaries a *translatio imperii* from Francia to Wessex took place, symbolized by the gifts of Hugh of the Franks to Æthelstan in 926.[70] These developments set the stage for the preoccupation with nation and empire that burgeons in Æthelstan's reign and continues to develop through the long tenth century and up to and beyond the Conquest. Such is the basis for a story of foreign contacts, landscapes, and empire-building that forms the subject matter of the essays in this volume.

A Note on the Maps

The specially commissioned maps in this volume are for illustrative purposes only, providing visual context for their relevant chapters. They are not intended for archaeological or navigational purposes.

Context'; Pezzarossa, 'Reading Orosius in the Viking Age'. On the theme of *cristendom* in the OE *Orosius*, see Harris, 'The Alfredian World History and Anglo-Saxon Identity'.

68 *The Old English History of the World*, ed. and trans. by Godden, pp. 56–58, 114–15. The translator considerably abbreviates Orosius's account of the Gothic invasions and softens the portrait of Alaric. Godden, 'The Anglo-Saxons and the Goths', connects this feature of the OE *Orosius* with Alfred's own Gothic ancestry, via his mother. For the suggestion that the translator may have found Orosius's account of the Carthaginian invasion of Italy a more useful historical parallel for Wessex's resistance of the Danes than the Gothic invasions, see Leneghan, 'Translatio imperii', pp. 690–94.

69 *The Old English History of the World*, ed. and trans. by Godden, p. 102.

70 See Wood, 'The Making of King Aethelstan's Empire'; Foot, *Æthelstan*, pp. 192–97.

Works Cited

Manuscripts

London, British Library, MS Cotton Tiberius, B V
London, British Library, MS Cotton Vitellius A XV
Oxford, Bodleian Library, MS Laud Misc. 636

Primary Sources

Adomnán, 'De Locis Sanctis', ed. by L. Bieler, in *Itineraria et alia geographica: Itineraria Hierosolymitana, Itineraria Romana, Geographica*, ed. by P. Geyer, O. Cuntz, A. Francheschini, R. Weber, L. Bieler, J. Fraipont, and F. Glorie, CCSL, 175 (Turnhout: Brepols, 1965), pp. 185–234

Aldhelm, *The Poetic Works*, trans. by Michael Lapidge and James Rosier, with an appendix by Neil Wright (Cambridge: D. S. Brewer, 1985)

Alfred the Great: Asser's 'Life of Alfred' and Other Contemporary Sources, ed. and trans. by Simon Keynes and Michael Lapidge (Harmondsworth: Penguin, 1983)

The Anglo-Saxon Chronicle: A Collaborative Edition, III: *MS A*, ed. by Janet Bately (Cambridge: D. S. Brewer, 1986)

The Anglo-Saxon Chronicle: A Collaborative Edition, VII: *MS E*, ed. by Susan Irvine (Cambridge: D. S. Brewer, 2004)

Asser's Life of King Alfred, together with the Annals of Saint Neots Erroneously Ascribed to Asser: New Imprint with Article on Recent Work by Dorothy Whitelock, ed. by William H. Stevenson (Oxford: Clarendon Press, 1959)

Bede, 'De Locis Sanctis', ed. by J. Fraipont, in *Itineraria et alia geographica: Itineraria Hierosolymitana, Itineraria Romana, Geographica*, ed. by P. Geyer, O. Cuntz, A. Francheschini, R. Weber, L. Bieler, J. Fraipont, and F. Glorie, CCSL, 175 (Turnhout: Brepols, 1965), pp. 251–80

——, *Bede's Ecclesiastical History of the English People*, ed. and trans. by Bertram Colgrave and R. A. B. Mynors, 2 vols (Oxford: Clarendon Press, 1969)

——, *The Ecclesiastical History of the English People*, trans. by Roger Collins and Judith McClure (Oxford: Oxford University Press, 1994)

——, *The Ecclesiastical History of the English People*, trans. by David Hugh Farmer, R. E. Latham, and Leo Sherley-Price (London: Penguin, 1990)

——, *Bedae Opera de Temporibus*, ed. by C. W. Jones (Cambridge, MA: Mediaeval Academy of America, 1943)

——, *Venerabilis Baedae Opera Historica*, ed. by Charles Plummer, 2 vols (Oxford: Clarendon Press, 1896)

——, *The Reckoning of Time*, trans. by Faith Wallis (Liverpool: Liverpool University Press, 2004)

King Alfred's Book of Laws: A Study of the Domboc and its Influence on English Identity, with a Complete Translation, ed. and trans. by Todd Preston (Jefferson, NC: McFarland and Company, 2012)

The Nowell Codex (British Museum Cotton Vitellius A.XV. Second MS), ed. by Kemp
   Malone, Early English Manuscripts in Facsimile, 12 (Copenhagen: Rosenkilde
   and Bagger, 1963)
The Old English and Anglo-Latin Riddle Tradition, ed. and trans. by Andy Orchard,
   DOML, 69 (Harvard: Harvard University Press, 2021)
The Old English History of the World: An Anglo-Saxon Rewriting of Orosius, ed.
   and trans. by Malcolm R. Godden, DOML, 44 (Cambridge, MA: Harvard
   University Press, 2016)
Old English Lives of Saints: Ælfric, ed. and trans. by Mary Clayton and Juliet Mullins,
   DOML, 58–60, 3 vols (Cambridge, MA: Harvard University Press, 2019)
The Riddles of Aldhelm, ed. and trans. by James Hall Pitman, Yale Studies in English,
   67 (New Haven, CT: Yale University Press, 1925)
Saint Aldhelm's Riddles, trans. by A. M. Juster (Toronto: University of Toronto
   Press, 2015)
'Vita Willibaldi Episcopi Eichstetensis', ed. by O. Holder-Egger, in MGH:
   Scriptores, 15.1 (Hanover, 1887), pp. 86–106

Secondary Sources

Anderson, Benedict, *Imagined Communities: Reflections on the Origin and Spread of
   Nationalism*, rev. edn (London: Verso, 1991)
Anlezark, Daniel, 'The Anglo-Saxon World View', in *The Cambridge Companion to
   Old English Literature*, 2nd edn, ed. by Malcolm Godden and Michael Lapidge
   (Cambridge: Cambridge University Press, 2013), pp. 66–81
Appleton, Helen, 'The Northern World of the Anglo-Saxon *mappa mundi*', ASE, 47
   (2018), 275–305
Baker, John, Stuart Brookes, and Andrew Reynolds, eds, *Landscapes of Defence
   in Early Medieval Europe: Anglo-Saxon England and Comparative Perspectives*,
   SEM, 28 (Turnhout: Brepols, 2013)
Banton, Nicholas, 'Monastic Reform and the Unification of Tenth-Century
   England', *Studies in Church History*, 19 (1982), 71–82
Beckett, Katharine Scarfe, *Anglo-Saxon Perceptions of the Islamic World*, Cambridge
   Studies in Anglo-Saxon England, 33 (Cambridge: Cambridge University Press,
   2003)
Bintley, Michael D. J., *Settlements and Strongholds in Early Medieval England: Texts,
   Landscapes, and Material Culture*, SEM, 45 (Turnhout: Brepols, 2020)
Breed, Brennan, 'The Politics of Time: Epistemic Shifts and the Reception History
   of the Four Kingdoms Schema', in *Four Kingdom Motifs before and beyond the
   Book of Daniel*, ed. by Andrew Perrin and Loren T. Stuckenbruck, Themes in
   Biblical Narrative, 28 (Leiden: Brill, 2020), pp. 300–328
Cameron, M. L., *Anglo-Saxon Medicine*, Cambridge Studies in Anglo-Saxon
   England, 7 (Cambridge: Cambridge University Press, 1993)
Carver, Martin, ed., *The Age of Sutton Hoo: The Seventh Century in North-Western
   Europe* (Woodbridge: Boydell, 1992)

——, *Sutton Hoo: Burial Ground of Kings?* (Philadelphia: University of Pennsylvania Press, 1998)

Clarke, Catherine A. M., *Literary Landscapes and the Idea of England, 700–1400* (Cambridge: D. S. Brewer, 2006)

Deutscher, Guy, *Through the Language Glass: Why the World Looks Different in Other Languages* (London: Heinemann, 2010)

Discenza, Nicole Guenther, *Inhabited Spaces: Anglo-Saxon Constructions of Place*, Toronto Anglo-Saxon Series, 23 (Toronto: University of Toronto Press, 2017)

Discenza, Nicole Guenther, and Paul E. Szarmach, eds, *A Companion to Alfred the Great*, Brill's Companions to the Christian Tradition, 58 (Leiden: Brill, 2014)

Edson, Evelyn, *Mapping Time and Space: How Medieval Mapmakers Viewed their World*, The British Library Studies in Map History, 1 (London: British Library, 1997)

Ekwall, Eilert, *The Concise Oxford Dictionary of English Place-Names*, 4th edn (Oxford: Clarendon Press, 1960)

Fanning, Steven, 'Bede, *Imperium*, and the Bretwaldas', *Speculum*, 66 (1991), 1–26

Featherstone, Peter, 'The Tribal Hidage and the Ealdormen of Mercia', in *Mercia: An Anglo-Saxon Kingdom in Europe*, ed. by Michelle P. Brown and Carol Ann Farr (Leicester: Leicester University Press, 2001), pp. 23–34

Fern, Chris, Tania Dickinson, and Leslie Webster, eds, *The Staffordshire Hoard: An Anglo-Saxon Treasure* (London: Society of Antiquaries of London, 2019)

Foot, Sarah, *Æthelstan: The First King of England* (New Haven, CT: Yale University Press, 2011)

——, 'The Making of *Angelcynn*: English Identity before the Norman Conquest', *Transactions of the Royal Historical Society*, 6th Ser., 6 (1996), 25–49; repr. in *Old English Literature: Critical Essays*, ed. by Roy M. Liuzza (New Haven, CT: Yale University Press, 2002), pp. 51–78

Gebhardt, Torben R., 'From Bretwalda to Basileus: Imperial Concepts in Late Anglo-Saxon England?', in *Transcultural Approaches to the Concept of Imperial Rule in the Middle Ages*, ed. by Christian Scholl, Torben R. Gebhardt, and Jan Clauß (Frankfurt: Peter Land, 2017), pp. 157–83

Gelling, Margaret, *Place-Names in the Landscape: The Geographical Roots of Britain's Place-Names* (London: J. M. Dent, 1984)

Gelling, Margaret, and Ann Cole, *The Landscape of Place-Names*, 2nd edn (Donington: Shaun Tyas, 2014)

Gellner, Ernest, *Nations and Nationalism* (Oxford: Blackwell, 1983)

Godden, Malcolm R., 'The Anglo-Saxons and the Goths: Rewriting the Sack of Rome', *ASE*, 31 (2002), 47–68

——, 'The Old English *Orosius* and its Context: Who Wrote it, for Whom, and Why?', *Quaestio Insularis*, 12 (2012), 1–30

Harris, Stephen J., 'The Alfredian World History and Anglo-Saxon Identity', *JEGP*, 100 (2001), 482–510; repr. in his *Race and Ethnicity in Anglo-Saxon Literature* (New York: Taylor & Francis, 2003), pp. 83–106

Higham, N. J., *An English Empire: Bede and the Early Anglo-Saxon Kings* (Manchester: Manchester University Press, 1995)

Hooke, Della, *The Anglo-Saxon Landscape: The Kingdom of the Hwicce* (Manchester: Manchester University Press, 1985)

Hoskins, W. G., *The Making of the English Landscape* (London: Hodder and Stoughton, 1955)

Howe, Nicholas, *Migration and Mythmaking in Anglo-Saxon England* (New Haven, CT: Yale University Press, 1989; repr. Notre Dame: University of Notre Dame Press, 2001)

——, 'Rome: Capital of Anglo-Saxon England', *Journal of Medieval and Early Modern Studies*, 34 (2004), 147–72

——, *Writing the Map of Anglo-Saxon England: Essays in Cultural Geography* (New Haven, CT: Yale University Press, 2008)

Ingold, Tim, *The Perception of the Environment: Essays on Livelihood, Dwelling and Skill* (London: Routledge, 2000)

John, Eric, '*Orbis Britanniae* and the Anglo-Saxon Kings', in *Orbis Britanniae and Other Studies* (Leicester: Leicester University Press, 1966), pp. 1–63

Jones, Richard, *Sense of Place in Anglo-Saxon England* (Donington: Shaun Tyas, 2012)

Kesling, Emily, *Medical Texts in Anglo-Saxon Literary Culture*, Anglo-Saxon Studies, 38 (Cambridge: D. S. Brewer, 2020)

Keynes, Simon, 'Alfred the Great and the Kingdom of the Anglo-Saxons', in *A Companion to Alfred the Great*, ed. by Nicole Guenther Discenza and Paul E. Szarmach, Brill's Companions to the Christian Tradition, 58 (Leiden: Brill, 2014), pp. 13–46

——, 'Edward, King of the Anglo-Saxons', in *Edward the Elder, 899–924*, ed. by N. J. Higham and David Hill (Abingdon: Routledge, 2001), pp. 40–66

Kirby, D. P., *The Earliest English Kings* (London: Unwin, 1991)

Kolen, Jan, and Hans Renes, 'Landscape Biographies: Key Issues', in *Landscape Biographies: Geographical, Historical and Archaeological Perspectives on the Production and Transmission of Landscapes*, ed. by Jan Kolen, Hans Renes, and Rita Hermans (Amsterdam: Amsterdam University Press, 2015), pp. 21–47

Lapidge, Michael, 'The Anglo-Latin Background', in *A New Critical History of Old English Literature*, ed. by Stanley B. Greenfield and Daniel G. Calder (New York: New York University Press, 1986), pp. 5–37

——, '*Beowulf*, Aldhelm, the *Liber Monstrorum* and Wessex', *Studi Medievali*, 3rd Ser., 23 (1982), 151–92

Lavezzo, Kathy, *Angels on the Edge of the World: Geography, Literature, and English Community, 1000–1534* (Ithaca, NY: Cornell University Press, 2006)

Leneghan, Francis, 'Dishonouring the Dead: *Beowulf* and the Staffordshire Hoard', *Quaestio Insularis*, 21 (2020), 1–32

——, *The Dynastic Drama of 'Beowulf'*, Anglo-Saxon Studies, 39 (Cambridge: D. S. Brewer, 2020)

——, '*Translatio imperii*: The Old English *Orosius* and the Rise of Wessex', *Anglia*, 133 (2015), 656–705

Levison, Wilhelm, *England and the Continent in the Eighth Century: The Ford Lectures Delivered in the University of Oxford in the Hilary Term, 1943* (Oxford: Clarendon Press, 1946)

Loyn, Henry R., 'The Imperial Style of the Tenth Century Anglo-Saxon Kings', *History*, 40 (1955), 111–15

McGurk, Patrick, 'The Macrobian Zonal Map', in *An Eleventh-Century Anglo-Saxon Illustrated Miscellany: British Library Cotton Tiberius B.V Part 1, Together with Leaves from British Library Cotton Nero D.II*, ed. by P. McGurk, D. N. Dumville, M. R. Godden, and Ann Knock, Early English Manuscripts in Facsimile, 21 (Copenhagen: Rosenkilde and Bagger, 1983), pp. 65–66

——, 'The Mappa Mundi', in *An Eleventh-Century Anglo-Saxon Illustrated Miscellany: British Library Cotton Tiberius B.V Part 1, Together with Leaves from British Library Cotton Nero D.II*, ed. by P. McGurk, D. N. Dumville, M. R. Godden, and Ann Knock, Early English Manuscripts in Facsimile, 21 (Copenhagen: Rosenkilde and Bagger, 1983), pp. 79–87

Michelet, Fabienne L., *Creation, Migration, and Conquest: Imaginary Geography and Sense of Space in Old English Literature* (Oxford: Oxford University Press, 2006)

Mittman, Asa Simon, *Maps and Monsters in Medieval England* (New York: Routledge, 2006)

Mittman, Asa Simon, and Susan M. Kim, *Inconceivable Beasts: The 'Wonders of the East' in the 'Beowulf' Manuscript* (Tempe: Arizona Center for Medieval and Renaissance Studies, 2013)

Molyneaux, George, *The Formation of the English Kingdom in the Tenth Century* (Oxford: Oxford University Press, 2105)

——, 'Why Were Some Tenth-Century English Kings Presented as Rulers of Britain?', *Transactions of the Royal Historical Society*, 21 (2011), 59–91

Naismith, Rory, 'Islamic Coins from Early Medieval England', *Numismatic Chronicle*, 165 (2005), 193–222

Neville, Jennifer, *Representations of the Natural World in Old English Poetry*, Cambridge Studies in Anglo-Saxon England, 27 (Cambridge: Cambridge University Press, 1999)

Ong, Walter J., *The Presence of the Word: Some Prolegomena for Cultural and Religious History* (New Haven, CT: Yale University Press, 1967; repr. Minneapolis: University of Minnesota Press, 1981)

Orchard, Andy, 'Aldhelm's Library', in *The Cambridge History of the Book in Britain*, I: *c. 400–1100*, ed. by Richard Gameson (Cambridge: Cambridge University Press, 2012), pp. 591–605

——, *Pride and Prodigies: Studies in the Monsters of the 'Beowulf'-Manuscript* (Cambridge: D. S. Brewer, 1995)

Ortenberg, Veronica, '"The King from Overseas": Why Did Æthelstan Matter in Tenth-Century Continental Affairs?', in *England and the Continent in the Tenth Century: Studies in Honour of Wilhelm Levison (1876–1947)*, ed. by David Rollason, Conrad Leyser, and Hannah Williams, SEM, 37 (Turnhout: Brepols, 2010), pp. 211–36

Pelteret, David A. E., 'Eleventh-Century Anglo-Saxon Long-Haul Travelers: Jerusalem, Constantinople, and Beyond', in *The Maritime World of the Anglo-Saxons*, ed. by Stacy S. Klein, William Schipper, and Shannon Lewis-Simpson (Tempe: Arizona Center for Medieval and Renaissance Studies, 2014), pp. 75–129

Pezzarossa, Lucrezia, 'Reading Orosius in the Viking Age: An Influential Yet Problematic Model', *Filologia Germanica*, 5 (2013), 223–40

Pratt, David, *The Political Thought of King Alfred the Great* (Cambridge: Cambridge University Press, 2007)

Rackham, Oliver, *The History of the Countryside* (London: Weidenfeld and Nicholson, 1986)

Rollason, David, Conrad Leyser, and Hannah Williams, eds, *England and the Continent in the Tenth Century: Studies in Honour of Wilhelm Levison (1876–1947)*, SEM, 37 (Turnhout: Brepols, 2010)

Scales, Len, and Oliver Zimmer, 'Introduction', in *Power and the Nation in European History*, ed. by Len Scales and Oliver Zimmer (Cambridge: Cambridge University Press, 2005), pp. 1–30

Smith, Scott T., *Land and Book: Literature and Land Tenure in Anglo-Saxon England* (Toronto: University of Toronto Press, 2012)

Snook, Benjamin, *The Anglo-Saxon Chancery: The History, Language and Production of Anglo-Saxon Charters from Alfred to Edgar*, Anglo-Saxon Studies, 28 (Woodbridge: Boydell, 2015)

Stevenson, Jane, *The 'Laterculus Malalianus' and the School of Archbishop Theodore*, Cambridge Studies in Anglo-Saxon England, 14 (Cambridge: Cambridge University Press, 1995)

Talbot, C. H. *The Anglo-Saxon Missionaries in Germany: Being the Lives of SS. Willibrord, Boniface, Sturm, Leoba and Lebuin, Together with the Hodoeporicon of St Willibald and a Selection from the Correspondence of St Boniface* (London: Sheed and Ward, 1954)

——, *Medicine in Medieval England* (London: Oldbourne, 1967)

Thomson, S. C., *Communal Creativity in the Making of the 'Beowulf' Manuscript: Towards a History of Reception for the Nowell Codex*, Library of the Written Word, 67, The Manuscript World, 10 (Leiden: Brill, 2018)

Tinti, Francesca, ed., *England and Rome in the Early Middle Ages: Pilgrimage, Art, and Politics*, SEM, 40 (Turnhout: Brepols, 2014)

Van Nuffelen, Peter, *Orosius and the Rhetoric of History* (Oxford: Oxford University Press, 2012)

Watts, Victor, ed., *The Cambridge Dictionary of English Place-Names* (Cambridge: Cambridge University Press, 2004)

Wilkinson, John, *Jerusalem Pilgrims before the Crusades* (Jerusalem: Ariel Publishing House, 1977)

Wood, Michael, 'The Making of King Aethelstan's Empire: An English Charlemagne?', in *Ideal and Reality in Frankish and Anglo-Saxon Society: Studies Presented to J. M. Wallace-Hadrill*, ed. by Patrick Wormald, with Donald Bullough and Roger Collins (Oxford: Blackwell, 1983), pp. 250–72

Woodward, David, 'Medieval *Mappaemundi*', in *The History of Cartography*, I: *Cartography in Prehistoric, Ancient, and Medieval Europe and the Mediterranean*, ed. by J. B. Harley and David Woodward (Chicago: University of Chicago Press, 1987), pp. 286–370

Woolf, Alex, 'Reporting Scotland in the Anglo-Saxon Chronicle', in *Reading the Anglo-Saxon Chronicle: Language, Literature, History*, ed. by Alice Jorgensen, SEM, 23 (Turnhout: Brepols, 2010), pp. 221–39

Wormald, Patrick, 'Bede, the *Bretwaldas* and the Origins of the *Gens Anglorum*', in *The Times of Bede, 625–865: Studies in Early English Christian Society and its Historian*, ed. by Stephen Baxter (Oxford: Blackwell, 2006), pp. 106–34

Wylie, John, *Landscape* (London: Routledge, 2007)

Yorke, Barbara, *Kings and Kingdoms of Early Anglo-Saxon England* (London: Taylor and Francis, 1990)

Zacher, Samantha, *Imagining the Jew in Anglo-Saxon Literature and Culture*, Toronto Anglo-Saxon Series, 21 (Toronto: University of Toronto Press, 2016)

Part I

Here, There, and Everywhere

DANIEL ANLEZARK

Alfred and the East

Asia was central to the spiritual geography of all Anglo-Saxon Christians, as the continent on which Christ was born, where he lived most of his life, and where the Christian Church was founded. Asia was the place where many early martyrs died, and where the relics of many still rested. Anglo-Saxon maps placed Jerusalem (at the western extremity of Asia) at the centre of the world, and despite the difficulty of the journey, pilgrims from England and other western Europeans made their way there to visit the sites of Christ's passion and resurrection.[1] Asia was also important to the Anglo-Saxon social elite in a more mundane way as a source of luxury goods.[2] These included expensive spices, such as pepper, used to flavour food and also in medical recipes, as well as gemstones, such as garnets, which could make their way from Sri Lanka to Britain via trade routes which had been in place more or less since Antiquity.[3] A group of Old English texts dating from the late ninth and early tenth centuries offers us insights into some ways in which people living in England across these decades conceptualized the faraway continent of Asia. Informative among these are the Old English translations of *The Wonders of the East*, *Alexander's Letter to Aristotle*, and Orosius's *History against the Pagans*, as well as the esoteric poem *Solomon and Saturn II*. Other texts known to the Anglo-Saxons also include insights into the geography and peoples of Asia, notably in legends of the saints, and especially in the Old English *Martyrology*.[4]

---

1 See Morris, *The Sepulchre of Christ and the Medieval West*, pp. 90–133. On Anglo-Saxon journeys to the East more than a century later, see Pelteret, 'Eleventh-Century Anglo-Saxon Long-Haul Travelers'. On Anglo-Saxon maps, see the chapter by Helen Appleton in this volume.

2 For an overview of the early medieval trade in luxury goods, see McCormick, *Origins of the European Economy*, pp. 708–28.

3 See Hamerow, 'The Circulation of Garnets in the North Sea Zone'. On the role of Jewish traders on these routes from the East, which came to the Mediterranean either via the Persian Gulf or around the Arabian Peninsula and up the Red Sea, see Gil, 'The Rādhānite Merchants', and Adler, *Jewish Travellers*, pp. 2–3.

4 Various vernacular saints' lives in verse and prose also have action set in Asia, for example the poems *Andreas*, *Fates of the Apostles*, and *Elene*, and the prose *Life of St Christopher*.

Daniel Anlezark (daniel.anlezark@sydney.edu.au) is the McCaughey Professor of Early English Literature and Language at the University of Sydney, Australia. His research interests include Alfred the Great and early English prose, and early English biblical literature.

Ideas of the World in Early Medieval English Literature, ed. by Mark Atherton, Kazutomo Karasawa, and Francis Leneghan, SOEL 1 (Turnhout: Brepols, 2022)   pp. 43–67
BREPOLS ❦ PUBLISHERS   DOI 10.1484/M.SOEL.5.130556

The books of the Bible and commentaries on these would also have provided significant information about the Holy Land — what had been ancient Israel, later was the Roman province of Palestine, and in the late ninth century was contested territory between the Abbasid Caliphate based in Baghdad and the Tulunid rulers of Egypt.[5]

Most of the Old English texts that have just been mentioned — *Wonders of the East, Alexander's Letter to Aristotle*, Orosius's *History against the Pagans, Solomon and Saturn II* — were produced in the decades around the year 900.[6] The focus of *Wonders* and *Alexander's Letter* is almost entirely on Asia, while *Solomon and Saturn II* takes Asia as its geographical reference point, and sets its debate in Jerusalem.[7] The geographical preface to Orosius's *History* includes a comprehensive description of Asia, and a significant part of the universal history that it narrates is also set there.[8] The Old English *Martyrology* is a calendrical compendium of saints' lives and their resting places, and a great many of these are also set in Asia. No doubt Asia loomed large in the imagination of the reader of Old English texts across these decades, and beyond. In this context and against this background, we find two references to King Alfred the Great's interest in Asia. There is clear evidence that Alfred corresponded with Elias, patriarch of Jerusalem, while an entry in some versions of the Anglo-Saxon Chronicle under the year 883 indicates that he sent envoys with alms 'on Indea to sancte Thome and to sancte Bartholomeae' (into India to St Thomas and to St Bartholomew; D text). This essay will examine the evidence for Alfred's Asian diplomacy and interrogate the range of contexts within which it took place. This will involve a clarification of the nature and scope of the journey of the two Anglo-Saxon travellers, Sigehelm and Athelstan, who set out for 'India', and the connection between this embassy and the retaking of London from the Vikings which occasioned it.

---

5 See Gil, *A History of Palestine*, pp. 279–334.

6 On the date of *Wonders* and *Alexander's Letter*, see Sisam, *Studies in the History of Old English Literature*, pp. 65–98; see also Simon Thomson's essay in this volume. *The Old English Orosius*, ed. by Bately, pp. lxxxvi–cxiii, suggests a late ninth-century date for this work, though it may have been made within the following decades; see Godden, 'The Old English *Orosius* and its Context'. Anlezark (*The Old English Dialogues of Solomon and Saturn*, ed. and trans. by Anlezark, pp. 49–57) suggests a date for *Solomon and Saturn II* sometime between the late ninth and early tenth centuries. Rauer (*The Old English Martyrology*, ed. and trans. by Rauer, pp. 1–4), suggests a date range of *c.* 800–*c.* 900 for the creation of this work.

7 On *Wonders* and *Alexander's Letter*, see Simon Thomson's chapter in this volume. On *Solomon and Saturn II*, see O'Brien O'Keeffe, 'The Geographic List of *Solomon and Saturn II*', and Powell, 'Orientalist Fantasy', who discusses the poem's imaginative configuration of the East. See further the chapter by Rachel Burns in this volume.

8 On the Old English *Orosius*, see also the essays of Helen Appleton, Ryan Lavelle, and Francis Leneghan in this volume.

Jerusalem

In the late ninth century, Jerusalem was for Christians the most important city in the East. However, Christian populations could be found across the Islamic world, especially in the arc extending from Alexandria in Egypt to what is now western Turkey, but which at the time was the kingdom of Armenia. Jerusalem held symbolic potency as the site of Christ's death and resurrection and was also the seat of one of the four patriarchates of the Eastern Church.[9] It has long been noted that Alfred maintained a correspondence with Patriarch Elias III of Jerusalem (*c.* 878–907).[10] The exchange of letters between the king and the patriarch is mentioned directly by Asser in his *Life of King Alfred*:

> Quid loquar de frequentibus contra paganos expeditionibus et bellis et incessabilibus regni gubernaculis? De cotidiana nationum, quae in Tyrreno mari usque ultimum Hiberniae finem habitant? Nam etiam de Hierosolyma ab Elia patriarcha epistolas et dona illi directas vidimus et logimus.
>
> > (What shall I say of his frequent expeditions and battles against the pagans and of the unceasing responsibilities of government? What of his daily involvement with the nations from the Mediterranean to the furthest limit of Ireland? — for I have seen and read letters sent to him with gifts from Jerusalem by the patriarch Elias.)[11]

It is known that Elias sent letters to at least two other Western rulers during his tenure in Jerusalem, asking for money to restore churches in the Holy Land and to ransom captive monks.[12] The earlier of these letters reached the emperor Charles the Fat in 881, carried by Elias's envoys, the monks Gispert and Rainard, whose names imply that they were Lombards or Franks resident in Jerusalem. It is unlikely that Asser is referring to letters at this same time, given that he did not come to Alfred's court until the mid-880s, probably in early 885, after the southern Welsh kings had accepted Alfred as overlord; this does not preclude the possibility that Alfred's exchanges with Elias had begun before Asser's arrival.[13]

---

9 The others were Antioch, Alexandria, and Constantinople.

10 Meaney, 'Alfred, the Patriarch and the White Stone'. On Elias's career, see Gil, *A History of Palestine*, pp. 461–62. Elias was a member of the prominent Christian Mansour family, and a descendant of Mansour ibn Sarjun (grandfather of St John of Damascus), a high-ranking civil servant of Emperor Heraclius who had been a member of the delegation that surrendered Damascus to Khalid ibn al-Walid in 635, and later served as a high-ranking civil servant in the new Islamic government; see Griffith, 'The Manṣūr Family and Saint John of Damascus'. Elias's kinsman Sergius (I) had been patriarch of Jerusalem from 842 to 855.

11 *Asser's Life of King Alfred*, ed. by Stevenson, ch. 91, pp. 76–77; see *Alfred the Great*, trans. by Keynes and Lapidge, p. 101, and their assessment of the evidence for a journey to India (p. 270).

12 Gil, *A History of Palestine*, p. 454; Meaney, 'Alfred, the Patriarch and the White Stone', p. 67.

13 See *Alfred the Great*, trans. by Keynes and Lapidge, pp. 26–27.

Elias's correspondence was not only with kings. A surviving letter to Elias from Pope John VIII (872–882), written in May 879, records the arrival of Elias's emissaries, the monks Theodosius, David, and Saba, and expresses the pope's regret that he cannot send a gift of greater value to the patriarch for 'fear of the Muslims'.[14] Elias's active diplomacy with the West and his requests for funds coincide with the rise to power of Ahmad ibn Tulun, governor of Egypt, who in 873 declared independence from Abbasid rule. Ahmad wrested control of Palestine from the caliphate based in Baghdad, apparently appointing a Christian governor either in Ramla, the seat of government for the province, or perhaps in Jerusalem.[15] Tulunid rule, which lasted in Palestine until 906, when the Abbasids regained control of the Holy Land, offered Christians of the region a period of respite from the more restrictive (for non-Muslims) Abbasid regime, a moment which was marked by the renovation of churches in Jerusalem. Elias's contact with the Western Christian rulers and requests for funds to restore churches in Palestine represents a moment when the churches of Asia could not only restore damaged property, but also attend to links with the West. The late ninth century also saw a resurgence of Byzantine power under the rule of Basil I (r. 867–886) and his successors in the Macedonian dynasty. The victories of Basil and his predecessor, Michael II (r. 839/49–867), against the fractured Abbasids in western Asia Minor also led to renewed diplomacy between emperors in the East and West. This bore fruit in Basil's successful military cooperation with the forces of Emperor Louis II (d. 875) in the destruction of the Emirate of Bari in southern Italy in 871.[16]

It is probable that Alfred, like Charles the Fat, was asked for money to help Elias's restoration projects. However, Alfred's engagement with Elias went further than simple requests for (and probably the sending of) alms; indeed, Asser's reference to plural 'letters' implies an ongoing exchange. Bald's *Leechbook*, a collection of medical texts possibly compiled during Alfred's reign, includes a set of medical recipes, concerning which we are told: 'Þis eal het þus secgean ælfrede cyninge domne helias patriarcha on gerusalem' (Dominus Elias, patriarch of Jerusalem, ordered all this to be told to King Alfred).[17] A number of leaves have been lost from the manuscript so that the chapter's opening is no longer extant, though a full indicative list in the table of contents survives. The remedies sent by the patriarch offer help with, among other disorders, constipation, pain in the spleen, diarrhoea, and more vaguely 'internal tenderness'. Also included was a recipe for the use of 'White Stone for all unknown illnesses'.[18] It would be very surprising if the

---

14 See Gil, *A History of Palestine*, p. 454.
15 See Gil, *A History of Palestine*, pp. 307–08.
16 Kreutz, *Before the Normans*, pp. 40–45. By the end of the century both Carolingian and Byzantine power had been displaced in southern Italy.
17 *Leechdoms, Wortcunning, and Starcraft*, ed. by Cockayne, Bk II, ch. 64, II, pp. 174–75, 288–91. On the *Leechbook*, see Kesling, *Medical Texts in Anglo-Saxon Literary Culture*, pp. 123–56.
18 See Meaney, 'Alfred, the Patriarch and the White Stone'.

patriarch had sent these recipes unsolicited (neither of his surviving letters asking for alms proffered unsought medical advice), inviting the plausible conclusion that Anglo-Saxon visitors to Jerusalem, perhaps alms bearers also carrying letters, brought news of Alfred's difficult medical condition, which is also mentioned by Asser.[19] The recipes itemized include some that would have assisted the treatment of the symptoms described by Asser. It is unlikely that information about the king's delicate illness could have reached the patriarch without having been brought by English pilgrims to Jerusalem, either by word of mouth or by letter. The wider historical context of Elias's requests is Charlemagne's great interest in and benefaction of the Christian holy places in Palestine nearly a century earlier, which established ongoing links between the Jerusalem patriarchate and the Western Empire, though these had diminished across the course of the ninth century.[20] In this context, Asser's Alfred emerges in the 880s and 890s as a latter-day Charlemagne, interested in the affairs of Jerusalem as the Carolingian dynasty faded away.[21]

The glimpse of Anglo-Saxon pilgrims in Jerusalem from the 880s into the 890s emerges in the context of very scant evidence of travel from western Europe to the eastern Mediterranean at the time. It is noteworthy in this context that the three Irish pilgrims who washed ashore in Wessex in 891, after visiting Alfred's court, intended later to set out for Rome with the ambition of then travelling on to Jerusalem, an added detail concerning their visit to the king reported uniquely in Æthelweard's *Chronicon*:

> in quorum aduectum cum rege pariter sinclitus ouat. Deinde Romam uestigia legunt ut soliti crebro Christi magistri petitum. Mentes ab inde Hierosolimis ire prætendunt.
>
> (the witan rejoiced equally with the king at their arrival. Then they directed their course to seek Rome as Christ's teachers are accustomed frequently to do. Their minds proposed going from there to Jerusalem.)[22]

The Irish monks brought news to Alfred of the death of the great Irish scholar and Clonmacnoise monk Suibhne, son of Máel Umai, apparently as the king was holding court in a formal meeting with his council in the west of Wessex.[23] The convergence in the *Chronicon*'s account of Alfred's contact with the furthest limits of Ireland and the plan of these monks from his court to make their way to Jerusalem presents a strikingly concrete analogue to Asser's description of Alfred at the centre of the daily business of government, while in contact with both furthest Ireland and Jerusalem.

---

19 See Pratt, 'The Illnesses of King Alfred the Great'.

20 See McCormick, *Charlemagne's Survey of the Holy Land*; Nelson, *King and Emperor*, pp. 449–53. See also Ottewill-Soulsby, "Abbāsid-Carolingian Diplomacy".

21 See MacLean, *Kingship and Politics*.

22 *Chronicon Æthelweardi*, ed. and trans. by Campbell, p. 48.

23 See *The Chronicle of Ireland*, ed. and trans. by Charles-Edwards, I, p. 338; Smyth, *Alfred the Great*, pp. 495–98.

A Mission to India?

Alfred's interest in Asia is also signalled by the entry *s.a.* 883 in the Anglo-Saxon Chronicle. The record does not appear in all the Chronicle versions, and where it does, the text has been disturbed in transmission, while even the date of the event it describes is a matter of discussion. Nevertheless, the annal points to an extraordinary journey undertaken by two English travellers at the end of the ninth century (D text):

> And Marinus papa sende þa lignum Domini Ælfrede cyninge, and þy ilcan geare lædde Sighelm and Æþelstan þa ælmessan to Rome þe Ælfred cyning gehet þyder, and eac on Indea to sancte Thome and to sancte Bartholomeae, þa hi sæton wið þone here æt Lundenne, and hy þær, Godes þances, swyðe bentigðe wurdon æfter þam gehatum.

> (And Pope Marinus sent some wood of the Cross to King Alfred. Sigehelm and Athelstan took to Rome — and also into India to St Thomas and to St Bartholomew — the alms which King Alfred had vowed to send there when they besieged the army in London; and there, by the grace of God, their prayers were well answered after those vows.)[24]

The entry is absent from the A version, which does not report the mission of Sigehelm and Athelstan, though A does record the restoration of the Mercian city of London in the annal for 886; the pope's gift and his death are recorded in A's annal for 885, which is also found in the other versions.[25] There is undoubtedly some confusion about the chroniclers' dates for events in the mid-880s, and while most versions here repeat the reference to his gift to King Alfred, it is now also noted for the first time in the A version (D text):

> Ðy ilcan geare forðfærde se goda papa Marinus, se gefreode Angelcynnes scole be Ælfredes bene, Westseaxena cyninges, and he sende him micla gifa and þære rode dæl þe Crist on þrowode.

> (In that same year the good pope Marinus died, who had freed the English school from taxation at the request of Alfred, king of the West Saxons, and he sent him great gifts and a part of the Cross on which Christ suffered.)

The Chronicle versions which included the 883 mission to India do not agree on all details: the closely related B and C texts do not include the

---

24 *The Anglo-Saxon Chronicle: MS D*, ed. by Cubbin, p. 28.
25 The journey is reported in the B, C, D, E, and F texts of the Chronicle, but not by Asser, St Neots, or Æthelweard; this pattern of agreement and divergence implies the absence of the detail from the common stock, and its inclusion not long after the A text diverged from the traditions represented by BCDE(F). See *The Anglo-Saxon Chronicle: MS A*, ed. by Bately, p. cvii.

phrase recording King Alfred's vow, and name *Iudea* rather than India as the destination. Richard Abels has noted that the events described in the 885 annal must predate 15 May 884, when Pope Marinus died.[26] Simon Keynes has argued that while the Chronicle versions appear to provide two separate dates for the taking of London (883 and 886), this can be accounted for by the possibility that London was successfully captured from the Danes in 883, and rebuilt in or by 886.[27] Three elements of the reported embassy of Sigehelm and Athelstan point to its reliability, despite the confusion of the Chronicles at this point: the annal's association of the journey with a known historical event — the taking of London from the Danes (in 883); the sending of alms to Rome, which conforms to (and may have initiated)[28] Alfred's known practice of sending annual gifts to Rome; and the association of the vow with the gift of the relic of the Cross to Alfred, indicative not only of his piety, but also of the spiritual dimension of both his campaign against the Danes and his international diplomacy.

I have suggested elsewhere that in the case of Bartholomew at least, the Mercian connection was strong, with indications, most notably in Felix's *Life of St Guthlac*, that Bartholomew was something of a patron saint in Mercia.[29] Thomas is not as easily explained. The 883 annal is not the only occasion on which the Chronicle indicates that a battle could be fought and won in alliance with powerful saints. In the account of the battle for London in 994, an occasion when the English were the defenders and the Danes the attackers, the Chronicle author (in the CDE versions) describes the unsuccessful assault made by Olaf Tryggvason and Swein Forkbeard on the Feast of the Nativity of St Mary (8 September) (C text):

> Ac hi þær geferdon maran hearm and yfel þonne hi æfre wendon þæt him ænig buruhwaru gedon sceolde. Ac seo halige Godes modor on þam dæge hire mildheortnesse þære buruhware gecydde and hi ahredde wið heora feondum.
>
> > (but there they suffered more harm and injury than they ever thought any citizens would do to them. For the holy Mother of God showed her mercy to the citizens on that day and saved them from their enemies.)[30]

In this light, is it possible that the references to Bartholomew and Thomas imply a reference to days of certain significance in the siege of London in 883?

---

26 Abels, *Alfred the Great*, p. 191, suggests the identification of Sigehelm with an ealdorman of Kent (and beneficiary of charter S 350) by the same name, and Athelstan with a court priest by the same name mentioned by Asser (ch. 77). Sigehelm of Kent became father-in-law of Edward the Elder (S 1211). Athelstan *sacerdos* attests S 350 and a number of other charters of Alfred and Edward.

27 Keynes, 'King Alfred and the Mercians', pp. 21–24.

28 As suggested by Abels, *Alfred the Great*, p. 190.

29 Anlezark, *Alfred the Great*, p. 56.

30 *The Anglo-Saxon Chronicle: MS C*, ed. by O'Brien O'Keeffe, p. 87.

St Bartholomew's Day is 24 August and St Thomas's 21 December, though we have no idea when during the year the campaign happened, or how long it took.[31] Nevertheless, there can be no doubt that the context of the retaking of London from Viking control is crucial to understanding what the mission of Sigehelm and Athelstan was about, and that the association of this victory with the patronage of the two apostles is not accidental.

Where Was 'India'?

While it is safe to assume that Sigehelm and Athelstan set out for 'India', a degree of caution must be exercised about where and what they and the Chronicler thought 'India' was, and whether they believed that both St Bartholomew and St Thomas might be found there. William Wordsworth's fantasy of Alfred as a precursor to nineteenth-century British imperialism simply equates the Chronicle's 'India' with that of his own imagining (Ecclesiastical Sonnets, no. xxvi, 'Alfred'):

> Though small his kingdom as a spark or gem
> Of Alfred boasts remote Jerusalem,
> And Christian India, through her widespread clime,
> In sacred converse gifts with Alfred shares.[32]

Alfred's kingdom was indeed small, but his 'India' was much larger than Wordsworth's and encompassed much of western Asia. It is difficult for us to know whether Anglo-Saxon readers drew a distinction between the more imaginative representations of Asia, such as those found in *Wonders* and *Alexander's Letter*, and more technical descriptions of Asia, such as that found in the geographic prologue to Orosius's *History*. Were these varying accounts read in different ways, some as fanciful imaginings of a faraway place, others as more credible? There is a discernible difference between, on the one hand, accounts of long ago, such as *Alexander's Letter* and *Solomon and Saturn II*, and on the other, *Wonders* and the Orosian geography, which claim to describe Asia in the present. But the line between these is not a demarcation between the sensational and the scientific.

In the early medieval geographical imagination 'India' covered far more territory than the Indian subcontinent, and in fact included much of north-western Asia. The Old English *Orosius* presents a full, if confusing, picture:

> Þæt sint India gemæro þær þær Caucasus se beorg is be norþan, and Indus seo ea be westan, and seo Reade Sæ be suþan ond garsecg be eastan. On Indea londe is xliiii þeoda buton þæm iglande Taprabane, þæt hæfð on him x byrg, buton oðerum monegum gesetenum iglondum. Of þære ie

---

31 See Keynes, 'King Alfred and the Mercians', p. 23.
32 Cited in Abels, *Alfred the Great*, p. 192.

Indus, þe be westan eallum þæm lande ligeð, betux þære ie Indus and þære þe be westan hiere is, Tigris hatte, þa flowað buta suþ on þone Readan Sæ, and betux þæm twæm ean sindon þas land: Arocasia and Parthia and Asilia and Persiða and Meðia, þeh þe gewrito oft nemnen eal þa lond Meðia oþþe Asiria; and þa lond sindon swiþe beorhtte, and þær sint swiþe scearpe wegas and stanihte; Þara landa norþgemæro sindon æt ðæm beorgum Caucasus, and on suþhealfe se Reada Sæ; and on ðæm londe sindon twa micla ea, Iþaspes and Arbis. On ðæm londe is xxxii þeoda. Nu hæt hit mon eall Parthia.

(The limits of India are the Caucasus mountains in the north, and the River Indus to the west, and the Red Sea to the south, and the ocean to the east. In the land of India there are forty-four nations, not including the island of Taprabane [Sri Lanka], which has in it ten cities, not including many other inhabited islands. From the Indus River, which flows on the western side of that entire land, and the river that lies to the west of it, called the Tigris, which both flow south into the Red Sea, are these lands: Arachosia, Parthia, Assyria, Persia, and Media, though texts often designate the whole land Media or Assyria. Those lands are very mountainous, and the roads there are rough and stony. The northern limits of those lands are the Caucasus Mountains, and on the south boundary is the Red Sea, and in that land there are two great rivers, the Hydaspes and the Arbis. There are thirty-two nations in that land. People now call it Parthia.)[33]

The Old English text greatly expands on the summary of world geography in the Latin original, drawing on a range of sources, at times with confusion.[34] The omission here of any reference to the Ganges (which is described in the Latin original) means that only the western part of 'India' (an arc extending from modern Pakistan through Iran to Turkey) is described.[35] However, neither the Indus (which empties into the Arabian Sea) nor the Tigris (which empties into the Persian Gulf) flows into the Red Sea as suggested, the imagined location of which cannot correlate to its actual geographical position. 'India' does not incorporate Asian lands west of the Tigris, including Babylonia, Chaldea, and Mesopotamia, which lie between the Tigris and the Euphrates, bounded to the north by the Taurus and the Caucasus Mountains, and south by the Red Sea. The Red Sea was understood to lie alongside Arabia, though from a modern viewpoint the various locations implied for the Red Sea are impossible. The region of 'Syria', which included Palestine, Damascus, Judea, and 'Saracene', was understood to lie south and west of Mesopotamia. To the

---

33 *The Old English Orosius*, ed. by Bately, i.i, pp. 9–10.
34 See *The Old English Orosius*, ed. by Bately, p. lxvi.
35 See *Orose: Histoires contre les païens*, ed. by Arnaud-Lindet, 1.2.9, I, p. 15.

north of this region and across the Taurus Mountains lay Armenia, and to the west of Armenia, Cappadocia and Asia Minor.

The Asian geography of the Old English *Orosius* offers a useful reference point for other accounts of 'India' in Old English texts. The geographic catalogue at the opening of *Solomon and Saturn II* — discussed in detail by Rachel Burns in her chapter in this volume — describes this Chaldean prince's wide wanderings in search of wisdom, first listing *Indea mere* (the land of the Indians, l. 8). All that is necessarily implied, however, is a crossing of the Euphrates from his home in Chaldea to the 'Indian' side of the river. The geographic account of *Wonders* includes greater detail than the Orosian geography about the more exciting creatures and peoples to be found in parts of Asia, though the two accounts harmonize. The description in *Wonders* of the geographical origin of pepper vaguely locates its production in the enlarged India of the medieval imagination (§ 6):

On sumon lande assan beoð akende þa habbað swa micle hornas swa oxan. Þa syndon on ðam mæstan westene þæt is on ða suð healfe fram Babilonia. Þa bugað to þære Readan Sæ, for ðæra næddrena mænigeo þe in ðam stowum beoð þa hattan Corsias. Ða habbað swa micle hornas swa weðeras. Gyf hi hwylcne monn sleað oððe æthrinað þonne swylt he sona. On ðam londum byð piperes genihtsumnys. Þone pipor þa næddran healdað on hyra geornfulnysse. Ðone pipor mon swa nimeð þæt mon þa stowe mid fyre onæleð ond þonne ða næddran of dune on eorðan þæt hi fleoð; forðan se pipor byð sweart. Fram Babilonia oð Persiam þa burh ðær se pipor weaxet is þæs læssan milgetæles þe stadia hatte eahta hund milia. Of þam is geteald þæs miclan milgetæles þe leuua hatte syx hund ond III ond XX ond I healf mil. Seo stow is unwæstmberendlicu for þæra næddrena menigeo.

(In a certain land donkeys are born which have great horns like oxen. They are in the vast desert that is in the southern region of Babylonia. They escape to the Red Sea because of the multitude of snakes called Corsias which are in those areas. They have great horns like rams. If they hit or touch anyone, then he immediately dies. In those lands there is a great abundance of pepper. The snakes guard that pepper because of their desire. To take the pepper a fire is kindled in that place and the snakes flee the fire down under the ground; that is why pepper is black. From Babylon to the city in Persia where the pepper grows is eight hundred units of the smaller measurement called *stadia*. It is calculated at six hundred and twenty-three and half units of the bigger measurement called *leuuae*. The place is infertile because of the multitude of snakes.)[36]

---

36 Orchard, *Pride and Prodigies*, pp. 186–88.

The author's grasp of the geography involved is loose, and it is unclear whether Persia is imagined to lie north or south of Babylonia, though the area described corresponds with the 'India' of the Old English *Orosius*, which undoubtedly includes Persia, lying between the Tigris and the Indus Rivers.

The Apostles and India

The Chronicle entry for 883 implies a number of associations, which in turn leave us with an important question: What is the association between the saints to whom Alfred made his vow and the siege of London, and what is these apostles' association with 'India'? It is possible that their feast days were of significance, but such a coincidence might not necessarily justify a pilgrimage to the other end of the world. Indeed, what is the implied destination of the two travellers, that is, where were the resting places of Bartholomew and Thomas,[37] is a question which seems to have caused some confusion in the BC text of the Chronicle (which places them in Judea). The two apostles were closely associated in apocryphal legend as missionaries to India. Their entries in the ninth-century Old English *Martyrology* give us an indication of how they might have figured in contemporary historical, ecclesiastical, and geographic imagination. Legend reports that St Thomas (21 December) set out from Jerusalem after Christ's ascension (Luke 24, Acts 1) and travelled across the large 'India' of medieval geography, converting pagans and overthrowing idols before his martyrdom:

> And æfter Crystes upastigennysse he gelærde monige þeode to Crystes geleafan, Warðwara and Medware and Perswaren and Hyrcanas and Bactrianas and twa Indea mægðe. And he þurhferde hæðenre þeode eorð and myddangeardes eastdæl [...]. Ac on oðre Indea mægðe Mygdæg se cyning and hys ealdorman se wæs on naman Caritius, he nydde þysne Thomum þæt he weorðode sunnan deofolgyld [...]. Þa þome þæder in eode, þa eode þær egeslic deofol ut of þam goldgeweorce and stod beforan hym, and þæt goldgeweorc eall todreas, swa swa weax gemylt æt fyre. Þa þæra hæðenra bysceopa sum ofsloh þone Crystes þegn, and gewrytu secgað hwylum þæt he wære myd sweorde þurhstungen, hwylum hig secgað þæt he wære mid sperum ofsticod. He þrowode in Calamina on Indea ceastre, and hys lychama wæs alæded of Indeum on þa ceastre þe ys nemned Edyssa.

> (And after Christ's ascension he instructed many nations in Christ's faith: the Parthians and the Medes and the Persians and the Hyrcanians and the Bactrians and two Indian nations. And he travelled through the lands of pagan people and the eastern part of the world [...].

---

37 On early medieval English interest in the cult of St Thomas, see the chapter by Luisa Ostacchini in this volume.

But in another Indian country King Mygdeus and his governor, whose name was Caritius, forced this Thomas to worship the devil-idol of the sun […]. When Thomas went in there, a horrible devil came out from the golden structure and stood before him, and the golden structure completely disintegrated, just as wax melts near a fire. One of the pagan bishops then killed the servant of Christ, and the texts sometimes say that he was stabbed with a sword, sometimes they say he was stabbed with spears. He suffered in the city of Calamina in India, and his body was removed from India to the city that is called Edessa.)[38]

The places in India now associated by tradition with Thomas are Muziris on the Malabar Coast (in modern Kerala State), where he is believed to have landed, and Mylapore (Chennai), the place of his martyrdom.[39] The Edessa referred to in the *Martyrology* is a city that was then placed in Syria, and now the site of the Turkish city of Urfa. By Late Antiquity, Edessa was an important centre of the Syriac church, and it is probably here that the first *Acts of Thomas* were created by the third of fourth century at the latest; there is inconclusive evidence that these build on traditions composed in the second century.[40] The *Acts* describe Thomas's mission to India and his martyrdom there, before the translation of his relics to Edessa in the third century. The tomb of St Thomas in Edessa was visited by the late fourth-century traveller Egeria (from Gaul), who reports that his whole body rested there ('ubi corpus illius integrum positus est').[41] Egeria reports the *martyrium* that she saw:

> peruenimus in nomine Christi Dei nostri Edessam. Vbi cum peruenissimus, statim perreximus ad ecclesiam et ad martyrium sancti Thomae. Itaque ergo iuxta consuetudinem factis orationibus et cetera, quae consuetudo erat fieri in locis sanctis, nec non etiam et aliquanta ipsius sancit Thomae ibi legimus. Ecclesia autem, ibi que est, ingens et ualde pulchra et noua dispositione, et uere digna est esse domus Dei; et quoniam multa erant, quae ibi desiderabam uidere, necesse me fuit ibi statiua triduana facere.

> (we reached Edessa in the name of Christ our God. When we arrived, we immediately proceeded to the church and tomb of Saint Thomas. There, according to custom, prayers are offered and the other things customary in the holy places were done, and we also read certain things about Saint Thomas himself. The church there is enormous and very beautiful and of new construction, and truly worthy to be a house of God, and as there was much which I desired to see, it was necessary for me to stay there for three days.)[42]

---

38 *The Old English Martyrology*, ed. and trans. by Rauer, p. 167.
39 See Frykenberg, *Christianity in India*, pp. 92–110.
40 See Frykenberg, *Christianity in India*, p. 93.
41 'Itinerarium Egeriae', ed. by Francheschini and Weber, XVII.2, p. 58.
42 'Itinerarium Egeriae', ed. by Francheschini and Weber, XIX.2–3, p. 59.

The city was long under the rule of Roman and then Byzantine emperors, but came under the dominion of the Rashidun Caliphate in 638 and after this remained under Muslim rule, though it was besieged by a Byzantine army in 944.[43] In the late ninth century it would have been a difficult destination for Western pilgrims, though not an impossible one. Strictly speaking, Edessa, certainly in Asia, was not located in India according to early medieval geography, but rather in Mesopotamia, between the upper reaches of both the Tigris and Euphrates Rivers. However, as we have seen, Anglo-Saxon geographic awareness did not always map precisely.

Nevertheless, the association of St Thomas with the land that we now call India was maintained,[44] and the places associated with his martyrdom and first burial near Chennai still draw pilgrims. Gregory of Tours (d. 594) records a visit to this locale in the later sixth century, relying on the direct report of a traveller who had been to India:

> Thomas apostolus, secundum passionis eius historiam, in India passus esse declaratur. Cuius beatum corpus post multum tempus assumptum in civitate, quam Syriae Edissam vocant, translatum est, ibique sepultum. Ergo in loco regionis Indiae, quo prius quievit, monasterium habetur, et templum mirae magnitudinis, diligenterque exornatum atque compositum […]. Hoc Theodorus qui ad ipsum locum accessit, nobis exposuit.
>
> (The apostle Thomas, according to the history of his passion, is said to have suffered in India. After a great amount of time, his blessed body was taken to the city called Edessa in Syria, moved and buried there. In that region of India where he had first been buried there are a monastery and a church that is spectacularly large and carefully decorated and constructed […]. Theodorus, who visited the spot, told this to me.)[45]

Gregory is careful to distinguish the place in India where Thomas was martyred from his resting place in Edessa in Syria. Theodorus's name strongly implies that he was Greek, and his reason for visiting the Indian subcontinent is not given, though most likely it was connected with trade.

Apocryphal traditions describe Bartholomew journeying to 'India' and dying there, with some vagueness about where his martyrdom took place. The Old English *Martyrology* describes his work converting the inhabitants of India (including a king), followed by the destruction of idols, which leads to the apostle's death:

---

43 Treadgold, *A History of the Byzantine State and Society*, pp. 484–85.

44 For example, Aldhelm reports Thomas's martyrdom in India, with no reference to his final resting place: Aldhelm, *De virginitate*, ed. by Ehwald, pp. 211–323, at p. 255, ll. 16–25.

45 Gregory of Tours, *Libri miraculorum*, col. 733; Gregory of Tours, *Glory of the Martyrs*, ed. and trans. by Van Dam, p. 51. The work was finished *c*. 590.

Se wæs Cristes ærendwreca in India mægþe, seo is ealra eorðena seo ytemyste, ond on oþre healfe ys þystre land, on oþre healfe se sæ Oceanum, þæt is garsecg. [...] Þa foron ða hæþnan bisceopas ond ðæt wregdon to ðæs kyninges breþer, se wæs on oþrum kynerice ond he wæs yldra ðonne he. Þa het se forþon Bartholomeus ðone Cristes þegen cwicne beflean. Ða com se gelyfeda kyning mid micle folce ond genom his lichaman ond hine þanon alædde mid micle wuldre ond hine gesette in wundorlice micle cyrcean. Ond se cyng awedde se þe hine cwellan het, ond ealle ða hæþenan bisceopas aweddan ond swulton þa ðe in þære lare wæron.

> (He was Christ's missionary in the country of India, which is the outermost of all the regions, on whose one side lies the dark land, on whose other side lies the world Ocean, that is *garsecg*. [...] Then the pagan bishops went and complained about that to the king's brother; he was in another kingdom, and he was older than he was. He therefore ordered Bartholomew, the servant of Christ, to be flayed alive. Then the believing king came with many people and took his body and transported it away with great splendour, and put it in a fantastically large church. And the king became insane, who wanted him killed, and all the pagan bishops became insane and died, who had reported him.)[46]

The account in the Roman *Martyrology*, followed by Bede, offers more details, describing Bartholomew travelling to 'Albania', that is, Armenia, where he was martyred.[47] This version of events is included the Old English *Fates of the Apostles* (ll. 42–48a):

Huru, wide wearð   wurd undyrne
þæt to Indeum   aldre gelædde
beaducræftig beorn,   Bartholameus!
Þone heht Astrias   in Albano,
hæðen ond hygeblind,   heafde beneotan,
forþan he ða hæðengild   hyran ne wolde,
wig weorðian.

> (Certainly, it has widely been no secret that Bartholomew, a soldier skilled in battle, went to live among the people of India. In Armenia, the heathen and spiritually blind Astrages ordered him to be beheaded, because he would not listen to heathendom, worship an idol.)[48]

However, the place of Bartholomew's martyrdom is a moot point; the question is, where in the late ninth century could he be found? Bartholomew's relics

---

46 *The Old English Martyrology*, ed. and trans. by Rauer, p. 227.
47 *Edition practique des martyrologes de Bede*, ed. by Dubois and Renaud, p. 223.
48 *Andreas and the Fates of the Apostles*, ed. by Brooks, p. 57.

were as restless as those of Thomas, though they enjoyed a more complicated and fantastic journey westwards. Again, Gregory of Tours is informative:

> Bartholomaeum apostolum apud Indiam passum, agonis ipsius narrat historia. Post multorum vero annorum spatia de passione eius, cum iterum Christianis persecutio advenisset, et viderent gentiles omnem populum ad eius sepulcrum concurrere, eique deprecationes assidue et incensa deferre, invidia illecti, abstulerunt corpus eius, et ponentes in sarcophagum plumbeum, proiecerunt illud in mare, dicentes: Quia non seduces amplius populum nostrum. Sed providentia Dei cooperante per secretum operis eius, sarcophagum plumbeum a loco illo aquis subvehentibus sublevatum, delatum est ad insulam, vocabulo Liparis. Revelatumque est Christianis, ut eum colligerent: collectumque ac sepultum, aedificaverunt super cum templum magnum. In quo nunc invocatus, prodesse populis multis virtutibus ac beneficiis manifestat.

> > (The history of his struggles states that the apostle Bartholomew was martyred in Asia. Many years after his martyrdom another persecution troubled the Christians. The pagans saw that everyone rushed to the tomb of Bartholomew and regularly offered prayers and incense. Blinded by jealousy, the pagans stole his body and put it into a sarcophagus made of lead. As they threw the sarcophagus into the sea, they said: 'No longer will you mislead our people'. But the providence of God was at work in his marvellous benevolence. The lead sarcophagus was carried by the waves and floated from that land until it came to an island called Lipari. It was revealed to the Christians that they acquire the sarcophagus; having done so, they buried it and built a large church over it. Whenever Bartholomew is invoked in this church, it is obvious from the many miracles and blessings that he assists the people.)[49]

The island of Lipari, however, was not to be Bartholomew's final resting place. The *Chronicle of Salerno*, a history of the Duchy of Salerno for the period 774 to 974, provides an account of the translation of Bartholomew's relics from Lipari to the city of Benevento in 838. The main actor was the notorious Prince Sikard of Benevento, the local ruler of Lipari (832–839), which was under threat from Muslim pirates (and with whom he was at times willing to cooperate): 'atque per idem tempus ex insula Liparitana Bartholomei beati apostoli corpus Beneventum cum magno tripudio deferri iussit' (and around the same time, he commanded the transfer of the body of the blessed Apostle Bartholomew with great pomp from the island of Lipari to Benevento).[50] Today Benevento, the principal city of the ancient Duchy of Beneventum,

---

49 Gregory of Tours, *Libri miraculorum*, col. 734; Gregory of Tours, *Glory of the Martyrs*, ed. and trans. by Van Dam, pp. 55–56.
50 *Chronicon salernitanum*, ed. by Westerberg, p. 71; Rose, 'Reinventing the Apostolic Tradition', p. 133.

is a regional centre in the mountains behind Naples, and St Bartholomew's reputed relics remain there. In the early Middle Ages it lay on the Appian Way, the principal route south through central Italy; at Benevento the Way divided, and the traveller could either reach a southern port by continuing on the Appian Way to Taranto and Brindisi, or reach the Adriatic coast more directly by taking the Via Traiana to Bari. From this port the traveller had access to all routes east across the Mediterranean.

The legends of both Thomas and Bartholomew focus on overthrowing idolatry, converting kings, and winning people for Christ. Both accounts offer a broad parallel to the historical action of the Christian Anglo-Saxons retaking London from the pagan Danes, engaged in an analogous spiritual battle. The adoption of these saints as patrons of the siege presents a spiritual context for the siege, harmonizing with an ideological element evident in an earlier first phase of Alfred's successful military campaign, which culminated in the baptism of King Guthrum at Whitsunday in 878. Alfred's wars against the Vikings included an evangelical element, winning both people and territory for Christ. The adoption of these two saints as patrons of the siege of London may be understood in this light, though this alignment of purpose does not offer a full explanation given that many other saints, apostles among them, broke idols and converted pagans.

To date there has been no discussion of where Sigehelm and Athelstan might have intended to find St Bartholomew, and there is confusion about where they might have looked for St Thomas.[51] The phrasing of the 883 Chronicle entry is ambiguous on this point, though perhaps not intentionally: the travellers will journey to Rome, and then 'on Indea to sancte Thome and to sancte Bartholomeae' (into India to St Thomas and to St Bartholomew). As we have seen, in the West in the late ninth century neither of these apostles rested in India according to either a medieval or modern understanding of geography, though Thomas's tomb in Edessa lay close to 'India', near the geographic meeting point of Syria, Mesopotamia, and 'India'. The Old English *Martyrology* entry makes it clear that the removal of St Thomas's body to Edessa meant that it left India, though there is no reason to assume that the geography implied was fully or widely understood. It would be surprising if St Bartholomew's final resting place in the city of Benevento was unknown to the Anglo-Saxon traveller. It is likely not only that the annal for 883 records the historical fact that the two Anglo-Saxon travellers set out on their journey, but that the intention to bring a gift to St Bartholomew also provides a clue about their itinerary: after delivering the gift in Rome (a payment probably tied to releasing English traders from local taxation), they then travelled through central Italy down the Appian Way to Benevento, before making their way to the Adriatic port of Bari, where they could join a ship for the East.

---

51 See Abels, *Alfred the Great*, p. 192.

A comparable pilgrimage is described in the itinerary of the Frankish monk Bernard, who travelled to Jerusalem at the end of the 860s on a route which took him through Rome and southern Italy, then across the Mediterranean to Alexandria, and ultimately to Jerusalem.[52] Bernard makes no mention of passing through Benevento — the Italian part of his journey after leaving Rome is not fully described — though one of his companions was from the city.[53] On his return Bernard produced an itinerary, providing many useful tips for the pilgrim, including the cost of various imposts to be paid to local officials, and noting their relative value for securing safe travel. Bernard and his companions sailed east from Bari, then under Muslim rule. As has been noted above, the Emirate of Bari was destroyed in 871 through the combined efforts of Emperor Louis II and a Byzantine fleet. This change of local rulers in Bari did not alter the shape of the southern, maritime route to Jerusalem, via Alexandria and 'Babylon in Egypt' (that is, the city of Fustat, now absorbed by modern-day Cairo), then north across Gaza and into Palestine. The passage and route of pilgrims, Christian and Muslim, was tightly controlled by local authorities, and Bernard's itinerary details how to travel it, including a description of the large camel rental market at al Farama. The politics of the region shifted around the time of Bernard's journey, with the appointment of Ahmad ibn Tulun as governor of Egypt in 868. Ibn Tulun quickly established an independent Egyptian army, founded his own capital at al-Qata'i, north of Fustat, and began to defy the authority of the Abbasid Caliphate. As has been noted, ibn Tulun's declaration in Egypt of independence in 873 significantly altered the treatment of Christians in this part of the Islamic East. This development offers a meaningful context for the correspondence between Patriarch Elias and King Alfred and other Western rulers.

We cannot be completely certain, however, that Alexandria would have been the first eastern destination of Sigehelm and Athelstan. If they indeed intended to visit St Thomas in Edessa, then a northern route to Asia Minor might have been followed. The *Hodoeporicon* of St Willibald, written in the 780s, describes his pilgrimage to the Holy Land in the mid-720s.[54] Both Willibald and the author of the *Hodoeporicon*, the nun Huneberc, were English missionaries in Germany. Willibald's narration describes his journey from Rome, first down the west coast of Italy to Naples, a maritime route which had become perilous by the late ninth century. In southern Italy Willibald joined a ship from Egypt which took him to Sicily, and then Greece and Asia Minor, where they visited the tomb of St John the Evangelist at Ephesus. After reaching Mount Chelidonium (modern Cape Gelidonya), his group turned

---

52 Wilkinson, *Jerusalem Pilgrims before the Crusades*, pp. 261–69. See Halevi, 'Bernard, Explorer of the Muslim Lake'.

53 Wilkinson, *Jerusalem Pilgrims before the Crusades*, p. 261, 'Blessed Vincentius of Beneventum'.

54 'The Hodoeporicon of St Willibald', ed. and trans. by Talbot, pp. 159–62. See Limor, 'Pilgrims and Authors'.

south to Cyprus, after which they crossed to Palestine. This route bypassed the northern Syrian ports that might have given access to Edessa, and the paucity of evidence means we have no way of knowing if such a route was even viable for the Western pilgrim in the 880s.

The pilgrimage route across the Mediterranean to Alexandria was better established at the time, as Bernard attests. If this is where Sigehelm and Athelstan headed, we can only speculate where they might have planned to go next, given that we are uncertain about where they though St Thomas might be found. Their more likely direction from Alexandria would be east and north towards Jerusalem, with the hope of reaching St Thomas either in Edessa by travelling through Syria, or in India via the Persian Gulf, on a well-established trade route.[55] On such a journey they would have relied on the hospitality of the Christian communities found throughout the region, and perhaps letters of introduction provided by Patriarch Elias, whose personal connections as a member of the prominent Mansour family would have been extensive across the region. Alternatively, but perhaps less likely, they could have travelled east and south, via the Red and Arabian Seas, to St Thomas and the Indian subcontinent. However, a remarkable account survives of the Irish pilgrim Fidelis, who visited the Red Sea sometime before the year 825, probably around the year 800, and reported his journey to the Irish Carolingian scholar Dicuil.[56] Dicuil's *Liber de mensura orbis terrae* briefly describes Fidelis's journey from Italy to Egypt with a group of pilgrims bound for Jerusalem. After arriving in Egypt, however, Fidelis travelled south as far as the Red Sea, though maybe no further than the Gulf of Aqaba. If the two Anglo-Saxon travellers went this way, they could have headed south from Fustat, following the caravan route south to the Red Sea. Sailing south, they probably would not have disembarked at Jeddah with Muslim pilgrims, but could have continued around the Arabian coast, and finally across the Arabian Sea, as far as the Malabar Coast of India. This route was one of those used by Jewish traders bringing goods from India to France.[57]

Why the Journey?

There is no doubt that the taking of London represented an important strategic victory for King Alfred. The 883 Chronicle entry presents this victory in a context which invites a spiritual reading of the course of events, not only with reference to the king's vow to the two apostles, but also through the association of this moment with the gift from Pope Marinus to Alfred of a

---

55 See Hall, 'International Trade and Foreign Diplomacy'.
56 Dicuil, *Liber de Mensura*, ed. by Tierney, VI.12–18, p. 62. McCormick, *Origins of the European Economy*, pp. 692, 911, notes the journeys of Sigehelm and Athelstan with this connection.
57 As described by Ibn Khordadbeh, see Adler, *Jewish Travellers*, pp. 2–3; see also Gil, 'The Rādhānite Merchants'.

ALFRED AND THE EAST

fragment of Christ's victorious Cross. The Chronicle's second entry about the taking of London strikes a different note (D886):

> Her for se here eft west þe ær east gelende, and þa up on Sigene, and þær wintersetl namon æt Paris þære byrig. Ðy ilcan geare gesette Ælfred cyning Lundenburh, and him eall Ængelcyn to gecyrde þæt butan Dæniscra manna hæftnede wæs, and he þa befæste þa burh Æþelrede ealdorman to healdenne.
>
> > (In this year the [Danish] army which had previously gone east went west again, and then up the Seine, and seized winter quarters there at the city of Paris. In the same year King Alfred established the city of London, and all the people of the Angles [or 'English'], except those subjugated by the Danes, submitted to him, and he entrusted the city to ealdorman Æthelred's control.)[58]

As noted above, Keynes has argued that the annals for 883 and 886 probably represent two distinct moments: the military victory, and the restoration of the city. The taking and re-establishment of the important Mercian port, brought under the shared dominion of the West Saxon king and his Mercian ealdorman son-in-law, offered new possibilities for trade and wealth for London's citizens and those who taxed them.[59] We catch a glimpse of the importance of trade in Alfred's renewal of the English economy in the annal for 885, which reports both the death of Pope Marinus and with it the pope's promise to release the English Quarter in Rome from taxation. Richard Abels has convincingly suggested that the exchanges between pope and king should be dated to 883, and that the 'gift' sent to Rome was part of a settlement in which a tax exemption was granted to the English Quarter in Rome, compensated by an annual gift to the Holy See.[60]

English trade across the Alps into Italy appears to have been alive and well at the time, and Michael McCormick has noted that there is evidence that 'in the later ninth century, Anglo-Saxon merchants still traded with northern Italy, and perhaps as far south as Rome'.[61] The *Honorantie civitatis Pavie*, drawn up around the year 1000, details the operations and rights of the royal treasury of the kingdom of the Lombards. The *Honorantie* reports that English merchants once rioted when forced to open their baggage at the customs crossing into the kingdom. The English king negotiated a general customs duties exemption for English merchants entering Italy, which included an annual fee of fifty

---

58 See Naismith, *Citadel of the Saxons*, p. 107, on the meaning of *gesette* in this context. Asser, close to the event, and using the Chronicle as his source, describes how Alfred 'restored' ('restauravit') the city, and adds that Alfred made it 'habitable again' ('habitabilem fecit').

59 On the varying fortunes of London as a trading centre across the eighth and ninth centuries, see Naismith, *Citadel of the Saxons*, pp. 90–103. Keynes, 'King Alfred and the Mercians', pp. 21–24.

60 Abels, *Alfred the Great*, p. 191.

61 McCormick, *Origins of the European Economy*, p. 679.

pounds of refined silver, among other things. McCormick notes that the phrasing of the document implies that this king was either Alfred or Edward the Elder, and argues that Alfred's negotiation of a tax exemption in Rome in the early 880s 'reinforces the likelihood that the treaty stems from this time'.[62] The king's willingness to ease international trade is noteworthy, while Pope Marinus himself benefited from a trade network that extended across the Mediterranean as far east as Byzantium.[63] Alfred's interest in international trade is also likely to be indicated by the accounts of the northern travellers Ohthere and Wulfstan, incorporated into the geographical preface of the Old English version of Orosius's *History*. In the *Orosius*, Ohthere's description of trade routes and commodities along the Norwegian coast and as far as the White Sea is framed as a report to 'his lord Alfred'.[64]

The restoration of London signalled in the annal for 886 was an ongoing project, and trade was an important motivation, as shown by two charters, one from 889 and the other from a decade later.[65] The later of the two, datable to either 898 or 899, records a meeting concerning 'the restoration of the city of London' ('de instauratione urbis Lundonie') held at Chelsea between Alfred, Ealdorman Æthelred, the Lady Æthelflæd (Alfred's daughter and Æthelred's wife), and the Bishops of Canterbury and Worcester, reflecting the balance of Mercian and southern interests in control over London that is also found in the annal for 886.[66] Together, the charters of 889 and 898/99 describe large land grants to the bishops, either side of what is called the 'public street' ('uia publica') running north–south between them, and bisected by the city walls running east–west. The estate of the Bishop of Worcester described in the earlier charter was situated around an 'old stone building' ('antiquum petrosum ædificium') extending to a 'public street' and grants the bishop rights to tolls on trade in the street and on the 'mercantile rivershore' ('ripa emtorali').[67] The later charter describes the location of these estates as *Ætheredeshythe* (Æthelred's 'hythe', or landing-place). The charter describes an important moment in the process of rebuilding the port of London, now provided with a new dock, with the bishops granted access to and revenue from the renewed trade.[68]

---

62 McCormick, *Origins of the European Economy*, pp. 622, 679.

63 McCormick, *Origins of the European Economy*, p. 607.

64 *The Old English Orosius*, ed. by Bately, I.i, p. 13, l. 29.

65 See Naismith, *Citadel of the Saxons*, pp. 122–23.

66 Naismith, *Citadel of the Saxons*, p. 122.

67 Naismith, *Citadel of the Saxons*, p. 123.

68 See Naismith, *Citadel of the Saxons*, pp. 75–76, who notes this is 'the very area where waterfront excavations have found traces of Alfredian-period building' (p. 123).

Conclusion

If we accept that Alfred sent Sigehelm and Athelstan on a journey through Italy to 'India', it is important to ask why he did so. There is no doubt that piety played a role. But for Alfred piety, politics, and economics were not easily separated. This blend of the material and the transcendent is seen in Alfred's most tangible connection with Asia, the priceless fragment of Christ's Cross given to him by Pope Marinus, a gift also full of spiritual significance. Alfred was interested in trade, and the mission to the east emerges directly from the English recapture of Mercia's principal trading port. The first important port of call for Sigehelm and Athelstan was Rome — as it was for all travellers to the east. The monetary gift that they brought to Rome emerges as part of a wider strategy being implemented by the king to facilitate trade between England and Italy. It is in this economic context that gifts of alms to St Bartholomew and St Thomas might also be understood. St Bartholomew rested in the principal city of Lombard Benevento on the important trade route through southern Italy, on the way to the trading port of Bari, at a time when Carolingian control of the region was collapsing and Byzantine dominance was waning. We cannot be sure exactly where the two Anglo-Saxons intended to go next, but their general intention of travelling to 'India', an important source of luxury goods, invites the conclusion that their pilgrimage was designed to mix matters of business with the divine. This is certainly the assumption of William of Malmesbury, who more than two centuries later (probably mistakenly) identified the pilgrim Sigehelm as a later bishop of Sherborne:

> Sigehelmus trans mare causa elemosinarum regis et etiam ad sanctum Thomam in Indiam missus, mira prosperitate, quod quiuis hoc seculo miretur, Indiam penetrauit, indeque rediens exotici generis gemmas, quarum illa hums ferax est, reportauit. Nonnullae illarum adhuc in aecclesiae ornamentis uisuntur.

> > (Sigehelm was sent across the seas, to further the almsgiving of the king and also to visit St Thomas in India, successfully completing a journey that anyone nowadays might well regard with wonder. He brought back with him exotic gems of the kind abundant in that land; and some of them can be seen still, set in objects ornamenting the church.)[69]

The association between India and luxury goods in William's and his informants' minds is unsurprising, and was undoubtedly shared by King Alfred himself. Whether or not Alfred was an interested reader of *The Wonders of the East* or *Alexander's Letter*, we cannot know. Alfred's 'Asia' was a country of the mind,

---

69 William of Malmesbury, *Gesta Pontificum Anglorum*, I, ed. by Winterbottom, II.80.2, pp. 278–79. On the identification, see William of Malmesbury, *Gesta Pontificum Anglorum*, II, ed. by Thomson, pp. 122–23.

and may well have included the kind of wondrous elements found in these texts. However, we do know that the king was interested in trading with the world beyond his kingdom, small 'as a spark or gem', an interest that was far from abstract. We cannot know if Sigehelm and Athelstan succeeded in reaching St Thomas in India, or wherever they might have hoped to find him. But if they managed to return from their difficult journey, we can be sure that whatever else they might have reported to the king, they would have had much to say about the routes they had followed, and the merchandise that moved along them.

Works Cited

Primary Sources

Aldhelm, *De virginitate*, in *Aldhelmi opera*, ed. by Rudolf Ehwald, MGH: Auctores antiquissimi, 15 (Berlin: Weidmann, 1919), pp. 9–323

Alfred the Great: Asser's 'Life of Alfred' and Other Contemporary Sources, ed. and trans. by Simon Keynes and Michael Lapidge (Harmondsworth: Penguin, 1983)

Andreas and the Fates of the Apostles, ed. by Kenneth R. Brooks (Oxford: Clarendon Press, 1961)

The Anglo-Saxon Chronicle: A Collaborative Edition, III: *MS A*, ed. by Janet Bately (Cambridge: D. S. Brewer, 1986)

The Anglo-Saxon Chronicle: A Collaborative Edition, V: *MS C*, ed. by Katherine O'Brien O'Keeffe (Cambridge: D. S. Brewer, 2001)

The Anglo-Saxon Chronicle: A Collaborative Edition, VI: *MS D*, ed. by G. P. Cubbin (Cambridge: D. S. Brewer, 1996)

Asser's Life of King Alfred, together with the Annals of Saint Neots Erroneously Ascribed to Asser: New Imprint with Article on Recent Work by Dorothy Whitelock, ed. by W. H. Stevenson (Oxford: Clarendon Press, 1959)

The Chronicle of Ireland, ed. and trans. by T. M. Charles-Edwards, 2 vols, Translated Texts for Historians, 44 (Liverpool: Liverpool University Press, 2006)

Chronicon Æthelweardi (The Chronicle of Æthelweard), ed. and trans. by A. Campbell (London: Thomas Nelson, 1962)

Chronicon salernitanum, ed. by Ulla Westerberg, Studia latina Stockholmiensia, 3 (Stockholm: Almqvist and Wiksell, 1956)

Dicuil, *Liber de Mensura Orbis Terrae*, ed. by James J. Tierney, Scriptores Latini Hiberniae, 6 (Dublin: Institute of Advanced Studies, 1967)

Edition practique des martyrologes de Bede, de l'Anonyme lyonnais et de Florus, ed. by J. Dubois and G. Renaud (Paris: Editions du Centre national de la recherche scientifique, 1976)

Gregory of Tours, *Glory of the Martyrs*, ed. and trans. by Raymond Van Dam (Liverpool: Liverpool University Press, 1988)

——, *Libri miraculorum*, PL, 71 (Paris: Garnier, 1879), cols 705–828

'The Hodoeporicon of St Willibald', ed. and trans. by C. H. Talbot, in *The Anglo-Saxon Missionaries in Germany: Being the Lives of SS. Willibrord, Boniface, Sturm, Leoba and Lebuin, Together with the Hodoeporicon of St Willibald and a Selection from the Correspondence of St Boniface* (London: Sheed and Ward, 1954), pp. 153–77

'Itinerarium Egeriae', ed. by A. Francheschini and R. Weber, in *Itineraria et alia geographica: Itineraria Hierosolymitana, Itineraria Romana, Geographica*, ed. by P. Geyer, O. Cuntz, A. Francheschini, R. Weber, L. Bieler, J. Fraipont, and F. Glorie, CCSL, 175 (Turnhout: Brepols, 1965), pp. 37–90

Leechdoms, Wortcunning, and Starcraft of Early England, ed. by T. O. Cockayne, 3 vols (repr. New York: Kraus, 1965)

The Old English Dialogues of Solomon and Saturn, ed. and trans. by Daniel Anlezark, Anglo-Saxon Texts, 7 (Cambridge: D. S. Brewer, 2009)

The Old English Martyrology: Edition, Translation and Commentary, ed. and trans. by Christine Rauer (Cambridge: D. S. Brewer, 2013)

The Old English Orosius, ed. by Janet Bately, EETS SS, 6 (London: Oxford University Press, 1980)

Orose: Histoires contre les païens, ed. by Marie-Pierre Arnaud-Lindet, Collection des Universités de France, 3 vols (Paris: Les Belles Lettres, 1990–1991)

William of Malmesbury, *Gesta Pontificum Anglorum*, I: *Text and Translation*, ed. by Michael Winterbottom (Oxford: Clarendon Press, 2007)

——, *Gesta Pontificum Anglorum*, II: *Introduction and Commentary*, ed. by R. M. Thomson (Oxford: Clarendon Press, 2007)

Secondary Sources

Abels, Richard, *Alfred the Great: War, Kingship and Culture in Anglo-Saxon England* (New York: Longman, 1998)

Adler, E. N., *Jewish Travellers in the Middle Ages* (New York: Dover, 1987)

Anlezark, Daniel, *Alfred the Great* (Kalamazoo: ARC Medieval Press, 2017)

Frykenberg, R. E., *Christianity in India: From the Beginnings to the Present* (Oxford: Oxford University Press, 2008)

Gil, Moshe, *A History of Palestine, 634–1099*, trans. by E. Broido (Cambridge: Cambridge University Press, 1992)

——, 'The Rādhānite Merchants and the Land of Rādhān', *Journal of the Economic and Social History of the Orient*, 17 (1974), 299–328

Godden, Malcolm, 'The Old English *Orosius* and its Context: Who Wrote it, for Whom, and Why?', *Quaestio Insularis*, 12 (2012), 1–30

Griffith, S. H., 'The Manṣūr Family and Saint John of Damascus: Christians and Muslims in Umayyad Times', in *Christians and Others in the Umayyad State*, ed. by A. Borrut and F. M. Donner (Chicago: The Oriental Institute of the University of Chicago, 2016), pp. 29–51

Halevi, Leor, 'Bernard, Explorer of the Muslim Lake: A Pilgrimage from Rome to Jerusalem, 867', *Medieval Encounters: Jewish, Christian and Muslim Culture in Confluence and Dialogue*, 4 (1998), 24–50

Hall, Kenneth R., 'International Trade and Foreign Diplomacy in Early Medieval South India', *Journal of the Economic and Social History of the Orient*, 21 (1978), 75–98

Hamerow, H., 'The Circulation of Garnets in the North Sea Zone, ca. 400–700', in *Gemstones in the First Millennium AD: Mines, Trade, Workshops and Symbolism*, ed. by A. Hilgner, S. Greiff, and D. Quast (Mainz: Römisch-Germanisches Zentralmuseum, 2017), pp. 71–86

Kesling, Emily, *Medical Texts in Anglo-Saxon Literary Culture*, Anglo-Saxon Studies, 38 (Cambridge: D. S. Brewer, 2020)

Keynes, Simon, 'King Alfred and the Mercians', in *Kings, Currency and Alliances: History and Coinage of Southern England in the Ninth Century*, ed. by Mark A. S. Blackburn and David N. Dumville, Studies in Anglo-Saxon History, 9 (Woodbridge: Boydell, 1998), pp. 1–45

Kreutz, Barbara M., *Before the Normans: Southern Italy in the Ninth and Tenth Centuries* (Philadelphia: University of Pennsylvania Press, 1992)

Limor, Ora, 'Pilgrims and Authors: Adomnán's *De locis sanctis* and Hugeburc's *Hodoeporicon Sancti Willibaldi*', *Revue Bénédictine*, 114 (2004), 253–75

MacLean, Simon, *Kingship and Politics in the Late Ninth Century: Charles the Fat and the End of the Carolingian Empire* (Cambridge: Cambridge University Press, 2003)

McCormick, Michael, *Charlemagne's Survey of the Holy Land: Wealth, Personnel, and Buildings of a Mediterranean Church between Antiquity and the Middle Ages* (Washington, DC: Dumbarton Oaks, 2011)

——, *Origins of the European Economy: Communications and Commerce, AD 300–900* (Cambridge: Cambridge University Press, 2001)

Meaney, Audrey L., 'Alfred, the Patriarch and the White Stone', *Journal of the Australasian Universities Language and Literature Association*, 49 (1978), 65–79

Morris, Colin, *The Sepulchre of Christ and the Medieval West: From the Beginning to 1600* (Oxford: Oxford University Press, 2005)

Naismith, Rory, *Citadel of the Saxons: The Rise of Early London* (London: I. B. Tauris, 2018)

Nelson, Janet, *King and Emperor: A New Life of Charlemagne* (Oakland: University of California Press, 2019)

O'Brien O'Keeffe, Katherine, 'The Geographic List of *Solomon and Saturn II*', *ASE*, 20 (1991), 123–41

Orchard, Andy, *Pride and Prodigies: Studies in the Monsters of the 'Beowulf'-Manuscript* (Cambridge: D. S. Brewer, 1995)

Ottewill-Soulsby, Samuel, '"Abbāsid-Carolingian Diplomacy in Early Medieval Arabic Apocalypse', *Millennium: Jahrbuch zu Kultur und Geschichte des ersten Jahrtausends nach Christus*, 16 (2019), 213–32

Pelteret, David A. E., 'Eleventh-Century Anglo-Saxon Long-Haul Travelers: Jerusalem, Constantinople, and Beyond', in *The Maritime World of the Anglo-Saxons*, ed. by Stacy S. Klein, William Schipper, and Shannon Lewis-Simpson (Tempe: Arizona Center for Medieval and Renaissance Studies, 2014), pp. 75–129

Powell, Kathryn, 'Orientalist Fantasy in the Poetic Dialogues of *Solomon and Saturn*', *ASE*, 34 (2005), 117–43

Pratt, David, 'The Illnesses of King Alfred the Great', *ASE*, 30 (2001), 39–90

Rose, Els, 'Reinventing the Apostolic Tradition: Transition and Appropriation in the Medieval Commemoration of the Apostles', in *Devising Order: Socio-religious Models, Rituals, and the Performativity of Practice*, ed. by Bruno Boute and Thomas Småberg (Leiden: Brill, 2012), pp. 123–44

Sisam, Kenneth, *Studies in the History of Old English Literature* (Oxford: Clarendon Press, 1953)

Smyth, Alfred P., *Alfred the Great* (Oxford: Oxford University Press, 1995)

Treadgold, Warren, *A History of the Byzantine State and Society* (Stanford: Stanford University Press, 1997)

Wilkinson, John, *Jerusalem Pilgrims before the Crusades*, rev. edn (Warminster: Aris and Phillips, 2002)

RACHEL A. BURNS

The Wanderings of Saturn: Psychogeography, Psalms, and *Solomon and Saturn*

Introduction

In the Old English poem *Solomon and Saturn II* (*SolSatII*), an educated pagan named Saturn arrives in Jerusalem to engage in a wisdom contest with the biblical King Solomon.[1] Saturn's pursuit of book learning has taken him on far-reaching travels through an array of Mediterranean, East European, Central Asian, Middle Eastern, and North African sites:[2]

> Land eall geondhwearf,
> Indea mere,　　East Corsias,
> Persea rice,　　Palestinion,
> Niniuen ceastre,　　ond norð Predan,
> Meda maððumselas,　　Marculfes eard,
> Saulus rice,　　swa he suð ligeð
> ymbe Geallboe　　and ymb Geador norð,
> Filistina flet,　　fæsten Creta,

1　Daniel Anlezark discusses medieval wisdom literature in relation to the dialogues of Solomon and Saturn (*The Old English Dialogues of Solomon and Saturn*, esp. pp. 12–23). All quotations from the dialogues are from *The Old English Dialogues of Solomon and Saturn*, ed. and trans. by Anlezark (hereafter Anlezark, *Dialogues*), and I follow his titular abbreviations; translations are my own unless otherwise stated, and I have consulted Anlezark's translations. The history of the term 'wisdom poetry' and problems of that category are addressed by John D. Niles in *God's Exiles and English Verse*, pp. 77 n. 21, 111. Anlezark identifies Jerusalem as the setting of the debate (*Dialogues*, p. 39). For an alternative view, see O'Neill, 'On the Date, Provenance and Relationship', p. 146.

2　On the literary traditions which represent Saturn as a traveller and associate him with wisdom, see Anlezark, *Dialogues*, pp. 31–39. Anlezark interprets 'East Corsias' ('East Corsias', 8b) as 'East Cossias', and 'North Predan' ('norð Predan', 10b) as 'the North Parthians' (pp. 78–79). For further discussion of difficult names and these terms as corruptions, and for extensive discussion of possible sources for the geographic list, see O'Brien O'Keeffe, 'The Geographic List of *Solomon and Saturn II*', p. 136. I have utilized these discussions of names in my own translation.

Rachel A. Burns (rachel.burns@ell.ox.ac.uk) is a lecturer in medieval English at Hertford College, University of Oxford.

Ideas of the World in Early Medieval English Literature, ed. by Mark Atherton, Kazutomo Karasawa, and Francis Leneghan, SOEL 1 (Turnhout: Brepols, 2022)　　pp. 69–101
BREPOLS ❧ PUBLISHERS　　　　　　　　　　　DOI 10.1484/M.SOEL.5.130557

wudu Egipta,   wæter Mathea,
cludas Coreffes,   Caldea rice,
Creca cræftas,   cynn Arabia,
lare Libia,   lond Syria,
Pitðinia,   Buðanasan,
Pamphilia,   Pores gemære,
Macedonia,   Mesopotamie,
Cappadocia,   Cristes eðel
Hieryhco, Galilea   Hierusalem.   *(SolSatII, ll. 7b–23)*

> ([Saturn] roamed throughout the land completely: the sea of India,
> East Corsias, the kingdom of Persia, Palestine, the city of Ninevah,
> North Predan, the treasure-halls of the Medes, the land of Marculf,
> Saul's kingdom, as it lies south by Gilboa and north by Gadara, the
> hall of the Philistines, the fortress of Crete, the wood of Egypt, the
> waters of Midia, the cliffs of Horeb, the kingdom of Chaldea, the arts
> of the Greeks, the Arabian race, the lore of Libya, the land of Syria,
> Bithinia, Buthanasan, Pamphilia, the border of Porus, Macedonia,
> Mesopotamia, Cappadocia, Christ's native country, Jericho, Galilee,
> Jerusalem.)

SolSatII and its sister poem, *Solomon and Saturn I* (*SolSatI*), are attested
together in Cambridge, Corpus Christi College, MS 422 (hereafter, CCCC,
MS 422), alongside prose text and a verse fragment (*SolSatFrag*), which
together constitute the Old English dialogues of Solomon and Saturn. The
poems were probably composed in the early tenth century, possibly by the same
author or by authors in the same circle of influence.[3] In *SolSatI*, Saturn, rather
than the narrator, delivers a reduced version of the account of Saturn's travels:

Hwæt! Ic iglanda   eallra hæbbe
boca onbyrged,   þurh gebregdstafas
larcræftas onlocen   Libia and Greca,
swylce eac istoriam   Indea rices.   *(SolSatI, ll. 1–4)*

> (Listen! I have tasted the books of every island, through cunning
> letters unlocked the lore-crafts of Libya and Greece, and so also the
> history of the kingdom of India.)[4]

Saturn's ranging travels show his extensive learning, but he is also associated
with pagan knowledge and a deficiency of understanding that must be
rectified by Christian means.[5] This shorter list foregrounds Saturn's pursuit of

---

3 Anlezark, *Dialogues*, pp. 1–2, 11–12, 49–57.

4 Punctuation here altered from Anlezark's edition. He describes the short list of *SolSatI* as a
'summary' of the longer list in *SolSatII* (*Dialogues*, p. 99).

5 On the relationship between Saturn's travels and his learnedness, see O'Neill, 'On the Date,
Provenance and Relationship', p. 143; O'Brien O'Keeffe, 'The Geographic List of *Solomon*

THE WANDERINGS OF SATURN   71

wisdom; his journeying is figured as having taken place between the learnings of various Eastern cultures ('boca', 'larcræftas', 'istoriam'). These learnings stand metonymically for the geographic sites themselves, but the image may also have appealed to the medieval English reader whose studies took them to places they could not physically visit, including the Jerusalem of *SolSatII*.

If the geographic list of *SolSatII* is an itinerary of Saturn's journey prior to his arrival in Jerusalem, it is a haphazard one. Some of the sites are listed in a geographically proximate order: from line 10b, we move westward from Parthia into Media, and then south-west into Chaldea (in modern-day Iran).[6] The list then jumps to the Holy Land ('Saulus rice', l. 12a), and such cross-regional transition is found throughout the list (e.g. from Persia to Palestine in l. 9, or between Syria and Bithynia in ll. 18b–19a). The list leapfrogs areas that it has already named or later returns to: Egypt is mentioned in line 15, and is then passed over in the movement from Arabia to Libya in lines 17b–18a, while Mesopotamia is skipped over between Chaldea and Israel (ll. 11b–12a), but appears later in line 21b. The list also transitions between continents, crossing the Mediterranean Sea between Crete and Egypt in lines 14–15 and moving across the land-border between Europe and Asia in line 20. This spatial disorganization is reflected in the grammatical construction of the list: some of the place names are direct objects of *geondhwearf* (roamed throughout, l. 7b); others are possessive modifiers of objects, which are either topographical (such as 'wudu', woods, 'cludas', cliffs, and 'lond', land), relate to human settlement (e.g. 'rice', kingdom, or 'cynn', people), or else refer to a nation's knowledge ('cræftas', arts; 'lare', lore); all (bar 'Geallboe' and 'Geador') are in apposition to 'land eall'.[7]

It has been suggested that the arrangement of the sites in the 'geographic list' is not particularly meaningful and is determined primarily by the needs of alliterative metre.[8] However, between lines 8 and 23 there are only seven

---

and Saturn II', p. 126; Heckman, 'The Order of the World', p. 41. On Saturn's association with pagan learning, and the insufficiency of this, see Anlezark, *Dialogues*, pp. 13, 36–37; Wilcox, 'Eating Books', p. 115; Powell, 'Orientalist Fantasy'. On his deficient understanding, see below, notes 67 and 83.

6 For the suggestion that *norð Predan* indicates Parthia and that *Marculfes eard* corresponds with Chaldea, and on the textual corruptions which add difficulty to identifying many of the list's sites, see O'Brien O'Keeffe, 'The Geographic List of *Solomon and Saturn II*', pp. 136–38. On the identification of *Pores* with India, see O'Brien O'Keeffe, 'The Geographic List of *Solomon and Saturn II*', p. 138; other sites have been identified following the translation in Anlezark, *Dialogues*. The descriptions of movement provided in this chapter follow the locations of these antique nations and peoples on modern maps.

7 O'Brien O'Keeffe writes: 'Syntactically, the thirty-two items in the list are in apposition to *land* and should be variations on it. Yet not every item is a land; some are people, and some, oddly, are neither people nor places but abstractions such as "Creca *cræftas*" and "*lare* Libya". Towards the end of what remains of the list there are simply place-names without modifiers of any sort' ('The Geographic List of *Solomon and Saturn II*', p. 127).

8 O'Brien O'Keeffe, 'The Geographic List of *Solomon and Saturn II*', p. 130, 140.

full lines in which a place name in the on-verse alliterates with a place name in the off-verse, while many of the words which take alliterative stress are not themselves place names. For example, in lines 14–15, 'Filistina' alone of the four place names takes metrical alliteration, while 'flet', 'fæsten', 'wudu', and 'wæter' carry the alliterative framework across the two lines. By using place names as possessive modifiers of alliterating nouns, the poet has given himself the ability to flexibly arrange the sites in a variety of different orders. Furthermore, Saturn's non-linear movement is not reflected in the account of the travels of Apollonius of Tyana given by Jerome's *Epistula* 53.4, which Anlezark persuasively proposes as a model for this section of *SolSatII*.[9] Although Apollonius's journey may be characterized as meandering, moving northwards out of Persia and around the Black Sea before coming back across the continent towards India, it can certainly be read as a reasonably coherent path, followed by more episodic travels with different Middle Eastern groups, before moving into Egypt and then south to Ethiopia. The Old English poet's stylistic control of metrical alliteration, and his distinct approach from the model in Jerome's *Epistula*, together suggest that the geographical disorganization of the list is purposeful.

Indeed, while the individual transitions between sites from half-line to half-line may appear meandering and chaotic, a sense of salvific direction emerges when these are considered as a whole. The list repeatedly returns to locations within the Holy Land (ll. 9b, 12–13, 14a, and 22b–23),[10] and the majority of

---

9 Anlezark, *Dialogues*, pp. 36–37. I give here the translation of Jerome's letter from *St Jerome: Letters and Select Works*, ed. and trans. by Fremantle, p. 97: 'He entered Persia, traversed the Caucasus and made his way through the Albanians, the Scythians, the Massagetae, and the richest districts of India. At last, after crossing that wide river the Pison, he came to the Brahmans […]. After this he travelled among the Elamites, the Babylonians, the Chaldeans, the Medes, the Assyrians, the Parthians, the Syrians, the Phoenicians, the Arabians, and the Philistines. Then returning to Alexandria he made his way to Ethiopia to see the gymnosophists and the famous table of the sun spread in the sands of the desert. Everywhere he found something to learn, so that as he was always going to new places, he became constantly wiser and better'. Numerous sources have been proposed for the geographical locations named in the list of Saturn's travels, on which see O'Brien O'Keeffe, 'The Geographic List of *Solomon and Saturn II*'. Various scholars have addressed the likelihood that the travels of Aethicus Ister in Jerome's *Cosmographia*, and of a euhemerized version of the pagan god Saturn in Lactantius's *Institutiones Diuinae*, are also sources for this passage. See, for example, Anlezark, *Dialogues*, pp. 34–36; O'Neill, 'On the Date, Provenance and Relationship', pp. 146–47, 151–52; Beechy, who notes that 'the otherness of the not-holy land seems to open up a space of play for the writer' in the *Cosmographia*, 'Wisdom and the Poetics of Laughter in the Old English *Dialogues of Solomon and Saturn*', p. 142.
10 We might include in this list 'cludas Coreffes' (l. 16a), which O'Brien O'Keeffe reads as 'rocks of Horeb' ('The Geographic List of *Solomon and Saturn II*', pp. 127, 133). Horeb is another name for Mount Sinai, which, while located in Egypt, is a site of great significance in the Old Testament, being the location at which Moses received the Ten Commandments (Exodus 19 and 20). Anlezark notes the list's focus on Palestine (*Dialogues*, p. 99), and the use of biblical and Christ-related place-names is noted by such scholarship as O'Brien O'Keeffe, 'The Geographic List of *Solomon and Saturn II*', p. 130; O'Neill, 'On the Date,

the other sites named are located in the Turkish, Middle Eastern, and North African countries which surround this area. There is a scattering of outliers: two references to sites in modern-day India, one reference to Libya, and two references to mainland Europe in the form of Greece and Macedonia. It is these 'outliers' which are named in *SolSatI*, lines 1–4, suggesting a geographic frame which holds the collected learnings of the extended list. Jerusalem is not just Saturn's ultimate destination, it is a centre of gravity in his long and ranging travels. The placement of Jerusalem at the centre of the world is a common feature of many late medieval *mappae mundi*, arising from geographic schemes informed by 'religious or devotional intent'.[11] In his chapter of this volume, Daniel Anlezark discusses the symbolic position of Jerusalem, both as the city of Christ's crucifixion and resurrection and as an authoritative centre of the Eastern Church.[12] Israel's centrality in the travels of *SolSatII* is analogous to such cartographic practice, and other aspects of the list's organization imply that the poet is exploiting the anagogical significance specific to this Eastern geography: within the references to Israel and its immediate neighbours, there is a shift from the evocation of Old Testament geography ('Saulus rice', l. 12a, and 'cludas Coreffes', l. 16a) to that of the New Testament ('Cristes eðel', l. 22b, 'Galilea', l. 23a, 'Hierusalem', l. 23b). Furthermore, geographical coherence is restored at line 22 when Saturn at last reaches 'Christ's native country' and makes his way through the biblical landscape. However, while modern-day Jericho and Jerusalem are only twenty-five kilometres apart, the list takes a detour between them to Galilee in the north of Israel. This may be an extension of the non-linear journeying of the list, or it may suggest that in a spiritual sense, Galilee, as the region of Christ's birth, is closer than Jericho to Jerusalem.[13]

Whether lines 7b–23 give an account of a route undertaken by Saturn, or whether they simply summarize various journeys undertaken at different times, the configuration of sites arises from a sense of geography as something defined spiritually as well as spatially.[14] For an early medieval English author looking East, physical movement towards Jerusalem could also be read as

---

Provenance and Relationship', p. 143; Powell, 'Orientalist Fantasy', p. 138; and Bisher, 'Heterogeneous Religious Expression', who notes a link with the forty years of wandering endured by the Hebrews (108–09). Dane notes a correspondence between the poem's list and the Pentecostal catalogue in Acts 2. 5ff. ('The Structure of the *Old English Solomon and Saturn II*', p. 593). This is all the more interesting in light of Anlezark's association of Saturn's wanderings with the dispersal of humanity at Babel (*Dialogues*, p. 46).

11 Appleton, 'The Northern World of the Anglo-Saxon *mappa mundi*', p. 282. Appleton notes, however, that this is not the case with the Anglo-Saxon *mappa mundi*, where it is 'the scale of the world' that the map emphasizes, rather than any one human settlement.

12 Further, on the 'symbolic' importance of Jerusalem and the Temple to Lactantius and Jerome, whose writings may have influenced the poet of *SolSatII*, see Anlezark, *Dialogues*, p. 37.

13 Note also that Christ visits Jericho directly before his arrival in Jerusalem (Luke 18 and 19).

14 See O'Brien O'Keeffe, 'The Geographic List of *Solomon and Saturn II*', p. 130.

spiritual movement towards salvation, bestowed by the divine and ecclesiastical authority of the city.[15]

The act of wandering and the role of authority in delineating the spaces occupied by individuals are core interests of the modern philosophical field of psychogeography, which examines the interactivity of environment with human mentality.[16] Psychogeography has generally been studied in the context of its twentieth-century origins and its later practitioners, but it has been proposed that a tradition of psychogeographical literature stretches back at least as far as the work of Daniel Defoe.[17] In this chapter, I will draw on the concerns and interests of psychogeographical practice, literature, and criticism to ask new questions about the intersection of space, mentality, and authority in *SolSatI* and *SolSatII*. I will argue that the geographic list deliberately presents Saturn's disordered wanderings as a spatialized metaphor for the senselessness of his pursuit of pagan wisdom. I will examine the affinities between the geographic list and three other episodes in the Old English dialogues which are concerned with the act of wandering, thereby locating Saturn's waywardness within a broader theological scheme in which physical and mental stillness are critical moral virtues.[18] I will locate the poem's consistent association of wandering with sin and mental distress in the context of influential patristic and biblical literature on the vice of *acedia*; specifically, I will argue that the poem models its psychological treatment of wandering on the extended travel metaphor used in Psalm 118 (i.e. Psalm 119 in the Hebrew numbering used in most Protestant Bibles). We will find that the dialogues share with certain later psychogeographical literature a recognition of the subversive potential of wandering. However, this subversiveness held different implications for medieval Christians (and for monks in particular) than it has held for many modern psychogeographers who celebrate resistance to authority. For medieval readers of the Solomon and Saturn dialogues, mental and physical wanderings represent resistance to the earthly authority of monastic institutions and the divine authority of God. Ultimately, the dialogues observe the biblical

---

15 Powell argues that the Solomon-figure of the dialogues represents specifically Christian and English forms of wisdom, '[supporting] a fantasy of English superiority relative to a foreign and pagan Other' ('Orientalist Fantasy', esp. pp. 119, 143).

16 Further, on the field of psychogeography, its interests, and the relevance of wandering in the form of the *dérive*, see below.

17 Coverley, *Psychogeography*, esp. pp. 18–20, 37–41; note also Coverley's analysis of Peter Ackroyd and 'a buried Catholic tradition' (p. 37). Ackroyd quotation from 'The Englishness of English Literature', p. 19.

18 Relevant to Saturn's wandering, but not discussed here, is the episode of the 'weallende Wulf', where 'weallende' is read as 'wandering' by Menner ('Nimrod and the Wolf in the Old English "Solomon and Saturn"', p. 353) and Bisher ('Heterogeneous Religious Expression', pp. 162, n 22, 117–18), the latter of whom connects wandering with anger and exile both here and in other Old English texts (pp. 53, 100–101). Kemble links Saturn and the wandering pagan god Woden (*The Dialogue of Salomon and Saturnus*, p. 131); cf. Bisher, 'Heterogeneous Religious Expression', p. 131.

injunction that the 'law' ('lege') of God is a 'way' ('via') which must be followed (Ps. 118. 1), and wandering is presented as a danger to the soul.[19] In a reinforcement of monastic values and practice, *SolSatII* presents holy books and texts as the cure for a wandering mind.

Psychogeographical Criticism and Old English Verse

Psychogeography is a varied and continuously developing area of theory and practice, stimulating research in disciplines related to arts, social sciences, and technology. The heterogeneity of the field in recent decades has made comprehensive definition impossible, but overviews from a range of practitioners and commentators give a sense of the priorities which continue to emerge in psychogeographic activity.[20] In his seminal 1955 essay, 'Introduction to a Critique of Urban Geography', Guy Debord defines psychogeography as 'the study of the precise laws and specific effects of the geographical environment, consciously organized or not, on the emotions and behavior of individuals'.[21] Tina Richardson writes that 'psychogeography is about crossing established boundaries', and Merlin Coverley defines it broadly as 'the point at which psychology and geography collide, a means of calibrating the impact of place'.[22] These definitions foreground an interest in the intersection of individual, subjective mentalities with the organization of space, and the *motion* of these mentalities through such spaces is critical to both the earliest and the newest engagements with psychogeographic theory. The practice of the *dérive* (trans., 'drift' or 'drifting') is a playful form of travel undertaken by one or more people through an urban landscape, characterized by 'randomness'. It was developed by the radical left-wing group Situationists International (SI) in the 1950s and 1960s, who were among the earliest practitioners of psychogeography.[23] Participants observe the 'psychogeographical contours'

---

19 Francis Leneghan addresses the intersection of wandering thoughts, demonic wandering, and individual exile, as well as the sinfulness of misery, in his discussion of *The Wanderer* ('Preparing the Mind for Prayer'), all of which elements will come into play in this reading of the dialogues.

20 Bonnet, 'Psychogeography', gives an overview of the changing history and distinct phases of psychogeographical work. Richardson notes that the discipline of psychogeography 'is hard to pin down in any formalised way', being characteristically 'disruptive, unsystematic, random' ('Introduction', p. 1), and discusses aspects which unify psychogeographers (pp. 17–18). Coverley, *Psychogeography*, summarizes the 'bewildering array of ideas', p. 14, referred to by the term 'psychogeography' in his literary analysis of psychogeographic writing and film from the eighteenth century to the twenty-first.

21 Debord, 'Introduction to a Critique of Urban Geography', p. 8.

22 Richardson, 'Introduction', p. 2; Coverley, *Psychogeography*, p. 10.

23 The quotations here and above, including the translation of *dérive*, are from Debord, 'Theory of the *Dérive*'; see also Bonnet, 'Psychogeography'; Richardson, 'Introduction', pp. 1–2. For a critique of Debord's idea of the *dérive*, see Coverley, *Psychogeography*, pp. 123–27. On other

of an area (for example, connections and 'fissures' between 'neighbourhoods', 'axes of passage', points of entry and exit). This exercise in wandering was one of a number of strategies used by the SI to challenge the delineation of space for certain purposes by authorities and by capitalist interests; reinterpreted in different ways by modern practitioners, the *dérive* continues to hold significant currency in psychogeographical work. Where the SI's objectives were 'revolutionary' and 'anti-literary', psychogeography in the twenty-first century includes an explicitly literary tradition led by such figures as W. G. Sebald, Will Self, and Iain Sinclair.[24] This new tradition both extends and alters the radical, anti-authoritarian concerns of the situationists, as for example the resistance to the authority of automation or gentrification posed by Self's walk to New York in *Psychogeography* (2007), or Sinclair's retrospective on the changing face of the city in *The Last London* (2018).[25]

Psychogeography has been critiqued as a relatively 'undertheorized' field in itself,[26] and so it is not surprising to find that it remains underdeveloped as a literary-critical approach. A small but wide-ranging collection of studies has made inroads in this area using aspects of psychogeographical thought to examine Chaucer's metropolitan London and Troy, the engagement of Romantic poets with the geography and tourist culture of the Wye Valley, the village setting of Agatha Christie's detective fiction, and the city in works of Paul Aster and Martin Amis.[27] In the field of Old English, scholars have examined the intersection of their own experiences with the geographies described in literature: in *Landscape of Desire*, Gillian R. Overing and Marijane Osborn travel through Scandinavia, immersed in the landscape of *Beowulf* and the Old Norse sagas; Christopher Abram explores the fenland topography which is the home both of the character Grendel and of the author.[28] This theoretical approach is particularly suitable for early medieval vernacular wisdom poetry, which, as J. S. Ryan notes, makes frequent use of journeying motifs to represent the internal movement towards wisdom.[29] Critical analysis has traced literary 'precursors' of modern psychogeography as far back as the early eighteenth century, and Coverley has identified a

---

early practitioners who influenced the development of psychogeography, see Richardson, 'Introduction', p. 3.

24 Quotation from Richardson, 'Introduction', pp. 2–3; see also Hay, 'Transforming Psychogeography'; Mudie, 'Convulsions of the Local', pp. 206–07; Sebald, *The Rings of Saturn*.

25 Self, *Psychogeography*; Sinclair, *The Last London*; Day, 'The Last London by Iain Sinclair Review'.

26 Mudie, 'Convulsions of the Local', p. 207.

27 Thompson, 'London's Chaucer'; Davies and Fulford, 'Introduction'; Martin, 'Psychogeography and the Detective'; Ross, 'Developing a Method of Literary Psychogeography in Postmodern Fictions of Detection'.

28 Overing and Osborn, *Landscapes of Desire*; Abram, 'At Home in the Fens with the Grendelkin'. Although Overing and Osborn do not themselves discuss psychogeography, Christopher Abram calls the book 'the most successful psychogeographical approach to *Beowulf* yet undertaken' (p. 139).

29 Ryan, 'Old English Wisdom Poetry', p. 263.

range of the typical features of this literature, including the portrayal of walking as a subversive act and anti-authoritarianism.[30]

Crucially, this critique need not handle only that writing which follows on from the works of the Situationists or other early practitioners and influencers of psychogeography, nor need it seek to identify the same radical or ideological motivations found in much (though not all) modern psychogeographical writing. Rather, a psychogeographical method of critique asks questions about the way texts formulate key aspects of psychogeographical concern, and these questions may be applied to texts of any place or period. These questions may be as varied as the heterogenous field they arise from, and some broad concerns which resonate in a range of psychogeographical work suggest some immediate questions which will inform my own approach in this chapter. Richardson characterizes the practice of psychogeography as 'a method of walking that responds to and critiques the terrain' and notes the interest literary psychogeography takes in both the emotional effect of place upon human subjects and the 'power structures' which are imposed upon place.[31] Following this, we might ask how the terrains or topographies of a text are shaped or given meaning by human powers; how they constrain or enable human activity; whether they give rise to an emotional response in characters; how the motion of characters or narrative affects or is affected by the terrain it moves through. We might begin this process by looking to textual representations of those 'psychogeographical contours' identified by Debord and the ways they are navigated: routes, 'attractions', 'microclimates'. Accounts from Will Self and Rebecca Solnit of walks made on foot in the age of mechanical transport point to the specificity of material conditions which can make walking into an act of resistance.[32] We might then conclude our examination by asking what material conditions pertinent to contemporary readers or writers of the given text help us to interpret its presentation of space and movement, and whether there is an ideological outlook at play. We can further ask whether this presentation or outlook is unique to a particular community or represents something broader about the epoch of composition or, especially in the context of medieval manuscript collections, collation.

These kinds of approaches prompt many possibilities for new readings of Old English verse texts. Such concerns of psychogeographical literature as the distinction between *walker* and *voyeur*, the exploration of neglected 'non-places', or the practice of mental travel from physical confinement may give rise to new perspectives on such well-studied episodes as Grendel's

---

30 Löffler (*Walking in the City*) applies psychogeographical analysis to eighteenth-century literary texts as early as Tom Browne's *Amusements Serious and Comical* (1700); Coverley argues that Daniel Defoe's account of London in *Journal of the Plague Year* (1772) is 'the prototype psychogeographical report' (*Psychogeography* pp. 18–20, 37–41). On features typical of psychogeographical literature, see Coverley, *Psychogeography*, p. 16.

31 Richardson, 'Introduction', esp. pp. 4–7.

32 Self, *Psychogeography*; Solnit, *Wanderlust*, Introduction; Richardson, 'Introduction', p. 8.

voyeurism towards Heorot from the hinterland of the moor in *Beowulf*, the imaginative travel of the Seafarer, or the threat and promise of Wulf's desired entry to the speaker's island-prison in *Wulf and Eadwacer*.[33] Such research would build on an enormous body of existing scholarship, and it is impossible to summarize succinctly here the breadth of work in the field of Old English verse which pertains to the varied concerns of psychogeography.[34] Themes of particular relevance to this chapter — the relationship between physical and mental journeying, and the intersection of physical place and human mentality — have stimulated research which, while not explicitly psychogeographic in its outlook, nevertheless forms a formidable body of psychogeographically aligned criticism.[35]

It is my contention that *SolSatI* and *SolSatII* occupy a yet earlier position in the tradition of psychogeographical writing, and that they represent how such a tradition manifested in England long before the Reformation, in an environment of early medieval monastic literacy. I will begin by examining the mental and physical behaviours of each wandering subject, locating these in the context of theological thought on sadness and the vice of *acedia*. I will go on to consider the implications of sinful wandering for monastic communities, and how the poems' perspectives on wandering correspond with patristic literature known in early medieval England.

---

33 On these concerns, see Coverley, *Psychogeography*.

34 For example, a psychogeographical analysis of Grendel's movement between mere and hall, across the non-space of the moors, would follow a number of papers handling the spatial organization and representation of power in *Beowulf*'s landscape, including Appleton, 'The Role of Æschere's Head'; Langeslag, 'Monstrous Landscape in Beowulf'; Elden, 'Place Symbolism and Land Politics in *Beowulf*; Gelling, 'The Landscape of *Beowulf*.

35 The interrelation of space and identity has been explored in a range of Old English texts. For example, Powell's 'Orientalist Fantasy' examines the role of 'geography, power and knowledge' in establishing a 'fantasy of English cultural superiority and stability' in the dialogues (quotations from pp. 120, 142). See also Dendle, 'The Role of the Devil in Old English Narrative Literature', pp. 80, 177, on geographic representations of moral and spiritual states; Michelet's *Creation, Migration, and Conquest*; Major, 'Saturn's First Riddle in *Solomon and Saturn II*'. Neville's *Representations of the Natural World in Old English Poetry* is an important precursor to much recent work in the realm of ecocriticism, especially chap. 3, 'Constructing Society: Outside and Inside, Powerlessness and Control', pp. 53–88. For an overview of scholarship on the early medieval English literary environment which precedes recent ecocritical approaches to Old English texts, including Neville's book, see Estes, *Anglo-Saxon Literary Landscapes*, pp. 28–31. Estes's book also offers fresh ground for examining the relationship between lived environments and their human occupants. Mental and physical wanderings in such poems as *The Seafarer* and *The Wanderer* are the subjects of several important scholarly essays: Clemoes, 'Mens absentia cogitans', esp. pp. 66–67, 69–70; Leneghan, 'Preparing the Mind for Prayer'; Harbus, 'Travelling Metaphors and Mental Wandering in Old English Poetry', pp. 117, 123 (and on metaphors of the wandering mind in the context of *The Wanderer*, esp. pp. 124–26); Harbus, *Cognitive Approaches to Old English Poetry*, pp. 45–46; North, 'Heaven Ahoy!' (and on Augustinian influence on the poem's depiction of journeying, pp. 9–10 n. 7).

Wandering through the Dialogues:
A Thematic Comparison of Four Passages

Including the geographic list, there are four passages in the two poetic texts of the dialogues which feature episodes of wandering. In each case, the act of wandering is connected to distress, ignorance, and sin. The first of these passages is from *SolSatI*, where Solomon compares a person who does not know the words of the Pater Noster to a wandering beast:

> Unlæde bið on eorþan,   unit lifes,
> wesðe wisdomes,   *weallað swa nieten,*
> *feldgongende   feoh* butan gewitte,
> se þurh ðone cantic ne can   Crist geherian
> *worað* he windes full
> [...]
> Fracoð he bið ðonne and fremede   frean ælmihtigum,
> englum ungelic   *ana hwearfað.*

> (*SolSatI*, ll. 21–25a, 34–35, emphases added)

> > (He is unhappy on earth, useless in life, empty of wisdom, *roams like an animal, field-faring cattle* without wits, he who cannot glorify Christ through the canticle, *wanders* full of wind [...] he is vile and strange to the almighty Lord, unlike the angels *he wanders alone.*)

The wandering of the man is invoked four times in this passage, twice to compare him to an animal (ll. 22, 23), once to say he is 'full of wind' (l. 25), and once to show him as outcast from the heavenly company of angels (l. 35).[36] It has been noted that the image of the field-going cattle is also found in the Old English *Soul and Body* poems: in these texts of the Vercelli Book and Exeter Book respectively, the soul berates the prostrate body for its sins, saying that it would have been better if the body had been made a mindless animal rather than a baptized man, now that damnation awaits him (*Soul and Body I*, ll. 76–87; *Soul and Body II*, ll. 71–81).[37] This may signal that the ignorant man of *SolSatI*, lines 21–35, is understood to face this same judgement as a result of his spiritual deficiency. The connection between such deficiency and the act of wandering is emphasized by the alliterative scheme, which binds three of the four verbs of motion with a noun in the series of similes and metaphor: 'wesðe' (waste) and 'weallað' (roams); 'feldgongende' (field-faring) and

---

36 This section is also discussed by Anlezark, *Dialogues*, pp. 41–42, 101. On wandering here as an exclusion from heavenly and human speech-communities, and on connections with other Old English exile-poetry, see Heinmiller, 'Orality, Literacy, and Dialogue', p. 71 n. 40, 72.

37 Wright, *The Irish Tradition in Old English Literature*, p. 256; see also Anlezark, *Dialogues*, p. 101. This episode has also been linked with the animal-like wanderings of King Nebuchadnezzar in the biblical book of Daniel (Anlezark, *Dialogues*, p. 101; Nelson, 'King Solomon's Magic', p. 27).

'feoh' (cattle); 'worað' (wanders) and 'windes' (wind).[38] The internal vacancy of the subject suggested by 'waste' and 'wind' is further emphasized by the paired alliteration on the prefix 'un-' in both on-verse and off-verse of line 21 ('unlæde', unhappy, l. 21a; 'unit', useless, l. 21b).[39] This has the further effect of emphasizing those qualities which are ideal in a person, and which in each case have been inverted by the 'un-' prefix: a man should be both happy ('-læde') and useful ('-nit').[40] In this account, sadness and vacancy are not in conflict; rather, the apposition of *unlæde*, *unit*, and *wesðe* suggests that these states are different aspects of the same deficiency.[41]

A more detailed account of personal misery in connection with wandering occurs in *SolSatII*, when Saturn poses a difficult question to Solomon: Why do apparently equal people suffer unequal fortunes in the world? Solomon replies with an affecting vignette of a mother watching her son grow up to become an exile:[42]

> Modor ne rædeð   ðonne heo magan cenneð,
> *hu him weorðe geond worold*   *widsið sceapen.*
> [...]
> Heo ðæs afran sceall   oft ond gelome
> grimme greotan,   ðonne he *geong færeð,*
> hafað wilde mod,   werige heortan,
> sefan sorgfullne,   *slideð geneahhe*
> werig, wilna leas,   wuldres bedæled.
> Hwilum higegeomor   *healle weardað,*
> *leofað leodum feor;*   locað geneahhe
> fram ðam unlædan,   ægen hlaford.

> (*SolSatII*, ll. 193–94, 198–205, emphases added)

> (A mother, when she gives birth to a son, doesn't determine *how his long journey will come to be shaped for him through the world.* [...] Again and again, she must weep bitterly for that son, when, young, he *goes off*, has a wild mood, a weary heart, a sorrowful mind. *Often he falls* weary, empty of desire, deprived of glory. Sometimes, sad-spirited,

---

38 Anlezark emends *worað* from MS *warað* on grounds of sense; see *Dialogues*, p. 101.

39 On the metrical flexibility of the *un-* prefix in *Beowulf*, see Kendall, 'The Prefix un- and the Metrical Grammar of *Beowulf*.

40 This pairing of qualities is evocative of Augustine's precept on man's interaction with the physical world in *De doctrina Christiana 1*, in which he argues that the things of the world are made to be enjoyed or used (or else, both). On the relationship of this idea in Augustine to wandering, see below.

41 Anlezark notes that 'Unlæde' is the first word spoken by Saturn in *SolSatI*, and that this corresponds with 'a pervasive concern with understanding the nature of the failure and unhappiness of the *unlæde* ("unhappy", "unfortunate") man' in *SolSatII* (*Dialogues*, pp. 50, 56, 101, 102, 131–32, 138).

42 For a discussion of this passage, see also Shippey, *Poems of Wisdom and Learning in Old English*, p. 22.

he watches the hall, lives far from people; often his own lord looks away from the unhappy man.)[43]

The woman's son goes on a journey ('geong færeð', l. 199), but like the ignorant man of *SolSatI*, lines 21–35, he has no stated destination. Rather, his route is described in terms of being away from both hall and people in an implicit state of exile. As in the passage on the ignorant man in *SolSatI*, this episode presents a detailed and appositive account of the wanderer's mood: wild, weary, sad, empty, and inglorious. It is unclear whether this despair arises from or has brought about the son's exile; cause and effect are tangled together, with references to his wandering (ll. 199b, 201b, 203b–204a) enveloping descriptions of his variant moods and emotions (ll. 200–201a, 202–03a).

The last of the four passages describes a man led astray by the devil:

Ðonne hine ymbegangað   gastas twegen;
oðer bið golde glædra,   oðer bið grundum sweartra,
oðer cymeð   ***
            ofer ðære stylenan helle,
oðer hine læreð   ðæt he lufan healed
Metodes miltse   ond his mæga ræd,
oðer hine tyhteð   ond on tæso læreð,
yweð him ond yppeð   earmra manna
misgemynda,   ond ðurh ðæt his mod hweteð,
læded hine ond læceð   ond hine geond land spaneð
oððæt his ege bið   æfðancum full,
ðurh earmra scyld   yrre geworden.

                    (*SolSatII*, ll. 308–19, emphases added)

(Then two spirits come about [the doomed man], one is as bright as gold, the other as dark as the earth; one comes *** the other from steely hell; one teaches him that he should hold love for God's mercy, and the teaching of his kin; the other tempts him and directs him towards injury, reveals to him and shows the more shameful of men's misunderstandings, and through this whets his mind, *leads him and abducts and entices him throughout the land* until his eyes are full of spite/offence/envy, through miserable sins he has become wrathful/gone astray.)[44]

---

43 Anlezark translates l. 203b as 'he is wary in the hall' (*Dialogues*, p. 89); *weardian* is defined as 'to watch, guard, keep, protect, preserve', s.v. *weardian*, Clark Hall, *A Concise Anglo-Saxon Dictionary*, p. 399.

44 Note the productive ambiguity of 'æfðancum' and 'yrre geworden', which offer multiple perspectives on the emotions experienced by the wandering man (*DOE*, s.v. *æf-þanca*, *æf-þunca*; Bosworth and Toller, *An Anglo-Saxon Dictionary*, s.v. *æf-þanc*; *of-þanc*; *irre*). For this reason, I have here presented multiple concurrent translations for each, separated by a forward slash.

Line 317, 'lædeð hine ond læceð | ond hine geond land spaneð' ([he] leads him and abducts and entices him throughout the land), calls back to Saturn's own cross-continental travels and echoes in particular *SolSatII*, line 7b ('Land eall geondhwearf', [he] roamed throughout the land completely).[45] Inflectional rhyme on -*eð* in this passage, and full rhyme between the verbs of line 315a, and between those of 317a, creates an aural pathway through the demon's processes. Firstly he misdirects in thought ('tyhteð', 'læreð', 'yweð', 'yppeð'), and secondly he misdirects in space ('lædeð', 'læceð', 'spaneð'). These lines bookend what remains of the poem with episodes of geographical meandering, and so hint at a demonic aspect to Saturn's own travels.[46] Again, the psychology of the wandering sinner comes into detailed focus in the highly physical and affecting image of line 318, where the eyes of the wandering man are full of spite, offence, or jealousy ('his ege bið | æfðancum full'). This passage makes the most explicit connection between wandering and sinfulness of the four and is the only one to introduce an aspect of spiritual or demonic interference.

The clearest correspondence between these four passages is the association of wandering with detailed and heterogenous accounts of mental distress, partaking of aspects of despondency, sadness, weariness, ignorance, and even anger.[47] In the case of the geographic list, the expression of associated mental distress follows in lines 57b–62 of *SolSatII* (as briefly discussed above):[48]

> Mec ðæs on worolde full oft
> fyrwit frineð, fus gewiteð,
> mod gemengeð. Naenig manna wat,
> haeleða under hefenum, hu min hige dreoseð,
> bysig aefter bocum. Hwilum me bryne stigeð,
> hige heortan neah haedre wealleð. (*SolSatII, ll. 57b–62*)

> (Very often curiosity asks me that in the world, departs with haste, confuses the mind. No man knows, of warriors under heavens, how

---

45 Furthermore, Anlezark (*Dialogues*, p. 49) sees a connection between this passage and that of the young exile discussed above, suggesting that '[the] character of the tempted man recalls and extends the characterisation of the unhappy twin in the hall, turning away from the wisdom offered by his kinsman'.

46 Note that the imperfect ending of *SolSatII* on p. 26 of CCCC, MS 422 means that the poem survives in an incomplete form (on which, see Anlezark, *Dialogues*, p. 2). Cf. Job 1. 7: 'cui dixit Dominus unde venis qui respondens ait circuivi terram et perambulavi eam' (And the Lord said to him: Whence comest thou? And he answered and said: I have gone round about the earth, and walked through it); from the Vulgate, with Douay-Rheims translation. There has been much work on demons in the dialogues; of particular interest from a psychogeographical vantage is Dendle, 'The Demonological Landscape of the "Solomon and Saturn" Cycle'.

47 On the manifold nature of *acedia* in early Christian thought, see Wenzel, *The Sin of Sloth*.

48 Leslie Lockett also discusses 'mental distress' in this passage in the context of the hydraulic model of the mind (Lockett, *Anglo-Saxon Psychologies*, pp. 64, 73). O'Neill writes about the torment of curiosity in this passage and elsewhere in the text, 'On the Date, Provenance and Relationship', p. 144.

my mind drips away, busy after books. Sometimes a burning ascends within me, the mind near the heart, wells up oppressively.)[49]

Saturn's cross-continental pursuit of book-learning has brought him not peace, but anxiety (see also *SolSatI*, ll. 11b–18a).[50] The secrecy which he has previously maintained around his state of mind is suggestive of shame; this sense that sadness is shameful is made concrete in *SolSatII*, when Solomon declares, 'Unlæde bið ond ormod se ðe a wile | geomrian on gihðe; se bið Gode fracoðast' (Unhappy and hopeless is the one who always wants to be sad in care. He is most hateful to God, ll. 73–74). Despair has been recognized as a psychological sin in Christian thought at least since the writings of the fourth-century hermit and mystic Evagrius Ponticus, who adopted the classical Greek term ἀκηδία (*acedia*, 'lack of care') as one of the eight vices.[51] In the writings of both Evagrius and his contemporary John Cassian, we find *acedia* linked to an account given in Psalm 90. 6 of the 'Demon of Noontide'; this demon attacks the isolating monk at midday and compels him to wander out of his cell in search of stimulation.[52] The 'noontide demon' may be associated with the dark spirit who leads the sinner astray in *SolSatII*, lines 308–19, while the monk's need for stimulation chimes with the 'fyrwit' (curiosity) which drives Saturn to travel the world.[53] *Acedia* is a complex term, incorporating

---

49 Note that there are a number of differences between the two manuscript variants of this text; for example, MS A (CCCC, MS 422) reads 'dreoseð' (falls, drips away, l. 60b), where MS B (CCCC, MS 41) reads 'dreogeð' (strives). See further Anlezark, *Dialogues*, pp. 1–6, 96–98, 104.

50 As noted and discussed by Nelson, 'King Solomon's Magic', p. 25, and also discussed by Beechy, 'Wisdom and the Poetics of Laughter in the Old English *Dialogues of Solomon and Saturn*', p. 148.

51 Wenzel, *The Sin of Sloth*, pp. 1–2. The complex history of this term is discussed further later in Wenzel. On sadness as sin and methods for consolation in the dialogues and elsewhere, see Wehlau, '"Seeds of Sorrow"', pp. 1–3 (including n. 8); Harbus, 'The Situation of Wisdom in *Solomon and Saturn II*', pp. 100–101; Wallis, 'Patterns of Wisdom in the Old English *Solomon and Saturn II*', p. 225; Persson, 'Job, Ecclesiastes and the Mechanics of Wisdom in Old English Poetry', pp. 201–02, including n. 585. John Cassian links *acedia* with the related theme of *tristitia* ('dejection', or 'sorrow'), and Gregory the Great combines the two into the single vice of sloth in his reformed list of seven vices (Irvine, '*Acedia, Tristitia* and Sloth', p. 96; Leneghan, 'Preparing the Mind for Prayer', p. 124 n. 9; see also Wenzel, *The Sin of Sloth*, p. 25). Gregory writes of the twofold sinfulness of *tristitia*: it represents a sinner's fear of punishment after death, and causes them to turn to worldly comforts (*Moralia in Iob*, Book XXXI). Ælfric's treatise on *The Vices and Virtues*, written at the turn of the eleventh century, addresses the vice of *tristitia* differently, as being a sadness that emerges from the loss of worldly goods, experienced by someone who loved them too much (see Leneghan, 'Preparing the Mind for Prayer', p. 127). On the knowledge of Evagrian thought in early medieval England, through material imported by Theodore of Tarsus and Hadrian, and through the works of Cassian, see Leneghan, 'Preparing the Mind for Prayer', pp. 126–27. See also the chapter in this volume by Eleni Ponirakis.

52 Irvine, '*Acedia, Tristitia* and Sloth', p. 95; Wenzel, *The Sin of Sloth*.

53 The noonday demon is discussed in the context of *Guthlac A* in Anlezark, '"Stand Firm"', pp. 263, 270; and by Bailey in 'Misinterpretation and the Meaning of Signs in Old English Poetry', p. 44.

aspects of both slothfulness and despondency,[54] and this polysemous history of meaning is perhaps reflected in the appositive construction of ranging emotions expressed in the four Old English passages on wandering.

SolSatI makes its interest in *acedia* yet more explicit through a direct allusion to Psalm 118. 28. In the Greek translation of the Septuagint Bible, this verse reads as follows: ἔσταξεν ἡ ψυχή μου ἀπὸ ἀκηδίας' (my spirit has dripped away because of *acedia*).[55] In the Vulgate, the term *acedia* is replaced by the word *stultitia* (foolishness, weakness), but the body of the Psalm verse is otherwise much the same: 'destillavit anima mea prae stultitia' (my soul has dripped down because of *stultitia*).[56] Saturn paraphrases this verse in *SolSatI*, lines 59b–61a, when he says that 'no man knows [...] how my mind drips away, busy after books'. As well as anchoring Saturn's character and his wandering pursuit of knowledge to the vice of *acedia*, this allusion exposes a host of further correspondences between the Old English texts and Psalm 118. The psalm is structured around a sustained metaphor of travel in which obedience to the laws of God is configured as a foot-journey on correct 'ways' (*viae*), while acts of wandering or straying (*errare*) are associated with sin and disobedience.[57] The psalm opens with a benediction for those who 'ambulant in lege Domini' (walk in the law of the Lord, Ps. 118. 1), and closes with the singer's plea for help, as he has lost his way like a sheep ('erravi quasi ovis perdita', Ps. 118. 176).[58] It is the first-person singing voice of the psalm which undertakes the metaphorical journeying in the text, often expressed as requests, for example, 'deduc me in semita mandatorum tuorum' (lead me in the path of your commandments, Ps. 118. 35), or as declarations of faith, for example, 'recogitavi vias meas et converti pedes meos ad testimonia tua' (I have reflected upon my ways, and I have turned back my feet towards your testimonies, Ps. 118. 59).[59] Crucially, the metaphorical pathways do not

---

54 Wenzel, *The Sin of Sloth*.

55 Greek text from *Septuagint*, ed. by Rahlfs.

56 Vulgate quotations throughout are from *Biblia sacra iuxta vulgatam versionem*, ed. by Weber and Gryson. This is the wording of the *Hebraicum*, Jerome's third and final translation of the Book of Psalms. Both the *Romanum* and *Gallicanum* versions of the Psalter were more widely attested in early medieval England, but on the availability of the *Hebraicum* from at least as early as the beginning of the eighth century, see Keefer and Burrows, 'Hebrew and the *Hebraicum* in Late Anglo-Saxon England'. Both the *Romanum* and *Gallicanum* versions read 'dormavit' (slept) in place of 'destillavit' (dripped down), with the verse reading, 'My soul slept because of *tædio*'. Latin *tædio* has varied meanings including 'weariness', 'boredom', 'suffering', 'disgust' (s.v. *tædio*, *The Dictionary of Medieval Latin from British Sources*, ed. by Latham, Howlett, and Ashdowne, and s.v. *tædio*, *A Latin Dictionary*, ed. by Lewis and Short).

57 In service of this metaphor, the text makes repeated use of a small set of verbs and nouns related to travel: various conjugations of *ambulare*, to walk; *quaerere*, to seek; *currere*, to run; *reverti*, to return; *errare*, to stray; and the nouns *semitae*, pathways; *viae*, ways or roads; *pedes*, feet.

58 Note also the association here, but not in all cases throughout the Psalm, of wandering with field animals, as in *SolSatI*.

59 In his commentary on Psalm 118, which was known in England and survives in North-umbrian manuscripts of the eighth century, Cassiodorus suggests that the psalm is narrated

represent virtues, but rather the 'laws' (*mandati*) and 'commandments' (*leges*) of God, which are themselves virtuous; the direction of the singer's journey is governed by God's unquestionable authority.

At several points, the experiences of the singer of Psalm 118 correspond closely with those of Saturn in the dialogues. The singer is not just a traveller, but one who travels widely in search of God's teaching, drawn by authority towards knowledge; early in the psalm he describes himself as an outsider who needs God's truth to be revealed to him.[60] This aligns with Saturn's multinational pursuit of learning, and his inevitable movement towards the sacred authority of Jerusalem in search of the knowledge that will truly satisfy him: the Pater Noster prayer (*SolSatI*, ll. 1–12). Solomon does indeed teach Saturn about the prayer, which he characterizes as a song to be invoked ('singan soðlice', *SolSatI*, l. 85a). The Psalm itself is intended to be sung, and the singer also promises to 'utter a hymn' ('fundant [...] hymnum') in response to receiving God's teachings (Ps. 118. 171), and even alludes to this song being sung after long travels.[61] Solomon tells Saturn that knowledge of the Pater Noster will be 'leofre ðonne eall ðeos leohte gesceaft | gegoten fram ðam grunde goldes and silofres' (more beloved to him than all this bright creation founded from the earth, of gold and of silver, *SolSatI*, ll. 30–31), which echoes the praise of Psalm 118. 72: 'melior mihi est lex oris tui super milia auri et argenti' (better to me is the law of your mouth, above thousands of gold and of silver). The context of the wisdom debate itself might draw upon Psalm 118. 23, 'sedentes principes adversum me loquebantur' (seated princes spoke against me), particularly in the description of Solomon and Saturn as 'middangeardes ræswum' (princes of middle-earth, *SolSatII*, l. 2b).[62]

The extent of the engagement between the two main poems of the dialogues and Psalm 118 has not been previously noted, to the best of my knowledge.[63]

---

by a 'chorus' of voices (Cassiodorus, *Explanation of the Psalms*, ed. and trans. by Walsh, pp. 174–75). See also 'lucerna pedi meo verbum tuum et lux semitae meae' (your words are an oil-lamp for my feet, and a light for my paths, Ps. 118. 105).

60 'Et ambulabo in spatioso quia praecepta tua quaesivi' (and I will walk in wideness, because I have sought for your teachings, Ps. 118. 45); 'advena ego sum in terra ne abscondas a me mandata tua' (I am a foreigner on the earth, do not conceal your commandments from me, Ps. 118. 19). The word *advena* means literally, 'one who arrives', which is how the geographic list presents Saturn following the poem's formulaic introduction, as discussed above.

61 'Carmina erant mihi praecepta tua in domo peregrinationis meae' (your teachings were my song in the house of my pilgrimage, Ps. 118. 54).

62 See also Ps. 118. 61, 'principes persecuti sunt me sine causa' (princes have pursued me without reason).

63 In addition to what is discussed above, a further possible correspondence may exist between the numerous references to the sinfulness and punishment of 'the proud' in Psalm 118 (*superbi*, verses 21, 51, 69, 78, 122), and the two descriptions of Saturn's people, the Chaldeans, as proud (*SolSatII*, ll. 30b, 149a). A few further connections between Psalm 118 and the dialogues have been previously noted by scholarship. In *SolSatI* the Pater Noster is credited with the ability to rescue souls from hell, and Godel ('Irish Prayer in the Early Middle Ages II', p. 74) notes that this ability is usually attributed to Psalm 118 (see also Anlezark,

Furthermore, the importance of this biblical text to the fabric of *SolSatI* and *SolSatII* suggests something important and perhaps unexpected about the fate of their pagan protagonist, Saturn. Anlezark notes that Saturn is 'sincere' in his pursuit of Christian knowledge,[64] and we have already observed that Jerusalem has exerted a repeated and almost gravitational pull on his travels. Psalm 118 suggests that even a traveller who has strayed from God's truth will achieve salvation if he seeks out the correct path: 'tuus ego sum salva me quoniam praecepta tua quaesivi' (I am yours, save me since I have sought your teachings, Ps. 118. 94). Manuscript lacunae obscure the endings of both *SolSatI* and *SolSatII*, but in the verse fragment which sits between the two longer poems in CCCC, MS 422, Solomon is declared to have overcome Saturn.[65] This defeat prompts Saturn to express joy, 'Næfre ær his ferhð ahlog' (Never before had his heart laughed, *SolSatFrag*, l. 9b), while the text reminds us that he had 'feorran gefered' (travelled from far off, *SolSatFrag*, l. 9a).[66] This signals a great change from the distress expressed by Saturn earlier in the debate and associated with his wanderings more generally. Despite Saturn's intellectual deficiencies,[67] it appears that his pursuit of Christian knowledge may allow him to achieve salvation; his straying and wandering have become correct and Christian movement through exposure to a sacred text.

I have spoken both of a gravitational 'pull' exerted by Jerusalem upon Saturn and also of his active wanderings, and this tension raises a question about the agency of the four wandering figures in the poems. Saturn's challenge to Solomon implies that his journey has been undertaken voluntarily (*SolSatI*, ll. 13–20); however, a pagan tradition of Saturn as an exile is reproduced in the *Institutiones* of Lactantius, which has parallels in the dialogues and may

---

Dialogues, p. 26). Wright draws attention to a connection between 'drops' and Psalm 118, not in connection with *SolSatI*, ll. 59b–62, but in connection with an earlier passage on torments faced by the devil (*The Irish Tradition in Old English Literature*, p. 238; see also Anlezark, *Dialogues*, pp. 102–03). See also Wright, "The Three "Victories" of the Wind', p. 22 n. 45; von Vincenti, *Die altenglischen Dialoge von Salomon und Saturn*, p. 59; Hill, 'Tormenting the Devil with Boiling Drops', p. 166 n. 15. Notker III of St Gall (950–1022) makes the first known reference to Solomon and his debate partner Marcolf in exegetical writing on Psalm 118 (Anlezark, *Dialogues*, p. 13, where he also writes further on the Solomon-Marcolfus tradition; Ziolkowski, *Solomon and Marcolf*, pp. 8, 317–20; von Vincenti, *Die altenglischen Dialoge von Salomon und Saturn*, p. 17). While not explicitly linking the poem and the psalm, Veronka Szőke and Megan Cavell each treat these texts together in their respective studies 'Nearu and its Collocations in Old English Verse' and 'Formulaic Friþuwebban', pp. 365–66.

64 Anlezark, *Dialogues*, p. 13.
65 For a theory that this fragment was originally the conclusion to *SolSatII*, see Anlezark, 'The Stray Ending in the Solomonic Anthology'; Anlezark, *Dialogues*, pp. 45, 49.
66 On Saturn's laughter, see further Beechy, 'Wisdom and the Poetics of Laughter in the Old English *Dialogues of Solomon and Saturn*'.
67 On which, see Wilcox, 'Eating Books', pp. 116–17; Powell, 'Orientalist Fantasy', esp. pp. 122–24; Anlezark, *Dialogues*, pp. 41, 101; Beechy, 'Wisdom and the Poetics of Laughter in the Old English *Dialogues of Solomon and Saturn*', esp. pp. 139–40.

have been known in early medieval England.[68] Saturn's mental distress adds nuance to the idea of agency, for his suffering appears to be the result of his 'curiosity', and it is this 'curiosity' which appears to exert control: it asks Saturn questions and is eager to set out in the world (*SolSatI*, ll. 57b–58b). The impression that Saturn is compelled in his travels by forces beyond his control is further suggested by the parallel between his worldwide wanderings and the wanderings of the sinner led across many lands by a demon in *SolSatII*, lines 308–19, as discussed above. The wanderings of the ignorant man in *SolSatI* (ll. 21–25, 34–35) represent his lack of Christian knowledge, and while he is not driven, the subject is presented as possessing no more autonomy or agency than an animal. The young exile of *SolSatII* (ll. 193–94, 198–205), like Saturn, seems to depart independently (*geong færeð*, 199). His displacement is figured not, as in the other passages, by where he wanders to, but by where he has wandered from: he exits the hall, he lives away from people, and his lord looks away from him.[69] The angels ('englum', *SolSatI*, l. 35a) in the account of the ignorant man and the lord ('hlaford', *SolSatII*, l. 205b) in the account of the young exile represent parallel models of authority. This analogy between secular, heroic hierarchy and heavenly order is a typical trope in Old English verse. As well as representing the sinfulness of spiritual wandering in material and social terms, the comparison points to the sinfulness of challenging divinely appointed authorities on earth, or absconding from the spaces they rule over.

Approaching Acts of Wandering as a Monastic Concern

The dialogues were most likely written in the context of early tenth-century monastic reform, composed for a learned religious audience.[70] I have previously explored pedagogical function in *SolSatI*, arguing that the poem incorporates exercises designed to train readers in exegetical analysis, and identifying the dialogues as participants in 'a monastic poetics'.[71] These contexts provide

---

68 Anlezark, *Dialogues*, pp. 31, 35–36.
69 Harbus writes that this episode 'explicitly link[s] unhappiness and misfortune with a lack of mental direction' ('The Situation of Wisdom in *Solomon and Saturn II*', p. 100).
70 Anlezark has persuasively argued that the author of the dialogues is likely to have been St Dunstan or one of his circle at Glastonbury during the reign of King Æthelstan (*Dialogues*, pp. 49–57). For alternative arguments proposing composition during the Alfredian period, see O'Neill, 'On the Date, Provenance and Relationship'; Wade, 'Language, Letters and Augustinian Origins'. In his introduction, Anlezark contextualizes the dialogues, addressing a number of sources and related genres with teaching functions, see *Dialogues*, esp. pp. 16–17, 24, 36–37; on the 'learned' character of the dialogues, see Anlezark, *Dialogues*, 'Introduction'.
71 Burns, 'Solomon and Saturn I, 89 a, "prologa prim"'; I follow Winfried Rudolf's comments on the pedagogical function of medieval riddles in teaching exegetical skills ('Riddling and Reading', esp. p. 501). 'Monastic poetics' is a term used by O'Camb ('Toward a Monastic Poetics' and '*Exeter Maxims, The Order of the World*, and the Exeter Book'); see also Niles, *God's Exiles and English Verse*.

a rationale for the texts' concern with mental aberration in the pursuit of knowledge, with the four metaphorical episodes of wandering providing distinct exempla of what such straying might look like to someone with access to a monastic library: the pursuit of pagan knowledge or purposeless engagement with non-Christian literature (Saturn's wanderings); ignorance of Christian learning (the episode of the ignorant man); deviation from figures and standards of authority (the exile of the young man); and the risk of following bad teachings over good ones (the episode of the sinner led by a demon). The dialogue structure of both *SolSatI* and *SolSatII* further lends to the poem the pedagogical aspect of famous dialogue literature circulating in early medieval England, such as Boethius's *De consolatione philosophiae* and Gregory's *Dialogues*.[72] Indeed, in Book II of his *Dialogues*, on the life of St Benedict, Gregory tells a story about sin and wandering in a monastic setting (emphases on aspects related to wandering added):[73]

> In uno autem ex eis monasteriis quae circumquaque construxerat, quidam monachus erat qui ad orationem stare non poterat: sed mox ut se fratres ad studium orationis inclinassent, ipse egrediebatur foras, *et mente vaga terrena aliqua et transitoria agebat*.

> (Also, in one out of those monasteries which [Benedict] had built all around, there was a certain monk who was not able to remain at prayers: but as soon as the brothers turned to the study of prayers, he would go outside, *and with a wandering mind occupied himself with something earthly and transitory*.)

The monk was sent to St Benedict for correction, but when this failed to have a permanent effect, Benedict came himself to the monastery:

> Cumque vir Dei venisset ad idem monasterium, et constituta hora, expleta psalmodia sese fratres in orationem dedissent, *aspexit quod eumdem*

---

72 Note that Solomonic dialogues are a distinct and heterogeneous tradition, which Anlezark summarizes (*Dialogues*, pp. 12–15).

73 Liber II, Caput iv; Latin text from PL, 66, col. 112. Irina Dumitrescu discusses this story in the context of *SolSatI* in *The Experience of Education in Anglo-Saxon Literature*, pp. 56–57. Another episode of demonic wandering in patristic writing, which may provide an analogue to Saturn's wanderings in *SolSatI*, occurs in Evagrius's *On Thoughts*, Book IX, 'There is a demon known as the one who leads astray ['wanderer'], who especially at dawn presents [himself] to the brothers, and leads around the mind of the solitary from city to city, from house to house, from village to village' (translation from *Evagrius Ponticus*, ed. by Casiday, p. 96). For discussion of this passage, see also Leneghan, 'Preparing the Mind for Prayer', pp. 124–25. Links between *SolSatII* and the writings of Gregory have been observed by Hill ('Two Notes on Solomon and Saturn', pp. 218–19), who notes that the account of the damned sinner in *SolSatII* draws from Gregory's description of the stages of sin in his *Moralia in Iob*, and Anlezark, who points to a shared interest in 'psychological process' between the two texts (*Dialogues*, p. 138). This attention to 'psychological process', then, seems to be part of a broader association between wandering, sinfulness, and misery made across the dialogues and ultimately drawn from patristic tradition.

*monachum qui in oratione manere non poterat, quidam niger puerulus per
vestimenti fimbriam foras traheret.*

> (And when the man of God went to that same monastery, and the
> hour was established when the singing of psalms was completed and
> the brothers gave themselves to prayer, *[Benedict] noticed that a certain
> dark little boy drew that same monk who was not able to remain in prayer
> outside by the border of his vestments.*)

In this anecdote about Benedict's encounter with a restless monk, wandering
is both physical (the monk would leave the place of prayer) and mental (his
'wandering mind' was concerned with 'earthly and transitory' things). The
passage is concerned particularly with the interrelated governance of both
space and time by communal rules: at the time the brethren must kneel
down inside, the aberrant monk walks outside, and it is at the particular
time between the singing of psalms and the saying of prayer that the devil
appears to lead him astray. The problem of wandering is here presented as
a subversive violation of the monastic rhythms required for both individual
devotion and collective organization. Mary Carruthers reads this episode as
an example of the patristic vice of *curiositas*, 'a kind of wandering about' and
'distraction' of the mind which ought to be focused, expressed by John Cassian
using 'locational' metaphors.[74] Saturn's 'fyrwit' (curiosity) corresponds with
this model and reflects broader anxieties about wandering minds. Gregory
addresses the more abstracted issue of the 'wandering mind' in Book XIX
of his *Moralia in Iob*: a wandering mind is a symptom of a deficiently 'light'
(*leves*) soul, easily lifted into motion by a force like wind; virtuous advice can
provide weight, steadfastness, and constancy.[75] Gregory's reference to 'wind'
may have influenced the episode of the ignorant man (*SolSatI*, l. 25a) who
wanders 'windes full' (full of wind). Elsewhere in the *Moralia*, Gregory notes
that the rigour of habit and ritual is not enough to guarantee salvation, for
mental wandering may be a precursor to sin (emphases added):[76]

> Nam saepe corde perverso necdum processit usque ad effectum operis
> deliberatio cogitationis, et adhuc fortasse per habitum intus astringitur,
> *qui iam mente foris vagatur.*

> > (For often, the heart being corrupted, but the deliberation of thought
> > not yet advanced all the way to an effected action, and perhaps even
> > now through religious life [he] is internally constrained, *who already
> > wanders outside in [his] mind.*)

---

74 Mary Carruthers, *The Craft of Thought*, pp. 83–84; see pp. 83–99 and 188–90; see also Irina
Dumitrescu, *The Experience of Education in Anglo-Saxon Literature*, pp. 56–57.

75 Liber XIX, Caput viii; Latin text from PL, 76, col. 100.

76 Liber XXV, Caput viii; Latin text from PL, 76, col. 331.

St Benedict himself addresses material and administrative concerns around practices of wandering in his *Rule*. He criticizes the itinerant order of 'Girovagi' monks, who are 'semper vagi et numquam stabiles et propriis voluptatibus et gule illecebris servientes' (always wandering and never stable, serving their own pleasures and the enticements of gluttony, Chapter I).[77] Here, wandering is not a compulsion brought on by the vice of *acedia*, but is rather an action that enables the pursuit of ungodly gratifications. As part of the instruction for the organization of a monastery, Benedict advises: 'Ad portam monasterii ponatur senex sapiens [...] et cuius maturitas eum non sinat vagari' (At the gate of the monastery let one be placed who is old and wise [...] and whose maturity does not permit him to wander, Chapter LXVI). In this instance, wandering is a problem that might affect monastic administration. Much of the *Rule* concerns temporal organization of the monastery's inhabitants, particularly those chapters dedicated to the Offices (see Chapters VII–XVII), but spatial organization is also key, such as the instructions for monks' sleeping arrangements (Chapter XXII), methods of punishment (Chapter XXIV), and guidance on whether monks who leave a monastery should be allowed to return (Chapter XXIX). As Benedict notes, other orders had different spatial and temporal systems of organization, for example, the isolation of anchorites, or the constant movement of Girovagi. Literary-pedagogical warnings against the perils of physical and mental wandering therefore have as much of a role for collective organization as for individual salvation. The spatialization of authority which we encounter both in Saturn's circuitous route to Jerusalem and in the episode on the young exile who abandons the hall may have emphasized for the reader that the spatial and temporal arrangement of monastic life was not to be strayed from.

Books as an Antidote to the Wandering Mind in the Dialogues

While warning the reader about the perils of wandering away from wisdom and authority, the poems also offer an antidote which can bring fixity and stillness to the mind: the power of holy books and texts.[78] Leneghan has

---

77 Latin text from St Benedict, *The Rule*, ed. by Logeman, p. 11.

78 Harbus writes on emotion and the moderating power of books ('The Situation of Wisdom in *Solomon and Saturn II*', for example, p. 99); Beechy, 'Wisdom and the Poetics of Laughter in the Old English *Dialogues of Solomon and Saturn*', sees books in the poem as 'the source both of wisdom and of happiness' (pp. 144–45) and as an 'authoritative means of disciplining the mind' (p. 146). The power of books in the poem has been noted by several scholars, for example Anlezark, 'Poisoned Places'; O'Neill, 'On the Date, Provenance and Relationship', p. 143. Powell writes that the poem 'fetishizes books' ('Orientalist Fantasy', p. 122); see also Dumitrescu, *The Experience of Education in Anglo-Saxon Literature*, p. 52. Distinct but relevant approaches to books in the dialogues include Christie on 'anxiety about

written about a similar process at work in the composition of *The Wanderer*, which is intended as a 'meditative tool' for monks, drawing upon treatises by Evagrius and Cassian on the achievement of *hesychasm*, 'stillness in prayer'.[79] God's disdain for wilful ignorance, and the power of Christian literature to overcome such ignorance with spiritual learning, is enshrined in the gnomic verse wisdom of the Exeter Book poem *Instructions for Christians* (ll. 63–65, 83–86):[80]

Swa hwilc man swa mæg   and nu nele
Geleornian hwaet-hwugo,   he bið lað Gode,
And his saul bið   swið scyldig.
[...]
Se ðe leornunge   longe fyligeð
Halgum bocum   her on worulde,
Heo ðone gelaeredon   longe gebetað
And þone unlaerdan   eac gelaereð.

> (So, if a man may but does not now wish to learn something, he will be hateful to God, and his soul will be very guilty. [...] He who for a long time attends to learning, through holy books here in the world, he will long amend the learned, and also teach the unlearned.)

Benedict's own stipulations regarding monastic reading in the *Rule* imply that engagement with books has a curative and even penitential aspect (by association with the season of Lent) for brethren:[81]

> Otiositas inimica est anime et ideo certis temporibus occupari debent fratres in labore manuum certis iterum horis in lectione divina.

> (Idleness is the enemy of the soul, and therefore the brothers ought to be occupied at certain times in manual labour, and at certain times in divine reading.)

> (Chapter XLVIII.1)

> In quadragesime vero diebus a mane usque ad tertiam plenam vacent lectionibus suis [...]. In quibus diebus quadragesime accipiant omnes singulos codices de bibliotheca quos per ordinem ex integro legant.

---

the materiality of writing and the ability to discern spiritual reality through this medium' ('By Means of a Secret Alphabet', p. 150); Wilcox, 'Eating Books'; Nelson, 'King Solomon's Magic', on the importance of written text in the poem (p. 20) and on words as a 'remedy', which corresponds with the idea of 'antidote' here (p. 27) and Wade, 'Language, Letters and Augustinian Origins', on anxiety around books corresponding with an Alfredian period of composition.

79 Leneghan, 'Preparing the Mind for Prayer', esp. pp. 123–24, 139–40.
80 Old English from *Old English Shorter Poems*, ed. and trans. by Jones, p. 143.
81 Latin text from *The Rule*, ed. by Logeman, pp. 81–83.

(Truly, in the days of Lent, from morning until the completion of the third hour let them have time for their readings [...]. During those days of Lent, let everyone receive a book from the library, which they are to read in order in its entirety.)

(Chapter XLVIII.14–16)

In the dialogues, books repeatedly feature two characteristics which demonstrate their role as antidote: they explicitly encourage virtue; and they espouse a fixed spatiality to counter wandering motion.[82] This association arises in one of the riddlic exchanges of *SolSatII*:

SATVRNVS CVAEÐ:
Ac hwæt is se dumba,   se ðe on sumre dene resteð?
Swiðe snyttrað,   hafað seofon tungan,
hafað tungena gehwylc   . xx . orda,
hafað orda gehwylc   engles snytro,
ðara ðe wile anra hwylc   uppe bringan,
*ðæt ðu ðære gyldnan gesiehst   Hierusalem
weallas blican   ond hiera winrod lixan,*
soðfæstra segn.   Saga hwæt ic mæne.

SALOMON CVAEÐ:
Bec sindon breme,   *bodiað geneahhe
weotodne willan   ðam ðe wiht hygeð,
gestrangað hie ond gestaðeliað   staðolfæstne geðoht,
amyrgað modsefan   manna gehwylces*
of ðreamedlan   ðisses lifes.

(*SolSatII*, ll. 52–64, emphases added)

(SATURN SAID: But what is that voiceless thing, which rests in a certain valley? It is very wise and has seven tongues, each tongue has twenty points, each point has the wisdom of an angel, each and every one of these will bring you up *so that you see the golden walls of Jerusalem shining*, and the joyful chorus gleaming, a sign of the righteous. Say what I mean.

SOLOMON SAID: Books are illustrious, *they earnestly announce the fixed mind to anyone who thinks at all, it strengthens and establishes firm-fixed thought, cheers the mind of each man* from the mental strife of this life.)

---

82 Powell comments briefly on the power of books in relation to journeying in *SolSatII*, writing that 'books are a place one can go to seek shelter — or in this case, wisdom — during an intellectual or spiritual storm before leaving again on one's own educational journey' ('Orientalist Fantasy', p. 125).

The subject of this exchange is not known until Solomon responds, 'Bec' (books, l. 60). His response precisely mirrors the sequence of attributes which Saturn uses in his riddle: each speaker first addresses the greatness of books and the way books speak, before moving to consider the power of books, both to counter wandering with fixed spatiality and also to counter sadness. This mirroring by Solomon shows him responding to every aspect of Saturn's puzzle in a display of his superior, God-granted wisdom. The exchange aligns geographical and mental fixedness: Saturn states that books have the power to raise up a reader until they can see Jerusalem — the setting of the poem and the seat of biblical learning — and Solomon responds that a book 'strengthens and establishes firm-fixed thought'. It is fitting that Saturn, who is limited by his pagan outlook throughout the poems, and whom critics have often described as overtly literal in his understanding, sees only the material, geographical aspects of fixedness.[83]

There are several such references to texts across the two poems, two of which occur in *SolSatI*:

> Þonne him bið leofre   ðonne eall ðeos leohte gesceaft
> gegoten fram ðam grunde   goldes and silofres,
> *feðerscette* full   fyrngestreona,
> gif he æfre ðæs organes   owiht cuðe.
>
> (SolSatI, ll. 30–33, emphasis added)

> (Then it will be more beloved to him than all this bright creation founded from the earth, of gold and silver, *the four corners* full of ancient treasure, if he ever knew anything of that song [the Pater Noster].)

> Forðon hafað se cantic   ofer ealle Cristes bec
> widmærost word;   he gewritu læreð,
> *stefnum steoreð,*   *ond him stede healdeð*
> *heofona rices.*
>
> (SolSatI, ll. 49–52a, emphasis added)

> (Therefore, the canticle has, above all the books of Christ, the most far-famed words; it teaches the scripture, *steers voices, and keeps an appointed place for them in the kingdom of heaven.*)

The canticle, or the Pater Noster, is variously imagined in *SolSatI* as a written and an oral text; in the second of these two extracts we can see it compared

---

83 For the argument that *SolSatII*, l. 89a and the subsequent episode of the Pater Noster battle can be read as training for monks to read both literally and spiritually, see Burns, 'Solomon and Saturn I, 89 a, "prologa prim"'. For interpretations of Saturn as a character who interprets too literally, see Powell, 'Orientalist Fantasy', p. 128; Wilcox, 'Eating Books'. Olsen, 'Shining Swords and Heavenly Walls', pp. 211–13; Dane, 'The Structure of the *Old English Solomon and Saturn II*', esp. pp. 593–96.

superlatively to 'the books of Christ', but also described as steering 'voices'.[84] In each extract, the Pater Noster is linked to imagery suggestive of fixed spaces and destinations: in lines 30–33, the favourable comparison of the Pater Noster to a map-like description of creation, with its 'four corners'; in lines 49–52, the power of the prayer to 'steer voices', which we are led to believe must belong to mortal souls, for the prayer also 'keeps an appointed place for them in [...] heaven', spatializing their salvation. This image draws on a tradition of early medieval cartography in which maps were used to communicate spiritual and political messages, as discussed by Helen Appleton in her chapter of this volume. Another example of the spatial representation of grace in Old English verse comes at the end of *The Wanderer*, where the final image that the speaker gives us of the hope he has in heavenly salvation is that of *fæstnung* ('fixity') in heaven, 'the place of God'.[85] A metaphor of books as guardians of sea travellers occurs early in *SolSatII*: 'Sige hie onsendað soðfæstra gehwam, | hælo hyðe, ðam ðe hie lufað' (They send victory to each of the righteous, *safety through a port*, for those who love [books], ll. 67–68). I have argued elsewhere that aspects of the Pater Noster battle in *SolSatI* are intended to provide monastic readers with exempla of the practice of *lectio divina*, or divine reading, and affirmations of its value.[86] Anlezark has argued that *SolSatI* may have been intended as a 'sequel' to *SolSatII*, with the Pater Noster battle offering a salvific answer to the problem of the wandering sinner at the end of *SolSatII*.[87] Ultimately, knowledge of the Pater Noster is the truth which Saturn seeks to be satisfied by after his long travels (*SolSatI*, l. 18a). It would certainly be fitting if the first poem in the sequence (*SolSatII*) proffered the antidote of books to the wandering mind, and the second poem (*SolSatI*) gave advice on how best to read them.[88]

Conclusions

The psychogeographical contours affecting the wandering figures of the dialogues draw a contrast between established practices or communal knowledge on the one hand, which are figured as spatially fixed and psychologically curative, and movement at odds with such practices or authority on the other hand, which are figured as spatially aberrant and haphazard, as well as mentally

---

84 O'Brien O'Keeffe argues that the battle of the letters engages with a tradition of 'tension' between written and spoken language (*Visible Song*, pp. 51–59).

85 Leneghan, 'Preparing the Mind for Prayer', p. 131, and see also p. 137.

86 Burns, 'Solomon and Saturn I, 89 a, "prologa prim"'.

87 Anlezark, *Dialogues*, p. 56.

88 Anlezark also notes of Jerome's description of travelling pagans in *Epistula liii*: 'Reading the book is not enough, as its meanings are enigmatic, and only with the "key" can the mystery be understood', a reference perhaps linked to Saturn's unlocking of books in *SolSatII* (*Dialogues*, p. 38). On runes in *SolSatI*, see further Birkett, 'Unlocking Runes?', esp. pp. 108–09.

distressing. Named structures and spaces appear in the dialogues — field, hall, and temple — but the episodes of wandering, much like source material in the discussed patristic literature, expend more focus on describing motion towards or away from members of a social or Christian community, and the psychology of the wanderers. Spiritual and mental peace are to be found by engaging with holy texts which, map-like, will help the reader reach fixity of both thought and place.

Modern psychogeographical writing shares with the dialogues of Solomon and Saturn an appreciation of the subversive potential of the act of wandering, but where such subversion and resistance is celebrated within the modern tradition, it is connected with sin and exile in the medieval poems. Whereas for Debord and his contemporary psychogeographers, the individual's resistance to received definitions of space was a means of rescuing both the city and the individual from authoritarian and capitalist domination, for St Dunstan and his contemporaries, such resistance would have certainly meant damnation for the individual and threatened the community as a whole. This is perhaps not so much a distinct outlook on the act of wandering, as on pleasure and the value of subjective experience. As influential a contemporary as Augustine is acutely aware of the pleasure an individual finds in the earthly wanderings of human life, and he makes it clear that such pleasure is entirely misplaced:

> Quomodo ergo, si essemus peregrini, qui beate vivere nisi in patria non possemus, eaque peregrinatione utique miseri et miseriam finire cupientes, in patriam redire vellemus […] quod si amoenitates itineris, et ipsa gestatio vehiculorum nos delectaret, et conversi ad fruendum his quibus uti debuimus, nollemus cito viam finire, et perversa suavitate implicati alienaremur a patria, cuius suavitas faceret beatos: sic in huius mortalitatis vita peregrinantes a Domino.
>
> > (Therefore how would it be, if we were travellers abroad, who were not able to live happily unless in our homeland, and in any case were feeling miserable through travel and desiring to end our misery, we might desire to return to our homeland […] but if the pleasantness of the journey and the conveyance of the vehicles themselves delight us, and having inverted that which we ought to use into what is to be enjoyed, we are unwilling to quickly finish the course, corrupted and embraced by sweetness, we are alienated from the homeland whose sweetness would make us truly happy: so it is in this mortal life, wandering away from God.)[89]

Thus, this highly intellectual Old English verse collection grapples with issues which have continued to trouble philosophers some thousand years

---

89 *De doctrina Christiana*, I. iv; Latin text from PL, 34, cols 20–21. On the metaphor of life-as-journey, Augustinian thought, and the 'Christian imperative to travel purposefully', see Harbus, 'Travelling Metaphors and Mental Wandering in Old English Poetry', pp. 128–29.

later: the interaction of spatiality and human mentality, and the control and definition of communal spaces by authorities. The subversive act of wandering has a literary history that goes back further than Defoe, indeed to the earliest centuries of English writing.

Works Cited

Manuscripts

Cambridge, Corpus Christi College, MS 41, <https://parker.stanford.edu/parker/catalog/qd527zm3425> [accessed 18 May 2021]
Cambridge, Corpus Christi College, MS 422, <https://parker.stanford.edu/parker/catalog/fr610kh2998> [accessed 18 May 2021]

Primary Sources

Augustine of Hippo, *Sancti Aurelii Augustini Hipponensis Episcopi Opera Omnia*, PL, 34 (Paris, 1841)
Benedict, *The Rule of S. Benet*, ed. by H. Logeman, EETS OS, 90 (London: Trübner, 1888)
Biblia sacra iuxta vulgatam versionem, ed. by Robert Weber and Roger Gryson, 5th edn (Stuttgart: Deutsche Bibelgesellschaft, 2007)
Cassiodorus, *Explanation of the Psalms*, ed. and trans. by P. G. Walsh, Ancient Christian Writers, 53 (New York: Paulist Press, 1990–1991)
The Dialogue of Salomon and Saturnus: With an Historical Introduction, ed. by John M. Kemble (London: Richard and John Taylor, 1848)
The Dictionary of Medieval Latin from British Sources, ed. by R. E. Latham, D. R. Howlett, and R. K. Ashdowne (London: British Academy, 1975–2013)
Evagrius Ponticus, ed. by Augustine Casiday, Early Church Fathers (London: Routledge, 2006)
Gregory the Great, *Sancti Benedicti Monachorum Occidentalium Patris, Opera Omnia*, PL, 66 (Paris: Garnier Fratres, 1866)
——, *Sancti Gregorii Papæ I, Cognomento Magni, Omnia Opera*, PL, 76 (Paris: Garnier Fratres, 1878)
Jerome, *Letters and Select Works*, ed. and trans. by William H. Fremantle, A Select Library of Nicene and Post-Nicene Fathers: 2nd series, 6 (repr. Grand Rapids, MI: Wm. B. Eerdmans, 1954)
A Latin Dictionary, Founded on Andrews' Edition of Freund's Latin Dictionary, ed. by Charlton T. Lewis and Charles Short (Oxford: Clarendon Press, 1879)
The Old English Dialogues of Solomon and Saturn, ed. and trans. by Daniel Anlezark, Anglo-Saxon Texts, 7 (Woodbridge: Boydell & Brewer, 2009)
Old English Shorter Poems, 1: Religious and Didactic, ed. and trans. by Christopher A. Jones, DOML, 15 (Cambridge, MA: Harvard University Press, 2012)

Septuagint: Id est Vetus Testamentum Graece iuxta LXX interpretes, ed. by
Alfred Rahlfs, 2nd rev. edn, ed. by Robert Hanhart (Stuttgart: Deutsche
Bibelgesellschaft, 2006)

Secondary Sources

Abram, Christopher, 'At Home in the Fens with the Grendelkin', in *Dating Beowulf:
Studies in Intimacy*, ed. by Daniel C. Remein and Erica Weaver, Manchester
Medieval Literature and Culture, 30 (Manchester: Manchester University
Press, 2019), pp. 120–44

Ackroyd, Peter, 'The Englishness of English Literature', in *Proceedings of the XIXth
International Conference of ADEAN* (Vigo: Departamento de Filoloxía Inglesa e
Alemana da Universidade de Vigo, 1996), pp. 11–19

Anlezark, Daniel, 'Poisoned Places: The Avernian Tradition in Old English Poetry',
ASE, 36 (2007), 103–25

——, '"Stand Firm": The Descent to Hell in Felix's Life of Saint Guthlac', in
Darkness, Depression, and Descent in Anglo-Saxon England, ed. by Ruth Wehlau
(Kalamazoo: Medieval Institute Publications, 2019), pp. 255–76

——, 'The Stray Ending in the Solomonic Anthology in Cambridge, Corpus
Christi College, MS 422', *MÆ*, 80 (2011), 201–16

Appleton, Helen, 'The Northern World of the Anglo-Saxon *mappa mundi*', *ASE*, 47
(2018), 275–305

——, 'The Role of Æschere's Head', *RES*, 68 (2017), 428–47

Bailey, Hannah McKendrick, 'Misinterpretation and the Meaning of Signs in Old
English Poetry' (unpublished doctoral dissertation, University of Oxford, 2015)

Beechy, Tiffany, 'Wisdom and the Poetics of Laughter in the Old English *Dialogues
of Solomon and Saturn*', *JEGP*, 116 (2017), 131–55

Birkett, Tom, 'Unlocking Runes? Reading Anglo-Saxon Runic Abbreviations
in their Immediate Literary Context', *Futhark: International Journal of Runic
Studies*, 5 (2015), 91–114

Bisher, Franklin E, 'Heterogeneous Religious Expression in the Old English
"Solomon and Saturn" Dialogues' (unpublished doctoral thesis, State
University of New York at Buffalo, 1988)

Bonnet, Alastair, 'Psychogeography', *Oxford Bibliographies*, 2013, <https://www.
oxfordbibliographies.com/view/document/obo-9780199874002/obo-
9780199874002-0020.xml> [accessed 17 May 2021]

Bosworth, Joseph, and T. Northcote Toller, eds, *An Anglo-Saxon Dictionary* (London: Oxford University Press, 1882–1898); T. Northcote Toller, ed., *Supplement
to An Anglo-Saxon Dictionary Based on the Manuscript Collections of the Late
Joseph Bosworth* (Oxford: Clarendon Press, 1921), <https://bosworthtoller.com>

Burns, Rachel A., '*Solomon and Saturn I*, 89 a, "prologa prim": An Exercise in
Monastic Reading Practice', *Anglia*, 138 (2020), 618–48

Carruthers, Mary, *The Craft of Thought: Meditation, Rhetoric, and the Making of
Images, 400–1200* (Cambridge, Cambridge University Press 2000)

Cavell, Megan, 'Formulaic Friþuwebban: Reexamining Peace-Weaving in the Light of Old English Poetics', *JEGP*, 114 (2015), 355–72

Christie, E. J., 'By Means of a Secret Alphabet: Dangerous Letters and the Semantics of Gebregdstafas (*Solomon and Saturn I*, Line 2b)', *Modern Philology*, 109 (2011), 145–70

Clark Hall, J. R., *A Concise Anglo-Saxon Dictionary*, 4th edn (Toronto: University of Toronto Press, 1960)

Clemoes, Peter, 'Mens absentia cogitans', in *Medieval Literature and Civilization Studies in Memory of G. N. Garmonsway*, ed. by D. A. Pearsall and R. A. Waldron, Bloomsbury Academic Collections: English Literary Criticism (London: Athlone Press, 1969), pp. 62–77

Coverley, Merlin, *Psychogeography*, 3rd edn (Oldcastle Books, 2018)

Dane, Joseph A., 'The Structure of the *Old English Solomon and Saturn II*', *Neophilologus*, 64 (1980), 592–603

Davies, Damian Walford, and Tim Fulford, 'Introduction: Romanticism's Wye', *Romanticism*, 19.2: *The Wye Valley* (2013), 115–25

Day, John, '*The Last London* by Iain Sinclair Review — an Elegy for a City now Lost', *The Guardian*, 27 September 2017, <https://www.theguardian.com/books/2017/sep/27/last-london-iain-sinclair-review> [accessed 15 January 2022]

Debord, Guy, 'Introduction to a Critique of Urban Geography' (1955), in *Situationist International Anthology*, ed. by Ken Knabb (Berkeley: Bureau of Public Secrets, 2006), pp. 8–11

——, 'Theory of the *Dérive*', in *Situationist International Anthology*, ed. by Ken Knabb (Berkeley: Bureau of Public Secrets, 2006), 62–67

Dendle, Peter, 'The Demonological Landscape of the "Solomon and Saturn" Cycle', *English Studies*, 80 (1999), 281–92

——, 'The Role of the Devil in Old English Narrative Literature' (unpublished doctoral thesis, University of Toronto, 1998)

Dumitrescu, Irina, *The Experience of Education in Anglo-Saxon Literature* (Cambridge: Cambridge University Press, 2018)

Elden, Stuart, 'Place Symbolism and Land Politics in *Beowulf*', *Cultural Geographies*, 16 (2009), 447–63

Estes, Heide, *Anglo-Saxon Literary Landscapes: Ecotheory and the Environmental Imagination*, Environmental Humanities in Pre-modern Cultures (Amsterdam: Amsterdam University Press, 2017)

Gelling, Margaret, 'The Landscape of *Beowulf*', *ASE*, 31 (2002), 7–11

Godel, Willibrord, 'Irish Prayer in the Early Middle Ages II', *Milltown Studies*, 5 (1980), 85–96

Harbus, Antonina, *Cognitive Approaches to Old English Poetry*, Anglo-Saxon Studies, 18 (Cambridge: D. S. Brewer, 2012)

——, 'The Situation of Wisdom in *Solomon and Saturn II*', *Studia Neophilologica*, 75 (2003), 97–103

——, 'Travelling Metaphors and Mental Wandering in Old English Poetry', in *The World of Travellers: Exploration and Imagination*, ed. by Kees Dekker, Karin

Olsen, and Tette Hofstra, Mediaevalia Groningana, n.s. 15, Germania Latina, 7 (Leuven: Peeters, 2009), pp. 117–32

Hay, Duncan, 'Transforming Psychogeography: From Paris to London', *Walled City* (2008)

Heckman, Christina M., 'The Order of the World: Boethius's Translation of Aristotle's "Categoriae" and the Old English "Solomon and Saturn" Dialogues', *Carmina Philosophiae*, 22 (2013), 35–64

Heinmiller, Mary Gene, 'Orality, Literacy, and Dialogue: Cultural and Stylistic Context for the Old English Solomon and Saturn' (unpublished doctoral thesis, University of Rochester, 1991)

Hill, Thomas D., 'Tormenting the Devil with Boiling Drops: An Apotropaic Motif in the Old English "Solomon and Saturn I" and Old Norse-Icelandic Literature', *JEGP*, 92 (1993), 157–66

——, 'Two Notes on *Solomon and Saturn*', *MÆ*, 40 (1971), 217–21

Irvine, Ian, '*Acedia*, *Tristitia* and Sloth: Early Christian Forerunners to Chronic Ennui', *Humanitas*, 21.1 (1999), 89–103

Keefer, Sarah Larratt, and David R. Burrows, 'Hebrew and the *Hebraicum* in Late Anglo-Saxon England', *ASE*, 19 (1990), 67–80

Kendall, Calvin B., 'The Prefix un- and the Metrical Grammar of *Beowulf*', *ASE*, 10 (1981), 39–52

Langeslag, Paul S., 'Monstrous Landscape in Beowulf', *ES*, 96 (2015), 119–38

Leneghan, Francis, 'Preparing the Mind for Prayer: *The Wanderer*, *Hesychasm* and *Theosis*', *Neophilologus*, 100 (2016), 121–42

Lockett, Leslie, *Anglo-Saxon Psychologies in the Vernacular and Latin Traditions* (Toronto: University of Toronto Press, 2011)

Löffler, Catharina, *Walking in the City: Urban Experience and Literary Psycho-geography in Eighteenth-Century London* (Wiesbaden: J. B. Metzler, 2017)

Major, Tristan, 'Saturn's First Riddle in *Solomon and Saturn II*: An Orientalist Conflation', *Neophilologus*, 96 (2012), 301–13

Martin, Sarah, 'Psychogeography and the Detective: Re-evaluating the Significance of Space in Agatha Christie's *A Murder Is Announced*', *Clues*, 36 (2018), 20–29

Menner, Robert J., 'Nimrod and the Wolf in the Old English "Solomon and Saturn"', *JEGP*, 37 (1938), 332–54

Michelet, Fabienne L., *Creation, Migration, and Conquest: Imaginary Geography and Sense of Space in Old English Literature* (Oxford: Oxford University Press, 2006)

Mudie, Ella, 'Convulsions of the Local: Contemporary British Psychogeographical Fiction', in *Twenty-First Century British Fiction and the City*, ed. by Magali Cornier Michael (Cham: Palgrave MacMillan, 2018), pp. 205–31

Nelson, Marie, 'King Solomon's Magic: The Power of a Written Text', *Oral Tradition*, 5 (1990), 20–36

Neville, Jennifer, *Representations of the Natural World in Old English Poetry*, Cambridge Studies in Anglo-Saxon England, 27 (Cambridge: Cambridge University Press, 1999)

Niles, John D., *God's Exiles and English Verse: On the Exeter Anthology of Old English Poetry* (Exeter: University of Exeter Press, 2019)

North, Richard, 'Heaven Ahoy! Sensory Perception in *The Seafarer*', in *Sensory Perception in the Medieval West: Manuscripts, Texts, and Other Material Matters*, ed. by Simon Thomson and M. J. Bintley, Utrecht Studies in Medieval Literacy, 34 (Turnhout: Brepols, 2016), pp. 7–26

O'Brien O'Keeffe, Katherine, 'The Geographic List of *Solomon and Saturn II*', *ASE*, 20 (1991), 123–41

——, *Visible Song: Transitional Literacy in Old English Verse*, Cambridge Studies in Anglo-Saxon England, 4 (Cambridge: Cambridge University Press, 1990)

O'Camb, Brian, '*Exeter Maxims*, *The Order of the World*, and the Exeter Book of Old English Poetry', *PQ*, 93 (2014), 409–33

——, 'Toward a Monastic Poetics: Exeter Maxims and the Exeter Book of Old English Poetry' (unpublished doctoral dissertation, University of Wisconsin, Madison, 2009)

O'Neill, Patrick P., 'On the Date, Provenance and Relationship of the "Solomon and Saturn" Dialogues', *ASE*, 26 (1997), 139–68

Olsen, Karen Edith, 'Shining Swords and Heavenly Walls: In Search of Wisdom in "Solomon and Saturn II"', in *Calliope's Classroom: Studies in Didactic Poetry from Antiquity to the Renaissance*, ed. by Annette Harder, Alasdair A. MacDonald, and G. Reinink (Leuven: Peeters, 2007), pp. 203–20

Overing, Gillian R., and Marijane Osborn, *Landscapes of Desire: Partial Stories of the Medieval Scandinavian World* (Minneapolis: University of Minnesota Press, 1994)

Persson, Karl Arthur Erik, 'Job, Ecclesiastes and the Mechanics of Wisdom in Old English Poetry' (unpublished doctoral thesis, University of British Columbia, 2014)

Powell, Kathryn, 'Orientalist Fantasy in the Poetic Dialogues of *Solomon and Saturn*', *ASE*, 34 (2005), 117–43

Richardson, Tina, 'Introduction: A Wander through the Scene of British Urban Walking', in *Walking Inside Out: Contemporary British Psychogeography*, ed. by Tina Richardson (London: Rowman & Littlefield International, 2015), pp. 1–30

Ross, Kent Chapin, 'Developing a Method of Literary Psychogeography in Postmodern Fictions of Detection: Paul Auster's *The New York Trilogy* and Martin Amis's *London Fields*' (unpublished doctoral dissertation, Texas A&M University-Commerce, 2013)

Rudolf, Winfried, 'Riddling and Reading: Iconicity and Logographs in Exeter Book *Riddles* 23 and 45', *Anglia*, 130 (2012), 499–525

Ryan, J. S., 'Old English Wisdom Poetry (review)', *Parergon*, 17 (1999), 261–64

Sebald, W. G., *The Rings of Saturn* (London: Harvill, 1998)

Self, Will, *Psychogeography* (London: Bloomsbury, 2007)

Shippey, Thomas A., *Poems of Wisdom and Learning in Old English* (Cambridge: D. S. Brewer, 1976)

Sinclair, Iain, *The Last London: True Fictions from an Unreal City* (London: Oneworld, 2018)

Solnit, Rebecca, *Wanderlust: A History of Walking* (London: Verso, 2001)

Szőke, Veronka, 'Nearu and its Collocations in Old English Verse', *Linguistica e Filologia*, 34 (2014), 53–93

Thompson, John J., 'London's Chaucer: A Psychogeography', in *Geoffrey Chaucer in Context*, ed. by Ian Johnson (Cambridge: Cambridge University Press, 2019), pp. 363–70

Vincenti, Arthur Ritter von, *Die altenglischen Dialoge von Salomon und Saturn* (Leipzig: A. Deichert, 1904)

Wade, Erik, 'Language, Letters and Augustinian Origins in the Old English Poetic *Solomon and Saturn I*', *JEGP*, 117 (2018), 160–84

Wallis, Mary V., 'Patterns of Wisdom in the Old English *Solomon and Saturn II*' (unpublished doctoral thesis, Ottawa, Ontario, 1991)

Wehlau, Ruth, '"Seeds of Sorrow": Landscapes of Despair in *The Wanderer*, Beowulf's Story of Hrethel, and *Sonatorrek*', *Parergon*, 15 (1998), 1–17

Wenzel, Siegfried, *The Sin of Sloth: Acedia in Medieval Thought and Literature* (Chapel Hill: University of North Carolina Press)

Wilcox, Jonathan, 'Eating Books: The Consumption of Learning in the Old English Poetic *Solomon and Saturn*', *American Notes & Queries*, n.s. 4 (1991), 115–18

Wright, Charles, *The Irish Tradition in Old English Literature*, Cambridge Studies in Anglo-Saxon England, 6 (Cambridge: Cambridge University Press, 1993)

——, 'The Three "Victories" of the Wind: A Hibernicism in the "Hisperica Famina, Collectanea Bedae", and the Old English Prose "Solomon and Saturn" Pater Noster Dialogue', *Ériu*, 41 (1990), 13–25

Ziolkowski, Jan, *Solomon and Marcolf* (Cambridge, MA: Harvard University Press, 2008)

S. C. THOMSON

Otherwheres in the Prose Texts of the Nowell Codex: Here and Otherwhere

In common with other chapters in this volume — those, for instance, by Mark Atherton, Rachel Burns, Caitlin Ellis, and Ryan Lavelle — this discussion is interested in the association between *where* something is and *what* it is in early medieval English texts. The places being considered here are all 'otherwheres'; that is, places that are defined by being in a location different from the reader's. This chapter argues that the three texts under consideration are explicitly interested in the otherness of these places and of those beings to be found there, not for their own sake, but because it is in that space of difference that the self can develop. Developmental psychologists might talk about this as a reflective or relational space, or more broadly as the world of play; phenomenologists as a form of Martin Heidegger's *Miteinandersein* or Maurice Merleau-Ponty's 'movement to and fro of existence'; sociologists as an expression of rhizomatic, networked life; psychologists as a 'dyadic expansion of consciousness'; and so on.[1] A broader discussion of different conceptualizations and applications of this dynamic is beyond the bounds of both this chapter and my capacity. Here, I simply seek to claim that a trio of texts from an eleventh-century English manuscript is interested in encounters with 'otherness' (very broadly conceived), which it locates in embodied forms that occupy otherwheres.[2]

---

* This discussion has benefitted significantly from comments from members of the Anglistik 1 Research Colloquium at HHU. I am also very grateful to the editors for their thoughtful management of this wider project under such difficult conditions, and specifically for their insightful comments on an earlier draft of this chapter. I am also indebted to Miriam Edlich-Muth, Anne-Katrin Röseler, Niamh Kehoe, and Brepols's external reviewer for their careful readings, comments, and suggestions.

1 See, respectively and as examples only, Winnicott, 'Mirror Role of Mother and Family'; Heidegger, *Being and Time*; Merleau-Ponty, *Phenomenology of Perception*; Deleuze and Guattari, *A Thousand Plateaus*; Latour, *Reassembling the Social*; Tronick, 'Dyadically Expanded States of Consciousness'.

2 For related discussions of place and otherness in these and other texts (though excluding *Passion of St Christopher*), which have influenced my own thinking in ways too far-reaching to acknowledge in individual footnotes, see Howe, *Writing the Map of Anglo-Saxon England*; Mittman, *Maps and Monsters*; and Discenza, *Inhabited Spaces*.

S. C. Thomson (thomson@hhu.de) is Senior Lecturer in Medieval English Language and Literature at Heinrich-Heine-Universität, Düsseldorf.

Ideas of the World in Early Medieval English Literature, ed. by Mark Atherton, Kazutomo Karasawa, and Francis Leneghan, SOEL 1 (Turnhout: Brepols, 2022)   pp. 103–126
BREPOLS ❧ PUBLISHERS   DOI 10.1484/M.SOEL.5.130558

These texts do not seek to acknowledge or connect with the subjectivity of that which is different — to, in Emmanuel Levinas's terminology, 'approach the face of the other' — but rather to use the space between 'here' and 'there', between 'subject' and 'object', to the benefit of the self.[3] I suggest that in these texts, we can identify a process of racialization: the active construction of particular groups as 'different' and, implicitly, as subordinate to 'the default identity around which all other bodies and experiences are organised'.[4] The unspoken 'default' self that produces and consumes these texts is therefore an unreflective one: an identity that is never called upon to consider the contexts and networks within which it exists, still less to conceptualize its own being as an object to others.

The three texts to be discussed here are usually called the *Passion of St Christopher*, *The Wonders of the East*, and *Alexander the Great's Letter to Aristotle*.[5] These works of prose translation are more well known as a group than in their own rights; the collective is best known because it is preserved in London, British Library, MS Cotton Vitellius A XV or 'the Nowell Codex', which is itself more famous as the manuscript containing *Beowulf* and *Judith*. It would be possible to extend most of the arguments made in this chapter to the poetic works; the scholarly work of reading all five texts together has only just begun.[6] But the three prose texts provide more than enough material for individual and collective discussion; what is more, they enable a productive focus on the eastern and southern borders of the world known to the English: to consider the specific fantasies of otherness that were projected onto these spaces.[7]

---

3 Levinas, 'Being-Toward-Death', p. 135.
4 On racialization, see for example Hochman, 'Racialization'. The quotation is from Rambaran-Olm, Leake, and Goodrich, 'Medieval Studies'.
5 The three texts are transcribed and lightly edited together by Rypins in *Three Old English Prose Texts*, and edited and translated together by Robert Fulk in *The 'Beowulf' Manuscript*. Fulk, though, presents a different text of *Wonders*; the only edition and translation of the Nowell Codex version is that by Elaine Treharne in *Old and Middle English*, pp. 173–81. The standard editions of *Wonders* and *Alexander*, each preceded by the closest Latin texts, are edited and translated by Andy Orchard in *Pride and Prodigies*, at pp. 183–203 and 224–53 respectively; that of *Christopher* is Phillip Pulsiano's 'Passion of Saint Christopher'. Pulsiano also prints a related Latin text, but as briefly discussed in note 10 below, this is not particularly closely related to the Old English translation.
6 See Thomson, *Communal Creativity in the Making of the 'Beowulf' Manuscript*, at pp. 1–4 and 13–15, with fuller references than space allows here. On racialization in *Beowulf*, see most recently Miyashiro, 'Homeland Insecurity'.
7 Within this volume, see also Daniel Anlezark's discussion of actual journeys from England to southern Europe and to Asia, and Helen Appleton's exploration of early medieval English world maps.

These Texts in *This* Manuscript

It is worth noting that, beyond their collective inclusion in a single, unusual, manuscript, there is relatively little to bind these three works together.[8] *Christopher* is a hagiography, an Old English translation which was likely made in the later tenth century somewhere in southern England, and which also appeared in at least one larger collection of mostly Ælfrician lives of saints.[9] The first two thirds of the Old English text are now missing, so the bulk of the story has to be recreated by comparison with Latin analogues. Latin copies, in astonishingly diverse forms, are widespread in western Europe: they occasionally appear with non-hagiographical texts, but are overwhelmingly witnessed in legendaries of one form or another.[10] *Wonders of the East* is also a translation from Latin, but this time of a catalogue. This translation is likely earlier and from further north than that of *Christopher*; *Wonders*, too, existed

---

8 I borrow the phrasing for the subheading from Asa Simon Mittman and Susan Kim's determination to consider *Wonders* in its presentation in Nowell, as discussed in *Inconceivable Beasts*, p. 5.

9 On the translation and its copies, see Thomson, 'Telling the Story'. The Ælfrician collection was the badly burnt BL, MS Cotton Otho B X, of which little survives; the parts of the incipit and explicit that have come down to us are printed in various places, most accessibly in 'The Passion of Saint Christopher', ed. by Pulsiano, p. 168, and Orchard, *Pride and Prodigies*, pp. 12–13.

10 I know of approximately 115 pre-1200 copies of the text, which the Bollandists divide into fifteen versions (*BHL* 1764–*BHL* 1778). These are quite widely variant, and there is often much inconsistency within each of the Bollandists' versions. I would subdivide these into 'Decius' and 'Dagnus' branches (named after the saint's antagonist), comprising *BHL* 1764–65 and *BHL* 1766–78 respectively. The only extant Anglo-Latin copy from the early medieval period is a partial one in BnF, MS lat. 5574 (s. x^{in}, ?England), fols 1^r–7^r, currently classified by the Bollandists as a copy of *BHL* 1768 though I would reassign it to *BHL* 1770. As discussed in Thomson, 'Telling the Story', the Old English translation is closest to *BHL* 1769, specifically to a version in Munich, Bayerische SB, MS Clm. 22242 (s. xii, Windberg), fols 67^r–69^v. For a productive reading of the English materials, see also Hooper, 'The Missing Women of the *Beowulf* Manuscript'. Publication of the Latin texts is itself quite complex: *BHL* 1764 and *BHL* 1766 have been published by the Socii Bollandiani in *Analecta Bollandiana* 10 (1891), 393–405, and *Acta Sanctorum*, XXXIII (*Iulii*, VI), pp. 146–49, respectively; Rosenfeld prints an idiosyncratic collated edition in *Der hl. Christophorus*, pp. 520–29; and a normalized transcription of an interesting copy of *BHL* 1768 in Turin, Bibl. Naz., MS D V 3 is printed by Monique Goullet and Sandra Isetta in *Le légendier de Turin*, pp. 229–43. I hope to produce a fuller collated edition, particularly in relation to the English Christopher tradition, in the near future. Walther of Speyer and Ratramnus of Corbie both worked with copies of the Dagnus branch, not (as is commonly assumed for both) with *BHL* 1764. Supplementing this confusion, the well-known redaction in the Old English *Martyrology* stands apart from both later recensions, and likely relies upon an earlier transmission to Ireland; see Thomson, 'The Overlooked Women of the Old English *Passion of Saint Christopher*'. Christopher is not always explicitly dog-headed in the western European tradition, but there is no clear distinction between those versions that present him as *cananeus/canineus* ('of the dog-heads') and as *chananeus* ('Canaanite'); these two (or three) different labels slide into one another in ways too complex to discuss here.

in at least one other roughly contemporary English manuscript, as discussed by Helen Appleton in this volume.[11] The Latin text was known in England from an early date and is also widely witnessed throughout western Europe in a number of different forms; outside the Nowell Codex, it generally appears (as it does in London, British Library, MS Cotton Tiberius B V) alongside other catalogues of encyclopaedic knowledge.[12] *Alexander's Letter*, another translation from Latin, and the longest by some distance, was probably made at some mid-point between the other two, around the end of the ninth century and — as Daniel Anlezark points out in this volume — would fit well with the wider Alfredian translation project of that period.[13] The Latin text was, once again, well known across western Europe and was known in England for some time before its translation. There is clear evidence that it had previously travelled, not with the 'other' prose pieces, but with *Beowulf*; indeed, it seems very likely to be the case that these three works were set next to one another for the first time in this manuscript in a boldly creative — or dunderheaded — decision.[14]

Whether or not they function as a unit, it is clear that the texts were not brought together carelessly. The Nowell Codex is a project founded on sophisticated and creative thinking, demonstrating — like any thoughtfully edited collective volume — that different units can be woven together into a collective singularity without losing their individual integrity. Given their relative scarcity in Old English texts, and their appearance in all three of Nowell's extant prose pieces (albeit fleetingly in *Alexander's Letter*, as discussed below), it has been observed before that dog-heads can be read as a sub-theme that unites the three texts.[15] The extent to which the manuscript's production team read the texts with one another is, I think, most strikingly demonstrated in the illustration of the Cynocephali (OE Conopenae) in *Wonders*. Section 7, on fol. 97(99) (BL100)^r, describes the creatures perfectly clearly: 'Hy habbað horses mana ond eofores tuxas ond hunda heafdu, ond heora oroð bið swylce fyres leg' (They have the manes of a horse and the

---

11 For a full discussion of the text in its different English manuscripts, see Ford, *Marvel and Artefact*.

12 Aside from Nowell, the only exception that I know of is an Old French translation alongside an Alexander text and a history of the kings of France in Brussels, KBR, Royale MS 14561–64. For this, and a full discussion of *Wonders*, see '*Wonders of the East*', ed. by Knock.

13 The strongest argument for a connection with Alfred is made by Khalaf, 'The Old English *Letter of Alexander to Aristotle*', as part of a much subtler discussion of the text and its translation than I attempt here. On its translation as related to the reading of *Beowulf*, see Orchard, *A Critical Companion to 'Beowulf'*, esp. pp. 23–35.

14 On the manuscript as the first to bring these texts together, with full references, see Thomson, *Communal Creativity in the Making of the 'Beowulf' Manuscript*, esp. ch. 2, pp. 65–102.

15 See for example Orchard, *Pride and Prodigies*, pp. 14, 27; Thomson, *Communal Creativity in the Making of the 'Beowulf' Manuscript*, pp. 44–45.

Figure 3.1. Cynocephali in Tiberius B V and Vitellius A XV. Left: London, British Library, MS Cotton Tiberius B V, fol. 80ʳ. Mid-eleventh century. Right: London, British Library, MS Cotton Vitellius A XV, fol. 97(99) (BL100)ʳ. Early eleventh century. © British Library Board.

tusks of a boar and dogs' heads and their breath is like the blaze of a fire).[16] Poisonous breath is illustrated elsewhere in the text, deployed threateningly by the two-headed snakes of § 5 (on fol. 96(98) (BL99)ᵛ) against the text above them. But there is no attempt to depict flaming breath here, or any other threatening element of the dog-heads' appearance. Instead, the individual shown is charming — handsome, even — and dressed to impress in fulsome, flamboyant, full-colour robes. One hand seems to hold these robes, and the other is perhaps tucked inside them, in a pose of confident self-containment (as opposed, for instance, to the many figures in Nowell whose arms open wide in vague gestures). As shown in Figure 3.1, it is worth comparing this with the depiction of the same creatures in Cotton Tiberius B V. There is no fiery breath here either (the Tiberius artist is less creative, if more refined, in their choices, so the omission is not surprising), but here, too, the dog-head is unthreatening: it eats leaves off a tree in a manner reminiscent of a giraffe.

---

16 Quotations from *Wonders* are from *Old and Middle English*, ed. and trans. by Treharne, but section numbers are from Orchard, *Pride and Prodigies*. Translations are my own, but with reference to the different translations cited in note 5 above. The foliation policy for BL, Cotton Vitellius A XV is as discussed in Thomson, *Communal Creativity in the Making of the 'Beowulf' Manuscript*, pp. xix–xx, following Kevin Kiernan's discussion in *'Beowulf' and the 'Beowulf' Manuscript*, pp. 91–110.

The collective resistance of two quite different artists to the text's implication that these beings are alarming is worth noting. It may recall a separate tradition of dog-heads as peaceful rural tribes, or indeed have been influenced by other near-contemporary accounts of Cynocephalic communities: the missionary and later bishop Rimbert reported to his colleague Ratramnus of Corbie that dog-heads in Scandinavia lived in civilized villages, even dressed in cloth rather than hides.[17] But in Cotton Tiberius B V, the being's nakedness at least makes it clear that it is to be read as uncivilized and bestial. The Nowell image is a world away, presenting a fellow citizen whom one could take home to meet one's mother. This is not in line with Augustine of Hippo's view of Cynocephali: if it looks like a dog then it barks like a dog, and if it cannot speak like a human, then it cannot think like one.[18] Either way, the immediate point here is straightforward: there is no textual or external reason to make the Nowell dog-head look so fine, with the single exception of, in this manuscript, the text before it. In *Christopher*, a dog-head is, ironically, more civilized and much more like 'us' (early medieval English Christians) than the people he confronts. In its elegance, the picture must recall his equanimity and eloquence: although it stands in *Wonders*, the image illustrates Saint Christopher.

Alexander encounters a tribe of Cynocephali in § 29 of his *Letter*, but, once a few arrows are shot in their direction, 'hie sona onweg aflymdon ða hie eft on þone wudu gewiton' (they immediately ran away and went back into the woods).[19] It is one of the least interesting moments of his *Letter*; indeed, the next sentence notes a particularly barren period of the journey during which he encountered 'noht wunderlices ne mærlices' (nothing wonderful or remarkable). If the texts were drawn together because they featured dog-heads, the connection is tenuous and its significance slight. As proposed at the outset of this chapter, the productive nature of their interaction lies not in this recollection of specific details, but in their interest in the construction of selfhood through encountering others. I will, then, explore how each of the three works explores these ideas in different ways, before seeking to bring this rather open-ended but hopefully productive discussion together.

Alexander's Letter

Alexander's fleeting meeting with dog-heads provides a straightforward example of how space works in his *Letter*. The king's own body provides a centre around which his soldiers coalesce, meaning that space is a relative

---

17 'Quod verenda non bestiarum more detegant, sed humane velent verecundia, quae res pudoris est indicium; quod in usu tegminis non solum pelles, verum etiam et vestes eos habere scripsistis' (this is Ratramnus's summary of Rimbert's report to him), Ratramnus of Corbie (d. 870), *Epistola de Cynocephalis ad Rimberterum Presbyterium Scripta*, ed. by Dümmler, pp. 155–57.

18 See Augustine, *De civitate Dei* XVI.8; cf. Isidore, *Etymologiae* XL.iii.15 and XII.ii.32.

19 Quotations and section numbers are from Orchard, *Pride and Prodigies*.

entity defined by his body. The soldiers have comparatively little agency of their own but function as external expressions of their general's self, which thereby expands itself through space.[20] This is presented most spectacularly in § 11, where Alexander has had his men cover their weapons and armour with the gold they have acquired for him; looking at them, he sees 'mine gesælinesse ond min wuldor ond þa fromnisse minre iuguðe ond gesælignisse mines lifes' (my prosperity and my glory and the success of my youth and the prosperity of my life). The lexical repetition and repetitive structure serve to reinscribe the way Alexander looks outwards only to see more of himself. A similar, but more chilling, expression of the same principle comes in § 20, in which a rampaging rhinoceros attacks the camp. Alexander tells us that 'hit ofsloh sona minra þegna . xxvi . ane ræse, ond . lii . hit oftræd, ond hie to loman gerenode þæt hie mec nænigre note nytte beon meahton' (in a single charge, it swiftly killed twenty-six of my men and trampled fifty-two, making them disabled so that they could no longer be of any use to me). Only a little later, in § 22, he has the legs of native guides by whom he feels betrayed broken so they can be left for dead; to be of no use to Alexander means, in his world, to be worthless.

The space Alexander occupies is itself firmly boundaried: each night, the borders to his camp are threatened and have to be re-established with violence; each day, they move with him, carving their way through different landscapes in a continuous process of incorporation of others into his own being. Alexander does not grow or change; does not enter into the lives of others or allow them into his own. And he reads all boundaries that are not his, all selves that are not him, as existing only in relation to him: any boundary exists solely to keep him out, and so must be violated in order to assert the integrity and primacy of his subjectivity. We therefore witness Alexander hearing about an endless succession of different enclosed spaces, and relentlessly shoving his way into them. In a minor but telling example in § 25, he hears about some golden statues of Hercules and Bacchus. Immediately, he tells us,

> wolde ic witan hwæþer ða gelicnissa wæron gegotene ealle swa he sæde. Het þa þurhborian þa wæron hie buta of golde gegotene, ða het ic eft þa ðyrelo þe hiora mon þurh cunnode mid golde forwyrcean ond afyllon.

> (I wanted to know whether these statues were cast precisely as he had said. Then I commanded that they be drilled into, and they were made entirely of gold, then I commanded that those holes that had been drilled to be filled up and replaced with gold.)

---

20   There are exceptions to this, with the soldier Seferus marked out for his positive behaviour at § 12, and the men more broadly condemned for their reaction to desperate thirst at § 13. As in note 13, above, Khalaf's reading of the text, particularly in relation to its source, is significantly more nuanced than mine here, and he discusses some of the same details that I explore below, 'The Old English *Letter of Alexander to Aristotle*', pp. 661–65.

Likewise, the whole purpose of a significant and destructive leg of Alexander's journey in § 26 is 'þy læs me owiht in þæm londe beholden oððea bedegled wære' (in case anything in that land had been hidden or concealed from me). The integrity of his own body and sanctity of his space are affirmed through the repeated violation of those of others. The only possible purpose of a closed door is to keep him out; there is no subjectivity outside his. *Alexander's Letter*, then, shows us the imposition of the self onto all others, and expects us to be contemptuous of such a performance.

This image of Alexander as a destructive force is in line with some of the other literature circulating about him in the period: he could be constructed as either a positive example of exploration and adventure, or extremely negatively as a violent murderer.[21] The negative presentation arguably reaches a peak in the Old English adaptation of Orosius's *Historiarum adversum paganos libri VII*, in which (despite a certain awestruck tone in describing some of his activities), Alexander is monstrous: 'sinþyrstende mannes blodes' (continuously thirsting for man's blood) and ultimately judged as having 'þisne middangeard under him þrysmde and egsade' (oppressed and terrified this world).[22] The *Letter*'s first-person account, covering essentially the same events, offers us less a universal catastrophe than a self-centred commander, inviting the reader to stand at an ironizing and perhaps mocking distance rather than presenting a condemnatory judgement. Read in the wider context of the Nowell Codex, Alexander's behaviour stands in line with that of God's enemies as represented in *Judith* and *Christopher* and indeed many other hagiographical texts.[23] His intense focus on physical forms of wealth, of power, and of meaning-making — and indeed his somewhat desperate desire to know everything when his ignorance is in fact a product of his own inability to look effectively — demonstrate some consequences of his lack of spiritual wisdom.

In the temporal context of an early medieval reader, Alexander could be seen to have failed: the Old English *Orosius* says that his was the second of the four great empires of the past. But for those trapped in the same world as him, the only defence against the Alexander of this *Letter* is the same violence that he deploys: space is only sacrosanct, can only remain itself, if

---

21 Fully discussed by Bunt, *Alexander the Great in the Literature of Medieval Britain*.

22 The narrative of Alexander's reign and conquests are in III.9; judgement of him is sustained in the reflections on the activities of his successors in III.11. Quotations here are from *The Old English History of the World*, ed. and trans. by Godden, III.9.11 and III.11.3 respectively; my translations are based on his. The Old English translator is here broadly following the tone of their Latin source: from the moment of his birth in III.7, Alexander is 'atrocissimus turbo totius orientis' (the most appalling whirlwind for the whole of the east).

23 As I have argued on primarily codicological grounds, *Communal Creativity in the Making of the 'Beowulf' Manuscript*, pp. 93–95, it seems likely that the Nowell Codex as first produced had a clearer balance between hagiographical and more secular texts. I am grateful to Niamh Kehoe for calling my attention to the value of reading the *Letter* in the context of hagiography.

OTHERWHERES IN THE PROSE TEXTS OF THE NOWELL CODEX   111

it is defended with force. But even here, Alexander does not take risk upon himself: it is his soldiers' bodies that are desperately thirsty, torn to pieces, poisoned, torn, trampled and disabled, wounded, tortured, killed, frozen, and burnt (§ 14, § 15, § 18, § 19, § 20, § 21, § 22, § 27, § 30). This is why, for all his movement, he himself never changes. The form of the text, composed in a continuous present moment, presents the same resistance to any dispersion of the self as his actions perform. It asks Aristotle to read it, and then re-present it to others: to Alexander's mother and sisters (§ 5, § 24). The outcome of all of this reading is — Alexander hopes — that these readers will be able to abandon their own selfhoods and enter into his, seeing with his eyes and exulting in his exultations.[24] In § 41, this unalterable self is finally projected into eternity: 'ecelice min gemynd stonde' (my memory will stand forever). As Orchard notes, the translator's response to the Latin is characteristic.[25] The source has Alexander reporting the creation of a memorial to courage (§ 41: 'virtutibus monimentum') as a way of simultaneously generating a form of immortality for both Alexander and Aristotle (§ 41: 'immortalitas esset perpetua et nobis opinio'), and representing a virtue (§ 41: 'animi industriae […] indicium'). The Old English Alexander still writes to his former tutor, but does not desire to blend their memories, and the whole idea of creating a solid, static monument which indicates something beyond itself is gone. It is Alexander's own memory, his own self, representing only itself, that will endure. And it will be eternally alone: at the very end of § 41, he casts off the bounds of fleshly confinement even as he rejects any parity with other kings, now and forever: his 'þrym ond […] weorðmynd maran wæron þonne ealra oþra kyninga þe in middan-gearde æfre wæron' (glory and honour were greater than that of any of the other kings who have ever been in the world). The compilers of the Nowell Codex, in a move that may use Alexander's absurdity to ironize the opening of *Beowulf* (a reading that would in turn ironize much of the subsequent glory of the poem), designed their book so that, when open, these self-aggrandizing words face the poem's memorialization of the *þrym* of the Danish kings and Scyld's brutal forging of a Danish space through the destruction of the homes of others.[26] Given that Alexander spends some time in this final section worrying about who he can trust, and how his army will collapse if they know the truth of the prophecy he

---

24 For a more nuanced reading of the relationships constructed by the text, see Kim, '"If One Who Is Loved Is Not Present, a Letter May Be Embraced Instead"'.

25 Orchard, *Pride and Prodigies*, pp. 138–39.

26 On fols 128 (BL131)ᵛ and 129 (BL132)ʳ. Orchard comments on this juxtaposition as inviting comparison of the presentation of the worlds of men and monsters, *Pride and Prodigies*, p. 139; and suggests the responsibility modern readers have of understanding the relationship that this layout constructs, *A Critical Companion to 'Beowulf'*, p. 39. I have discussed the parallels constructed by the Nowell Codex between the *Letter* and *Beowulf* in more detail than space here allows in *Communal Creativity in the Making of the 'Beowulf' Manuscript*, pp. 59, 152, and 198–201.

has heard, the *Letter* shows us that a leader like him does not bind an empire together, but weakens the all-important bonds of loyalty between lord and followers. The *Beowulf*-poet no doubt composed the opening of their poem as glorious, but the manuscript seems to problematize it, striking the same note of decay and loss as Beowulf's own funeral ultimately does. The worlds of Alexander and of Scyld, these modes of being, have failed, placing them in a temporal space now unreachably distant from their audience.

Where, then, is the reading self in this text, the *we* that so confidently opens *Beowulf*? Alexander's aggressive construction of himself through difference, defined ultimately as exceeding all others, and the epistolary form that creates a self-enclosed world for the *Letter*, seals 'us' off from him and those to whom he writes. 'We' are safe at home, watching not only the places he visits but also his encounters with them. Alexander has a sociopathic lack of empathy but is anything but unreflective: he obsesses about how he is perceived and watches his own performances of greatness. This allows the reader to participate in his gaze even as we diverge from his assessment of himself — always and only looking at or with him, and never at ourselves. This defines him as exceptional, as objectified, almost othered within his own text, consigning him to the sort of barbaric spectacular past that (as Helen Appleton discusses in this volume) Orosius's *History* constructs, and thereby firmly places him far away from the reader who is invited to look without seriously reflecting on their own selfhood or behaviour.

Wonders of the East

The definition of Alexander as different from the reader is also part of the project of *Wonders*. And, if it is possible to read the abbreviated end of the *Letter* as meaningfully speaking to the opening of *Beowulf* which it faces in the open codex, it is even more tempting to think that the omission of four final sections which exist at the end of the Cotton Tiberius B V text may have been intentional in Nowell, because they result in the text's second mention of Alexander facing the opening of his *Letter*.[27] Certainly, his portrayal in *Wonders* broadly reinforces (or sets up, if read in manuscript sequence) the image of the king as an uncontrollable maniac. He slaughters a tribe of hybrid women in § 27, and in § 30 his reaction to a tribe of generous men is to resist his evidently overwhelming instinct to murder: 'ne wolde he hi cwellan ne him nan lað don' (he didn't want to kill them or do them any harm at all). As Mittman and Kim observe, the text resists his genocidal approach: the women he sought to destroy are in the present tense and clearly depicted as still existing (unlike Alexander himself, who is firmly confined to the

---

27 On fols 103 (BL106)ᵛ and 104 (BL107)ʳ.

past).[28] The value to the text of introducing Alexander in relation to these two groups is, I suggest, twofold. On the one hand it provides a reaction to the wonders which the text is otherwise reluctant to offer and illustrates further a specifically human inclination to cross borders and damage the homelands of others. On the other, it allows the text to portray Alexander himself as a 'wonder of the east', as a being who exists to be objectified. However, unlike the other beings of this text, he is not bonded to a particular part of the world; as suggested above, his relentless movement is a crucial feature of his identity, and it can of course only be shown here by illustrating his interactions with more than one group.

This runs counter to the general approach taken by *Wonders*, which is to firmly tie each of its beings to specific physical spaces. These may once have had some connection with geographical space as we would recognize it, but they are garbled beyond all recognition, leaving only the impression that the world is divided into specific places, each of which contains a set of beings that belong there. Again and again, the catalogue opens a section by identifying a place. This might have a name, like Lentibelsina, or Ciconia; or it might be described in relation to the previous place with numerical distances or vague relative phrases (*þa* — 'then' — is the most frequent, with occasional more specific directions such as 'east from there', or 'by the ocean'). And the specific beings that inhabit that place are apparently restricted to that location: even the ravenous and polylingual Donestre does not leave its island in the Red Sea. Travelling is for 'us', not 'them'.

This is curious; it is as though, first, the desire to expand beyond the boundaries of the self is a specifically human characteristic. But it also expresses a fear that one can go too far, that otherness can prove too attractive, taking us too far out of our selves; like Prufrock, if we linger in the chambers of the sea, we risk drowning. As has been widely discussed, this is one of the roots of the horror of anthropophagi (those who consume humans): that which consumes us undoes the fabric of our being and incorporates us into them.[29] As noted above, such a threat is never personally confronted by Alexander, who plays with the selfhood of others but jealously guards his own. In *Wonders*, though, it is a persistent risk to the traveller: two beings eat any humans who enter their regions (the Hostes in § 13 and Donestre in § 20), and two others burn or kill anyone who touches them (§ 4, § 6). But the risk of losing oneself is balanced by the opportunity of enrichment: three sections present trees that grow precious materials (§ 19, § 24, § 31), and other valuable non-living goods include pepper in § 6, gold in § 9, and jewels in § 25, to say nothing of the chances of receiving the free gift of a woman (§ 30). This is indeed a world teeming with fruitful possibility — a plenitude that is also disturbingly chaotic, to borrow Discenza's description of contemporary

---

28　Mittman and Kim, *Inconceivable Beasts*, p. 30.

29　See for instance Cohen, 'Monster Culture', p. 14.

accounts of the earth's atmosphere — but it is also one in which nothing can be gained without cost: § 6, indeed, explicitly associates the danger from the snakes (called Corsiae) with the opportunity of acquiring pepper if that risk is confronted.[30] This is not (quite) as simplistic as the world being presented as a human plaything, and nor is it the invitation to conquer that Alexander sees in every thing he encounters: it is a world that is full of other places which can be visited and exploited, but not colonized or occupied, because they fundamentally — perhaps essentially — belong to the beings already there.

In contrast with Luisa Ostacchini's reading of Ælfric's *Life of St Thomas* in this volume, there is, then, no possibility of building in these places or even establishing a concrete, comprehensible relationship with them. Objects can be taken from 'there' and brought 'here', but the source itself, the land, remains by definition unassimilable and is fundamentally unknowable, as the perpetual collapse of the text's system of measurement seems to indicate.[31] The space itself is other, spawning balsam and gold and pepper; the idea of 'the world' is that it is otherwise, defined by its difference from the reader's 'here'. This difference offers an unrolling list of opportunities which echo one another to the extent that they become one vast infinite quivering mass of fertile possibility.[32] Without wishing to insist on the point, it is worth suggesting that the only illustration of the riches of this world in Nowell — that of the gold pieces on fol. 98 (BL 101)[r] — seems to show them emerging from a vaginal, lozenge-formed, shape: the earth of *Wonders* may literally give birth to wealth.[33] As Daniel Anlezark shows in this volume, this forms a potent advert for trading possibilities; here, I want to suggest more broadly that otherwheres are constructed as free spaces in which the self can change, develop, become. But they carry a concomitant threat of dissipation, becoming only a foot brandished by a grinning Hostes, or a head wept over by a lonely Donestre.

If to be human in *Wonders* is to be capable of this form of expansion, then to what extent is it different from what it is to be Alexander in his *Letter*? In the reading presented here, it is located in precisely the idea of space and its intimate relationship with selfhood explored by so many chapters in this volume. Humans in *Wonders* do not travel on and relentlessly on, carrying their world and their glory with them, ignoring and overriding any boundary they come across: they move, like Bilbo and Frodo Baggins, 'there and back again', bringing a little of that which was 'there' back 'here'. The Old English translation of *Alexander's Letter* curtails its source text, leaving its narrator stranded at the furthest limits of his journey, naked and alone in the garden

---

30 Discenza, *Inhabited Spaces*, p. 27.

31 Mittman and Kim, *Inconceivable Beasts*, appendix A, p. 239.

32 Compare Abdelkarim, 'This Land Is Your Land', who argues for a range of English poetic texts of this period as celebrating the opportunities of movement.

33 Compare e.g. Riddle K-D 35 (as numbered and edited in *The Exeter Book*, ed. by Krapp and Dobbie), which says that earth 'of his innaþe [...] cende' (2: from its inside gave birth) to the metal used to make a mailcoat.

of the two trees unable to communicate with them or the old man who rules the place, as if he has sought a return to Eden and only ended up in a different form of exile. This seems designed to provide a contrast with the humans in *Wonders* who enter the domain of the snakes to take their pepper in § 6, or of the ants to take their gold in § 9, or of the generous men to receive a woman in § 30; or indeed with Beowulf and Judith who travel away to perform heroic deeds and then return home.

In *Wonders*, then, humans display Alexander's rapacious behaviour, but not for its own sake. The space they can occupy is not limitless — it is, in fact, unchanging; their homes are as clearly defined and delimited as those of the different creatures whose own homes they raid. Like the world map in Cotton Tiberius B V, the landscape of *Wonders* is scattered with isolated *land-bunessa* in § 1, § 2, § 10 (settlements) and *byrig* in § 2, § 6, § 7 (cities). The rest of the world is not there to be settled (indeed, some parts of it are, as in § 6, *un-wæstm-berend-lic* (barren)), and even the great kings of § 29 'þa habbaþ under monigfealde leodhatan' (who have many tyrants under them) have specified *landgemæru* (borders). In the light of Hannah Bailey's discussion of the significance of rivers as borders in this volume, it is worth noting how often bodies of water matter as border-markers, with frequent mentions of the Red Sea, and the Rivers Nile, 'Brixontes', 'Archoboleta', and 'Capi' (§ 4, § 6, § 9, § 10, § 13, § 15, § 20, § 28). This becomes most explicit in § 9, in which huge ants live beyond a river and spend their time digging up gold. The gold can be retrieved with three camels (perhaps acquired from the location between the Nile and Brixontes described in § 10). A young camel is tied on the human side of the river, and a male camel given to the ants for them to feast on. While that distracts them, the female camel is loaded up with gold; her maternal instincts overcome her care for the screams of her partner, and she can be taken back across the river. The fearsomeness of the ants in § 9 is communicated in one of the few moments in *Wonders* where the narrator is visible, noting laconically that they return 'swa hrædlice ofer þære ea þæt þa men wenað þæt hy fleogan' (so swiftly across that river that one would believe that they're flying). In Nowell, this scene is elegantly depicted in the text's largest image, which has flowing rivers dividing space from space and, in its comic-strip-like presentation of different stages of the story in a single image, time from time.[34]

The ants, the camels, and the gold of § 9 are not the unknowable but strongly selved 'some-things' of the Riddles with voices and opinions of their own. Like all of the beings and spaces of *Wonders*, they are pure objects: coming into being only as they are perceived by a subject; existing in order to be looked at, to be approached, to be used. Like Cohen's theorized monsters, they are

---

34 As discussed in Thomson, *Communal Creativity in the Making of the 'Beowulf' Manuscript*, pp. 115–16, where the image is replicated, much of the present messiness of the image has been caused by enthusiastic attempts to imitate parts of it.

pure culture, originating only from that which points towards them; one could say, invoking Bill Brown, that the text of *Wonders* rejects the thing-ness of the things — beings, places, plants — at which it looks, granting them the status of a purely objectified existence.[35] It is in this sense that they are racialized.[36] The narrating (and, by implication, reading) subject is 'normal', without need of definition, while that which is not the subject — existing anywhere other than where the subject reads — needs to be categorized.[37] The final section of the Nowell *Wonders*, § 32, tells us about a race (*moncynn*) who 'seondon sweartes hyiwes on onsyne' (are of black colour when looked at/in the face). The Latin describes them as 'valde nigrum' (very black) without the addition of *on onsyne*, which specifies the blackness as located in the face or produced through the process of looking at them. But what is worth noting in the immediate context is that the narrator does not construct themself as white in opposition to blackness. Three earlier beings are noted as having white skin: in § 11 the two-faced people have 'hwit lic' (white bodies); the Panopti of § 21 have 'lichoman swa hwite swa meolc' (bodies as white as milk); and the bodies of the women murdered by Alexander in § 27 are, perhaps reflecting their now-deathly pallor, 'on marmorstanes hiwnesse' (beautiful like marble).[38] The audience is not invited to construct itself in opposition to the features of these other groups of humans; we are, instead, assumed to be qualitatively different from them. 'They' are white or black or red or dog-headed or shining-eyed or barbaric or noble; 'we' are the default and uncategorizable normal. It is, though, important to note that the blackness of the Sigelwara is their only identifying feature: this colour on its own suffices to other a group, where whiteness is an additional characteristic of beings who are also distinguished from the 'normal' by their behaviour, culture, or

---

35 See Brown, 'Thing Theory'.

36 Race is a significant and complex process of categorization, and I am aware that I am nodding to rather than fully dealing with its complexities and challenges here. I use the term here broadly in line with its definition in Geraldine Heng's *Invention of Race*, at for instance p. 27, taking the text's account of different *mancynn* as being equivalent to its notion of *wild-deora cynn*, identifying 'races' of human-like beings and 'species' of beasts, both responding to the Latin idea of *genus*. Race in *Wonders* is itself a subject of considerable scholarly energy; the most comprehensive and thoroughly referenced overview is Mittman, 'Are the "Monstrous Races" Races?'. Mittman argues against using the term 'races' for these groups because of the problems it brings with it; I respectfully disagree here, because I see the text as working to construct precisely the sort of hierarchy of the 'superior normative' and 'inferior abnormal' that Mittman identifies as inherent to the term, and it is this interaction between the carefully constructed, objectified, racialized 'other' and unreflective 'self' to which I want to point.

37 Cf. the discussions in Mittman, *Maps and Monsters* at e.g. p. 208; and Discenza, *Inhabited Spaces*, at e.g. pp. 93–94, where she discusses the same issue of coloured skin that I comment on below.

38 One other being, the anthropagistic Hostes of § 13, is 'sweartes hiwes' (of black colour). The murdered women's bodies are of the *whiteness* of marble in the Latin ('quasi marmore candido') and in Tiberius's OE translation ('on marmorstanes hwitnysse').

physical appearance.[39] This assumption of the 'normal' allows the narrator of *Wonders* to be almost entirely invisible: the text poses, in a mode familiar from much current scientific discourse, as being neutrally observed objective statements of fact, with no interest in reflecting on the subjective self from which those observations are generated.

Passion of St Christopher

While it, too, reveals an interest in the otherness of the other and how that can be useful to the self, *Christopher* invokes these differences in order to collapse them. In some senses, it combines the approaches taken by *Alexander's Letter* — in distancing the reader from its protagonist and those he encounters — and by *Wonders*: constructing racialized groups at whom we can gaze in wonder and horror. But, having created that distance, it shows how figures within the text bridge it, before ultimately inviting readers to do the same. The reading self, watching a dramatic and violent story unfold on the bodies of strange others (a dog-head, sex workers, a deranged non-Christian king), is no more reflective than in the two secular texts discussed above. The text's final demand, though, takes us in a new direction: not to reflect on the constitution, location, or categorization of the self, but to let go of it altogether.

As Rachel Burns observes in this volume, solo wandering can be a radical act in early medieval texts, threatening borders and collapsing distinctions. At the outset of the text, we meet Christopher as just such a destabilizing wandering individual, when he simply appears at the outskirts of the city of Samos. The English translation says, 'sum man com on þa ceastre se wæs healf hundisces manncynnes' (a certain man came to that city; he was of the race of the dog-heads / of the half-dog people).[40] He is, then, from no place at all. This is a common way of introducing the saint, though he sometimes originates, as in the only surviving early medieval English Latin copy, 'genere cananeus, de insula quadam' (of the race of dog-heads, and from a certain island).[41] This vague gesture is the closest to a point of origin we receive because his origin does not really matter; like the marvels of *Wonders*, he exists purely in and for difference, an object to the multiple subjects to whom he comes,

---

39 I am indebted to Alicia Grimes, my student at HHU, for this observation.

40 This quotation is from the beginning to the Otho text; I seek to show that, with the exception of the coda in Nowell, the translation in BL, MS Cotton Otho B X and that in Nowell were the same in 'Telling the Story'.

41 My transcription from BnF, MS lat. 5574, fol. 1ʳ; translations from Latin are mine. As in note 10 above, the Christopher tradition is complex, and I focus here on that represented in Nowell, where possible quoting from the Old English text and otherwise from my transcriptions from the nearest Latin copy in Munich, Bayerische SB, MS Clm. 22242. Also as outlined in note 10 above, Christopher's dog-headedness is not entirely consistent; in pre-thirteenth-century English texts, however, he is always canine.

not a self-actualized thing. This is why Christopher resists interest in his race and place of origin. When Dagnus first sees him, he urgently demands 'Quis et tu, aut unde es, aut quid nomen tuum?' (What are you, and where are you from, and what is your name?). The saint responds to only the last: 'Ex nativitate mea "Reprobus" dictus sum; post baptismum "Christoforus" vocor' (At my birth I was named 'Reprobus' [Terrible]; after baptism I am called 'Christopher' [Christ-Bearer]). Due to the later popularity of the saint, his name does not feel unfamiliar; in context, however, it is more of a job description (Χριστό-φορος, Christo-phorus, 'Christ-Bearer') than an identity. He is a functionary, a container, rather than a subject with a self. His function is not to be comprehended, but to be an object encountered by subjects, enabling them, too, to let go of their selfhoods, their subjectivities, and be folded into the expanding empire of Christ.

In a parallel scene, then, when two sex workers are sent to Christopher in prison, he does not ask them where they come from or even what their names are, and focuses instead on what they do ('Quod est artificium vestram?'). Placed beside (and before) *Wonders*, *Christopher* points to the limitations of the catalogue form: 'What are they called and where do they come from?' are almost all that *Wonders* can offer. But, having called them into being, *Christopher* explicitly rejects place and race, abnegating individual selfhoods and collapsing them into a totalizing Christian universalism, a vision in line with that explored by Kazutomo Karasawa in this volume in relation to the crucifixion of Christ.

Such an aspiration gestures towards the apocalyptic totality of Paul's vision of the future in Colossians, in which there will be 'no longer Greek and Jew, circumcised and uncircumcised, barbarian, Scythian, slave and free; but Christ is all and in all' (3. 11; cf. Galatians 3. 28), an enforced similitude in which individual subjects no longer really exist at all. Within the text, the movement towards this state is figured by ever-widening circles of individuals and groups who convert (Christopher himself, a woman, a crowd, soldiers, the two sex workers, another crowd, and finally Dagnus himself), producing a staggering total of 'eaht ond feower þusenda manna ond hundteontig ond fiftyne' (l. 110: 48,000 people and 115).[42] But this is not enough: the text ends with Dagnus issuing the command at lines 126–29 'þætte nan mon þe to mines rices anwealde belimpe ne gedyrstlæce nan wuht do óngean þæs heofonlican Godes willan þe Cristoforus beeode' (that no one who is subject to the rule of my kingdom does anything against the heavenly will of the God whom Christopher followed), and if they do then, lines 130–31, 'on þære ylcan tide

---

42 Quotations from the Old English *Christopher* are from 'The Passion of Saint Christopher', ed. by Pulsiano, by line number. Fulk here prints *feowertig*; the manuscript reading is clear, though it is not clear what 'eight-and-four-thousand' means: 48,000 (as I have assumed here) or 12,000, or something else. The number of Christopher's converts varies widely, but 48,115 is the usual number for texts in this group (BnF, MS lat. 5574, in keeping with *BHL* 1770 texts, gives 49,120).

sy he mid swyrde witnode' (in that same hour let them be punished with a sword).[43] Here, as frequently in the text, God is identified through Christopher: the saint's remarkable face is removed and a window set in its place. But even this vision of evangelism does not suffice: the narrator circles back one final time to the image of Christopher praying in order to project out from the space and time of his story into the present moments (mine, and yours) in which the story is retold. God has already told him that his power reaches beyond any place associated with him:

> þeah þin lichama ne sy on þære stowe; swa hwyllce geleafulle men swa þines naman on heora gebedum [gebiddon] beoð gehælede fram hyra synnum ond swa hwæs swa hie rihtlice biddaþ for þinum naman ond for þinum geearningum hig hyt onfoð.
>
> > (ll. 100–105: even if your body is not in a place, any believers who offer their prayers in your name will be healed of their sins, and whatever they reasonably ask for in your name and because of your merits, they will receive it.)

And the coda to the text, at lines 145–46, tells us that Christopher asked God to 'syle gode mede þam þe mine þrowunga awrite ond þa ecean edlean þam þe hie mid tear[um] ræde' (give a true blessing to anyone who writes about my sufferings, and an eternal reward to any who read about them with tears). Unlike Alexander, who ends his text by seeking to stand still for eternity, Christopher seeks endless dispersion: he releases his selfhood so that he may become the otherness that can alter ours. Divisions between selves, times, and spaces are to be obliterated in the homogenizing process of creating an empire of servants of Christ. In the context of this chapter, then, we see Christopher's story as recognizing that identity is tied to race and place in the ways discussed above, but inviting us to — or demanding that we — abandon those bordered, individualized selves.

To this end, the hagiography repeatedly stages the drama of an encounter between self and other. The dynamic is illustrated in Figure 3.2, from a twelfth-century German manuscript of Usuard's *Martyrology*.[44] This presents Christopher, in the only image of this text that has a full side to itself, communicating the massive and all-consuming nature of his being, and with a face more leonine than canine. He has flat, iconic, emotionless features: his self is already gone, leaving only surface. The tiny people of the city at whose gates he stands gaze up at him with mobile, fluid, and individual reactions: their bodies and faces each have different shapes, expressing different movements and different emotional responses as they encounter his impassive otherness.

---

43 Cf. Daniel 3. 96, where Nebuchadnezzar issues a similar command; the Latin *Christopher* is closely associated with the scriptural Daniel.

44 I am extremely grateful to the Württembergischen Landesbibliothek for allowing me to use this image.

Figure 3.2. St Christopher Chananeus arriving at the city of Samos. Stuttgart, Württembergische Landesbibliothek, MS Cod. hist., fol. 415. Reproduced by permission.

But he stares out at us, uninterested in the world in which he stands. The inhabitants of Samos model our reaction for us, inviting our own multiple and affective responses; he, meanwhile, will gaze forever, beyond the possibility of change. As they are overwhelmed by the otherness of his face, he is able to — literally, in this image — get one foot into the door.[45] He is, in this sense and again making use of Brown's terminology, no 'thing' at all, but a pure object existing to be used.[46] His dog-headedness is, then, a functional part of his sanctity: it aids the human subject in objectifying him, calling attention to his otherness before effectively vanishing and pushing our attention towards that which he represents and its relationship with the beholder's own selfhood.[47] As a being without subjecthood, like those in *Wonders* he has moved beyond time into a permanent present: as long as there are subjects to behold him, he exists in the same state. The role of the reader (or, in this case, the viewer) is, in the different times and places in which they — we — exist, to objectify by looking and reacting.

This is precisely the process that we witness, repeatedly, in the text. In a sequence of individual and collective encounters with the saint, Christopher stands still (usually in prayer) and is looked at: first a woman leaving the city to worship idols (or gather flowers); then a crowd which she summons; then two separate groups of soldiers sent by Dagnus; then the king himself; then Nicaea and Aquilina, the two sex workers sent to him in prison; and finally Dagnus again. On each occasion, the experience of seeing Christopher is a radical shock. Individuals' own faces change in unspecified ways, or they collapse in a faint. Each individual and group ultimately reacts to the shock of such an encounter with radical otherness by abandoning their selves, collapsing their individualities into his driving mission.

Dagnus makes this process clearer than those he rules because he clings onto his selfhood. Like Alexander, it is not that he is immune to the impact of encountering otherness; both men simply resist any disruption to their own selfhoods. For the ruler of Samos, this comes in the form of being unwilling to let go of different external markers of his own identity: the social practice of sacrifice; his followers; his gods (associated by the text with his father). His determination to hold onto himself results in increasingly extreme assaults on his selfhood. As explored above, in his *Letter* it is not altogether easy to know how to respond to the excesses of Alexander, but there can be little doubt that in this text Dagnus's absurd resistance to this process is funny. His two faints occur in scenes that he has orchestrated: in a scene no longer extant in the Old English text, when Christopher is brought before him explicitly so that

---

45 I am grateful to Brepols's anonymous reviewer for calling my attention to the feet in this image.

46 See note 35 above.

47 For a wider discussion of the importance of his dog-headedness and the uses made of his otherness, see Thomson, 'Grotesque, Fascinating, Transformative'; Weinreich, 'How a Monster Means'.

he can be looked at, the king topples down 'a consistorio ubi sedebat' (from the high place where he was sitting); and later, when Christopher is being tortured in a fire, Dagnus looks at the saint's face and 'wæs swa abreged þæt he gefeol on eorðan ond þær læg fram þære ærestan tide þæs dæges oð ða nigoþan tide' (was so appalled that he fell to the earth and lay there from the first until the ninth hour of the day). The Old English translation is unique in saying at line 36 that Christopher contemptuously 'hyne het uparisan' (commanded him to get up), and these moments may have been particularly enjoyable for an English audience given that they are both included in the Old English *Martyrology*'s compressed summary. When the process of beholding Christopher is clearly not enough to overcome Dagnus's refusal to let go of himself, the idea of that which is seen entering the mind of the beholder is physicalized, with two arrows flying into his eyes. This invasion of selfhood is, at last, enough, with Dagnus rubbing both mud and Christopher's blood into his damaged eyes, taking both the saint and the physical space he occupied into himself. He finally accepts the inevitability of the change brought by the saint, following the example set by the women of his city by, as we have seen above, taking the message much further at line 126: 'geond eall min rice' (throughout my entire kingdom).

Suggestions

What, then, can be said about the prose texts of the Nowell Codex and the ways in which they invite readers to think about the world beyond England's shores? First, all three texts share a construction of that which is elsewhere as other, defined by its difference from the reading subject rather than in its own right. They therefore share an unreflective assumption that (in highly simplistic terms) place defines race: where a being is controls how it is constructed. Second, although they present the encounters in different ways, they are all interested in what happens when these boundaries between places are violated; or, when selved subjects encounter those that are different from them. Third — if we can read the negative presentation of Alexander in his *Letter* as pointing us away from his self-construction — they all construct a changing self as an inevitable, and essentially as a positive, phenomenon.

It is equally clear that they differ quite significantly in how they present this process. *Alexander's Letter* offers a (negative) case study of an individual who clutches himself to himself, parading his egocentrism, arrogance, and childishness. *Wonders* tells us that if we venture beyond our own places, we can encounter otherness and profit thereby; it also warns us that we must go back again if we are to retain our own subjecthood and not become subsumed by that which is not us. *Christopher* aspires towards precisely this sublimation, demanding that we look at its central figure's face of 'pure alterity' and see through it to God, abandoning our individual selfhoods in service to the empire of Christ.[48] The Nowell Codex does not bring texts together in pursuit of a single answer: it is not a sermon, but a playful collage, with texts interacting productively with one another and inviting the reader to participate in its communal creativity.[49] In a sense, then, its form echoes the interest explored here in what happens when fundamentally different entities are brought together and how a subject can benefit from encountering such difference.

This has wider implications for how we read manuscripts and indeed groups of texts together, but also for how we understand the construction and shaping of selfhood and community in early medieval England. When we think, for instance, of how poetic texts in the Anglo-Saxon Chronicles imagine the community of the *engla-cyn*, it is clear that they are a relatively complex composite, comprising (as in *The Battle of Brunanburh*) groups of Mercians and West Saxons and (as in *The Capture of the Five Boroughs*) those of English and those of Danish descent; or indeed of how *Judith* represents Bethulia as a city founded in communal strength at lines 162–70.[50] In the Chronicles and more widely, we can see, too, that this nascent English community is not only made up of people, but also of the places those people inhabit and the land they tread upon.[51] Further, though, as part of the community of Christendom, this composite subjecthood extends to communion with the wider worlds of Rome and Jerusalem. And such extra-corporeal being extends not only to the places with which they co-exist, but also through time, with the primary interest of many early English texts being (as expressed in genealogical lists) towards the past but always with an apprehension of an apocalyptic Christian future. We could say that selfhood was (and is) simultaneously here and now, but also otherwhere and otherwhen. To some degree, this sense of subjecthood as a composite complex — a form of matrix or network — returns us to where this chapter began; this time, though, subjecthood looks less constructed in the space between self and others and more as itself comprising such difference held together in a unity, what I have in a different context called an 'entangled self'.[52]

This is a position that could be pushed too far. Not all difference is embraced into the unity of English subjecthood in these texts. None of the three texts discussed here seek to comprehend that which is different from them: even the first-person narrator of *Alexander's Letter* is held at arm's length as an object; and the totalizing glare of *Christopher* uses the saint's difference to claim that all subjectivities are irrelevant in the divine scheme. The texts' categorization of difference has no interest in engaging with the subjective

---

48 The phrase 'pure alterity' is widely used, but I consciously cite it here from Levinas, 'Being-Toward-Death', p. 134.

49 Thomson, *Communal Creativity in the Making of the 'Beowulf' Manuscript*, pp. 14–15.

50 Compare M. D. J. Bintley's discussion, in *Settlements and Strongholds*, pp. 159–67.

51 Again, compare Bintley, *Settlements and Strongholds*, at e.g. pp. 116–18; and see also Discenza, *Inhabited Spaces*, esp. chs 2 and 3, who discusses the constructions of England and elsewhere in relation to English identity in much more detail than attempted here.

52 Thomson, 'The Composite Unity of the Entangled Self', with some of these phenomeno-logical ideas discussed in more detail pp. 206–11.

experience of those who are different, nor in recognizing their own selfhoods as objects to other subjects. As such, even as they work to shape a composite reading selfhood, the texts allow their audience's selves to remain unreflective, unexamined, and indeed unlocated. The prose texts of the Nowell Codex therefore participate in the production of a dynamic which — interested as they are in the interactions between self and other, in contrapuntal movement between 'here' and 'there' — ultimately reify the distances between them.

Works Cited

Manuscripts

Brussels, KBR, Royale MS 14561–64
London, British Library, MS Cotton Otho B X (excluding
    fols 29, 30, 51, 58, 61–64, 66)
London, British Library, MS Cotton Tiberius B V, fols 2–73 and 77–88
London, British Library, MS Cotton Vitellius A XV, fols 94–209 (the Nowell Codex)
Munich, Bayerische Staatsbibliothek, MS Clm. 22242
Paris, Bibliothèque nationale de France, MS latin 5574
Stuttgart, Württembergischen Landesbibliothek, MS Cod. hist. 415
Turin, Biblioteca Nazionale, MS D V 3

Primary Sources

The *'Beowulf' Manuscript: Complete Texts and 'The Fight at Finnsburg'*, ed. and trans.
    by Robert D. Fulk, DOML, 3 (Cambridge, MA: Harvard University Press, 2010)
The Exeter Book, ASPR, III, ed. by George Philip Krapp and Elliott Van Kirk
    Dobbie (New York: Columbia University Press, 1936)
Le légendier de Turin: MS D. V. 3 de la Bibliothèque Nationale Universitaire, ed. by
    Monique Goullet and Sandra Isetta (Florence: SISMEL-Edizioni del Galluzzo,
    2014)
Old and Middle English c. 890–c. 1450: An Anthology, ed. and trans. by Elaine
    Treharne (Oxford: Wiley-Blackwell, 2000; 3rd edn, 2009)
The Old English History of the World: An Anglo-Saxon Rewriting of Orosius, ed.
    and trans. by Malcolm R. Godden, DOML, 44 (Cambridge, MA: Harvard
    University Press, 2016)
'The Passion of Saint Christopher', ed. by Phillip Pulsiano, in *Early Medieval
    English Texts and Interpretations: Studies Presented to Donald G. Scragg*, ed. by
    Elaine Treharne and Susan Rosser (Tempe: Arizona Center for Medieval and
    Renaissance Studies, 2002), pp. 167–99
Ratramnus of Corbie, 'Epistola de Cynocephalis ad Rimberterum Prebyterium
    Scripta', in *Epistolae Karolini aevi*, IV, ed. by Ernst Dümmler, MGH: Epistolae, 6
    (Berlin: Weidmann, 1925), pp. 155–57
Rosenfeld, Hans-Friedrich, *Der hl. Christophorus, seine Verehrung und seine Legende*
    (Åbo: Harrassowitz, 1937)

Socii Bollandiani, 'De S. Christophoro Martyre Forte in Lycia', *Acta Sanctorum*, XXXIII: *Iulii*, VI (Paris: Palmé, 1868), pp. 125–49

——, 'Passio Sancti Christophori martyris ex cod. Paris. signato num. 2179 inter noviter acquisitos', *Analecta Bollandiana*, 10 (1891), 393–405

Three Old English Prose Texts: 'Letter of Alexander the Great', 'Wonders of the East', 'Life of St Christopher', ed. by Stanley Rypins, Early English Texts Society, 161 (London: Early English Texts Society, 1924)

'*Wonders of the East*: A Synoptic Edition of *The Letter of Pharasamanes* and the Old English and Old Picard Translations', ed. by Ann Knock (unpublished doctoral dissertation, University of London, 1981)

Secondary Sources

Abdelkarim, Sherif, 'This Land Is Your Land: Naturalization in England and Arabia, 500–100', *postmedieval*, 11 (2020), 396–406

Bintley, Michael D. J., *Settlements and Strongholds in Early Medieval England: Texts, Landscapes, and Material Culture*, SEM, 45 (Turnhout: Brepols, 2020)

Brown, Bill, 'Thing Theory', *Critical Inquiry*, 28 (2001), 1–22

Bunt, Gerrit H. V., *Alexander the Great in the Literature of Medieval Britain*, Mediaevalia Groninga, 14 (Groningen, 1994)

Cohen, Jeffrey Jerome, 'Monster Culture (Seven Theses)', in *Monster Theory: Reading Culture*, ed. by Jeffrey Jerome Cohen (Minneapolis: University of Minnesota Press, 1996), pp. 3–25

Deleuze, Gilles, and Félix Guattari, *A Thousand Plateaus*, vol. II of *Capitalism and Schizophrenia*, trans. by Brian Massumi (Minneapolis: University of Minnesota Press, 1993) [first published as *Capitalisme et Schizophrénie*, II: *Mille Plateaux* (Paris: Éditions de minuit, 1980)]

Discenza, Nicole Guenther, *Inhabited Spaces: Anglo-Saxon Constructions of Place*, Toronto Anglo-Saxon Series, 23 (Toronto: University of Toronto Press, 2017)

Ford, A. J., *Marvel and Artefact: The 'Wonders of the East' in its Manuscript Contexts* (Leiden: Brill, 2016)

Heidegger, Martin, *Being and Time*, trans. by J. M. Macquarrie and E. Robinson (Oxford, 1962) [first published as *Sein und Zeit* (Halle: M. Niemeyer, 1927)]

Heng, Geraldine, *The Invention of Race in the European Middle Ages* (Cambridge: Cambridge University Press, 2018)

Hochman, Adam, 'Racialization: A Defense of the Concept', *Ethnic and Racial Studies*, 42 (2019), 1245–62

Hooper, Teresa, 'The Missing Women of the *Beowulf* Manuscript', in *New Readings on Women and Early Medieval English Literature and Culture: Cross-Disciplinary Studies in Honour of Helen Damico*, ed. by Helene Scheck and Christine E. Kozikowski (York: ARC Humanities Press, 2019), pp. 161–78

Howe, Nicholas, *Writing the Map of Anglo-Saxon England: Essays in Cultural Geography* (New Haven, CT: Yale University Press, 2008)

Khalaf, Omar, 'The Old English *Letter of Alexander to Aristotle*: Monsters and *Hybris* in the Service of Exemplarity', *ES*, 94 (2013), 659–67

Kiernan, Kevin, *'Beowulf' and the 'Beowulf' Manuscript* (Ann Arbor: University of Michigan Press, 1981; rev. edn, 1996)

Kim, Susan M., '"If One Who Is Loved Is Not Present, a Letter May Be Embraced Instead": Death and the *Letter of Alexander to Aristotle*', *JEGP*, 109 (2010), 33–51

Latour, Bruno, *Reassembling the Social: An Introduction to Actor-Network Theory* (Oxford: Oxford University Press, 2005)

Levinas, Emmanuel, 'Being-Toward-Death', trans. by Andrew Schmitz, *Is It Righteous to Be? Interviews with Emmanuel Levinas*, ed. by Jill Robbins (Stanford, CA: Stanford University Press, 2001), pp. 130–39

Merleau-Ponty, Maurice, *Phenomenology of Perception*, trans. by Colin Smith (London: Routledge and Keegan Paul, 1962) [first published as *Phénoméno-logie de la perception* (Paris: Gallimard, 1945)]

Mittman, Asa Simon, 'Are the "Monstrous Races" Races?', *postmedieval*, 6 (2015), 36–51

——, *Maps and Monsters in Medieval England* (London: Taylor & Francis, 2006)

Mittman, Asa Simon, and Susan M. Kim, *Inconceivable Beasts: The 'Wonders of the East' in the 'Beowulf' Manuscript* (Tempe: Arizona Center for Medieval and Renaissance Studies, 2013)

Miyashiro, Adam, 'Homeland Insecurity: Biopolitics and Sovereign Violence in *Beowulf*', *postmedieval*, 11 (2020), 384–95

Orchard, Andy, *A Critical Companion to 'Beowulf'* (Cambridge: D. S. Brewer, 2003)

——, *Pride and Prodigies: Studies in the Monsters of the 'Beowulf'-Manuscript* (Cambridge: D. S. Brewer, 1985)

Rambaran-Olm, Mary, Breann Leake, and Micah James Goodrich, 'Medieval Studies: The Stakes of the Field', *postmedieval*, 11 (2020), 356–70

Thomson, S. C., *Communal Creativity in the Making of the 'Beowulf' Manuscript: Towards a History of Reception for the Nowell Codex*, Library of the Written Word, 67, The Manuscript World, 10 (Leiden: Brill, 2016)

——, 'The Composite Unity of the Entangled Self in Maria Dahvana Headley's *The Mere Wife*', *Studies in Medievalism*, 30 (2020), 203–27

——, 'Grotesque, Fascinating, Transformative: The Power of a Strange Face in the Story of Saint Christopher', *Essays in Medieval Studies*, 34 (2019), 83–98

——, 'The Overlooked Women of the Old English *Passion of Saint Christopher*', *Medievalia et Humanistica*, 44 (2018), 61–80

——, 'Telling the Story: Reshaping *Saint Christopher* for an Anglo-Saxon Lay Audience', *Open Library of Humanities*, 4 (2018), 1–32

Tronick, Edward Z., 'Dyadically Expanded States of Consciousness and the Process of Therapeutic Change', *Infant Mental Health Journal*, 19 (1998), 290–99

Weinreich, Spencer J., 'How a Monster Means: The Significance of Bodily Difference in the Christopher Cynocephalus Tradition', in *Monstrosity, Disability, and the Posthuman in the Medieval and Early Modern World*, ed. by Richard H. Godden and Asa Simon Mittman (Cham: Palgrave, 2019), pp. 181–207

Winnicott, Donald W., 'Mirror Role of Mother and Family in Child Development', in *Playing and Reality* (London: Tavistock, 1971; repr. London: Routledge, 2009), pp. 149–59 [first published in *The Predicament of the Family: A Psycho-Analytical Symposium*, ed. by P. Lomas (London: Hogarth, 1967)]

LUISA OSTACCHINI

Rome Away from Rome: India, Rome, and England in Ælfric's *Life of St Thomas*

England and Rome

No individual place loomed larger in the early medieval English imagination than Rome. The Eternal City, the source of both English Christianity and early medieval English dreams of empire, was ever-present in English texts and culture. It was from Rome, after all, that the pallium, papal decrees, and the Augustinian mission were carried over to English shores; from Roman foundations that many walled English towns such as Winchester were built; and from Rome that England would inherit the secular power, learning, and cultural achievements of the Roman empire via *translatio studii et imperii*.[1] Yet despite Rome's importance and constant presence in English thought, there was a considerable geographical and cultural distance between the two places. Whilst Rome stood at the centre of Christendom, England was frequently depicted as peripheral by classical sources, and this sense of a

---

* I am grateful to Francis Leneghan, Siân Grønlie, and Caroline Batten for their helpful comments on this chapter.

[1] A wealth of previous scholarship has sought to explore the close connection between England and Rome, and to highlight a sense of 'special relationship' between the two that endured over the centuries. For the eighth century, see Levison, *England and the Continent in the Eighth Century*, pp. 15–44; in the ninth century, see Pengelley, 'Rome in Ninth-Century Anglo-Saxon England'; in the tenth and eleventh centuries, see Ortenberg, *The English Church and the Continent*, pp. 127–97. For the Anglo-Roman relationship more generally, see Howe, 'Rome: Capital of Anglo-Saxon England' and Tinti, 'Introduction'. For the pallium, see Matthews, *The Road to Rome*, pp. 67–69; Tinti, 'The Archiepiscopal Pallium in Late Anglo-Saxon England'. For Roman walls and foundations in the early English landscape, see Bintley, *Settlements and Strongholds* and Atherton, *The Making of England*, p. 40. For *translatio imperii* and *studii*, see Curtius, *European Literature and the Latin Middle Ages*, pp. 28–29. For the resonances of these concepts in early medieval England, see Irvine, 'The Anglo-Saxon Chronicle and the Idea of Rome in Alfredian Literature'. For the concept of *translatio imperii* in the ASC, see Leneghan, '*Translatio imperii*', pp. 664–66. For Rome's role in the art and architecture of early medieval England, see Hawkes, 'Design and Decoration'; Ó Carragáin, 'The Periphery Rethinks the Centre'; Ó Carragáin, *The City of Rome and the World of Bede*. See also the chapters by Francis Leneghan, Helen Appleton, and Caitlin Ellis in this volume.

Luisa Ostacchini (luisa.ostacchini@ell.ox.ac.uk) is a college lecturer in medieval literature at the University of Oxford.

Ideas of the World in Early Medieval English Literature, ed. by Mark Atherton, Kazutomo Karasawa, and Francis Leneghan, SOEL 1 (Turnhout: Brepols, 2022)   pp. 127–147
BREPOLS ⹂ PUBLISHERS   DOI 10.1484/M.SOEL.5.130559

marginalized England persisted throughout the early medieval period in the works of English writers and cartographers.[2] This chapter examines the way that Ælfric of Eynsham, one of the most prolific writers and teachers of the tenth century, navigated the distance between his homeland and Rome in his *Life of St Thomas*.[3]

In his works, Ælfric often remarked on England's position at the geographic periphery, and on the fact that this peripheral location made it difficult for the English to replicate the practices of their Continental Christian counterparts. In his homily *On the Prayer of Moses* (part of the *Lives of Saints*) he describes England as being 'on uteweardan þære eorðan bradnysse' (at the extremity of the earth's surface, l. 107) and suggests that consequently, the English cannot fast as easily as those who live 'tomiddes, on mægenfæstum eardum' (in the middle [of the earth], in strong countries, l. 108).[4] Similarly, in his *Letter to the Monks of Eynsham*, he mentions that monks may adjust their psalm recitals from the Continental model in the summer, since the nights are shorter than in Italy: 'nos in Bryttannia degentes, breuiores noctes habentes estate Beneuentanis' (we who dwell in Britain, having shorter nights in the summer than those in Benevento).[5] For Ælfric, England's geographical location positions the country not only at a physical remove from Rome, but also at a cultural distance, since certain aspects of Christian praxis were observed differently between the two places. These differences between English and Roman Christianity were clearly a source of some anxiety for Ælfric, and he is keen to assure his vernacular audiences that England and its Christianity are deserving of a place on the world stage.[6] He reassures his readers and listeners that their history is a venerable one, telling them that 'nis Angel-cynn bedæled Drihtnes halgena' (the English people are not deprived of the Lord's

---

2 On the way that this was portrayed in maps, see Michelet, 'Centrality, Marginality and Distance'; Bridges, 'Of Myths and Maps'; Appleton, 'The Northern World of the Anglo-Saxon *mappa mundi*'. See also Helen Appleton in this volume. On the difficulties of travel between England and Rome, see Matthews, *The Road to Rome*; Pelteret, 'Not All Roads Lead to Rome'. On the cultural difference between England and Rome, and the sense of England as peripheral, see Discenza, *Inhabited Spaces*, pp. 67–68; Lavezzo, *Angels on the Edge of the World*, pp. 27–45.

3 For a summary of Ælfric's life and works, see Hill, 'Ælfric: His Life and Works'.

4 All references to the *Lives of Saints* in this chapter are taken from *Old English Lives of Saints: Ælfric*, ed. and trans. by Clayton and Mullins. Translations are my own.

5 Ælfric of Eynsham, *Letter to the Monks of Eynsham*, ed. and trans. by Jones, p. 138. For the relationship between England and Benevento, see Daniel Anlezark in this volume. Ælfric also refers to the difference in night length in his *De temporibus anni*, where he notes that 'on Italia, þæt is Romana rice, hæfð se dæg fiftyne tida. On Engla lande hæfð se lengsta dæg seofontyne tida' (in Italy, which is the kingdom of the Romans, that [longest] day has fifteen hours. In England the longest day has seventeen hours, ll. 268–69): Ælfric of Eynsham, *De Temporibus Anni*, ed. and trans. by Blake, pp. 86–88.

6 On Ælfric's monastic and lay audiences for the *Lives of Saints*, see Cubitt, 'Ælfric's Lay Patrons'; Wilcox, 'The Audience of Ælfric's Lives of Saints'; Gulley, *The Displacement of the Body in Ælfric's Virgin Martyr Lives*, pp. 7–8.

saints, *Life of Edmund*, l. 247), and that 'þa ða þis ig-land wæs wunigende on sibbe […] ure word sprang wide geond þas eorðan' (when this island was living in peace […] our fame sprang widely across this earth, *On the Prayer of Moses*, ll. 148–51).[7] Yet even these assurances acknowledge that England, as an *ig-land*, exists on the periphery and that, owing to this fact, the country might be expected not to benefit from the same relationship with the saints as places closer to the centre.

In his *Life of St Thomas*, a translation of the Latin *Passio S. Thomae* contained within the *Lives of Saints*, Ælfric confronts the challenged relationship between centre and periphery.[8] In the *Life*, the apostle Thomas builds a palace 'on Romanisce wisan' (in the Roman style, ll. 27 and 79) in India, a place on the distant periphery of the early medieval English world-view.[9] Through alterations that he made to his source material, Ælfric encourages his audiences to view India as a marginal and extremely foreign place, and as such emphasizes the country's distance from the Roman Christianity that Thomas is seeking to recreate there. By showing that the Roman palace has the power to transform the Indian landscape into a place of devout Christian sanctity, Ælfric demonstrates that the values and cultural heritage of places at the centre can be shared and replicated even on the edges of the world. In doing so, he uses India to explore the difficulties of mimicking Rome's practices in England.

The parallel that Ælfric draws between England and India relies on the sense that both were 'on uteweardan'. To some extent, the view of India as a place on the extreme geographic and cultural periphery already existed within the early medieval English textual tradition.[10] Texts such as *The Wonders of the East* and *Alexander's Letter to Aristotle* established the easternmost parts of the known world as being full of strange creatures and exoticized wealth.[11] Such extreme strangeness, however, would have been contrary to Ælfric's purposes. He states in the Latin preface to the *Lives of Saints* that he wishes to present the text in a manner that is easily understood and aligns the clarity

---

7 The phrase 'nis […] bedæled' (not deprived) has been subject to widely varying interpretations in recent scholarship. See, for example, Fell, 'Saint Æðelþryð', p. 18; McKinney, 'Creating a *Gens Anglorum*', pp. 209–10; Hurley, 'Communities in Translation', pp. 60–61.

8 The *Passio S. Thomae* (*BHL* 8136) was identified as the source material for the *Life of St Thomas* by Loomis, 'Further Sources of Ælfric's Saints' Lives'. See also Zettel, 'Ælfric's Hagiographic Sources and the Latin Legendary', pp. 259–62. The print edition closest to the version that Ælfric would have consulted in his version of the Cotton-Corpus Legendary is found in *Sanctuarium seu vitae sanctorum*, ed. by Mombritius, pp. 606–14. Page and line numbers given in this chapter correspond to Mombritius's edition. Quotes have been checked against the Cotton-Corpus versions in Hereford, Cath. Libr., MS P 7 VI, and Oxford, Bodl. Libr., MS Bodley 354 for variant readings.

9 Busbee, 'The Idea of India in Early Medieval England'. For the relationship between India and England, see the chapter by Daniel Anlezark in this volume. For the literary depictions of India, see Simon Thomson, also in this volume.

10 Busbee, 'The Idea of India in Early Medieval England'.

11 See the discussions of cynocephali and *Wonders of the East* by Simon Thomson in this volume, pp. 106–08.

of the text with its usefulness and instructiveness to its audience: 'diligenter curavimus vertere simplici et aperta locutione quatinus proficiat audientibus' (we have taken care to translate in a simple and clear style so that it will benefit listeners).[12] Though he is here referring to legibility of vernacular language and style, he was also concerned with clarity of content, and anything open to misinterpretation would have rendered a text un-useful in Ælfric's eyes in the same way that unclear language might have. As Malcolm Godden and Scott DeGregorio have noted, Ælfric was concerned with the ideas of believability and authenticity, and he consistently sought to combat the idea of *gedwyld* (error).[13] Within this framework, it would not have been suitable for Ælfric to include the strange monsters and miraculous happenings found in other Old English texts about distant places.

Instead, Ælfric utilizes subtle methods in order to convey the sense that the *Life of St Thomas* takes place on the edge of the world. To this end, there are three main ways that he makes India seem foreign or strange to his audience: (1) the Latin preface; (2) the use of rare or unusual vocabulary; and (3) the admission of untranslatability. This chapter will demonstrate how each of these three aspects worked to highlight India's marginality, before exploring how Ælfric represented Thomas's productive recreation of Rome in such a peripheral place, and suggesting that this episode seeks to assure an early medieval English audience that their distance from Rome did not render their relationship with Roman Christianity any less powerful.

India as a Place of Periphery

Ælfric first alerts his audiences to the foreignness of the *Life of St Thomas*'s setting through the text's preface, which not only represents a Latin disruption in an otherwise vernacular text, but also invokes the world of monsters through referencing a dog carrying a human hand. In this preface, Ælfric bemoans the fact that his patron, Æthelweard, has requested a vernacular version of the *Passio S. Thomae*, and states his reasons for hesitating to translate this text in the past, namely that Augustine has renounced the text as apocryphal on the basis of an episode concerning 'niger canis' (a black dog). Though there is a Latin preface to the *Lives of Saints* as a whole, the prefaces to individual items are always in the vernacular, and there are no other sustained pieces of Latin within the collection. The length and style of this preface set it apart from the rest of the *Lives of Saints* and merit its quotation here in full:

Dubitam diu transferre anglice passionem sancti Thomae apostoli ex quibusdam causis, et maxime eo quod Augustinus magnus abnegat de

---

12 *Old English Lives of Saints: Ælfric*, ed. and trans. by Clayton and Mullins, I, p. 4.
13 Godden, 'Ælfric's Saints' Lives and the Problem of Miracles'; DeGregorio, 'Ælfric, Gedwyld, and Vernacular Hagiography'.

illo pincerno cuius manum niger canis in convivium portare deberet. Cui narrationi, ipse Augustinus his verbis contradicens scripsit: 'Cui scripturae licet nobis non credere, non enim est in Catholico canone. Illi, tamen, eam et legunt et tamquam incorruptissimam uerissimamque honorant qui adversus corporales vindictas quae sunt in Veteri Testamento, nescio qua caecitate, acerrime saeviunt quo animo et qua distributione temporum factae sint omnino nescientes.' Et, ideo, volo hoc praetermittere et caetera interpretari quae in eius passione habentur, sicut Æþelwerdus, venerabilis dux, obnixe nos praecatus est.

(Ælfric, Thomas, preface)

> (For a long while I was in doubt about translating the Passion of St Thomas the apostle into English, for various reasons, particularly because the great Augustine rejects the story concerning a cupbearer whose hand a black dog is said to have carried to a feast. In contradicting this story, Augustine himself wrote, in these words: 'we are allowed to disbelieve this narrative, for it is not in the Catholic canon. Nevertheless, there are those who both read and respect it as being most uncorrupted and true, and are very bitterly opposed to the bodily punishments described in the Old Testament — owing to I know not what kind of blindness — because they are wholly ignorant of the spirit in which these were inflicted, and of the dispensations of different times.' And therefore I wish to pass over that part, and to translate the other matters which are contained in his Passion, just as the venerable lord Æthelweard persistently requested me to.)

When the *Life of St Thomas* is considered in isolation, it is easy to consider this prologue as simply a characteristic feature of Ælfric's translation practice. Many of his other works have prefaces, often centred on discussions of translation.[14] Yet within the context of the *Lives of Saints*, only four of the other lives (*Agnes, George, Martin,* and *Edmund*) include any kind of text that might be considered a 'preface'. These are usually very short and discuss the sources of the text in some way. For example, the *Life of St George* contains a four-line preface in which Ælfric complains of apocryphal tales of the saint and announces that 'nu wille we eow secgan þæt soð is be ðam, | þæt heora gedwyld ne derige digellice ænigum' (now we will tell you what is true about him, so that their error may not secretly harm anyone, ll. 3–4). Further, while these other prefaces occasionally reference Ælfric's translation practice, they never mention specific episodes that will be omitted in the way that the preface to the *Life of St Thomas* does. Within the *Lives of Saints* Ælfric frequently removes aspects of his Latin texts that he deems problematic, but he usually does so silently. When he does alert his audience to his shortening of the text,

---

14 Ælfric's discussions of translation are explored in Stanton, 'Rhetoric and Translation in Ælfric's Prefaces'.

he does so vaguely, usually by suggesting that he is removing information for the sake of brevity.[15]

By contrast, in the prologue to the *Life of St Thomas*, Ælfric specifies that the problematic aspect is the incident in which a dog brought a cupbearer's hand to a wedding feast. Further, he misrepresents Augustine in order to do so: though Ælfric claims to be quoting Augustine, he is in fact misrepresenting his argument, which is that the entire life of Thomas, not only the dog episode, is apocryphal.[16] The 'niger canis' carrying the severed hand evokes the same kind of strange horror and danger found in the wild animals and monstrous races of the *Liber Monstrorum*, *Alexander's Letter to Aristotle*, and *The Wonders of the East*.[17] The reference to 'corporales vindictas' (bodily punishments) is also evocative of these texts, whose focus is often on the (in)human body and its potential for monstrosity.[18] Moreover, by quoting Augustine's statement that the passion of Thomas 'non […] est in Catholico canone' (is not in the Catholic canon), Ælfric aligns the *Life of St Thomas* with ideas of textual marginality and distance from the Christian centre. The preface, then, works as a sort of apophasis, in which, by specifically mentioning the episode that he disagrees with and refuses to translate, and emphasizing its apocryphal nature, Ælfric alerts his audience to the potential for strange happenings within the Indian landscape that they are about to experience.

Once the narrative has begun, Ælfric continues to suggest that the *Life of St Thomas* is one concerned with foreign or strange material through the use of rare vocabulary, much of which is concentrated at the beginning of the text. When Thomas is called to go to India, Christ promises the apostle the 'wuldor-beage martyrdomes' (glorious crown of martyrdom, l. 14), translating the Latin term *corona*, which Ælfric more usually translates as *cynehelm*.[19] Milfull and Gretsch suggest that *cynehelm* and *wuldorbeah*, both 'Winchester words', held different connotations: *cynehelm* denoted physical crowns, whilst *wuldorbeah* was used for more metaphorical ones. However, in the *Lives of Saints*, Ælfric frequently uses *cynehelm* to describe the spiritual crown of martyrdom, and uses *wuldorbeah* only three times.[20] As such, his choice of *wuldorbeah* in the *Life of St Thomas* and elsewhere ought to be

---

15 See, for example, his *Life of Maurus*, in which he alerts his audience to his abbreviation of the text by declaring of the saint's miracles that 'sume þære we secgað her, sume we forsuwiað' (some of these [miracles] we will tell here, some we will pass over silently, l. 50).

16 Biggs, 'Ælfric's Comments about the Passio Thomae'; Godden, 'Ælfric's Saints' Lives and the Problem of Miracles'.

17 See Simon Thomson in this volume.

18 For the bodily focus of *Wonders of the East*, see Oswald, *Monsters, Gender, and Sexuality*, pp. 27–65. See also Miyashiro, 'Monstrosity and Ethnography in Medieval Europe'.

19 The other two instances are in *The Forty Soldiers*, ll. 127–28, and the *Life of Cecilia*, l. 264.

20 Milfull, *The Hymns of the Anglo-Saxon Church*, p. 83; Gretsch, *The Intellectual Foundations of the English Benedictine Reform*, pp. 96–104. See, for example, 'kyne-helme martirdomes' (glorious crown of martyrdom, *Life of St Thomas*, l. 279) or 'wuldorfullan cyne-helm heora martyrdomes' (the glorious crown of their martyrdom, *Life of Vincent*, l. 43).

considered a stylistic choice as much as a connotative one. The infrequent usage of *wuldorbeah* throughout the *Lives of Saints* makes it unfamiliar to Ælfric's audiences, and so further encourages the sense that Thomas will experience unusual things in India. Similarly, when the Indian steward, Abbanes, asks Thomas to come to India to build a palace, Ælfric uses the rare compound *cyne-botl* (palace, l. 27) to translate the Latin word *palatium*. The term *cyne-botl* appears only twice in the Old English corpus: once in the *Life of St Thomas* and once in Ælfric's *Glossary*. Ælfric more usually translates *palatium* as *gebytlu* (which is the term he uses in all eight of the other instances within the *Life of St Thomas*), or as *botl*.[21] Ælfric places this rare word emphatically at the very end of Abbanes's address to Thomas, which comprises the first piece of direct speech made by an Indian person in the entirety of the *Lives of Saints*. This speech also includes the rare adjective *gecwemlic*, which occurs only fourteen times across the extant corpus, predominantly in glosses.[22] In including rare terms in Abbanes's direct speech, Ælfric presents Indian speech as foreign and unusual to an English audience. Though the effect of these rare terms is minimal in isolation, together they contribute to a pattern of unusual diction at the opening of the text and heighten the sense that the *Life of St Thomas* is set apart from the rest of the collection.

Bringing Rome to the Periphery

Ælfric's Latin preface to the *Life of St Thomas* and the inclusion of unusual vocabulary, then, work to present India as a foreign, peripheral place, distinct from other locations within the *Lives of Saints*. Yet despite this extreme geographical distance from the Christian centre, in the *Life of St Thomas*, India becomes the home of a Roman-style palace. This building serves as the focal point for Thomas's missionary activity: it is through the palace that the Indian king is converted, that his brother is resurrected from the dead, and that his people turn to Christianity. Through this episode, Ælfric shows that the power of Rome could successfully be recreated even in the remotest parts of the world. In doing so, he encouraged reflection on England's relationship with Rome, suggesting that despite the distance between the two places, England could nonetheless share Rome's imperial and Christian achievements. Moreover, he demonstrated that Rome could be at once strange

---

21 Ælfric translates *palatium* as *gebytlu* in the *Life of St Thomas*, ll. 60, 80, 84, 126, 129, 163, 173, and 176. For Ælfric's translations of *botl* for *palatium*, see for example 'ðæs cynincges botl' (the king's palace, *Book of Kings*, l. 172) or 'þam heofonlicum botle' (the heavenly palace, l. 162) in his homily for the Assumption in his *Catholic Homilies* I.

22 'On stane cunnon and gecwemlice on treowe' (skilful with stone and pleasing with wood, l. 26). The adverbial form, *gecwemlice*, is also rare, recorded in only twelve extant instances. Data taken from the *DOE Corpus*.

and familiar, and emphasized England's unique and paradoxical relationship with the Eternal City.

The depiction of Roman architecture in the *Life of St Thomas* celebrates Roman cultural achievement and demonstrates its power to enhance Christian faith. The description of the palace clearly held great significance for Ælfric, since he removes the entire preceding episode about the chaste marriage of Dionysius and Pelagia found in his Latin source.[23] This is particularly striking given Ælfric's usual reformist interest in chaste marriage on display elsewhere in the *Lives of Saints* and the *Catholic Homilies*.[24] Through the removal of the Dionysius and Pelagia episode, Ælfric's account places greater emphasis on the episode of the Roman-style building — planning and erecting the palace becomes Thomas's first narrated act once he reaches India, and as such represents the first moment of his missionary effort. Ælfric describes the Roman palace at great length:

> and Thomas eode metende mid anre mete-gyrde þone stede,
> and cwæð þæt he wolde wyrcan þa healle
> ærest on east-dæle, and þa oþre gebytlu
> bæftan þære healle: bæð-hus and kycenan,
> and winter-hus and sumor-hus and wynsume buras,
> twelf hus togædere, mid godum bigelsum.
> Ac swylc weorc nis gewunelic to wyrcenne on Englalande,
> and forþy we ne secgað swutellice heora naman.
>
> (Ælfric, *Thomas*, ll. 82–89)

> (And Thomas went about measuring the site with a measuring rod, and said that he intended to build the hall first on the east side, and the other buildings behind the hall: the bath-house and kitchen, and winter house and summer house, and beautiful chambers, twelve buildings altogether, with good arches. But it is not customary to make such buildings in England, and therefore we will not say their names clearly.)

Here, Ælfric presents Rome's material culture as both distant from and close to his audience. In particular, his use of vocabulary to describe the Roman palace balances familiarity with strangeness. The palace is described with an abundance of compounds that are unusual or otherwise unattested, but which bring together common, well-known elements, highlighting the ways in which the building is both foreign and recognizable to an English audience. Ælfric uses a wealth of terms that are found in three or fewer instances across the extant corpus of Old English Literature: *mete-gyrde* (measuring stick);

---

23 *Passio S. Thomae*, 606.48–608.9.

24 This interest has been noted by Upchurch, 'For Pastoral Care and Political Gain'; and Gretsch, *Ælfric and the Cult of Saints in Late Anglo-Saxon England*, pp. 4, 9.

sumor-hus (summer house); *winter-hus* (winter house); and *bæð-hus* (bath-house). However, all of these compounds build upon common lexis: the word *hus*, for example, has over two thousand attestations, and *gyrd* over four hundred. Moreover, the concepts that these compounds describe were not unknown to English audiences. Measuring rods or perches, which were most often described as *gyrd*, were commonplace in medieval England, and would constitute a familiar tool for building surveillance.[25] Similarly, the idea of a complex comprised of buildings for different purposes or utilized at different times of year would be familiar to English monastic and high-status audiences alike.[26] Ælfric, then, depicts the buildings of the palace in terms that reflect the way that Rome was at once foreign and recognizable to his audiences, bringing common ideas and root words into relatively unusual compounds.

The word *bigels* (arch) is unusual and was not part of the standard Old English architectural lexis.[27] The term is attested in eighteen extant instances, four of which are Ælfrician, and the remaining fourteen of which are in glossaries, where *bigels* is used to gloss the Latin *arcus* or *fornix*. More commonly, these Latin lemmata are glossed with the Old English *boga* or *hrof*, which are comparatively more common terms compared to *bigels*. Ælfric's use of this term usually describes abundant, fetishized, non-European material wealth. For example, in his *De falsis diis* (a text which is included alongside the *Lives of Saints* in London, British Library, MS Cotton Julius E VII) the term is used to describe an idol of the Egyptian god Serapis, 'ænlice geworht | of ælcum antimbre þe of eorþan cymð' (beautifully made from each material that comes from the earth, ll. 527–28), which is 'betwux þam bigelsum gefæstnod' (fastened between the arches, l. 534). Similarly, in his homily on Simon and Jude, Ælfric describes how Xerxes built a church to house the bodies of the apostles in Babylon, 'and beworhte ða bigelsas mid gyldenum læfrum' (and decorated the arches with gold plates, l. 268).[28] His word choice in the *Life of St Thomas*, then, gestures to the idea of the palace's tempering of foreignness and familiarity by utilizing a term that is both strange (owing to its relatively infrequent use in Old English literature) and recognizable (since Ælfric repeatedly uses the term to describe non-European wealth in his works).

Ælfric draws attention to the relative unfamiliarity of his vocabulary choices and of the palace itself with his statement that the Roman palace is untranslatable: 'swylc weorc nis gewunelic to wyrcenne on Englalande, | and forþy we ne secgað swutellice heora naman' (it is not customary to make such buildings in England, and therefore we will not say their names clearly, ll. 88–89). This admission of translation difficulty is unusual within the *Lives*

---

25 Blair, 'Grid-Planning in Anglo-Saxon Settlements', pp. 19–20.

26 See Blair, *Building Anglo-Saxon England*, pp. 365–72, 400–401; Blair, *The Church in Anglo-Saxon Society*, p. 203.

27 The term *bigels* is absent from Biggam's consideration of Old English vocabulary used for building work ('Grund to Hrof').

28 'The Passion of Simon and Jude', in *Ælfric's Catholic Homilies: The Second Series*, ed. by Godden.

of Saints. It is in stark contrast to, for example, Ælfric's translation of the *Chair of Saint Peter*, where he states that 'nu synd sume men þe nyton hwæt se nama getacnað: | *cathedra* is gereht "bisceop-stol" on Englisc' (now, since there are some men who do not know what the name signifies: *cathedra* means 'bishop's throne' in English, ll. 3–4). Similarly, in his *Life of Agatha*, Ælfric writes that the volcano is full of '*sulphore*, þæt is swæfel on Englisc' (*sulphore*, that is 'sulphur' in English, l. 219). The only other instance when he references an untranslatable concept within the *Lives of Saints* is the description of an elephant in *The Maccabees*, where he notes that 'sumum menn wile þincan syllic þis to gehyrenne | forþan þe ylpas ne comon næfre on Englalande' (some men will think this strange to hear, because elephants have never come to England, ll. 565–66). However, this is immediately followed by an explanation, drawing upon Ambrose's *Hexameron* and Isidore's *Etymologiae*.[29] Indeed, Ælfric explains what an elephant is in great detail: how it is 'ormæte nyten, mare þonne sum hus' (an enormous animal, larger than a house, l. 567), that it 'næfre ne lið' (never lies down, l. 569), and that it lives 'þreo hund geara' (three hundred years, l. 571). Indeed, the explanation is so detailed that Ælfric even informs his audiences of the gestation period for an elephant, 'feower and twentig monða gæð seo modor mid folan' (the mother is with foal for twenty-four months, l. 570). He ensures that his audience knows what he is referring to, even though it is likely to be foreign to them. Further, as Edward Christie notes, Ælfric removes all of the more fantastic lore that his sources contain, and expresses only the material that he considers will be believable to his audience.[30] By contrast, the Roman-style buildings of St Thomas are left a mystery, and Ælfric's comment that 'swylc weorc nis gewunelic to wyrcenne on Englalande' increases rather than diminishes the strangeness of these buildings to an English audience.

Ælfric, then, is adapting Roman architecture for his audiences, synthesizing familiar and strange aspects in much the same way that Ó Carragáin notes that early medieval English and Irish ecclesiastics selectively adapted Roman ceremonies and liturgy for their respective audiences.[31] In this, Ælfric was perhaps reflecting on the real variance between English and Roman customs. For example, whereas Roman royal palaces were primarily built from stone, there is no evidence, save for one mysterious description in Asser's *Life of King Alfred*, that stone-built royal vills were ever constructed in pre-Conquest England.[32] Yet monumental stone buildings were not unfamiliar to the early medieval English, whose landscape was filled with Roman stone remains and whose churches were often constructed of stone.[33] By employing unusual yet

---

29 These sources are identified in Cross, 'The Elephant to Alfred, Ælfric, Aldhelm and Others'.
30 Christie, 'The Idea of an Elephant', pp. 469–70.
31 Ó Carragáin, 'The Periphery Rethinks the Centre', esp. pp. 63–65.
32 Blair, *Building Anglo-Saxon England*, pp. 84–86.
33 Bintley, *Settlements and Strongholds*, pp. 44–62; Godfrey, *The Church in Anglo-Saxon England*, pp. 362–65.

ultimately recognizable terms to describe the architecture of the palace and also emphasizing the untranslatability of Roman architecture, Ælfric balances the real tension between foreignness and familiarity that underlined the English relation to Roman practices.

Moreover, Ælfric emphasizes that, despite its potential to sometimes appear unfamiliar or confusing, Rome's material culture merited his audience's attention. The anonymous *Passio S. Thomae*, which Ælfric used as his source, includes the names of each of the twelve buildings, including the *epicaustoria*, the *hippodromos*, and the *gymnasium*.[34] Whilst Ælfric omits some of these buildings from his account, he nonetheless retains a significant amount of information about the construction of the palace. Patrizia Lendinara describes this passage as 'quite simplified' from the Latin, particularly owing to the repetition of *gebytle*.[35] However, this description is unusually extensive for Ælfric: elsewhere in the *Lives of Saints*, he omits almost all the information about Roman geography and buildings found in his sources, whilst here he depicts Roman architecture closely. It has often been noted that Ælfric aspired to *brevitas* in his translations and aimed to present clear teaching material by streamlining his Latin sources both stylistically and narratively.[36] This retention of detail, then, indicates not only an interest in Roman architecture but also a desire to describe it to his audiences, and suggests that Ælfric considered the stylistic aspects of Rome to carry didactic value.

The sense that Roman materiality could contribute to Christian teaching was not unique to Ælfric. The careful recitation of the aspects of the Roman palace is in some ways reminiscent of Roman stational liturgy as found in early medieval England, in which familiarity with the major feast days of the Church went hand in hand with familiarity with the material city of Rome, its shrines and basilicas.[37] Similarly Bede, in his praise of Benedict Biscop, notes that the gifts that Benedict brought back from Rome 'non ad ornamentum solummodo ecclesiae uerum et ad instructionem intuentium proponerentur aduexit uidilicet ut qui per litterarum lectionem non possent opera domini et saluatoris nostri per ipsarum contuitum discerent imaginum' (are displayed not simply to ornament the church, but also for the instruction of viewers, so that those who cannot learn the works of our Lord and Saviour through letters may do so by looking at the images, *Hom.* 1.13.12).[38] In the same way, Roman materiality, for Ælfric, is symbolic of Roman practices more broadly, and a vital teaching tool.

Indeed, Ælfric uses the palace's materiality to demonstrate the value of replicating Roman practices in places on the periphery. A key force in Gad's

---

34 *Passio S. Thomae*, 608.14–17.

35 Lendinara, 'Minimal Collections of Glosses', p. 196.

36 See, for example, Whatley, 'Lost in Translation'; Stanton, *The Culture of Translation in Anglo-Saxon England*, pp. 144–71, esp. pp. 163–66; Nichols, 'Ælfric and the Brief Style'.

37 On the stational liturgy, see Ó Carragáin, *The City of Rome and the World of Bede*, pp. 9–15.

38 Bede, *Homeliarum evangelii libri II*, p. 93.

and Gundophorus's conversions is a heavenly vision of Thomas's palace from the angels of God. Ælfric's account emphasizes the important role played by this image of Rome:

> Min sawl wæs gelæd soþlice to heofonum
> þurh Godes englas, and ic þær geseah
> þa mæran gebytlu þe Thomas þe worhte
> on þære gelicnysse þe he hit gelogode her,
> mid gym-stanum gefrætewod, fægere geond eall.
> Mid þam þe ic sceawode þa scinendan gebytlu,
> þa sædon me þa englas: 'Þis synd þa gebytla
> þe Thomas getimbrode þinum breðer on eorðan.'

(Ælfric, *Thomas*, ll. 124–31)

(My soul was truly led to heaven by God's angels, and I saw there the glorious buildings that Thomas made for you, in the likeness of how he made it here, adorned with gemstones, beautiful everywhere. While I was examining the shining buildings, the angels said to me: 'These are the buildings which Thomas built for your brother on earth'.)

Upon hearing about this vision, Gad's brother Gundophorus is also converted: 'þa gesohte Gundoforus þone Godes apostol, | biddende miltsunge his misdæda georne' (then Gundophorus sought God's apostle, asking earnestly for mercy for his sins, ll. 152–53). Owing to Ælfric's omission of the previous episodes in the Latin *passio*, the conversion of India more generally also seems to hinge on the Roman palace. When rumour of Thomas spreads 'geond þæt land wide' (widely throughout that land, l. 184), it is claimed that the apostle 'mihte gehælan mid his handa hrepunge | deafe and blinde and þa deadan aræran' (could, with the touch of his hands, heal the deaf and the blind and raise the dead, ll. 186–87). However, in Ælfric's account, the apostle has performed none of these miracles — his only recorded act in India is the construction of Gundophorus's palace. In the vernacular translation, then, Roman material culture takes centre stage in Thomas's conversion efforts and prompts widespread Christianity across India.

Ælfric presents the palace's materiality as central to its power as a tool of conversion. The wonder of the material palace is highlighted through Ælfric's ornamental prose style, in which the chiastic alliteration of '**gym**-stanum gefrætewod, f**æ**gere **g**eond eall' and insistent repetition of *gebytlu* centres the physical aspect of the palace. In Ælfric's account, this physicality is shared between the angelic version of the palace and its real counterpart. The Latin text revels in the description of the palace's gemstones but clearly demarcates the difference between the vision and the reality. Gad describes how he saw a palace just like the one built by Thomas, 'sed tota fabrica ex lapidibus smaragdinis et hiacynthinis et prasinis et albis instructa est intus et foris' (but it was totally made from emerald jewels and jacinths and onyxes and white precious stones inside and out, 608.39–40). Though Ælfric removes the reference to

ROME AWAY FROM ROME   139

specific jewels, he does not translate the word *sed* (but), suggesting that the
real palace is also 'mid gym-stanum gefrætewod', and thereby representing
Roman material culture as being equally wonderous as Gad's dream vision.

Moreover, Ælfric does not criticize the material wealth conveyed by the
'scinendan gebytlu'. Writing in the context of the late tenth century, in which
the landowning aristocracy aided the establishment and maintenance of
monastic communities, and working under the patronage of two such wealthy
men, Æthelweard and Æthelmær, Ælfric did not always entirely condemn
wealth.[39] However, he was keen to distinguish between riches used for spiritual
betterment and those used for personal greed.[40] Within the *Lives of Saints*, the
word *gymstan* is often linked to this greed mentality and to the unfavourable
aspects of materialism. In the *Life of Æthelthryth*, for example, the saint decries
the toxic nature of her previously materialistic life: 'þonne me nu þis geswel
scynð for golde | and þæs hata bryne for healicum gym-stanum' (when this
tumour now shines for me in the place of gold, and this hot burning for
precious gemstones, ll. 59–60). Ælfric also warns against the harmful nature
of riches in the *Life of Chrysanthus and Daria*, where Ælfric describes Daria
attempting to lure Chrysanthus to heathenism. She appears 'geglenged mid
golde, to þam cnihte, | and scinendum gym-stanum swilce sun-beam færlice'
(to the young man, adorned with gold and brightly shining gemstones like
a sunbeam, ll. 89–90). In both these instances, Ælfric denounces physical
wealth, suggesting that it is inferior to spiritual wealth and actively harmful
to both the body and soul. However, in the *Life of St Thomas*, Ælfric does not
attach negative connotations to the dream vision of Thomas's palace. Thomas
encourages Gundophorus and Gad to donate their material goods to the poor
and states that 'magon eowre æhta yrnan eow ætforan, | and hi ne magon
folgian on forð-siðe eow' (your possessions can go before you, but they will
not follow you after death, ll. 179–80), but the gemstone-embellished palace
itself is never subject to direct criticism. Rather, its materiality is presented
as a reflection of its spiritual glory, and the wonder that it evokes allows it to
become an effective tool of conversion, just as Rome's monumental materiality
was effective in strengthening the faith of its early medieval English viewers.[41]

Ælfric perhaps presented the palace in such material terms not only because
it leads to spiritual ends, but also because it occurred in India. India was a
place which a vernacular audience already associated with exoticized wealth
through texts like *Wonders of the East*, which portrays distant places as being
filled with rich material resources such as gold and jewels.[42] This trope was
specifically linked to India on the so-called Cotton *mappa mundi*, discussed

---

39   Godden, 'Money, Power and Morality in Late Anglo-Saxon England'. For Ælfric's patrons,
      see Cubitt, 'Ælfric's Lay Patrons'.
40   Gulley, *The Displacement of the Body in Ælfric's Virgin Martyr Lives*, pp. 55–57.
41   See, for example, Ó Carragáin's exploration of the Ruthwell Cross, *The City of Rome and the
      World of Bede*, pp. 31–34.
42   On this text, see the chapter by Simon Thomson in this volume.

by Helen Appleton elsewhere in this volume, where India has within its boundaries the 'mons aureus' (mountain of gold).[43] In India, then, such things are expected for an early medieval English audience. The gemstone-studded palace of the *Life of St Thomas* is part of an existing textual tradition, and so does not seem as out of place or questionable as it might have been in the *Life* of an insular or Continental saint. In having the most extensive description of Roman material culture in the whole *Lives of Saints* in a life set in India, Ælfric was able to foster a sense of wonder at Rome's rich heritage without contradicting his teaching regarding materialistic and spiritual wealth.

Further, Ælfric's interest in the material aspect of the palace is entrenched in the idea of imperial Rome. Earl Anderson has read Ælfric's architectural descriptions in the *Life of St Thomas* as primarily symbolic, writing that 'Thomas's architectural skill symbolizes his mission to build "cristes getimbrunge" in India', but notes that Ælfric's comparison of Roman and English architecture also reveals an appreciation for Roman building.[44] Indeed, when compared with its Latin source, it becomes clear that Ælfric's text demonstrates a particular interest in the workmanship itself, and in the idea of Roman authority. This is visible in the way that he shifts the emphasis of the Latin source in his translation. For example, in the Latin text, the palace's orientation takes on symbolic significance, with Thomas saying that 'ianuas in isto loco disponam ab ortu solis ingressum' (in this place I will place doors according to the entry of the rising sun, 608.14). The *passio* conveys a symbolic importance of the palace's orientation that relies upon the rising sun, reflecting the entry of the risen Christ, and the light of Christianity, to India through the palace. This reflects the juxtaposition of mission and craftmanship in Thomas's earlier statement that 'facio exhedras et fenestras ut domus lumen numquam deficiat' (I make halls and windows so that light of the house never diminishes, 606.38), translated by Ælfric as 'þa egðyrle macige þe alteowe beoð | þæt þam huse ne bið wana þæs healican leohtes' (I will make windows that will be well-finished, so that the house will not lack the heavenly light, ll. 57–58).

By contrast, the phrase that Ælfric uses to describe the palace's orientation, 'he wolde wyrcan þa healle | ærest on east-dæle' (he intended to build the hall first on the east side), suggests precise workmanship and the importance of correct placement. The symbolic meaning is no longer explicit here. Instead, Ælfric's text seems to celebrate the orderly nature of the Roman construction, made with a 'mete-gyrde', with all of its buildings set in their correct place ('on east-dæle') and order ('ærest', 'bæftan'). The careful manner of Thomas's work is further highlighted by the repetition of the verb 'metan' (to measure) in the collocation of 'metende' with 'mete-gyrde', which emphasizes the importance of measurement and precise construction. This styling is absent from the Latin text, which gives: 'Thomas autem appraehendens harundinem coepit

---

43 BL, MS Cotton Tiberius B V, fol. 56ᵛ.
44 Anderson, 'The Uncarpentered World of Old English Poetry', p. 70.

metiri' (Thomas then, grasping a reed, began to measure, 608.13). Thomas's positioning of each of the different Roman-style buildings re-enacts the Roman stational system, which Ó Carragáin suggests celebrated the unity of the Church on a microcosmic scale.[45] Clemoes has argued that Ælfric's prose style was intended to mirror cosmic order.[46] Here, then, we see this desire manifested not only in Ælfric's use of alliteration or rhythmical prose, but also in his translation practice: in his choice of omissions, reworkings, and re-emphasis of a Latin text.

The most extensive description of Roman architecture in the entire *Lives of Saints*, then, is one that presents it as a cultural achievement because of its well-ordered craftsmanship. This draws upon the image of imperial Rome, a political and cultural power against whose authority the rest of Christendom can be ordered. In the Old English *Orosius*, time is ordered by Rome, with each chapter opening by setting the year it concerns against either 'ær ðam þe Romeburh getimbred wæs' (before the city of Rome was built) or 'æfter ðam þe Romeburh getimbred wæs' (after the city of Rome was built).[47] Rome is used as a structuring device, in order to make sense of the chronology of the rest of Christendom. Ælfric's presentation of the Roman method of construction may be seen to operate in a similar way, in that it uses Rome as an authoritative means of creating order. In Ælfric's *Thomas*, Rome's power, its ability to seem wondrous to its audience and to convey authority, stem from its orderliness of craftsmanship. To Ælfric, a Benedictine, this orderly construction no doubt granted a sense of prestige to the Roman palace, since the *Regula Benedicti* stresses the importance of orderliness within the monastery — 'ælc endebyrdnes on mynstre sceal beon gehealden and gefadod be heora gecyrrednesse and be lifes geearnunge' (every rank in the minster must be observed and arranged by their [time of] turning [to the monastic life] and by their life's merit, LXIII) — and the correct layout of the monastery itself: 'se sylfa geatweard sceal cytan habban wið þæt geat, þæt þa cuman, þe mynster geseceað, simle gearone hæbban and andwyrde þæra ærenda underfo' (this porter himself must have a cell close to the gate, so that those who come seeking the minster may always find someone ready, and receive answers to their questions, LXVI).[48] As such, Ælfric's presentation of Thomas's palace as being carefully organized may be seen as a sort of model for Christian architecture and lifestyle more generally. By focusing on the craftsmanship rather than the symbolic potential of the passage, he employs the image of imperial Rome to teach the importance of order to his English vernacular audiences, both monastic and lay.[49]

---

45 Ó Carragáin, *The City of Rome and the World of Bede*, pp. 26–27.

46 Clemoes, *Rhythm and Cosmic Order in Old English Christian Literature*, pp. 16–21.

47 *The Old English History of the World*, ed. and trans. by Godden.

48 *Die angelsächsichen Prosabearbeitungen der Benediktinerregel*, ed. by Schröer, pp. 112–13, 126.

49 Gatch and Wilcox both note that vernacular texts were used alongside Latin ones in some monastic houses, and that the *Lives of Saints* may have been used in monastic contexts

That this episode occurs in India allows Ælfric to demonstrate the didactic potential of Rome and its culture, whilst also acknowledging its potential foreignness to an English Christian milieu. Though the palace is a source of great conversion and a testament to imperial achievement, it is nonetheless acknowledged by Ælfric as 'nis gewunelic' (not customary). The palace is as untranslatable and strange to an English audience as it is to the Indian landscape in which it finds itself reconstructed. Yet because this episode takes place in India, a place whose foreignness Ælfric is at pains to stress through his vocabulary and preface, this untranslatability does not emphasize England itself as a place of periphery. In the *Life of St Thomas*, then, India becomes a place where Ælfric can acknowledge the difficulties of following Roman customs in a faraway place, without distancing his readers from the city that was so foundational to English religious practice and political ambitions.

Conclusion

When compared to other descriptions of India in the Old English corpus, the markers of strangeness used by Ælfric in his *Life of St Thomas* are admittedly subtle. There are no monstrous races, and the fetishized wealth presented in the Latin *Passio* is largely minimized. However, this speaks to Ælfric's desire to create a text that was ultimately believable for his English readers. Adam Miyashiro suggests that *The Wonders of the East*, with its array of depictions of monstrosity according to the Plinian model, 'establishes a template for imagining peripheral communities in Africa and India'.[50] The India of Ælfric's *Life of St Thomas* belongs to a very different genre, and so expresses this sense of the 'peripheral' in a different way. Within the *Lives of Saints*, marvels are saintly miracles, not monstrous races or strange sights.[51] However, India's distance from early medieval England and from the Christian centre are nonetheless made apparent. Ælfric strikes a balance between the strange and the foreign by inserting a Latin preface, employing commonplace nouns in rarely occurring compounds, and depicting exoticized wealth. In doing so, he establishes an expectation of India as somehow esoteric without compromising the didactic power of the text.

Through this foreignization of India, we see Ælfric reflecting on England's similarly peripheral position. In the palace-building episode, Ælfric suggests to his audiences that just as Rome can be physically recreated on Indian soil, so

---

as well as lay ones: Gatch, *Preaching and Theology in Anglo-Saxon England*, p. 41; *Ælfric's Prefaces*, ed. and trans. by Wilcox, p. 50.

50 Miyashiro, 'Monstrosity and Ethnography in Medieval Europe', pp. 41–44.

51 Even the saintly miracles themselves sometimes provide a problem. As Malcolm Godden has demonstrated, Ælfric shows a clear concern that his hagiography should distinguish between true and false stories, and that he should include nothing too spectacular: 'Ælfric's Saints' Lives and the Problem of Miracles', pp. 87–88.

too can the city's authority and practices be recreated in tenth-century England. In Ælfric's version of the *Life of St Thomas*, the Roman palace episode becomes a parable about reconciling England's physical and temporal distance from Rome with a religious practice that takes Rome as its centre. Busbee sees the *Life of St Thomas* as a text which 'offers particular insights into Anglo-Saxon anxieties about India'.[52] However, as this chapter has argued, Ælfric uses the palace-building narrative as a place to express and assuage anxieties not only about India, but also about Rome and his native England. By presenting India as distant, esoteric, and yet still very much part of a community of Christianity, strongly linked to Rome, Ælfric encourages his audience to celebrate and reflect upon their own Roman past whilst also acknowledging their separation from it. Through this, he demonstrates the potential for peripheral places to enjoy a close relationship with central ones. That the Roman building is so untranslatable is in many ways an open acknowledgement that England is set aside from Rome: it might still follow the Roman psalter, or enjoy the hagiography of Roman martyrs, but it is *not* Rome.

The *Life of St Thomas* is the final item in the *Lives of Saints* as it stands in its main manuscript witness, BL, MS Cotton Julius E VII.[53] Indeed, the date of Saint Thomas's death, 21 December, marks his feast as the last major feast before Christmas in the Western *sanctorale*. It stands, then, at the periphery of the collection. Its position on the edge, in placement and content, made it an ideal vessel for Ælfric to reflect on England's own perceived peripheral position in the world, and to close his collection with the reminder that tenth-century England was not the remote island portrayed by classical sources, but a part of a global Christian community.

---

52 Busbee, 'A Paradise Full of Monsters', p. 60.

53 BL, MS Cotton Julius E VII (Ker, *Catalogue of Manuscripts Containing Anglo-Saxon*, § 162) is the closest extant manuscript to the *Lives of Saints* as originally compiled by Ælfric, in terms of both its date (s. xi[in]) and its content, although it had already seen some anonymous interpolations by this stage. See Kleist, *The Chronology and Canon of Ælfric*, pp. 235–36. It has provided the basis for both Skeat's and Clayton and Mullins's editions of the *Lives of Saints*. The *Life of St Thomas* occupies fols 224[r]–230[r], after which the manuscript includes two other Latin works, *Interrogationes Sigewulfi in Genesin* and *De falsis diis*, which, although both by Ælfric, are unrelated to the *Lives of Saints*.

Works Cited

Manuscripts

Hereford, Cathedral Library, MS P 7 VI
London, British Library, MS Cotton Julius E VII
London, British Library, MS Cotton Tiberius B V
Oxford, Bodleian Library, MS Bodley 354

Primary Sources

Ælfric of Eynsham, *Ælfric's Catholic Homilies: The Second Series, Text*, ed. by
    Malcolm R. Godden, EETS SS, 5 (Oxford: Oxford University Press, 1979)
——, *Ælfric's De Temporibus Anni*, ed. and trans. by Martin Blake (Cambridge:
    D. S. Brewer, 2009)
——, *Ælfric's Letter to the Monks of Eynsham*, ed. and trans. by Christopher Jones
    (Cambridge: Cambridge University Press, 1998)
——, *Ælfric's Lives of Saints*, ed. by W. W. Skeat, 2 vols (London: Kegan Paul,
    Trench, Trübner, 1881–1885)
——, *Old English Lives of Saints: Ælfric*, ed. and trans. by Mary Clayton and Juliet
    Mullins, DOML, 58–60, 3 vols (Cambridge, MA: Harvard University Press,
    2019)
——, *Ælfric's Prefaces*, ed. and trans. by Jonathan Wilcox (Durham: Durham Medi-
    eval Texts, 1994)
Die angelsächsichen Prosabearbeitungen der Benediktinerregel, ed. by Arnold Schröer
    (Darmstadt: Wissenschaftliche Buchgesellschaft, 1964)
Bede, *Homeliarum evangelii libri II*, in *Beda Venerabilis, Opera homiletica, Opera
    rhythmica* ed. by David Hurst and J. Fraipont, CCSL, 122 (Turnhout: Brepols,
    1955), pp. 1–378
The Old English History of the World: An Anglo-Saxon Rewriting of Orosius, ed.
    and trans. by Malcolm R. Godden, DOML, 44 (Cambridge, MA: Harvard
    University Press, 2016)
Sanctuarium seu vitae sanctorum, ed. by Bonino Mombritius, vol. II (Paris:
    Albertum Fontemoing, 1910)

Secondary Sources

Anderson, Earl, 'The Uncarpentered World of Old English Poetry', *ASE*, 20 (1991),
    65–80
Appleton, Helen, 'The Northern World of the Anglo-Saxon *mappa mundi*', *ASE*, 47
    (2018), 275–305
Atherton, Mark, *The Making of England: A New History of the Anglo-Saxon World*
    (London: I. B. Tauris, 2017)
Biggam, Carole P., 'Grund to Hrof: Aspects of the Old English Semantics of
    Building and Architecture', *Architectural History*, 45 (2002), 49–65

Biggs, Fred, 'Ælfric's Comments about the Passio Thomae', *N&Q*, 52 (2005), 5–8

Bintley, Michael D. J., *Settlements and Strongholds in Early Medieval England: Texts, Landscapes, and Material Culture*, SEM, 45 (Turnhout: Brepols, 2020)

Blair, John, *Building Anglo-Saxon England* (Princeton, NJ: Princeton University Press, 2018)

——, *The Church in Anglo-Saxon Society* (Oxford: Oxford University Press, 2005)

——, 'Grid-Planning in Anglo-Saxon Settlements: The Short Perch and the Four Perch Module', *Anglo-Saxon Studies in Archaeology and History*, 18 (2013), 18–61

Bridges, Margaret, 'Of Myths and Maps: The Anglo-Saxon Cosmographer's Europe', in *Writing and Culture*, ed. by Balz Engler, Swiss Papers in English Language and Literature, 6 (Tübingen: Gunter Narr Verlag, 1992), pp. 69–84

Busbee, Mark Bradshaw, 'The Idea of India in Early Medieval England', in *India in the World*, ed. by Cristina M. Gámez-Fernández and Antonia Navarro-Tejero (Newcastle: Cambridge Scholars, 2011), pp. 1–16

——, 'A Paradise Full of Monsters: India in the Old English Imagination', *LATCH: A Journal for the Study of the Literary Artifact in Theory, Culture, or History*, 1 (2008), 51–72

Christie, Edward J., 'The Idea of an Elephant: Ælfric of Eynsham, Epistemology, and the Absent Animal of Anglo-Saxon England', *Neophilologus*, 98 (2014), 465–79

Clemoes, Peter, *Rhythm and Cosmic Order in Old English Christian Literature: An Inaugural Lecture* (Cambridge: Cambridge University Press, 1970)

Cross, James E., 'The Elephant to Alfred, Ælfric, Aldhelm and Others', *Studia Neophilologica*, 37 (1965), 367–73

Cubitt, Catherine, 'Ælfric's Lay Patrons', in *A Companion to Ælfric*, ed. by Hugh Magennis and Mary Swan, Brill's Companions to the Christian Tradition, 18 (Leiden: Brill, 2009), pp. 165–93

Curtius, Ernst Robert, *European Literature and the Latin Middle Ages*, trans. by Willard R. Trask, Bollingen Series, 180, new edn (Princeton: Princeton University Press, 2013)

DeGregorio, Scott, 'Ælfric, Gedwyld, and Vernacular Hagiography: Sanctity and Spirituality in the Old English Lives of SS Peter and Paul', in *Ælfric's Lives of Canonised Popes*, ed. by Donald Scragg (Kalamazoo: Medieval Institute Publications, 2011), pp. 75–98

Discenza, Nicole Guenther, *Inhabited Spaces: Anglo-Saxon Constructions of Place*, Toronto Anglo-Saxon Series, 23 (Toronto: University of Toronto Press, 2017)

Fell, Christine, 'Saint Æðelþryð: A Historical-Hagiographical Dichotomy Revisited', *Nottingham Medieval Studies*, 38 (1994), 18–34

Gatch, Milton McC., *Preaching and Theology in Anglo-Saxon England: Ælfric and Wulfstan* (Toronto: University of Toronto Press, 1977)

Godden, Malcolm, 'Ælfric's Saints' Lives and the Problem of Miracles', *Leeds Studies in English*, 16 (1985), 83–100

——, 'Money, Power and Morality in Late Anglo-Saxon England', *ASE*, 19 (1990), 41–65

Godfrey, John, *The Church in Anglo-Saxon England* (Cambridge: Cambridge University Press, 1962)

Gretsch, Mechthild, *Ælfric and the Cult of Saints in Late Anglo-Saxon England*, Cambridge Studies in Anglo-Saxon England, 34 (Cambridge: Cambridge University Press, 2006)

——, *The Intellectual Foundations of the English Benedictine Reform*, Cambridge Studies in Anglo-Saxon England, 25 (Cambridge: Cambridge University Press, 1999)

Gulley, Alison, *The Displacement of the Body in Ælfric's Virgin Martyr Lives* (Farnham: Ashgate, 2006)

Hawkes, Jane, 'Design and Decoration: Re-visualizing Rome in Anglo-Saxon Sculpture', in *Rome across Time and Space: Cultural Transmission and the Exchange of Ideas, c. 500–1400*, ed. by Claudia Bolgia, Rosamund McKitterick, and John Osborne (Cambridge: Cambridge University Press, 2011), pp. 203–21

Hill, Joyce, 'Ælfric: His Life and Works', in *A Companion to Ælfric*, ed. by Hugh Magennis and Mary Swan, Brill's Companions to the Christian Tradition, 18 (Leiden: Brill, 2009), pp. 35–65

Howe, Nicholas, 'Rome: Capital of Anglo-Saxon England', *Journal of Medieval and Early Modern Studies*, 34 (2001), 147–72; repr. in his *Writing the Map of Anglo-Saxon England: Essays in Cultural Geography* (New Haven, CT: Yale University Press, 2008), pp. 101–24

Hurley, Mary Kate, 'Communities in Translation: History and Identity in Medieval England' (unpublished doctoral thesis, Columbia University, 2013)

Irvine, Susan, 'The Anglo-Saxon Chronicle and the Idea of Rome in Alfredian Literature', in *Alfred the Great: Papers from the Eleventh-Centenary Conferences*, ed. by Timothy Reuter (Aldershot: Ashgate, 2003), pp. 63–78

Ker, Neil R., *Catalogue of Manuscripts Containing Anglo-Saxon* (Oxford: Clarendon Press, 1957)

Kleist, Aaron, *The Chronology and Canon of Ælfric of Eynsham*, Anglo-Saxon Studies, 37 (Cambridge: D. S. Brewer, 2019)

Lavezzo, Kathy, *Angels on the Edge of the World: Geography, Literature, and English Community, 1000–1534* (Ithaca, NY: Cornell University Press, 2006)

Lendinara, Patrizia, 'Minimal Collections of Glosses: The Twelve Rooms of Thomas' Palace', in *Anglo-Saxon Micro-Texts*, ed. by Ursula Lenker and Lucia Kornexl, Anglia Book Series, 67 (Berlin: De Gruyter, 2019), pp. 175–202

Leneghan, Francis, '*Translatio imperii*: The Old English *Orosius* and the Rise of Wessex', *Anglia*, 133 (2015), 656–705

Levison, Wilhelm, *England and the Continent in the Eighth Century: The Ford Lectures Delivered in the University of Oxford in the Hilary Term, 1943* (Oxford: Clarendon Press, 1946)

Loomis, Grant, 'Further Sources of Ælfric's Saints' Lives', *Harvard Studies and Notes in Philology and Literature*, 13 (1931), 1–8

Matthews, Stephen, *The Road to Rome: Travel and Travellers between England and Rome in the Anglo-Saxon Centuries*, British Archaeological Reports International Series, 1680 (Oxford: British Archaeological Reports, 2007)

McKinney, Windy A., 'Creating a *Gens Anglorum*: Social and Ethnic Identity in Anglo-Saxon England through the Lens of Bede's *Historica Ecclesiastica*' (unpublished doctoral thesis, University of York, 2011)

Michelet, Fabienne, 'Centrality, Marginality and Distance: Britain's Changing Location on the Map of the World', in *The Space of English*, ed. by David Spurr and Cornelia Tschichold (Tübingen: Gunter Narr, 2005), pp. 51–68

Milfull, Inge B., *The Hymns of the Anglo-Saxon Church: A Study and Edition of the 'Durham Hymnal'*, Cambridge Studies in Anglo-Saxon England, 17 (Cambridge: Cambridge University Press, 1996)

Miyashiro, Adam, 'Monstrosity and Ethnography in Medieval Europe: Britain, France, Iceland' (unpublished doctoral dissertation, Pennsylvania State University, 2006)

Nichols, Ann Eljenholm, 'Ælfric and the Brief Style', *JEGP*, 70 (1971), 1–12

Ó Carragáin, Éamonn, *The City of Rome and the World of Bede*, Jarrow Lecture ([n.p.]: [n.pub.], 1994)

——, 'The Periphery Rethinks the Centre: Inculturation, "Roman" Liturgy and the Ruthwell Cross', in *Rome across Time and Space: Cultural Transmission and the Exchange of Ideas, c. 500–1400*, ed. by Claudia Bolgia, Rosamund McKitterick, and John Osborne (Cambridge: Cambridge University Press, 2011), pp. 63–83

Ortenberg, Veronica, *The English Church and the Continent in the Tenth and Eleventh Centuries: Cultural, Spiritual, and Artistic Exchanges* (Oxford: Oxford University Press, 1992)

Oswald, Dana, *Monsters, Gender, and Sexuality in Medieval English Literature* (Cambridge: D. S. Brewer, 2010)

Pelteret, David, 'Not All Roads Lead to Rome', in *England and Rome in the Early Middle Ages: Pilgrimage, Art, and Politics*, ed. by Francesca Tinti, SEM, 40 (Turnhout: Brepols, 2014), pp. 17–41

Pengelley, Oliver, 'Rome in Ninth-Century Anglo-Saxon England' (unpublished doctoral thesis, University of Oxford, 2010)

Stanton, Robert, *The Culture of Translation in Anglo-Saxon England* (Cambridge: D. S. Brewer, 2002)

——, 'Rhetoric and Translation in Ælfric's Prefaces', *Translation and Literature*, 6 (1997), 135–48

Tinti, Francesca, 'The Archiepiscopal Pallium in Late Anglo-Saxon England', in *England and Rome in the Early Middle Ages: Pilgrimage, Art, and Politics*, ed. by Francesca Tinti, SEM, 40 (Turnhout: Brepols, 2014), pp. 307–42

——, 'Introduction', in *England and Rome in the Early Middle Ages: Pilgrimage, Art, and Politics*, ed. by Francesca Tinti, SEM, 40 (Turnhout: Brepols, 2014), pp. 1–15

Upchurch, Robert, 'For Pastoral Care and Political Gain: Ælfric of Eynsham's Preaching on Marital Celibacy' *Traditio*, 59 (2004), 39–78

Whatley, E. G., 'Lost in Translation: Omission of Episodes in Some Old English Prose Saints' Legends', *ASE*, 26 (1997), 187–208

Wilcox, Jonathan, 'The Audience of Ælfric's Lives of Saints and the Face of Cotton Caligula A. xiv, fols 93–130', in *Beatus Vir: Studies in Early English and Norse Manuscripts in Memory of Phillip Pulsiano*, ed. by Alger Nicolaus Doane and Kristen Wolf, Medieval and Renaissance Texts and Studies, 319 (Tempe: Arizona Center for Medieval and Renaissance Studies), pp. 229–63

Zettel, Patrick, 'Ælfric's Hagiographic Sources and the Latin Legendary Preserved in B.L. MS Cotton Nero E I + CCCC MS 9 and other manuscripts' (unpublished doctoral thesis, University of Oxford, 1980)

KAZUTOMO KARASAWA

Christ Embracing the World: Ælfric's Description of the Crucifixion in 'De Passione Domini'

When describing Christ on the cross in the homily for Palm Sunday in the second series of his *Catholic Homilies*, Ælfric writes:

> Drihten wæs gefæstnod. mid feower nægelum. to westdæle awend. and his wynstra heold. ðone scynendan suðdæl. and his swiðra norðdæl. eastdæl his hnol. and he ealle alysde middaneardes hwemmas. swa hangiende.[1] ('De Passione Domini')
>
>> (The Lord was fastened with four nails, turned to the west part; and his left held the shining south part, and his right the north part, the east part the crown of his head; and he redeemed all the regions of the world, thus hanging.)[2]

Modern readers may well be confused about what posture Ælfric envisages Christ being in on the cross. Malcolm Godden suggests that 'Ælfric imagines Christ raised on the cross, facing west but with the crown of his head [...] somehow tilted to point to the east'.[3] Yet if he faces west, it is unlikely that the crown of his head was tilted so as to point east (which must be why Godden adds the word 'somehow'), because then the shaft of the cross would be right behind his head and it would have been almost impossible for him to bend his neck backward. It is iconographically unusual too, as Godden admits that 'none of the visual representations that' he has 'seen match such an image: they show Christ's head either upright or bent in the direction of one arm'.[4]

---

1   All the quotations from 'De Passione Domini' are based on *Ælfric's Catholic Homilies: The Second Series*, ed. by Godden. This passage is quoted from p. 145.
2   This translation of 'De Passione Domini' is taken from *The Homilies of the Anglo-Saxon Church*, ed. by Thorpe, II, pp. 255 and 257.
3   Godden, *Ælfric's Catholic Homilies: Introduction, Commentary, and Glossary*, p. 483.
4   Godden, *Ælfric's Catholic Homilies: Introduction, Commentary, and Glossary*, p. 483. Many images of paintings and sculptures of the Crucifixion from the Anglo-Saxon period are included in Raw, *Anglo-Saxon Crucifixion Iconography*, between pages 116 and 117, but none of them match such an image as Godden suggests.

Kazutomo Karasawa (kazutomo_karasawa@rikkyo.ac.jp) is Professor of English Philology at Rikkyo University, Tokyo.

Ideas of the World in Early Medieval English Literature, ed. by Mark Atherton, Kazutomo Karasawa, and Francis Leneghan, SOEL 1 (Turnhout: Brepols, 2022)   pp. 149–163
BREPOLS ❧ PUBLISHERS   DOI 10.1484/M.SOEL.5.130560

Moreover, even if it is not impossible physically and/or iconographically for his head to be somewhat tilted to point to the east, it seems still unlikely that such a feature of his posture would be highlighted and juxtaposed with the other three much more obvious and prominent features. There may, therefore, be a better way of understanding the passage.

As Godden suggests, the passage seems to be inspired by the following verses of Caelius Sedulius in *Carmen paschale* V, ll. 188–95:[5]

> Neue quis ignoret speciem crucis esse colendam,
> Quae dominum portauit ouans, ratione potenti
> Quattuor inde plagas quadrati colligat orbis:
> Splendidus auctoris de uertice fulget Eous;
> Occiduo sacrae lambuntur sidere plantae;
> Arcton dextra tenet; medium laeua erigit axem.
> Cunctaque de membris uiuit natura creantis,
> Et cruce complexum Christus regit undique mundum.

> > (Lest anyone forget that the form of the cross which carried the Lord
> > In triumph is to be cherished, with cogent reasoning let him
> > Infer from it the four regions of the four-cornered world:
> > The shining east gleams down from the head of its creator;
> > The soles of his holy feet are licked by the western star;
> > His right hand holds the north; and his left raises up the southern heaven.
> > All nature derives life from the limbs of its creator,
> > And Christ rules a world everywhere embraced by the cross.)[6]

Godden writes that 'Sedulius's description of the hands pointing north and south, and the head and feet pointing west and east, would seem to view Christ in a prone position',[7] but this is unlikely since Sedulius has in mind Christ on the cross, not lying down. Here Sedulius must follow a Christian symbolic tradition of associating the four quarters of the world (or the four cardinal directions) with the four ends of the cross and/or with the four body parts of Christ on the cross. The same tradition is also reflected in the following passage from Paulinus of Nola's *Carmen* XIX.640–42:

---

5   Godden, *Ælfric's Catholic Homilies: Introduction, Commentary, and Glossary*, p. 483. Michael Lapidge includes Sedulius's *Carmen paschale* in staple patristic texts that the typical Anglo-Saxon library housed. See Lapidge, *The Anglo-Saxon Library*, p. 127. For this passage, see also Ó Carragáin, *Ritual and the Rood*, pp. 4–7.

6   The original text and its translation are both taken from Sedulius, *The Paschal Song and Hymns*, ed. by Springer, pp. 152–53; chapter and line numbers are those in this edition. Bede accurately quotes these verses in his *Commentarius in Lucam* VI.1537–44. For the original text, see Bede, *Commentarius in Lucam*, ed. by Hurst, p. 401.

7   Godden, *Ælfric's Catholic Homilies: Introduction, Commentary, and Glossary*, p. 483.

Qui cruce dispansa per quatuor extima ligni
quatuor adtingit dimensum partibus orbem,
ut trahat ad uitam populos ex omnibus oris.[8]

> (It is His cross He extends in the four extremities of the wood, and so touches the world in its division of four regions, so as to draw the peoples of every land into life.)[9]

Figure 5.1. An eleventh-century example of a T-O Map. London, British Library, MS Royal 6 C I, fol. 108ᵛ. © British Library Board.

The four regions mentioned here refer to the east, west, north, and south quarters of the world, each of which corresponds to each of the four ends of the cross. Paulinus does not specify which cardinal direction corresponds to which end of the cross, but as Sedulius states, there is a tradition associating the top and bottom ends holding Christ's head and feet with east and west respectively, while associating the shafts holding Christ's right and left arms with north and south respectively.

The east orientation of the cross in this tradition corresponds to that in the medieval T-O map of the world traditionally associated with Isidore of Seville (Fig. 5.1),[10] in which the T was regarded as 'a crucifix superimposed

---

8 This passage is quoted from *Sancti Pontii Meropii Paulini Nolani Carmina*, ed. by de Hartel, p. 140.
9 The translation is taken from St Paulinus of Nola, *The Poems*, trans. by Walsh, p. 153.
10 The T-O map is often recorded in the manuscripts of Isidore of Seville's *Etymologiae* or *De natura rerum*. The earliest T-O map is recorded on fol. 24ᵛ of the seventh-century manuscript of his *De natura rerum*, Escorial, Real Bibl., MS R.II.18. See Bede, *On the Nature of Things and On Times*, trans. by Kendall and Wallis, pp. 10–12 and 164. The T-O map in Fig. 5.1 is recorded with Isidore's *Etymologiae* in BL, MS Royal 6 C I (s. xi², St Augustine's Canterbury), fol. 108ᵛ; the image is taken from the following website by courtesy of the British Library:

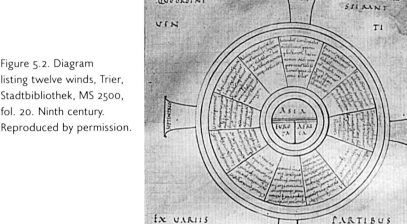

Figure 5.2. Diagram listing twelve winds, Trier, Stadtbibliothek, MS 2500, fol. 20. Ninth century. Reproduced by permission.

on the spherical earth, symbolizing its salvation by Christ's sacrifice';[11] this interpretation of the T in T-O maps reflects a very similar idea to that underlying Sedulius's verses quoted above.

Similarly, many medieval *mappae mundi* including the Anglo-Saxon one preserved on fol. 56ᵛ of London, British Library, MS Cotton Tiberius B V (s. xi²/⁴),[12] adopt the east orientation, and in some of them, the head, hands, and feet of Christ are depicted at the ends of the corresponding four cardinal directions with Jerusalem placed at the centre of the world.[13] In the ninth-century manuscript attributed to Reims or Laon, Trier, Stadtbibliothek, MS 2500 (c. 840), fol. 20 (Fig. 5.2), a diagram centred on a T-O map and listing twelve winds is recorded as a frontispiece of Bede's *De natura rerum*, and it is superimposed on a cross at whose four ends the Latin terms for the

---

<https://www.bl.uk/picturing-places/articles/world-maps-before-1400>. For more information about T-O maps, see Woodward, 'Medieval *Mappaemundi*', pp. 301–03. See also Helen Appleton in this volume.

11 Edson, *Mapping Time and Space*, p. 5.
12 For this manuscript, see Gneuss and Lapidge, *Anglo-Saxon Manuscripts*, p. 297. For the Anglo-Saxon *mappa mundi*, see McGurk, 'The Mappa Mundi', and Appleton, 'The Northern World of the Anglo-Saxon *mappa mundi*'. See also Helen Appleton in this volume.
13 The best example of this type of *mappae mundi* with representations of Christ's body parts in the four cardinal directions is said to be the thirteenth-century Ebstorf Map. Unfortunately, it was destroyed during World War II and no longer exists, but its black-and white photographs and also colour facsimiles made before it was destroyed are available. For this type of *mappae mundi* and the Christian symbolism reflected therein, see Woodward, 'Medieval *Mappaemundi*', p. 290. See also Kupfer, 'Reflections in the Ebstorf Map', and Edson, *Mapping Time and Space*, p. 5. In addition, cruciform churches whose east end corresponds to the top end of the cross may also well be viewed as reflecting the same idea.

CHRIST EMBRACING THE WORLD   153

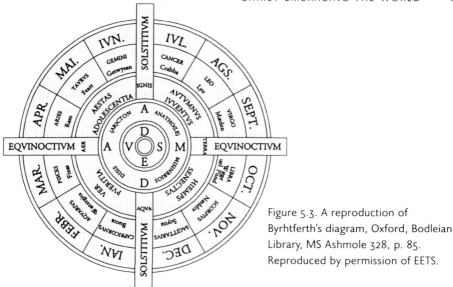

Figure 5.3. A reproduction of Byrhtferth's diagram, Oxford, Bodleian Library, MS Ashmole 328, p. 85. Reproduced by permission of EETS.

four cardinal directions are inscribed with *oriens* (east) at the top, associating the four cardinal directions with the four ends of the cross which embraces the world.[14]

In some of the Byrhtferth's diagrams illustrating the concord of the four elements with, for example, the seasons, solar turning points (i.e. solstices and equinoxes), and ages of man, the four cardinal directions are mentioned with east at the top.[15] One of them, namely, the one recorded on page 85 of Oxford, Bodleian Library, MS Ashmole 328 (s. xi[med.], Christ Church Canterbury?; Fig. 5.3),[16] consists of several concentric circles with a Greek cross overlapping. In the central position, each letter of the Latin word for God, *Deus*, is placed in alignment with one hand of the cross with the initial *D* at the top, whereas in the next layer of circle, capital letters *A*, *D*, *A*, and *M* are also placed in alignment with the hands of the cross. These letters represent

---

14   For this diagram, see Kühnel, *The End of Time in the Order of Things*, pp. 156–57, and Obrist, 'Wind Diagrams and Medieval Cosmology', pp. 49–53. A very similar diagram is also recorded in the ninth-century Berlin, Deutsche SB, MS Phillipps 1830, fol. 3[v], where the diagram was added later in the eleventh century. This image of the diagram in Trier, SB, MS 2500 is taken from Kühnel, *The End of Time in the Order of Things*, p. 338, where an image of the analogous diagram in Berlin, Deutsche SB, MS Phillipps 1830 is also available.

15   The best-known diagram of this kind ascribed to Byrhtferth is the so-called 'Diagram of the Physical and Physiological Fours' preserved in Oxford, St John's College, MS 17, fol. 7[v], and in BL, MS Harley 3667, fol. 8[r]. It is reproduced in *Byrhtferth's Enchiridion*, ed. by Baker and Lapidge, p. 374.

16   For the details of the manuscript, see Gneuss and Lapidge, *Anglo-Saxon Manuscripts*, pp. 420–21. This reproduction of the diagram is taken from *Byrhtferth's Enchiridion*, ed. by Baker and Lapidge, p. 76. Its facsimile version is available in *Byrhtferth's Manual*, ed. by Crawford, p. 87.

not only the name of the first man but also the four cardinal directions as actually indicated in the same circle; they are the initials of the (Latinized) Greek words for the four cardinal directions, *anathole* (east), *disis* (west), *arcton* (north), and *misinbrios* (south), and *A* representing *anathole* (east) is placed at the top. As pointed out by Faith Wallis, 'Adam' in the diagram can also be conceived of as the generic name of mankind, and Adam in this sense and Deus in combination may well represent Christ the God-Man.[17] Moreover, the capital letters in the central portion of the diagram are arranged in order to make the sign of a cross, and this cruciform design is obviously intended to represent the crucifix. In this diagram, therefore, we can see a schematized version of the idea underlying Sedulius's verses quoted above: Christ-God on the cross whose ends are associated with the four cardinal directions, east being at the top. In relation to this diagram, it is also noteworthy that in those verses Sedulius uses the Greek word *arcton* (north) rather than its Latin correspondent to refer to the north; this may betray some remote connection with the tradition lying behind Byrhtferth's diagram, where Greek words are used since it is ultimately based on the Greek notion about the four elements and the number four.

Inspired by Sedulius's verses, Ælfric, in the above-quoted passage, seems basically to follow the symbolic tradition of associating the four ends of the cross or the four body parts of Christ with the four cardinal directions or the four quarters of the world. Used collectively, the words *eastdæl*, *westdæl*, *norððæl*, and *suððæl* are reminiscent of the quarters of the world, especially when they are used with the word *middaneardes* (of the world) as in the passage in question.[18] The four quarters of the world are all mentioned here to highlight symbolically Christ on the cross as a redeemer of the whole world. Ælfric may also well associate this tradition with the symbolism of the number 'four', in line with the importance given by the Greeks to the number four, as reflected in the above-quoted Byrhtferth's diagram,[19] and possibly also in Sedulius's use of the word *arcton* (north), since Ælfric seems

---

17 See Wallis, 'Computus Related Materials: 20. Byrhtferth's Diagram'. In a literary tradition regarding the six ages of the world, which is closely associated with the seven days of the creation, Adam created on the sixth day of the creation and Christ, whose coming is regarded as the beginning of the sixth age of the world, are associated with each other, as is reflected, for instance, in Bede's 'Hymn on the Work of the First Six Days and the Six Ages of the World', stanzas 13–14. For the original text, see Bede, *Liber Hymnorum*, ed. by Fraipont, pp. 407–10, and Bede, 'Hymnus über das Sechstagewerk und die Weltalter', ed. by Rädle, pp. 59–62. Its English translation is found in Bede, *On the Nature of Things and On Times*, trans. by Kendall and Wallis, pp. 180–84.

18 As in the Ælfrician passage in question, these words can be used to represent the four quarters of the world, while *eastdæl* and *westdæl* can also be used to refer to the eastern and western halves of the world. As we shall see below, *eastdæl*, *norððæl*, and *suððæl* can also represent Asia, Europe, and Africa respectively. Thus these words are closely associated with the notion of the divisions of the world.

19 Byrhtferth deals with the symbolism of the number four in Part 4 of his *Enchiridion*, where

to emphasize the significance of the number four, not only by writing that Christ was crucified with four nails but also by writing just before the passage in question that 'dældon ða cwelleras. cristes reaf on feower. heora ælcum his dæl' (the executioners parted Christ's garments into four, to each of them his part) .[20] The reference to the garments parted into four is based on John 19. 23–24, while the earliest reference to the four nails used for the Crucifixion in literary works is found in Gregory of Tours, Chapter 6 'De gloria martyrum' in his *Libri Miraculorum*.[21] Ælfric combines these originally separate literary traditions together and composes a passage where the reference to the *four* parts of Christ's garments divided by the *four* executioners who crucified Christ with *four* nails precedes the reference to the *four* quarters of the world redeemed by Christ. As Raw points out, Ælfric throughout this homily sees symbolism in each detail of Christ's passion,[22] and his description of the scene of the Crucifixion itself may well reflect his symbolic understanding of it.

Unlike Sedulius, Ælfric does not mention Christ's feet in association with the west quarter of the world, but writes instead that Christ faced the west part of the world. This may well be because it occurs in a narrative describing the process up to the Crucifixion rather than in an account explaining its symbolic meaning; if he wrote in this context that Christ's head and feet held the east and west parts of the world respectively, that would sound as if he were saying that Christ was in a prone position in an east–west orientation (as Godden actually conjectures in his above-quoted comment on Sedulius's account). Instead of creating an awkward context by suddenly shifting from a realistic narrative to a symbolic account, Ælfric seems to combine these two with a gradual shift from one to the other. Thus the first part, where Christ is said to be nailed to the cross facing west, is in line with a realistic narrative

---

the number four is regarded as the controlling number of the cosmos. For the original text and its translation, see *Byrhtferth's Enchiridion*, ed. by Baker and Lapidge, pp. 198–203.

20 The original text is based on *Ælfric's Catholic Homilies: The Second Series*, ed. by Godden, p. 145, while the translation is taken from *The Homilies of the Anglo-Saxon Church*, ed. by Thorpe, II, p. 255.

21 For the relevant passage, see Gregory of Tours, *Libri miraculorum*, ed. by Migne, col. 710. As reflected in early medieval Crucifixion iconography, there seems to have been a strong tradition of four, rather than three, nails used for the Crucifixion in the earlier Middle Ages. Regarding the reference to the four nails in the passage in question, Godden writes that 'the shift to three nails probably started too late to be an issue here'. See Godden, *Ælfric's Catholic Homilies: Introduction, Commentary, and Glossary*, p. 483. In many of the paintings of the Crucifixion included in Raw, *Anglo-Saxon Crucifixion Iconography*, between pages 116 and 117, Christ is crucified with four nails, whereas I cannot find any example of the Crucifixion with three nails there.

22 Raw mentions, for instance, Christ's red robe symbolizing his death, his crown of thorns symbolizing man's sins, the bitter drink as a symbol of the bitterness of death, the seamless robe as a sign of the unity of the Church, and two thieves crucified with Christ representing the Jews and the Gentiles. See Raw, *Anglo-Saxon Crucifixion Iconography*, p. 181. Christ's red robe and crown of thorns symbolizing his death and man's sins respectively are also mentioned in his source text, namely, Sedulius's *Carmen paschale*, 5.

continuing from the preceding part. Then in the next part, where Christ's left and right hands are said to have held the south and north parts (of the world), the description starts to take on a symbolic trend with the references to *suðdæl* and *norðdæl* in response to *westdæl* in the previous part, though this is still understandable as a realistic description since Christ's left and right hands must point southward and northward respectively, if he faces west on the cross. Then Ælfric writes that the crown of Christ's head held *eastdæl* and concludes that he redeemed 'ealle [...] middaneardes hwemmas' (all the corners of the world), at which point it should clearly be understood that the words *westdæl*, *suðdæl*, *norðdæl*, and *eastdæl* in this passage symbolically refer to the four quarters of the world, and that the whole passage has a symbolic meaning. This also explains why Ælfric mentions Christ's head last, unlike Sedulius, who mentions it first. Where a realistic narrative gradually shifts to a symbolic account, the least realistic and the most symbolic part needs to come last.

Following the symbolic tradition reflected in Sedulius's account, Ælfric, when composing the passage in question, seems to visualize a flat image of the Crucifixion based on the same 3D-to-2D conversion system underlying those *mappae mundi* superimposed upon the (partial) image of the Crucifixion or in the diagrams mentioned above; if Christ faces west in an image of the Crucifixion which is depicted as seen from in front, as is usual, the lower part of the image, below the bottom of the cross, is understood as the direction of west, whereas the upper part, behind the cross, is the direction of east. When Ælfric writes that the crown of the head of Christ held the east part, he means that his head is located at the top of the cross, which corresponds to the eastern division of the world according to the symbolic tradition. Ælfric is therefore describing a standard image of the Crucifixion in a symbolic context, where Christ is on the cross with his head either upright or a little bent in the direction of one arm.

As reflected in the repeated reference to the number four as well as in the actual reference to the four quarters of the world, Ælfric obviously had in mind the quadruple division of the world when composing the passage. However, he deviates from the tradition when omitting the reference to the feet of Christ associated with the west quarter of the world. Although the probable reason for his deviation is explained above, there is another way of interpreting this feature of the text, which I shall discuss here before concluding this chapter.

In Ælfric's account, Christ's hands and head are associated with the south, north, and east quarters of the world, whereas only the west quarter lacks any link with one of Christ's body parts, which may make its connection with Christ seem weaker than that of the others. Yet from the perspective of an Anglo-Saxon idea of the world, it may well be possible to interpret Ælfric's account as saying that all the parts of the world are in a sense equally associated with Christ's body parts. Apart from the quadruple division of the world mentioned in the passage in question, Ælfric may have had in mind at the same time another tripartite division of the world, which may justify the unequal treatment of the west quarter of the world. As summarily indicated in the T-O map, in the Middle Ages, the inhabited world or *oikoumene* was conceived of as consisting of three parts: Asia, Europe, and Africa.[23] The idea of the tripartite division of the world in which Asia occupies the eastern half of the world while Europe and Africa occupy the north and south halves of the western half of the world was also current in Anglo-Saxon England,[24] as Bede points out in Chapter 51 of his *De natura rerum*:

> *Terrarum orbis uniuersus*, Oceano cinctus, *in tres diuiditur partes: Europam, Asiam, Africam. Origo ab occasu solis et Gaditano freto, qua irrumpens Oceanus Athlanticus in maria interiora diffunditur — hinc intranti dextera Africa, laeua est Europa; inter has Asia* magnitudine compar est aliis duabus.[25]

> (The whole circle of lands, girded by the Ocean, is divided into three parts: Europe, Asia, and Africa. It takes its starting-point from the West and the Straits of Cadiz, where the Atlantic Ocean bursting in floods into the interior seas. For one entering from this direction, Africa is on the right, and Europe is on the left. Asia is between them, and is comparable in size to the other two taken together.)[26]

A similar account of the division of the world is found at the beginning of the Old English *Orosius*:[27]

> Ure ieldran ealne þisne ymbhwyrft þises middangeardes, cwæþ Orosius, swa swa Oceanus utan ymbligeþ, þone [mon] garsæcg hateð, on þreo todældon ond hie þa þrie dælas on þreo tonemdon: Asiam ond Europem ond Affricam, þeah þe sume men sæden þæt þær nære buton twegen dælas: Asia ond þæt oþer Europe. Asia is befangen mid Oceano þæm garsecge

---

23 The tripartite division of the world was already current at the time of Herodotus in the fifth century BC. In those days, however, Europe seems to have often been regarded as occupying a half of the whole inhabited world, while Asia and Libya (Africa) occupy the other half; Herodotus makes a comment disagreeing with this tradition because he believes that in it Europe is oversized. By the time of Dicaearchus in the third century BC, the proportion of the three components of the inhabited world had been modified. For the developments of ancient cartographic traditions and the idea of the tripartite world, see Harley and Woodward, eds, *The History of Cartography*, pp. 130–76.

24 The topic is dealt with by Isidore of Seville in his *Etymologiae* (Bk XIV, Ch. 2) and in *De natura rerum* (Ch. 48), as well as by Augustine of Hippo in his *De civitate Dei* (Bk XVI, Ch. 17). These three works were among 'a small core of staple patristic texts, scarcely exceeding twenty titles', that the typical Anglo-Saxon library housed. See Lapidge, *The Anglo-Saxon Library*, p. 127.

25 This passage is quoted from Bede, *De natura rerum*, ed. by Jones and Lipp, pp. 233–34; italics are the editors'. Here Bede is based on Pliny, *Naturalis historia*, 3.1.3. See Bede, *On the Nature of Things and On Times*, trans. by Kendall and Wallis, pp. 103 and 163.

26 This translation is quoted from Bede, *On the Nature of Things and On Times*, trans. by Kendall and Wallis, pp. 102–03.

27 The corresponding passage in Orosius's original is found in *Historiarum adversus paganos libri septem*, I.2.

suþan ond norþan ond eastan ond swa ealne middangeard from þæm eastdæle healfne behæfð.[28] (i.i)

> (Orosius said that our ancestors divided the whole expanse of this world into three parts, surrounded by the sea called Oceanus, and they called the three parts Asia, Europe and Africa, although some people said that there were only two parts, Asia and Europe. Asia is bounded by the sea called Oceanus on the south, north and east, and so occupies the eastern side of the whole world.)[29]

Ælfric follows this notion of the tripartite world in a passage in his treatise 'On the Old and New Testament' (in his letter to Sigeweard),[30] as well as in the following passage in his Old English version of Alcuin's *Interrogationes Sigeuulfi in Genesin*:

> Se yldesta Noes sunu Sem gestrynde mid his sunum seofon ond twentig suna ond hi gebogodan þone east dæl middaneardes þe is gehate Asia. Se oðer Noes sunu Cham gestrynde mid his sunum þrittig suna, ond hy gebogodan þone suðdæl þe is gehaten Affrica. Se þridda Noes sunu Iafeth gestrynde mid his sunum fiftyne suna ond þa gebogodan norðdæl þe is gehaten Europa.[31]

> (The oldest son of Noah, Shem, and his sons procreated twenty-seven sons and they inhabited the east part of the world, which is called Asia. The second son of Noah, Ham, and his sons procreated thirty sons, and they inhabited the south part, which is called Africa. The third son of Noah, Japheth, and his sons procreated fifty sons, who inhabited the north part, which is called Europe.)[32]

Here the components of the tripartite world, Asia, Europe, and Africa, are referred to as *eastdæl*, *norðdæl*, and *suðdæl* respectively, while *westdæl* is not mentioned. Alcuin's original Latin text does not specify which part of the world Asia, Europe, and Africa occupy and so this is an addition made by Ælfric himself.[33] In his treatise 'On the Old and New Testament', he also uses

---

28 This passage is quoted from *The Old English Orosius*, ed. by Bately, p. 8. In this chapter, I have replaced all the Tironian signs in Old English texts with *ond* (and).

29 This translation is quoted from *The Old English History of the World*, ed. and trans. by Godden, p. 25.

30 For the relevant passage in the original text, see *The Old English Version of the Heptateuch*, ed. by Crawford, p. 27; and Ælfric of Eynsham, *Letter to Sigeweard*, ed. by Swain, p. 95.

31 This passage is quoted from Ælfric of Eynsham, *Anglo-Saxon Version of Alcuini Interrogationes Sigeuulfi Presbyteri in Genesin*, ed. by MacLean, pp. 95–97.

32 My translation. In Genesis 9. 24, Ham is said to be the youngest son of Noah, but both in this passage and a similar passage in the treatise 'On the Old and New Testament', Ælfric regards Japheth as the youngest. In Alcuin's original Latin version, Noah's sons are not ranked by age, and so Ælfric himself is responsible for it. See Ælfric of Eynsham, *Letter to Sigeweard*, ed. by Swain, pp. 135–36.

33 The following is the corresponding part in Alcuin's original Latin version: 'Sem, ut

norðdæl and *suðdæl* for Europe and Africa respectively, while for Asia he uses another term to represent the eastern part of the world, *eastrice*,[34] without any reference to the western part.[35]

The use of these appellations for the three components of the tripartite world (based on their geographic distribution, *eastdæl/eastrice*, *norðdæl*, and *suðdæl*) is not unique to Ælfric, but seems to have been generally current in Anglo-Saxon England, as reflected in several glosses where *europe/europam* is glossed as *norðdæl* or *norð*,[36] *assiam* as *east*, and *africam* as *suut* (< *suð*).[37] Moreover, the gloss *suðdæl* for *africum* in the Stowe Psalter 77.26 may well reflect the glossator's misunderstanding of *africum* (south-west wind) as *africam* (Africa).[38] The word *westdæl* can be used to mean the west half of the world, as opposed to *eastdæl* referring to Asia or the east half of the world, yet in the Anglo-Saxon terminological tradition, it is not regarded as one of the primary components of the world when the tripartite structure of the world is mentioned; and as far as I can find, *westdæl* is never used for either Europe or Africa alone, but belongs to a secondary category, and is a combination of the two primary components, *norðdæl* 'Europe' and *suðdæl* 'Africa'.

If we take this tradition into account when we read Ælfric's passage in question, it may be possible to give it an alternative interpretation. According to this reading, the whole world is equally associated with one of Christ's body parts; his head is associated with *eastdæl* or Asia, and his left and right hands with *norðdæl* or Europe and *suðdæl* or Africa, respectively. Interpreted in this way, all the regions of the world are equally associated with Christ's body parts,[39] while Christ's facing *westdæl* agrees with this tradition and may

---

æstimatur, Asiam, Cham, Africam, Japhet Europam sortitus est. De Japhet nati sunt filii quindecim. de Cham triginta, de Sem viginti septem'. This text is quoted from Ælfric of Eynsham, *Anglo-Saxon Version of Alcuini Interrogationes Sigeuulfi Presbyteri in Genesin*, ed. by MacLean, pp. 95–97.

34 See *DOE*, s.v. *eastrice*, definition 1.b., where it is defined as 'the eastern part of the world, the East, the Orient' and the relevant part of the passage in question is quoted.

35 For the original text, see *The Old English Version of the Heptateuch*, ed. by Crawford, p. 27, and Ælfric of Eynsham, *Letter to Sigeweard*, ed. by Swain, p. 95.

36 These examples are recorded in some glosses for Aldhelm's *De laudibus virginitatis*. See glosses 2001 and 4447 in *The Old English Glosses of MS. Brussels, Royal Library, 1650*, ed. by Goossens, pp. 277 and 435, and glosses 2032 and 4566 in *Old English Glosses*, ed. by Napier, pp. 55 and 118.

37 These glosses for *assiam* and *africam* are recorded in a collection of Old English glosses for Bede's *Historia ecclesiastica gentis Anglorum*. See glosses 170 and 171 in '4. Beda, Historia Ecclesiastica' in *Old English Glosses*, ed. by Meritt, p. 10.

38 See *The Stowe Psalter*, ed. by Kimmens, p. 148. According to the *DOE Corpus*, *africum* here is glossed in other psalter glosses as *westansuðanwind* (PsGlA, PsGlC), *suðan westan wind* (PsGlB), *suðenwestenwind* (PsGlE), *suðanwestan wind* (PsGlG) 'southwest wind', *suðerne wind* (PsGlD, PsGlH, PsGlJ, PsGlK) 'southern wind', or *wind ł norðerne wind* (PsGlI) 'wind or northern wind'.

39 The concept of *totus Christus*, according to which Christ is the head while Christians are the members of his body, may be somewhat comparable to the idea of the world embraced

also imply that his grace is directed to the west half of the world to which Ælfric and his readers and audience belong.

When writing the passage on the Crucifixion in the homily for Palm Sunday in the second series of his *Catholic Homilies*, Ælfric seems to have had in mind the symbolic interpretation of the Crucifixion as explained in Sedulius's verses. Based on the tradition followed by Sedulius, Ælfric mentions the four quarters of the world, but he deviates from the tradition when he fails to associate Christ's feet or the end of the cross holding them with the west quarter of the world. His deviation from the tradition reflects his effort to achieve a good balance between a realistic narrative and a symbolic account; he avoids shifting suddenly to a symbolic account, which would cause confusion in his audience, but he gradually shifts to it, while hinting at the symbolic significance of the number four at the same time. Thus his statement that Christ on the cross faced the west part of the world is in line with the preceding mainly realistic narrative, but it does not contradict the symbolic account since Christ is supposed to face west based on the 3D-to-2D conversion system underlying the symbolic tradition.[40] His reference to Christ's hands holding the north and south parts of the world can still be understood as part of a realistic narrative but begins to sound more than that, chiefly because of the use of group terms, *westdæl*, *suðdæl*, and *norðdæl* in rapid succession, which naturally leads to the reference in the next part to the other quarter of the world, *eastdæl*. His concluding statement just after the reference to *eastdæl*, that Christ by hanging thus redeemed all the corners of the world, makes it clear that the foregoing part is not just a realistic narrative but a symbolic account at the same time, and this allows the word *eastdæl* to represent the top part of the image of the Crucifixion; when Ælfric writes that the crown of Christ's head held the east part, he meant that the top end of the cross held his head. This also explains why Ælfric mentions Christ's head last, unlike Sedulius, who mentions it first.

Following the symbolic tradition, Ælfric mentions the four quarters of the world in the passage in question, but it is also possible that the Anglo-Saxon idea of the tripartite world allowed him to deviate more readily from the tradition of associating Christ's feet with the west quarter of the world. The

---

by Christ on the cross in that the (Christian) world is conceived of as interconnected by the body of Christ. Augustine repeatedly mentions the concept in his commentaries on the Psalms, and Ælfric also occasionally mentions it in his works as in *Catholic Homilies* I.17, I.19, I.26, II.15, II.28, and 'Sermo ad populum in octavis Pentecosten dicendus'. For *totus Christus* in Ælfric's *Catholic Homilies*, see Kramer, *Between Earth and Heaven*, pp. 160–67. In his *Ritual and the Rood*, pp. 44–46, Ó Carragáin argues that the early eighth-century Bewcastle Cross, which seems to antedate the closely related Ruthwell Cross, embodies the concept of *totus Christus* (the cross faces east, and in this respect, it does not match the literary tradition discussed in this chapter).

40 Compare Christ depicted as facing north in Jerusalem in the Ebstorf Map, where Christ is illustrated in a south–north orientation with his head on the right and his feet on the left.

idea of the tripartite world itself was handed down from ancient times and was widely diffused in early medieval Christendom, but in Anglo-Saxon England, it developed a peculiar terminological tradition, with *eastdæl* (east part), *norðdæl* (north part), and *suðdæl* (south part) to refer to the three components of the world, Asia, Europe, and Africa; according to this tradition, *westdæl* (west part) of the world consists of *norðdæl* (Europe) and *suðdæl* (Africa) occupying the west half of the world. If this notion of the division of the world is applied to the passage in question, each component of the world is equally associated with Christ's body parts, that is, Asia with his head, Europe with his right hand, and Africa with his left hand. The different treatment of *westdæl* may well be justified since it is not a basic component of the world equal to the other three in the Anglo-Saxon idea of the tripartite world. This alternative way to understand the passage may have made it easier for Ælfric to deviate from the tradition, though basically following it at the same time. The passage can be understood in two ways, based on the idea of a quadripartite or tripartite world, but both readings have the same meaning: all the regions of the world were redeemed by Christ on the cross and they are all equally in his embrace.

Works Cited

Manuscripts and Archival Sources

Berlin, Deutsche Staatsbibliothek, MS Phillipps 1830
Escorial, Real Biblioteca, MS R.II.18
London, British Library, MS Cotton Tiberius B V
London, British Library, MS Harley 3667
London, British Library, MS Royal 6 C I
Oxford, Bodleian Library, MS Ashmole 328
Oxford, St John's College, MS 17
Trier, Stadtbibliothek, MS 2500

Primary Sources

Ælfric of Eynsham, *Ælfric's Anglo-Saxon Version of Alcuini Interrogationes Sigeuulfi Presbyteri in Genesin*, ed. by George Edwin MacLean (Halle: E. Karras, 1883)
——, *Ælfric's Catholic Homilies: The Second Series, Text*, ed. by Malcolm R. Godden, EETS SS, 5 (Oxford: Oxford University Press, 1979)
——, *Ælfric of Eynsham's Letter to Sigeweard: An Edition, Commentary, and Translation*, ed. by Larry J. Swain (Troy, AL: Witan Publishing, 2020)
Bede, *Commentarius in Lucam*, in *Beda Venerabilis, Opera Exegetica*, III: *In Lucae evangelium expositio, In Marci evangelium expositio*, ed. by D. Hurst, CCSL, 120 (Turnhout: Brepols, 1960), pp. 1–425
——, *De natura rerum*, ed. by C. W. Jones and F. Lipp, in *Beda Venerabilis, Opera didascalica*, I: *De orthographia, De arte metrica et de schematibus et tropis*,

De natura rerum, ed. by C. W. Jones, C. B. Kendall, M. H. King, and F. Lipp, CCSL, 123A (Turnhout: Brepols, 1975), pp. 173–234

——, 'Bedas Hymnus über das Sechstagewerk und die Weltalter', ed. by Fidel Rädle, in *Anglo-Saxonica: Beiträge zur Vor- und Frühgeschichte der englischen Sprache und zur altenglischen Literatur. Festschrift für Hans Schabram zum 65. Geburtstag*, ed. by Klaus R. Grinda and Claus-Dieter Wetzel (Munich: Wilhelm Fink, 1993), pp. 53–75

——, *Liber Hymnorum, Rhythmi, Variae Preces*, ed. by J. Fraipont, in *Beda Venerabilis, Opera homiletica, Opera rhythmica*, ed. by D. Hurst and J. Fraipont, CCSL, 122 (Turnhout: Brepols, 1955), pp. 405–70

——, *On the Nature of Things and On Times*, trans. by Calvin B. Kendall and Faith Wallis, Translated Texts for Historians, 56 (Liverpool: Liverpool University Press, 2010)

Byrhtferth's Enchiridion, ed. by P. S. Baker and Michael Lapidge, EETS SS, 15 (Oxford: Oxford University Press, 1995)

Byrhtferth's Manual, ed. by S. J. Crawford, EETS OS, 177 (London: Oxford University Press, 1929)

Gregory of Tours, *Libri miraculorum*, PL 71 (Paris: Garnier, 1879), cols 705–828

The Homilies of the Anglo-Saxon Church: The First Part Containing the Sermones Catholici or Homilies of Ælfric in the Original Anglo-Saxon, with an English Version, ed. by Benjamin Thorpe, 2 vols (London: Ælfric Society, 1844–1846)

Old English Glosses: A Collection, ed. by Herbert Dean Meritt (New York: Modern Language Association of America, 1945)

Old English Glosses Chiefly Unpublished, ed. by Arthur S. Napier (Oxford: Clarendon Press, 1900)

The Old English Glosses of MS. Brussels, Royal Library, 1650 (Aldhelm's De Laudibus Virginitatis) Edited with an Introduction, Notes and Indexes, ed. by Louis Goossens (Brussels: Paleis der Academiën, 1974)

The Old English History of the World: An Anglo-Saxon Rewriting of Orosius, ed. and trans. by Malcolm R. Godden, DOML, 44 (Cambridge, MA: Harvard University Press, 2016)

The Old English Orosius, ed. by Janet Bately, EETS SS, 6 (Oxford: Oxford University Press, 1980)

The Old English Version of the Heptateuch, Ælfric's Treatise on the Old and New Testament and his Preface to Genesis, ed. by S. J. Crawford, EETS OS, 160 (1922; repr. with the text of two additional manuscripts transcribed by N. R. Ker, Oxford: Oxford University Press, 1969)

Paulinus of Nola, *The Poems of St Paulinus of Nola*, trans. by P. G., Walsh, Ancient Christian Writers: The Works of the Fathers in Translation, 40 (New York: Newman Press, 1975)

Sancti Pontii Meropii Paulini Nolani Carmina, ed. by Guilelmus de Hartel, Corpus Scriptorum Ecclesiasticorum Latinorum, 30.2 (Vienna: F. Tempsky, 1899)

Sedulius, *The Paschal Song and Hymns*, ed. by Carl P. E. Springer, Writings from the Greco-Roman World, 35 (Atlanta: Society of Biblical Literature, 2013)

The Stowe Psalter, ed. by Andrew C. Kimmens (Toronto: University of Toronto Press, 1979)

Secondary Sources

Appleton, Helen, 'The Northern World of the Anglo-Saxon *mappa mundi*', *ASE*, 47 (2018), 275–305

Edson, Evelyn, *Mapping Time and Space: How Medieval Mapmakers Viewed their World*, The British Library Studies in Map History, 1 (London: British Library, 1997)

Gneuss, Helmut, and Michael Lapidge, *Anglo-Saxon Manuscripts: A Bibliographical Handlist of Manuscripts and Manuscript Fragments Written or Owned in England up to 1100*, Toronto Anglo-Saxon Series, 15 (Toronto: University of Toronto Press, 2014)

Godden, Malcolm R., *Ælfric's Catholic Homilies: Introduction, Commentary, and Glossary*, EETS SS, 18 (Oxford: Oxford University Press, 2000)

Harley, J. B., and David Woodward, eds, *The History of Cartography*, 1: *Cartography in Prehistoric, Ancient, and Medieval Europe and the Mediterranean* (Chicago: University of Chicago Press, 1987)

Kramer, Johanna, *Between Earth and Heaven: Liminality and the Ascension of Christ in Anglo-Saxon Literature* (Manchester: Manchester University Press, 2014)

Kühnel, Bianca, *The End of Time in the Order of Things: Science and Eschatology in Early Medieval Art* (Regensburg: Schnell & Steiner, 2003)

Kupfer, Marcia, 'Reflections in the Ebstorf Map: Cartography, Theology and *dilectio speculationis*', in *Mapping Medieval Geographies: Geographical Encounters in the Latin West and Beyond, 300–1600*, ed. by Keith D. Lilley (Cambridge: Cambridge University Press, 2013), pp. 100–126

Lapidge, Michael, *The Anglo-Saxon Library* (Oxford: Oxford University Press, 2006)

McGurk, Patrick, 'The Mappa Mundi', in *An Eleventh-Century Anglo-Saxon Illustrated Miscellany: British Library Cotton Tiberius B.V Part 1, Together with Leaves from British Library Cotton Nero D.II*, ed. by P. McGurk, D. N. Dumville, M. R. Godden, and Ann Knock, Early English Manuscripts in Facsimile, 21 (Copenhagen: Rosenkilde and Bagger, 1983), pp. 79–87

Obrist, Barbara, 'Wind Diagrams and Medieval Cosmology', *Speculum*, 72 (1997), 33–84

Ó Carragáin, Éamonn, *Ritual and the Rood: Liturgical Images and the Old English Poems of the Dream of the Rood Tradition* (London: British Library, 2005)

Raw, Barbara C., *Anglo-Saxon Crucifixion Iconography and the Art of the Monastic Revival*, Cambridge Studies in Anglo-Saxon England, 1 (Cambridge: Cambridge University Press, 1990)

Wallis, Faith, 'Computus Related Materials: 20. Byrhtferth's Diagram', <http://digital.library.mcgill.ca/ms-17/folio.php?p=7v&showitem= 7r_2ComputusRelated_20ByrhtferthsDiagram#note39> [accessed 24 December 2020]

Woodward, David, 'Medieval *Mappaemundi*', in *The History of Cartography*, 1: *Cartography in Prehistoric, Ancient, and Medieval Europe and the Mediterranean*, ed. by J. B. Harley and David Woodward (Chicago: University of Chicago Press, 1987), pp. 286–370

PART II

A Place in the World

DANIEL THOMAS

Babel and Beyond:
Thinking through Migration in *Genesis A*

The 'Anglo-Saxon' world begins, notionally at least, with the *adventus Saxonum* — the arrival in Britain, traditionally dated to 449 AD, of Germanic tribes and their warlike leaders. Notionally, because the *adventus* represents, in Simon Keynes's memorable phrase, 'the first recorded non-event in English history'.[1] Understood as a single dramatic occurrence which would change the destiny of the lands that would become England, the *adventus* has its origins in Gildas's *De excidio Britanniae*. This account, which was most likely composed in the mid-sixth century, famously records the arrival of three boatloads of Germanic mercenaries summoned to defend the British people whom they were subsequently to betray.[2] In reality, events were probably very different and very much more complicated. The scale and nature of the Germanic settlement of England is a matter of ongoing and multidisciplinary investigation. Since the mid-twentieth century, scholars have increasingly grown suspicious of the idea that large-scale migration facilitated wholesale conquest and displacement over a relatively short period of time.[3] But the myth of the *adventus* first recorded by Gildas was to occupy a powerful

---

1   Keynes, '*Adventus Saxonum*', p. 6.
2   Gildas, *De excidio Britanniae*, ed. and trans. by Winterbottom, ch. 23. Cf. Coumert, 'Gildas'.
3   See especially White, 'Changing Views of the *Adventus Saxonum*'; Sims-Williams, 'Gildas and the Anglo-Saxons'; and Sims-Williams, 'The Settlement of England'. Much of the scholarly debate on this topic has focused on a divide between a 'maximalist' view of large-scale migration and settlement and a 'minimalist' view of elite migration followed by a process of acculturation. In recent years, however, theoretical developments relating to the study of ethnicity and culture have posed further challenges for both interpretations of available literary, linguistic, and archaeological evidence. See, for example, Hills, 'Overview: Anglo-Saxon Identity'; Brugmann, 'Migration and Endogenous Change'. Both main interpretative models — large-scale migration and elite replacement — are rejected by Susan Oosthuizen, *The Emergence of the English*, who emphasizes instead continuity across the longue durée of post-Roman Britain.

Daniel Thomas (daniel.thomas@ell.ox.ac.uk) is Departmental Lecturer in Old and Early Middle English at the University of Oxford.

Ideas of the World in Early Medieval English Literature, ed. by Mark Atherton, Kazutomo Karasawa, and Francis Leneghan, SOEL 1 (Turnhout: Brepols, 2022)   pp. 167–201
BREPOLS ❧ PUBLISHERS   DOI 10.1484/M.SOEL.5.130561

place in the historical *imaginaire* of the early English inhabitants of Britain throughout the early medieval period.[4]

Gildas's dramatic account of the arrival of the barbarian mercenaries 'like wolves into the fold' ('quasi in caulas lupi') must be read in the context of the text's particular polemical purpose.[5] Written to rebuke the contemporary British population and its rulers, the *De excidio* draws upon models from scripture, and particularly the Old Testament prophetic books, to present an analogy between the suffering of the British at the hands of their 'Saxon' persecutors and the many tribulations suffered by the tribes of Israel as a divine judgement.[6] In drawing this analogy, Gildas established a connection to Christian history by interpreting insular history in relation to the Old Testament *populus Israhel* paradigm of apostasy, fall, repentance, and redemption.[7] The people of Britain are thus constituted as a 'latter-day Israel' ('praesentem Israelem'), and the historical moment of the *adventus* is located within a recurrent and essentially cyclical pattern in the history of humanity and its relationship with God.[8]

This providential view of fifth- and sixth-century British history, adopted and adapted in Bede's *Historia ecclesiastica*, underlies the importance of the *adventus* for early English authors. Writing from an early eighth-century perspective, Bede effectively reverses the polarity of Gildas's polemic by recasting the migratory tribes — not the British whom they displace — in the role of the 'chosen people'. Reimagining the *adventus* in these terms, Bede emphasizes not only the sinfulness of the British, but particularly their failure

---

4 Gildas's description of the arrival of the Saxons in three ships seems to reflect 'a core origin myth that was common to many Indo-European societies' which attributed the founding of royal dynasties to legendary figures arriving by sea with a small group of followers in the lands they were destined to rule by virtue of conquest (Yorke, 'Anglo-Saxon Origin Legends', p. 28; cf. Brooks, *Anglo-Saxon Myths*, pp. 78–89). Bede provides a more developed version of this myth — which Gildas may have encountered in an early, perhaps oral, form — by adding to the narrative taken from Gildas the information that the leaders of the first mercenaries were Hengest and Horsa, legendary founders of the Kentish royal dynasty (Bede, *HE*, I.15). This Kentish origin myth is repeated in the Anglo-Saxon Chronicle (*s.a.* 449) which also provides similar foundation legends for the kingdoms of Sussex (*s.a.* 477), Wessex (*s.a.* 495), southern Hampshire (*s.a.* 501), and the Isle of Wight (*s.a.* 514). In contrast to the providential view of history so prominent in Gildas's account of the *adventus*, the Chronicle's account has been shown to serve a contemporary ideological purpose, justifying the late ninth-century political situation by producing a migrationist narrative that legitimized West Saxon dominance in the southern regions of Britain. See especially, Kleinschmidt, 'What Does the "Anglo-Saxon Chronicle" Tell Us about "Ethnic" Origins?'; Konshuh, 'Constructing Early Anglo-Saxon Identity'. See also discussion of the *adventus* above, Introduction, pp. 12–14.

5 Gildas, *De excidio Britanniae*, ed. and trans. by Winterbottom, ch. 23.1.

6 See especially Higham, *The English Conquest*, pp. 67–89, and Perkins, 'Biblical Allusion and Prophetic Authority'.

7 Scheil, *The Footsteps of Israel*, pp. 143–47; Coumert, 'Gildas', pp. 28–31.

8 Gildas, *De excidio Britanniae*, ed. and trans. by Winterbottom, ch. 26.1. On Gildas and the influence of the *De excidio Britanniae*, see the comments of Caitlin Ellis in this volume, esp. pp. 336–38.

to fulfil God's will by converting the pagan newcomers to the Christian faith.[9] In so doing, Bede provided a model upon which later writers such as Alcuin and Wulfstan, writing centuries apart but both under the shadow of Viking threat, could draw in recasting the attackers as agents of divine displeasure and issuing a call for repentance and reform in order to avoid the fate which, between them, Gildas and Bede ascribe to the British.

The *adventus*, as it is imagined in these texts, exerts a powerful influence on modern scholarship. The idea of the *adventus* and its importance as a foundational 'non-event' continues to shape our reconstruction of the early English peoples' own sense of identity, and their understanding of the world and their place in it. In particular, since the publication in 1989 of Nicholas Howe's landmark study of *Migration and Mythmaking in Anglo-Saxon England*, it has become a critical commonplace to talk in terms of an early English 'migration myth'.[10] By positing a common origin for the disparate and heterogenous populations of the lands that were to become England, the *adventus* myth 'gave the English as a folc a common identity'.[11] But it also, Howe suggested, helped to form their understanding of their place in relation to specifically Christian ideas of the world by establishing a connection between the early English and the chosen people of Israel more specific than Gildas's appeal to the *populus Israhel* tradition, identifying the former as a people specially favoured by God above even other Christian peoples. According to Howe, the core of the migration myth was an imaginative or typological equivalence between the Germanic migrations to Britain of the fifth and sixth centuries and the biblical migrations of the tribes of Israel on their journey to the Promised Land. The key to this identification, Howe proposed, was an understanding of the *adventus* in relation to the Exodus story: Christian writers from the eighth century onwards were able to interpret the pre-Christian Continental origins of the early English peoples in terms of 'a common geographical pattern of an exodus from a place of spiritual bondage across the water to a land of spiritual salvation'.[12] Although this typological connection is not given direct expression in any surviving early medieval texts, Howe contends that a 'deeply absorbed sense' of the myth can be discovered not only in texts which concern or refer to the *adventus* directly, but also in other texts — such as the Old English poetic *Exodus* or *Beowulf* — in which the myth provides an invisible subtext informing the meaning of the work in ways that would have been evident to an early medieval audience.[13]

---

9 Bede, *HE*, I.22.
10 Howe, *Migration and Mythmaking*.
11 Howe, *Migration and Mythmaking*, p. 179. Cf. Wormald, 'The Venerable Bede and the "Church of the English"' and Wormald, '*Engla Lond*'.
12 Howe, *Migration and Mythmaking*, p. 179.
13 Howe, *Migration and Mythmaking*, p. 2. For Howe, the migration myth facilitates the *Beowulf*-poet's engagement with the Germanic past, enabling the poem's audience to make an 'imaginative journey back to the continental homeland' and thus 'appreciate how conversion

Howe's work was greeted on publication with a mixture of appreciation and scepticism, and various elements of his thesis have been challenged in the decades since.[14] These objections notwithstanding, however, Howe's thesis has come to occupy an important place in scholarship on early medieval England. In particular, Howe's formulation of the migration myth has exerted a significant influence on subsequent studies of Old English poetry in general, and vernacular biblical verse in particular.[15] In fact, as I will argue further below, the notion of the migration myth has — by dint of repetition — become so central a part of critical study and discourse relating to the pre-Conquest period of British literary history that its existence is more often than not taken for granted. For many of us, the migration myth is presented early in our engagement with early medieval literature and culture as an established fact and is absorbed as such into our critical thought-world, lending a lasting colour to our understanding of the *adventus* and its meaning for early medieval writers. Such scholarly commonplaces must, however, be susceptible to scrutiny or run the risk of becoming the critical equivalent of self-fulfilling prophecies. In this spirit, the wider argument of the following chapter is that the migration myth, as a paradigm of modern critical thought, may have assumed too much significance in early English studies, becoming at times a distorting rather than illuminating lens through which to view texts from this period.

The more immediate focus of the chapter is on the Old English poem *Genesis A*, a long biblical paraphrase which has received particular attention for its sustained thematic engagement with ideas of migration.[16] The impor-

---

altered their condition as a Germanic people' (*Migration and Mythmaking*, p. 176). His suggestion that *Exodus* plays a seminal role in the construction of the migration myth by establishing 'the parallel between the first exodus and the tribal migrations across the North Sea' (*Migration and Mythmaking*, p. 72) is discussed further below.

14 See, for example, reviews by Bremmer, Crick, Jacobs, Russom, Schoening, and Stacey (full details in the Works Cited). The notion of English exceptionalism central to Howe's reading of the *Historia ecclesiastica* has been strongly refuted by Molyneaux, 'The Old English Bede' and Molyneaux, 'Did the English Really Think They Were God's Elect?'; Merrills has argued that Howe's identification of the *Historia ecclesiastica* as the foundational text in development of the migration myth is undermined by the absence of any 'sense of ethnic cohesion and narrative coherence' in Bede's account of the *adventus* (*History and Geography in Late Antiquity*, pp. 300–307; quotation at p. 303). Howe's reading of the 'appositive geography' of *Beowulf* has also been challenged by Hiatt, who notes his tendency 'to adapt the poem to the argument of his book' ('*Beowulf* Off the Map', p. 38).

15 See, for example, Michelet, *Creation, Migration, and Conquest* and Michelet, 'Lost at Sea'; Zacher, *Rewriting the Old Testament*; Trilling, *The Aesthetics of Nostalgia*, esp. pp. 133–43; Zollinger, 'Cynewulf's *Elene* and the Patterns of the Past'; Harris, *Race and Ethnicity*, pp. 157–84; Estes, *Anglo-Saxon Literary Landscapes*, esp. pp. 61–87; Fitzgerald, *Rebel Angels*, pp. 4–5; Barajas, *Old English Ecotheology*, pp. 14–15.

16 The poem is cited by line number from *Genesis A, Revised*, ed. by Doane. I have added capital letters where appropriate. Translations from the poem, except where otherwise noted, are from *Old Testament Narratives*, ed. and trans. by Anlezark.

BABEL AND BEYOND   171

tance of this theme in the poem — which reflects the similar importance of migration in the biblical source text — has been most comprehensively, and most influentially, analysed by Paul Battles, in an important article that seeks to both draw upon and extend Howe's work on the cultural importance of migration for the early medieval English imagination.[17] The main contention of Battles's article is that the poet of *Genesis A* draws upon an existing migration myth in order to establish an implicit parallel between the *adventus* and the migrations described in the Genesis story. Attractive as this interpretation of the poem undoubtedly is, a re-examination of the evidence seems to me to raise question marks over the presence of such an intended analogy in the poem. The desire to read *Genesis A* in these terms may, I suggest, say more about the continuing power of Howe's formulation of the migration myth as an interpretative model than about the poem itself. It may, in other words, reveal more about our own scholarly interests and preoccupations than about those of the poem's long-dead author or his or her original audience.

Sohton rumre land: The Tower of Babel as Migration Myth?

In his discussion of the 'migration myth' in *Genesis A*, Battles identifies eight passages in the poem that describe migrations of various sizes. Highlighting similarities of content and diction between the passages, he argues that they bear witness to the presence in the poem of a traditional or formulaic theme which he calls simply 'Migration'.[18] The existence of this formulaic theme had been noted previously by the poem's editor, A. N. Doane, but Battles's analysis builds on the earlier treatment by identifying the theme in passages not considered by Doane and by providing a more detailed analysis of the elements of which the theme consists.[19] Battles identifies six key motifs from which the Migration passages are constructed: '(1) "departure"; (2) "with household"; (3) "leading possessions"; (4) "travelling"; (5) "in search of more spacious territory"; and (6) "settling the green plains"'.[20] He also catalogues

---

17 Battles, '*Genesis A* and the Anglo-Saxon "Migration Myth"'. For the influence of this work on subsequent studies of the poem, see, for example, Liuzza, 'The Tower of Babel', pp. 1–5; Trilling, *The Aesthetics of Nostalgia*, pp. 96–101; Wright, '*Genesis A* ad litteram', pp. 169–70.

18 Battles, '*Genesis A* and the Anglo-Saxon "Migration Myth"', pp. 44–45 and passim. The passages from *Genesis A* identified by Battle are the account of the building of Tower of Babel (ll. 1649–67; 1694–99a), three consecutive descriptions of Abraham's departure in search of Canaan (ll. 1730–38a; 1746–52a; 1767–90a), his subsequent journey into Egypt (ll. 1816–19; 1844–47a), his departure from that land (ll. 1873–79), the account of Lot's separation from Abraham (ll. 1890–1931a), and finally Abraham's departure into the land of Abimelech (ll. 2621–23a).

19 *Genesis A*, ed. by Doane, pp. 81–82. The comments are repeated, with reference to Battles's argument, in the revised edition (*Genesis A, Revised*, ed. by Doane, pp. 106–07 and n. 128).

20 Battles, '*Genesis A* and the Anglo-Saxon "Migration Myth"', p. 55.

the repeated vocabulary that appears in connection with these motifs across the different iterations of the theme.[21]

As both Doane and Battles note, examination of the Migration theme clearly shows the *Genesis A*-poet engaging in formulaic poetics, sometimes at the expense of strict fidelity to the details of the scriptural source, throwing light upon the poet's compositional practices. But, for Battles, the use of this theme also frames the poet's depiction of biblical migrations in relation to the cultural migration myth, establishing an 'implicit analogy' between the migrations described in the first book of the Bible and the historical Germanic migrations to England.[22]

Central to this argument is Battles's reading of the account of the Tower of Babel episode in *Genesis A*, which he characterizes as 'the first, longest, most detailed, and least "biblical"' of the poem's migration scenes (ll. 1649–1701).[23] The introduction of the Migration theme in this episode is of particular importance because it represents a significant departure from the biblical source.[24] The poet's attention to this episode suggests that, where Howe focuses on Exodus as the point of imaginative connection between ancestral and biblical histories, it was the Babel episode that offered the *Genesis A*-poet an opportunity to exploit the migration myth as a means of 'situating the Anglo-Saxons' immediate, regional-tribal history within the larger framework of universal Christian history'.[25]

In the Vulgate text of Genesis, the account of how the descendants of Noah settle the plain of Shinar prior to the building of the tower occupies just one verse.[26] In the Old English poem, by contrast, twelve lines are devoted to a description of this relocation and of the charms of the newly settled land:

Gewiton him þa eastan	**æhta lædan**,	*departure; leading possessions*
feoh and **feorme**.	Folc wæs anmod.	
Rofe rincas	**sohton rumre land**	*seeking spacious lands*
oð þæt hie becomon	corðrum miclum,	
folc **ferende**,	þær hie fæstlice	*travelling*

---

21 Battles, '*Genesis A* and the Anglo-Saxon "Migration Myth"', p. 56 (fig. 2).

22 Battles, '*Genesis A* and the Anglo-Saxon "Migration Myth"', p. 66.

23 Battles, '*Genesis A* and the Anglo-Saxon "Migration Myth"', p. 62.

24 Battles, '*Genesis A* and the Anglo-Saxon "Migration Myth"', pp. 45–51.

25 Battles, '*Genesis A* and the Anglo-Saxon "Migration Myth"', p. 65.

26 Genesis 11. 2, 'cumque proficiscerentur de oriente invenerunt campum in terra Sennaar et habitaverunt in eo' (And when they removed from the east, they found a plain in the land of Sennaar, and dwelt in it). I cite the Vulgate here and throughout as the poet's source. Studies by Doane (*Genesis A, Revised*, pp. 79–87) and Remley (*Old English Biblical Verse*, pp. 94–149; 'The Latin Textual Basis of *Genesis A*') have established that the *Genesis A*-poet was most likely working closely with a continuous textual source which consisted of a predominantly Vulgate text marked by 'a limited but conspicuous admixture' of Old Latin variants (*Genesis A, Revised*, ed. by Doane, p. 79). In considering the relationship between the Old English and the probable Latin source, I have also consulted the Old Latin variants recorded in *Vetus Latina*, ed. by Fischer.

æðelinga bearn,	**eard genamon**.	*settling...*
Gesetton þa Sennar	sidne and widne	
leoda ræswan	leofum mannum	
heora geardagum.	**Grene** wongas	*... the green plains*
fægre **foldan**	him forðwearde	
on ðære dægtide	duguðe wæron,	
wilna gehwilces	weaxende sped.	

(ll. 1649–60, emphasis added)

(Then they departed to the east, leading their possessions, cattle and goods. That folk was resolute; brave warriors sought a more spacious land, until the migrating people arrived in great multitudes, where they, the children of princes, seized the territory. Then the leaders of the people settled Shinar, broad and wide; in their ancient days they were green fields for dear men, at that time a beautiful earth for the troop, henceforth an increasing abundance of each good thing for them.)

The contrast with the brevity of the Latin source is indeed striking. As Battles points out, the description of a large nation seeking out a more spacious dwelling place fits uncomfortably with the fact that this episode occurs in Genesis shortly after the Flood, the descendants of Noah being, by this point, insufficiently numerous to make population pressures a reasonable motivation for the search for a more spacious dwelling.[27] The departure from the Vulgate in this passage suggests to Battles that here and in subsequent Migration passages the *Genesis A*-poet is working under the influence of a well-established, traditional poetic theme associated with large-scale movement of peoples. As the annotation provided above shows, this passage contains five of the six motifs Battles identifies as constituting the Migration theme (omitting only the idea of travelling 'with household') and includes several of the repeated lexical items associated with the expression of this theme (marked here in bold emphasis).

Following the internal logic of this traditional theme over that of the source narrative, the poet provides a 'surprisingly positive' description of the protagonists of the episode, to the extent of presenting the dispersal 'in universas terras' following the confusion of tongues in a 'less ignominious' fashion than the biblical account.[28] This is suggested by comparison of two passages which, taken together, seem to imply that the dispersal was a result of the builders' own volition rather than a direct result of divine punishment as depicted in the biblical account. In the first of these passages, the poet expresses the builders' intention to construct a city and tower

---

27 Battles, '*Genesis A* and the Anglo-Saxon "Migration Myth"', pp. 46–47.
28 Battles, '*Genesis A* and the Anglo-Saxon "Migration Myth"', pp. 47, 51.

> æwere seo mengeo eft
geond foldan bearn   tofaran sceolde,
leoda mægðe   on landsocne.   (ll. 1663b–65)

> (before the multitudes later should move away across the earth's bosom, the tribes of people in search of land.)

The hint at future migration in search of land in these lines apparently presents the building project as a precursor rather than an alternative to continued migration. Subsequently, following the confusion of tongues, the poet employs strikingly similar terms to describe the dispersal:

> Wæs oðere   æghwilc worden
> mægburh fremde   siððan metod tobræd[29]
> þurh his mihta sped   monna spræce.
> Toforan þa   on feower wegas
> æðelinga bearn   ungeþeode
> on landsocne.   (ll. 1694–99a)

> (Each tribe had become foreign to the other, after the creator split the languages of human beings by his mighty ability. The disunited sons of princes scattered into four directions in search of land.)

In this account of the dispersal, the builders are presented as the grammatical subject of an active verbal construction. This departure from the Vulgate source — in which God as grammatical subject scatters the builders across the face of the earth ('divisit eos Dominus […] in universas terras', Genesis 11. 8) — suggests to Battles a deliberate intention on the part of the poet to recast the dispersal as a continuation of the voluntary, heroic migration which resulted in the settlement of Shinar.[30] By effecting this change, the poet establishes the dispersal as a suitable parallel for the *adventus*, understood

---

29 The poet's use of the verb *tobregdan* — which might best be rendered 'to (cause to) disperse, to thrust apart' — may be significant here. The prefixed form of the verb denotes sudden and forceful action on the part of the subject, but the root *bregdan* equally carries spatial connotations of moving, pulling, or throwing. The poet's depiction of God violently sundering the speech of the builders stands in contrast to the Vulgate account, in which the confusion of tongues is anticipated and referred to retrospectively, but not actually narrated (Genesis 11. 7–9). The repetition of the *to-* prefix in the following lines ('tofaran þa on feower wegas') may imply a direct causal link between the confusion of tongues and the sudden dispersal 'in universas terras', presenting the latter event as a direct consequence of God's agency. I am grateful to Mark Atherton for bringing this point to my attention.

30 Battles, '*Genesis A* and the Anglo-Saxon "Migration Myth"', pp. 50–51: 'Noah's descendants separate of their own accord (or rather discord), with the now alienated members of the tribe continuing their migration in search for land (*on landsocne*), a motif introduced even before their arrival at Shinar (they *sohton rumre land*, 1651).' A similar understanding of the building project as a precursor to onward migration is evident in comments by Michelet ('they decide to build the tower as a commemorating token before they scatter over the face of the earth', *Creation, Migration, and Conquest*, p. 205) and Scheil ('the Tower of Babel is

in similarly heroic terms, and 'places the biblical and Germanic migrations within a single historical continuum'.[31]

This is an elegant and persuasive argument. The Babel episode in Genesis — with its explanation of the origin of linguistic diversity and its depiction of the descendants of Noah departing 'in universas terras' to populate the earth — was an important source for early medieval writers invested in popular *origines gentium* myths which traced the ancestry of particular medieval peoples to biblical figures generally and the descendants of Noah in particular.[32] Just such a myth is famously enshrined in the West Saxon royal genealogies which trace the ancestry of Æthelwulf of Wessex to the legendary Germanic figure Sceaf, identified as the apocryphal fourth, ark-born son of Noah, and it is by no means impossible that 'a similar fusion of native and biblical origin myths' might explain a positive presentation of the dispersal as a heroic migration.[33]

That *Genesis A* offers such a presentation is, however, by no means certain. Much of the weight of Battles's argument rests upon his interpretation of the builders' motivations in constructing the tower and of the statement that the builders sought to undertake their project 'ær seo mengeo eft [...] tofaran sceolde [...] on landsocne'. The point at issue here is the precise force of the conjunction *ær*. Battles — translating the phrase 'before this host [...] would thereafter scatter in different directions [...] in search of land' — assigns a purely temporal function to the conjunction.[34] In rendering the text thus, he is in agreement with each of the translations of the poem that I have consulted.[35] Nevertheless, it seems to me that translating *ær* as 'before' in this instance distorts — in fact, reverses — what was probably the intended sense of the lines.

Alongside its temporal function, the conjunction *ær* can — as Eric Stanley points out — denote preference, particularly in relation to a choice of alternatives.[36] Examples of such constructions — in which the force of the

---

built [...] as a sign of unified glory and power before their kin should scatter over the earth', *The Footsteps of Israel*, p. 154).

31 Battles, '*Genesis A* and the Anglo-Saxon "Migration Myth"', p. 65.

32 Cf. Reynolds, 'Medieval *Origines Gentium*'; Major, *Undoing Babel*, pp. 53–59.

33 Battles, '*Genesis A* and the Anglo-Saxon "Migration Myth"', p. 65. See below, note 62.

34 Battles, '*Genesis A* and the Anglo-Saxon "Migration Myth"', p. 50 n. 27.

35 Anlezark's recent translation ('before the multitudes later should move away [...] in search of land') is cited above. Cf. *Cædmon's Metrical Paraphrase*, ed. and trans. by Thorpe, p. 100 ('ere *the* multitude again [...] should journey [...] in search of land'); *Genesis A*, trans. by Mason, p. 26 ('before the masses of the people should scatter again [...] in search of land'); *The Cædmon Poems*, trans. by Kennedy, p. 58 ('before their multitude [...] should be scattered again [...] in search of land'); 'A Critical Edition of the Old English *Genesis A*', ed. and trans. by Wells, p. 129 ('before the many again could scatter [...] on a land-hunt'). Williamson's recent poetic rendering of *Genesis A*, though much freer than those cited above, shows a similar understanding of the force of the conjunction: 'Before the tribes were scattered once more | In their restless search for a richer land' (*The Complete Old English Poems*, trans. by Williamson, p. 81).

36 Stanley, 'Old English *Ær* Conjunction'. Cf. Sievers, 'Zum Beowulf', pp. 329–31; Mitchell, *Old*

conjunction is best captured by translating it not 'before' but 'rather than' — can be found in a number of extant Old English poems.[37] In each case, the clause introduced by the conjunction *ær* expresses a hypothetical alternative less preferable than the action proposed in the main clause. A good example of this use of the conjunction can be found elsewhere in *Genesis A*, when Lot offers his daughters to the inhabitants of Sodom and urges them to commit the supposedly lesser crime by directing their sexual violence against these women *rather than* against his male, angelic visitors:

> Her syndon inne   unwemme twa
> dohtor mine.   Doð swa ic eow bidde
> — ne can þara idesa   owðer gieta
> þurh gebedscipe   beorna neawest —
> and geswicað þære synne.   Ic eow sylle þa
> *ær* ge sceonde   wið gesceapu fremmen,
> ungifre yfel   ylda bearnum.
>
> (ll. 2466–72, emphasis added)

> (Here inside are my two unblemished daughters. Do as I offer you — neither of these ladies knows anything of the experience of men in bed — and desist from this sin. I give them to you, before you do shame against creation, a harmful evil against the sons of men.)

Notwithstanding Anlezark's translation of line 2471 as 'before you do shame against creation', a purely temporal understanding of the conjunction *ær* is impossible here — as it is in other examples of this construction. As the subjunctive verb forms 'sylle' and 'fremmen' indicate, Lot's speech sets out hypothetical alternatives and, in Stanley's words, the construction with *ær* 'excludes the realization of the alternative notion'.[38] The use of this construction in these lines may, in fact, reflect the proviso clause introduced by the conjunction *dummodo* in the equivalent passage in the Vulgate, where Lot promises to give his daughters to the mob *on condition that* they do not interfere with the visitors.[39] The comparison of Latin and Old English here suggests how strongly the sense of (negative) preference expressed by the *ær* clause might have been felt by a contemporary audience.

English Syntax, II, pp. 376–78 (§ 2721, § 2724), pp. 644–45 (§ 3252); *DOE*, s.v. *ær*, III. C.

37   See, for example, *Juliana*, ll. 253–56a, *Elene*, ll. 441–47, 673b–677a, *Andreas*, ll. 1352–56a, 1437b–1440, *Daniel*, ll. 589–92, *Beowulf*, ll. 251b–254a. With a correlative adverb in the construction *ær … ær …*, see also *Beowulf*, ll. 1368–72a, and *The Battle of Maldon*, ll. 60–61. All Old English poems other than *Genesis A* are cited by line number from the relevant volume of *ASPR*. Translations from these texts are my own.

38   Stanley, 'Old English Ær Conjunction', p. 12.

39   Genesis 19. 8: 'educam eas ad vos et abutimini eis sicut placuerit vobis dummodo viris istis nihil faciatis mali' (I will bring them out to you, and abuse you them as it shall please you, so that [i.e. 'provided that'] you do no evil to these men).

The phrase 'ær seo mengeo eft [...] tofaran sceolde [...] on landsocne' is best understood as another example of this construction. The building of the tower and city is presented as a favoured choice as against an alternative of continued migration. When the phrase in question is viewed in this light, the adverb *eft* would seem to refer to frequency ('again') rather than time ('afterwards'), and the full force of necessity expressed by the modal auxiliary *sculan* in the phrase 'tofaran sceolde' becomes apparent. My suggestion is that the phrase does not mean 'before the multitude would afterwards disperse in search of land', but 'rather than that the multitude should have to disperse once more in search of land'. As in the case of Lot's daughters, moreover, the poet's use of the construction with *ær* 'rather than' seems to arise from careful attention to the language of the biblical source.[40] In the Vulgate text, the descendants of Noah propose to undertake their building project 'antequam dividamur in universas terras', which the Douay-Rheims translation gives as 'before we be scattered abroad into all lands'. Like the Old English *ær*, however, the Latin conjunction *antequam* can have more than just temporal force. Accompanied (as here) by a subjunctive verb form, the conjunction can introduce a subordinate clause the realization of which is prevented by the action of the main clause.[41] The poet's understanding of the meaning of this verse seems, in this instance, closer to that of the King James reading ('lest we be scattered abroad upon the face of the whole earth') than to the Douay-Rheims version. The passage as a whole delineates hypothetical alternative futures involving either continued migration or the building of tower and city (reflected again in the subjunctive verb forms 'sceolde', 'geworhte', 'arærde') and, through the use of *ær* (rather than), expresses preference for the latter alternative.[42]

As presented in *Genesis A*, the building of Babel makes more sense as an alternative to continued migration than as a memorial that will be built and immediately, voluntarily, abandoned. As Battles points out, the description in the poem of the settlement of Shinar expands considerably upon the terse Vulgate account. The chief difference, however, lies in the sense of purpose that is introduced to the poetic narrative. The sequence of finite verbs in the passage defines a process of journeying ('gewiton'), seeking ('sohton'), arriving ('becomon'), and settling ('gesetton'). In contrast to the simple statement in the Vulgate that the descendants of Noah dwelt in Shinar ('habitaverunt in eo'), the poem depicts them establishing a permanent residence ('fæstlice [...] eard genamon').[43] The subsequent description characterizes this settlement

---

40 Cf. Remley's observation that 'there can be little doubt that the poet of *Genesis A* was a competent Latinist' (*Old English Biblical Verse*, p. 114 n. 56).

41 Hullihen, *Antequam and Priusquam*, p. 39.

42 On the subjunctive forms in this passage, see Bloomfield, 'Old English Plural Subjunctives'.

43 Cf. *DOE*, s. v. *fæstlice* adv., 2.A.II and s.v. *eard* noun, 1.B.I.

as both expansive ('sidne and widne') and durative ('heora geardagum', 'forðwearde', 'on ðære dægtide').

Such details support the suggestion that, as the poet of *Genesis A* conceived the narrative, the building of the city and tower was a project intended to mitigate against the need for further migration. The poet's description of how, following the division of speech, the builders 'toforan þa […] on landsocne' need not, after all, imply that the dispersal (a direct result of the sundering of their speech) was an act of *volition* rather than *necessity* on the part of the builders.[44] Their determination to build the tower and city that they need not scatter in search of land is frustrated by God's intervention. There is an ironic appropriateness, therefore, to the fact that the builders suffer precisely that fate that they hoped to avoid.

The builders' lack of desire for further migration in fact establishes a contrast with the account of the earlier arrival at Shinar. While Battles is surely right to note the poet's positive, heroic depiction of those who settle the plains as resolute and bold warriors ('anmod'; 'rofe rincas'), the builders' actions are, by contrast, characterized as excessive ('ofer monna gemet', l. 1677a), motivated by pride and recklessness ('for wlence and for wonhygdum', l. 1673). The poet subtly distances the builders from the earlier settlers: where the Vulgate account suggests that the building of the tower follows directly upon the settlement of Shinar, the Old English poet implies a passage of time by stating that the builders chose Shinar as the site of the tower because their ancestors ('þa yldestan', l. 1670a) — the 'most powerful leaders of the nation' ('foremeahtige folces ræswan', l. 1669) — had previously dwelt happily there. The introduction of this delay seems to present the building project as marking a decline in a society whose heroic achievements are now conspicuously located in the past.[45] From the initial heroism of the settlers, through the pride of the builders, the episode ends with the tribes dispersing 'wretchedly' ('earmlice', l. 1692b) following God's intervention. While the initial settlement of Shinar might be viewed as admirable, heroic behaviour, the dispersal itself cannot.[46]

---

44 It is useful by way of comparison to note that Ælfric — whose condemnation of the builders as idolaters is explicit — consistently employs a third-person plural form of the weak verb *toferan* in active constructions to describe the dispersal. Cf. Major, *Undoing Babel*, pp. 175–98, esp. pp. 183–84.

45 Scheil reads this passage in relation to the narrative arc of the *populus Israhel* tradition noting that 'the Hebrews in this passage shift without warning from the noble seekers of a homeland to boastful criminals' (*The Footsteps of Israel*, p. 154). Major notes that the poet establishes verbal parallels between the description of the Tower and both Sodom and Cain's proto-city which 'point not so much towards their wickedness per se but rather urban progression that ends in inevitable destruction' (*Undoing Babel*, p. 222).

46 Olsen, '"Him þæs grim lean becom"', argues that the pride of the builders is intended to recall the *superbia* of the rebel angels in the opening episode of *Genesis A*: noting that the reference to the builder's *wrohtscipe* ('criminal behaviour', l. 1672b) forms a verbal connection to the description of the angelic rebellion as a *wrohtgeteme* ('series of crimes', l. 45b), Olsen

BABEL AND BEYOND   179

Under earce bord:
The Migration Theme in the Flood Episode

For the reasons outlined above, it seems unlikely that the poet of *Genesis A* intended to promote the dispersal 'in universas terras' as a scriptural paradigm through which the inhabitants of early England might interpret their ancestral history. But there is another passage in the poem which might offer such a paradigm. The Babel episode is not, in fact, 'the earliest and most extensive migration passage in *Genesis A*'.[47] The origins of the Migration theme lie not in the settlement of Shinar, but in the poet's adaptation of the Flood narrative. Though dispersed over a longer portion of the poem, the account of the Flood contains each of the elements that Battles identifies as constituting the Migration theme, some of them reiterated several times.

The passage with which I am concerned extends from the moment that God orders Noah to enter the ark to the point at which he and his family leave it again (*Genesis A*, ll. 1330–1496). The narrative of the Flood is, as Phyllis Portnoy has shown, marked by the poet's extensive use of patterned verbal and ideational repetition forming a sequence of sometimes-overlapping envelope patterns.[48] The passage currently under discussion is delineated by a 'double' envelope pattern formed around the idea of departure with household. The passage begins with God addressing Noah and commanding him to lead his family into the ark, which command he subsequently obeys:

> Ða to **Noe** cwæð   **nergend** usser:
>   ['...]   **Læd** swa ic þe **hate**
> **under earce bord**   eaforan þine,
> frumgaran þry,   and eower feower **wif**. [...]
> **Gewit** þu nu mid hiwum   on þæt hof gangan
> gasta **werode**. [...]
> Him þa **Noe gewat**   swa hine **nergend het**
> **under earce bord**   eaforan lædan,

---

argues for the presence in the poem of a pattern for the depiction of sin whereby 'recurrent images of infertility [...] recall with each transgression and punishment on earth Lucifer's rebellion and fall in heaven' (p. 128). The verbal connections that Olsen notes might be pushed still further. The simplex *wroht* ('crime') appears in the successive accounts of the rebellion (l. 83b), the Fall (ll. 911a, 932a), and the murder of Abel (l. 991b), while the term *unræd* ('bad counsel') is used to describe the sinful desires of the rebel angels (l. 30a), the builders (l. 1682b), and the people of Sodom (l. 1937a). The related term *unræden* ('evil action', l. 982b) also describes the murder of Abel. Even the description of how the builders abandon the city and tower standing in their paths as they disperse throughout the world ('him on laste [...] stod', ll. 1699–1701) recalls both the angels leaving behind them their heavenly homes ('him on laste [...] stodan', ll. 86b–87) and the locking of paradise behind the departing Adam and Eve ('him on laste beleac', l. 945a).

47   Battles, '*Genesis A* and the Anglo-Saxon "Migration Myth"', pp. 59–60.
48   Portnoy, *The Remnant*, pp. 128–45. See also Stévanovitch, 'Envelope Patterns'.

weras on wægþæl   and heora **wif** somed
    [...]   swa him ælmihtig
weroda Drihten   þurh his word abead.

(ll. 1330–62, emphasis added)

(Then our saviour said to Noah: ['...] Lead under the deck of the ark, as I command you, your heirs, the three chieftains, and your four wives. [...] Now get going with your companions into the building, with the troop of souls [...'].) Noah then went, as the saviour commanded him, leading his children under the deck of the ark, men onto the vessel, together with their wives [...] as the almighty Lord of hosts had commanded them by his word.)

As the bold typeface here shows, this passage forms a local envelope pattern based around a sequence of repeated words and phrases detailing the command and its fulfilment.[49] The wider passage as a whole, however, also forms an extended envelope pattern with the subsequent account of God's command to *leave* the ark and Noah's obedient compliance:

Þa to **Noe** spræc   **nergend** usser,
heofonrices weard,   halgan reorde:
    ['...]   Gewit on freðo gangan
ut of earce,   and on eorðan bearm
of þam hean hofe   hiwan **læd** þu [...']
He fremede swa   and frean hyrde,
stah ofer streamweall,   swa him seo stefn bebead,
lustum miclum,   and **alædde** þa
of wægþele   wraðra lafe.
Þa **Noe** ongan   **nergende** lac
rædfæst, reðran.

(ll. 1483–98a, emphasis added)

(Then our saviour, the guardian of the kingdom of heaven, spoke to Noah, in a holy voice: ['...] Go walking safely out of the ark, and from the tall building lead your household [...'].) He did so and obeyed the Lord, with great eagerness climbed over the current-wall, as the voice commanded him, and then led from the vessel the survivors of the rages. Then Noah, the prudent one, prepared a sacrifice [for the saviour].)

This latter passage again forms a self-contained envelope pattern. While the extent of the verbal repetition is less striking than in the former passage, the core of the passage is the repetition of the motif of leading the household (described in the second instance as the survivors of the Flood), together with Noah's obedience to the voice of the Lord ('halgan reorde'; 'seo stefn').

---

49   Cf. Portnoy, *The Remnant*, pp. 135–37.

BABEL AND BEYOND   181

But the two passages together also form an envelope encompassing the sojourn in the ark. This is marked most clearly by the double repetition in each passage of both the 'Noe [...] nergend(e)' collocation and the twofold use of *(a)lædan* in the 'leading household' motif. The paralleling is further enforced, however, by the repetition across the passages of the departure formula 'gewit [...] gangan', the alliterative collocation of *hof* and *hiwan*, and the reference to Noah obeying God's word ('swa him [...] þurh his word abead'; 'swa him seo stefn bebead'), as well as through the opposition of the phrases 'on wægþæl' and 'of wægþele'.

The double envelope structure demarcating this part of the poem may have been inspired, in general terms, by the biblical source. The equivalent passages in the Vulgate text similarly feature a doubling of command and fulfilment for both entering and leaving the ark, and parallel phrasing in these passages performs a similar enveloping function. In the first case, God commands Noah 'ingredere tu et omnis domus tua arcam' (go in, thou and all thy house, into the ark, Genesis 7. 1), a verse which (as Doane notes in his apparatus) the poet seems to have conflated with the earlier pronouncement that Noah will have to enter the ark to escape the Flood: 'ingredieris arcam tu et filii tui uxor tua et uxores filiorum tuorum tecum' (thou shalt enter into the ark, thou and thy sons, and thy wife, and the wives of thy sons with thee, Genesis 6. 18). Following this command, the actual moment of entering the ark is recounted in a perfect passive construction: 'ingressus est Noe et filii eius uxor eius et uxores filiorum eius cum eo in arcam' (Noe went in and his sons, his wife and the wives of his sons with him into the ark, Genesis 7. 7). This same pattern is repeated later when God commands Noah to leave the ark using an imperative verb form — 'egredere de arca tu et uxor tua filii tui et uxores filiorum tuorum tecum' (go out of the ark, thou and thy wife, thy sons and the wives of thy sons with thee, Genesis 8. 16) — before the action is again described in a perfect passive construction: 'egressus est ergo Noe et filii eius uxor illius et uxores filiorum eius cum eo' (so Noe went out, he and his sons: his wife, and the wives of his sons with him, Genesis 8. 18).

It seems likely that this parallel phrasing inspired the double envelope pattern found in the Old English poem. The poet has, however, simplified the *ingredior/egredior* opposition in the Latin by substituting in each case the 'leading' motif using the verb *(a)lædan* which features so prominently in the poem's depictions of migration.[50] There is, moreover, an additional use of this 'leading' motif in the account of the Flood which is entirely without parallel in the biblical source. In treating the Resting of the Ark (Genesis 8. 4–5), the poet introduces a non-biblical, but decidedly naturalist detail by

---

50 It is possible that the use of this motif was encouraged by the use of the verb *educo* in Genesis 8. 17 when God commands Noah to 'bring out with thee' ('educ tecum') the livestock within the ark — though there seems no warrant in the Vulgate for the emphasis in the poem on Noah leading his household specifically.

emphasizing the impatience of the passengers to leave their confinement within the ark:[51]

> Hæleð langode,
> wæglidende,   swilce wif heora
> hwonne hie of nearwe   ofer nægledbord
> ofer streamstaðe   stæppan mosten
> and of enge ut   æhta læden.   (ll. 1431b–35)

> (The hero, the wave-travelers and also their wives longed for when they might step out from their constraint over the nailed boards and across the stream-shore, and bring their possessions out from confinement.)

The inclusion of this detail not only provides yet another iteration of the 'leading' motif, but also specifically introduces the idea of leading possessions, featuring the identical half-line found in the account of the journey to Shinar ('æhta læden').

The description here of the passengers in the ark as 'wæglidende' presents them specifically as travellers. As we have seen, the poet introduces the departure motif to the account of Noah's entry into the ark, notably when rendering the Latin passive construction 'ingressus est' with the active construction 'him þa Noe gewat'. In contrast to the biblical source, the sojourn in the ark is, in the poem, consistently depicted as a journey, variously characterized as dangerous ('frecenra siða', l. 1427b) and troublesome ('earfoðsið', l. 1476a).[52] Where the Latin text simply says that the waters began to abate after 150 days (Genesis 8. 3), the Old English poem specifies this as the period during which the 'foamy ship' travelled on the water ('for famig scip', l. 1417a). The verb *feran*, used here to describe the ship's passage, constitutes the key repeated lexical item for the 'departure' motif that constitutes part of the Migration theme. The casual personification of the ship as a traveller in this half-line is evident in more developed form, again employing the verb *feran*, when the poet elaborates on the statement in the Vulgate that the ark was 'carried upon the waves' ('arca ferebatur super aquas', Genesis 7. 18) by depicting the ark instead as a traveller bearing goods:

> Siððan wide rad   wolcnum under
> ofer holmes hrincg   hof seleste
> for mid fearme.   (ll. 1392–94a)

> (Then the most excellent craft rode widely under the clouds across the expanse of the sea, travelled with the cargo.)

---

51 Anlezark points out that the naturalistic desire to leave the ark does not accord with traditional exegetical interpretations of the ark as a prefiguration of the Church (*Water and Fire*, p. 194). Cf. Michelet, *Creation, Migration, and Conquest*, p. 205. For analogues in ancient Jewish exegetical texts, see Mirsky, 'On the Sources', pp. 389–91.

52 Michelet, *Creation, Migration, and Conquest*, pp. 221–22.

The form *fearm* in this passage is interpreted by Doane as a uniquely attested noun meaning 'freight' or 'cargo' — reflected here in Anlezark's translation.[53] It would seem preferable, however, to see this as an error for or variant of the well-attested noun *feorm* (food, goods) which occurs in three other passages in the poem: once in the account of the settlement of Shinar describing the goods which the settlers lead with them ('feoh and feorme', l. 1650a), once in the first of the 'Abrahamic' migration scenes in the half-line 'feran mid feorme' (l. 1731a), and once when God warns Abimelech that he will perish 'mid feo and mid feorme' (l. 2660a) if he does not return Sarah to Abraham. Since *feorm* represents one of the repeated lexical items associated with the 'leading possessions' motif in *Genesis A*, and in view of the similarity with line 1731a in particular, positing a unique noun to account for the form 'for mid fearme' in line 1394a seems unnecessary.[54] This half-line would seem, in fact, to introduce another iteration of the 'leading possessions' motif, here in a striking doubly metaphorical construction in which the anthropomorphization of the ark as a traveller is paralleled by the objectification of the inhabitants as the 'goods' borne on the journey.

The journey in the ark culminates in the possession of a new homeland, specifically appointed by God as a rest from the long sea-voyage:

> Þe is eðelstol   eft gerymed,
> lisse on lande,   lagosiða rest,
> fæger on foldan.   (ll. 1484–86a)

> (A native seat is again opened up for you, delight on land, rest from the voyage, fair upon the earth.)

This passage, which does not derive from the Vulgate account of God's speech (Genesis 8. 16–17), frames the departure from the ark as the culmination of a search for a homeland.[55] But the motif of seeking spacious lands is, in the Flood episode, enacted primarily by non-human rather than human actors. The raven sent out from the ark to test the waters is tasked with finding land; its disobedience is defined specifically in terms of a refusal to undertake this search:

> Noe tealde   þæt he on neod hine
> gif he on þære lade   land ne funde
> ofer sidwæter   secan wolde
> on wægþele.   Eft him seo wen geleah
> ac se feonde gespearn   fleotende hreaw.
> Salwigfeðera   secan nolde.   (ll. 1443–48)

---

53 *Genesis A, Revised*, ed. by Doane, p. 419. Cf. *DOE*, 'fearm noun'.

54 The spelling *fearme* may, indeed, be evidence for the common Northumbrian confusion of <eo> and <ea>, on which, see *Genesis A, Revised*, ed. by Doane, p. 46.

55 Cf. Michelet, *Creation, Migration, and Conquest*, p. 210.

(Noah reckoned that if it could not find land on that excursion, in its need it would seek the wave-plank across the wide water. Afterward this hope deceived him, as the enemy perched on a floating corpse; the dark-feathered one did not wish to seek further.)

By contrast, the obedient dove, sent in search of green land ('grenre eorðan', l. 1454a), seeks far and wide in a search for land ('wide hire willan sohte | and rume fleah', ll. 1455b–1456a), returning only when it is unable to find a place to rest ('no hweðere reste fand', l. 1456b). Released a second time, the dove again flies widely ('wide fleah', l. 1465b) before discovering a branch on which to perch. In a passage which presages God's opening up a homeland for Noah as a place of rest, the dove is depicted rejoicing in the open spaces ('rumgal', l. 1466a) as it finds a fair resting-place ('reste stowe | fægere funde', ll. 1466b–1467a).[56] The third time it is released, the dove does not return, and the motif of settling the green plains is present in the added detail that the bird occupied the land and green groves ('land begeat, | grene bearwas', ll. 1479b–1480a).

The respective depictions of the raven and the dove in *Genesis A*, which elaborate freely on the terse biblical narrative (Genesis 8. 6–12), have been discussed by Britt Mize as 'a veritable study in the narrative technique of focalization'.[57] As Mize shows, the poet's use of focalization in these passages is characteristic of their practice throughout the poem, which, by comparison with the biblical source, 'consistently heightens the emphasis on mental and emotional states'.[58] But the use of this technique also allows the poet to recast the episode of the raven and the dove in terms of a purposive search for a green and spacious land.

Battles suggests that the first and most elaborate example of the Migration theme in *Genesis A* occurs during the Babel episode because the poet understood the dispersal as 'the *archetypal* migration of all humankind' and 'the "first precedent" for the Anglo-Saxons' own migration'.[59] As the foregoing analysis shows, however, the six motifs that constitute the Migration theme are also present in the earlier, more extensive account of the Flood, including substantial repetition of the key vocabulary found in the later iterations of the theme.[60] If, then, the poet intends us to understand migration in the poem in relation

---

56 Anlezark points out that the emphasis on (need for) rest in the Flood episode recalls the biblical etymology of Noah's name as 'rest' or 'comfort' (*Water and Fire*, pp. 192–95). For contrasting views regarding the possible allegorical significances of the raven and the dove, see *Genesis A, Revised*, ed. by Doane, pp. 337–39, and Wright, '*Genesis A* ad litteram', pp. 137–40.

57 Mize, *Traditional Subjectivities*, p. 37.

58 Mize, *Traditional Subjectivities*, p. 79.

59 Battles, '*Genesis A* and the Anglo-Saxon "Migration Myth"', p. 65 (emphasis original).

60 Cf. Battles, '*Genesis A* and the Anglo-Saxon "Migration Myth"', p. 56 (fig. 2). Following Battles's schema, the key vocabulary associated with Migration found in the Flood episode would be: (1) departure — *him þa [...] gewat*; (2) with household — *wif*; (3) leading possessions — *læd, lædan, alædde, æhta, fearme*; (4) travelling — *for*; (5) in search of more

to a culturally specific origin myth, it seems likely that the 'first precedent' is to be found in the account of the Flood, rather than the Babel episode.

Wera eðelland: The Flood Episode as Migration Myth?

In many ways, the narrative of the Flood presents a more plausible point of imaginative intersection between biblical and ancestral history than does the dispersal. Presented as a journey undertaken by sea, the sojourn in the ark provides a closer analogy to the *adventus* than the dispersal 'in universas terras'. The redemptive aspects of the Flood narrative, moreover, offer a more positive point of comparison than the punitive dispersal in the Babel episode. The preservation of Noah and his family potentially fits more closely with the ideas of early English exceptionalism seen by Howe as a central tenet of the migration myth than does the punishment of the builders: identification with Noah, recipient of special divine favour, could suggest that the early English people possessed a similar status as God's elect for whom the 'Promised Land' of Britain was reserved.[61] And though it seems unlikely that the *Genesis A*-poet would have known of the mythical connection between the West Saxon royal family and an ark-born son of Noah, the poet would presumably have been familiar with the more commonplace notion that the population of Europe descended ultimately from Noah's biblically attested son Japheth (though no trace of this idea is evident in the poem itself).[62]

An analogy between the *adventus* and journey of the ark and its passengers to a new homeland would fit, moreover, with the ideological dimensions of the migration myth as recently delineated by Catherine Karkov. In an important study of ideas of 'Anglo-Saxon England' through time, Karkov stresses the importance of the migration myth as an expression of supremacist and colonialist thinking in the early medieval period and beyond. The 'exodus

---

spacious territory — *secan, sohte, gerymed, rumgal, rume, land*; (6) settling the green plains — *grenre (eorðan), grene (bearwas), (fæger on) foldan*.

61 Cf. Howe, *Migration and Mythmaking*, p. 46.

62 The adaptation of the West Saxon genealogies to include the ark-born son Sceaf seems to have taken place in the late ninth century, probably during the reign of Alfred, and appears not to have gained widespread or lasting acceptance (see, especially, Anlezark, 'Sceaf, Japheth and the Origins of the Anglo-Saxons' and Anlezark, *Water and Fire*, pp. 241–90; Cronan, '*Beowulf* and the Containment of Scyld'). The composition of *Genesis A* is usually held to have taken place in the eighth or early ninth century in an Anglian (perhaps Northumbrian) linguistic environment (see *Genesis A, Revised*, ed. by Doane, pp. 42–55; Fulk, *A History of Old English Meter*, pp. 391–92). On these grounds, it seems unlikely that the tradition of the ark-born ancestor could have influenced the poem. On the other hand, Estes has suggested that *Genesis A* might have formed part of the translation programme attributed to Alfred the Great in the late ninth century, arguing that the poem 'was copied and adapted in Alfred's circle, with specific details in the language of the poem echoing contemporary events' ('Abraham and the Northmen in *Genesis A*', p. 10).

186 DANIEL THOMAS

myth' (as she calls it) partakes of colonial violence by replacing a presumed reality of invasion and conquest with a teleological narrative of divinely ordained migration to a promised land. The myth, Karkov says, rewrites the displacement of the existing population of Britain by presenting the early English ancestors as a chosen people claiming their always already appointed homeland as a rightful inheritance. The trauma and violence of conquest is thus silenced and 'encrypted' within a narrative which, though culturally powerful and indicative of a strong exceptionalist ideology, lacks 'legitimacy' and can 'only ever have emptiness at its core'.[63] Like Howe, Karkov argues that the vitality and centrality of this myth means that we can discern its presence in places where it is not explicitly announced.[64]

Karkov's analysis of the migration myth offers a powerful way of reading of the Flood narrative in *Genesis A* as an 'encrypted' narrative of the *adventus*. Unlike the account of the dispersal 'in universas terras', the Flood narrative culminates not in the loss of land but in the possession of a new, divinely appointed home.[65] This new homeland is produced through violence, death, and destruction which results in the displacement of the existing holders of the land. But this violence is sanitized and justified as a divine rather than human act. The heroic element that Battles sees as key to the theme of migration is largely absent from the Flood narrative as regards Noah and his family: the passengers in the ark are described at embarkation as a troop of souls ('gasta werode', l. 1346a) and at disembarkation as brave-minded heroes ('hæleð hygerofe', l. 1550a), but during the sojourn itself they are (as we have seen) presented as anxiously enduring hardship. The heroic note is rung, however, by the strikingly martial depiction of God as a powerful and vengeful lord.[66] The Flood itself is repeatedly anthropomorphized as God's 'water-army' ('wægþreat', l. 1352b; 'egorhere', l. 1402a) and the drowning of all living creatures without the ark is presented in terms of a powerful warlord attacking the inhabitants of a homeland:

> Strang wæs and reðe
> se ðe wætrum weold,   wreah and þeahte
> manfæhðu bearn,   middangeardes,
> wonnan wæge,   wera eðelland.
> Hof hergode,   hygeteonan wræc

---

63 Karkov, *Imagining Anglo-Saxon England*, p. 112.

64 See, for example, Karkov's suggestion that, through its juxtaposition of narratives from legendary Germanic, Roman, and biblical history, the Franks Casket 'deflects the violence of its own past, the violence that took place on the geographical island of Britain, onto the foundation stories and origin legends of those other times and places' (*Imagining Anglo-Saxon England*, pp. 99–100).

65 Cf. Howe's suggestion that 'the enduring fact of migration is that it is remembered as a transit between two places, between a home that has been left behind and the one that has been found or, more likely, seized on arrival' (*Writing the Map of Anglo-Saxon England*, p. 50).

66 Anlezark, *Water and Fire*, pp. 189–91.

metod on monnum.　　　Mere swiðe grap
on fæge folc　　feowertig daga,
nihta oðer swilc.　　Nið wæs reðe,
wællgrim werum.　　Wuldorcyninges
yða wræcon　　arleasra feorh
of flæschoman.　　　　　　　　　　(ll. 1376b–1386a)

> (He who wielded the waters was strong and fierce; he covered and hid the children of the feud of middle-earth, the homeland of men, with a dark wave; the creator destroyed buildings, malevolently inflicted revenge on humanity. The sea quickly grasped at the doomed people for forty days, and also by night. The hate was fierce, slaughter-grim for men; the king of glory's waves drove out the life of the graceless ones from the body.)

Read in this way, the account of the Flood can be seen (*pace* Karkov) to reveal violent realities that underlie the myth of migration to a promised land. The problem with such an interpretation, however, is that, unless we accept the presence in the episode of an otherwise unrepresented traditional theme of Migration which had a sufficiently strongly felt connection with the migration myth that its mere presence in the poem would be enough to spark an association with the *adventus*, there is nothing in the text of *Genesis A* to suggest or promote such a reading.[67]

The identification of the constituent elements of Migration in the narrative of the Flood provides an opportunity to rethink the nature and origins of this theme. The succinct and stylized expression of the account of the settlement of Shinar, departing significantly from the biblical source, led Battles to conclude that Migration must have been a well-established traditional theme, despite the lack of surviving evidence for its currency outside the poem, and it is on this assumption that the argument for an 'implied analogy' between biblical and ancestral history rests.[68] But the appearance of the elements of the theme in more dispersed, less stylized fashion across the longer, earlier account of the sojourn in the ark does not seem so indicative of a poet engaging with a well-established, coherent traditional theme. It may suggest

---

67　It might be observed more generally in response to Karkov's discussion of the migration myth that her analysis tends to privilege what is not said about the *adventus* over what is said in early English texts, particularly in accounts such as those preserved in the Anglo-Saxon Chronicle which appeal directly to the violence of invasion and conquest in order to legitimize claims of ownership over the land. These claims, as Francis Leneghan demonstrates in his chapter in this volume, reflect an imperial theme evident more widely throughout the Chronicle (below, esp. pp. 414–19).

68　Battles, '*Genesis A* and the Anglo-Saxon "Migration Myth"', p. 61: 'It is unfortunate, of course, that no other extant Old English poem preserves the theme, a state of affairs that may beg the question of how a single poem can provide evidence for the existence of an entire tradition. [...] Of course, if "Migration" is indeed a traditional theme, such poems must once have existed.'

instead that the concise iterations of the theme later in the poem represent the condensation of elements from the longer narrative of the Flood through a process of formulaic development. This would support Doane's view that the theme was constructed by the *Genesis A*-poet in response to the nature of the source material: 'the recurring textual need led to the development of the theme from occurrence to occurrence [...] affording us a view in fast-forward mode of the way a formulaic thematic nexus develops'.[69] If this is the case, then any connection between biblical and ancestral migrations depends upon inference rather than implication.[70] The reading of the Flood narrative as an encrypted narrative of migration outlined above remains plausible, but there is no good reason to suppose that the poet intended or facilitated such a reading, just as there is no evidence to suggest that any previous reader of the poem interpreted the episode in these terms.

In fact, such evidence as there is tends to point the poem's audience towards a rather different understanding of the connection between the events of the poem and their own experience. The presentation of the sojourn in the ark as a migratory journey to a new homeland does certainly represent a significant adaptation of the biblical source, but it is one that seems to reflect wider concerns within the poem that do not seem to relate to the ancestral history of the early English peoples. By focusing exclusively upon passages that deploy a developed Migration theme, we risk losing sight of how this theme relates to a narrative pattern that operates throughout *Genesis A*. As Renée Trilling explains, the pervasive message of the poem — the need for obedience to God's will — is expressed through a repeated paradigm whereby 'exile is the punishment for sin [and] the promise of the homeland is the reward for virtue'.[71] This paradigm is established at the beginning of the poem through the inclusion of the non-biblical account of how God condemned the rebel angels to occupy an 'exile-place' ('wræcstowe', l. 90a) and created man in order to repopulate the 'native seats' ('eðelstaðolas', l. 94a) in heaven. The paradigm can subsequently be traced through major events in the poem, including the Fall, the murder of Abel, the Flood, the Babel episode, the destruction of Sodom, and the migratory journeys that punctuate the Abrahamic narrative. And it is, as Trilling points out, in the context of loss of land — rather than the search for land — that the poet twice interrupts the narrative of the poem to make

---

69 *Genesis A, Revised*, ed. by Doane, p. 106 n. 128.

70 For a similar argument regarding the widespread notion of early English exceptionalism, see Molyneaux, 'Did the English Really Think They Were God's Elect?', p. 724.

71 Trilling, *The Aesthetics of Nostalgia*, pp. 96–101 (p. 100). Cf. Smith, 'Faith and Forfeiture'. On the importance of obedience as a governing theme in the poem, see Lucas, 'Loyalty and Obedience'. Discussing *Genesis A* as an *ad litteram* rendition of the biblical text, Wright notes that 'Old Testament history is sacred because it recounts the deeds — the *gesta* — of both the righteous and the wicked in the first ages of the world, as well as the corresponding temporal rewards and punishments that God meted out to each' ('*Genesis A* ad litteram', pp. 154–55).

emotive appeals to the anticipated audience. The first of these interruptions occurs in the account of the Fall, following God's injunction that Adam and Eve should 'seek another home' ('oðerne eðel secean', l. 927) on account of their disobedience:

> Hwæt, we nu gehyrað   hwær us hearmstafas
> wraðe onwocan   and woruldyrmðo.   (ll. 939–40)

> (Listen! We hear now where the sorrows and worldly misery cruelly awoke for us.)

The second interruption emphasizes the implications of the murder of Abel as the first sinful act in the postlapsarian world and as a re-enactment of the original transgression, just before God condemns Cain to turn from the land ('of earde', l. 1019a) and go into exile ('on wræc hweorfan', l. 1014b):

>   We þæt spell magon,
> wælgrimme wyrd,   wope cwiðan
> nales holunge.   Ac us hearde sceod
> freolecu fæmne   þurh forman gylt
> þe wið metod æfre   men gefremeden.   (ll. 995b–99)

> (Not at all in vain can we lament that story with weeping, the slaughterous fate; but the elegant woman hurt us hard by that first crime that people ever committed against the creator.)

The dramatic intrusion of the narrator at these moments is characteristic of traditional vernacular poetics, but through the use of the first-person plural and the emphasis on the spiritual needs of poet and audience it is also essentially homiletic. It is the postlapsarian human condition — characterized by exile from paradise and a longing to establish a permanent home in heaven — rather than ancestral history to which the poet appeals directly in drawing a connection between narrative past and the audience's present experience.[72]

Conclusions: Rethinking the Migration Myth

Early medieval ideas of the world were, as the essays collected in this volume show, complex and multifarious. There is significant danger, therefore, in allowing any one scholarly narrative — such as the idea of a migration myth — to loom too large in our modern attempts to reconstruct and understand these ideas. If we prioritize our understanding of the migration myth in reading a poem like *Genesis A* over interpretations that the text itself seems to promote, we inevitably run the risk of appropriating the text for our own scholarly agendas rather than listening closely to what the poem itself has to

---

72   Cf. Trilling, *The Aesthetics of Nostalgia*, p. 99.

say. There is, I suggest, nothing in the text of the poem that encourages an audience to see an analogy or typological link between the various scenes of migration which, following the biblical source, the poem describes and the myth of the *adventus* as an originary moment as it was formulated from the time of Gildas onwards. Such a reading of the text depends less on what the poem itself actually says, therefore, than it does on a modern critical conception of the ubiquity of the early English 'migration myth' first described by Howe. Allowed to speak for itself, *Genesis A* emerges as a poem less concerned with an imagined Germanic past than with the present and future needs of its intended Christian audience.

The idea of the migration myth has come to be central to modern critical ideas of early medieval England, conditioning how we conceive of the early English understanding of the world and their place in it. In this way, the migration myth is, in essence, also a central myth of contemporary scholarship, exerting a significant influence over how we construct 'Anglo-Saxon England'. Applied in ever more contexts and with increasingly little need for explanation or justification, the myth has accrued its own formidable explanatory power. If the early English used the migration myth to think through, to justify, and to exceptionalize their ancestral history, the myth is equally a monolith of modern scholarship authorizing one of the dominant narratives through which we view the surviving artefacts of early English culture. We know it as, in Karkov's words, an 'ever-present' feature of early English thought, and the danger is that we therefore tend to see it everywhere.[73]

But in its scholarly iteration also the migration myth might be said to 'have emptiness at its core'.[74] As has been noted already, no surviving artefact from early medieval England articulates the myth in anything very like the terms in which Howe defines it.[75] In fact, surviving accounts of the *adventus* — particularly those in Gildas, Bede, and the Anglo-Saxon Chronicle — are, as Fabienne Michelet has pointed out, marked by a curious lack of attention to the actual journey which the Germanic tribes undertook to reach England. Commenting upon the 'silence' of these texts regarding 'the central part of the Anglo-Saxons' myth of cultural identity', Michelet notes that 'the Germanic tribes' journey to Britain is not emphasised; it is hardly even mentioned'.[76]

---

73 Karkov, *Imagining Anglo-Saxon England*, p. 109. Cf. Michelet, *Creation, Migration, and Conquest*, p. 231 ('the Anglo-Saxons never forgot that they only reached England after a group journey from the Continent'); Davies, 'Hengist and Horsa at Monticello', p. 168 ('The history of the Anglo-Saxons is a history of migration').

74 See above, note 63.

75 Howe argues that 'fine writers rarely announce the central myth of their culture, but instead explore it as it exists at the very core of their audience's imaginative and historical being' (*Migration and Mythmaking*, p. xvii). This may be so, but it is disconcerting to have so little evidence that any such core ever existed. Cf. Molyneaux, 'Did the English Really Think They Were God's Elect?', p. 737.

76 Michelet, 'Lost at Sea', p. 78. See also p. 65: 'both Gildas and Bede inscribe the Anglo-Saxon migration in a providential scheme of history and could therefore have elaborated in biblical

Faced with the question of 'why [...] the "founding event" of Anglo-Saxon identity [is] thus downplayed', Michelet suggests that the migratory journey itself was of less importance to early English identity than 'the fact that the Anglo-Saxons' ancestors originated from elsewhere and that they took control [of] and appropriated the territory they now inhabit'.[77]

This observation strikes at the heart of the scholarly migration myth. Howe's formulation of the myth identified the poem *Exodus* as a foundational text which 'allow[ed] the Anglo-Saxons to align their history with the Old Testament, through the model of migration'.[78] Central to his thesis was the suggestion that an understanding of *Exodus* in these terms explains the poem's concentration on the crossing of the Red Sea, at the expense of much of the rest of the biblical account, and the insistent use of nautical language to describe a journey undertaken on foot. For the poet, Howe observes, 'the crossing is the exodus' and the close focus on this event represents the poet's 'most daring attempt to contain ancestral history'.[79] The wider biblical narrative, including the arrival in the Promised Land, is extraneous because it is in the sea-crossing that 'the inescapable correspondence between Israelites and Anglo-Saxons' lies.[80] But this correspondence looks less inescapable in light of Michelet's observation that early English writers typically understood the *adventus* in spatial terms as invasion and conquest of land rather than as migration per se.[81] Comparison with surviving accounts of the *adventus* would, in fact, tend to suggest that — viewed as a migration myth — *Exodus* puts the irrelevancies in the centre and the serious things on the outer edges.

A similar picture is suggested by consideration of the only surviving Old English poem that makes direct reference to the *adventus*. Celebrating the historical victory of the forces of King Æthelstan and his brother Edmund against an alliance of their Dublin Norse, Scottish, and Strathclyde Welsh opponents, the poem known as *The Battle of Brunanburh* — preserved as the Anglo-Saxon Chronicle entry for the year 937 — draws directly upon

---

and Christian terms on the sea journey to highlight the coming of the Germanic tribes as an event willed by God. They could also have elaborated on the sea crossing in heroic terms to enhance the courage and martial prowess of the protagonists. But neither chose to do so.'

77 Michelet, 'Lost at Sea', pp. 66, 78–79. Michelet's conclusions were anticipated by Jacobs's observation in relation to Howe's thesis that 'it is not always the migration itself which is primarily significant' ('[Review]', p. 452). See also Yorke's suggestion that the core of the early English origin myth was the shared knowledge that 'we came from overseas as a group' ('Anglo-Saxon Origin Legends', p. 22).

78 Howe, *Migration and Mythmaking*, p. 106.

79 Howe, *Migration and Mythmaking*, pp. 102–03.

80 Howe, *Migration and Mythmaking*, p. 103.

81 Compare Caitlin Ellis's observation, in her chapter in this volume, that the Anglo-Saxon Chronicle's failure to name the leaders of the British tribes against whom the Germanic newcomers fought made of the land 'a blank canvas [...] onto which to project early English kingdoms' (below, p. 342).

the *adventus* as a point of comparison against which the magnitude of the violence inflicted upon their enemies might be measured:

>   Ne wearð wæl mare
> on þis eiglande   æfre gieta
> folces gefylled   beforan þissum
> sweordes ecgum,   þæs þe us secgað bec,
> ealde uðwitan,   siþþan eastan hider
> Engle and Seaxe   up becoman,
> ofer brad brimu   Brytene sohtan,
> wlance wigsmiþas,   Wealas ofercoman,
> eorlas arhwate   eard begeatan.   (ll. 65b–73)

> (Never was there greater slaughter in this island, nor yet before this more people felled by the edges of the sword, as the books tell us, old scholars, since the Angles and Saxons, proud war-smiths, glory-eager warriors, came hither out of the east, sought Britain over the broad sea, overcame the Welsh, won the land.)

As per Michelet's observations, the significance of the *adventus* according to this account consists almost entirely in the success of the invaders' violent conquest and seizure of land. The actual journey across the broad sea ('ofer brad brimu') — the literal exodus of the Germanic tribes from their Continental homelands — is treated here with conspicuous brevity, uninflected by any salvific or redemptive overtones. Indeed, the meaning of these lines depends not upon a shared awareness of a cultural migration myth but on their context within the poem in which they appear.

Paul Cavill, elsewhere in this volume, demonstrates that the rhetoric of *Brunanburh* originates in the propaganda of Æthelstan's reign.[82] The picture of the king presented in the opening lines of the poem comes straight from the world of heroic poetry. He is not only a king, but a lord of warriors, a ring-giver, and a defender of land and treasure:

> Her Æþelstan cyning,   eorla dryhten,
> beorna beahgifa,   and his broþor eac,
> Eadmund æþeling,   ealdorlangne tir
> geslogon æt sæcce   sweorda ecgum
> ymbe Brunanburh.   Bordweal clufan,
> heowan heaþolinde   hamora lafan,
> afaran Eadweardes,   swa him geæþele wæs
> from cneomægum,   þæt hi æt campe oft
> wiþ laþra gehwæne   land ealgodon,
> hord and hamas.   (ll. 1–10a)

---

82 Paul Cavill below. See also the discussion of the poem in Caitlin Ellis's chapter (below, pp. 349–50).

(Here King Æthelstan, lord of warriors, ring-giver to men, and his brother also, Edmund the prince, won long-lasting glory at battle with the edges of swords, around Brunanburh. The sons of Edward split the shield-wall, hewed the battle-wood with the hammers' remnant, as was natural to them on account of their ancestors, so that they always defended the land, treasure and homes, in battle against every enemy.)

The description of the glory which Æthelstan and Edmund win through violent deeds recalls the famous account of the career of Scyld Scefing in the opening passages of *Beowulf* as a man who terrorized warriors ('egsode eorlas') and forced obedience from his neighbours ('ymbsittend') by military domination (*Beowulf*, ll. 4–11).[83] In both poems, violent persecution of enemies is presented as habitual, almost constitutive action. The success of Æthelstan and Edmund 'æt campe oft' is paralleled in the *Beowulf*-poet's description of how Scyld repeatedly subjugated his enemies ('oft […] meodosetla ofteah', ll. 4–5). But if the beginning of *Brunanburh* reveals generic similarities with the beginning of *Beowulf*, elevating Æthelstan from the historic plane to the level of heroic legend, the two accounts are nevertheless different in important ways. In *Beowulf*, Scyld is an originating figure, the founding foundling who establishes a royal dynasty.[84] In *Brunanburh*, by contrast, emphasis is placed on Æthelstan and Edmund's royal heritage as sons of Edward ('afaran Eadweardes') whose successes derive from their ancestry as much as from their exceptional personal qualities ('swa him geæþele wæs | fram cneomægum').[85] Accordingly, while Scyld is celebrated for conquest and for expanding his authority across the seas, the West Saxon princes are praised instead for their defence of an existing territorial arrangement.

For a modern scholar, writing with the benefit of a long historical perspective, the events that took place 'ymbe Brunanburh' in 937 might be perceived as a moment of significant, even dramatic political change — in Sarah Foot's memorable phrase, the moment 'when English becomes British', a key development in the West Saxon imperialist ambitions discussed by Francis Leneghan elsewhere in this volume — but the poem itself celebrates the victory as a moment of heroic continuation and as the defence of an existing status quo.[86] It is in this context that the comparison to the violence of the *adventus* must be considered. As Paul Cavill discusses in his chapter in this volume, the account of the *adventus* at the end of the poem is linked to the opening praise of Æthelstan and Edmund through a series of verbal echoes

---

83 Francis Leneghan, in this volume, sees similar parallels with the account of Scyld Scefing in another Chronicle poem, *The Death of Edward*. See below, pp. 423–24.

84 Leneghan, *The Dynastic Drama of 'Beowulf'*, pp. 139–51.

85 It is possible, of course, that Æthelstan may have considered Scyld himself as part of this noble and heroic lineage. Cf. Cronan, '*Beowulf* and the Containment of Scyld' and above, n. 62.

86 Foot, 'Where English Becomes British'.

forming an envelope pattern. The description in the first line of Æthelstan as 'lord of warriors' ('eorla dryhten', l. 1b) is picked up in the final line in the reference to the 'glory-eager warriors' ('eorlas arhwate', l. 73a); in both contexts, glory is achieved by the edge of the sword ('sweorda ecgum', l. 4b; 'sweordes ecgum', l. 68a); the defence of land at Brunanburh parallels the winning of land at the *adventus* ('land ealgodon', l. 9b; 'eard begeatan', l. 73b); the reference to metalworking in the description of weapons as 'the hammers' remnant' ('hamora lafan', l. 6b) is recalled in the description of the invading tribes as 'proud warsmiths' ('wlance wigsmiþas', l. 72a). The connections thus forged invite us to connect the two historical moments, clearly drawing upon the origin myths associated with the *adventus* in order to justify the continuation of West Saxon authority. The poet simultaneously celebrates the great slaughter of the *adventus*, associated here with the displacement of existing populations, as the grounds for Æthelstan's later, inevitable, successes and presents the victory at Brunanburh as a triumphant reiteration of that originary violence. In doing so, the poet collapses the temporal distance between the two events. Though it appeals to the authority of books ('bec') and old scholars ('ealde uðwitan') for the events of the *adventus*, the poem itself becomes a superior witness to those events by incorporating a new awareness of how Æthelstan's victory reinscribes the meaning of the *adventus*.[87] Events of the fifth and the tenth centuries are compounded as part of a single, complex, and continuous heroic moment.[88]

What is obviously missing from *Brunanburh* is any sense of a providential understanding of the events it recounts. In *Migration and Mythmaking*, Howe reads in the poem a narrative of how the English armies 'battle a force of heathen invaders, such as they had once been', arguing that the events become 'spiritually significant' when viewed within 'a larger vision of insular history'; seen from such a perspective, 'the English victory could be set in the cycle of events that reveals the divinely appointed destiny of the island'.[89] The poem, however, makes no concession to such an interpretation. Howe's description

---

87 Donald Scragg suggests that, if the poem were written specifically for inclusion in the Chronicle, the phrase 'ealde uðwitan' could be intended self-referentially, revealing the poet's consciousness of his or her role in determining the meaning of events ('A Reading of *Brunanburh*', p. 118).

88 The repeated description of the battlefield at Brunanburh as a 'place of slaughter' ('wælstow', l. 43a; 'wælfeld', l. 51b) perhaps performs a similar operation in conflating the place of the *adventus* with that of the battle. For another reading of the historical and temporal perspectives within the poem, see Trilling, *The Aesthetics of Nostalgia*, pp. 195–98. Trilling suggests elsewhere in her important monograph that the vernacular historiography represented in the appositive approach of legendary-historical poems like *Beowulf* 'forges thematic links between people and events of the past and those of the present, resulting in a view of history as a constitutive element of the present rather than as a prelude to it' (p. 23). This description seems to me to fit admirably the historiographic approach evident in *Brunanburh*, though I would emphasize that the present represented in the poem also has a constitutive influence on the meaning of the historically prior event.

89 Howe, *Migration and Mythmaking*, p. 31.

of the forces defeated at Brunanburh as 'heathen[s]' is historically suspect, but it also represents an imposition of meaning upon the text. The poet never describes the vanquished in such a way, nor are the victors described in specifically Christian terms. With the exception of a single, rather stereotyped reference to the sun as 'the bright candle of God, of the eternal lord' ('godes condel beorht, | eces drihtnes', ll. 15b–16a), religious and spiritual concerns play no part in the account of the battle.[90] And while it is clear that the arrival of the Dublin Norse from across the sea represents a threatened repetition of the Germanic invasion (as the poem presents it), this possibility is shut down in a manner which not only celebrates its failure but also renders its success unthinkable. The poem's historiography thus in fact rejects the sort of cyclical or providential thinking that Howe's reading seeks to impose upon it.

In the introduction to *Migration and Mythmaking*, Howe draws a comparison between the typological understanding of the *adventus* which he identifies as the heart of the early English migration myth and the myths about migration 'which shaped prerevolutionary America'.[91] Noting Thomas Jefferson's never-realized proposal that the seal of the United States should depict, on one side, the tribes of Israel led by the pillars of cloud and fire and, on the other, the figures of Hengist and Horsa, legendary founders of the Kentish royal dynasty, Howe writes that 'the histories of the Israelites and of the Anglo-Saxons anticipated the geographical imperative of America, since each of these nations had made its migration across the sea to a promised land'.[92] In drawing this connection, Howe builds upon a historical and cultural narrative according to which early Puritan colonists and settlers (in particular) appealed to the Book of Exodus to develop a typological identity as the new chosen people: Exodus was 'the informing book of the Bible [...] because it sanctioned their migration to the new Jerusalem and proved they were a people set apart by divine election'.[93] This understanding of Puritan self-fashioning drew upon an established historiographical trend evident, particularly, in the work of scholars such as Perry Miller and Sacvan Bercovitch (whose work Howe cites).[94] In hindsight, it is in fact striking the extent to which Howe's discussion of early English memories and myths of migration reproduces in an early medieval British context characteristic scholarly discourses of typology, myth, and divine election found in then-contemporary studies of the so-called 'Great Migration' of the early seventeenth century.[95]

---

90 As Paul Cavill notes, the reference to the sun — a 'noble creation' ('aþele gesceaft') — participates in the poet's extended wordplay on the name Æthelstan. See below, p. 388.
91 Howe, *Migration and Mythmaking*, p. 2.
92 Howe, *Migration and Mythmaking*, p. 1.
93 Howe, *Migration and Mythmaking*, p. 1.
94 Miller, *Errand into the Wilderness*; Bercovitch, *The Puritan Origins of the American Self*.
95 Perhaps not only with hindsight: cf. Julia Crick's comments in an early review of *Migration and Mythmaking* that the exodus story 'presents an image less appropriate to the Anglo-Saxon migration of the fifth century than to that of the seventeenth' ('[Review]', p. 695).

It is particularly interesting, therefore, to note how scholarship has, in the decades since Howe's book was published, moved away from what is sometimes referred to as the 'puritan origins thesis'.[96] The field of New Puritan Studies has more recently demonstrated the extent to which Puritan exceptionalism and typological theology are constructs of nineteenth-century nationalistic discourse and twentieth-century historiography.[97] In a curious way, Howe's conception of the early English migration myth might be thought to represent a parallel development out of this same historical thinking about the supposed origins of America in the seventeenth century.[98] I have suggested already that the migration myth as delineated by Howe is itself a scholarly myth, in much the same way as the puritan origins thesis has been shown to be.[99] There may be benefits to the field of early medieval studies in recognizing it as such. By moving away from a static and monolith understanding of the Puritan migrations, New Puritan Studies has already allowed scholars to discover more clearly than previously the complexity and multiplicity of contemporary seventeenth-century attitudes to migration and to consider the experience of the English settlers in America in broader and more diverse and connected geographical and cultural contexts.[100] Rethinking what we think we know about early English attitudes to the *adventus* might be similarly productive.

---

96 The appearance of *Migration and Mythmaking* in 1989 coincided with the publication of Andrew Delbanco's *The Puritan Ordeal*, described by Abram van Engen as 'in many ways the scholarly swan song of the puritan origins thesis' ('Prologue: Pilgrims, Puritans, and the Origins of America', p. 31).

97 Cf. Traister, 'Introduction', p. 2: 'What New England Puritanism actually was as a historical object both informs and misinforms the stories we have told about the country's Puritan past, and continue to tell about that past today. That is, both scholarly and popular readers today rely a great deal on histories and narratives told by earlier readers of the Puritan past.' See more generally: Traister, ed., *American Literature and the New Puritan Studies*; Bross and van Engen, eds, *A History of American Puritan Literature*. To describe these narratives of Puritan history as constructs is not, of course, to deny their continued currency or their ideological force. For an important recent discussion of the legacies of English and American exceptionalism, and its roots in medieval studies and reception, see Karkov, *Imagining Anglo-Saxon England*, esp. pp. 195–239.

98 In his discussion of *Brunanburh*, for example, Howe cites approvingly Roberta Frank's passing suggestion that the poem presents 'a historical perspective reminiscent of manifest destiny' ('The *Beowulf* Poet's Sense of History', p. 63; quoted in *Migration and Mythmaking*, p. 31). The word 'destiny' recurs like a leitmotif throughout the course of Howe's monograph.

99 Compare van Engen's suggestion that 'the evidence that puritans thought of themselves as commissioned with a solitary, divine mission to save the world turns out to be rather scant — at best' ('Prologue: Pilgrims, Puritans, and the Origins of America', p. 33).

100 Van Engen, 'Prologue: Pilgrims, Puritans, and the Origins of America', pp. 33–34. Howe suggests that the migration myth did not survive the Norman Conquest of 1066 'because it could not respond to a more complex relation between England and the continent' (*Migration and Mythmaking*, p. 180). Conversely, we might think that the scholarly migration myth potentially masks the complex realities of early English relationships with the wider world. See, for example, Daniel Anlezark's chapter in this volume.

Works Cited

Primary Sources

Bede, *Bede's Ecclesiastical History of the English People*, ed. and trans. by Bertram Colgrave and R. A. B. Mynors, 2 vols (Oxford: Clarendon Press, 1969)

The Cædmon Poems, Translated into English Prose, trans. by Charles W. Kennedy (London: George Routledge & Sons, 1916)

Cædmon's Metrical Paraphrase of Parts of the Holy Scriptures in Anglo-Saxon, ed. and trans. by Benjamin Thorpe (London: Society of Antiquaries of London, 1832)

The Complete Old English Poems, trans. by Craig Williamson (Philadelphia: University of Pennsylvania Press, 2017)

'A Critical Edition of the Old English *Genesis A* with a Translation', ed. and trans. by David M. Wells (unpublished doctoral thesis, University of North Carolina, 1969)

Genesis A: A New Edition, ed. by A. N. Doane (Madison: University of Wisconsin Press, 1978)

Genesis A: A New Edition, Revised, ed. by A. N. Doane (Tempe: Arizona Center for Medieval and Renaissance Studies, 2013)

Genesis A, Translated from the Old English, trans. by Lawrence Mason (New York: Henry Holt & Co., 1915)

Gildas, *De excidio Britanniae*, in Gildas, *The Ruin of Britain and Other Works*, ed. and trans. by Michael Winterbottom (London: Phillimore, 1978)

Old Testament Narratives, ed. and trans. by Daniel Anlezark, DOML, 7 (Cambridge, MA: Harvard University Press, 2011)

Vetus Latina: Die Reste der altlateinischen Bibel nach Petrus Sabatier neu gesammelt und herausgegeben von der Erzabtei Beuron, II: *Genesis*, ed. by Bonifatius Fischer (Freiburg: Herder, 1949–1954)

Secondary Sources

Anlezark, Daniel, 'Sceaf, Japheth and the Origins of the Anglo-Saxons', *ASE*, 31 (2002), 13–46

——, *Water and Fire: The Myth of the Flood in Anglo-Saxon England* (Manchester: Manchester University Press, 2006)

Barajas, Courtney Catherine, *Old English Ecotheology: The Exeter Book* (Amsterdam: Amsterdam University Press, 2021)

Battles, Paul, '*Genesis A* and the Anglo-Saxon "Migration Myth"', *ASE*, 29 (2000), 43–66

Bercovitch, Sacvan, *The Puritan Origins of the American Self* (New Haven, CT: Yale University Press, 1975)

Bloomfield, Leonard, 'Old English Plural Subjunctives in -*E*', *JEGP*, 29 (1930), 100–113

Bremmer, Jr, Rolf H., '[Review of Nicholas Howe, *Migration and Mythmaking in Anglo-Saxon England*]', *ES*, 73 (1992), 479–80

Brooks, Nicholas, *Anglo-Saxon Myths: State and Church, 400–1066* (London: Hambledon Press, 2000)

Bross, Kristina, and Abram van Engen, eds, *A History of American Puritan Literature* (Cambridge: Cambridge University Press, 2020)

Brugmann, Birte, 'Migration and Endogenous Change', in *The Oxford Handbook of Anglo-Saxon Archaeology*, ed. by Helena Hamerow, David A. Hinton, and Sally Crawford (Oxford: Oxford University Press, 2011), pp. 30–45

Coumert, Magali, 'Gildas', in *Medieval Historical Writing: Britain and Ireland, 500–1500*, ed. by Jennifer Jahner, Emily Steiner, and Elizabeth M. Tyler (Cambridge: Cambridge University Press, 2019), pp. 19–34

Crick, J. C., '[Review of Nicholas Howe, *Migration and Mythmaking in Anglo-Saxon England*]', *English Historical Review*, 108 (1993), 694–95

Cronan, Dennis, '*Beowulf* and the Containment of Scyld in the West Saxon Royal Genealogy', in *The Dating of Beowulf: A Reassessment*, ed. by Leonard Neidorf (Cambridge: D. S. Brewer, 2014), pp. 112–37

Davies, Joshua, 'Hengist and Horsa at Monticello: Human and Nonhuman Migration, Parahistory and American Anglo-Saxonism', in *American/Medieval Goes North: Earth and Water in Transit*, ed. by Gillian R. Overing and Ulrike Wiethaus (Göttingen: V & R Unipress, 2019), pp. 167–88

Delbanco, Andrew, *The Puritan Ordeal* (Cambridge, MA: Harvard University Press, 1989)

Estes, Heide, 'Abraham and the Northmen in *Genesis A*: Alfredian Translations and Ninth-Century Politics', *Medievalia et Humanistica*, 33 (2007), 1–13

——, *Anglo-Saxon Literary Landscapes: Ecotheory and the Environmental Imagination* (Amsterdam: Amsterdam University Press, 2017)

Fitzgerald, Jill, *Rebel Angels: Space and Sovereignty in Anglo-Saxon England* (Manchester: Manchester University Press, 2019)

Foot, Sarah, 'Where English Becomes British: Rethinking Contexts for Brunanburh', in *Myth, Rulership, Church and Charters: Essays in Honour of Nicholas Brooks*, ed. by Julia Barrow and Andrew Wareham (Aldershot: Ashgate, 2008), pp. 127–44

Frank, Roberta, 'The *Beowulf* Poet's Sense of History', in *The Wisdom of Poetry: Essays in Early English Literature in Honour of Morton W. Bloomfield*, ed. by Larry D. Benson and Siegfried Wenzel (Kalamazoo: Medieval Institute Publications, 1982), pp. 53–65

Fulk, R. D., *A History of Old English Meter* (Philadelphia: University of Pennsylvania Press, 1992)

Harris, Stephen J., *Race and Ethnicity in Anglo-Saxon Literature* (New York: Routledge, 2003)

Hiatt, Alfred, '*Beowulf* Off the Map', *ASE*, 38 (2009), 11–40

Higham, N. J., *The English Conquest: Gildas and Britain in the Fifth Century* (Manchester: Manchester University Press, 1994)

Hills, Catherine, 'Overview: Anglo-Saxon Identity', in *The Oxford Handbook of Anglo-Saxon Archaeology*, ed. by Helena Hamerow, David A. Hinton, and Sally Crawford (Oxford: Oxford University Press, 2011), pp. 3–12

Howe, Nicholas, *Migration and Mythmaking in Anglo-Saxon England*, paperback edn (Notre Dame: University of Notre Dame Press, 2001)

———, *Writing the Map of Anglo-Saxon England: Essays in Cultural Geography* (New Haven, CT: Yale University Press, 2008)

Hullihen, Walter, *Antequam and Priusquam with Special Reference to the Historical Development of their Subjunctive Usage* (Baltimore: The Lord Baltimore Press, 1903)

Jacobs, Nicolas, '[Review of Nicholas Howe, *Migration and Mythmaking in Anglo-Saxon England*]', *N&Q*, 37 (1990), 452–53

Karkov, Catherine E., *Imagining Anglo-Saxon England: Utopia, Heterotopia, Dystopia* (Woodbridge: Boydell, 2020)

Keynes, Simon, 'Adventus Saxonum', in *The Wiley Blackwell Encyclopedia of Anglo-Saxon England*, 2nd edn, ed. by Michael Lapidge and others (Chichester: John Wiley & Sons, 2014), p. 6

Kleinschmidt, Harald, 'What Does the "Anglo-Saxon Chronicle" Tell Us about "Ethnic" Origins?', *Studi Medievali*, 3rd Ser., 42 (2001), 1–40

Konshuh, Courtnay, 'Constructing Early Anglo-Saxon Identity in the *Anglo-Saxon Chronicles*', in *The Land of the English Kin: Studies in Wessex and Anglo-Saxon England in Honour of Professor Barbara Yorke*, ed. by Alexander James Langlands and Ryan Lavelle, Brill's Series on the Early Middle Ages, 26 (Leiden: Brill, 2020), pp. 154–79

Leneghan, Francis, *The Dynastic Drama of 'Beowulf'*, Anglo-Saxon Studies, 39 (Cambridge: D. S. Brewer, 2020)

Liuzza, R. M., 'The Tower of Babel: *The Wanderer* and the Ruins of History', *Studies in the Literary Imagination*, 36 (2003), 1–35

Lucas, Peter J., 'Loyalty and Obedience in the Old English *Genesis* and the Interpolation of *Genesis B* into *Genesis A*', *Neophilologus*, 76 (1992), 121–35

Major, Tristan, *Undoing Babel: The Tower of Babel in Anglo-Saxon Literature* (Toronto: University of Toronto Press, 2018)

Merrills, A. H., *History and Geography in Late Antiquity* (Cambridge: Cambridge University Press, 2005)

Michelet, Fabienne L., *Creation, Migration, and Conquest: Imaginary Geography and Sense of Space in Old English Literature* (Oxford: Oxford University Press, 2006)

———, 'Lost at Sea: Nautical Travels in the Old English *Exodus*, the Old English *Andreas*, and Accounts of the *adventus Saxonum*', in *The Sea and Englishness in the Middle Ages: Maritime Narratives, Identity, and Culture*, ed. by Sebastian I. Sobecki (Cambridge: D. S. Brewer, 2011), pp. 59–79

Miller, Perry, *Errand into the Wilderness* (Cambridge, MA: Belknap Press of Harvard University Press, 1956)

Mirsky, Aaron, 'On the Sources of the Anglo-Saxon *Genesis* and *Exodus*', *ES*, 48 (1967), 385–97

Mitchell, Bruce, *Old English Syntax*, 2 vols (Oxford: Oxford University Press, 1985)

Mize, Britt, *Traditional Subjectivities: The Old English Poetics of Mentality* (Toronto: University of Toronto Press, 2013)

Molyneaux, George, 'Did the English Really Think They Were God's Elect in the Anglo-Saxon Period?', *Journal of Ecclesiastical History*, 65 (2014), 721–37

——, 'The *Old English Bede*: English Ideology or Christian Instruction?', *English Historical Review*, 124 (2009), 1289–1323

Olsen, Karin, '"Him þæs grim lean becom": The Theme of Infertility in *Genesis A*', in *Verbal Encounters: Anglo-Saxon and Old Norse Studies for Roberta Frank*, ed. by Antonina Harbus and Russell Poole (Toronto: University of Toronto Press, 2005), pp. 127–43

Oosthuizen, Susan, *The Emergence of the English* (Leeds: ARC Humanities Press, 2019)

Perkins, Nicholas, 'Biblical Allusion and Prophetic Authority in Gildas's *De excidio Britanniae*', *Journal of Medieval Latin*, 20 (2010), 78–112

Portnoy, Phyllis, *The Remnant: Essays on a Theme in Old English Verse* (London: Runetree Press, 2005)

Remley, Paul G., 'The Latin Textual Basis of *Genesis A*', *ASE*, 17 (1988), 163–89

——, *Old English Biblical Verse: Studies in Genesis, Exodus, and Daniel*, Cambridge Studies in Anglo-Saxon England, 16 (Cambridge: Cambridge University Press, 1996)

Reynolds, Susan, 'Medieval *Origines Gentium* and the Community of the Realm', *History*, 68 (1983), 375–90

Russom, Geoffrey, '[Review of Nicholas Howe, *Migration and Mythmaking in Anglo-Saxon England*]', *Speculum*, 66 (1991), 893–95

Scheil, Andrew P., *The Footsteps of Israel: Understanding Jews in Anglo-Saxon England* (Ann Arbor: University of Michigan Press, 2004)

Schoening, Kari M., '[Review of Nicholas Howe, *Migration and Mythmaking in Anglo-Saxon England*]', *Comitatus*, 21 (1990), 128–32

Scragg, Donald, 'A Reading of *Brunanburh*', in *Unlocking the Wordhord: Anglo-Saxon Studies in Memory of Edward B. Irving, Jr.*, ed. by Mark C. Amodio and Katherine O'Brien O'Keeffe (Toronto: University of Toronto Press, 2003), pp. 109–22

Sievers, E., 'Zum Beowulf', *Beiträge zur Geschichte der deutschen Sprache und Literatur*, 29 (1904), 305–31

Sims-Williams, Patrick, 'Gildas and the Anglo-Saxons', *Cambridge Medieval Celtic Studies*, 6 (1983), 1–30

——, 'The Settlement of England in Bede and the *Chronicle*', *ASE*, 12 (1983), 1–41

Smith, Scott Thompson, 'Faith and Forfeiture in the Old English *Genesis A*', *Modern Philology*, 111 (2014), 593–615

Stacey, Robin Chapman, '[Review of Nicholas Howe, *Migration and Mythmaking in Anglo-Saxon England*]', *Journal of British Studies*, 30 (1991), 90–92

Stanley, E. G., 'Old English *Ær* Conjunction: "rather than"', *N&Q*, 39 (1992), 11–13

Stévanovitch, Colette, 'Envelope Patterns in *Genesis A and B*', *Neophilologus*, 80 (1996), 465–78

Traister, Bryce, ed., *American Literature and the New Puritan Studies* (Cambridge: Cambridge University Press, 2017)

——, 'Introduction: The New Puritan Studies', in *American Literature and the New Puritan Studies*, ed. by Bryce Traister (Cambridge: Cambridge University Press, 2017), pp. 1–20

Trilling, Renée R., *The Aesthetics of Nostalgia: Historical Representation in Old English Verse* (Toronto: University of Toronto Press, 2009)

Van Engen, Abram, 'Prologue: Pilgrims, Puritans, and the Origins of America', in *A History of American Puritan Literature*, ed. by Kristina Bross and Abram van Engen (Cambridge: Cambridge University Press, 2020), pp. 17–34

White, Donald A., 'Changing Views of the *Adventus Saxonum* in Nineteenth and Twentieth Century English Scholarship', *Journal of the History of Ideas*, 32 (1971), 585–94

Wormald, Patrick, '*Engla Lond*: The Making of an Allegiance', *Journal of Historical Sociology*, 7 (1994), 1–24

——, 'The Venerable Bede and the "Church of the English"', in *The English Religious Tradition and the Genius of Anglicanism*, ed. by Geoffrey Rowell (Wantage: Ikon, 1992), pp. 13–32

Wright, Charles D., '*Genesis A* ad litteram', in *Old English Literature and the Old Testament*, ed. by Michael Fox and Manish Sharma (Toronto: University of Toronto Press, 2012), pp. 121–71

Yorke, Barbara, 'Anglo-Saxon Origin Legends', in *Myth, Rulership, Church, and Charters: Essays in Honour of Nicholas Brooks*, ed. by Julia Barrow and Andrew Wareham (Aldershot: Ashgate, 2008), pp. 15–29

Zacher, Samantha, *Rewriting the Old Testament in Anglo-Saxon Verse: Becoming the Chosen People* (London: Bloomsbury Academic, 2013)

Zollinger, Cynthia Wittman, 'Cynewulf's *Elene* and the Patterns of the Past', *JEGP*, 103 (2004), 180–96

BRITTON ELLIOTT BROOKS

The Sound-World of Early Medieval England:
A Case Study of the Exeter Book Storm Riddle

Ideas of the world, whether medieval or modern, are complex, fluctuating, sometimes contradictory, and continually evolving, as the various chapters in this volume highlight. Such perceptions of the world are, in great part, reliant upon the embodied experience of the physical world, which is in turn reliant upon, and transformed by, those very perceptions. This chapter will examine the ways early medieval English peoples engaged with and represented one aspect of the world in their literary productions: the sound-world of inanimate forces.[1] Shane Butler defines this sonic category as 'geophony', the 'sound of the earth and its elements', which is part of the broader 'phonosphere' that also includes 'anthrophony' (sounds created by humans) and 'biophony' (sounds created by living organisms).[2] The use of geophony to create literary soundscapes relies on the interdependent relationship between embodied perception of sound stimuli and the contextual understanding of those stimuli.[3] This chapter will suggest that such geophonic soundscapes are

---

1 Following current developments in the field, I am employing the phrase 'early medieval English' to denote the various peoples more traditionally referred to as the 'Anglo-Saxons'. I will also be employing the phrase 'early medieval English literature' to refer to literature composed by the early medieval English, whether in Old English or Anglo-Latin. See, for example, the recent special issue of *postmedieval*, 11 (2020) on race, esp. Rambaran-Olm, Leake, and Goodrich, 'Medieval Studies', and Lomuto, 'Becoming Postmedieval'; see also Niles, *The Idea of Anglo-Saxon England*; Jones, *Fossil Poetry*; and Ellard, *Anglo-Saxon(ist) Pasts, postSaxon Futures*.

2 Butler, 'Principles of Sound Reading', pp. 236 and 240. It should be noted that Butler is employing these terms to analyse Virgilian poetry in terms of its multitude of sonorous effects, including not just the poetic 'virtuosity in daring acts of sensory mimeses', but also the ways in which the specific lines are 'not just representing but making sound' through classical rhetorical and literary devices such as homoeoteleuton and polysyndeton. Butler's sonic categories include not just the descriptive ones listed above, but also orality, vocality, musicality, theophony, sublimity, and logophony (p. 236).

3 The concept of 'soundscape', though coined by Schafer, can be best understood in its application here through Thompson's definition in *The Soundscape of Modernity*, that it 'is simultaneously a physical environment and a way of perceiving that environment' (p. 1).

Britton Elliott Brooks (brooks@flc.kyushu-u.ac.jp) is Assistant Professor of English at Kyushu University, Japan.

Ideas of the World in Early Medieval English Literature, ed. by Mark Atherton, Kazutomo Karasawa, and Francis Leneghan, SOEL 1 (Turnhout: Brepols, 2022)   pp. 203–222
BREPOLS ❦ PUBLISHERS   DOI 10.1484/M.SOEL.5.130562

utilized widely in the Old English corpus, in both poetry and prose. The extent to which Old English poets employed sound effects in the creation of soundscapes, however, is not without debate. Eric Stanley, for example, has argued against the presence of onomatopoeia in Old English verse, on the grounds that that the aural context of Old English poetry is irrecoverable.[4] In recent years, however, scholars have sought to demonstrate the important role of sonic materials, including onomatopoeia, in early medieval English literature, and it is in this trajectory that the present chapter will travel.[5] By examining the sonic mingling of water and wind in the Exeter Book Riddle 1, it will demonstrate that one of the primary uses of specifically geophonic literary soundscapes is to inspire awe at the expanse and strength of the elemental world, and in so doing, to encourage reflection upon the extraordinary strength of God to shape and restrain it.[6] In this riddle, geophonic sounds are paramount, from the crashing of wind-driven waves upon each other, to the ear-shattering din of thunder. Andy Orchard calls the riddle 'an extraordinary piece of storm-poetry' and notes numerous parallels with one of the only other lengthy treatments of storm in early medieval English literature: Aldhelm's *Carmen rhythmicum* (*CR*).[7] These parallels include depictions of lightning, waves crashing on the shore, as well as the poem's connection of the storm's power to the 'unknowable power of God'.[8] As I will

---

See also Schafer, *The Soundscape*. For a related discussion of this interdependent relationship between the physical world and ideas about that world, see Twomey and Anlezark, 'Introduction: Worlds of Water', esp. pp. 13–17.

4 See Stanley, *In the Foreground*, pp. 138–41.

5 See Stanton, 'Sound, Voice, and Articulation', pp. 93–94, who argues for onomatopoeia in several riddles, including Riddle 1, and Stanton, 'Bark Like a Man', esp. p. 99, for onomatopoeia more generally in relation to Old English literature and Aldhelm's *voces animatum* tradition. See also Warren, *Birds in Medieval English Poetry*, esp. p. 41, who discusses the onomastic practice of bird names stemming from their individual calls or songs, and Nelson, 'The Rhetoric of the Exeter Book Riddles', for a discussion of rhetorical techniques, including onomatopoeia, in the Riddles.

6 The numbering of the first riddle of the Exeter Book remains a subject of scholarly debate, with numerous editors dividing it into three separate poems, 1 (ll. 1–15), 2 (ll. 16–30), and 3 (ll. 31–104), and others presenting it as a single unified poem (with three linked sections). Williamson in his edition, *The Old English Riddles of the Exeter Book*, pp. 130–33, argues that it is a single poem based on a variety of reasons including the possibility of 'wind' as the solution for all three sections, given that all the events described in the riddle(s) can be caused by wind within the framework of medieval meteorology. Muir in his edition, *The Exeter Anthology of Old English Poetry*, pp. 576–77, though acknowledging Williamson and others, retains the more common division of three separate poems, while also highlighting that paleographically the text is presented as two poems rather than one or three. This chapter will follow Orchard's recent edition, *The Old English and Anglo-Latin Riddle Tradition*, which, like Williamson, presents it as a single riddle. All references to the Exeter Book Riddles are from Orchard's edition, in consultation with Williamson and Muir, and will follow Orchard's numbering.

7 Orchard, *A Commentary on the Old English and Anglo-Latin Riddle Tradition*, p. 330.

8 Orchard, *A Commentary on the Old English and Anglo-Latin Riddle Tradition*, p. 330.

THE SOUND-WORLD OF EARLY MEDIEVAL ENGLAND 205

discuss below, Riddle 1 is much more focused on geophonic description than Aldhelm's poem, employing soundscapes to evoke a sense of religious awe at the power of God.[9] This evocation of awe relies on embodied physicality, on the reality of sonic experience, as is most evident in the riddle's use of geophonic events such as thunder. The intensity of this type of sonic event is power made manifest, with soundwaves felt as much as they are heard, as the low-frequency sound produced can penetrate the body and resonate within it.[10] Such an elemental multimodal experience functions within the aural cultural soundscape of early medieval English literature as a reminder of the only being who is able to create and control such forces: God.[11]

Geophonic Soundscapes in Exeter Book Riddle 1

One of clearest uses of geophonic soundscapes in early medieval English literature is their employment to give form, depth, and weight to the elemental world. Wind, water, fire, earth are each vast categories, to a great degree beyond the scope of single human comprehension, and generally considered beyond human control by the medieval world. As James Paz recently noted in relation to Old English literature, such a concept is helpfully understood through Timothy Morton's notion of 'hyperobjects', which, as Paz defines them, 'challenge assumptions of human mastery and our powers of cognition [...] as hyperobjects cannot quite be grasped — either physically or intellectually'.[12] Aqueous soundscapes in early medieval English literature, for example, are sometimes used to describe the wild, untameable nature of water; how its

---

9 While Aldhelm's *CR* does include a substantial range of sonic description, the majority of the poem focuses on visual description. See, for example, ll. 29, 39, and 142–44 for aural depictions, and compare with ll. 54–105 in which the storm is primarily described for its obscuring qualities, and which is almost entirely visual in nature. All references to the text, including quotations and translations, are from Howlett, 'Aldhelmi Carmen Rhythmicum', and will be cited by line number following Howlett's edition.

10 Reybrouck, Podlipniak, and Welch, 'Music and Noise', p. 4, note that thunder's most audible frequency, between 40 and 100 Hz, is a range which has been shown to 'excite vibrations in the human body, particularly the chest region, which resonates in the range of 50–80 Hz'. See also Abegunawardana and others, 'Frequency Analysis of Thunder Features', p. 3, with reference to what they term the 'peal' of thunder: 'More than 80% of recorded frequencies are scattered around the frequencies between 40 to 100 Hz with accordance to the sample considered'; as well as Yuhua and Ping, 'Audible Thunder Characteristics', pp. 215–16, who note that while higher frequencies (~400 Hz) are heavily attenuated by distance (here they give a range of 5 km), humidity, and temperature, the attenuation of lower frequency sonic productions of thunder (in the 50–100 Hz range) by such factors is negligible. The audible portion of thunder, therefore, is most evident in the lower frequencies for the majority of human listeners.

11 See Novák, 'Sound in Literary Texts', p. 155, for a theoretical approach to the process of encoding intended sonic meaning in literary texts.

12 Paz, 'Mind, Mood, and Meteorology', p. 194.

fluidity, power, and in the case of the ocean, expanse, render human muscle and mind impotent.[13] A medieval hyperobject.[14] Such a presentation is tied to medieval theology, in which God is understood as the only one who can contain, bound, and direct the sheer elemental potency of the physical world, the only one who is able to take the chaos of pre-creation and shape Creation into being. As Jennifer Neville and other scholars have noted, the early medieval English conceived of God's creation of the universe primarily, though not universally, as an act of ordering, of structuring, of limiting and shaping, rather than creation *ex nihilo*.[15] In *Genesis A*, for example, the Creation narrative is retold with a clear emphasis on God setting the limits and boundaries of the oceans:

> Flod wæs *adæled*
> under heah-rodore   *halgum mihtum*,
> wæter of wætrum,   þam þe wuniað gyt
> under fæstenne   folca hrofes.
> [...]
> Frea engla *heht*
> *þurh his word* wesan   *wæter gemæne*,
> þa nu under roderum   *heora ryne healdað*,
> stowe *gestefnde*.   Ða stode hraðe
> holm under heofonum   *swa se halga bebead*,
> sid ætsomne,   ða *gesundrod* wæs
> lago wið lande.   (ll. 150b–153; 157b–163a).

(The flood was *divided* under the high sky *by holy powers*, water from waters, for those who still dwell under the firmament of the people's roof. [...] *By his word* the Lord of angels *commanded* the *waters to be gathered*, which now *hold their course* under the heavens, *fixed* in their place. Then the

---

13   For a recent discussion of the role of water, particularly the water in the ocean, in relation to human life, see Twomey and Anlezark, eds, *Meanings of Water*.

14   Michelet, 'Lost at Sea', p. 76, highlights this feature with relation to ll. 190–98a of the Old English poem *Andreas*: 'The contrast set up between Andrew's repeated claims to ignorance and the angel's mastery of the sea emphasises that the sea is a divine or angelic privilege quite out of reach for human beings. For Andrew, the sea is a vast and unmapped expanse which escapes his control'. The emphasis of the ocean's expanse and inexorable nature for humanity is also expressed in the miracles of medieval saints who, echoing Jesus's calming of the storm in the synoptic Gospels (Matt 8. 23–27, Mark 4. 35–40, and Luke 8. 22–25), reveal that God alone can calm the sea at storm (Michelet notes the connection between the passage in *Andreas* and Jesus's miracle). See, for example, the miracle of St Aidan calming an ocean at storm in Bede's *Vita metrica S. Cudbercti*, ll. 145–63. This humbling function of the ocean remained fairly consistent in the medieval period. For example, Clarke, 'Edges and Otherworlds', p. 82, argues that the depiction of King Cnut's attempt to command the sea in Henry of Huntingdon's *Historia Anglorum* 'calls attention to the limits of earthly laws when measured against the inexorable workings of nature and the ultimate power of God'.

15   Neville, *Representations of the Natural World in Old English Poetry*, pp. 61 and 140 n. 4.

THE SOUND-WORLD OF EARLY MEDIEVAL ENGLAND 207

ocean quickly stood, wide and united under the heavens *as the holy one commanded*, when the sea was *divided* from the land.)[16]

Bede likewise emphasizes the ordering nature of God's creative acts in his *In Genesim*: 'factam caeli aquarumque creationem ac dispositionem *non excessisse praescriptos sibi in uerbo Dei terminus*' (when the creation and arrangement of heaven and the waters were done, *they did not go beyond the boundary prescribed for them in the Word of God*).[17] Drawing from this theological conception of God as sole shaper of the elemental world, early medieval English literature utilizes geophonic soundscapes to reveal the magnitude of humanity's smallness before the vastness of Creation, and by contrast, God's strength.

Riddle 1 depicts its meteorological subject as a kind of medieval hyperobject, utilizing geophonic description of the elements to inspire awe in the audience, thereby leading them to reflecting on God.[18] The first five lines of Riddle 1 are a microcosm of this process, as well as representative of the remainder of the poem:

Hwylc is hæleþa þæs horsc   ond þæs hyge-cræftig
þæt þæt mæge asecgan   *hwa mec on sið wræce*
þonne ic astige strong,   stundum reþe,
þrym-ful þunie,   þragum wræcca
fere geond foldan.   (ll. 1–5a).

(What man is so brisk and so crafty in mind that he can tell *who drives me on my way* when I rise up strong, angry at times, *thunder full of power*, occasionally as an exile pass over the land.)

---

16 Text and translation from *Old Testament Narratives*, ed. and trans. by Anlezark. All translations of Latin and Old English, unless otherwise noted, are my own, and italics are added throughout for emphasis.

17 Bede, *In Genesim*, p. 11. See also a similar emphasis in *The Old English Boethius*, ed. and trans. by Godden and Irvine, *Metre II*, ll. 64–70, I, p. 431: 'Hæfð se ilca God eorðan and wætere | mearce gesette. Merestream ne dear | ofer eorðan sceat eard gebrædan | fisca cynne butan frean leafe, | ne hio æfre ne mot eorðan þryscwold | up ofersteppan, ne ða ebban þon ma | flodes mearce oferfaran moton' (The same God has established boundaries for land and water. The sea does not dare to spread its home for the species of fish over the earth's surface without the Lord's permission, nor may it ever step up over the earth's threshold, nor moreover may the tides cross the water's boundary) (II, p. 128).

18 Dale similarly notes how the poem is 'an engagement with the notion that humans cannot control or know everything about the created world', which she connects to the Book of Job. See Dale, *The Natural World*, p. 182. It should be noted, however, that Dale treats these as three separate riddles, rather than one, though she nonetheless connects them in her analysis. It should also be noted that the poem is clearly drawing from classical and medieval conceptions of meteorology. For a discussion of such influences, see Paz, 'Mind, Mood, and Meteorology', p. 195, who notes Pliny the Elder's *Historia naturalis* with reference to medieval cosmological understanding of storms, as well as Williamson's edition, *The Old English Riddles of the Exeter Book*, pp. 130–33, who gives numerous examples of meteorological texts, including Pliny's *Historia naturalis*, Lucretius's *De rerum natura*, Isidore's *De natura rerum*, and Bede's *De natura rerum*. See also Lapidge, 'Stoic Cosmology'.

The riddle object, given voice here, focuses not primarily on the question of its identity, but instead on the identity of the one who is able to direct it, on who ('hwa') is able to drive or press ('wræce') the riddle object on its way in line 2b. As Orchard notes, the riddle includes 'eight separate explicit challenges [...] which combine in a clearly patterned fashion to ask both the nature of the creature in question and the identity of the individual who controls it by alternately unleashing and confining it'.[19] Of these eight questions, only two ask about the identity of the riddle object, while the rest are focused on the question of who could control such an object: 'who unleashes?' (ll. 2b–6a, ll. 12b–14, and l. 103); 'who confines?' (l. 14b, l. 65b, and l. 104); 'what?' (l. 15 and l. 102b).[20] Lines 3–5a highlight the riddle object's power and, importantly, present this power primarily in terms of concrete phenomenal experience via sound, as depicted in line 4a, 'þrymful þunie' (thunder full of power).[21] The sonic verb employed here, *þunian*, has two distinct denotations, one visual and the other aural, though both intend an action that is meant to be easily perceived: 'to stand out, be prominent, be lifted up, stick up; to make a noise, to sound, resound, creak'.[22] While it should be noted that the verb's visual meaning is more common in Old English, it is employed sonically several times, including in an evocative line from *Beowulf* whose cause is likewise geophonic:

> Þa wæs be mæste   merehrægla sum,
> segl sale fæst;   *sundwudu þunede;*
> no þær wegflotan   wind ofer yðum
> siðes getwæfde.   (ll. 1905–08a)

> (The sail by the mast was rigged fast with ropes, a great sea-cloth; *the timbers resounded*, the wind over the sea did not hinder at all the wave-floater on its way.)[23]

---

19 Orchard, *A Commentary on the Old English and Anglo-Latin Riddle Tradition*, p. 330.

20 List summarized from Orchard, *A Commentary on the Old English and Anglo-Latin Riddle Tradition*, p. 330. Orchard notes that despite how the three sections (or three poems) are 'marked off as divisions within the manuscript in rather different ways [they all] focus on different aspects of a much larger issue: in a Christian context, the repeated question *hwa* ("who") that runs through all three sections' (pp. 328–29). He suggests that the answer can be God, but could also be Thor. It is this repetition which leads Orchard to categorize the riddle as a single text rather than three: 'Note the repeated *hwa*, found also at EXE 1.14b, 1.28a, 1.65b, 1.103a, and 1.104a, so binding the text together' (p. 335).

21 Orchard, *A Commentary on the Old English and Anglo-Latin Riddle Tradition*, p. 335 calls attention here to the 'string of finite verbs in successive a-lines' from ll. 3a–6a with '*stige* ... *þunie* ... *fere* ... [and] *reafige*' that all emphasize 'movement and power'.

22 *BT*, s.v. þunian 1 and 2. Note that Clark Hall, *A Concise Anglo-Saxon Dictionary*, gives 'to stand out, be prominent: be proud: roar, thunder, crash, groan'.

23 Text from *Klaeber's Beowulf*, ed. by Fulk, Bjork, and Niles; translation adapted from *Beowulf*, ed. and trans. by Liuzza. All references to *Beowulf* are from *Klaeber's Beowulf*, and all translations are adapted from Liuzza. The term also occurs as a gloss to Latin *tonare* (to thunder, resound) in a description of God producing such a sound in the Canticles of the

The vibrational resounding of the ship's beams, drenched and buffeted by gusts, mingles wind, water, and wood for aural effect. In sonic instances like this, the verb *þunian* is cognate with various words related to thunder (most of which alliterate with *þunian*), including the nouns *þunor* (thunder), the verb *þunrian* (to thunder), and the adjective *þunorlic* (thunderous, of thunder),[24] and it is this meteorological geophonic production that is intended in Riddle 1. While the visual imagery is highly non-specific, how the unknown riddle object 'rises up' and acts in some fashion described as 'angry', the alliterative phrase 'þrymful þunie' (thunder full of power), with its resonance of cognate aurality, produces a much more specific effect. It is a loud, powerful geophonic blast, one whose literary sounding relies on embodied experience of thunder, and whose sonic potency is meant to call attention to its inexorable nature for the hearing human audience. The depiction, as suggested above, is meant to direct attention to God, the only one powerful enough to control such forces.

The second section of Riddle 1 begins with the following:

> Hwilum ic gewite   (swa ne wenaþ men),
> under *yþa geþræc*   eorþan secan,
> gar-secges grund.   (ll. 16–18a)

> (Sometimes I travel (unexpectedly to men) beneath *the thrash of waves*, seeking the ground, the bottom of the deep.)

While this description is not focused on sonic information, the use of the noun *geþræc*, again with alliterative stress on 'þ', and meaning 'press, crowd, crush, tumult', or as Orchard translates, 'thrash', includes in its visual depiction an aural element.[25] This term focuses on bringing together into extreme proximity several objects, whose clash implies the creation of sonic information, as can be seen in *Elene*, line 114: 'Þær wæs borda *gebrec* ond beorna *geþræc*' (There was

---

Arundel Psalter, London, British Library, MS Arundel 60: 'Drihten strangiaþ wiþerwinnan his & ofer him on heofonum hi þuniaþ drihten demeþ endas eorþan & he silþ onweald kininge his & he gemærsaþ horn kininges his; *Dominum formidabunt aduersarii eius et super ipsos in caelis tonabit dominus iudicabit fines terre et dabit imperium regi suo et sublimabit cornu christi su*'. The text for the Arundel Psalter is from the *DOE*, which transcribes *Der altenglische Arundel-Psalter*, ed. by Oess.

24   For visual uses of *þunian*, see, for example, *Exodus*, ed. by Lucas, l. 160 'þufas þunian' (banners *unfurled*); Riddle 43, l. 2a, 'þindan ond þunian' (swelling and *surging*); and Psalm 54. 9 from the Old English *Metrical Psalms*: 'Þunie him gewinnes wearn ofer wealles hrof' (May a heap of trouble be *lifted up* over the rampart's summit), text and trans. from *Old English Psalms*, ed. and trans. by O'Neill. There is a potential for polysemous riddling here as the emphasis on thunder connects to the etymologically linked name of Þórr (Thor), the Norse god associated with thunder. See Orchard, *A Commentary on the Old English and Anglo-Latin Riddle Tradition*, p. 329. It should also be noted that God is referred to as the 'Thunderer' (*tonans*) several times in Anglo-Latin texts, including Bede's *Vita metrica S. Cudbercti*, l. 248 'Inque dies meritis crescenti summa tonantis', and in Aldhelm's *CR*, l. 190, 'Trini Tonantis famina'.

25   *BT*, *geþræc* 1.

the *crash* of shields and *tumult* of men). Here 'geþræc' in the b-line is collocated with the noun 'gebrec' in the a-line, with the collocation further emphasized through internal half-rhyme. The first term, *gebrec*, a sound noun meaning primarily 'a loud noise or crashing sound', is being employed to describe the sonic event of shields smashing together, and the second term, *geþræc*, is being used to describe an aurally similar event with the soldiers crashing together in battle.[26] This dual aural/visual potential for the term is also evident in lines 822–24 of *Andreas*, where it is applied to create a multimodal experience of the sea, as well as in line 7 of Riddle 20, in relation to waves:[27]

Andreas:

Þa gelædan het   lifes brytta
ofer *yþa geþræc*   englas sine,
fæðmum ferigean   on fæder wære.

(Then did the Giver of Life bid His angels convey over *the jostling of the waves*, ferry in their embrace into Father's covenant.)

Riddle 20:

atol *yþa geþræc*,   ofras hea,
streamas stronge.

(the dread *thrash of the waves*, steep shores, strong streams.)

The aural/visual noun *geþræc* is being used similarly in Riddle 1, with the waves crashing against one another, the image carrying with it sonic information.

Riddle 1's aqueous aurality continues in lines 20–21a, with three sound terms emphasized poetically by internal rhyme in line 20, and end rhyme in line 21a: 'hwæl-mere *hlimmeð*, hlude *grimmeð*, | streamas staþu *beatað*' (the whale-sea (*resounds*), loudly *howls*, | tides *batter* cliffs).[28] The first sonic term, the verb *hlimman*, is relatively rare in the Old English corpus, occurring only six times and only in poetry.[29] According to the *DOE*, the verb is used in *Judith* and Riddle 35 with the general meaning of 'to sound, resound, make a sound', while in its use here, as well as in *Andreas* and *The Seafarer*, to mean 'of the sea:

---

26 The *DOE* lists two other similar uses of *gebrec*: *Beowulf*, l. 2259, 'ofer borda gebræc bite irena' (the bite of iron over the crack of boards), and the *Battle of Maldon*, l. 295a, 'Da wearð borda gebræc' (Then there was the crash of shields).

27 Orchard, *A Commentary on the Old English and Anglo-Latin Riddle Tradition*, p. 337, calls attention to these comparisons.

28 Orchard's edition translates the verb *hlimman* here as 'growls', suggesting a semi-bestial sonic action, which he doubles with his translation of *grimman* as 'howl'. While I have maintained 'howl', with its potential for inanimate description, I have rendered *hlimman* with the less bestial 'resound' to suggest more clearly the geophonic nature of the sound. Orchard, *A Commentary on the Old English and Anglo-Latin Riddle Tradition*, p. 337, notes the unusual rhyme here between 'hlimmeð' and 'grimmeð', and suggests potential parallels to *Andreas*, l. 370a 'onhræred, hwælmere' and l. 392b 'Garsecg hlymmeð'. All references to *Andreas* are from *Andreas*, ed. by North and Bintley.

29 *DOE Corpus*.

THE SOUND-WORLD OF EARLY MEDIEVAL ENGLAND   211

to resound or roar'.[30] The strength of this tempestuous sea and the sounds it makes are doubled through the end rhyme of line 20b's 'hlude *grimmeð*', where the adjective *hlud* modifies the verb *grimman*. *Grimman* is also relatively rare, occurring only five times in the extant Old English corpus, but in each instance the verb is connected to notions of tumult, often directly describing the sonic information produced by such disturbance. In *Genesis B*, lines 792b–794a, for example, the poet expands the widely attested 'mouth of hell' motif beyond its primarily visual aspects to include the sonic accompaniment of a bestial mouth as doorway to hell:

> Gesyhst þu nu þa sweartan helle
> grædige and gifre.   Nu þu he *grimman* meaht
> heonane *gehyran*.

> (Do you now see the dark hell, greedy and gaping? Now you can *hear* it *roaring* from here.)[31]

The verb also occurs as a gloss to Latin *fremere* (to roar, resound, growl, murmur, rage, snort, howl) in the Blickling Psalter, Psalm 111. 10: 'dentibus suis *fremet*' (he will *gnash* with teeth). The familiar biblical notion of gnashing one's teeth expressed in the Old English *grimman*, therefore, carries with it an implicit sonic dimension.[32]

The sonic assault is not relegated to the wide ocean, but is also brought against the land itself with line 21a's 'streamas staþu *beata*' (tides *batter* cliffs). The verb *beatan*, while not specifically aural in meaning, carries with it sonic potential, as its range of denotations focuses on the act of one object striking another with great force, the completion of which nearly always creating sound waves.[33] The term appears, for example, in lines 23–24a of *The Seafarer* to describe the mingled elements of wind and water as storm beating cliffs, a sonic contribution figured as a vocalized conversation: 'Stormas þær stan-clifu *beotan* þær him stearn *oncwæð* | isig-feþera' (Storms *beat* the rocky cliffs where the icy-feathered tern | *answered* them);[34] it also appears in lines 1325–26 of

---

30 *DOE*, s.v. hlimman, 1. and 1b. respectively.

31 *Genesis B* text and trans. from *Old Testament Narratives*, ed. and trans. by Anlezark. All references to the text are from this edition.

32 The verb also occurs in the much-contested l. 306a of *Beowulf*, in which it potentially denotes the creating of a loud noise: 'guþmod *grummon*' (war-minded ones *clamoured*). This reading retains the form *grummon* from the MS, where *grummon* is taken as a preterite plural verb, though most editors emend this to *grimmon*, a dative plural, which instead yields a translation less aural: 'of the grim battle-minded ones'. See *Klaeber's Beowulf*, ed. by Fulk, Bjork, and Niles, pp. 136–37, for a discussion of this issue.

33 For the full range of definitions of *beatan*, see the *DOE*.

34 Text and trans. from *Old English Shorter Poems*, ed. and trans. by Bjork. All references to *The Seafarer* are from this edition. Shores, 'Sounds of Salvation', p. 116, likewise highlights the sonic role of the ocean in *The Seafarer*, noting how the 'echoing soundscape' here is 'almost claustrophobic', and that the 'materiality of the environment is crucial to the ways in which sensory experience creates emotional affect'.

the Old English poem *Genesis A* to describe the waves beating upon Noah's ark: 'symle bið þy heardra þa hit hreoh wæter, | swearte sæ-streamas swiðor *beatað*' (it always becomes harder when rough waters, dark streams, *beat* more vigorously against it). The primary role of sound in Riddle 1's depiction of waves here is highlighted when compared with a similar scene of waves crashing against the shore in Aldhelm's *Carmen rhythmicum*:[35]

Riddle 1:

hwæl-mere *hlimmeð*,   hlude *grimmeð*,
streamas staþu *beatað*.

(ll. 20–21a)

(the whale-sea (*resounds*),
loudly *howls*, tides *batter* cliffs.)

Carmen rhythmicum:

Sic turgescebat *trucibus;*
Pontus uentorum *flatibus;*
Inflegendo flaminibus;
Scopulosis marginibus.

(ll. 111–14)

(Thus did the sea swell with *harsh blowing* of winds, *dashing* with *blasts* against rocky shores.)

The two depictions are strikingly similar in their presentation of a stormy ocean, particularly in terms of the physical breaking of the sea upon stone, with Aldhelm's 'inflegendo' (dashing) carrying a potentially sonic meaning akin to Riddle 1's *beatan* (to beat). Yet the Old English text is focused primarily on sound, with each half-line emphasizing that element. It should also be noted that Aldhelm's lexical choice, *infligere* (from *infligo*), is rarely used in the medieval period with sonic meaning; instead it is most often employed with the sense of 'inflict'.[36] The three sonic terms in a row combine in Riddle 1, therefore, to produce the bone-vibrating roar of the ocean in storm. Such an interpretation is further justified by the use of the compound *hwælmere* in line 20a, a compound which occurs only twice in Old English, here and in *Andreas*, in which it is also used to describe a tempestuous sea.[37] The image

---

35 The comparison between scenes of waves crashing in these two poems was suggested by Orchard, though he compares Aldhelm's passage above with ll. 47–58a of Riddle 1, which I deal with below. He also does not discuss the comparison with relation to sonic terminology. See Orchard, *A Commentary on the Old English and Anglo-Latin Riddle Tradition*, pp. 331 and 339.

36 The *Dictionary of Medieval Latin from British Sources Online*, ed. by Latham, Howlett, and Ashdowne, gives only two uses of the form *infligere*: the first is the use by Aldhelm discussed above, and the second is from Goscelin's *Libellus contra inanes S. Mildrethae usurpatores*. The more common and non-sonic use of related *infligo* to mean something like 'inflict', however, has a number of attestations, including four uses in Bede's *HE* (1.22, 11.6, 11.9, and iv.16 [14]), as well as in the Old Testament, as seen in Leviticus 24. 20.

37 *Andreas*, ll. 368–70a: 'þæt hie þe eað mihton ofer yða geþring | drohtaþ adreogan þa gedrefed wearð, | onhræred, hwælmere' (that they might more easily over wave's throng | endure the life when disturbed it became, | when whale-deep was stirred). This comparison is suggested by Orchard, *A Commentary on the Old English and Anglo-Latin Riddle Tradition*, p. 337.

THE SOUND-WORLD OF EARLY MEDIEVAL ENGLAND   213

created in the riddle is one of extraordinary sonic wildness, a grandmother storm whose pressure bursting outward from wave upon wave of water punishes ear and body with its strength. It is an all-consuming type of aural event, eclipsing everything else as the primary sensory experience.

Geophonic information is employed in the text to highlight the power of the riddle object to create such noise with the ocean, with water driven by wind. But as both Corinne Dale and Orchard note, the text departs here from the usual riddle paradigm to ask not what the object is, but instead, who could possibly control the object:[38]

> Sund-helme ne mæg
> losian ær mec *læte*   se þe min *latteow* bið
> on siþa gehwam.
>
> Saga, þoncol mon,
> *hwa* mec *brægde*   of brimes fæþmum,
> þonne streamas eft   stille weorþað,
> yþa geþwære,   þe mec ær wrugon.   (ll. 25b–30)

> (My covering of liquid I cannot lose, before *he lets* me, *who is* my *leader* on every expedition. Say, learned man, *who draws* me from the wave's embrace, when the streams again grow still, the breakers calm, that concealed me before.)

The shift of the riddle formula that begins with the imperative verb *saga* refocuses the riddle not on the object itself, but instead on God. The poet's use of the phrase 'yþa geþwære' in line 30a draws a clear verbal parallel to the earlier 'yþa geþræc' in line 17a. It is God alone, the *lad-teow* (leader, guide, or a leader in war), who can lead the wind both to stir up the immensity of the ocean as experienced through its sonic actions ('yþa geþræc'), and also the one who can calm the wind and sea ('yþa geþwære'). That this calming is described with the adjective *geþwære* is important because it connects directly to the conception of God bringing about a harmonious and structured universe, with meanings including 'united', 'agreeing', 'mild', 'peaceful', but also 'harmonious', 'consonant', and 'concordant'.[39] The adjective glosses several words in Anglo-Latin texts related to notions of ordered harmony, of rightness, all with connection to God, including the adjectives *concors* (concordant, harmonious) and *consonus* (sounding in harmony), with the second term focused on aural unity. *Concors*, for example, is used by Aldhelm in his prose *De virginitate* to describe the harmonious nature of bees as a model for ideal monastic fellowship, and by Bede in his *In Genesim*, to describe the harmony

---

38 Dale highlights this shift and connects it to Job: 'This riddle does not end in the traditional way by asking what the subject is. Instead, we are asked to recognise God as the master of his subject, to recognise the powers of the Creator, just as Job says humbly to God, *scio quia omnis potes* "I know that thou canst do all things"' (*The Natural World*, p. 192).

39 *BT*, adj. *geþwære* 1.

of the prelapsarian world, while *consonus* is used by Bede in his *HE* to describe unity in song as Augustine settles with his comrades in Canterbury.[40]

In the third section of Riddle 1 geophonic information is utilized in a way that unites the theological vision of Creation outlined earlier with the meteorological understanding of the late antique and early medieval worlds. Here the riddle continues with a statement about the role of God as shaper and constrainer of the riddle object:

> Hwilum mec *min frea*   *fæste genearwað,*
> *sended* þonne   under sal-wonges
> bearm þone bradan,   ond on bid *wriceð,*
> *þrafað* on þystrum   þrymma sumne,
> *hæste on enge.*   (ll. 31–35a)

> (Sometimes *my lord tethers me tight, sends me* then beneath the lush land's broad bosom, and *forces me* to a standstill, *confines* in darkness a certain one of powers, with *harsh restraint*.)

The poem doubles up on this point just a few lines later:

>   Stille þynceð
> lyft ofer londe   ond lagu swige,
> oþþæt ic of enge   up aþringe,
> efne *swa mec wisaþ*   *se mec wræde on*
> æt frum-sceafte   furþum legde,
> *bende* ond *clomme,*   *þæt ic onbugan ne mot*
> *of þæs gewealde*   *þe me wegas tæcneð.*   (ll. 40b–46)

> (The sky seems still over the earth, and the sea is silent, until from constraint I catapult up, even as *he leads me who first laid on me shackles* from the very start, *bonds* and *bindings, so I might not budge from the power of him who guides my paths*.)

After further description of a stormy sea in lines 47–63a, the poem again emphasizes God's role, asking in line 65b 'Hwa gestilleð þæt?' (Who keeps that calm?). Immediately following this, the riddle constructs an extraordinary depiction of water being used to create a sonic event:

> Hwilum ic þurhræse   þæt me on bæce rideð,
> won *wæg-fatu,*   wide toþringe
> lagu-streama full,   hwilum læte eft
> slupan tosomne.   (ll. 66–69a)

---

40   For *concors*, see Aldhelm, *De virginitate*, p. 233, and Bede, *In Genesim*, pp. 29–30; for *consonus*, see Bede, *HE*, 1.25.

(Sometimes I rush through what rides on my back, dark *water vessels* [clouds], scatter wide the cup of liquid streams, sometimes allow them to slip back together again.)

The compound hapax 'wæg-fatu' is composed of the noun *wæg*, meaning 'waves or the sea' and *fæt*, a common term denoting essentially a container of some kind, whether closed or open, often for fluids, but also sometimes containers with specifically religious or ritual use.[41] The combination of the elements (water in motion + container) creates a striking depiction of a raincloud. Both terms are fairly widespread in Old English, and are often used as parts of compounds: for example, the noun *wæg* occurs in *Andreas*, line 923a, as *wæg-fær*, meaning 'sea-voyage', as well as *wæg-flota*, meaning 'wave-coaster, or ship', in both *Andreas*, line 487a, and *Elene*, line 246a, while *fæt* appears in the compounds *husel-fæt* (a sacrificial vessel, [Christian times] a sacramental vessel) and *ban-fæt* (the body, literally 'vessel of bones'), always in poetry.[42] The hapax *wæg-fæt* in Riddle 1 is relevant here not so much because of its prosaic parts, but because the image draws from early medieval understanding of meteorological events like clouds, rain, and thunder. As Bede highlights in his *De natura rerum*, drawing from traditions including Pliny and Pseudo-Isidore, clouds are made of tiny droplets of floating water, 'nubes coacto guttatim aere conglobantur' (Clouds are massed together into a ball drop by drop out of condensed air),[43] and rain occurs when those drops coalesce into larger ones.[44] For Bede, when these clouds collide with one another (as depicted also in Riddle 1) one of the most sonically intense geophonic events occurs — thunder:

---

41 *DOE*, '1. (open) vessel or container, mainly for fluids; 1.a. vessel made from specific materials; 1.b. vessel used for specific purposes; 1.b.i. vessel for ecclesiastical/religious use, etc. 2. (closed) vessel, receptacle or container'.

42 *Huselfæt* occurs, for example, twice in *Daniel*, ll. 704b and 748a; twice in the *Old English Version of Bede's Ecclesiastical History*, I. 16.88.32 and v. 18.466.14, hereafter, the *Old English Bede* (cited by paragraph no. following edn and line no. assigned by the *DOE*). *Banfæt* occurs five times in Old English, all in poetry: *Guthlac B*, ll. 1193 and 1265; *The Phoenix*, ll. 228b–29 and 519b–20a; and *Beowulf*, ll. 114–16a.

43 Bede, *De natura rerum*, XXXII, ed. by Jones and Lipp, p. 221; trans. from Bede, *On the Nature of Things*, trans. by Kendall and Wallis, p. 92.

44 Bede, *De natura rerum*, XXXIII, ed. by Jones and Lipp, pp. 221–22; trans. Bede, *On the Nature of Things*, trans. by Kendall and Wallis, p. 93: '*Imbres ex nubium concreti guttulis dum in maiores stillas coeunt, aeris amplius non ferente natura, nunc uento impellente nunc sole dissoluente, pluuialiter ad terras dilabuntur*' (*Rains are formed from the little drops of the clouds. As they coalesce into bigger drops, no longer supported by the nature of the air, sometimes driven by the wind, sometimes dissolved by the sun, they fall down in the form of rain to the earth*).

Tonitrua dicunt *ex fragore nubium generari*, cum et spiritus uentorum earum sinu concepti, sese ibidem uersando pererrantes et uirtutis suae mobilitate in quamlibet partem uiolenter erumpentes, magno concrepant murmure instar exilentium de stabulis quadrigarum, uel uesicae quae licet parua, magnum tamen sonitum displosa emittit.

> (They say *thunder is produced by the crash of clouds*, when gusts of winds conceived in their interior, stirring restlessly about in the same place and violently bursting out somewhere by the innate power of their mobility, resound with a great roar like four-horse teams bursting out from their stalls, or like a bladder which although small nevertheless emits a great noise when it bursts.)[45]

The image, then, of clouds as overflowing water-filled vessels whose clash produces thunder is both evocative as metaphor and supported by early medieval meteorology.

Riddle 1 employs this knowledge to produce one of the most striking depictions of thunder in medieval literature; a depiction saturated by sound, geophony employed to startling effect. This effect can once again be highlighted by comparison with Aldhelm's *Carmen rhythmicum*:[46]

> Riddle 1:
>
> Se bið *swega mæst*,
> *breahtma* ofer burgum,   ond *gebreca hludast*,
> þonne scearp cymeð   sceor wiþ oþrum,
> ecg wið ecge;   eorþan gesceafte,
> fus ofer folcum,   fyre swætað,
> blacan lige,   ond *gebrecu* ferað
> deorc ofer dreorgum   *gedyne micle*,
> farað feohtende,   feallan lætað
> sweart *swinsendu*   seaw of bosme,
> wætan of wombe.   (ll. 69b–78a)

> (That is the *mightiest of sounds, of clamouring* over townships, and the *loudest of collisions*, when one shower sharply connects with another, edge against edge; the murky creatures, striving forward over folk, stream with fire, bright flame, and *sounds of clashing* pass dark over the afflicted with *a mighty din*; they travel battling, they let fall dark moisture *roaring* from their bosom, juice from their belly.)

---

45 Bede, *De natura rerum*, xxviii, ed. by Jones and Lipp, p. 219; trans. Bede, *On the Nature of Things*, trans. by Kendall and Wallis, pp. 91.

46 Orchard, *A Commentary on the Old English and Anglo-Latin Riddle Tradition*, p. 331, briefly notes the parallel imagery of thunder and lightning in these two texts, but does not discuss their sonic components.

Aldhelm's *Carmen rhythmicum*:

Attamen *flagrant* fulmina
Late per caeli culmina
Quando pallentem pendula
Flammam *uomunt* fastigia
Quorum natura nubibus;
Procedit conlidentibus.   (ll. 93–98)

> (Nevertheless, lightning bolts *blaze* widely through the heights of heaven when their suspended jagged tips *belch* pallid flame, whose [i.e. lightning bolts] nature proceeds from colliding clouds.)

Riddle 1 depicts two water-filled vessels crashing together, the poem building the sonic event to a deafening cacophony, all caused by the violent bringing together of water droplets as clouds by wind. Aldhelm's *CR* presents a similar scene, yet it is one focused on visual description, the clashing clouds producing lightning rather than thunder. The only term that carries any sonic force in the *CR* is the verb *vomere* (to vomit, throw up), while the remainder all emphasize the visual effect of lightning caused by the collisions of clouds ('flagrant fulmina').[47] Riddle 1's narration, on the other hand, is almost entirely aural, its emphasis evidenced by the placement of the objects that are creating the sounds after the three half-lines of geophonic description, as well as by its use of variation in what Adeline Bartlett calls Parallel Patterning, specifically Repetition Parallels.[48] First, line 69b utilizes the noun *sweg* for the noise of thunder, 'se bið *swega mæst*' (that is the *mightiest of sounds*), a term whose semantic range includes 'unregulated, confused sound, noise, din, or crash'. Second, the poem builds on this sonic construction with line 70a's '*breahtma* ofer burgum' (*clamouring* over townships), with the noun *breahtm* furthering the volume and intensity of the sonic event because, as the *DOE* highlights, the exact sense of this term is 'difficult to determine'. This ambiguous semantic range, I would argue, is an intentional lexical choice; it is a word without clear distinction, noise in the sense of undefined and chaotic intensity.[49]

---

47 While Aldhelm's octosyllabic verse is aurally compelling with its consistent rhyme and frequent, if irregular, alliteration, these metrical features do not appear to be tied directly to the sonic meaning of the words involved. For a discussion of Aldhelm's poetry, particularly with regards to alliteration, see Orchard, *The Poetic Art of Aldhelm*, esp. pp. 43–54, and with regards to the *CR*, Aldhelm, *The Poetic Works*, trans. by Lapidge and Rosier, pp. 171–76.

48 Bartlett, *The Larger Rhetorical Patterns*, pp. 30–48, defines her system of Parallel Patterns as a 'correspondence of rhetorical or syntactical characteristics' in which a parallel group 'will have two or more parts with such a balance of structure or of phraseology as to give the effect of a close similarity of form' (p. 31). For Repetition Parallels, Bartlett sees variation with repetition of closely corresponding content, whereas for Balance Parallels, Bartlett sees variation in which the content is not similar, but whose parts 'form a pair or series of similar, or in some ways related, thoughts' (p. 33).

49 See the *DOE* whose primary definition includes the following statement: 'the exact sense in any particular context is often difficult to determine'. The potential lexical range of *breahtm*

The geophonic cacophony is then trebled by line 70b, 'ond *gebreca hludust*' (and *loudest of collisions*), with the word *gebrec* again focusing on the crashing nature of loud noises, and which is used here, and in both the Old English *Bede* and *The Letter of Alexander the Great to Aristotle*, with reference to storms.[50] The aural emphasis is likewise furthered by the grammatical and syntactical Parallel Repetition of lines 69b and 70b (genitive plural sound term + superlative modifier).[51] There is also potential for onomatopoeia in the three geophonic half-lines, with the alliterative 'b' sounds of the sonic terms creating a staccato effect not unlike successive booms of thunder. After describing lightning as a wound from this cumulonimbus war with 'fyre swætað' (stream with fire), Riddle 1 continues its sonic assault with three more geophonic descriptions: two depicting the low-frequency blast of thunder sounding out into the distance, '*gebrecu* ferað [...] *gedyne micle*' (*sounds of clashing* pass [...] with *a mighty din*, ll. 74b, 75b), and one describing the accompanying sonic contribution of heavy rain, 'feallan lætað | sweart sumsendu' (they let fall dark moisture *roaring*, ll. 76b–77a).[52] The strength of the geophonic event is the point; the piling up of sound terms for loudness is meant to engender, once more, fearful awe at the power of the elements. This use of geophony to focus the audience on God is evident once again at the end of the poem, which requires an answer both for the riddle object, but also, and more importantly, in terms of line length and emphasis, for the one who is able to control it:

<blockquote>

Saga hwæt ic hatte,

oþþe *hwa mec rære*,   þonne ic restan ne mot,

oþþe *hwa mec stæðþe*,   þonne ic stille beom.   (ll. 102b–104)

(Say what I am called, or *who raises me up*, when I may not rest, or *who makes me steady*, when I stand still.)
</blockquote>

---

includes 'sound, loud noise' (1.a.), along with the more specific assignation of sound to cause, including the sound of a horn (1.b.), the sound of songs or singing (1.c.), the 'noise' or 'uproar' of the wind (1.d.), and the 'trembling of the earth' (1.e.).

50 *Old English Bede*, v. 1.386.7: 'he gehyrde þæt gebrec þara storma & þæs weallendes sæs' (he heard the loud noise of the storms and the surging sea), and *Alexander's Letter to Aristotle* 30.3, 'Ða cwom þær semninga swiðe micel wind on gebræc' (Then suddenly a great wind and crashing [noise] came there). Text for the *Letter* from Orchard, *Pride and Prodigies*.

51 It should be noted, however, that the presence of such rhythmical patterning is not relegated to sections with specific sonic meaning, but throughout Riddle 1, including the more visual chiastic Repetition Parallel of ll. 71b and 72a ('sceo wiþ oþrum, | ecg wið ecge') and Balance Parallel of ll. 73a and 75a ('fus ofer folcum [...] deorc ofer dryhtum').

52 It should be noted that the adjective *sumsende* here is a hapax and has generally been translated, with reference to New German *sumsen*, as something akin to 'humming'. See *The Exeter Anthology of Old English Poetry*, ed. by Muir, p. 579. I follow Muir here for the translation.

Sounds, geophonic events created by the clashing of the inanimate elements, inscribed into text as overwhelming sonic information, are designed to produce awe in the audience, which should lead to rightful, and potentially ruminative, awe at the power of God, the only one whose hands shape and direct wind, water, and their geophonic creation, thunder.

Conclusion

The literary creation of soundscapes, drawing from various elements of the phonosphere, remains an area relatively unexplored with relation to early medieval English literature. These soundscapes rely not only on the embodied experience of the listener, but also on the interpretation of such events. The elemental world, from wind to water, was often encountered and treated in the medieval world as a kind of hyperobject, whose vastness, strength, and often inexplicable nature rendered it beyond human conception or control. In Riddle 1, geophonic soundscapes are employed with this structure in mind, focusing, uniquely in the Old English riddle tradition, not on the identity of the riddle object, but instead on the identity of the only one able to control such elemental potency. In this poem, sound is being used to remind humanity of its limitations by comparison with God's Creation, a comparison intended to elicit awe. The final purpose of such a textual creation is to direct the audience towards God himself, the shaper and structurer of wind, water, and storm.

Works Cited

Dictionaries and Databases

BT = *An Anglo-Saxon Dictionary Based on the Manuscript Collections of the Late Joseph Bosworth*, ed. by Thomas Northcote Toller (Oxford: Clarendon Press, 1898); *Supplement*, ed. by Thomas Northcote Toller (Oxford: Clarendon Press, 1921); *Revised and Enlarged Addenda*, ed. by Alistair Campbell (Oxford: Oxford University Press, 1972)

Clark Hall, J. R., *A Concise Anglo-Saxon Dictionary*, 4th edn with suppl. by Herbert D Merritt (Toronto: University of Toronto Press, 2008)

Dictionary of Medieval Latin from British Sources, ed. by R. E. Latham, D. R. Howlett, and R. K. Ashdowne (London: British Academy, 1975–2013)

Primary Sources

Aldhelm, *Carmen rhythmicum*, in David Howlett, 'Aldhelmi Carmen Rhythmicum', *Bulletin du Cange, Archivum Latinitatis Medii Aevi*, 53 (1995), 119–40

——, *De virginitate*, in *Aldhelmi opera*, ed. by Rudolf Ehwald, MGH: Auctores antiquissimi, 15 (Berlin: Weidmann, 1919; repr. 1961), pp. 350–471

——, *The Poetic Works*, trans. by Michael Lapidge and James Rosier, with appendix by Neil Wright (Woodbridge: D. S. Brewer, 1985; repr. 2009)

Der altenglische Arundel-Psalter: Eine Interlinearversion in der HS. Arundel 60 des Britischen Museums, ed. by Guido Oess (Heidelberg, 1910)

Andreas: An Edition, ed. by Richard North and Michael D. J. Bintley (Liverpool: Liverpool University Press, 2016)

Bede, *De natura rerum*, ed. by C. W. Jones and F. Lipp, in *Beda Venerabilis, Opera didascalica*, I: *De orthographia, De arte metrica et de schematibus et tropis, De natura rerum*, ed. by Charles W. Jones, C. B. Kendall, M. H. King, and F. Lipp, CCSL, 123A (Turnhout: Brepols, 2003), pp. 173–234

——, *Bede's Ecclesiastical History of the English People*, ed. and trans. by Bertram Colgrave and R. A. B. Mynors, 2 vols (Oxford: Clarendon Press, 1969)

——, *In Genesim, Beda Venerabilis, Opera exegetica*, I: *Libri quatuor in principium Genesis usque ad nativitatem Isaac et eiectionem Ismahelis adnotationum*, ed. by Charles W. Jones, CCSL, 118A (Turnhout: Brepols, 1967)

——, *On the Nature of Things and On Times*, trans. by Calvin B. Kendall and Faith Wallis (Liverpool: Liverpool University Press, 2010)

——, *Vita metrica S. Cudbercti*, in *Bede's Latin Poetry*, ed. by Michael Lapidge (Oxford: Oxford University Press, 2019), pp. 181–313

Beowulf, ed. and trans. by Roy Liuzza, 2nd edn (Peterborough: Broadview Press, 2013)

The Exeter Anthology of Old English Poetry: An Edition of Exeter Dean and Chapter MS 3501, ed. by Bernard J. Muir, 2nd rev. edn (Exeter: Exeter University Press, 2000)

Exodus, ed. by Peter J. Lucas (Liverpool: Liverpool University Press, 1994)

Klaeber's Beowulf and the Fight at Finnsburg, 4th edn, ed. by Robert D. Fulk, Robert E. Bjork, and John D. Niles (Toronto: University of Toronto Press, 2008)

The Letter of Alexander the Great to Aristotle, in Andy Orchard, *Pride and Prodigies: Studies in the Monsters of the 'Beowulf'-Manuscript* (Toronto: Toronto University Press, 2003), pp. 204–53

The Old English and Anglo-Latin Riddle Tradition, ed. and trans. by Andy Orchard, DOML, 69 (Cambridge, MA: Harvard University Press, 2021)

The Old English Boethius: An Edition of the Old English Versions of Boethius's 'De Consolatione Philosophiae', ed. and trans. by Malcolm Godden and Susan Irvine, 2 vols (Oxford: Oxford University Press, 2009)

Old English Psalms, ed. and trans. by Patrick P. O'Neill, DOML, 42 (Cambridge, MA: Harvard University Press, 2016)

The Old English Riddles of the Exeter Book, ed. by Craig Williamson (Chapel Hill: University of North Carolina Press, 1977)

Old English Shorter Poems, II: *Wisdom and Lyric*, ed. and trans. by Robert E. Bjork, DOML, 32 (Cambridge, MA: Harvard University Press, 2014)

The Old English Version of Bede's Ecclesiastical History of the English People, ed. by Thomas Miller, EETS OS, 95, 96, 110, 111, 4 vols (London: published for the Early English Text Society by the Oxford University Press, 1959–1963)

Old Testament Narratives, ed. and trans. by Daniel Anlezark, DOML, 7
  (Cambridge, MA: Harvard University Press, 2011)

Secondary Sources

Abegunawardana, Sidath, J. A. P. Bodhika, Sankha Nanyakkara, Upul Sonnadara,
  Mahendra Fernando, and Vernon Cooray, 'Frequency Analysis of Thunder
  Features', 33rd International Conference on Lightning Protection (Portugal,
  2016), <https://www.researchgate.net/publication/309982045_Frequency_
  Analysis_of_Thunder_Features>
Bartlett, Adeline Courtney, *The Larger Rhetorical Patterns in Anglo-Saxon Poetry*,
  Columbia University Studies in English and Comparative Literature, 112 (New
  York: Columbia University Press, 1935; repr. New York: AMS Press, 1966)
Butler, Shane, 'Principles of Sound Reading', in *Sound and the Ancient Senses*, ed. by
  Shane Butler and Sarah Nooter (London: Routledge, 2019), pp. 233–55
Clarke, Catherine A. M., 'Edges and Otherworlds: Imagining Tidal Spaces in
  Early Medieval Britain', in *The Sea and Englishness in the Middle Ages: Maritime
  Narratives, Identity, and Culture*, ed. by Sebastian I. Sobecki (Cambridge: D. S.
  Brewer, 2011), pp. 81–101
Dale, Corinne, *The Natural World in the Exeter Book Riddles* (Woodbridge: D. S.
  Brewer, 2017)
Ellard, Donna Beth, *Anglo-Saxon(ist) Pasts, postSaxon Futures* (New York:
  Punctum Books, 2019)
Jones, Chris, *Fossil Poetry: Anglo-Saxon and Linguistic Nativism in Nineteenth-
  Century Poetry* (Oxford: Oxford University Press, 2018)
Lapidge, Michael, 'Stoic Cosmology and the Source of the First Old English
  Riddle', *Anglia*, 112 (1994), 1–25
Lomuto, Sierra, 'Becoming Postmedieval: The Stakes of the Global Middle Ages',
  postmedieval, 11 (2020), 503–12
Michelet, Fabienne L., 'Lost at Sea: Nautical Travels in the Old English *Exodus*, the
  Old English *Andreas*, and Accounts of the *adventus Saxonum*', in *The Sea and
  Englishness in the Middle Ages: Maritime Narratives, Identity and Culture*, ed. by
  Sebastian I. Sobecki (Cambridge: D. S. Brewer, 2011), pp. 59–79
Nelson, Marie, 'The Rhetoric of the Exeter Book Riddles', *Speculum*, 49 (1974), 421–40
Neville, Jennifer, *Representations of the Natural World in Old English Poetry*,
  Cambridge Studies in Anglo-Saxon England, 27 (Cambridge: Cambridge
  University Press, 1999)
Niles, John D., *The Idea of Anglo-Saxon England, 1066–1901: Remembering, For-
  getting, Deciphering, and Renewing the Past* (Chichester: Wiley Blackwell, 2015)
Novák, Radomil, 'Sound in Literary Texts', *Neophilologus*, 104 (2020), 151–63
Orchard, Andy, *A Commentary on the Old English and Anglo-Latin Riddle Tradition*,
  DOML, Supplements (Cambridge, MA: Harvard University Press, 2021)
——, *The Poetic Art of Aldhelm* (Cambridge: Cambridge University Press, 1994)

Paz, James, 'Mind, Mood, and Meteorology in *þrymful þeow* (R.1–3)', in *Riddles at Work in the Early Medieval Tradition: Words, Ideas, Interactions*, ed. by Megan Cavell and Jennifer Neville (Manchester: Manchester University Press, 2020), pp. 193–210

Rambaran-Olm, Mary, Breann Leake, and Micah James Goodrich, 'Medieval Studies: The Stakes of the Field', *postmedieval*, 11 (2020), 356–70

Reybrouck, Mark, Piotr Podlipniak, and David Welch, 'Music and Noise: Same or Different? What Our Body Tells Us', *Frontiers in Psychology*, 10 (2019), article 1153, 1–13

Schafer, R. Murray, *The Soundscape: Our Sonic Environment and the Tuning of the World* (Rochester, VT: Destiny Books, 1993)

Shores, Rebecca, 'Sounds of Salvation: Nautical Noises in Old English and Anglo-Latin Literature', in *Meanings of Water in Early Medieval England*, ed. by Carolyn Twomey and Daniel Anlezark, SEM, 47 (Turnhout: Brepols, 2021), pp. 109–26

Stanley, Eric Gerald, *In the Foreground: Beowulf* (Cambridge: D. S. Brewer, 1994)

Stanton, Robert, 'Bark Like a Man: Performance, Identity, and Boundary in Old English Animal Voice Catalogues', in *Animal Languages in the Middle Ages: Representations of Interspecies Communication*, ed. by Alison Langdon (Basingstoke: Palgrave Macmillan, 2018), pp. 91–111

——, 'Sound, Voice, and Articulation in the *Exeter Book* Riddles', in *Riddles at Work in the Early Medieval Tradition: Words, Ideas, Interactions*, ed. by Megan Cavell and Jennifer Neville (Manchester: Manchester University Press, 2020), pp. 92–106

Thompson, Emily, *The Soundscape of Modernity: Architectural Acoustics and the Culture of Listening in America, 1900–1933* (Cambridge, MA: MIT Press, 2002)

Twomey, Carolyn, and Daniel Anlezark, 'Introduction: Worlds of Water', in *Meanings of Water in Early Medieval England*, ed. by Carolyn Twomey and Daniel Anlezark, SEM, 47 (Turnhout: Brepols, 2021), pp. 13–32

——, eds, *Meanings of Water in Early Medieval England*, SEM, 47 (Turnhout: Brepols, 2021)

Warren, Michael, *Birds in Medieval English Poetry: Metaphors, Realities, Transformations* (Woodbridge: Boydell and Brewer, 2018)

Yuhua, Ouyang, and Yuan Ping, 'Audible Thunder Characteristics and the Relation between Peak Frequency and Lightning Parameters', *Journal of Earth System Science*, 121 (2012), 211–20

ELENI PONIRAKIS

The Place of Stillness:
Greek Patristic Thought in Cynewulf's *Juliana*

The chapters in this volume explore the ideas that the people of early medieval England had of the world, ideas formed through direct contact and trade or through imaginative responses to received legends and narratives. Ideas about Greece and the Greek language came to England first and foremost through Christianity. Greek is one of the languages of the Bible, as Alfred notes in his preface to Gregory's *Pastoral Care,* and it is one of the languages of the cross.[1] Francis Leneghan notes in his chapter that the Greek Empire had been depicted as one of the four corners of the world, and the stories of Alexander the Great, founder of that empire, are discussed by Simon Thomson in his chapter on 'otherwheres'. Kazutomo Karasawa discusses the use of Greek in Ælfric's description of the east, and Paul Cavill notes that puns on Æthelstan's name play on the languages of Old English, Latin, and Greek. Evidence of the influence of Greek thinking is also to be found, and Rachel Burns identifies references to the Greek concept of *acedia* in the Old English poem *Solomon and Saturn II.* This chapter will demonstrate the presence of Greek thought in Cynewulf's *Juliana.*[2] I will argue, through close analysis of the poem and with special attention to the alterations made by Cynewulf to his primary source from the *Acta Sanctorum,* that Cynewulf is drawing on the writings of the Greek desert fathers and their teachings on the way of prayer, most specifically with Evagrian teaching on the methods of devils to distract the mind from prayer through the eight vices and wicked thoughts which Evagrius termed λογισμοὶ. The most relevant of Evagrius's teachings on the way of prayer are the *Chapters on Prayer* and the *Praktikos.*[3]

---

1   See Major, '*Awriten on þreo geþeode*'.
2   Quotations from *Juliana* are from *The Exeter Book,* ed. by Krapp and Dobbie. Translations are my own.
3   Quotations from the *Praktikos* are from Évagre, *Traité Pratique,* ed. and trans. by Guillaumont and Guillaumont; translations are my own made with reference to the French translations of the Guillaumonts. Quotations from all other Evagrian works are from Evagrius, *The Greek Ascetic Corpus,* ed. and trans. by Sinkewicz, unless otherwise stated.

Eleni Ponirakis (eleni.ponirakis3@nottingham.ac.uk) teaches Early English at the University of Nottingham.

Ideas of the World in Early Medieval English Literature, ed. by Mark Atherton, Kazutomo Karasawa, and Francis Leneghan, SOEL 1 (Turnhout: Brepols, 2022)   pp. 223–248
BREPOLS ❧ PUBLISHERS   DOI 10.1484/M.SOEL.5.130563

The arrival of Greek influence on medieval England can be dated to the seventh century. This was a time when Rome had close links with the Byzantine East and was home to several communities of oriental monks which included Maximus the Confessor and Theodore of Tarsus among their number.[4] This last was to become Archbishop of Canterbury in 668. Maximus the Confessor drew heavily on the works of Evagrius in his own writings, adapting them slightly to his own conception as has been demonstrated by Maximos Constas, among others.[5] This means that if Theodore was influenced by Maximus the Confessor, which seems quite likely, then he was indirectly influenced by a filtered form of Evagrian teaching. Michael Lapidge makes a convincing case for Theodore's participation in the Lateran Council of 649 which met to review the question of *monotheletism*.[6] Bede (*HE*, IV.1) notes that before preparing for his role as Archbishop of Canterbury, Theodore had to grow out his Eastern tonsure — in the Eastern Church monks shaved their whole heads — before receiving the Western tonsure.[7] Although Bede admired Theodore greatly, he was hesitant about his potential to import Eastern ideas, explaining that Pope Vitalian instructed Hadrian, 'uir natione Afir sacris litteris diligenter inbutus, monasterialibus simul et ecclesiasticis disciplinis institutus, Grecae pariter et Latinae linguae peritissimus' (a man of African origin assiduously steeped in the holy scriptures with experience in both monastic and ecclesiastical disciplines, equally expert in the Greek and Latin languages), to accompany him to support Theodore in his teaching and to ensure that he did not 'contrarium veritati fidei Graecorum more in ecclesiam cui praeesset introduceret' (introduce Greek customs contrary to the true faith into the church which he was to preside over).[8] It is not clear which Greek customs Bede was concerned about, but Greek ideas most certainly did make their way to Anglo-Saxon England. Indeed, the source for Bede's own history of the church was Abbot Albinus, a man trained by 'Theodoro archiepiscopo et Hadriano abbate, uiris uenerabilibus atque eruditissimus'

---

4 Michael Lapidge explains that the exodus of refugees from Syria and Palestine fleeing Persian and Arab invasions settled in southern Italy and Sicily, and as a result, 'many of the popes from the mid-seventh to the mid-eighth century were Greek speaking monks of Syrian origin', adding that 'it was at the time of these immigrations, in the mid-seventh century, that several monasteries of oriental monks were established in Rome'. Bischoff and Lapidge, *Biblical Commentaries*, pp. 65–66.

5 Constas, 'Nothing Is Greater than Divine Love'.

6 Lapidge, 'The Career of Archbishop Theodore', pp. 22–23. There was a disagreement as to whether Christ had one will or two. *Monotheletism* is the argument that Christ had only one divine will. This view was rejected at the Lateran Council of 649, which held that Christ had two wills, one human and one divine. This last view was notably defended by Maximus the Confessor, and Theodore was to reinforce this teaching in England.

7 Lapidge, 'The Career of Archbishop Theodore', p. 19.

8 Bede, *HE*, IV.1, ed. and trans. by Colgrave and Mynors, pp. 328 and 330 (all translations from Bede are my own, unless otherwise stated).

(Archbishop Theodore and Abbot Hadrian, men most learned and worthy of respect).[9]

It was also in the seventh century that the cult of Juliana became popular in England. The *Passio* of Juliana is included in Bede's *Martyrologium*, and her feast day on 16 February is mentioned in an eighth-century recension of the *Martyrologium Hieronymianum*. The reason for this may be that Juliana, despite being recorded as meeting her death at Nicomedia, was translated to Cumae near Naples, and devotion to her most probably came to England with Hadrian, as he had spent some considerable time in the Neapolitan area.[10]

England in the early medieval period was a society built around the Christian church and as such saw itself as extending a history and culture that included Palestine, Syria, Egypt, North Africa, Greece, Rome, and neighbouring Francia. Few of the founding fathers of the English church were English. They were Roman and Greek, African, and Irish, and those who were English spent time on the Continent and enriched their learning from cultural exchange. The people of early medieval England were well aware that their churches faced East and that they were part of an international community. Among the most important texts in English monasteries were Cassian's *Conlationes* (*The Conferences*) and *De institutis coenobiorum* (*The Institutes*), both of these based on the words of the desert fathers and most especially on the writings of Evagrius Ponticus of whom Cassian, a native of the Balkans, was a disciple.[11]

There is currently no consensus as to the dating of Cynewulf's life and work, but Fulk's argument based on the runic spelling of Cynewulf's name that his writing can be no earlier than *c.* 750 and no later than *c.* 850, has gained widespread acceptance.[12] It is clear from Cynewulf's signed output, *Christ II*, *The Fates of the Apostles*, *Juliana*, and *Elene*, that he has an interest in the history of the Church, an interest that has its focus on the East. Listing the poems in chronological order by subject, Cynewulf's output traces the

---

9   Bede, *HE*, 'Praefatio', ed. and trans. by Colgrave and Mynors, p. 2.

10 See Biggs, Hill, and Szarmach, eds, *Sources of Anglo-Saxon Literary Culture*, I, pp. 276–77. See also Bischoff and Lapidge, eds, *Biblical Commentaries*, pp. 97 and 166–67. It is now argued, based on evidence from the early martyrologies, that Juliana was in fact a local Cumae martyr and that the legend of her martyrdom in Nicomedia is a fabrication (Biggs, Hill, and Szarmach, eds, *Sources of Anglo-Saxon Literary Culture*, I, pp. 276–77). That the story has no basis in fact is not hard to imagine, given the role of the demon and the excessive number of torments meted out to her, but this does not invalidate her role as representative of the countless martyrs who did suffer these torments between them.

11 Cassian avoids naming Evagrius in his writings, most probably because of the uncomfortable associations with Origenism.

12 Fulk, 'Poet, Canon, Date', p. 16. See also Fulk, *A History of Old English Meter*; Conner, 'On Dating Cynewulf', pp. 23–56; and Neidorf, 'Lexical Evidence for the Relative Chronology', p. 39. Niles has recently argued for a tenth-century dating of Cynewulf, contemporary to the compilation of the Exeter Book, proposing that Cynewulf may even have been involved in the manuscript's compilation (*God's Exiles and English Verse*, pp. 82–83), but this view has yet to be widely adopted.

Church from its beginnings in Christ, through the spreading of the word by the apostles, the period of persecutions epitomized in *Juliana*, and the end of the persecutions, brought about by Constantine whose mother will find the true cross, signalling a fresh beginning.[13]

This chapter will argue that Cynewulf is using an adaptation of the *Passio S. Iulianae* to demonstrate the principles set out in the *Praktikos* of Evagrius for a monk's preparation for prayer, which in itself is a stage on the way to *theologia*, contemplation of the divine.[14] This chapter joins a growing number of studies demonstrating evidence of Greek thought, including Neoplatonic and Evagrian ideas, in Old English texts.[15] It is also not the first to see *Juliana* as a figural narrative. Joseph Wittig, for example, argues convincingly that 'a multi-term figural relationship operates in *Juliana* between Christ, the Church, the saint and the individual Christian soul'.[16] This chapter does not put Wittig's reading into doubt, but adds another figural layer whereby Juliana is also the figure of one engaged in the contemplative life, the ascetic soul.[17]

Before demonstrating through a close reading of the text exactly how Juliana's experience and behaviour demonstrates the Evagrian way of prayer, an overview of the *Praktikos* will be necessary, as will a brief consideration of Evagrius's life and influences. Evagrius Ponticus (*c*. 345–399) represents one of the most important figures of desert monasticism as the man who developed the idea of the perfection of prayer as a way towards knowledge of God (*gnosis*). We know certain facts about his life, as they were recorded not long after his death by Palladius in the *Historia Lausiaca*.[18] As a young man he met and became a disciple of the Cappadocian fathers, Basil the Great and Gregory of Nazianzus, this last becoming his spiritual master. In 380 he accompanied Gregory to Constantinople, where he fell in love with the wife of an important dignitary. Warned of the dangers of this in a vision or dream, Evagrius left Constantinople for Jerusalem, where he was

---

13 In *The Fates of the Apostles*, Cynewulf describes himself as *siðgeomor*, journey-weary, having travelled with the apostles in his imagination through Greece and Rome, to India and other parts of Asia, Ethiopia, Jerusalem, and Persia.

14 See Louth, *The Origins of the Christian Mystical Tradition*, p. 108: 'the mind *is* what it contemplates in *theologia*, contemplation of the Trinity'.

15 See Anlezark, 'The Soul in the Old English *Soliloquies*'; Flight, 'Through a Glass Darkly'; Flight, 'The *Dream of the Rood*'; Leneghan, 'Preparing the Mind for Prayer'; Mainoldi, 'The Reception of the Greek Patristic Doctrine of Deification in the Medieval West'; Ponirakis, 'Echoes of Eriugena'; Ritzke-Rutherford, 'Anglo-Saxon Antecedents of the Middle English Mystics'; Treschow, 'Echoes of the *Periphyseon* in the Third Book of Alfred's *Soliloquies*'.

16 Wittig, 'Figural Narrative in Cynewulf's *Juliana*', p. 148. See also Niles, *God's Exiles and English Verse*; Niles argues a degree of monastic identity to Juliana as one of *Godes cempan* (God's soldiers), p. 92.

17 See also Bdzyl, '*Juliana*'. Bdzyl argues that the poem works also on a literal and realistic level, and that Cynewulf has Juliana gradually dispel the devilish delusions presented in the opening of the poem, that the world is in the control of the forces of evil.

18 *The Lausiac History*, ed. by Clarke.

welcomed by Melania and Rufinus at Melania's monastery in the Mount of Olives. After being nursed by Melania through a terrible illness (which Russell interprets as more psychological than physical),[19] he was persuaded by her to take up the monastic life and went first to Nitria, one of the most famous centres of monasticism in Egypt at the time, and then on to the desert cells of Kellia, where he lived the remainder of his life, visiting from time to time Macarius of Egypt, one of the most famous of the desert fathers. Evagrius was influenced by the Cappadocian fathers on the one hand and the desert fathers on the other. The soon to be anathematized Origen was a major influence on his ideas, especially in the defence of allegorical exegesis in opposition to the idea of many monks who took an overly literal view of the Bible, attributing a human face to God (anthropomorphists). Evagrius was saved from the persecution meted out to the followers of Origen by his death in 399, but he was posthumously anathematized by the Fifth Ecumenical Council at Constantinople in 553, which meant that subsequently some of his works were lost in their original Greek. Fortunately, these were preserved in Syriac and Armenian. The monastic texts were, however, preserved by the Greeks as they held little evidence of Origenism, even if they tended to be attributed to St Nilus to bypass the opprobrium that was by now attached to Evagrius's name.[20]

The travels and ideas of a Greek thinker, writer, and ascetic may seem a long way from the early medieval England of Cynewulf,[21] but these ideas were to become the foundation of Western monasticism through the intermediary of John Cassian. During the time that Evagrius was at Kellia, Cassian, a young man most probably from eastern Europe in the Dobrudja, intent on following the spiritual life of the desert fathers, became a disciple of Evagrius and would take back with him the precepts on prayer that his master had perfected in the *Praktikos* and other writings.[22] These he would later write up in Latin at his monastery in Massilia (Marseille) as the *Institutes*. John Cassian's *Institutes* and his *Conferences* (reported conversations with the desert fathers) were required reading or listening in both Irish and English monasteries.[23]

There are also traces of Evagrius to be found in the *Canterbury Commentaries* made at the school of Theodore and Hadrian. For example, in the very first commentary there is a reference to three Greek authors who criticized Jerome's

---

19 Russell, *The Doctrine of Deification in the Greek Patristic Tradition*, p. 238.

20 For more details on the life of Evagrius and its significance to his work, see the introduction to the *Praktikos*, in Évagre, *Traité Pratique*, ed. and trans. by Guillaumont and Guillaumont, I, pp. 21–31; Russell, *The Doctrine of Deification in the Greek Patristic Tradition*, p. 238; and Evagrius, *The Praktikos*, ed. and trans. by Bamberger, pp. xxxv–xlviii.

21 The majority consensus for the dating for Cynewulf's poetry argues for a range between 750 and 850. See above.

22 See Chadwick, *John Cassian*, p. 9.

23 For the list of extant manuscripts of Cassian's works, including the *Institutes* and *Conferences*, see Lapidge, *The Anglo-Saxon Library*, pp. 295–96.

Vulgate translation, these being Rufinus, Cassian, and Evagrius. Evagrius, incidentally, was a friend to both Rufinus and Cassian, and both men translated his works.[24] Evagrius wrote extensively, both on biblical exegesis and monastic asceticism. Here we are particularly interested in the ascetic corpus, and we will focus on the *Praktikos*, a treatise on the practical life of the ascetic monk, with reference also to the *Chapters on Prayer* and *Foundations of the Monastic Life*. The aim of Evagrius's teaching is for the monk to progress to a state of *apatheia*, that is, a still mind, free from the distraction of vices, from which contemplation can arise, the first level being θεωρία φυσική (contemplation of God through his creation), and then the highest contemplation, θεωρία τῆς ἁγίας Τριάδος (contemplation of the Holy Trinity). *Apatheia* is the immobile state of the soul when free from the eight vices of *gastrimargia* (gluttony), *porneia* (fornication), *philarguria* (avarice), *lupe* (grief), *orge* (anger), *acedia* (accidie), *kenodoxia* (vainglory), and *hyperephania* (pride). Evagrius begins the *Praktikos* by explaining the three stages of the soul, *praktike*, *physike*, and *theologia*.[25] In *praktike*, the soul develops the practice of virtues through rejection of vices; this presupposes a state of *hesychia*, that is, a life of quiet and stillness both on the outside, through retirement to a cell and away from the temptations of the world and even other brothers, and an internal stillness that is brought about by a subjugation of the passions. This is where the monk must learn to fight with demons, to recognize the different kinds of demonic attack related to each of the eight vices and know how to counter them, to ultimately overcome all temptations and subdue the passions. Once the monk has successfully overcome the passions, he achieves the state of *apatheia*, which is a state of mental stillness through freedom from passions allowing an ability to pray, that is, to commune with God, without distraction, impassive to the violent torments meted out by devils. *On Prayer* ends with anecdotes of monks (the *apophthegmata*) who have achieved complete *apatheia*, praying undistracted whilst attacked by demons transformed into lions and devouring their cheeks or dragons feeding on their flesh and vomiting it back in their faces.[26] Evagrius offers a summary of the process in the prologue to the *Praktikos*:

---

24 Bischoff and Lapidge, eds, *Biblical Commentaries*, pp. 217–18. Bischoff and Lapidge conclude, 'the commentator apparently had knowledge of a dossier of materials containing attacks on Jerome which originated in fourth-century Jerusalem, and which may have been composed in Greek, but which has not survived' (p. 218).

25 See Louth, *The Origins of the Christian Mystical Tradition*, pp. 102–03. For a discussion of the transmission of the idea of the eight vices from Evagrius to Ælfric, see Clayton, 'Introduction'. See also Szarmach, 'The Vocabulary of Sin and the Eight Cardinal Sins'. Clayton points out that in his metrical *De virginitate*, Aldhelm, although mainly drawing on Cassian and Gregory, uses the term *kenodoxia* for vainglory, remarking that this is what the Greeks call it (Clayton, 'Introduction', p. 74). Aldhelm, as a student of the Canterbury School and a disciple of Hadrian, may have been exposed to a Greek version of the list of eight vices.

26 *On Prayer*, chapters 106–09, in Evagrius, *The Greek Ascetic Corpus*, ed. and trans. by Sinkewicz, pp. 204–05.

τὴν πίστιν, ὦ τέκνα, βεβαιοῖ ὁ φόβος ὁ τοῦ Θεοῦ, καὶ τοῦτον πάλιν ἐγκράτεια, ταύτην δὲ ἀκλινῆ ποιοῦσιν ὑπομονὴ καὶ ἐλπίς, ἀφ' ὧν τίκτεται ἀπάθεια, ἧς ἔγγονον ἡ ἀγάπη, ἀγάπη δὲ θύρα γνώσεως φυσικῆς ἣν διαδέχεται θεολογία καὶ ἡ ἐσχάτη μακαριότης.

> (Faith, children, is made steadfast by fear of God, and this in turn by self-control/continence; this is made unyielding by perseverance and hope, from which is born *apatheia*, which has love (*agape*) for issue, which is the door to knowledge of nature (created things) from which follows theology and at the end, bliss (beatitude).)[27]

The ultimate aim, then, of the *Praktikos* is a form of beatitude, found in contemplation of the divine. The process begins with the achievement of *apatheia* and is accompanied by contemplation (θεωρία). Once this is achieved, the monk may begin by understanding God through an understanding of the science of created things (γνώσεως φυσικῆς) before ridding his mind of all images and achieving contemplation of the Holy Trinity (θεωρία τῆς ἁγίας Τριάδος).[28]

Cynewulf presents an Evagrian approach to prayer in the poem in several ways. He establishes Juliana's state of *apatheia* when she is introduced, and this is confirmed in her lack of response to the temptations and torments offered by Affricanus and Heliseus. The devil's confessions are used to demonstrate the various ways devils attempt to move the minds of the righteous away from the place of prayer, in a way that reflects Evagrius's teaching in the *Praktikos* and other writings. Juliana's speech before her death provides a summary of this Evagrian teaching, which represents the achievement of a final union with God. Throughout the body of the poem there is a consistent pattern of mental imagery where Juliana's mind is shown in a state of stasis, fixed to God, in opposition to the devil's attempts to create mental movement away from God, illustrating the continued necessity to maintain *hesychasm*, or mental stillness. Finally, Cynewulf's signature embodies the advice to novice monks in *Foundations* to pray with compunction as if the poet has begun on the path of learning having contemplated the death of the saint and benefited from her teaching. In this, the poem's conclusion is not dissimilar to that of *The Dream of the Rood*, where the dreamer has learned from his vision and the words of the cross the way to salvation.[29]

It has long been assumed that the source for Cynewulf's *Juliana* is a version of the *Acta Sanctorum*. Michael Lapidge argues convincingly that Paris, Bibliothèque nationale de France, MS lat. 10861 represents a copy of

---

27 Greek text from Évagre, *Traité Pratique*, ed. and trans. by Guillaumont and Guillaumont, II, p. 492. Translation my own with reference to Guillaumont, and Souter, *A Pocket Lexicon to the Greek New Testament*.

28 See Russell, *The Doctrine of Deification in the Greek Patristic Tradition*, pp. 238–39.

29 See Flight, 'The Dream of the Rood', for a reading of that poem as a contemplative text which contains apophatic discourse, following Pseudo-Dionysius.

the *Passio S. Iulianae* 'very similar to, and possibly identical with the exemplar used by Cynewulf', and this is the version to which we will refer.[30]

Evagrian Approaches in *Juliana*

We will begin at the end. Just as the end of *The Dream of the Rood* is a beginning, when the newly enlightened dreamer finds himself transformed, so, in a way, Cynewulf's signature and prayer at the end of *Juliana* signals a beginning as the poet presents himself in the position of a novice. In his short treatise for novice monks, *Foundations*, Evagrius explains the importance of compunction as the most necessary element of prayer, especially for a beginner: 'Seated in your cell, gather together your mind, give heed to the day of your death, and then look at the dying of your body'. Cynewulf gives heed to the day of his death: 'min sceal of lice | sawul on siðfæt' (my soul must go on a journey [away] from my body, ll. 699b–700a). The gathering of the self in groups of runes suggests Cynewulf gathering together his dissipated mind — the Greek instruction is 'συνάγαγέ σου τὸν νοῦν' (gather together your mind); *νοῦσ* is the word for the mind or reasoning faculty.[31] Evagrius enjoins the novice to imagine the day of judgement, 'and at the judgement of sinners, groan, weep and put on the form of mourning, for fear lest you find yourself among them' (*Foundations* 9).[32] Cynewulf does this:

> Geomor hweorfeð
> ᛣ ᛝ ond ᛏ.   Cyning biþ reþe,
> sigora syllend,   þonne synnum fah
> ᛗ ᛈ ond ᚾ   acle bidað
> hwæt him æfter dædum   deman wille
> lifes to leane.   (ll. 703b–708a)

> (Sorrowing, C Y and N turn away. The King will be stern, Giver of Victories, when stained with sin E W and U terrified, await what will be judged to them for their lives in requital for their deeds.)

One should approach God with 'fear and trembling' (*Foundations* 11),[33] writes Evagrius, and so Cynewulf closes his signature terrified, as we have seen, and trembling: 'ᛏ, ᚠ beofað, | seomað sorg-cearig' (L and F tremble, and lie wretched, ll. 708b–709a). This is, of course, a prayer to Juliana for intercession and not a direct prayer to God, but nevertheless the correct attitude to compunction is

---

30 Lapidge, 'Cynewulf and the *Passio S. Iulianae*'. Quotations from the *Passio* will be from Lapidge's edition which is printed as an appendix at the end of his chapter.

31 *SS Patrum Aegyptiorum opera omnia*, ed. by Migne, col. 1262.

32 Evagrius, *The Greek Ascetic Corpus*, ed. and trans. by Sinkewicz, p. 9.

33 Evagrius, *The Greek Ascetic Corpus*, ed. and trans. by Sinkewicz, p. 11.

THE PLACE OF STILLNESS   231

shown in exactly the way indicated by Evagrius and summed up in *On Prayer* 42: 'prayer with perception involves the engagement of the mind accompanied by reverence, compunction, and suffering of soul, along with confessions of failings with unspoken groanings'.[34] It is interesting to note that the wording of the *Benedictine Rule* on the correct attitude to prayer, seems to be taken from Evagrius's *Foundations*.

Regula Benedicti XX *De reverentia orationis* reads:

> Si, cum hominibus potentibus volumus aliqua suggerere, non præsumimus nisi cum humilitate et reverentia, quanto magis Domino Deo universorum cum omni humilitate et puritatis devotione supplicandum est.[35]
>
> > (When we want to ask something of a powerful man, we do not presume to do so without humility and reverence; how much more is the Lord God of all things to be humbly beseeched with all humility and purity of devotion.)

Foundations XI reads:

> If then someone approaches a human king with fear, trembling, and vigilance (μετὰ φόβου καὶ τρόμου καὶ νήψεως) and presents a petition in this way, all the more should one not present himself in similar fashion to God the Lord of all and Christ the King of kings and Prince of princes and so make his petition and supplication?[36]

Regula Benedicti makes reference to purity of heart and tears of compunction — 'in puritate cordis et compunctione lacrimarum' —but not to

---

34 Evagrius, *The Greek Ascetic Corpus*, ed. and trans. by Sinkewicz, p. 197. Sinkewicz notes that in some recensions this is 'the quality of prayer' rather than 'prayer with perception'. See Evagrius, *The Praktikos*, ed. and trans. by Bamberger, p. 61, who translates as 'quality of prayer'.

35 *RB 1980*, ed. by Fry and others, p. 216. This is translated faithfully into Old English as: 'gif we mid rican mannan hwæt embe ure neode manian willað, þæt we ne gedystlæcat butan mid micelre eaðmodnesse; micle swyþor is to halsienne ealra gesceafta drihten mid ealre eaðmodnesse and mid ealre underþeodnesse and modes hlutternesse'. The source for this passage in *Regula Benedicti* is usually given as the *Asketikon* of Basil the Great (see *RB 1980*, ed. by Fry and others, p. 216, and Basil, *The Asketikon*, ed. by Silvas, p. 517). The passage in the *Asketikon* reads, 'for if when someone sees a ruler or officer and converses with him, he keeps his eyes intent, then how much more does one who prays to God keep his mind intent on him who searches hearts and inmost parts fulfilling what is written lifting up holy hands without anger and arguments'. There are clear similarities, but the wording and sense of *Regula Benedicti* is closer to Evagrius, relating to humility and compunction in prayer, more than maintaining focus or intent. As Evagrius was a disciple of Basil, it is to be supposed that the image of comparing God to a rich man or ruler did originate with Basil. It is also perhaps significant that both Evagrius and Basil were translated into Latin by Rufinus.

36 Evagrius, *The Greek Ascetic Corpus*, ed. and trans. by Sinkewicz, p. 11. Sinkewicz translates νῆψις as 'vigilance'; the literal meaning is 'sobriety', and it has a range of meanings including 'self-control', which might be more precise here. Greek from *SS Patrum Aegyptiorum opera omnia*, ed. by Migne.

trembling.[37] Cassian refers to an approach to God with trembling heart when we meditate on his power (*Conlationes* 1:xv), but it is Evagrius's descriptions of compunction in prayer — thinking of future death, being mindful of sins, and approaching God with fear and trembling — which most resembles that of Cynewulf's signature.[38] Cynewulf's signature certainly shows a clear influence of the Evagrian approach to prayer. We will now return to the beginning of *Juliana* and see how the persona of the saint also embodies the Evagrian ideal.[39]

The Latin *Passio* begins with only the briefest mention that the story of Juliana takes place during the time of Maximian's persecution of Christians. There is a great deal more detail in Cynewulf's version, and it must be supposed that he had access to a history of the early Church such as Lactantius's *De mortibus persecutorum*, or Eusebius's Ἐκκλησιαστική Ἱστορία (*Ecclesiastical History*), Book VIII, Chapter 2 of which describes the destruction of the churches and burning of books, while Chapters 3–5 outline the nature of the killings and torture, with a special focus on Nicomedia.[40] Cynewulf's reference to the burning of the 'boccræftig' (learned, 16) may even show his awareness that the officers of Diocletian and Maximian specifically sought out those men who had Christian books in their churches or houses as detailed, for example, in the *Gesta apud Zenophilum* for May 303.[41] Juliana's opening reference announcing that 'we ðæt hyrdon hæleð eahtian, | deman dædhwate' (we have heard warriors, bold in deeds, proclaim, ll. 1–2a) shows the narrator keen to demonstrate that he has sources for what follows. The principal source for the story, as we have said, is from a version of the *Acta Sanctorum*. In establishing Cynewulf's use of the story, and therefore his aim in composing the poem, it is most important to notice the differences between the Old English poem and the primary source.

The most obvious change is the removal of nearly all expressions or signs of emotion from *Juliana*. Rosemary Woolf remarks, somewhat acidly, that the lack of emotional and rhetorical emphasis in the poem leads to a monotony that is only relieved by some 'echoes of Latin warmth' in the passages where Affricanus and Heliseus lose their tempers, but finds that this does not fit with the 'bleaker atmosphere of the northern poem'.[42] Not all critics assign the lack of emotion to a bleak northern attitude. Bdzyl, for example, reads

---

37 *Puritas cordis* is Cassian's translation of Evagrius's *apatheia*. *Conlationes* 13:x also refers to Philippians 2. 12, 'with fear and trembling, work out your salvation'.

38 As noted above, this could also refer to Philippians 2. 12.

39 For other interpretations of Cynewulf's signature at the end of *Juliana*, see Clements, 'Reading, Writing and Resurrection', pp. 144–45 and 149–50.

40 Eusebius's Ἐκκλησιαστική Ἱστορία was translated into Latin as *Historia ecclesiastica*; there is a tenth-century copy in the library of Worcester Cathedral, MS Q28. For an overview of evidence of Cynewulf's access to a variety of source texts, see Anderson, *Cynewulf*, pp. 23–24.

41 See *A New Eusebius*, ed. by Stevenson, rev. by Frend, p. 309.

42 *Juliana*, ed. by Woolf, pp. 17–18.

Juliana's lack of emotion as representing the saint's rejection of the world, while Wittig sees it as an element of her symbolic role as figure of Christ and/or his Church.[43] As we shall see, the eradication of emotion in the persona of Juliana can most readily be accounted for by understanding that Cynewulf is showing the saint in a state, quite literally, of *apatheia*.

If we examine the words used by Cynewulf when he presents Juliana for the first time, we will see close parallels to Evagrius's summary of the *praktike* towards the end of his prologue cited above:

Hio in gæste bær

halge treowe,	hogde georne
þæt hire mægðhad	mana gehwylces
fore Cristes lufan	clæne geheolde.
Ða wæs sio fæmne	mid hyre fæder willan
welegum biweddad;	wyrd ne ful cuþe,
freondrædenne	hu heo from hogde,
geong on gæste.	Hire wæs godes egsa
mara in gemyndum,	þonne eall þæt maþþumgesteald
þe in þæs æþelinges	æhtum wunade.	(ll. 28b–37)

> (She carried in her soul, holy faith, focused her mind eagerly to keep her chastity clear of each of [the] sins for Christ's love. Then the maiden was by her father's will engaged to the rich one; he could not fully know the outcome, how she, young in spirit, rejected physical affection. To her, fear of God was greater in her mind than all that treasure that dwelt in this nobleman's possession.)

Juliana's faith ($\pi\acute{\iota}\sigma\tau\iota\varsigma$) and continence ($\dot{\varepsilon}\gamma\kappa\rho\acute{\alpha}\tau\varepsilon\iota\alpha$) is indicated by the fact that she keeps her chastity clean from each of the sins. The use of *gehwylc* (each) indicates a finite number of sins and is analogous with Evagrius's eight vices. Juliana's chastity is linked to Christ's love ($\dot{\alpha}\gamma\acute{\alpha}\pi\eta$), and over all this in her mind is fear of God ($\dot{o}\ \varphi\acute{o}\beta o\varsigma\ \tau o\tilde{v}\ \Theta\varepsilon o\tilde{v}$).[44] None of this is in the *Acta Sanctorum*, which is more concerned with the narrative of Juliana's speech and actions than what is taking place in her mind and soul.[45]

Before encountering a devil in person, Juliana must face human temptation in the form of Affricanus and Heliseus. Evagrius taught that beyond the hesychastic

---

43 Bdzyl, '*Juliana*'; Wittig, 'Figural Narrative in Cynewulf's *Juliana*', p. 150.

44 *Mana gehwylc* seems to be an expression unique to Cynewulf, appearing here and in *Elene*, l. 1317.

45 The *Acta Sanctorum* shows Juliana as a new Christian when we are introduced to her, asking herself if there is a true God who created heaven and earth, and going to church to pray and to learn the divine writings ('Iuliana […] hoc cogitabat apud se, quoniam uerus est Deus qui fecit caelum et terram. Et per singulos dies uacans orationi, concurrebat ad ecclesiam ut diuinam sapientiam intelligeret' (*Passio S. Iulianae*, ed. by Lapidge, p. 157)). Cynewulf's Juliana is already in an advanced state of *apatheia*. Both her faith and her ability to withstand temptation are firmly established.

solitude of the cell, devils used men to fight in their place (*Praktikos* 5) and when these men have the same levels of anger or wickedness as devils, then they *are* devils.[46] The heightening of emotive responses, especially of anger, in Juliana's antagonists would suggest, from an Evagrian perspective, that they themselves have become instruments of devils, if not devils themselves.

Juliana has little trouble resisting the temptations presented through the flattery which appeals to vainglory (*kenodoxia*); Affricanus calls her: 'seo dyreste | ond seo sweteste' (the dearest and the sweetest, ll. 93b–94a), Heliseus, 'min se swetesta sunna scima' (my sweetest brightness of the sun, l. 166). Appeals to avarice (*philarguria*) in Affricanus's insistence on the wealth of her suitor, or to conjugal pleasures (*porneia*) implied in *freondræden* (ll. 34 and 71) also produce no effect. Juliana is equally impassive in the face of the threat of pain. For Evagrius, fear is not a vice, but concern for the body's well-being is included in gluttony (*gastrimargia*), which for Evagrius has little or nothing to do with a desire for excessive amounts of food, rather the fear of bodily suffering brought on by abstinence and fasting. That the demons will provide torment and physical pain seems to be a given; the *apophthegmata* relate the stories of devils tormenting desert fathers who have achieved *apatheia* and continue to pray despite the worst kinds of torments.[47] In the *Acta Sanctorum*, Juliana is not impassive in response to all of this. She responds with anger and a certain sense of suffering expressed in her prayers for deliverance from torment. It can be surmised from this that the hagiographer of the *Acta Sanctorum* was presenting an entirely different lesson to the one provided by Cynewulf. Where the *Acta Sanctorum* portrays the opposition of good and evil and the power of faith, prayer, and the sacraments, Cynewulf is concerned with showing a more internal battle against emotion and against distraction from prayer. This last is made explicit in the nature of the devil's confessions, and may suggest that the primary audience for the poem was monastic. For Cynewulf, following the Evagrian ideal of *apatheia*, Juliana's anger (*lupe*) would be indicative of a soul that has not attained *apatheia*. In the Latin text, Juliana prays to God to have Heliseus sent to the underworld in the power of demons to be consumed by worms and brought to ridicule ('Et fac ipsum praefectum participem diis tartareis habitatorem consumptum uermibus, derisum plenum etiam super terram'), and she beats the devil with

---

46 See Évagre, *Traité Pratique*, ed. and trans. by Guillaumont and Guillaumont, ii, pp. 505–06: 'selon la métaphysique évagrienne, ce qui distingue les hommes et les demons, c'est, non pas une différence de nature, mais la surabondance de colère et de méchanceté chez ces derniers' (according to Evagrian metaphysics, that which distinguishes men from demons is not a difference of nature, but an excess of anger and wickedness in the latter). Cynewulf certainly stresses the excessive levels of anger in these two men.

47 See above. The painful torments meted out by the devils to the desert fathers allow them a form of martyrdom no longer available through human persecution. Indeed, the devil will include the persecutions in the long list of anti-Christian activities he confesses responsibility for.

the chains with which she was bound and finally throws him on a midden ('proiecit eum in loco stercore plenum').[48] All of this is expunged in the Cynewulfian version, leaving a woman who is remarkable for her impassivity and her steadfastness. Through the substantial alterations made to his primary Latin source, Cynewulf has transformed Juliana into an embodiment of the Evagrian monastic ideal of *apatheia*.

The Devil's Confessions

In both the *Acta Sanctorum* and Cynewulf, Juliana is hung up by her hair for six hours. In the Cynewulfian version, however, she is described as glowing with light while she undergoes this; she is 'seo sunsciene' (the one bright as the sun, l. 229), and later she is 'seo wlitescyne wuldres condel' (the beautifully radiant candle of glory, l. 454). Again, this feature can be accounted for by turning to the monastic thought of the Greek desert fathers. In the writings of the desert fathers, a face or body glowing with light, compared to the sun or a pillar of light, is a sign that the monk has achieved spiritual purity.[49] For Evagrius, it is a sign of *apatheia* when the soul (νοῦσ) sees its own light (*Praktikos* 64).[50] Further similarities with the teachings of Evagrius are to be found when Cynewulf describes Juliana as being in the presence of the Trinity. Evagrius argued that the highest form of spiritual purity leads to oneness with the Kingdom of God: 'Βασιλεία Θεοῦ ἐστι γνῶσις τῆς ἁγίας Τριάδος συμπαρεκτεινομένη τῇ συστάσει τοῦ νοός, καί ὑπερβάλλουσα τὴν ἀφθαρσίαν αὐτοῦ' (the Kingdom of God is spiritual knowledge of the Holy Trinity coextensively with the substance of the intellect and exceeding its incorruptibility).[51] In the *Acta Sanctorum*, when Juliana is shut in her prison cell she offers a prayer to God, at the end of which the devil Belial makes an appearance. Cynewulf removes the prayer and instead offers a description of Juliana in her prison cell where the description alternates between Juliana's cell and her mind, and where the Holy Trinity is present — indicative of Juliana's advanced state of spiritual understanding. This is the moment where Juliana's position most resembles that of a *hesychast* isolated in a cell (and the cell is symbolic of the body); she is focusing on the inside of her mind until it is not clear whether the scene is taking place in the cell or in her mind — or perhaps both:

---

48 *Passio S. Iulianae*, ed. by Lapidge, p. 159 and p. 162.
49 See Lemeni, '"You Can Become All Flame"', esp. pp. 16–22.
50 See Louth, *The Origins of the Christian Mystical Tradition*, pp. 106–07.
51 Évagre, *Traité Pratique*, ed. and trans. by Guillaumont and Guillaumont, II, p. 500, translation my own with reference to the translation and notes of the Guillaumonts, p. 501. The Guillaumonts comment here that for Evagrius, as for Gregory of Nazianzus, Βασιλεία, or kingdom, meant the knowledge or contemplation of God.

> Hyre wæs Cristes lof
> in ferðlocan   fæste biwunden,
> milde modsefan,   mægen unbrice.
> ða wæs mid cluster   carcernes duru
> behliden, homra geweorc.   Halig þær inne
> wærfæst wunade.   Symle heo wuldorcyning
> herede æt heortan,   heofonrices god,
> in þam nydclafan,   nergend fira,
> heolstre bihelmad.   Hyre wæs halig gæst
> singal gesið.   (ll. 233b–242a)

(Praise of Christ was firmly wound in her spirit, [her] gentle mind, an inviolate power. Then the cell door was bolted shut, the work of hammers; the holy one therein, faithful dwelled. She always praised the King of Glory in her heart, the God of the heavenly kingdom, in the prison, the Saviour of men, in the cover of darkness. The Holy Spirit was a constant companion to her.)

This is θεωρία τῆς ἁγίας Τριάδος (contemplation of the Holy Trinity), the highest form of *theoria*. Juliana has the Holy Trinity firmly entwined in her heart and mind, and this is a power that is *unbrice*, inviolate and therefore incorruptible. Juliana seems to be in a permanent state of prayer. Louth explains Evagrius's idea of prayer as being 'not so much an activity as a state (*katastasis*), not so much something that you do as something that you are'. This is true of Juliana; she has praise of God constantly (*symle*) and unshakeably (*fæst*) in her heart.[52] It is at this point, as Cynewulf establishes the achievement of absolute *apatheia*, where Juliana's mind is joined to God in Trinitarian form and finding her at last in a state of perfect *hesychasm*, not only spiritually but physically, that Juliana is visited by a devil in the form of an angel.

It is perhaps this element of the hagiography which encouraged Cynewulf to choose the story of Juliana in particular as a vehicle. The nature of devilish attacks on monks practising *hesychasm* in their cells is the very essence of the *Praktikos*; such attacks are a central feature of the lives of the desert fathers, and from there they became a commonplace of medieval hagiography. The appearance of devils in the form of angels, or even imitating God, is the danger faced by those anchorites who have successfully freed themselves from their passions and achieved *apatheia*. This would normally be an ultimate attempt at temptation through *kenodoxia* (vainglory, *On Prayer* 73), when the monk takes pride in his achievement. This does not seem to be the situation here, but Juliana does, for a moment, lose her complete state of *apatheiea* as she feels the emotion of fear: 'ða wæs seo fæmne for þam færspelle | egsan geaclad' (then the woman was petrified with fear by the sudden message, ll. 267–68a).

---

52   Louth, *The Origins of the Christian Mystical Tradition*, p. 109.

However, it is momentary, and she immediately repairs the damage — 'ongan þa fæstlice ferð staþelian' (she immediately began to make her spirit steadfast, l. 270) — and prays to God for help. The result is immediate, and although it is consistent with the source, it also fits very neatly with Evagrius's *On Prayer* 74: 'when the angel of God is present, with a single word he puts an end to every opposing activity within us and moves the light of the mind to an unerring activity'.[53] In this way, we see Cynewulf's saint moving through the stages of *hesychasm* as outlined by the desert fathers.

The angel tells Juliana to question the devil. The voice in the *Acta Sanctorum* tells Juliana to grab hold of it ('tu autem adprehende istum'), whilst Cynewulf's angelic voice tells her to hold it still, 'forfoh þone frætgan ond fæste geheald' (seize the wicked one and hold it firmly, l. 284). The importance of immobilizing the devil is added by Cynewulf and becomes part of the continued opposition between movement and stasis which we will discuss in more detail below. What follows becomes a guide to the manipulations of devils, in other words a version of the *praktike*, extricated through the experience of an advanced *hesychast* (Juliana) and confessed by one of the devils directly. The devil's confessions are given in sections in response to Juliana's questioning.[54] Damage to the Exeter Book manuscript means that we are missing the first part of the devil's confession. He gives a long list of the most important Christians, including Christ himself, and takes credit for their torments and deaths. In the *Acta Sanctorum* Belial's methods are either vague, a repeated 'ego sum qui feci [...]' (I am the one who made [...]), or else he refers to devilish possession: 'ego sum qui ad Nironem imperatorem ingressus sum' (I am the one who entered into the emperor Nero); in this way the acts are in fact the acts of the devil, and thus it is the devil who crucifies Peter and decapitates Paul.[55] In Cynewulf, the devil explains how he brought about these events through the mental manipulation of the pagan persecutors:

---

53 Evagrius, *The Greek Ascetic Corpus*, ed. and trans. by Sinkewicz, p. 210. In *On Prayer* 73, Evagrius explains how the devil 'by touching the spot just mentioned [a place in the brain, *On Prayer* 72], alters the light around the mind as he wishes' (*The Greek Ascetic Corpus*, ed. and trans. by Sinkewicz, p. 200). This method is used as a tool to create false visions of the divine. Being fooled by this is indicative of the passion of vainglory. See also *On Prayer* 94: 'Watch out lest the evil demons deceive you through some apparition; rather be mindful, turn to prayer, and call upon God, in order that, if the mental representation comes from Him, he may enlighten you, but if not, that he may quickly drive the deceiver from you.' Evagrius, *The Greek Ascetic Corpus*, ed. and trans. by Sinkewicz, p. 203.

54 Much has been written about Cynewulf's use of opposition in *Juliana*; see Nelson, '*The Battle of Maldon* and *Juliana*'. See also Frantzen, 'Drama and Dialogue in Old English Poetry', p. 110, who sees the exchanges between Juliana and the devil as establishing 'a theatre of penance within the poem'. Hill sees Juliana as representing the *miles Christi* ('The Soldier of Christ in Old English Poetry and Prose', p. 69); while Palmer sees the opposition between Juliana and her oppressors as 'allegorical representations of [...] contending forces' ('Characterization in the Old English *Juliana*', p. 14).

55 *Passio S. Iulianae*, ed. by Lapidge, p. 160.

'Ic Herode | in hyge bisweop' (I incited Herod in his mind, ll. 294b–295a); 'ic gelærde' (I taught, ll. 297 and 307); 'ic Neron bisweac' (I seduced Nero, l. 302). Each time the devil makes clear that it is through his interference in the mental processes of men that these evil actions were brought about. Cynewulf alters the description of devilish methods in the *Acta Sanctorum*, in such a way as to transpose the agency for the killing of notable Christians from action controlled by devils to indirect action brought out by devilish manipulation of the human mind in ways similar to those outlined by Evagrius in the *Praktikos*.

It will be worth looking at the central part of the devil's confession in some detail in both versions, in order to appreciate how Cynewulf's adaptations render the original more Evagrian in focus. In Chapter 9 of the *Acta Sanctorum*, the devil claims that he and his brothers enter into all men. When they find anyone standing firm in the work of God, they cause them to embrace a multitude of desires. This causes them to turn their minds towards the objects of their desire, leading them into error in their thoughts, and then they can neither animate themselves in prayer or persevere in good works. The devils also prevent their victims from attending church, mortifying themselves, or hearing divine scripture. When they find anyone doing these things, they immediately enter into their homes, preventing them from completing any good action. The demons are put to flight by anyone who listens to the holy scriptures or takes the sacrament.[56] This description pits good against evil, the temptations of the devil against the power of holy scripture and divine sacrament, and it has a domestic focus as indicated by the reference to the devils entering the *domus*, or home. This domestic detail suggests it was written for a general public who need only turn aside from vain thoughts and go to church. Cynewulf, on the other hand, focuses more specifically on 'the place of prayer'.

For Evagrius, the place of prayer, προσευχῆς τόπος, is a special term. Bamberger explains that it relates to τόπος θεοῦ, the place of God, and 'refers to the experience of God's presence'.[57] The image of burning is one Evagrius uses in relation to *porneia* (*Eight Thoughts* 16),[58] and he even uses it to describe his own shortcomings in the letter preceding *On Prayer*: 'when I was feverish with the burning of the impure passions, you restored me'.[59] The reference to perversions, lusts, and fantasies in the devil's confession suggests that this is a reference to the demon of lust, *porneia*. Evagrius writes about each of the vices in most of his works. In his letter to Eulogius, we find similarities:

---

56 Summarized from *Passio S. Iulianae*, ed. by Lapidge, pp. 160–61.

57 Evagrius, *The Praktikos*, ed. and trans. by Bamberger, p. 64 n. 30.

58 'Sometimes it [the demon of fornication] touches even the flesh, inducing within it an irrational burning', Evagrius, *The Greek Ascetic Corpus*, ed. and trans. by Sinkewicz, p. 163.

59 We do not know to whom this letter was addressed, but Bamberger makes a good case for Rufinus. See Evagrius, *The Praktikos*, ed. and trans. by Bamberger, p. 51.

THE PLACE OF STILLNESS   239

Little by little the demon [of lust] plots against the person who has relaxed his abstinence due to the flattery of pleasures, in order to become the familiar of his heart, so that once ignited by converse with vice it may be captured and its hatred for sin come to an end. [...] Do not accustom your thinking to a familiarity with the pleasures of the thoughts, for in the assemblage of evils there burns a fire.[60]

Similarly in *On Prayer* 10:

When the demons see you eagerly intent upon true prayer, then they suggest mental representations [...] they stir up your memory of these things, moving the mind to seek after them; and when it does not find them it becomes saddened and miserable. And when the mind stands at prayer, they remind it of the things sought after and the memories associated with them so that the mind, weakened at the knowledge of these things, may lose the fruitlessness of its prayer.[61]

In Cynewulf's version of the devil's confession, there is no mention of domesticity, nor is there reference to the Church, the scriptures, or the sacraments. Instead, the devil goes into a great deal more detail about how he turns the mind of steadfast Christians away from God and prevents them occupying the place of prayer:

þær ic hine finde   ferð staþelian
to godes willan,   ic beo gearo sona
þæt ic him monigfealde   modes gælsan
ongean bere   grimra geþonca,
dyrnra gedwilda,   þurh gedwolena rim.
Ic him geswete   synna lustas,
mæne modlufan,   þæt he minum hraþe,
leahtrum gelenge,   larum hyreð.
Ic hine þæs swiþe   synnum onæle
þæt he byrnende   from gebede swiceð,
stepeð stronglice,   staþolfæst ne mæg
fore leahtra lufan   lenge gewunian
in gebedstowe.
                                                        (ll. 364–76a)

(Where I find him fixing his spirit to God's will, I am immediately ready so that I can carry against him many lusts of the mind, horrible thoughts, dark delusions, through countless perversions. I sweeten for him the pleasures of sins, wicked fantasies,[62] until he quickly becomes

---

60 Evagrius, *The Greek Ascetic Corpus*, ed. and trans. by Sinkewicz, p. 48.
61 Evagrius, *The Greek Ascetic Corpus*, ed. and trans. by Sinkewicz, p. 194.
62 *Modlufu* (l. 370) is translated as 'affection' by both Woolf and Bjork. The context and association with *mæne* (wicked), make 'affection' an unsatisfying option. If we take the first part of the compound *mod* to imply the mind rather than the heart and *lufu* in the sense it

attached to my vices, obeys my teaching. I so greatly inflame him with sins, that he, burning, turns away from the place of prayer, firmly steps away, he can no longer remain steadfast, through love of my vices, in the place of prayer.)

This detailed description in *Juliana* of the devil's attempts to use vices to turn away the steadfast from the place of prayer is typically Evagrian, as is the reference to the place of prayer ('gebedstowe', l. 376) and the light of faith ('leohtes geleafan', l. 378).[63] Evagrius's 'flattery of pleasures' is echoed in Cynewulf's 'sweetening of desires' (l. 369), and the 'dyrnra gedwilda' (dark/ evil errors, l. 368) and the 'gedwolena rim' (countless perversions, l. 368) are suggestive of the impure passions and mental representations produced by the demon of lust. These may not be direct borrowings, but the way Cynewulf has adapted his primary Latin source shows a distinct transposition of the domestic and homiletic temptation of the original to a specifically monastic and Evagrian version of the operation of devils on the mind.

Cynewulf describes the devil's target in terms of the *miles Christi*, or warrior for Christ. Niles has recently argued that the Exeter Book engages in what he calls 'monastic poetics', that is, a 'hybrid poetics, based on Latinate and Germanic models' one of the aims of which, most notably in the case of the two signed poems by Cynewulf, was to 'reinforce the value system embedded in the Rule of St Benedict'.[64] Lines 382–89 of *Juliana* introduce the *miles Christi* (*metodes cempa*), a well-armed Christian who stands firm on the mental battlefield. From him the devils flee, humiliated (*heanmod*, l. 390), and seek out a weaker warrior. The first is able to withstand the arrows of temptation with a *haligne scyld* (holy shield, l. 386). This shield is a reference to 'the shield of faith' (Ephesians 6. 16), but it is also a symbol of *hesychasm*, mental stillness and physical isolation, as in Evagrius's *Eight Thoughts*: 'the one who loves stillness ever remains unwounded by the enemies' arrows' (*Thoughts* 2:6).[65] The weaker warrior is attacked under the *cumbolhagan* (shield wall, l. 395); this is the lower part of the mind that is influenced by the senses, as opposed to the higher, rational part of the mind.[66] According to Evagrius, devils attack the different parts of the mind in different ways, using sensual temptation for the lower part. For Evagrius, these weaker warriors become arms of the devils, they arm 'the more negligent among the brothers' (τοὺς ἀμελεστέρους τῶν ἀδελφῶν, *Praktikos* 5). Both Evagrius and Cynewulf use the image of a

---

is used to refer to Heliseus's feelings for Juliana at ll. 26, 41, and 114 (*brydlufu*), it presumably refers to sexual love in the mind, so 'fantasy' seems a more appropriate translation.

63 When the highest state of *theoria* (contemplation) is achieved, the soul sees its own light. See above.

64 Niles, *God's Exiles and English Verse*, p. 5, and the reference to the poems of Cynewulf, pp. 19–20. Niles credits O'Camb with coining the term. See also Leneghan, 'Preparing the Mind for Prayer', p. 123.

65 Evagrius, *The Greek Ascetic Corpus*, ed. and trans. by Sinkewicz, p. 76.

66 Augustine divides the mind in a similar way. See *The Trinity*, XII.1.

tower under assault to describe the mind under demonic attack: Evagrius describes the mind of the man who flees all worldly pleasure as a tower (πύργος) that is inaccessible to the demon of sadness (λύπη), a demon impossible to resist if we have any attachment to worldly things, because he will set his net and produce sadness there where he sees exactly where our inclination lies (*Praktikos* 19). Cynewulf describes the mind of the weaker warrior as a tower (*se torr*, l. 402) that is pierced by the wicked thoughts of the devil. Cynewulf's devils, like those of Evagrius, use all kinds of methods, including stirring up old memories of past passions, deeds, or grudges: 'þæt hy færinga | ealde æfþoncan edniwedan' (so that they suddenly renewed old grudges, ll. 484b–485). All of their methods attack the mind, however: 'εὐκίνητον γάρ τι πρᾶγμα ὁ νοῦς καὶ πρὸς τὰς ἀνόμους φαντασίας δυσκάθεκτον' (because the mind is a thing easily moved and hard to restrain from forbidden imaginings, *Praktikos* 48).[67] Cynewulf has adapted the more domestic and general description of devilish temptation and the methods used to combat them from the *Acta Sanctorum*, to one that is more specifically monastic in outlook. The images of burning, turning away from the place of prayer, and the description of the mind as a tower attacked by devils' arrows bring it closer to the Evagrian teaching of the *Praktikos* and *On Prayer* than to the *Acta Sanctorum*.

To attain *hesychasm*, the contemplative must still the mind by resisting the forces that aim to trouble it. This creates an opposition of movement and stasis in the mind. Stillness and fixity of the mind is brought about by isolating the self from worldly temptation and stilling the mind from all passionate thoughts that disturb it. There is a constant opposition between mental movement and stasis in *Juliana*. Juliana's mind is described using terms associated with fixity and stasis: *fæste, staþelian, staþol, staþolfæst*, and *soðfæst*. For example, 'Hio to gode hæfde | freondrædenne fæste gestaþelad' (She had firmly fixed [her] affection to God, ll. 106b–107); 'Ic to dryhtne min | mod staþelige' (I fix my mind to my Lord, ll. 221–22b); 'Hyre wæs Cristes lof | in ferðlocan fæste biwunden' (Praise of Christ was firmly wound in her spirit, ll. 233–34). The devil uses the same terms for the minds of the good Christians, for example, 'þær ic hine finde ferð staþelian | to godes willan' (where I find him to have fixed [his] heart to God's will, ll. 364–65a), or 'staþolfæst ne mæg | fore leahtra lufan lenge gewunian | in gebedstowe' (he cannot, for love of vices, remain long firm in the place of prayer, ll. 374b–376a). In the same way, verbs of movement, the *-cyrran* verbs, *ahwyrfan, hweorfan*, and *bugan*, are used in terms of what Juliana and other Christians are resisting. To give a few examples, Juliana asserts, 'ne þu næfre gedest þurh gedwolan þinne | þæt þu mec acyrre from Cristes lofe' (you will never accomplish through your delusion that you will turn me away from the praise of Christ, ll. 138–39); she asks God, 'þæt þu me ne læte of lofe hweorfan | þinre eadgife' (that you do not let me turn aside from your praise and your grace, ll. 275–76a). Affricanus demands,

---

67 Évagre, *Traité Pratique*, ed. and trans. by Guillaumont and Guillaumont, II, p. 608.

'onwend þec in gewitte' (turn yourself in your mind, l. 144), and Heliseus feels excessive shame that 'he ne meahte mod oncyrran | fæmnan foreþonc' (he could not turn the mind [or] the intention of the woman, ll. 226–27a). The devil claims that he is sent 'þæt we soðfæstra | þurh misgedwield mod oncyrren, | ahwyrfen from halor' (that we change the minds of the righteous, turn them from salvation through evil deceit, ll. 325b–327a). There are more examples, and all show the same opposition between mental movement and stasis typical of the struggles of the *hesychast*.

In *Praktikos* 43, Evagrius teaches that the monk must learn about the devils and study them, the better to be able to resist them: 'οὕτω γάρ ἄν αὐτοί τε ῥᾳδίως σὺν Θεῷ προκόπτωμεν, κἀκείνους θαυμάζοντας ἡμᾶς καὶ ὀδυνωμένους ἀποπτῆναι ποιήσωμεν' (for in this way, with the help of God we will easily make progress; as for them [the devils], we will make them fly off, full of admiration for us and perplexed).[68] Juliana uses her time in prison to learn about the methods of devils, and the devil is certainly admiring of her. He finds that

> næs ænig þæs modig   mon ofer eorþan
> þurh halge meaht,   heahfædra nan
> ne witgena.   (ll. 513–15a)

> (nor was any man on earth more brave through holy power, none of the patriarchs, nor the prophets.)

Having learned the wiles of the devil from his own confession, Juliana imparts her knowledge as a teacher to the watching crowd before she meets her final end. Although Juliana is subjected to more tortures, she remains unharmed, unlike her counterpart in the *Acta Sanctorum*, whose body is destroyed. In the *Acta Sanctorum*, Juliana addresses the crowd urging them to repent having sacrificed to idols and to build their houses on living stone: 'peniteat nos daemonibus immolare, et aedificate domus uestras super petram uiuam'. She urges them always to pray in church and obey the scriptures ('semper orate indeficienter in ecclesiam sanctam, et scripturas sanctas oboedite'), to love one another, to receive God's mercy, to sing, pray, and be penitent in heart. Finally, she asks the crowd to pray for her.[69]

While Cynewulf retains much of the original, there are some telling additions that are indicative of Cynewulf's debt to Evagrian models of monastic prayer. For example, Cynewulf's Juliana presents herself as a teacher: 'forþon ic, leof weorud, læran wille' (therefore, beloved people, I want to teach you, l. 647). As one who has achieved *apatheia* and has been tested in her combat

---

68 Évagre, *Traité Pratique*, ed. and trans. by Guillaumont and Guillaumont, II, p. 600, translated into English with reference to the translation by the Guillaumonts: 'De cette façon, nous progresserons facilement avec l'aide de Dieu; quant à eux, nous les ferons s'envoler, pleins d'admiration pour nous et consternés' (p. 601).

69 Summarized from *Passio S. Iulianae*, ed. by Lapidge, pp. 164–65.

THE PLACE OF STILLNESS 243

with a devil, she becomes a teacher to instruct others in the way (*praktike*). Cynewulf adapts the image from the *Acta Sanctorum* of building a house on living rock to protect it from the buffeting of storms, but he expands on the image, adding:

Weal sceal þy trumra
strong wiþstondan   storma scurum,
leahtra gehygdum.   (ll. 650b–652a)

(A strong wall must more firmly withstand showers of storms, thoughts of vices.)

The house built on living rock is a reference to Matthew 7. 24–27, but whereas in the *Acta Sanctorum* this is a question of putting faith in Christ addressed to people who have been worshipping idols, Cynewulf extends it into an instruction on *hesychasm*. The house is the mind, and the forces of the storm battering the walls are specifically 'leahtra gehygd' (thoughts of vices, l. 652) or λογισμοί. The house on firm foundations, able to withstand the attack of λογισμοί is the *hesychast* mind having attained *apatheia*. Juliana insists on the image of fixing the mind firmly and unshakeably to God: 'to þam lifgendan | stane stiðhydge staþol fæstniað' (to the living stone, fix firm foundations with unshakeable mind, ll. 653b–654), and this in 'leohte geleafan' (the light of faith, l. 653), which hints at the light of the soul (νοῦσ).[70] The end of this part of the prayer has a gnostic reference:

soðe treowe   ond sibbe mid eow
healdað æt heortan,   halge rune
þurh modes myne.   (ll. 655–57a)

(Hold true faith and peace with you in your heart, holy mystery through purpose of mind.)

The *halig run* (holy mystery or secret) is obtained through the Old English collocation *modes myne*, purpose of mind.[71] *Modes myne* is suggestive of *praktike* and the *halig run* the achievement of the *gnosis* of *theoria* (contemplation of the divine), the highest form of which is γνῶσις τῆς ἁγίας Τριάδος (the understanding of the Holy Trinity).

Evagrius resumes the idea of the *praktike* in Chapter 2, where he writes: 'βασιλεία οὐρανῶν ἐστιν ἀπάθεια ψυχῆς μετὰ γνώσεως τῶν ὄντων ἀληθοῦς'

---

70 See above, p. 235.

71 This collocation is earlier used by the devil at l. 376. *Myne* has a range of meanings, including mind, purpose, and desire. The devil can be presumed to be referring to 'desire of the mind', as it is one of his methods of temptation, but here 'purpose' seems more appropriate. There is a similar use in *Christ* 3, when Christ describes acts of charity to the poor, 'ge holdlice hyge staþeladon | mid modes myne' (you faithfully make firm their hearts through purpose of mind, ll. 1357–58).

(the kingdom of heaven is *apatheia* of the ψυχῆς with understanding of the true nature of beings, *Praktikos* 2). The ψυχή (psyche) can refer to appetite or desire, but according to Souter, 'the general use of the word in the Bible is in the sense of whatever is felt to belong most essentially to a man's life, when his bodily life has come to be regarded as a secondary thing. It comes near the modern conception, *self*.[72] Cynewulf's *Juliana* teaches that the way to the heavenly kingdom is achieved though resisting devilish attack, the wicked thoughts sent to turn the *hesychast* away from prayer which Evagrius calls λογισμοὶ:

> Wærlic me þinceð   þæt ge wæccende
> wið hettendra   hildewoman
> wearde healden,   þy læs eow wiþerfeohtend
> weges forwyrnen   to wuldres byrig.   (ll. 662–65)

> (It seems prudent to me that you, being vigilant, hold yourselves against the terrors of enemies, lest you be hindered in your way to the city of glory by the foe.)

The idea of vigilance against enemy attack, an attack which is a bar to reaching the heavenly kingdom, sums up the *praktike* in both aim and outcome. How to hold oneself vigilantly against the terrors of enemies is the entire subject of the *praktike*, and achieving the kingdom of glory, βασιλεία οὐρανῶν (the kingdom of heaven) or ultimately Βασιλεία Θεοῦ (the kingdom of God), is its aim, where the kingdom is, in fact, a mental state. This Evagrian idea of the kingdom of heaven being a state of mind achieved through *apatheia* is found not only in the *Praktikos*, but in Ælfric:

> Gesibsume sind þa on him sylfum, þe ealle heora modes styrunga mid gesceade gelogiað, and heora flæsclican gewilnunga gewyldað swa þæt hi sylfe beoð godes rice.[73]

> (They are peaceful in themselves, they who regulate in themselves all their mind's (e)motions with reason, and dominate their fleshly desires so that they become God's kingdom themselves.)

---

72 Souter, *A Pocket Lexicon to the Greek New Testament*, entry for ψυχή, p. 287. The Guillaumonts translate this word as *âme* (soul), Évagre, *Traité Pratique*, ed. and trans. by Guillaumont and Guillaumont, II, p. 499.

73 Ælfric of Eynsham, *Catholic Homilies: The First Series*, ed. by Clemoes, p. 494.

Conclusion

Whether or not Cynewulf had direct access to an Evagrian text, the evidence is overwhelming that he was applying Evagrian thought in his adaptation of *Juliana*. The principles of the *Praktikos* are present in the saint's extreme *apatheia*, in the repeated references to mental movement and stasis (*hesychasm*), in the explanation of the devil's methods to turn the faithful away from God through vices and wicked thoughts (λογισμοί), and in the references to the light of faith in the soul (νοῦσ). The evolution of the process is shown in its highest form in the presence of the Holy Trinity in Juliana's heart (indicative of the ultimate attainment for Evagrius, the Βασιλεία Θεοῦ — the kingdom of God), and the way towards attaining this is explained in Juliana's teaching. The poem ends at the beginning with the compunction of the novice in Cynewulf's signature. These elements suggest Cynewulf composed *Juliana* with a monastic audience in mind, or at least added a layer of meaning that only a monastic audience would understand.

Niles's recent volume on the Exeter Book offers a new and holistic evaluation of the collection of poems found within. These poems, including *Juliana*, represent what Niles terms 'monastic poetics', that is, works 'designed to reinforce the value system embodied in the Rule of St Benedict'.[74] This monastic context is built upon foundations laid by the desert fathers, perhaps the most influential being Evagrius Pontus. Niles's argument supports the work of Leneghan, who had earlier demonstrated the influence of monastic training 'as outlined by the Church Fathers Evagrius Ponticus and John Cassian' on *The Wanderer*.[75]

The adaptations made by Cynewulf to his source in the *Acta Sanctorum* demonstrate a detailed and informed knowledge of Greek monastic spirituality, a spirituality that found its way from the deserts of Egypt to early medieval England and which shows a continuity in the monastic ideal from East to West present from the earliest period of Anglo-Saxon Christianity.

---

74 Niles, *God's Exiles and English Verse*, p. 123.

75 Leneghan, 'Preparing the Mind for Prayer', p. 139.

Works Cited

Manuscripts and Archival Sources

Paris, Bibliothèque nationale de France, MS lat. 10861
Worcester Cathedral, MS Q28

Primary Sources

Ælfric of Eynsham, *Ælfric's Catholic Homilies: The First Series, Text*, ed. by Peter Clemoes, EETS SS, 17 (Oxford: Oxford University Press, 1996)

Augustine, *The Trinity (De Trinitate)*, trans. by Edmund Hill, ed. by John E. Rotelle (New York: New City Press, 1991)

Basil, *The Asketikon of St Basil the Great*, ed. by Anna M. Silvas, Oxford Early Christian Studies (Oxford: Oxford University Press, 2005)

Bede, *Bede's Ecclesiastical History of the English People*, ed. and trans. by Bertram Colgrave and R. A. B. Mynors, 2 vols (Oxford: Clarendon Press, 1969)

Cassian, John, *The Conferences*, ed. and trans. by Boniface Ramsay (New York: Newman Press, 1997)

——, *The Institutes*, ed. and trans. by Boniface Ramsey (New York: Newman Press, 2000)

Evagrius Ponticus, *Évagre le Pontique: Traité Pratique ou Le Moine*, ed. and trans. by A. Guillaumont and C. Guillaumont, Sources Chretiennes, 170–71, 2 vols (Paris: Les Éditions du Cerf, 1971)

——, *Evagrius of Pontus: The Greek Ascetic Corpus*, ed. and trans. by Robert E. Sinkewicz, Oxford Early Christian Studies (Oxford: Oxford University Press, 2003)

——, *Evagrius Ponticus: The Praktikos and Chapters on Prayer*, ed. and trans. by John Eudes Bamberger (Trapist: Cistercian Publications, 1972)

The Exeter Book, ASPR, III, ed. by George Philip Krapp and Elliott Van Kirk Dobbie (New York: Columbia University Press, 1936)

Juliana, ed. by Rosemary Woolf (London: Methuen, 1966)

The Lausiac History of Palladius, ed. by W. K. Lowther Clarke (London: Macmillan, 1918)

A New Eusebius: Documents Illustrating the History of the Church to AD 337, ed. by J. Stevenson and rev. by W. H. C. Frend (Grand Rapids, MI: Baker Academic, 2013)

The Passio S. Iulianae from Paris, BNF, lat. 10861, fols 113v–121r, ed. by Michael Lapidge, 'Cynewulf and the *Passio S. Iulianae*', in *Unlocking the Wordhord: Anglo-Saxon Studies in Memory of Edward B. Irving Jr.*, ed. by Mark C. Amodio and Katherine O'Brien O'Keeffe (Toronto: University of Toronto Press, 2003), pp. 156–71

Benedict, *RB 1980: The Rule of St Benedict*, ed. by Timothy Fry and others (Collegeville: Liturgical Press, 1981)

SS Patrum Aegyptiorum opera omnia: Praecedunt Philonis Carpasii, Asterii Amaseni, Nemesii Emeseni, Hieronymi Græci Scripta Quæe Supersunt, ed. by Jacques-Paul Migne, Patrologiae cursus completus, series Graeca, 40 (Paris: Traditio Catholica, 1863)

Secondary Sources

Anderson, Earl R., *Cynewulf: Structure, Style and Theme in his Poetry* (London: Associated University Presses, 1983)

Anlezark, Daniel, 'The Soul in the Old English *Soliloquies* and Ninth-Century Neoplatonism', in *Germano-Celtica: A Festschrift for Brian Taylor*, ed. by Anders Ahlqvist and Pamela O'Neill, Sydney Series in Celtic Studies, 16 (Sydney: University of Sydney, 2017), pp. 35–60

Bdzyl, Donald G., '*Juliana*: Cynewulf's Dispeller of Delusion', in *The Cynewulf Reader*, ed. by Robert E. Bjork (London: Routledge, 2001), pp. 193–206

Biggs, Frederick M., Thomas D. Hill, and Paul E. Szarmach, eds, *Sources of Anglo-Saxon Literary Culture*, 1: *Abbo of Fleury, Abbo of Saint-Germain-des-Prés, and Acta Sanctorum* (Kalamazoo: Medieval Institute Publications, 2001)

Bischoff, Bernhard, and Michael Lapidge, eds, *Biblical Commentaries from the Canterbury School of Theodore and Hadrian* (Cambridge: Cambridge University Press, 1994)

Chadwick, Owen, *John Cassian*, 2nd edn (Cambridge: Cambridge University Press, 1968)

Clayton, Mary, 'Introduction', in *Two Ælfric Texts: 'The Twelve Abuses' and 'The Vices and Virtues'. An Edition and Translation of Ælfric's Old English Versions of 'De duodecim abusivis' and 'De octo vitiis et de duodecim abusivis'*, ed. and trans. by Mary Clayton, Anglo-Saxon Texts, 11 (Woodbridge: D. S. Brewer, 2013), pp. 1–107

Clements, Jill Hamilton, 'Reading, Writing and Resurrection: Cynewulf's Runes as a Figure of the Body', *ASE*, 43 (2014), 133–54

Conner, Patrick W., 'On Dating Cynewulf', in *The Cynewulf Reader*, ed. by Robert E. Bjork (London: Routledge, 2001), pp. 23–56

Constas, Maximos, 'Nothing Is Greater than Divine Love: Evagrios of Pontos, St Maximos the Confessor, and the Philokalia', in *Rightly Dividing the Word of Truth: Studies in Honour of Metropolitan Kallistos of Diokleia*, ed. by Andreas Andreopoulos and Graham Speake (Oxford: Peter Lang, 2014), pp. 57–74

Flight, Tim, '*The Dream of the Rood*: A Neglected Contemplative Text', in *Mystical Doctrines of Deification: Case Studies in the Christian Tradition*, ed. by John Arblaster and Rob Faesen (London: Routledge, 2020), pp. 72–88

——, 'Through a Glass Darkly: Evidence for Knowledge of Pseudo-Dionysius in Anglo-Saxon England', *Journal of Medieval Religious Cultures*, 43 (2017), 1–23

Frantzen, Allen J., 'Drama and Dialogue in Old English Poetry: The Scene of Cynewulf's *Juliana*', *Theatre Survey*, 48 (2007), 99–119

Fulk, R. D., *A History of Old English Meter*, Middle Ages Series (Philadelphia: University of Pennsylvania Press, 1992)

——, 'Poet, Canon, Date', in *The Cynewulf Reader*, ed. by Robert E. Bjork (London: Routledge, 2001), pp. 3–22

Hill, Joyce, 'The Soldier of Christ in Old English Poetry and Prose', *Leeds Studies in English*, 12 (1981), 57–80

Lapidge, Michael, *The Anglo-Saxon Library* (Oxford: Oxford University Press, 2006)

——, 'The Career of Archbishop Theodore', in *Archbishop Theodore: Commemorative Studies on his Life and Influence*, ed. by Michael Lapidge (Cambridge: Cambridge University Press, 1995), pp. 1–29

——, 'Cynewulf and the *Passio S. Iulianae*', in *Unlocking the Wordhord: Anglo-Saxon Studies in Memory of Edward B. Irving Jr.*, ed. by Mark C. Amodio and Katherine O'Brien O'Keeffe (Toronto: University of Toronto Press, 2003), pp. 147–71

Lemeni, Daniel, '"You Can Become All Flame": Deification in Early Egyptian Monasticism', in *Mystical Doctrines of Deification: Case Studies in the Christian Tradition*, ed. by John Arblaster and Rob Faesen (London: Routledge, 2020), pp. 16–34

Leneghan, Francis, 'Preparing the Mind for Prayer: *The Wanderer, Hesychasm* and *Theosis*', *Neophilologus*, 100 (2016), 121–42

Louth, Andrew, *The Origins of the Christian Mystical Tradition: From Plato to Denys* (Oxford: Clarendon Press, 1999)

Mainoldi, Ernesto Sergio, 'The Reception of the Greek Patristic Doctrine of Deification in the Medieval West: The Case of John Scottus Eriugena', in *Mystical Doctrines of Deification: Case Studies in the Christian Tradition*, ed. by John Arblaster and Rob Faesen (London: Routledge, 2020), pp. 60–71

Major, Tristan, '*Awriten on þreo geþeode*: The Concept of Hebrew, Greek, and Latin in Old English and Anglo-Latin Literature', *JEGP*, 120 (2021), 141–76

Neidorf, Leonard, 'Lexical Evidence for the Relative Chronology of Old English Poetry', *SELIM: Journal of the Spanish Society for Medieval English Language and Literature*, 20 (2013–2014), 7–48

Nelson, Marie, '*The Battle of Maldon* and *Juliana*: The Language of Confrontation', in *Structures of Opposition in Old English Poems* (Amsterdam: Rodopi, 1989), pp. 137–52

Niles, John D., *God's Exiles and English Verse: On the Exeter Anthology of Old English Poetry* (Exeter: University of Exeter Press, 2019)

Palmer, R. Barton, 'Characterization in the Old English *Juliana*', *South Atlantic Bulletin*, 40 (1976), 10–21

Ponirakis, Eleni, 'Echoes of Eriugena in the *Old English Boethius*', *Neophilologus*, 105 (2021), 279–88

Ritzke-Rutherford, Jean, 'Anglo-Saxon Antecedents of the Middle English Mystics', in *The Medieval Mystical Tradition*, ed. by Marion Glasscoe (Exeter: University of Exeter Press, 1980), pp. 216–33

Russell, Norman, *The Doctrine of Deification in the Greek Patristic Tradition* (Oxford: Oxford University Press, 2009)

Souter, Alexander, *A Pocket Lexicon to the Greek New Testament* (Oxford: Clarendon Press, 1920)

Szarmach, Paul E., 'The Vocabulary of Sin and the Eight Cardinal Sins', in *Old English Lexicology and Lexicography: Essays in Honor of Antonette diPaolo Healey*, ed. by Maren Clegg Hyer, Haruko Momma, and Samantha Zacher, Anglo-Saxon Studies, 40 (Cambridge: D. S. Brewer, 2020), pp. 110–26

Treschow, Michael, 'Echoes of the *Periphyseon* in the Third Book of Alfred's *Soliloquies*', *N&Q*, 40 (1993), 281–86

Wittig, Joseph, 'Figural Narrative in Cynewulf's *Juliana*', in *The Cynewulf Reader*, ed. by Robert E. Bjork (London: Routledge, 2001), pp. 147–70

HANNAH M. BAILEY

St Rumwold in the Borderland

The textual evidence available to scholars of early medieval England tends to privilege *an* idea of the world — one which is Christian, literate, elite, and generally late in the chronology of the era that comes under the loose label of 'early medieval'. But this a long era of multiple revolutionary social changes that will have altered assumptions about the way the world works: not just major political moments such as the conversion and the spread of literacy and the particular view of the cosmos that came with it, or the consolidation of discrete communities into a unified kingdom and proto-nation, but also the subtler but no less significant transformations from gift economy to coin economy,[1] and from a presumption that dwellings are transient and moveable to a presumption of permanence and the beginnings of urbanization.[2] It is possible to see hints of the discrepancies between earlier and later understandings of the world — particularly changing assumptions about land use, geography, and elite domestic culture — in some later texts about the past, particularly in their moments of confusion or implausibility. The example treated in this chapter is the eleventh-century Latin *Vita sancti Rumwoldi*, which records a narrative about a conversion-era infant saint which on the surface is thoroughly implausible.[3] When read in conversation with physical geography and our knowledge of seventh-century patterns of elite culture, however, it appears that the *vita* may actually contain a kernel of truth about

---

[*] Thanks to Stefany Wragg for sharing resources and suggestions at an early stage of the research for this chapter, and to the Oxford Old English Work-in-Progress seminar for their feedback.

[1] See, for example, Jones, 'Transaction Costs, Institutional Change, and the Emergence of a Market Economy'.

[2] Blair, *Building Anglo-Saxon England*, pp. 64–67, 84–86, 104–13, 385–415. See also Sofield, 'Shaping Buildings and Identities'; Blair, *The Church in Anglo-Saxon Society*, pp. 279–81; Wickham-Crowley, 'Living on the Ecg'.

[3] *Vita sancti Rumwoldi*, in *Three Eleventh-Century Anglo-Latin Saints' Lives*, ed. and trans. by Love, pp. 91–115. In this chapter I use the spelling 'Rumwold' in deference to its being the most common of several spellings of the saint's name within scholarship, but where the saint is presently commemorated in the names of churches, holy wells, streets, a care home, and a housing development, the standard spelling is 'Rumbold'.

> **Hannah M. Bailey** (hannah.bailey@ell.ox.ac.uk) is a Lecturer in English at Wadham College, University of Oxford.

Ideas of the World in Early Medieval English Literature, ed. by Mark Atherton, Kazutomo Karasawa, and Francis Leneghan, SOEL 1 (Turnhout: Brepols, 2022)   pp. 249–272
BREPOLS ❧ PUBLISHERS   DOI 10.1484/M.SOEL.5.130564

past landscape use which has been both preserved and distorted through processes of social memory.[4]

That landscape itself can also be read as a historical document, as it both shapes and records patterns of human activity.[5] The role that watersheds have played in defining English 'cultural provinces' throughout history was established by Charles Phythian-Adams, who notes that drainage patterns will determine a region's 'directional logic — a broad underlying axis of activity', while 'however insignificant they may sometimes be in terms of altitude, watersheds represent identifiable lines of punctuation in the landscape'.[6] One of the key points developed by John Blair in his 2018 book *Building Anglo-Saxon England* is the cultural distinctiveness of the 'Eastern Zone', particularly (though certainly not exclusively) in the seventh century, when the life of Rumwold takes place.[7] Blair observes that the south-western limit of this Eastern Zone (which he notes is more or less coterminous with the 'North Sea Cultural Province' whose geography was established by Tom Williamson through different methodologies) is defined by the watershed of the rivers that flow into Wash.[8] More recently, Carolyn Twomey has also shown that patterns of practical and ritual landscape use as shaped by rivers and watersheds persisted from the late Iron Age through evangelization into the early medieval period.[9]

St Kenelm: Text and Landscape

These watershed boundaries may not have been consciously or overtly addressed by medieval writers in the way that political boundaries such as the one between Mercia and Wessex were, but the quotidian patterns of movement shaped by them do make their way into otherwise fantastical texts, such as the *Life of St Kenelm*.[10] According to the eleventh-century *Vita et miracula*,

---

4 On the concept of 'social memory', see Fentress and Wickham, *Social Memory*.
5 Cf. Everitt, *Continuity and Colonization*, p. 13. See also Rippon, Smart, and Pears, *The Fields of Britannia*.
6 Phythian-Adams, 'Introduction', pp. 10, 11. See also Phythian-Adams, 'Local History and Societal History'.
7 Blair, *Building Anglo-Saxon England*, especially pp. 10–11, 71–73, 116, 278.
8 The term 'watershed' is usually used for the dividing line between two drainage basins — for example, rain falling on one side of Edge Hill in Warwickshire will flow down to the Cherwell in the Thames Basin and on to the sea via London, whereas rain falling on the other side of Edge Hill will flow down to the Avon in the Severn Basin and out to the sea via the Bristol Channel — but it is also frequently used as a synonym for 'drainage basin', especially in North American English. In this article I will generally use it to refer to the dividing line between river basin districts, though some of the figures use it as a shorthand to label the river basin districts themselves.
9 Twomey, 'Rivers and Rituals', pp. 72–77.
10 *Vita et miracula sancti Kenelmi*, in *Three Eleventh-Century Anglo-Latin Saints' Lives*, ed. and trans. by Love, pp. 49–89.

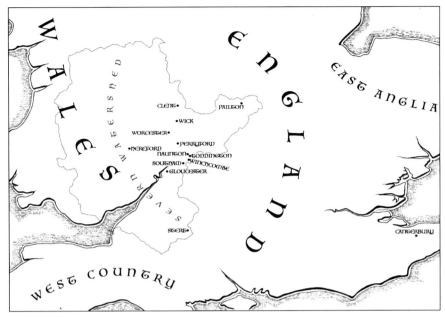

Figure 9.1. The Geography of the *Vita S. Kenelmi* and the Severn Basin. © 2021 Robin Alexander Lucas.

Kenelm was a seven-year-old Mercian child-king of the eighth century who was murdered on the orders of his wicked and greedy older sister. It is well known that this narrative is more fairy tale than fact; the Kenelm (Cynhelm) who appears in the historical record was never king, and was an adult — old enough to be witnessing charters — when he died.[11] But even the fairy-tale version of Kenelm's life carries some genuine social history in it, including geographical details that make it more useful to historians as a 'landscape biography' than a personal one.[12]

The *vita* makes some grand claims about the geographical extent of Kenelm's significance and influence. The pope in Rome and the archbishop in Canterbury both play a part in the recovery of his body. A Saxon man comes all the way to Winchcombe to seek a miraculous release from his iron bonds through Kenelm's intercession, and on Kenelm's feast day people 'ex tota Anglia […] confluerent' (flocked together from the whole of England).[13] But leaving aside the generic foreigner (the Saxon penitent is a hagiographical trope, as Love notes),[14] and the aspirational allusions to seats

---

11   *Three Eleventh-Century Anglo-Latin Saints' Lives*, ed. and trans. by Love, pp. lxxxix–xc.
12   On the concept of landscape biography, see the chapter by Mark Atherton in this volume, p. 274.
13   *Three Eleventh-Century Anglo-Latin Saints' Lives*, ed. and trans. by Love, pp. 78/79.
14   *Three Eleventh-Century Anglo-Latin Saints' Lives*, ed. and trans. by Love, p. 82 n. 1.

of ecclesiastical power, the locations actually mentioned in the *vita* proper are Winchcombe (Gloucestershire), Clent and Cowbach (presumably in the Clent Hills in Worcestershire), Worcester(shire), Gloucester(shire), and Perryford (between Winchcombe and Worcester).[15] Places named in the miracles which can be located with some certainty are Toddington (about three miles north of Winchcombe), Naunton (a farm just outside Toddington), Southam (about four miles south-west of Winchcombe), and Hereford.[16] Three other places mentioned in the miracles, *Peyletona*, *Stertel*, and *Wic*, cannot be certainly identified, but Rosalind Love proposes Pailton near Rugby, Stert in Wiltshire, and Droitwich as plausible candidates.[17] This is not *tota Anglia* — it is not even most of Mercia. What is most interesting about the distribution of these places is that not one is outside the Severn Basin (see Fig. 9.1).[18] They are spread across a range of about ninety miles north to south and seventy-five east to west, but as far as the *vita* is concerned no one of note made the five-mile journey to Winchcombe, the centre of Kenelm's cult, from the other side of the nearby Severn/Thames watershed. Excluding the three geographical outliers of Hereford, Stert, and Wick (the latter two of which are doubtful identifications anyway), we are left with a central cluster of places lying along a fifty-mile stretch of the Severn. Though the *vita* makes large claims for Kenelm's importance for all of England — and Christendom more widely — the shape and extent of the more limited social world of the hagiographer(s) is clearly visible. Their cultural province is the Severn drainage basin, and more particularly, the region Phythian-Adams designates 'Severn/Avon'.[19]

St Rumwold: The Text

St Rumwold is also a Mercian royal child with an eleventh-century *vita*. Unlike Kenelm, he cannot be identified with a recorded historical figure, though the fact that the cult was genuinely old and not an eleventh-century invention is confirmed by the presence of an entry in the list of saints' resting places known as the *Segan*, which says: 'Ðonne resteð sancte Rumwold on þare stowe, þe is gehaten Buccyngaham, neah þare ea Usan' (and Saint Rumwold rests in that place which is called Buckingham, near the River Ouse).[20] In D. W. Rollason's analysis of the *Segan* he notes that the section in which

---

15 *Three Eleventh-Century Anglo-Latin Saints' Lives*, ed. and trans. by Love, pp. 63 n. 7, 69 n. 5.

16 *Three Eleventh-Century Anglo-Latin Saints' Lives*, ed. and trans. by Love, pp. 74 n. 1, 84 n. 1.

17 *Three Eleventh-Century Anglo-Latin Saints' Lives*, ed. and trans. by Love, pp. 76 n. 2, 79 n. 5, 84 n. 4.

18 The Severn Basin includes all rivers that come out at the Severn Estuary, not just the Severn itself. For detailed maps of England's river basin districts, see Environment Agency, *Catchment Data Explorer*.

19 Phythian-Adams and Carter, eds, *Societies, Cultures and Kinship*, fig. 1.1, p. xvii.

20 Liebermann, *Die Heiligen Englands*, p. 13, item 19. Translation mine.

Rumwold appears looks to be pre-Viking in origin and goes out of its way to associate saints with rivers. He also observes that the majority of the places named in this section are known sites of religious foundations, one of three exceptions being Rumwold's resting place of Buckingham, 'about which in the pre-Conquest period virtually nothing is known'.[21] There is no historical record of a real person who can be plausibly identified with Rumwold as Cynhelm can with Kenelm, but I approach the text from the premise that it did not arise ex nihilo. While it seems unlikely that it preserves accurate information about specific persons and events, I suspect that it does reflect a tradition of knowledge regarding social practices and landscape use in the seventh century.

According to the *vita*, Rumwold is the grandson of Penda, the king of Mercia. The story begins with Penda getting himself baptized before marrying. He has a daughter who is raised a Christian; she marries an unnamed pagan king of Northumbria and insists that he convert to Christianity before consummating their marriage. Several months later when Rumwold's mother is heavily pregnant, Penda invites the couple to come to a meeting with him to 'publicas res ciuiles equo discrimine constituerent' (establish civil administration by a fair division).[22] Rumwold's mother goes into labour en route, so the servants pitch a camp in a field full of lilies and roses, and St Rumwold is born. He immediately cries out three times: 'Christianus sum' (I am a Christian).[23] Fortunately, there are two priests on hand, Widerin and Eadwald, who lead the party in singing a hymn. Rumwold explains that he will only live for three days so they must baptize him straight away. He requires a font, and gives instructions to the servants to go and fetch a particular hollow stone lying in a hut 'humide adiacentis uallicule' (in the marshy valley nearby).[24] They cannot lift it, but the two priests miraculously can. The baptism is accomplished, the Mass is celebrated, and baby Rumwold gives a lengthy sermon — his preaching and the audience's pious responses to it take up about a third of the *vita*.[25] At the end of the sermon, Rumwold reminds those assembled that he will only live for three days and tells them that he has determined that his bones should remain in the place where he was born for one year, then reside in Brackley for two years, and then 'requiescant in loco qui uocabitur quandoque Buccingaham omni tempore' (rest for all time in the place which will sometime be known as Buckingham).[26]

---

21 Rollason, 'Lists of Saints' Resting-Places', p. 67.

22 *Three Eleventh-Century Anglo-Latin Saints' Lives*, ed. and trans. by Love, pp. 96/97. Love speculates on what might be implied by this expression but notes that 'the hagiographer is characteristically vague on historical detail'.

23 *Three Eleventh-Century Anglo-Latin Saints' Lives*, ed. and trans. by Love, pp. 98/99.

24 *Three Eleventh-Century Anglo-Latin Saints' Lives*, ed. and trans. by Love, pp. 100/101.

25 One of the themes of the sermon is the Trinity; as David Parsons notes, 'the legend is pervaded by the symbolism of the number three' ('The Mercian Church', p. 59).

26 *Three Eleventh-Century Anglo-Latin Saints' Lives*, ed. and trans. by Love, pp. 112/13.

The narrator goes on to explain:

> Istorum autem locorum nomina non erant eo tempore nota, sed post multorum temporum curricula inuenta uel cognita sunt. Sunt quoque nunc uille in illis locis site, fertiles segetibus, iugerum multorum habentes copiam, atque dense hominum habitatione. Vocatur autem locus in quo natus est Suthtunus, alius uero Braccalea, tertius quoque Buccinghaham.
>
>> (Now, the names of those places were not known at the time, but after the passage of many years they have been discovered or recognized. Now also there are towns sited in those places, which are rich in crops, have many acres of land, and are densely populated by men. The place in which he was born is called (King's) Sutton, the second place is called Brackley, and the third Buckingham.)[27]

Even after making allowances for the miraculous, there is still much about this story that is unlikely. The religious affiliations seem reversed; Penda did have a daughter, Cyneburh, who married a Northumbrian sub-king, Alhfrith, but by Bede's account Penda was famously pagan while Alhfrith was the son of the Christian king Oswiu and an ally of Bishop Wilfrid. As Love observes, the conventional hagiographical roles of pagan husband and Christian wife are more appropriate to the marriage of Cyneburh's brother Peada to Alhfrith's sister Alhflæd.[28]

The story also takes place at the wrong border. Rumwold is born in Kings Sutton, by the River Cherwell, on the present Oxfordshire/Northamptonshire border. It seems a strange choice for a king of Mercia meeting with a Northumbrian ally (and asking his heavily pregnant daughter to travel to the meeting as well) to arrange for that meeting to happen just about as far from their mutual border as it is possible to get without spilling over into Wessex. The fact that Rumwold's parents have to stop and set up a hasty camp en route suggests that the intended meeting point with Penda was somewhere even further south, though the *vita* is somewhat confused on this point. After they have made camp, Penda abruptly appears in the story making a suggestion for a baptismal vessel, which Rumwold dismisses. His presence (or absence) is then never mentioned again.

I am prepared to accept that *somebody* existed whose death or commemoration provided the grit around which the pearl of narrative was built — though, like Love, I am not convinced that the historical Rumwold was really Penda's grandson and still less persuaded that he was the son of a reigning Northumbrian sub-king. It is certainly plausible that events like those described in the *vita*

---

27 *Three Eleventh-Century Anglo-Latin Saints' Lives*, ed. and trans. by Love, pp. 112/13.
28 *Three Eleventh-Century Anglo-Latin Saints' Lives*, ed. and trans. by Love, pp. clxii–clxiii, 96 n. 3. On Alhfrith, and on the marriages between children of Penda and children of Oswiu, see also Yorke, *Kings and Kingdoms of Early Anglo-Saxon England*, pp. 79, 82.

might have taken place during Penda's reign. The presupposition that there was not yet a minster at Kings Sutton,[29] that conversion was ongoing, and that the impromptu baptism and subsequent death of the child of socially prominent parents was sufficiently out of the ordinary to be a noteworthy event, are all details that suit the story's seventh-century setting. But Penda has a suspiciously large number of saintly progeny — Thacker counts at least eleven.[30] As Barbara Yorke puts it:

> The number of Penda's daughters appears to be legion and no historian would wish to go to his or her death defending all these attributions as historically accurate, but their cumulative effect is to suggest that the promotion of the cults of members of the royal house was part of the Mercian policy for strengthening control of the satellite provinces.[31]

Yorke notes that there is evidence that some of such provinces were controlled directly by members of the Mercian royal house, while others were not.[32] It is possible that Rumwold's parents were relations of Penda who had been placed in charge of a satellite province located somewhere in or near the area associated with Rumwold's cult, though it is unlikely that Rumwold's mother was one of the legitimate daughters of Penda known to the historical record. Alternatively, Rumwold's parents might have been among the ruling elite of a satellite province whose kin relationship with Penda was constructed retrospectively, either as propaganda legitimizing Mercian expansionism or through the simplifying and snowballing tendencies of social memory — the same cultural force that results in the attribution of so many dubious inspirational quotations to Abraham Lincoln and Marilyn Monroe. As James Fentress and Chris Wickham observe, 'the natural tendency of social memory is to suppress what is not meaningful or intuitively satisfying in the collective memories of the past, and interpolate or substitute what seems more appropriate or more in keeping with their particular conception of the world'.[33] Kings Sutton's 'rival' in the etymological sense (i.e. its neighbour on the opposite bank of the river) is Adderbury, which credits its name and monastic foundation to Penda's daughter Eadburg;[34] this could be what provided the initial impetus for Kings Sutton to associate itself (or assume itself to be associated) with Penda as well.

---

29 The date of the foundation at Kings Sutton is unknown, but highly unlikely to be any earlier than 650–850, the period which John Blair refers to as the 'golden age of minsters'. Blair, 'A Saint for Every Minster?', p. 456.

30 Thacker, 'Kings, Saints and Monasteries', p. 1.

31 Yorke, *Kings and Kingdoms of Early Anglo-Saxon England*, p. 110. For her comments on Rumwold, see p. 101.

32 Yorke, *Kings and Kingdoms of Early Anglo-Saxon England*, p. 108.

33 Fentress and Wickham, *Social Memory*, pp. 58–59. An example they give is Charlemagne's battle with Basque forces at Roncevaux being remembered at the time of the Crusades as a battle with Saracens.

34 Blair, 'A Handlist of Anglo-Saxon Saints', p. 525.

It is also plausible that Rumwold genuinely was the issue of a marriage alliance intended to reinforce ties between Mercia and one of its satellites or sub-kingdoms, but the belief that Rumwold's father was a king of Northumbria is almost certainly a fiction of social memory. The idea that Mercia was a stable kingdom of relatively fixed geographical scope, with a single powerful king whose (legitimate) progeny made alliances with rulers of other stable major kingdoms of the Heptarchy and went on to establish half the region's monastic foundations, is more in keeping with eleventh-century ideals of kingship and understandings of English history than with the messier reality of the seventh century. This was a time when different dynasties were vying for control of the major kingdoms, and (as documents like the Tribal Hidage hint) those kingdoms were overlaid on top of smaller sub-kingdoms or cultural units.[35] Barbara Yorke describes the late seventh-century saint Frideswide (who lived about twenty-five miles south of St Rumwold, in or near Oxford), as one of the 'dependent rulers on the fringes of the Mercian Kingdom'.[36] It seems far more likely that one or both of Rumwold's parents belonged to a milieu that could also be described in these terms than that he was the child of Alhfrith of Northumbria.

St Rumwold: The Landscape

Leaving aside the long journey from Northumbria to southern Mercia that Rumwold's parents supposedly made, what we are left with in the *vita*'s geography is a local journey from west to east made by the saint's remains. From Kings Sutton to Brackley is a distance of just over five miles as the crow flies, and Buckingham is a further seven miles beyond that. Rumwold may have allowed three years for his body to reach Buckingham, but a person travelling by foot (assuming they're unencumbered by baggage or boggy ground) could cover the distance in as little as 4.5 hours.

Much of the scholarship on this *vita* has attempted to find some rationale for the invocation of these three places that is rooted in royal or ecclesiastical administrative units. For Brackley to have been within the same (royal or ecclesiastical) administrative unit as Kings Sutton would be consistent with later practice (they are in the same hundred and deanery), but Buckingham is in a separate county and lacks an obvious administrative link to Kings Sutton, so it is the connection between Kings Sutton and Buckingham which attracts the most speculation.

Some historians have attempted to explain the movement of the *vita* in terms of royal estates; David Parsons for one takes the *vita* as evidence that

---

35 On the Tribal Hidage, see Yorke, *Kings and Kingdoms of Early Anglo-Saxon England*, pp. 9–15, 106–07; Featherstone, 'The Tribal Hidage and the Ealdormen of Mercia'.

36 Yorke, *Nunneries and the Anglo-Saxon Royal Houses*, p. 21.

Kings Sutton was part of a vast seventh-century royal estate that stretched as far as Buckingham.[37] There is a danger of circular argument here, however, since the *vita* itself is the only evidence that an estate centred on Kings Sutton (1) extended that far at that date and (2) was royal at that date. One reason for caution in interpreting Kings Sutton as an early royal estate is, paradoxically, its status as a later one: what John Blair has demonstrated about the co-evolution of minsters and royal vills is the fundamental instability of royal sites prior to the ninth century, such that continuity between pre-Viking royal vills and those recorded by Domesday is a rare exception.[38] He also argues that the common assumption that minsters were constructed on pre-existing sites of secular power often gets the sequence the wrong way around.[39] Even if the area around Kings Sutton did have very early royal associations, it is also important not to assume that this made it a royal *residence*. Jill Bourne's work on the place name 'Kingston' has demonstrated that in most cases, the name does not refer to a town in which the king dwells, but to a town that serves the function of monitoring and regulating communication routes and the movement of goods and people *on behalf of* the king.[40] Kings Sutton is not exactly a 'Kingston' (the manor at Sutton is held by the king in the Domesday book, though the prefix 'Kings' is not attested until late in the thirteenth century),[41] but Bourne's discoveries have shaken prior scholarly assumptions about both royal relationships to the landscape and also 'functional' and 'directional' place names ending in *-tūn* more generally.[42] In short, attempting to explain the movement of Rumwold's body as evidence for the territory of an early royal vill raises more questions than it answers.

Other historians have tried to explain the geography of the *vita* through details of ecclesiastical bureaucracy that link Kings Sutton to Buckingham. Many such connections do exist, but they cannot be convincingly traced back to the seventh century, nor do they seem sufficient to explain the need to invent a story like this in the eleventh. Such studies often allude to an article in which M. J. Franklin states that in his unpublished PhD dissertation he was 'able to argue that its [Kings Sutton's] *parochia* covered a considerable area, at one time at least as far as Watling Street some fifteen miles to the north-east and possibly as far as Buckingham the same distance across the county boundary in the other direction'.[43] The dissertation is in fact much more circumspect,

---

37 Parsons, 'The Mercian Church', p. 59. Curiously the suggestion of discrete but *linked* holdings does not arise; see the chapter by Mark Atherton in this volume, pp. 296–97, on the lines of communication that linked lands belonging to Byrhtnoth and his relatives.

38 Blair, *The Church in Anglo-Saxon Society*, pp. 266–81.

39 Blair, *The Church in Anglo-Saxon Society*, p. 266.

40 Bourne, *The Place-Name Kingston and Royal Power*.

41 Gover, Mawer, and Stenton, *The Place Names of Northamptonshire*, p. 58.

42 See Blair, *Building Anglo-Saxon England*, pp. 193–228, discussed further below. See also Mark Atherton in this volume, pp. 284–86.

43 Franklin, 'The Identification of Minsters', p. 81.

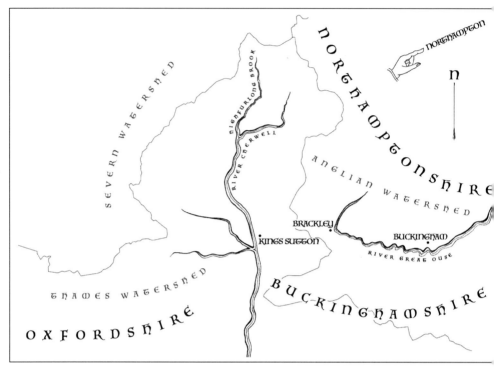

Figure 9.2. The Resting Places of St Rumwold. © 2021 Robin Alexander Lucas.

however, and describes the actual formal ecclesiastical links between Kings Sutton and Buckingham as 'a piece of administrative convenience rather than evidence of a huge *parochia*'.[44] While Love is committed to the premise that details of the *vita* are more likely to be explicable in terms of eleventh-century concerns than seventh-century ones, she concedes that 'the tie between Rumwold's three supposed resting-places seems to elude definition'.[45]

Neither the 'royal estate' nor the 'church politics' hypothesis is entirely persuasive in articulating a relationship between Kings Sutton, Brackley, and Buckingham which is reflected by the *vita*. However, the connection between these three places does not need to take the form of a royal or ecclesiastical administrative unit. Instead of attempting to explain the tale in these top-down cultural terms, it is more productive to look for the seams of compromise between that authoritative layer of culture, the narrative conventions of hagiography, and underlying local memory. John Blair argues that many of

---

44 Franklin, 'Minsters and Parishes', pp. 266, 263. Alan Thacker expresses some doubt about the Buckingham connection as proposed by Franklin but admits the possibility that 'all the foci of Rumwold's cult were originally the interconnected ecclesiastical centres of a large royal estate'. Thacker, 'Kings, Saints and Monasteries', p. 7.

45 *Three Eleventh-Century Anglo-Latin Saints' Lives*, ed. and trans. by Love, p. clix.

the literate hagiographies of the eleventh and twelfth centuries which took as their subject local saints from the first golden age of minsters (650–850) may be 'repositories of folklore motifs captured at a relatively early date, of evidence for vernacular cult practice, and even of genuine information about landscapes, sites, and events'.[46] He notes that posthumous journeys of saints' bodies are a common narrative convention of southern Mercian *vitae*, but points out that 'the fact that the sites do often mark stages along routes may point to more organic origins, whether in specific journeys by individuals or in the general importance of certain lines of communication'.[47] Looking at Rumwold's journey in these terms, the most striking thing about it is that it is a journey that crosses a watershed (see Fig. 9.2). Kings Sutton sits beside the River Cherwell, whose catchment forms the northernmost protrusion of the Thames River Basin. Kings Sutton to Brackley is the shortest possible overland route from a major tributary of the Thames to the River Great Ouse; Buckingham is a short way downriver, further into that culturally distinctive Eastern Zone.

As well as being a logical overland crossing point for someone who was travelling primarily by water where possible,[48] Kings Sutton is also where people travelling across the Cherwell Valley overland towards Brackley and points east would have crossed the river (see Fig. 9.3).[49] The most striking feature of the geography of Kings Sutton is how it stands on a slight rise above the flood plain, not quite as high as other neighbouring hills, but perfectly situated to command a clear view of the Twyford (i.e. 'double-ford') crossing a mile upriver to the north. Building upon Bourne's demonstration that most Kingstons are positioned to monitor and regulate communication, Blair has shown that most Burtons are named not because they are themselves fortified but because they stand on high ground *near* a fortified burh, in a position to keep watch over a broader swathe of the landscape, and he furthermore argues that this is just one component of a systematic use, beginning in Mercia, of *-tūn* place names in relation to royal sites and aristocratic itineration.[50] Although the role directional *-tūnas* such as Sutton have in this system has not yet been fully elucidated, the insight into the importance of viewpoints and sight lines in naming practices leads me to the hypothesis that it is the sight line between Kings Sutton and the

---

46 Blair, 'A Saint for Every Minster?', p. 478.

47 Blair, 'A Saint for Every Minster?', pp. 484, 485.

48 The extent to which these rivers were navigable is still debated, but water levels in England were generally higher in the Middle Ages. See Twomey, 'Rivers and Rituals', p. 67.

49 The Cherwell routinely floods in the winter, and Franklin cites an episode from a life of Osyth as evidence that the Cherwell was, in the Middle Ages, a 'considerable barrier'; 'Minsters and Parishes', p. 332. See also Wickham Steed, 'Roman Roads of the Banbury District', p. 17, on the difficulties of crossing the Cherwell.

50 Bourne, *The Place-Name Kingston and Royal Power*; Blair, *Building Anglo-Saxon England*, pp. 193–228, esp. pp. 197–99.

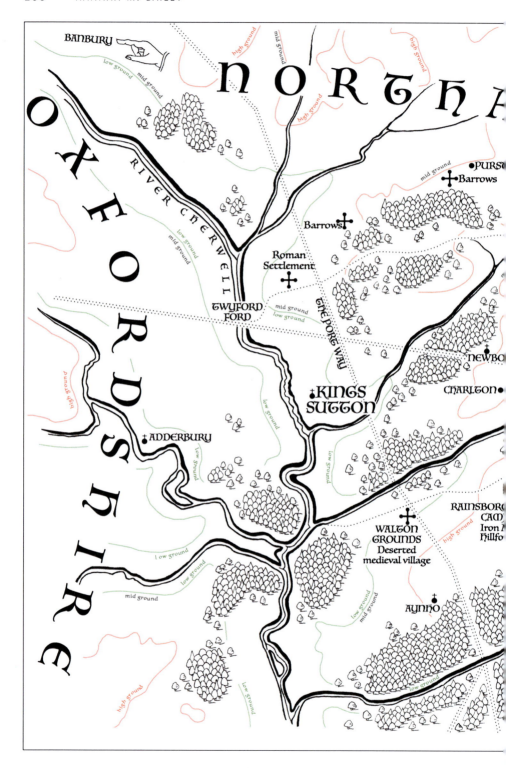

ST RUMWOLD IN THE BORDERLAND

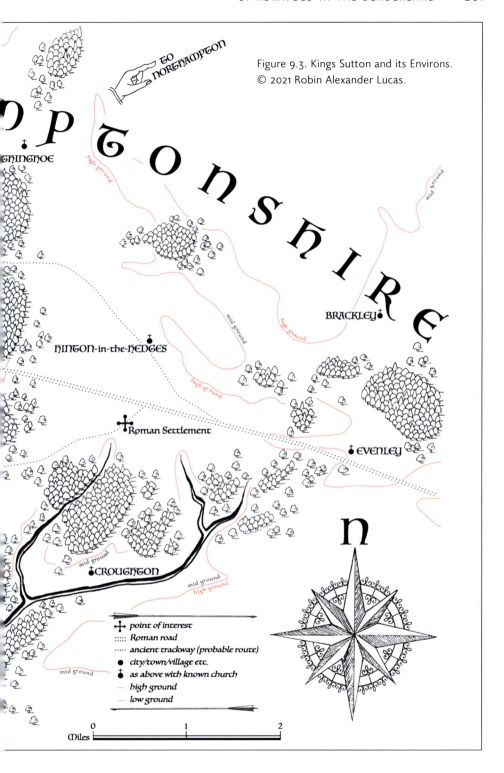

Figure 9.3. Kings Sutton and its Environs. © 2021 Robin Alexander Lucas.

ford — specifically, the view of the village *from* the ford — which was the origin of the place name 'Sutton' (south -*tūn*).[51]

D. Hayward has proposed in a recent archaeological report that this crossing at Twyford is on the route of an ancient trackway that diverged from the Jurassic Way at Great Rollright (which stands not far from the Rollright stone circle and almost exactly on the point where the drainage basins of the Cherwell, Evenlode, and Severn Avon meet), and proceeded across the Cherwell Valley, crossing the river at Twyford and from there either through Kings Sutton itself or along the promontory just north of the village (which is the site of 'Extensive Neolithic, Bronze Age, Iron Age and Romano-British activity') and on to Evenley, which is a 'probable inter-tribal ritual trading site at the head of the Ouse':

> This location has significant coin deposits from at least four Iron Age tribes, the Trinovantes, Dobunni, Corieltauvi and Catuvellauni. This grouping of coins, coupled with other factors (including Evenley's location at the edge of the River Ouse, close to its headwaters and at the interface of three of these tribes), would make it an ideal 'neutral' zone for high status inter-tribal trading together with ritual feasting or similar activity.[52]

The later Roman road that ran west–east through this area is also thought to have crossed the river at Twyford,[53] and possibly to have continued beyond Evenley (which is adjacent to Brackley) to Thornborough (which is just beyond Buckingham).[54]

In explaining the mechanics of the spread of Rumwold's cult, what is important is not the relationship between Kings Sutton, Brackley, and Buckingham as actual established places per se, but as points along a line of communication. On its route to Buckingham, Rumwold's body might have been translated via Brackley, or it could just as well have been translated via Evenley with later memory reassigning the story to the adjacent population centre once that had been established (or 'discovered' as the hagiography puts it). Deborah Hayter also raises the possibility that 'the translation of his remains reflected the decline of Sutton and the growth of Brackley

---

51 Franklin suggests that the name distinguishes between two royal estates, (Kings) Sutton and (Greens) Norton, some seventeen miles north-east ('Minsters and Parishes', p. 256). The English Place-Name Society suggests that the name refers to its position relative to Purston, but the three 'priest-towns' (now Buston Farm, Little Purston, and Great Purston) in the north of the parish are small peripheral places, probably farms supporting the minster community at Kings Sutton, and it seems unlikely that the central place of the parish would take its name relative to them (Gover, Mawer, and Stenton, *The Place Names of Northamptonshire*, p. 58). On the oddities of Purston, see RCHM, *An Inventory of the Historical Monuments*, pp. 94–95.

52 Hayward, 'Appendix 1: Notes on Early Trade Paths and Communication Routes', p. 42.

53 See the map on p. 116 of Wickham Steed, 'Roman Roads of the Banbury District' and RCHM, *An Inventory of the Historical Monuments*, p. 179.

54 Rosevear, 'Turnpike Roads to Banbury', section 1.1.

and Buckingham'.[55] Whatever the chronology or veracity of the translation of Rumwold's remains, the bigger picture is that his cult moved a short distance along an established route of communication.[56] This journey would hardly have attracted the speculation it has if not for the fact that it crosses explicit boundaries of jurisdiction — and the unspoken boundary between cultural zones.

The space between the Cherwell and its watershed boundary is very narrow at Kings Sutton. From where the present-day village begins on the edge of the Cherwell flood-plain to Charlton House Farm on the edge of the Cherwell Basin (and on the Roman Road to Evenley) is a distance of only three miles. This gives Kings Sutton and its hinterlands an odd liminality which endures to the present — it is a Northamptonshire village with an Oxfordshire post code, where Anglian Water supplies the taps, but Thames Water maintains the drains. Formal political boundaries claim Kings Sutton as an outpost of the River Great Ouse culture zone: it stands at the south-westernmost limit of Northamptonshire and the western margin of the hundred to which it gives its name.[57] But its viewscapes are orientated inward towards the Cherwell (as the -hoh element in the names of the villages of Farthinghoe and Aynho attests, the area features several low promontories running perpendicular to the river with views across the valley and up the river to Banbury and the high ground beyond),[58] and culturally it belongs to 'Banburyshire', the term used in recent centuries to refer to the cultural province constituted by a constellation of North Oxfordshire, Northamptonshire, and Warwickshire villages in the upper Cherwell Basin which look to Banbury as their commercial centre rather than their respective county seats.[59] The orientation towards Banbury specifically is

---

55 Hayter, 'King's Sutton', p. 20.
56 Lines of communication determined by physical geography may also explain a great deal about the distribution of Rumwold's cult beyond its centre at Kings Sutton/Brackley/Buckingham. Outside this area, Love identifies ten churches with possible dedications to Rumwold, though she notes that any of these could potentially refer instead to the missionary martyr Rombaut (*Three Eleventh-Century Anglo-Latin Saints' Lives*, ed. and trans. by Love, pp. cli–cliv). Romaldkirk in North Yorkshire she classes as a 'doubtful case'. Of those that remain, four might be explained by transmission along Roman roads. Watling Street crosses the Ouse eight miles downstream of Buckingham and proceeds to London; four of the churches with dedications to Rumwold are near the coasts on Roman roads that fan out from London. (Clockwise, these are Colchester, Kent, Chichester, and Winchester.) The remaining five are three churches in Dorset, one in Stoke Doyle, Northamptonshire, and one in a suburb of Lincoln. These three locations — and also the heartland of Rumwold's cult — are connected by the shallow inverted-s diagonal line of Jurassic limestone bedrock which traces a string of uplands (British Geological Survey, *Geological Map of the British Islands*). These uplands might possibly be a route of transmission (along the postulated prehistoric Jurassic Way) but they might be better interpreted as a limit on the spread of Rumwold's cult, as apart from the unlikely Romaldkirk, there is no evidence of his cult north-west of this line.
57 See Anderson, *English Hundred-Names*, pp. 126–27.
58 See Gelling and Cole, *The Landscape of Place-Names*, pp. 186–90.
59 The borders of Banburyshire have never been officially defined, but there is a great deal of

due to its later development as a market town (reinforced by the construction of the canal and railroad running parallel to the Cherwell), but Kings Sutton's dependent chapelries at Horley and Hornton up to the sixteenth century are evidence of earlier links across the river.[60] Hayter suggests that Kings Sutton in early medieval times may have belonged to a border region between Wessex, Mercia, and the Danelaw and that it may have been 'separated from part of its river-valley territory' by the drawing up of the county boundary between Oxfordshire and Northamptonshire in the tenth century.[61] She also considers the evidence that this was an area of contested territory in the sixth century, before the region came under Mercian hegemony. The many Iron Age hillforts on high ground in the district — including Rainsborough Camp just two miles from Kings Sutton — suggest that the perimeter of the Cherwell River Basin was also the site of even earlier disputes over territorial boundaries.

Evidence for a vast and early royal estate stretching from Kings Sutton to Buckingham does not extend much beyond the existence of the cult of Rumwold in those places. More persuasive is the more limited claim which Frances Brown and Chris Taylor make (on place-name and archaeological evidence) that the three adjoining modern parishes of Kings Sutton, Newbottle, and Farthinghoe show evidence of having constituted a single interdependent 'estate' originating in Roman times, or the late Iron Age.[62] Hayter has some criticisms of their use of recent parish boundaries in their map of this estate and offers a revised interpretation of the territory (see Fig. 9.4) that puts three of its four boundaries at watercourses; she describes the 'core estate' at Kings Sutton as being 'contained on one side by the river Cherwell and on two other sides by brooks' (north of Purston and south of Aynho).[63]

Though neither Hayter nor Brown and Taylor specifically mention the watershed, it clearly influences the patterns of affiliation and land use which shaped their interpretations of the eastern limit of this territory. The watershed runs south through the centre of the present village of Farthinghoe and then (through several stepwise, almost right-angled turns) to the south-east between Charlton and Hinton-in-the-Hedges, and between Croughton and Evenley, where it makes a sharp turn back to the west. Hayter's map includes Farthinghoe, Hinton-in-the-Hedges, and Evenley, and so proposes

---

continuity between the shape of the bulge the Cherwell catchment adds to the north of the broader Thames Basin and the limits of certain maps of Banburyshire; compare the map of Roman Banburyshire in Bromley, 'Roman "Banburyshire"', p. 104, to those available through Environment Agency, *Catchment Data Explorer*.

60 Lobel and Crossley, 'Parishes: Horley and Hornton'.

61 Hayter, 'King's Sutton', pp. 18–20.

62 Brown and Taylor, 'Settlement and Land Use in Northamptonshire', pp. 85–89. See also RCHM, *An Inventory of the Historical Monuments*, p. 94, fig. 82. On the continuity of land use and field systems between the late Roman and early medieval periods, see Rippon, Smart, and Pears, *The Fields of Britannia*.

63 Hayter, 'King's Sutton', p. 15, fig. 6.

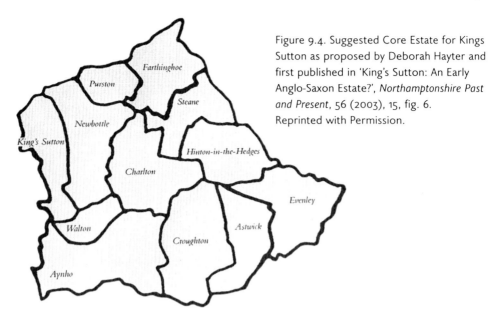

Figure 9.4. Suggested Core Estate for Kings Sutton as proposed by Deborah Hayter and first published in 'King's Sutton: An Early Anglo-Saxon Estate?', *Northamptonshire Past and Present*, 56 (2003), 15, fig. 6. Reprinted with Permission.

an eastern boundary for the estate that just overlaps the Ouse watershed, closely following its swing south-east and sharp turn south-west at Evenley. Brown and Taylor's estate map also overlaps the watershed at Farthinghoe and runs just up to the watershed at the Newbottle parish boundary between Charlton and Hinton-in-the-Hedges.

The term 'estate' is used for convenience, but it does carry anachronistic connotations that are unlikely to have applied in the period in question. Whether or not this area was the unitary holding of a particular individual or institution in the early seventh century in some sense does not matter. It is sufficient to say that the Cherwell to the west and its watershed to the east, the lands adjacent to an ancient trackway to the north, and the lands adjacent to an Iron Age hill fort to the south — containing between them the intersection of two significant medium-distance Roman roads — define the (approximate, porous) limits of a landscape that meets many of the criteria of a 'persistent place' as defined by Sarah Schlanger and applied to seventh-century English elite sites by John Blair.[64]

This is also just the sort of landscape in which one might expect to find an assembly site (or perhaps multiple assembly sites serving different

---

64 Blair, *Building Anglo-Saxon England*, p. 111. Everitt allows for similar ambiguity in his discussion of Kentish settlement when he states that he uses the term 'estates' in a sense that 'is not intended to imply any specific form of social organization, still less any theory of property'. He goes on to argue that the *regiones* developed from 'primitive agrarian estates': that they were not the result of administrative authority imposed from above on a blank canvas, but of interaction between that authority and already embedded perceptions and practices. *Continuity and Colonization*, pp. 8, 10.

purposes or periods of time). The fact that Kings Sutton gives its name to the hundred in which it is situated is suggestive, though not conclusive. John Baker and Stuart Brookes have outlined criteria which can be used to assess the probability of a place being an assembly site, under the headings of 'accessibility, distinctiveness, functionality/practicality, and territorial centrality/liminality'.[65] The area in which Kings Sutton is situated certainly combines territorial liminality with accessibility, being on the border between two distinct cultural provinces but readily accessible from both directions due to the trackway running from Great Rollright to Evenley, which takes advantage of a ford that makes Cherwell passable just at a point where there is also a comparatively gentle climb over the watershed to the east. There is also a Portway running north–south through the area, which 'appears to link a series of hillforts and other prehistoric and early Romano-British features'.[66] Under the heading of 'distinctiveness', Baker and Brookes note that assembly sites were often located in 'upland locations with commanding views over surrounding districts', and that many are at or in proximity to distinctive landscape features, including manmade ones such as hill forts.[67] Kings Sutton itself has significant sight lines as discussed previously, and its hinterlands include several promontories of even greater elevation, which feature both commanding views up the Cherwell Valley and proximity to prehistoric monuments (see Fig. 9.3). There is Rainsborough Camp itself,[68] but there is also a ridge between the fort and the village which has direct sight lines to both Rainsborough Camp and the present-day village, and is in closer proximity to the crossroads and to Walton Grounds, a deserted medieval village which is the less unlikely of two places identified in local legend as the 'actual' birthplace of Rumwold. (The alternative claim that Rumwold was born in Astrop, an adjacent hamlet which in modern times has been absorbed into the eastern end of Kings Sutton, seems conveniently to have arisen at precisely the moment that a spa developed around a 'St Rumbold's Well' there.) The place name Walton might refer to *wealas* (i.e. serfs) or Welsh (i.e. a persisting Romano-British community),[69] but it could also be *weallas* (i.e. the ruins of Roman walls); this combined with its position in a dip around a brook make it at least remotely plausible as a boggy area in which a convenient stone for

---

65 Baker and Brookes, 'Identifying Outdoor Assembly Sites', p. 12. See also Twomey, 'Rivers and Rituals', pp. 69–74, on rivers and their peripheries as 'neutral' sites for interaction between leaders of different territories — including baptisms — and high ground, hill forts, barrows, and views over rivers as important factors in the location of cemeteries, assembly sites, and early churches.

66 Hayward, 'Appendix 1: Notes on Early Trade Paths and Communication Routes', p. 41.

67 Baker and Brookes, 'Identifying Outdoor Assembly Sites', p. 15.

68 On the reuse of Iron Age hill forts as hundredal assembly sites, see also Pantos, 'The Location and Form of Anglo-Saxon Assembly-Places'. For more information on Rainsborough Camp, its viewshed, and communication routes, see the site report by Aveling and Close, 'Rainsborough Camp, Aynho Northants'.

69 On early medieval English attitudes to the Welsh, see the chapter by Caitlin Ellis in this volume.

a font might have been found, though as Twomey has shown that baptism directly in rivers was the common practice at the time it is quite likely that the entire font episode is a later fiction.[70] Perhaps the most plausible site for assembly, however, apart from the location of the present village itself (which is certainly a possibility), is the ridge above the ford to the north, which Hayward proposed as a possible route of the ancient trackway towards Evenley. The high ground here offers views clear across Banbury, and there is a great deal of evidence of Roman and prehistoric activity in the vicinity.[71] Of particular relevance is the discovery of a Saxon burial in close proximity to (since destroyed) barrows that stood along this route;[72] this is the sort of practice Sarah Semple considers to be suggestive of an assembly site.[73]

The *vita* does not actually claim that Kings Sutton was a royal estate; it is very insistent that Rumwold was born in 'ameno prato' (a pleasant field),[74] and that that field was not in any sense *home*. I would suggest that the claims of the hagiography combined with what is known about the history and features of the landscape in which the story is set point to a (distorted) memory of territory around Kings Sutton being a liminal location for assembly in earlier centuries. The royal assemblies of later centuries left substantial documentary evidence,[75] but comparatively little is known about the functions of earlier and more local assembly sites. However, Aliki Pantos has made a strong case for the probability (which may be confirmed by future archaeological work) that assemblies were often polyfocal sites, with space not only for formal acts of governance but for games, trade, and exchange.[76] It is easy to imagine local elites — who may have been as itinerant as kings, if on a smaller scale — habitually residing for a while in the vicinity of such a site, thus reinforcing the area's status as a 'persistent place' and setting the stage for its later development as a monastic, then royal, site.[77]

For the eleventh-century hagiographer, the presence of Rumwold's parents in tents in a field near Kings Sutton is something that needs to be explained by the emergency of Rumwold's mother going into labour while on her way somewhere else. John Blair has shown that the eleventh century was a tipping point in a gradual process of change in building practice and landscape use: towns were growing, elite dwellings were increasingly fixed in space, and the legal vocabulary of landholding began to associate units of

---

70 Twomey, 'Rivers and Rituals', pp. 59–66.

71 See the Archaeological Data Service entries referenced in the Works Cited.

72 RCHM, *An Inventory of the Historical Monuments*, pp. 92–93.

73 Semple, 'Locations of Assembly'.

74 *Three Eleventh-Century Anglo-Latin Saints' Lives*, ed. and trans. by Love, pp. 98/99.

75 On royal assembly, see Roach, *Kingship and Consent*.

76 Pantos, 'The Location and Form of Anglo-Saxon Assembly-Places', esp. p. 166.

77 Blair borrows this term from Sarah Schlanger's work on Anasazi settlement systems: 'Recognising Persistent Places in Anasazi Settlement Systems'.

land with fixed domestic dwellings on them.[78] Commerce was moving into towns, and gatherings and assemblies, particularly of guilds, were moving indoors.[79] This was, as Blair has shown, a radical conceptual change from earlier centuries, when elite culture was both more rural and more *moveable*, with many high-status dwellings being by choice transient and transportable;[80] even great hall complexes were only expected to be used for a few decades before being destroyed and replaced by some other structure — not in exactly the same place, but at some other nearby point in the landscape.[81] It is true that royal itineration persisted well beyond the eleventh century, but ideas about the world had changed. The fact that the hagiography treats Rumwold's birth in a tent rather than a town, minster, manor, or *burh* as something noteworthy and unexpected implies a mismatch between the received narrative and the hagiographer's own cultural expectations.

Conclusions

If we approach the story of St Rumwold through the lens of social memory, presuming that it may preserve — though in profoundly altered form — genuine information about cultural provinces and lines of communication, its landscape becomes far more intelligible.

Rumwold almost certainly was not the son of a Christian daughter of Penda who converted a pagan king of Northumbria, but he may have been a child of local dependent rulers — perhaps from two different communities, as his story is set at the point of interface between two distinct topographically defined cultural zones — whose relationship to Penda was retrospectively simplified, if not outright invented. Though he may not have preached on the Trinity as an infant, he might have been a child or young person (not necessarily a newborn) who was given an impromptu baptism shortly before his death at a time and place when such a thing was sufficiently out of the ordinary to be memorable. The story about the religious disagreement between his mother and father is, of course, a hagiographical trope, but there is a chance that this *particular* hagiographical trope became connected to the story because of an actual memory of adjacent communities navigating differences in their religious practices.

There are a number of plausible explanations for the translation of Rumwold's relics that do not require the hypothesis of a seventh-century royal estate stretching from Kings Sutton to Buckingham. Perhaps one or both of his parents counted 'home' to be in the vicinity of the River Great Ouse and

---

78 Blair, *Building Anglo-Saxon England*, p. 400.
79 Blair, *Building Anglo-Saxon England*, pp. 383–408.
80 Blair, *Building Anglo-Saxon England*, pp. 51–67.
81 Blair, *Building Anglo-Saxon England*, p. 123.

genuinely did have his remains moved in the years following his death. Perhaps the Mercian royal house saw an opportunity to extend their influence eastward by sponsoring the translation. Perhaps there never was any translation, and it was only the cult itself that spread with the itineration of local elites, or shifted over a longer period as various minsters and population centres waxed and waned in prominence. There are many unanswered questions here (some of which may hopefully be answered in part by future archaeological work),[82] but what is clear is that the simplest explanation for the link between Kings Sutton, Brackley, and Buckingham is that they lie along an established line of communication. It is not necessary to posit a huge pre–Viking Age royal estate or to turn to the mechanics of ecclesiastical bureaucracy to explain the link between the three places mentioned in the *vita*.

The interplay of physical and cultural geographies at Kings Sutton makes it an excellent candidate to have hosted some kind (or kinds) of assembly site in the seventh century; for local elites to set up temporary dwellings and stay there for a week, or a month, or a season, need not in itself have been anything out of the ordinary, although a crisis involving a novel religious practice and the death of a child might have made one particular visit to that spot memorable.[83] Over time, as views of the world changed, that memory was adapted to fit new patterns of hagiographical narrative and new assumptions about kingdoms, elite culture, and landscape use so that the child of some dependent rulers who quite naturally were spending a season at an assembly site, living in mobile dwellings — because that is what seventh-century elites did — became reinterpreted as the child of a Mercian princess who was passing through on her way to some town or *burh*. Social memory and changing ideas of the world imposed a narrative about kings and kingdoms and long journeys from north to south on top of one that had originally been about short journeys carrying new ideas and religious practices over a topographical boundary between east and west.

---

82 See Foard, 'An Archaeological Resource Assessment of Anglo-Saxon Northamptonshire', esp. pp. 12–15, 19, 20, 25.

83 Cf. Blair, *The Church in Anglo-Saxon Society*, p. 280.

Works Cited

Primary Sources

Three Eleventh-Century Anglo-Latin Saints' Lives: Vita S. Birini, Vita et miracula S. Kenelmi, and Vita S. Rumwoldi, ed. and trans. by Rosalind C. Love (Oxford: Clarendon Press, 1996)

Secondary Sources

Anderson, O. S., *English Hundred-Names*, Lunds Universitets Årsskrift, 30.1 (Lund: Lunds Universitet, 1934)

Archaeology Data Service, Untitled Record (Historic England) <https://archaeologydataservice.ac.uk/archsearch/record?titleId=1049653> [accessed 4 January 2021]

——, Untitled Record (Historic England) <https://archaeologydataservice.ac.uk/archsearch/record?titleId=1050797> [accessed 4 January 2021]

——, Untitled Record (Historic England) <https://archaeologydataservice.ac.uk/archsearch/record?titleId=1050799> [accessed 4 January 2021]

Aveling, Jim, and Rob Close, 'Rainsborough Camp, Aynho Northants', in *The Atlas of Hillforts of Britain and Ireland Hillfort Survey*, ed. by Gary Lock and Ian B. M. Ralston (Community Landscape Archaeology Survey Project, 2013) <https://www.claspweb.org.uk/large_pdf_files/CLASP%20Hillfort%20survey%20form%20-%20Rainsborough%20Camp,%20Aynho.pdf> [accessed 4 January 2021]

Baker, John, and Stuart Brookes, 'Identifying Outdoor Assembly Sites in Early Medieval England', *Journal of Field Archaeology*, 40.1 (2015), 3–21

Blair, John, *Building Anglo-Saxon England* (Princeton, NJ: Princeton University Press, 2018)

——, *The Church in Anglo-Saxon Society* (Oxford: Oxford University Press, 2005)

——, 'A Handlist of Anglo-Saxon Saints', in *Local Saints and Local Churches in the Early Medieval West*, ed. by Alan Thacker and Richard Sharpe (Oxford: Oxford University Press, 2002), pp. 495–565

——, 'A Saint for Every Minster? Local Cults in Anglo-Saxon England', in *Local Saints and Local Churches in the Early Medieval West*, ed. by Alan Thacker and Richard Sharpe (Oxford: Oxford University Press, 2002), pp. 455–94

Bourne, Jill, *The Place-Name Kingston and Royal Power in Middle Anglo-Saxon England: Patterns, Possibilities and Purpose* (Oxford: BAR Publishing, 2017)

British Geological Survey, *Geological Map of the British Islands Based on the Work of the Geological Survey*, 5th edn (2010) <https://www.bgs.ac.uk/data/maps/maps.cfc?method=viewRecord&mapId=12059> [accessed 19 August 2020]

Bromley, V., 'Roman "Banburyshire"', *Cake and Cockhorse: The Magazine of the Banburyshire Historical Society*, 2 (1964), 103–14

Brown, Frances, and Chris Taylor, 'Settlement and Land Use in Northamptonshire: A Comparison Between the Iron Age and the Middle Ages', in *Lowland Iron Age Communities in Europe*, ed. by Barry Cunliffe and Trevor Rowley, BAR International Series (Supplementary), 48 (Oxford: BAR, 1978), pp. 77–89

Environment Agency, *Catchment Data Explorer*, updated 17 September 2020, <https:// environment.data.gov.uk/catchment-planning/> [accessed 4 January 2021]

Everitt, Alan, *Continuity and Colonization: The Evolution of Kentish Settlement* (Leicester: Leicester University Press, 1986)

Featherstone, Peter, 'The Tribal Hidage and the Ealdormen of Mercia', in *Mercia: An Anglo-Saxon Kingdom in Europe*, ed. by Michelle P. Brown and Carol Ann Farr, Studies in the Early History of Europe (London: Leicester University Press, 2001), pp. 23–34

Fentress, James, and Chris Wickham, *Social Memory* (Oxford: Basil Blackwell, 1992)

Foard, Glenn, 'An Archaeological Resource Assessment of Anglo-Saxon Northamptonshire (400–1066)', <https://archaeologydataservice. ac.uk/researchframeworks/eastmidlands/attach/County-assessments/ NorthantsSaxon.pdf> [accessed 4 January 2021]

Franklin, M. J., 'The Identification of Minsters in the Midlands', *Anglo-Norman Studies*, 7 (1984), 69–88

——, 'Minsters and Parishes: Northamptonshire Studies' (unpublished doctoral dissertation, University of Cambridge, 1982)

Gelling, Margaret, and Ann Cole, *The Landscape of Place-Names* (Stamford: Shaun Tyas, 2000)

Gover, J. E. B., Allen Mawer, and F. M. Stenton, *The Place Names of Northamptonshire*, English Place-Name Society, 10 (Cambridge: Cambridge University Press, 1975)

Hayter, Deborah, 'King's Sutton: An Early Anglo-Saxon Estate?', *Northamptonshire Past and Present*, 56 (2003), 7–21

Hayward, David, 'Appendix 1: Notes on Early Trade Paths and Communication Routes', in G. W. Hatton, 'Iron Age Hillforts Survey (Northamptonshire): Analysis of the Individual Hillfort Reports' (Community Landscape Archaeology Survey Project, 2016), pp. 41–47, <https://www.claspweb.org.uk/large_ pdf_files/CLASP%20IA%20Hillforts%20analysis%20report.pdf> [accessed 18 August 2020]

Jones, S. R. H., 'Transaction Costs, Institutional Change, and the Emergence of a Market Economy in Later Anglo-Saxon England', *Economic History Review*, 46 (1993), 658–78

Liebermann, F., *Die Heiligen Englands: Angelsächsisch und lateinisch* (Hanover: Hahn, 1889)

Lobel, D., and Alan Crossley, 'Parishes: Horley and Hornton', in *A History of the County of Oxford*, IX: *Bloxham Hundred*, ed. by Mary D. Lobel and Alan Crossley (London: Victoria County History, 1969), pp. 123–39, <https://www. british-history.ac.uk/vch/oxon/vol. 9/pp. 123–39> [accessed 4 January 2021]

Pantos, Aliki, 'The Location and Form of Anglo-Saxon Assembly-Places: Some "Moot Points"', in *Assembly Places and Practices in Medieval Europe,* ed. by Aliki Pantos and Sarah Semple (Dublin: Four Courts Press, 2004), pp. 155–80

Parsons, David, 'The Mercian Church: Archaeology and Topography', in *Mercia: An Anglo-Saxon Kingdom in Europe*, ed. by Michelle P. Brown and Carol Ann Farr, Studies in the Early History of Europe (Leicester: Leicester University Press, 2001), pp. 51–68

Phythian-Adams, Charles, 'Introduction: An Agenda for English Local History', in *Societies, Cultures and Kinship, 1580–1850: Cultural Provinces and English Local History*, ed. by Charles Phythian-Adams and Mary Carter (Leicester: Leicester University Press, 1993), pp. 1–23

——, 'Local History and Societal History', *Local Population Studies*, 51 (1993), 30–45

Phythian-Adams, Charles, and Mary Carter, eds, *Societies, Cultures and Kinship, 1580–1850: Cultural Provinces and English Local History* (Leicester: Leicester University Press, 1993)

RCHM (Royal Commission on Historical Monuments), *An Inventory of the Historical Monuments in the County of Northamptonshire*, IV: *Archaeological Sites in South-West Northamptonshire* (London: Her Majesty's Stationery Office, 1982), pp. 94–95

Rippon, Stephen, Chris Smart, and Ben Pears, *The Fields of Britannia: Continuity and Change in the Late Roman and Early Medieval Landscape* (Oxford: Oxford University Press, 2015)

Roach, Levi, *Kingship and Consent in Anglo-Saxon England, 871–978: Assemblies and the State in the Early Middle Ages* (Cambridge: Cambridge University Press, 2013)

Rollason, D. W., 'Lists of Saints' Resting-Places in Anglo-Saxon England', *ASE*, 7 (1978), 61–93

Rosevear, Alan, 'Turnpike Roads to Banbury (through Bicester, Brackley, and Buckingham)', in *Roads of the Upper Thames Valley* Booklet 14 (Wantage: A. Rosevear, 2002), <http://www.turnpikes.org.uk/RUTV14%20Banbury%20 Turnpikes.htm> [accessed 4 January 2021]

Schlanger, S. H., 'Recognising Persistent Places in Anasazi Settlement Systems', in *Space, Time, and Archaeological Landscapes*, ed. by J. Rossignol and L. Wandsnider (New York: Plenum Press, 1992), pp. 91–112

Semple, Sarah, 'Locations of Assembly in Early Anglo-Saxon England', in *Assembly Places and Practices in Medieval Europe*, ed. by Aliki Pantos and Sarah Semple (Dublin: Four Courts Press, 2004), pp. 135–54

Sofield, Clifford, 'Shaping Buildings and Identities in Fifth- to Ninth-Century England', *Leeds Studies in English*, 48 (2017), 105–23

Thacker, Alan, 'Kings, Saints and Monasteries in Pre-Viking Mercia', *Midland History*, 10 (1985), 1–25

Twomey, Carolyn, 'Rivers and Rituals: Baptism in the Early English Landscape', in *Meanings of Water in Early Medieval England*, ed. by Carolyn Twomey and Daniel Anlezark, SEM, 47 (Turnhout: Brepols, 2021), pp. 59–84

Wickham-Crowley, Kelley Marie, 'Living on the Ecg: The Mutable Boundaries of Land and Water in Anglo-Saxon Contexts', in *A Place to Believe In: Medieval Monasticism in the Landscape*, ed. by Clare A. Lees and Gillian R. Overing (University Park: Pennsylvania State University Press, 2006), pp. 85–110

Wickham Steed, Violet, 'Roman Roads of the Banbury District', *Cake and Cockhorse: The Magazine of the Banburyshire Historical Society*, 2 (1964), 116–19

Yorke, Barbara, *Kings and Kingdoms of Early Anglo-Saxon England* (London: Routledge, 1997)

——, *Nunneries and the Anglo-Saxon Royal Houses* (London: Continuum, 2003)

MARK ATHERTON

The World of Ealdorman Byrhtnoth: A Landscape Biography

What kind of world did an ealdorman inhabit in the tenth century? This chapter considers the borders and limits and features of such a world from the perspective of arguably one of the most famous figures of tenth-century England: Ealdorman Byrhtnoth, leader of the East Saxon forces and their supporters who fought the Vikings at Maldon in Essex on 10 or 11 August of the year 991, celebrated afterwards in the now canonical Old English commemorative poem *The Battle of Maldon*, as well as in at least four other contemporary accounts of that battle. In this chapter I will offer some close readings of the documentary sources of the period in order to establish the locations and to analyse the names and functions of the places that Byrhtnoth owned, the ultimate aim being to 'map out' the East Anglian and East Saxon world that the ealdorman knew and inhabited.

Despite his fame in his own time, there is no contemporary *vita* of Byrhtnoth. Nor has any modern biographer attempted any extensive life writing on the hero of Maldon, presumably because the main sources for biographical information are impersonal administrative documents.[1] A similar problem has been faced also by recent biographers who have tackled the lives of even the leading figures of the period such as King Æthelstan or Æthelred the Unready,[2] for there is a distinct dearth of private letters or other personal writings in the records of the time. In short, Byrhtnoth as a human being, as a personality, is only glimpsed fitfully in the written sources that survive.

---

*   I am grateful to Robin Lucas for creating the maps in Figures 10.1 and 10.2, on which this chapter depends.

1   Abels, 'Byrhtnoth', is a brief entry in the *Oxford Dictionary of National Biography* that mentions a few of the main events of Byrhtnoth's life: his marriage, appointment as ealdorman, and final battle at Maldon; Abels also emphasizes his support of the Benedictine Reform, his importance as the leading ealdorman of the kingdom, and the significance of the battle. But, perhaps necessarily, there is no outline as such of Byrhtnoth's career.

2   Foot, *Æthelstan*; Keynes, *The Diplomas of King Ethelred 'the Unready'*; Roach, *Æthelred the Unready*.

Mark Atherton (mark.atherton@regents.ox.ac.uk) is Senior Lecturer in English at Regent's Park College, University of Oxford.

Ideas of the World in Early Medieval English Literature, ed. by Mark Atherton, Kazutomo Karasawa, and Francis Leneghan, SOEL 1 (Turnhout: Brepols, 2022)   pp. 273–305
BREPOLS ❦ PUBLISHERS   DOI 10.1484/M.SOEL.5.130565

However, given all the data on lands and estates associated with our subject, this suggests another path of enquiry: to uncover more of the life world that Byrhtnoth inhabited by studying the relevant parts of the *landscapes* he lived, worked, and moved in, drawing on the geographical and historical perspectives of place-name studies. The starting point will be the idea of 'landscape biography', as presented in theoretical writings and case studies by historical geographers and archaeologists who are interested in landscape and cultural heritage. The approach of Kolen and Renes, in a volume of essays entitled *Landscape Biographies*, 'starts from the assumption that landscapes are essentially *human* life worlds, and that people and their life worlds produce and transform each other in an ongoing dialectical movement'.[3] For Kolen and Renes, then, the landscape is not simply something separate, to be viewed from a distance, for human beings were involved in creating it and shaping it and giving it a history. It follows that scholars who study the life worlds of the past have to engage with them both imaginatively and physically, by experiencing them: by walking the paths and retracing the rivers and ditches and other landmarks that originally defined these lands and estates. Pioneers of this approach to landscape include historians such as W. G. Hoskins, author of the classic *The Making of the English Landscape* (1955), or theory-inspired archaeologists such as Chris Tilley in his influential *A Phenomenology of Landscape* (1997). Other schools of thought prefer a more data-driven and objective approach, and Hoskins and Tilley have been criticized for their subjectivity, which ultimately derives, so it is argued, from the Romantic approaches to nature of the early 1800s, when poets and painters such as William Wordsworth or John Constable projected new sensibilities and ideologies onto their environment.[4] But the accusations of being too Romantic may be unfair, for anthropologists, geographers, and archaeologists of all persuasions still agree on the need for experiential fieldwork, both as a source of data and as a corrective of theory. Most of the locations mentioned in this chapter were personally visited by the present writer, if once and only briefly, but travel restrictions prevented any subsequent revisit.

Coincidentally, the notion of 'life world' promoted by geographers like Kolen and Renes, which ultimately derives from the German 'Lebenswelt' of phenomenologists like Husserl, neatly reflects the original *temporal* meaning of the English noun 'world'. As the OED shows, the primary meaning (sense

---

3   Kolen and Renes, 'Landscape Biographies', p. 25. For a psychogeographical reading of the Old English poem *Solomon and Saturn II*, see the chapter by Rachel Burns in this volume, and more generally for such approaches Smith, *Land and Book*. The importance of human action on the medieval East Anglian landscape is treated in Pestell, *Landscapes of Monastic Foundation* and Wareham, *Lords and Communities in Early Medieval East Anglia*.

4   Johnson, *Ideas of Landscape*, offers a critique of the 'underlying discourse of cultural Romanticism'. Nevertheless, in his more recent 'Phenomenological Approaches in Landscape Archaeology' he concedes in his conclusion on p. 84 that 'understanding human experiences of landscapes will continue to be a vibrant and important part of archaeological discourse'.

1) is 'human existence' or 'a period of human existence', from Old English *woruld* meaning 'age of man', originally a compound of *wer* ('man') and a variant of the adjective *ald/eald* (Germanic cognates include Old Saxon *werold* and Old High German *weralt*). Thus the idea of a life world entails the subjective involvement of people over time in the landscape itself. Two obvious examples of such interaction from the English tenth century are the building and maintenance of bridges (often a legal requirement) and the founding of monasteries in particular localities (an act of piety and patronage). Such activities had immense influence on both the physical and the cultural landscape and were usually put into practice by members of the ruling elite, figures such as Æthelwold, bishop of Winchester, or Æthelwine, ealdorman of East Anglia. In a similar way Byrhtnoth and his wife, as well as his father-in-law and sister-in-law, were also closely involved in the administration, defence, and religious life of their local region. In my discussion, the initial focus will be on Cambridge and Ely, and thereafter on southern Suffolk and Essex, where the relevant estates and vills held by Byrhtnoth accumulate. Essentially, the single perspective of the man Byrhtnoth will become the common denominator linking these disparate lands together.

A Toponymic Approach to the Sources

Three areas stand out as worth exploring for further insights and information on Byrhtnoth. First, there are the many (mainly West Saxon) charters from the reigns of the four successive kings Eadwig, Edgar, Edward, and Æthelred covering the years from Byrhtnoth's first promotion under Eadwig in 956 to Byrhtnoth's death in 991: some of these charters are land transactions in which Byrhtnoth was a beneficiary;[5] more commonly his name features in the witness list. Accounts of Byrhtnoth's life might therefore be supplemented further by studying these witness lists and tracing his whereabouts at various moments in his career. Such a wide-ranging task, however, is beyond the remit of this essay, which will limit its focus to Byrhtnoth's Essex and East Anglian interests.

Secondly, there are well-known monastic writings associated with Ramsey and Ely, respectively Byrhtferth of Ramsey's contemporary *Vita S. Oswaldi* and the twelfth-century cartulary-chronicle known as the *Liber Eliensis* (The Book of Ely), which incorporates a range of tenth-century documents, including the charters and lawsuits of the *Libellus Æthelwoldi Episcopi* (The Little Book of Bishop Æthelwold). Here Byrhtnoth the administrator comes to the fore, the arbitrator of land disputes and the supporter of the Benedictine monasteries. The basic events and details of the lawsuits have been covered

---

5   For example, S 750; *Charters of Abingdon Abbey*, ed. by Kelly, no. 106; discussed in Baines, 'Ealdorman Byrhtnoth and the Brayfield Charter of 967'.

by legal historians,[6] while, in addition, further research into the context of late tenth-century Ely and Cambridge also promises to yield results.[7]

Thirdly, there are the vernacular wills of the nobility, particularly of male and female landowners, thegns, and ealdormen, many of these documents dating to Byrhtnoth's lifetime. Byrhtnoth's last will and testament is summarized in Latin in the *Liber Eliensis*, though the original Old English document, if it existed, is no longer extant. Significantly, however, we have copies of the three wills of Byrhtnoth's family by marriage: his father-in-law, sister-in-law, and wife;[8] these are informative on their attitudes to land and landholding, and show how members of this family attempted to shape and influence the way future generations would own and use their lands and estates. Once more it is fair to say that some excellent studies already exist, and the basic historical patterns of the family's landholding and kindred relations have been traced; and recently historians have turned out some detailed histories of the landscape of the region.[9]

What is still lacking, however, is a more integrated approach, in which the cultural history of the lands held by Byrhtnoth is connected more closely with the study of the toponyms, the actual Old English words and phrases used in the place names. One of the turns in place-name studies in recent decades is the insight, promoted especially in the writings of Margaret Gelling and confirmed by more recent research, that toponyms are accurate and precise descriptors of the landscape, and hence historically valuable.[10] And naturally it is not sufficient to work simply with modern translations and equivalents.

Present-day English *hill*, to cite a pertinent case-study, is rather vague and generic, whereas Old English *dun*, usually the second element in the relevant toponyms, very consistently denotes 'a low hill with a fairly level and fairly extensive summit which provided a good settlement-site in open country',[11] a definition with obvious relevance to discussions of Maldon and the topography of the Blackwater estuary, which features a number of such

---

6 Kennedy, 'Law and Litigation in the *Libellus Æthelwoldi Episcopi*'; Wormald, 'Handlist of Lawsuits'.

7 For a discussion of the role of the Cambridge thegns' guild in the tenth century and its possible relevance to the Maldon campaign, see Atherton, *The Battle of Maldon*, pp. 105–17.

8 The documents are the will of Ælfgar (S 1483) and the wills of Byrhtnoth's sister-in-law Æthelflæd (S 1494) and of his widow Ælfflæd (S 1486); *Anglo-Saxon Wills*, ed. and trans. by Whitelock, nos II, pp. 6–9; XIV, pp. 34–37; XV, pp. 38–43.

9 Hart, 'The Ealdordom of Essex', in *The Danelaw*; Locherbie-Cameron, 'Byrhtnoth and his Family'; Tollerton, *Wills and Will-Making in Anglo-Saxon England*, pp. 93–95, 233–36; Rippon, *Beyond the Medieval Village*; Williamson, *Environment, Society and Landscape in Early Medieval England*.

10 Gelling, *Place-Names in the Landscape*; Gelling and Cole, *The Landscape of Place-Names*; Watts, ed., *The Cambridge Dictionary of English Place-Names*; recent work in this field includes Baker, 'The Language of Anglo-Saxon Defence', and Baker and Brookes, 'Signalling Intent'.

11 Gelling and Cole, *The Landscape of Place-Names*, p. 164.

THE WORLD OF EALDORMAN BYRHTNOTH   277

names in -*dun* (see Fig. 10.2 below). For instance, east of Maldon and south of Northey Island, not far from the fields that are a likely site of the Maldon battle,[12] is Latchingdon (OE *Læcendune*), the element *Læcen-* (watercourses) perhaps referring to the streams that flow down past Mundon to Lawling Creek. Incidentally, Lawling itself (OE *Lellinge*) is named in the will of Byrhtnoth's wife Ælfflæd.[13] Another example is the low hill that is listed as Munduna (security hill) in Domesday Book: the security that Mundon offers seems to be protection from flooding of the marshland in which it stands prominently.[14] There is a fourteenth-century wooden church on the site, which is notable also for its field of petrified oaks, each about nine hundred years old.[15] The woodland is emblematic of the larger pattern here: saltmarsh to the east around the creeks and coastline, and various woods inland to the west, some of which still present on the ground, and indicated by the various *leigh* and *wood* names around Maldon itself.

Of the *leigh*-names the most significant is Purleigh, as a contemporary document — just possibly — may refer to the famous Wulfstan who defended the 'bridge' in *The Battle of Maldon* (ll. 74–83). Coincidentally, a certain Wulfstan is named as the family father in the will of Leofwine of Purleigh (near Maldon) who in the year 998 grants his estates at *Hnutlea*, that is, Notley (nut-wood), and Kelvedon (Cynelaf's valley) to two churches, as well as the manor house or 'chief building' (OE *heafodbotl*) at Purleigh to his paternal aunt Leofwaru (see Fig. 10.2 below).[16] Like a number of Byrhtnoth's properties (or those held later by his wife), Purleigh itself is situated on a hill in well-established farmland, but overlooking the saltmarshes of the Blackwater estuary; its name means 'bittern or snipe wood or clearing' and refers to two similar species of bird that are found commonly on marshland.[17] There may be no direct connection with the poem, but such documents form the necessary context for the present study, and there are indeed connections with our subject, for Byrhtnoth's wife held properties on Stane Street near Notley and Kelvedon.

Before proceeding, I have one more point to recapitulate from a previous publication for its possible relevance to the present discussion, and I aim to return to this point later in the chapter. This is the toponym *Mæl-dun* itself, which could mean literally 'hill of the sign', but as careful comparison of

---

12   I discuss the disputed location of the battle in Atherton, *The Battle of Maldon*, pp. 3–6.

13   S 1486; *Anglo-Saxon Wills*, ed. and trans. by Whitelock, pp. 40–41, 145.

14   Watts, ed., *The Cambridge Dictionary of English Place-Names*: on Latchingdon, p. 362; on Mundon, p. 426.

15   For online images of Mundon and the trees, see 'Witch Hunting around the Petrified Oaks of Mundon, Essex', *Essex Explored* (blog), 3 October 2020, <https://essexexplored.com/petrified-oaks-mundon-essex/> [accessed 2 June 2021].

16   The main text of this will is printed with a translation in Atherton, *The Battle of Maldon*, pp. 200–201. The will was originally edited by Napier and Stevenson in *The Crawford Collection*.

17   For a brief discussion of the location, see Watts, ed., *The Cambridge Dictionary of English Place-Names*, p. 485.

the uses of this noun shows, the usual meaning is 'hill of the cross'.[18] The suggestion, based on patterns in the naming of battle sites in the Old English records, and prevailing mentalities that may be inferred from Bede and other writers, is that the battle-site may even have been chosen for its auspicious name, appropriate for one such as Byrhtnoth, who is leading the East Saxon defence-force to protect 'Æthelred's land' against pagan invaders (*The Battle of Maldon*, l. 53).[19] And as the poet has Byrhtnoth say to these hostile incomers on the occasion of that battle: 'God ana wat | hwa þære wælstowe wealdan mote' (God alone knows who may control this place of battle, ll. 94b–95).

To reiterate, then, the aim of this chapter is to offer close readings of the language, style, and content of the relevant source texts on Byrhtnoth's landholdings and to explore the meaningful patterns of their names and toponyms. Such an approach would not have been unfamiliar to the local monk and teacher Byrhtferth of Ramsey, one of the very few named contemporary writers who possibly knew Byrhtnoth personally. In fact, Byrhtferth in his *Vita S. Oswaldi* also employs a topographical and toponymic method: as a good monk of Ramsey Abbey he cites a Latin poem by his great teacher Abbo of Fleury, the Frankish grammarian, computist, and poet who spent time at Ramsey in the years 985–987, when Byrhtferth was a student at the monastery school. The context is Byrhtferth's account in the *Vita S. Oswaldi* (III.18) of the meeting in 965 between Bishop Oswald and the ealdorman of East Anglia, Æthelwine (later a close friend of Ealdorman Byrhtnoth), who declares to Oswald that he has 'a suitable place' for the site of a new monastery, that is, Ramsey, an offer that Oswald joyfully accepts.[20] Next, Byrhtferth evokes the riches of this location: the island setting, the meadows and woodland, the teeming fish of the great mere (drained in the nineteenth century), and his citing of Abbo's poem adds further lustre as it praises 'Ramesiga cohors' (the noble throng of Ramsey, i.e. the monks, l. 1), and evokes 'vasta palus' (the vast fen, l. 3), exploring the etymology of the constellations in the starry skies (ll. 5–9) that are stretched out above 'insula pulchra' (the exquisite island, l. 6) with its 'land-bridge (*pons*) accessible to all the English' (l. 8).[21] Appropriately, Byrhtferth offers the following response to the themes of Abbo's poem:

---

18   For more detailed reflections on the name *Mældun*, see Gelling and Cole, *The Landscape of Place-Names*, p. 170; Rumble, 'The Cross in English Place-Names'; Atherton, *The Battle of Maldon*, pp. 28–32.

19   For this and subsequent citations of the poem *The Battle of Maldon*, see the critical editions by Scragg or by Gordon. Dr Mark Griffith is working on a new critical edition of the poem. And for a discussion of battle sites and the choice of where to fight, see Williams, 'The Place of Slaughter'.

20   For the background to the foundation of Ramsey Abbey, see Byrhtferth of Ramsey, *The Life of St Oswald*, ed. and trans. by Lapidge, pp. xvii–xx.

21   Text and translation of this poem in Byrhtferth of Ramsey, *The Life of St Oswald*, ed. and trans. by Lapidge, pp. 92–93; see also the text and discussion in Clarke, *Literary Landscapes*, pp. 84–89.

THE WORLD OF EALDORMAN BYRHTNOTH   279

Hec de loci positione ab illo theophilo dicta sufficient; nos uero aliquid de nomine ipsius loci disputemus. 'Nisi enim nomen scieris, cognitio', ut magister Hieronimi ait, 'rerum perit.'[22]

> (Let these words suffice, said by that lover of God, concerning the location of the place; for our part we shall discuss something about the name of the place. For as the teacher of Jerome said, 'Unless you know the name, all knowledge of things perishes.')

Suitably equipped with this grammatical authority, Byrhtferth now devotes himself to exploring the etymology of *Ramesige* and *Rammesmere* (III.19), by which he seems to mean Whittlesey Mere (which existed until 1840, when it was drained for agriculture). The consensus among place-name specialists would interpret the first of these names as being *hramsa* (ramson, wild garlic) + *eg* (island) + *mere*, although other 'Ram-type' names (e.g. Ramsey Island in Essex) may derive from *ram(m)* (ram) or, with assimilation of *fn* to *mn*, from *hræfn* (raven) — or even from the personal name Hræfn, just as Whittlesey is *Witles eg* (Witel's island).[23] Strikingly, Byrhtferth does not opt in his etymology for the nearest obvious right-sounding homonym *ramm* (ram, male sheep). Instead, he cites local opinion that 'all those familiar with it call it *Ramere*', implying an origin in Old English *ra* (roe-deer), and his own observation that roe-bucks and hinds and 'stags of astonishing size' live near the lake. But Byrhtferth's method is flexible: he freely ranges between languages, and noting the mighty trees that surround the island he finds more significance in the alternative etymology of Latin *ramis* (tree branches), because now he can bring in biblical associations and the spiritual message of 'Shoot ye forth your branches, and yield your fruit' (Ezekiel 36. 8). It might even be said that Byrhtferth has returned to his point of departure, citing Jerome's words: 'Unless you know the name, all knowledge of things perishes.'

Employing the different emphases and more precise findings of modern etymology and toponymy, this chapter will seek to emulate Byrhtferth's dictum. To the insights of landscape history and archaeology, then, I will aim to add a contribution from language, literary criticism, and place-name studies.

---

22 Lapidge (Byrhtferth of Ramsey, *The Life of St Oswald*, p. 93 n. 181) traces the origin of this quotation via Donatus Ortigraphus and Isidore of Seville to 'Jerome's teacher', i.e. the Roman grammarian Aelius Donatus.

23 These various toponyms are discussed in Watts, ed., *The Cambridge Dictionary of English Place-Names*, pp. 491 and 675.

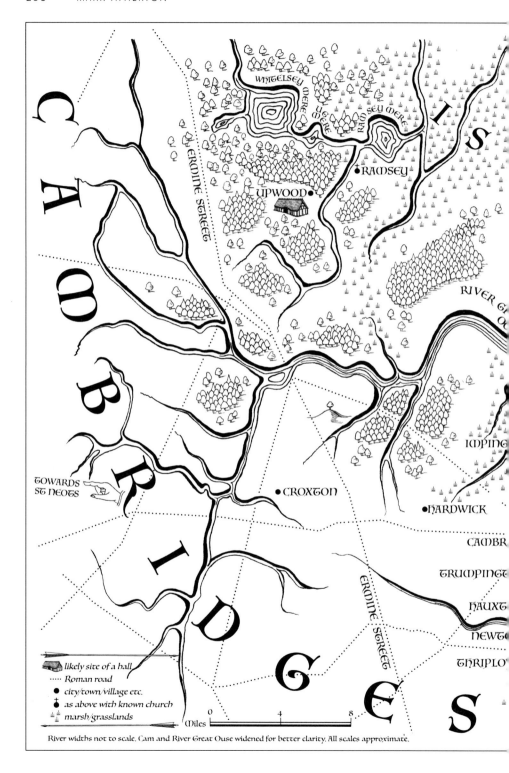

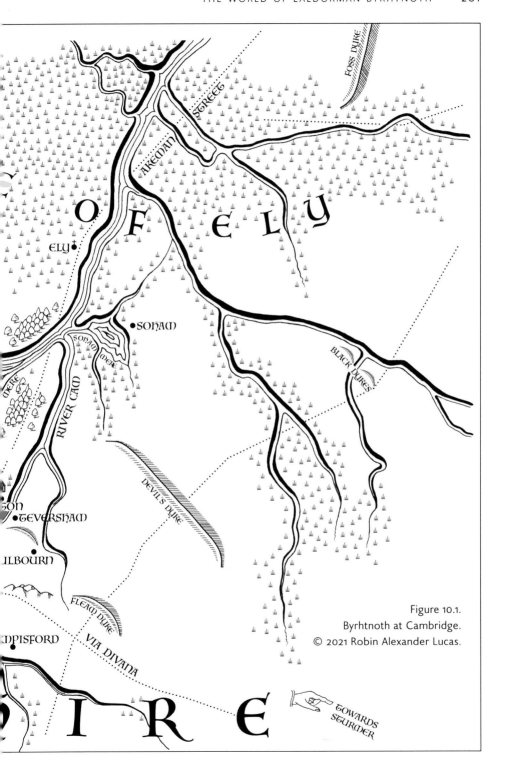

Figure 10.1.
Byrhtnoth at Cambridge.
© 2021 Robin Alexander Lucas.

The Archive of Ely and the Lands around Cambridge

As told in the twelfth-century cartulary-chronicle *Liber Eliensis*, at the moment near the end of his life when news came of renewed Viking incursions in Essex, Byrhtnoth was not in situ to confront them. The plain reason being — so the *Liber* asserts — that he was the 'very valiant leader [Latin *dux*] of the Northumbrians',[24] and at the time of the invasion he is described as being back home in Northumbria. Of course, the Ely cartularist's misidentifying the region of Byrhtnoth's jurisdiction should make us suspicious of the whole account in the *Liber Eliensis*, were it not for two considerations. First, both Byrhtnoth's landholdings and his area of governance were not simply confined to the borders of present-day Essex, and may well have extended into northern territory.[25] As we will see, he was buried at the abbey in Ely, where he held some land near the town; he also owned a circle of estates around Cambridge (see Fig. 10.1), while, starting at Bury St Edmunds in Suffolk, a whole chain of his lands extends southwards down the Stour valley to the coast (see Fig. 10.2 below). And as four of the chapters of *Liber Eliensis* also attest (II.25, II.27, II.33, II.46), Byrhtnoth was involved in settling a number of land disputes in the Cambridge region, thus assisting or complementing the work of his friend and colleague Æthelwine, ealdorman of East Anglia. Rather pointedly, the Latin text of *Liber Eliensis* describes these two regional governors as *ealdormen* (in the sense of 'earl' or *dux*), consciously taking pains to explain the Old English term, which had become archaic by the twelfth century, when the work was compiled.[26]

Byrhtnoth's journey south during the Maldon campaign, as narrated in *Liber Eliensis*, has another notable scene. As he and his men reach Ramsey Abbey (situated in the north-west of the region) Byrhtnoth petitions the abbot for board and lodging to billet his men:

> When, during the march, he approached the abbey of Ramsey and sought hospitality and provisioning from Abbot Wulfsige for himself and his men, the reply was given to him that the place had not resources sufficient for such a multitude, but that, so that he should not go away entirely rejected, Wulfsige would provide what he was requesting for Byrhtnoth himself and seven of his men. (II.62)

Abbot Wulfsige's counteroffer is not generous, and Byrhtnoth gently rejects it:

---

24 *Liber Eliensis*, ed. by Blake, pp. 133–36; *Liber Eliensis*, trans. by Fairweather, pp. 160–63. I follow Fairweather's translation and occasionally quote from the Latin when relevant.

25 Cyril Hart, in 'Byrhtnoth and the Northumbrian Eorldom', in his *The Danelaw*, pp. 138–40, makes the case that Byrhtnoth had jurisdiction in Northamptonshire, which at the time was regarded as being part of Northumbria.

26 *Liber Eliensis*, trans. by Fairweather, discusses the compilation of the cartulary at pp. xiii–xxiii.

THE WORLD OF EALDORMAN BYRHTNOTH   283

To this, Byrhtnoth is said to have made the elegantly phrased response, 'Let the lord Abbot know that I will not dine alone without the men you refer to, because I cannot fight alone without them.' (ii.62)

The elegance of his reply is heard especially in the textures and rhythms of the original Latin. Stylistically one might note, in Byrhtnoth's rhetoric, the use of artful repetition, parallelism, and alliteration on the 'q', 's', 'i', 'n', and 'p' sounds:

Ad quod fertur eleganter respondisse: 'Sciat dominus abbas, **q**uod solus sine istis **n**olo **p**randere, **q**uia solus sine illis **n**equeo **p**ugnare.' (ii.62)

We might again speculate that if it had been turned into Old English verse, such a dialogue would have made a suitably dramatic opening scene for the poem on the battle at Maldon, presenting Byrhtnoth as loyal to the men of his retinue, just as they prove loyal to him in the latter half of the extant heroic poem.

But all this of course may be an invention or embellishment by a local patriot, namely the author of the *Liber Eliensis*, for he goes on to show how Byrhtnoth and his retinue proceed to Ely Abbey, where, in contrast to those inhospitable monks of Ramsey, the brothers receive them with great generosity and hospitality 'fit for a king'. Certainly this reflects where Byrhtnoth's loyalties lay. In his gratitude, he decides to repay the Ely monks handsomely. Attending next day in the chapter house to receive membership of the fraternity (a traditional way in which a layman could receive monastic support in prayer), he takes the opportunity to adjust and reaffirm his last will and testament:

and, giving thanks to the abbot and the community for their charity — so liberal was it — gave to them, there and then, in recompense for their generosity, these capital estates: Spaldwick and Trumpington, Rettendon and *Hesberie*, Soham and Occold. Explaining the business which was the objective of his journey, he granted other estates too, namely Fulbourn, Teversham, Impington, Pampisford, Croxton and Finborough, Triplow, Hardwick, and Somersham with its appurtenances, and, in addition, thirty mancuses of gold and twenty pounds of silver, on the condition that, if by chance he should die in battle, they should bring his body here and give it burial. In addition, by way of investiture of this gift to the church of Ely, he supplemented it with two golden crosses and two borders of his cloak, woven with costly work in gold and gems, and a pair of skillfully made gloves. Then, commending himself to the prayers of the brothers, he hastened with his men to battle.[27]

What hardly needs emphasis in the above is the manifest piety of the ealdorman, for not only does he give various religious artefacts, in particular the gold crosses, to the abbey at Ely, but he also grants all these lands and estates.

---

27   *Liber Eliensis*, trans. by Fairweather, p. 162; see also the discussion in Hill, 'The *Liber Eliensis* "Historical Selections" and the Old English *Battle of Maldon*'.

And there is every reason to give credit to the information contained in this statement, since most of these gifts are confirmed elsewhere. For example, Soham and Rettendon are mentioned in the last will of Byrhtnoth's wife, to be discussed shortly, while most of the other lands feature in a document (S 1051) from Ely Abbey written in the 1080s.[28] In this charter, King Edward the Confessor (who ruled 1042–1066; the forgery was made some twenty years after his reign) purportedly confirms a long list of estates as the legitimate property of Ely: probably Edward made no such confirmation at any time in his reign, but the spurious charter is nevertheless good evidence for attitudes to the land held or claimed by Ely Abbey in the early decades of the Norman Conquest; by fair means or (slightly) foul, the monks were determined to hold on to the lands which ultimately they had acquired from the family of Byrhtnoth and others. Other monastic centres behaved similarly: Christ Church Canterbury also fabricated documents to prove their right to own property that had once belonged to Ealdorman Byrhtnoth.[29]

To understand more easily the East Anglian landscape that Byrhtnoth inhabited we need to study closely the distribution of his lands, as well as looking for patterns in the meanings of their names. Figure 10.1 traces the properties that Byrhtnoth names in his will, as cited in *Liber Eliensis*, along with a few other properties recorded in his name in the same source. Immediately striking is that these form a ring of properties encircling the larger town; the following is a list of the relevant names in Old English, with interpretations of their meanings, based mostly on Watts:[30]

Impington, OE *Impintune* (Impa's estate) in S 1051

Fen Ditton, OE *æt Dictunæ* (ditch settlement)

Teversham, OE *Teuuresham*; the meaning is uncertain — either based on OE *teafor* (red, red lead, purple) or on a hypothetical occupational term **teafrere* (a painter) or an unrecorded personal name (i.e. Tever's village).

Fulbourn, OE *Fuulburne* (brook frequented by birds)[31]

Pampisford, OE *Pampesuuorde* (Pampi's enclosure)

Finborough, nr Stowmarket, Suffolk, OE *Fineberga* DB (woodpecker's hill)[32]

Thriplow, OE *Tripelaue* (Tryppa's mound)

Trumpington (Trump's estate)

---

28 For the text of the lady Ælfflæd's will, see *Anglo-Saxon Wills*, ed. and trans. by Whitelock, no. 15; S 1486.

29 *Charters of Christ Church Canterbury*, ed. by Brooks and Kelly, no. 132; S 1637.

30 Watts, ed., *The Cambridge Dictionary of English Place-Names*.

31 Ekwall, *The Concise Oxford Dictionary of English Place-Names*, p. 189.

32 Ekwall, *The Concise Oxford Dictionary of English Place-Names*, p. 179.

THE WORLD OF EALDORMAN BYRHTNOTH   285

Hauxton, OE *Hauekestune* (Hawk's estate) in S 1051

Newton, OE *Neutune* (new estate) in S 1051

Hardwick, OE *Hardwic* (herd trading-place) in S 1051

Croxton, OE *Crochestune* (Croc's estate), may even derive from the Old
Norse personal name Krokr; located further away, on the road from
Cambridge to St Neots

What do these properties have in common? Can their etymologies throw
light on their use as working estates and villages?

It may be noted that certainly five and perhaps seven of the twelve
place-names seem to have been coined after an original owner, for example,
'Pampi's enclosure'. In this respect, 'Hawk's estate' is ambiguous. It could
refer to a literal hawk, a reminder of the falconry that was practised by the
tenth-century elite,[33] but as with *Hræfn* mentioned above, *Hafoc* (Hawk) could
also be a personal name, and like nearby *Crochestune* (Croxton, i.e. Croc's
or — if Old Norse — Krokkr's estate) and *Trumpintune* (Trumpington, i.e.
Trump's estate), which also end in -*tun*, it may be the name of a thegn whom
an earlier king had rewarded with the grant of an estate. As Gelling showed in
an important publication, this use of personal name + -*tun* probably reflects
the increase in bookland grants that accompanied the development of the new
and much larger thegnly class within the hierarchy of the English kingdom.[34]

Perhaps the most straightforward item in the list of the ealdorman's
Cambridge lands is the functional name Hardwick, that is, *heorde-wic*, which
Watts defines as 'that part of a manor devoted to livestock', the contrast in
this definition being with the *Barton*, that is, 'a corn farm, an outlying grange,
a demesne farm, especially one retained for the lord's use and not let to
tenants'.[35] But since Coates's study of the element *wic* as implying specialized
agriculture, it makes sense to follow Ann Cole's recent argument that the
Hardwick-names are distributed on or near drove roads for cattle, and that
-*wic* implies a place for trade and exchange; Hardwick near Cambridge fits
this pattern well, perhaps a place where drovers brought their stock to graze
and fatten up after the long journey and before sale at markets.[36]

---

33 Cf. the phrase 'hafoc wið þæs holtes' (hawk towards the woodland) in *The Battle of Maldon*,
l. 8a; for contemporary references to falconry, see Atherton, *The Battle of Maldon*, pp. 40–50;
and Owen-Crocker, 'Hawks and Horse-Trappings'.

34 Gelling, *Signposts to the Past*, pp. 177–84; Blair, *Building Anglo-Saxon England*, p. 354; Watts,
ed., *The Cambridge Dictionary of English Place-Names*, pp. 173, 629. For a study of the rise and
development of the thegnly class in the tenth century, see Williams, 'A Bell-House and a
Burh-Geat'; for the importance of this class of men in the action of the poem, see also Busse
and Holtei, 'The Battle of Maldon'.

35 Watts, ed., *The Cambridge Dictionary of English Place-Names*, pp. 279 and 39.

36 Coates, 'New Light from Old Wicks'; Cole, 'Searching for Early Drove Roads', pp. 75 ff. and
esp. p. 85. I am grateful to Paul Cavill for drawing my attention to this article.

Of the six names in -*tun* in the above list, however, two, namely Ditton and Newton, belong to what John Blair and others have termed 'functional place names in -*tun*' that refer to 'specialised and defined mono-functional foci', such as a Roman road or a river (e.g. Stretton, Eaton), and often appear in clusters at Mercian locations.[37] Blair is particularly concerned with the development in Mercia in the eighth century of the name Burton (*burh-tun*), which he convincingly argues represents an outpost or 'guard-station' for the nearby *burh*. Similarly the name *Chesterton* (OE *ceaster*) may denote the same sort of outpost outside a former *chester* or Roman town, as may arguably be the case with Chesterton just north of Cambridge (the Roman origins of Cambridge are seen in the place name Grantchester to the west of the main town, on a Roman road that connects with the more famous north–south route of Ermine Street). Other likely functional -*tun* names around Cambridge include a Kingston and a Milton, the latter occurring in S 1051 as *fram Middeltune* (from the middle estate), a classic case of a 'directional -*tun*', which elsewhere is also matched by a Norton and Sutton, or, as in the case of the old hundred assembly at Leighton Bromswold in north-west Cambridgeshire, by the directional names Old Weston and Easton.

A key place is Ditton, nowadays called Fen Ditton, located just to the north of Cambridge, which is mentioned not only in the *Liber Eliensis* but also in the three wills of Byrhtnoth's family. Originally Old English *Dictun* (ditch estate),[38] the name must refer to the early strategic feature known as the Fleam Dyke, a seven-to-eight-metre-high bank with ditch which once marked the boundary of Flendish hundred and still runs for three miles from Fulbourn to Balsham. Interestingly, beyond Balsham is Haverhill and then *Sturmer* (the only place name that features in *The Battle of Maldon*), which in turn is close to Baythorne, an estate owned by Byrhtnoth's father-in-law Ælfgar and then later by Byrhtnoth's widow, Ælfflæd (see Fig. 10.2 and discussion below).

As the legal disputes recorded in *Liber Eliensis* show, Byrhtnoth seems to have used Ditton as an administrative base, as seen in the following narrative from II.33 about his dispute with Leofsige, an untrustworthy priest, who had in fact deceived him on a previous occasion (there are shades here, one might feel, of the deceitfully persuasive Vikings of *Maldon*, l. 86):

> After these transactions, the priest Leofsige mentioned previously bought from the priest Leofstan a hide and a field for a hundred shillings. Even though he had previously broken the agreement which he had had with Ealdorman Byrhtnoth, once more he offered him one hide as a gift, and another for sale. But, just as before, it was now proved that he was telling a complete pack of lies. When, therefore, Ealdorman Byrhtnoth realized that the priest had deceived him with the lies and treachery with

---

37 ˙Blair, *Building Anglo-Saxon England*, pp. 193–231.

38 The estate of *Dictun* occurs in the wills of Byrhtnoth's sister-in-law Æthelflæd (S 1494) and of his widow Ælfflæd (S 1486).

THE WORLD OF EALDORMAN BYRHTNOTH 287

which he was replete, he ordered him to be summoned and, coming to Ditton, he there proceeded to set out and explain the actions and claims, agreements and broken compacts which he held against him, by means of the testimony of many lawmen.

All turns out well for Byrhtnoth on this occasion. Leofsige is unable to summon enough supporters to clear himself with an oath (which was a common legal practice in the period), and it is decided that he should be evicted and that Byrhtnoth should be given possession of both hides of land:

This same was decreed a second time on another occasion, at Cambridge. When it was done, Ealdorman Byrhtnoth granted these lands to St Æthelthryth.

Since St Æthelthryth was the local saint traditionally linked with Ely (as told in Bede), the last statement entails that Byrhtnoth granted the property to Ely. But what this anecdote reveals is a characteristic of the *Liber Eliensis*, its main purpose being to record donations of land to the abbey. It might be compared with another dispute over two estates south of Cambridge, namely Hauxton and Newton, as narrated in II.27. Here Byrhtnoth intervenes at Ely on behalf of the abbot, who has failed to gain the assistance of Ealdorman Æthelwine (as noted above, Æthelwine was the officially appointed ealdorman of East Anglia). Once more settling the dispute positively, Byrhtnoth again presents the charters of the two estates to Ely Abbey.[39]

In short, then, Byrhtnoth owned administrative and other estates in and around Cambridge, and the narrative in the *Liber Eliensis* (II.62) of his last days sees him granting these estates to Ely Abbey. And as a kind of coda to this account of Byrhtnoth's last will and testament, a short chapter follows in this same Ely cartulary (II.63), listing the five properties that Byrhtnoth's wife also bequeathed to the abbey:

This man's wife, indeed, the Lady Ælfflæd by name, at the time when her husband was killed and buried, gave to this church an estate at Rettendon, which formed part of her marriage-portion, and land at Soham, which is by a mere adjoining Ely, and Ditton, and a hide at Cheveley, and a golden torque, and a hanging (Latin *cortina*) woven upon and embroidered with deeds of her husband, in memory of his probity.[40]

Unlike her husband's will, Ælfflæd's last wishes have survived in full in their original language: they are recorded in documents preserved originally in the archive of the monastery at Bury St Edmunds in Suffolk; it is to these that we now turn.

---

39 For analysis of the various legal cases contained in *Liber Eliensis*, see Kennedy, 'Law and Litigation in the *Libellus Æthelwoldi Episcopi*'.

40 *Liber Eliensis*, trans. by Fairweather, p. 163. There is discussion of the (lost) Byrhtnoth Tapestry and its possible appearance, with references, in Atherton, *The Making of England*, pp. 126, 137, 166–69.

The Archive of Bury St Edmunds

In 1020 the secular minster at *Bedricesweorth* in Suffolk, now known as Bury St Edmunds, underwent a radical transformation, similar to what had taken place in previous generations at Winchester, Worcester, and Canterbury: previously run by secular clerics, the church was refounded by Cnut, the new Anglo-Danish king of England, as a Benedictine monastery, and the clerics were replaced by monks. However, not everything was overturned, for their patron saint, who was the undoubted spiritual focus of Bury, remained the same: since the Viking wars of the late ninth century and the Danish conquest and settlement of East Anglia, the region's last king, Edmund, had been venerated there as a martyr saint; and in the early tenth century his mortal remains had been translated to a special shrine at the minster. Much later, the great Frankish scholar Abbo of Fleury — during or shortly after his residence at Ramsey Abbey in the 980s — wrote an elaborate account of King Edmund's martyrdom.[41] Now, in the 1020s, the Benedictine monastery, with a newly built church to honour the royal martyr, became an economic boost to the region, and a town rapidly developed outside its monastic gates. Around the same time, and probably not coincidentally, a copy of two tenth-century wills (S 1494 and S 1486) was added to the Bury archive; the testators whose last wills were thus preserved for posterity were the two daughters of Ælfgar, ealdorman of Essex (946–951): Æthelflæd of Damerham, who married King Edmund in 944 and who died 975x91, and Ælfflæd (died c. 1002), wife of Byrhtnoth. A later copy of the will of Ælfgar their father (S 1483) also survives in the Bury archive.[42]

By the 1020s, various properties mentioned in these wills now belonged to Bury, and the new abbey was probably keen to establish on a firm footing its credentials and its right to own these estates. It seems fitting and appropriate that the documents were preserved at Bury St Edmunds, for King Edmund of East Anglia had died in battle against invading Viking forces, as had Byrhtnoth the hero of Maldon; indeed there are various parallels to be drawn in the accounts of Edmund's heroic martyrdom as told by Abbo of Fleury and of Byrhtnoth's pious death in battle as told in the *Liber Eliensis* and *The Battle of Maldon*.[43] Moreover, the three wills, composed at different times and for different contexts, can be read as the basis of a landscape biography of Byrhtnoth's family involvement in the life and culture of the region.

For our purposes, the importance of the monastic archive at Bury St Edmunds lies in the fact that it has preserved the three aforementioned wills, thus affording many insights into the landholdings of Ealdorman Byrhtnoth in a large area that covers southern Suffolk and northern Essex. But before

---

41 For detailed discussion, see Cavill, 'The *Passio S. Eadmundi* and *The Battle of Maldon*'.
42 Hart, 'The Ealdordom of Essex', in *The Danelaw*, pp. 127–31, 134.
43 Cavill, 'The *Passio S. Eadmundi* and *The Battle of Maldon*'.

THE WORLD OF EALDORMAN BYRHTNOTH   289

continuing, I think it may be helpful to highlight some of the differences in style, tone, and content between the three texts. Most obviously, they vary in length. Though broadly covering the same region there is a chronological development, for each document in turn becomes progressively longer and more complex than its predecessor. Commentators usually agree that thematically the three wills are united in their promotion of Stoke-by-Nayland as the minster church for the region (see centre of the map in Fig. 10.2). This was the ecclesiastical community that Ælfgar and his daughters aimed to support as patrons, and they speak in their wills of their concern to honour the burial place of their 'ancestors' (OE *yldran*) at Stoke. When Byrhtnoth joined the family by marriage, he must have become involved in this project.[44] But despite the shared aim of the three members of the family, there are differences in their wills, and some perceptive comments by Cyril Hart can be developed further, for they point to significant differences in content and tone between the three texts.[45]

Byrhtnoth's marriage to Ælfflæd took place around 951. Since his wife was the daughter of the Ealdorman of Essex, he found himself on course for inheriting the ealdordom itself, a goal he eventually achieved in the year 956, when King Eadwig promoted him to that position on the demise or retirement of a certain Byrhtferth (probably Byrhtnoth's uncle), who had held the position after Ælfgar.[46] Later, as the religious life of the nation changed under the Benedictine Reform promoted by King Edgar after his full succession in 959, Byrhtnoth must have shifted his allegiance away from the Suffolk minster of Stoke-by-Nayland that his father-in-law Ælfgar had so zealously promoted. This was the attraction of the recently founded great fenland abbeys of Ramsey and Ely, the latter becoming his spiritual home and eventually his final resting place, as we have seen.

The shift to the Benedictines signalled the decline of Stoke as an institution. As Ælfflæd's will reveals, various properties which should have been donated to the local church at Stoke remained in the family until after her death. For example, her father Ælfgar had stipulated in his will (*c.* 951) that Ditton should pass as a life interest to her sister Æthelflæd, who would then donate it to a minster of her choice. But we have already seen that Byrhtnoth was using Ditton as an administrative base for his jurisdiction in Cambridge. This suggests that Æthelflæd had in fact given it to the married couple, her sister and husband. Ælfflæd's will of 1002 confirms this, for only now does she bequeath Ditton to the Church, and her choice falls on Ely Abbey rather than Stoke.

---

44 Wareham, *Lords and Communities in Early Medieval East Anglia*; Tollerton, *Wills and Will-Making in Anglo-Saxon England*, pp. 233–36.

45 Hart, 'The Ealdordom of Essex', in *The Danelaw*.

46 *Charters of Abingdon Abbey*, ed. by Kelly.

Another set of properties received similar treatment. In his will, Ælfgar had twice (and even rather emotively) insisted that his elder daughter Æthelflæd should do more to promote the family minster at Stoke:

> And I grant to my daughter Æthelflæd the estates at Cockfield and Ditton and that at Lavenham after my death on condition that she be the more zealous for the welfare of my soul and of her mother's soul and of her brother's soul and of her own; and then after our lifetime I grant the estate at Cockfield to St Edmund's foundation at Bedericesworth. And it is my wish that Æthelflæd shall grant the estate at Ditton after her death to whatever holy foundation seems to her most advisable, for the sake of our ancestors' souls. And I grant the estate at Lavenham after our lifetime to my daughter's child if it be God's will that she have any, unless Æthelflæd wishes to grant it to him before; and if she has no child, the estate is to go to Stoke for our ancestors' souls.[47]

Ælfgar had also declared that after his daughter Æthelflæd's time, Cockfield should revert to Bury St Edmunds, while Lavenham, Peldon, Mersea, and Greenstead should go to Stoke-by-Nayland, but Æthelflæd in *her* will (*c.* 975) keeps these five estates firmly in the family and grants their use to her sister Ælfflæd and brother-in-law Byrhtnoth instead. It is only in Ælfflæd's will of 1002 that we see her attempt to honour the wishes of her father. In fact, the text reveals that Ælfflæd was anxiously trying to recruit Ealdorman Æthelmær — the founder of Eynsham Abbey and the patron of Abbot Ælfric the Homilist — to safeguard the will of her family. But Æthelmær was unwilling or unsuccessful in his endeavours. By 1042, as we will see, Mersea was owned by Edward the Confessor, who gave it to the community of St Ouen in Rouen in Normandy,[48] while by the time of the Domesday Survey of 1086, Peldon was in the hands of Swein, son of Robert Fitzwymarc, sheriff of Essex under both Edward the Confessor and William the Conqueror.[49]

The emotional colouring, the note of insistence, in the above quotation is not hard to miss. In both their wills Ælfgar and his younger daughter Ælfflæd share a certain anxiety about the status of the family and about the chances of their monastic project ever coming to fruition. One experience that the sisters Ælfflæd and Æthelflæd had in common was that both had been widowed by the violent deaths of their husbands, and eleven years after the fight at Maldon, Ælfflæd still appeals to the king 'for the sake of God's love, the love of my husband's soul and the love of my sister's soul'; still calls to mind with affection the abbey, naming the five saints honoured at Ely, 'þer mines hlafordes lichoma rest' (where my lord's body rests); and renews the promise to give the three lands to the abbey 'þe wit buta geheotan Gode'

---

47 Full text and translation in *Anglo-Saxon Wills*, ed. and trans. by Whitelock, no. 2, pp. 6–9.
48 S 1015; Hart, *The Danelaw*, pp. 504–07.
49 Barker, 'Peldon in the Domesday Book'.

THE WORLD OF EALDORMAN BYRHTNOTH   291

(which we-two both promised to God), the dual pronoun *wit* emphasizing that this was a joint action carried out by both her husband and herself. She even finds the matching arm-ring to the one given for Byrhtnoth's 'soul-payment' and grants this second ring to the abbey.

Her sister has a different perspective. To use a biblical analogy, if — of the two sisters — Ælfflæd is the affectionate Mary, then Æthelflæd is the practical Martha. Admittedly the murder of her husband King Edmund in 946 is more remote in time (and one source suggests she may have remarried); nevertheless Æthelflæd writes more plainly than her sister: 'And I grant the estate at Damerham to Glastonbury for King Edmund's soul and for King Edgar's and for mine'. She is also more involved, it would seem, with the details of kindred and the people of the household. It is only Æthelflæd who remembers a range of people, of differing ranks, in the final clauses of her will: her kinsman, her reeve, her servant (*cniht*), her two priests, her kinswoman; half the slaves on her estates are to be freed; the villages are to be given half her livestock.

Two of the names of these extra figures are intriguingly resonant for readers of *The Battle of Maldon*, for the *cniht* (an upcoming rank in the tenth century connected with squire-like duties and horsemanship) is a certain Brihtwold. Now if this will was composed quite late in the period 975x91 (the date of Æthelflæd's death is not known more precisely), the question arises: could this Brihtwold be Byrhtwold, the *eald geneat* (suitably aged and now higher in rank, but also a horseman), the man who makes the final speech of fortitude and perseverance that ends the extant text of the poem (*Maldon*, ll. 309–19)? This admittedly is speculation. But more convincing, perhaps, is the name of the 'kinsman', *Sibriht*, recalling the 'noble companion' of the poem *The Battle of Maldon* (ll. 280–82) whose name is *Æþeric* [*sic*], and whose brother is said to be *Sibyrht*, essentially the same name as Sibriht but for the metathesis of the 'r' (cf. *Byrhtnoth* in the poem and *Brihtnoth* in the documents). As Scragg points out, it is 'worth noting' that the poet nowhere states that Ætheric died in the battle;[50] and in a case recorded in a contemporary will and charter, another Essex man of the same name, Ætheric, was involved in a notorious accusation of treason and involvement in a plot to invite King Swegn of Denmark to invade.[51] The home of this Ætheric was Bocking, situated on Stane Street in the middle of our region, not far from properties at Rayne, Notley, and Kelvedon that were left in another contemporary will by Leofwine, son of Wulfstan. As we have seen, this Wulfstan may just possibly be the Wulfstan of the poem who successfully defended the bridge.[52]

---

50   The comment appears in the 'Glossary of Proper Names' in *The Battle of Maldon*, ed. by Scragg, p. 108.

51   Brooks, 'Treason in Essex in the 990s'; for an alternative edition and translation of the texts, see also Atherton, *The Battle of Maldon*, pp. 194–98; the critical edition is found in *Charters of Christ Church Canterbury*, ed. by Brooks and Kelly, nos 136 and 137, pp. 999–1010.

52   S 1522. For the text of Leofwine's will, with some commentary, see Atherton, *The Battle of Maldon*, pp. 199–201.

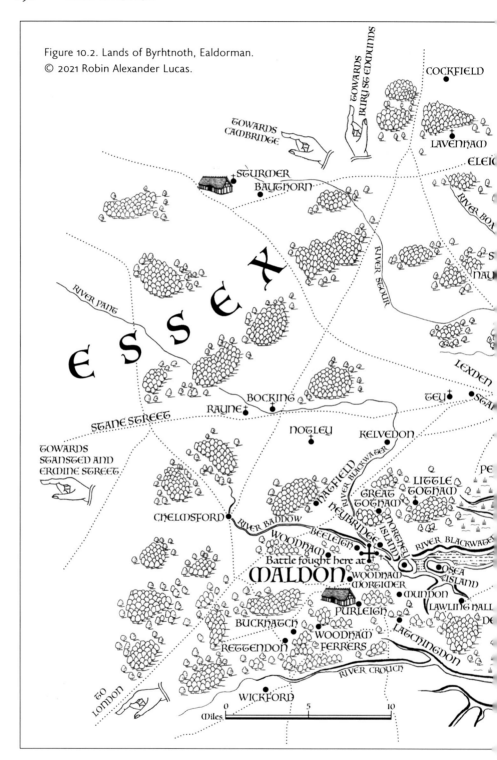

Figure 10.2. Lands of Byrhtnoth, Ealdorman.
© 2021 Robin Alexander Lucas.

THE WORLD OF EALDORMAN BYRHTNOTH 293

Moreover, further to the east along the same Roman road to Colchester are the estates of Tey, Stanway, and Lexden, all owned by Byrhtnoth himself — the proximity of such estates that is revealed by visualizing their locations on a map (see Fig. 10.2) makes real connections between these figures seem distinctly more credible. In other words, Byrhtnoth and his wife, Leofwine son of Wulfstan, and Ætheric of Bocking were all neighbours.

Let us pause to take stock. The aim of this section has been to introduce the three wills of Byrhtnoth's family and to identify other documents that name relevant locations. It is time now to examine the patterns and distribution of these names and explore ways in which they might contribute to the interpretation of the landscape as it existed in Suffolk and Essex in the course of Byrhtnoth's lifetime. Plotting the locations of Byrhtnoth's lands on a map (Fig. 10.2), we see that there are definite patterns, and that very broadly speaking his territory divides into four regions:

1) the lands along the Stour

2) the central region: the Roman road of Stane Street

3) the fields and woodlands around Maldon

4) the waterways of the Blackwater Estuary.

These divisions are as much conceptual as they are actual physical regions, and there are certainly overlaps between them, but in the rest of this chapter I propose to employ them as a kind of ad hoc 'mental geography' which I hope will help to visualize the ways in which Byrhtnoth interacted and engaged with his physical surroundings.

Byrhtnoth's Lands in Suffolk and Essex

Byrhtnoth began his path to the ealdordom of Essex in the region of the river Stour, 'the boundary between Essex and East Anglia'.[53] This pastoral, tree-lined river-valley landscape will already be familiar to most readers of the present chapter, even if they have never visited the region, for it has been immortalized in the work of the Romantic period painter John Constable (1776–1837), in paintings such as *The Vale of Dedham* (1802), *Flatford Mill* (1816), *The Hay Wain* (1821), or *Stoke-by-Nayland* (1836). It was the latter locality in particular, namely *Stoke*, that is, Stoke-by-Nayland (the place on the island), that attracted the spiritual and material investments of Byrhtnoth's family. And although it may seem incongruous to think of the *har hilderinc* — the grey-haired veteran warrior of *Maldon*, a man described in the same language as that of *Beowulf* — as active in a landscape of this kind, it is nevertheless

---

53 Reaney, *The Place-Names of Essex*, p. xxvi.

THE WORLD OF EALDORMAN BYRHTNOTH

a valuable corrective to mental images of 'Anglo-Saxon England' that we may still harbour in our heads. The present-day landscape of Suffolk is very traditional, and not overly affected by eighteenth-century enclosures or other such nationwide changes, other than the obvious historical developments in architecture. And for some writers, notably the mid-twentieth-century essayist and historian of folklore George Ewart Evans, its rural culture and folk-life have long-standing roots.[54] In this sense it is even possible to claim that, at least for periods of time, Byrhtnoth lived in 'Constable country', since he no doubt visited his many estates in the Stour valley, and probably helped to administer and manage them.

One feature that the present-day Suffolk region in particular has inherited from the early medieval period is the prevalence of 'hall-and-church' clusters in 'prime valley side locations close to a water supply'.[55] This seems to reflect the living conditions of the thegnly class of tenth-century England: a broadly square area demarked by a ditch and fence, containing a church, a manor, and *burhgeat* (manor gate).[56] The term *burhgeat*, which scholars have borrowed from the much quoted thegnly Promotion Law, is reflected in such place names as Burgate in Suffolk,[57] and there are also many Essex examples: Reaney cites *Burgateslongeredenes* in Chigwell, *Burgatefeld* in Great Sampford, *Burgatesstrete* in Woodford, *Burgettfeild* in Rivenhall. None of these appear in our particular sources, but there is a possible connection here with Byrhtnoth, for he gave his wife Ælfflæd the estate of Rettendon as her morning-gift, presumably a manor with land attached, and nearby there is Buckhatch (see the south-west of the map in Fig. 10.2), which Reaney links to the name *Burgatesfeld* recorded in 1336, justifying the phonetic change as Burgates > Burgatch > Buckhatch.[58]

For examples of 'hall-and-church' clusters in the region of the Stour a good starting point is Byrhtnoth's estate at Polstead, OE *Polstede* (the pool place), situated in the valley of the Box not far from the Stour; the Ordnance Survey map of Polstead of 1885 shows a deer park with woodland, in which Polstead Hall (sixteenth century) is marked as adjacent to St Mary's Church

---

54 One might compare the ritual 'placed deposits' of early Anglo-Saxon buildings with those of early twentieth-century rural Suffolk; see Blair, *Building Anglo-Saxon England*, pp. 86–87, and Evans, *The Pattern under the Plough*, pp. 52–60.

55 'Suffolk Landscape Character Assessment: Hall-and-Church', Suffolk County Council, <https://suffolklandscape.org.uk/glossary/hall-and-church/> [accessed 6 May 2021].

56 For discussion of such thegnly residences, see Reynolds, *Late Anglo-Saxon England* and Blair, *Building Anglo-Saxon England*.

57 Skeat, *The Place-Names of Suffolk*, p. 40.

58 Reaney, *The Place-Names of Essex*, p. 263. For a similar figure to the lady Ælfflæd in her 'morning-gift' residence at Rettendon, see the discussions of her contemporary the lady Wynflæd, who has also left a will to document her lands and who owned tapestries rather like that commissioned by Ælfflæd; Wynflæd's morning-gift at Faccombe Netherton is mentioned in her will, and archaeologists have now excavated and studied the remains of her hall and residence; Blair, *Building Anglo-Saxon England*, pp. 365–69; Weikert, 'The Biography of a Place'.

(twelfth century), with an ancient Gospel Oak located between them.[59] Just to the north across the main road are two fish ponds labelled Polstead Ponds. The documentary evidence helps to fill out the picture, for Ælfflæd's will rather unusually singles out this area, as though it is special, by providing a description of the bounds of the estate (normally this practice is reserved for charters rather than wills). Not all the toponyms can be identified, but it is clear that the land covers a large area of woodland and waterways between Stratford St Mary and Chelsworth in which there are the following features: two clearings (OE *leah*), one covered in heath (present-day Hadleigh), the other on a shelf or slope (Shelley); there is a *hnutstede*, 'a place where nuts grow' (Nurstead), an unlocated *wudemannestun* (woodman's estate), and a *hlig-ham*, 'shelter homestead' (Layham); the waterways include the rivers Brett and Stour, and the text mentions a 'cress-island', that is, 'water-cress' (present-day Kersey), as well as the 'Ford of the Gyddingas' (now Gifford's Hall). If Byrhtnoth and his wife ever mounted their horses to survey the bounds of their estate then this is the kind of landscape they moved and worked in.

Examples of other hall-and-church clusters occur still further north in our region at the villages of Lavenham, OE *Lauanham* (Lafa's homestead), later a centre of the wool trade with many fine fifteenth-century buildings still extant; Monk's Eleigh, OE *Illanlege* (Illa's wood or clearing); and Chelsworth, OE *Ceorlesweorð* (Ceorl's or the peasant's enclosure); all three have the requisite hall-and-church clusters. Chelsworth was originally a gift of King Edgar to his kinswoman Æthelflæd (Byrhtnoth's sister-in-law), who was Edgar's stepmother (since he was a son of King Edmund). Notably, the charter thus issued is the oldest Suffolk charter, since most extant charters originate in Wessex.[60]

Communication between Cambridge and the Stour region must have been easy for Byrhtnoth, for the Roman road from Cambridge to Colchester passes through the Stour valley not far from Sturmer, where Leofsunu of *The Battle of Maldon* had his home.[61] And Sturmer is close to a property mentioned in Ælfflæd's will as 'þes landes æt Babbingþyrnan' (the land at the thorn-bush of Babba's people), still known today as Baythorne, though the solitary hawthorn

---

59 OS reference: TL991381. Local tradition claims a great age for this oak, going back to St Cedd: 'An oak (*Quercus*) tree which grows in the grounds of Polstead Hall, near the church at Polstead, Suffolk is associated with St Cedd, a Saxon missionary. According to tradition the saint preached under the original tree in 753 A.D. For many years it was believed that this was no more than a "picturesque legend", but when the tree collapsed in 1953 a cut through its trunk revealed over 1,400 annual growth rings, indicating that the tree would have been a mature 200 year old in 753.' See 'Polstead Gospel Oak', *Plant-Lore: Collecting the Folklore and Uses of Plants*, <https://www.plant-lore.com/plantofthemonth/polstead-gospel-oak/> [accessed 2 June 2021].

60 S 703; Hart, *The Danelaw*, p. 479; brief discussion of the bounds of the charter occurs in Atherton, *The Battle of Maldon*, pp. 11–12.

61 For discussion of Sturmer (Stour Pond) and its context, see Atherton, *The Battle of Maldon*, pp. 62–64.

that marked its location is long gone.[62] If Byrhtnoth passed this way on his last ride from Ely to Maldon, then there was ample opportunity to stay the night at the estate then visit Sturmer in order to muster Leofsunu (and his men?) to the *fyrd* before proceeding further southwards.

Another easy line of communication is the Roman road of Stane Street, which passes from Colchester westwards across the region (see Fig. 10.2). In fact, two of the properties owned by Byrhtnoth and Ælfflæd signal their location on this road by their name: Stanway or 'æt Stanwægun' (at the stoney ways) appears on Stane Street, its toponym revealing the flat stones with which these roads were paved, while further north is *Stredfordæ* (Stratford St Mary), where another Roman *strata via* (paved road) crosses the River Colne. Near Stane Street too are the couple's lands at Lexden and Tey, the latter clearly some kind of farm or *teag* (enclosure), while further to the west is Bocking, home to the disgraced-then-reprieved thegn Ætheric of Bocking mentioned above. From Bocking, the old road from Bury leads southwards towards London, crossing the Chelmer at another ford, Chelmsford.

In a land of rivers and deep tidal estuaries that often constituted formidable obstacles, the fords and crossing places were — and still are — vitally important. It is clear that there were more fords than there were bridges — these tended to come later and often replaced the ford at the same location.[63] The older name of the town at Heybridge (high bridge) just across the river from Maldon was *Tidwoldingtun* (Tidwold's estate), while the bridge itself, given the later name Fullbridge Road, was probably *ful brycg* (foul or muddy bridge), so called because it was regularly flooded by the tidal estuary. We may recall that the Latin for 'land-bridge' in Byrhtferth's *Vita S. Oswaldi* is *pons*, suggesting that even through the medium of Anglo-Latin the early medieval English concept of 'bridge' could signify either an actual bridge or a causeway, as in *The Battle of Maldon* (ll. 74, 78, 81, 88). Instances of place names occur where 'bridge' can denote a causeway, examples in Essex being compounds with *hris* (brushwood) to give *hrisbrycg* (brushwood causeway), as in Risebridge in Romford and Rice Bridge in Little Clacton near Harwich. Otherwise, bridges in the period could also be timber planks resting on either caissons or stone piers.[64] With these practicalities in mind, it is worth pointing out that a narrow muddy bridge, or perhaps a causeway combined with a narrow bridge over the actual course of the river, would be a far more plausible location for a successful defence than a modern broad causeway wide enough for a National Trust Land Rover to cross with ease. Such a scenario would give due credit to Wulfstan and his two companions

---

62 On solitary trees as landmarks in the early medieval landscape, see Hooke, *Trees in Anglo-Saxon England*, pp. 174–84; and more generally Bintley, *Trees in the Religions of Early Medieval England*.

63 On *brycg* and *ford*, see Gelling and Cole, *The Landscape of Place-Names*, pp. 67–80.

64 Gelling and Cole, *The Landscape of Place-Names*, p. 68; Blair, *Building Anglo-Saxon England*, pp. 190, 191 (fig. 65), and 220–21.

298   MARK ATHERTON

being able to resist successfully the full might of the Danish army coming at them in single file (*Maldon*, ll. 74–83).

I have already mentioned the ford where the Roman road crosses the Stour at Stratford St Mary, while another ford owned by Byrhtnoth and Ælfflæd is Alresford (Ægel's ford) to the east of the Colne estuary. Otherwise there is Wickford, which Æthelflæd gave to her kinsman Sibriht; the place name indicates the presence of a *wic* (market or trading place). A distribution map published by Reaney with his *Place-Names of Essex* shows that the -*wic* names gather in dense clusters along the coast of eastern Essex; as seen in Figure 10.2 there is Ipswich at the head of the Orwell, or Harwich at the mouth of the Stour. The latter name, OE *herewic*, suggests a place where an earlier Danish *here* (raiding army) might have lodged and traded, and there are Scandinavian names nearby at Kirby (Old Norse *kirkja* + *by*) and possibly Thorpe.[65] Their presence in this part of Essex was a memory in the 990s, but no doubt a warning too. The Anglo-Saxon Chronicle (version A) reports that back in the year 894, during the reign of Alfred the Great, the invading Viking army evaded the defence force sent to attack it and escaped to Essex, where they set up for the winter on this island:

> Þa hie ða eft ut of Norðwealum wendon mid þære herehyðe þe hie ðær genumen hæfdon, þa foron hie ofer Norðhymbra lond 7 Eastengla, swa swa seo fird hie geræcan ne mehte, oþþæt hie comon on Eastseaxna lond easteweard, on an igland þæt is ute on þære sæ, þæt is Meresig haten.[66]
>
> > (When they left Wales with the raiding-plunder that they had taken there they travelled across Northumbria and East Anglia, as the *fyrd* (defence force) was not able to intercept them, until they came to the eastern part of Essex, to an island out on the sea which is called Mersea.)

Almost a hundred years earlier than the battle at Maldon, this annal captures another scene in the ongoing drama of invasion and defence in the Blackwater estuary in this period. For readers of *Maldon*, however, the major interest of this text must lie in the fact that the island it names was later owned by Byrhtnoth and his family. Later still, it came into royal hands, and a charter from the reign of Edward the Confessor gives the bounds of the property:

> Þis is þæt landgemere æt meresege þæt is ærest on pantan streame oð hit cymð to ðam dican betwyx east meresege and west <meresege>. Ðonne of ðam dican into ðam fleote. Ðonne of ðam fleote into ðære stræte þæt hit cymð to ðære petan. Þonne on fingringaho <æt> ðam stane fram

---

65 Reaney, *The Place-Names of Essex*, pp. 341, 353. It is possible that Harwich represents an East Saxon military mustering place rather than a Viking trading place; see the discussion in Baker and Brookes, 'Explaining Anglo-Saxon Military Efficiency', esp. at pp. 242–48.

66 Cited from *The Anglo-Saxon Chronicle: MS A*, ed. by Bately.

ðam stane to bricsfleotes orde æft fram ðam stane to mannanbricse fram
mannanbricse to peltandunes meowte.[67]

> (These are the bounds of the estate at Mersea: that is first from the
> River Panta until it comes to the dykes between East Mersea and West
> Mersea. Then from the dykes to the Pyefleet channel. Then from the
> channel to the Roman road until it comes to Pete Bridge [i.e. an area
> of peatland]. Then to the stone at Fingringhoe; from the stone to the
> spit on Bridge River; back from the stone to Manwood Bridge, and
> from Manwood Bridge to Peldon boundary.)[68]

This document can function as confirmation of the river name in the poem:
line 68 of *Maldon* also refers to *Pantan stream*, while line 98 describes the
Vikings crossing 'west ofer Pantan, ofer scir wæter' (west over Panta, over the
bright water). The boundary clause describes land on Mersea and the Roman
road which leads from Mersea northwards across the Pyefleet via the early
medieval causeway (later known as The Strood) that separates Mersea from
the mainland. The road then heads up through the parish of Fingringhoe (it
eventually leads to the old Roman town of Colchester).

This landscape north of the Pyefleet Channel and on either side of the
Colne estuary is marshy, and this fact is clearly signalled by the names of
the estates that Byrhtnoth held here, as recorded in Ælfflæd's will (S 1486).
The most expressive is 'æt fulan pettæ' (at the foul pit) 'referring to the
marshy hollow above which the hamlet stands'; the pejorative appellation
was replaced in the twelfth century by *Bealmont* and then *Beaumont*
(beautiful hill) — the name it still sports to this day.[69] What is striking is
that Byrhtnoth's other estates here are situated on markedly higher ground,
above the reaches of the marsh. West of the River Colne is Fingringhoe, a
hill-spur on a broad 'finger of land' between Roman river (a tributary of
the Colne) and Geeton creek. Even more prominently, Peldon, later known
as Pelden in le Plaish (OE *plæsc*, marsh), is nowadays a steep climb up a
lane from the main road between Mersea and Colchester, located on a hill
overlooking the salt marshes on three sides, its eleventh-century origin
church clearly visible, mentioned incidentally for its crooked tower in the
gothic novel *Mehalah, a Story of the Salt Marshes* (1880) by the Victorian
writer Sabine Baring-Gould, who was rector of East Mersea. In its Old
English form, *Peltandun* has two possible interpretations: it could be named
after a man Pylta or be derived from a conjectural verb **pyltan* (to thrust,
drive), hence descriptive of the steep hill.

---

67 Text edited in Cyril Hart, 'The Mersea Charter of Edward the Confessor', in his *The Danelaw*,
     pp. 495–508, at p. 505.
68 My translation, based on Hart's commentary in *The Danelaw*, pp. 498–500. The noun *meowte*
     may be a scribal error for *mearce*.
69 Watts, ed., *The Cambridge Dictionary of English Place-Names*, p. 45; Reaney, *The Place-Names
     of Essex*, pp. 327–28.

Its general situation might be compared with Hatfield Peverel and the two Tothams (Great and Little) further to the west (see Fig. 10.2). In her will Ælfflæd pointedly mentions 'þonæ wuda æt Hæþfælda þæ min swystar gæuþæ. 7 mine yldran' (the wood at Hatfield which my sister and my forefathers gave) and 'þæt wudæland æt Totham þæ min fæder geuþæ into Myresiæ' (the woodland at Totham which my father granted to Mersea). In general, these names present a pattern for the landscape moving west to east, namely: open fields and clearings – hills and woodland – marshland – coast. Significantly, the name Totham itself contains the element *toot*, which the OED defines as 'an isolated conspicuous hill suitable as a place of observation; a lookout hill; perh. short for toot-hill'. A 'Beacon Hill' with views southwards down to the Blackwater estuary is situated not far from Great Totham.

As it turns out, the original name of the Blackwater, the Pant (Welsh: valley) fits a standard pattern: there is a Celtic or older pre-English origin for several other major rivers of the region, notably Colne (also the name of one of Byrhtnoth's family estates, at what is now Colne Engaine), Orwell, and Rayne.[70] A comparably ancient name is that of Byrhtnoth's estate at Dovercourt, OE, *æt Douorcortæ*, on the slope overlooking the sea near Harwich. As Reaney points out, the second element is obscure, but the first element is Celtic, and related to *Dover* in Kent, and must refer to a stream flowing past Great Oakley nearby; the Welsh cognate is *dwfr* (water).[71]

The Chelmer (mentioned above), the name of the river which flows through Chelmsford and then into the Blackwater at Maldon, is an example of a later medieval back-formation, a process by which local speakers misinterpreted the name of the crossing-place Ceolmær's Ford as 'Ford over the Chelmer', thus coining a new toponym. Originally, however, the river was named the Baddow, which has an uncertain, complex, and ultimately fascinating etymology, one which brings us full circle back to the reflections on the name Maldon with which we opened this essay. Though Ekwall and Watts are cautious, Reaney makes a valiant attempt to find a valid etymology for the Baddow, which is preserved in the names of the villages Great Baddow and Little Baddow. The earliest recorded spelling in a will of *c.* 975 is *to beadewan ea* (to Baddow River) which Reaney sees as a derivative of OE *beadu*, genitive *beadwe*, 'battle', that is, 'the battle river' with possibly also Celtic cognates and parallels.[72] Here again the question is raised of the practice of choosing places to fight on the basis of their auspicious or favourable names; did Byrhtnoth choose to fight his good fight at 'battle river', outside a city wall, in view of the 'hill of the cross'?

---

70 See Watts, ed., *The Cambridge Dictionary of English Place-Names* on Colne, p. 151; on Orwell (the swift one), pp. 19, 453; on Rayne (wet, moisten, water), p. 494.

71 Reaney, *The Place-Names of Essex*, p. 337; on the name Dover, see Watts, ed., *The Cambridge Dictionary of English Place-Names*, p. 192.

72 Reaney, *The Place-Names of Essex*, p. 234.

Reflections and Conclusions

Stretching from Cambridge to Harwich, from Colchester to Chelmsford, from Maldon to Wickford, the two maps in this chapter present the following picture of the life and world of Ealdorman Byrhtnoth. Findings must be expressed with caution, but include the following.

The main pattern is one of highly descriptive 'speaking names', toponyms providing evidence to the kind of land he held and its qualities: its use for travel, communication, agriculture, woodland, the arrangements of social hierarchy, trade, religion, defence. There is ease and speed of travel and communication, for Byrhtnoth's estates are never more than a day's journey apart and distributed in patterns, a ring of property around Cambridge, lines or chains of adjacent lands along the old Roman roads and the rivers, in particular the line of the Stour and the two sides of the Blackwater estuary — where possible at strategic points the fords are marked, though not the bridges.

If Cambridge was important for trade, Essex must have been important for its woods, its water, its coast. Woodland must have been important as an economic resource, for timber and fuel — along the Blackwater the pattern from west to east is field, woodland, marsh. The non-human life world is sometimes evoked, for example, Purleigh. High ground is often chosen, and the modern descendants of Byrhtnoth's villages are located at the tops of hills, with the church and sometimes also the hall occupying the highest point. Hills serve as look-out posts, beacons, or even protection perhaps from flood as well as invasion. For the traveller to Essex, it is striking to see many of Byrhtnoth's properties located on hilltops, alongside churches.

We can extrapolate various narratives that may emerge from such studies, for instance the story of the revolutionary Benedictine Reform and its impact on the career of Byrhtnoth and his household. Place-name studies may thus provide insights into the everyday life of Byrhtnoth and his family as well as into his political allegiances, his planning for defence and war. There are even personal stories, emotions of love and devotion, allegiances and loyalties to be gleaned from the documents we have studied.

In short, Byrhtnoth's East Anglian and East Saxon world was bound by fenland abbeys in the north, by coastline in the east, by river and road, hill and woodland in the south; it was conditioned by his personal relations, his religious allegiances, his administration of trade and justice, and his concern for military defence and communications. Moreover, it may be argued, many of these landscape features relate to topographical themes and motifs which recur in that heroic poem which finally established his fame for posterity.

Works Cited

Primary Sources

The Anglo-Saxon Chronicle. A Collaborative Edition, III: *MS A*, ed. by Janet Bately (Cambridge: D. S. Brewer, 1986)

Anglo-Saxon Wills, ed. and trans. by Dorothy Whitelock (Cambridge: Cambridge University Press, 1930)

The Battle of Maldon, ed. by E. V. Gordon (London: Methuen, 1937)

The Battle of Maldon, ed. by D. G. Scragg (Manchester: Manchester University Press, 1981)

Byrhtferth of Ramsey, *The Life of St Oswald*, in *The Lives of St Oswald and St Ecgwine*, ed. and trans. by Michael Lapidge (Oxford: Clarendon Press, 2009), pp. 1–203

Charters of Abingdon Abbey, ed. by S. E. Kelly, 2 vols (Oxford: Oxford University Press, 2000–2001)

Charters of Christ Church Canterbury, ed. by Nicholas P. Brooks and Susan E. Kelly, 2 vols (Oxford: Oxford University Press, 2013)

The Crawford Collection of Early Charters and Documents, ed. by A. S. Napier and W. H. Stevenson (Cambridge: Cambridge University Press, 1895)

Liber Eliensis, ed. by E. O. Blake, Camden Third Series, 92 (London: Royal Historical Society, 1962)

Liber Eliensis: A History of the Isle of Ely, trans. by Janet Fairweather (Woodbridge: Boydell, 2005)

Secondary Sources

Abels, Richard, 'Byrhtnoth [Brihtnoth] (d. 991), Magnate and Soldier', in *Oxford Dictionary of National Biography* (2004), <https://ezproxy-prd.bodleian.ox.ac.uk:2102/10.1093/ref:odnb/3429> [accessed 28 April 2021]

Atherton, Mark, *The Battle of Maldon: War and Peace in Tenth-Century England* (London: Bloomsbury, 2020)

——, *The Making of England: A New History of the Anglo-Saxon World* (London: I. B. Tauris, 2017)

Baines, A. H. J., 'Ealdorman Byrhtnoth and the Brayfield Charter of 967', *Records of Buckinghamshire*, 24 (1992), 30–45

Baker, John, 'The Language of Anglo-Saxon Defence', in *Landscapes of Defence in Early Medieval Europe: Anglo-Saxon England and Comparative Perspectives*, ed. by John Baker, Stuart Brookes, and Andrew Reynolds, SEM, 28 (Turnhout: Brepols, 2013), pp. 65–90

Baker, John, and Stuart Brookes, 'Explaining Anglo-Saxon Military Efficiency: The Landscape of Mobilization', *ASE*, 44 (2015), 221–58

——, 'Signalling Intent: Beacons, Lookouts and Military Communications', in *The Material Culture of the Built Environment in the Anglo-Saxon World*, ed. by

M. Clegg Hyer and G. Owen-Crocker (Liverpool: Liverpool University Press, 2015), pp. 216–34

Barker, Elaine, 'Peldon in the Domesday Book', Mersea Museum website, <http://merseamuseum.org.ukmmresdetails.php?pid=PH01_DMS&ba=mmpeldon.php&rhit=4> [accessed 8 May 2021]

Bintley, Michael D. J., *Trees in the Religions of Early Medieval England*, Anglo-Saxon Studies, 26 (Woodbridge: Boydell and Brewer, 2015)

Blair, John, *Building Anglo-Saxon England* (Princeton, NJ: Princeton University Press, 2018)

Brooks, Nicholas, 'Treason in Essex in the 990s: The Case of Æthelric of Bocking', in *Royal Authority in Anglo-Saxon England*, ed. by Gale Owen-Crocker and Brian W. Schneider, BAR British Series, 584 (Oxford: Archaeopress, 2013), pp. 17–27

Busse, W. G. and R. Holtei, '*The Battle of Maldon*: A Historical, Heroic and Political Poem', *Neophilologus*, 65 (1981), 614–21; repr. in *Old English Shorter Poems: Basic Readings*, ed. by Katherine O'Brien O'Keeffe (New York: Garland, 1994), pp. 185–97

Campbell, James, 'England, *c.* 991', in *The Battle of Maldon: Fiction and Fact*, ed. by Janet Cooper (London: Hambledon Press, 1993), pp. 1–17

Cavill, Paul, 'The *Passio S. Eadmundi* and *The Battle of Maldon*', in *The Hero Recovered: Essays on Medieval Heroism in Honor of George Clark*, ed. by Robin Waugh and James Weldon (Kalamazoo: Western Michigan Publications, 2010), pp. 110–24

Clarke, Catherine A. M., *Literary Landscapes and the Idea of England, 700–1400* (Cambridge: D. S. Brewer, 2006)

Coates, Richard, 'New Light from Old Wicks', *Nomina*, 22 (1999), 75–116

Cole, Ann, 'Searching for Early Drove Roads: *hryðer, mersc-tun*, and *heord-wic*', *Journal of the English Place-Name Society*, 47 (2015), 55–88

Ekwall, Eilert, *The Concise Oxford Dictionary of English Place-Names*, 4th edn (Oxford: Clarendon Press, 1960)

Evans, George Ewart, *The Pattern under the Plough: Aspects of the Folk-Life of East Anglia* (London: Faber and Faber, 1966)

Foot, Sarah, *Æthelstan: The First King of England* (New Haven, CT: Yale University Press, 2011)

Gelling, Margaret, *Place-Names in the Landscape: The Geographical Roots of Britain's Place-Names* (London: J. M. Dent, 1984)

——, *Signposts to the Past: Place-Names and the History of England* (London: Dent, 1978)

Gelling, Margaret, and Ann Cole, *The Landscape of Place-Names*, new edn (Donington: Shaun Tyas, 2014)

Hart, Cyril, *The Danelaw* (London: Hambledon Press, 1992)

Hill, Thomas D., 'The *Liber Eliensis* "Historical Selections" and the Old English *Battle of Maldon*', *JEGP*, 96 (1997), 1–25

Hooke, Della, *Trees in Anglo-Saxon England: Literature, Lore and Landscape* (Woodbridge: Boydell, 2010)

Johnson, Matthew H., *Ideas of Landscape* (Oxford: Blackwell, 2007)

Kennedy, Alan, 'Law and Litigation in the *Libellus Æthelwoldi Episcopi*', ASE, 24 (1995), 131–83

Keynes, Simon, *The Diplomas of King Ethelred 'the Unready', 978–1016: A Study in their Use as Historical Evidence* (Cambridge: Cambridge University Press, 1980)

——, 'Ely Abbey, 672–1109', in *A History of Ely Cathedral*, ed. by Peter Meadows and Nigel Ramsay (Woodbridge: Boydell Press, 2003), pp. 3–58

Kolen, Jan, and Hans Renes, 'Landscape Biographies: Key Issues', in *Landscape Biographies: Geographical, Historical and Archaeological Perspectives on the Production and Transmission of Landscapes*, ed. by Jan Kolen, Hans Renes, and Rita Hermans (Amsterdam: Amsterdam University Press, 2015), pp. 21–47

Locherbie-Cameron, Margaret A. L., 'Byrhtnoth and his Family', in *The Battle of Maldon, AD 991*, ed. by Donald G. Scragg (Oxford: Basil Blackwell, 1991), pp. 253–62

Owen-Crocker, Gale, 'Hawks and Horse-Trappings', in *The Battle of Maldon, AD 991*, ed. by Donald G. Scragg (Oxford: Basil Blackwell, 1991), pp. 220–37

Pestell, Tim, *Landscapes of Monastic Foundation: The Establishment of Religious Houses in East Anglia, c. 650–1200* (Cambridge: Cambridge University Press, 2004)

Reaney, P. H., *The Place-Names of Essex* (Cambridge: Cambridge University Press, 1935)

Reynolds, Andrew, *Late Anglo-Saxon England: Life and Landscape* (Stroud: Tempus, 1999)

Rippon, Stephen, *Beyond the Medieval Village: The Diversification of Landscape Character in Southern Britain* (Oxford: Oxford University Press, 2008)

Roach, Levi, *Æthelred the Unready* (New Haven, CT: Yale University Press, 2016)

Rumble, Alexander R., 'The Cross in English Place-Names: Vocabulary and Usage', in *The Place of the Cross in Anglo-Saxon England*, ed. by Catherine E. Karkov, Sarah Larratt Keefer, and Karen Louise Jolly (Woodbridge: Boydell Press, 2006), pp. 29–40

Skeat, Walter W., *The Place-Names of Suffolk* (Cambridge: Cambridge Antiquarian Society, 1913)

Smith, Scott T., *Land and Book: Literature and Land Tenure in Anglo-Saxon England* (Toronto: University of Toronto Press, 2012)

Tilley, Christopher, *A Phenomenology of Landscape: Places, Paths and Monuments* (Oxford: Berg, 1997)

Tollerton, Linda, *Wills and Will-Making in Anglo-Saxon England* (Woodbridge: Boydell and Brewer, 2011)

Wareham, Andrew, *Lords and Communities in Early Medieval East Anglia* (Woodbridge: Boydell and Brewer, 2005)

Watts, Victor, ed., *The Cambridge Dictionary of English Place-Names* (Cambridge: Cambridge University Press, 2004)

Weikert, Katherine, 'The Biography of a Place: Faccombe Netherton, Hampshire, ca 900–1200', *Anglo-Norman Studies*, 37 (2015), 257–84

——, 'Ely Cathedral and the Afterlife of Ealdorman Byrhtnoth', in *The Land of the English Kin: Studies in Wessex and Anglo-Saxon England in Honour of Professor Barbara Yorke*, ed. by Alexander James Langlands and Ryan Lavelle, Brill's Series on the Early Middle Ages, 26 (Leiden: Brill, 2020), pp. 555–81

Williams, Ann, 'A Bell-House and a Burh-Geat: The Lordly Residences in England before the Norman Conquest', in *Medieval Knighthood*, IV, ed. by Christopher Harper-Bill and Ruth Harvey (Woodbridge: Boydell, 1992), pp. 221–40

Williams, Thomas J. T., 'The Place of Slaughter: Exploring the West Saxon Battlescape', in *Danes in Wessex: The Scandinavian Impact on Southern England, c. 800–c. 1100*, ed. by Ryan Lavelle and Simon Roffey (Oxford: Oxbow, 2016), pp. 35–55

Williamson, Tom, *Environment, Society and Landscape in Early Medieval England: Time and Topography*, Anglo-Saxon Studies, 19 (Woodbridge: Boydell, 2013)

Wormald, Patrick, 'Handlist of Lawsuits', *ASE*, 17 (1988), 247–81

PART III

Nation and Empire

HELEN APPLETON

Mapping Empire: Two World Maps in Early Medieval England

Introduction

Theodulf, bishop of Orleans during the reigns of Charlemagne and Louis the Pious, produced a poem about a magnificent table map (Carmen 47), which states: 'Totius orbis adest breviter depicta figura, | Rem magnam in parvo corpore nosse dabit' (Here is the figure of the entire world depicted succinctly and it will allow you to know a great thing in a small body, ll. 49–50).[1] As Patrick Gautier Dalché observes, 'le Moyen Age a laissé une profusion de mappemondes, mais guère de textes qui puissent nous renseigner sur leur fabrication, leur perception et leur usage' (the Middle Ages left a profusion of world maps, but hardly any texts which can inform us about their manufacture, their perception, and their use), which makes Theodulf's poem especially valuable.[2] Theodulf's words offer an insight into the importance of cartography as both powerful transmitter of knowledge and reflection of status; his edifying table map, whether real or imagined, reveals a tradition of exploiting the spiritual and temporal value of displaying images of the world in Carolingia. Across the Channel in what is now England, in the succeeding centuries, world maps were produced with a similar aim to communicate more than geography. The images of the world that these maps present complement the textually constructed worlds of English literatures. The maps are conveyors of both worldly and spiritual knowledge, neatly placing their viewer in the position of one 'þam þurh wisdom woruld ealle con | behabban on hreþre' (who through wisdom knows how to encompass the entire world in their mind), as the Exeter Book's *Order of the World* (ll. 9–10a) imagines the enlightened.[3] The most complex surviving examples of early medieval English cartography exhibit a tendency towards innovation

---

1 *Poetae Latini Aevi Carolini*, ed. by Dümmler, p. 548. Translation from Alexandrenko, 'The Poetry of Theodulf of Orleans', p. 270.

2 Gautier Dalché, 'De la glose à la contemplation', p. 693.

3 *The Exeter Anthology of Old English Poetry*, ed. by Muir, p. 260.

> **Helen Appleton** (helen.appleton@humanities.ox.ac.uk) is a member of the Faculty of English, University of Oxford.

Ideas of the World in Early Medieval English Literature, ed. by Mark Atherton, Kazutomo Karasawa, and Francis Leneghan, SOEL 1 (Turnhout: Brepols, 2022)   pp. 309–334
BREPOLS ❧ PUBLISHERS   DOI 10.1484/M.SOEL.5.130566

and an independence from their manuscripts' other contents that potentially frustrates analysis of how they were employed and the insights that they were designed to communicate. Yet, by examining both what they represent and how they represent it, alongside scholarly insights on the Carolingian practice which they emulate, a picture of these maps' manufacture, perception, and use emerges. This chapter focuses on two world maps preserved in an eleventh-century codex, London, British Library, MS Cotton Tiberius B V, in order to consider what great things these succinct representations of the world enabled their audience to know.

The maps in Cotton Tiberius B V offer both a view of the world and an insight into the early medieval world view. The manuscript, which was probably produced at Canterbury around 1025–1050, contains both a zonal map of the globe (Fig. 11.1, below) and a detailed map of the *oikoumene* (Fig. 11.2, below), the inhabited temperate zone of the northern hemisphere. A map of the heavens was also present but is now lost. The two world maps are both distinctive, suggesting an innovative engagement with mapmaking in England in this period.[4] By examining the Cotton Tiberius B V maps in dialogue with the surviving corpus of early medieval English maps, and examples from the Carolingian centres on which they evidently depend, they can be placed in a broader cartographic context. In early medieval Francia, as Theodulf's writing shows, large-scale map making was political, educational, and/or spiritual — often all three concerns can be seen as shaping the production and reception of cartography. This chapter argues that the same is also true of these two English manuscript maps, and their interest in urban space and the translation of imperial power from east to west is examined to highlight the ambition, and the limitations, that they invite people to contemplate in visual form.[5]

To Know a Great Thing in a Small Body

Perhaps the most famous owner and user of cartography in early medieval Europe was Charlemagne, who, according to his biographer Einhard, possessed metallic maps of Constantinople, Rome, and the whole universe.[6] These maps, which the emperor bequeathed in his will, are an evident statement of imperial power.[7] Possession of a map indicated that one assumed knowledge and by extension some control over the area depicted; the precious materials

---

4 McGurk, 'The Macrobian Zonal Map'; Edson, 'World Maps and Easter Tables', p. 35; Hiatt, 'The Map of Macrobius before 1100', p. 170 n. 46. On the way both BL, MS Cotton Tiberius B V maps problematize standard schemes, see Edson, 'Isidore, Orosius, and the Medieval Image', p. 220 n. 5.

5 See further Francis Leneghan's chapter in this volume.

6 Einhard, *Vita Karoli Magni*, XXXIII, ed. by Holder-Egger and Pertz, p. 40.

7 See also Albu, 'Imperial Geography and the Mediaeval Peutinger Map', pp. 139–40.

and artistic skill used to render the image only served to increase the owner's prestige. Cartography is obviously and easily connected with imperialism, yet in early medieval Europe it is most often found being produced and used in religious contexts. Church and empire obviously intersect, but their interpretation of cartography differs; Charlemagne's maps are a statement of worldly power, but for Theodulf a map is a statement that worldly power is temporally limited. Carmen 47 describes how the map could be a tool for perceiving greatness, but also that greatness passes. The poem connects the seats of worldly and ecclesiastical power with the fixed seat of the earth — and by implication the seats around the table. The result is a playful, yet pointed musing on impermanence:[8]

> Per sedes etiam mundi signantur honores,
> Perpetuo quod eos nemo habiturus adit.
> Alter in alterius gaudet residere cathedra,
> Hic sedet, hic sedit, hic it, et ille redit. (ll. 27–30)[9]

> (The honours of the world are signified by the seat also, because none will have them eternally. One rejoices to sit in the seat of another: this one sits, this one sat; this one goes, and that one returns.)[10]

Theodulf's polyptoton suggests rule is rather like a game of musical chairs. The synchronic view of time provided by the map shows the movement of human power by affording the viewer a God-like perspective. The map's fabulous materiality conveys not only status, but also worldliness. This table map, from which guests derive both physical and spiritual sustenance, may be entirely imagined, but it offers a useful insight into what the uniquely distanced perspective afforded by a map could communicate about the magnificence and mutability of the world. Could this be how the maps are to be read in Cotton Tiberius B V? Gautier Dalché has persuasively argued that the ability of cartography to replicate the perspective of a divine vision was key to its popularity in the high medieval period, as, especially in a manuscript context, it allowed the viewer to occupy a position like that of the enlightened soul beholding the world from above, as in the vision of Benedict in Gregory's *Dialogues* II.35 — a text well known in early medieval England, and translated into Old English by Bishop Wærferth.[11] Whilst Gautier Dalché suggests that this way of using cartography in a manuscript, as opposed to on a wall, as a contemplative tool flourished from the twelfth century, he acknowledges that earlier examples of codex maps with evident contemplative function

---

8 Theodulf's Carmina 46 and 47 are discussed by Kupfer, 'Medieval World Maps', pp. 265–67. On the identification of the subject as a map, see Vidier, 'La mappemonde de Théodulfe et la mappemonde de Ripoll (ixe–xie siècle)'.

9 *Poetae Latini Aevi Carolini*, ed. by Dümmler, p. 548.

10 Trans. by Alexandrenko, 'The Poetry of Theodulf of Orleans', p. 269.

11 Gautier Dalché, 'De la glose à la contemplation', esp. pp. 753–57.

exist, and that the fragmentary nature of the corpus makes assessing trends difficult. The two Tiberius maps, with their evident focus on synchronous representations of human power alongside geographical information, and notable independence of the manuscript's other contents, show that the contemplative potential of manuscript cartography was understood and exploited in eleventh-century England.

The two Cotton Tiberius B V world maps are not the only world maps surviving from early medieval England. Loredana Teresi has produced a provisional survey of the corpus which identifies some twenty-four items.[12] Given the limited survival of manuscripts, this number of maps suggests cartographic images were relatively readily available in English intellectual centres. All twenty-four of the maps Teresi lists are the product of monastic scriptoria, most are schematic, and many are relatively conventional, occurring in copies of texts with an established tradition of cartographic illustration, such as Isidore's *De natura rerum*. This is to be expected of early medieval cartography, as maps, as part of broader geographical and historical knowledge, were, alongside the seven liberal arts, core to monastic education. In his *Institutiones* (I.XXV.1–2) Cassiodorus famously encourages monks to make a study of the world so that they can understand scriptural geography and travel with their minds to holy places that they cannot and should not physically reach.[13] The geography which Cassiodorus recommends is not focused specifically on the locations of holy places; the recommended works are much more general. Evidently a broad knowledge of the world was to be encouraged, allowing sacred places to be imagined in a wider context and the wonder of creation to be appreciated. As Gautier Dalché notes in his discussion of this passage, there is, for Cassiodorus, a difference in nature and utility between text and map, and the map is subordinated to the textual geographies.[14] This is the relationship between text and map that we expect to see in manuscripts in the early medieval period, and it holds true for the majority of the English examples that Teresi identifies. Yet, as Teresi also highlights, there are some innovative items from the eleventh century where the relationship of priority between text and image shifts.

A small group of maps found in English manuscripts present a notable development of the classic T-O design to incorporate a more obviously spiritual element, presenting the world as dominated by God's power. These English maps follow the general trend towards high-medieval cartography as independent contemplative tool that Gautier Dalché shows in a distinctive way. T-O maps schematically represent the three continents of the northern hemisphere surrounded by the O-shaped world ocean and trisected by a

---

12 Teresi, 'Anglo-Saxon and Early Anglo-Norman "Mappaemundi"'.

13 Cassiodorus, *Institutiones*, ed. by Mynors, p. 66; Cassiodorus, *Institutions of Divine and Secular Learning; and, On the Soul*, trans. by Halporn, pp. 157–58.

14 Gautier Dalché, 'De la glose à la contemplation', p. 696.

T-shaped sea. Oxford, St John's College, MS 17 (*c.* 1110, Thorney, fol. 6ʳ) and London, British Library, MS Harley 3667 (s.xii²ᐟ⁴, Peterborough, fol. 8ᵛ) both contain diagrammatic T-O maps which are unusual in listing cities, often rather inaccurately located, in the three continents and in having Jerusalem written in large letters across the crossbar of the T; Teresi terms this unique design the 'Jerusalem T-O map'.[15] Much of the legend on these maps is biblical, and Greek and Latin names are used for the cardinal directions to achieve the word 'ADAM' encircling the world, as in Byrhtferth's diagram which accompanies the map in both manuscripts.[16] Clearly, the originator of this design, whom Martin Foys suggests was in the school of Byrhtferth, desired to fuse catalogue-like information on cities with a schematic representation of the world to create profound spiritual meaning.[17] Cartographic tradition is being adapted to communicate more effectively a particular perspective on the world to these manuscripts' monastic readers.

The St John's and Harley manuscripts are both *computus* compilations containing other texts and diagrams that spread the same kind of spiritual and geographical knowledge that their T-O maps convey. In this context the cartography is an obvious complement to other kinds of geographical, computistical, and spiritual information. However, there is a third copy of this map in a slightly different context which shows the map operating entirely independently of relevant texts and suggests that manuscript cartography, like larger wall maps, was being valued for its ability, as Theodulf noted, to communicate a great deal of information in a small space. Cambridge, Corpus Christi College, MS 265 (Worcester, s.xi²) contains an unfinished *mappa mundi* on p. 210 which belongs to the same family as the maps in the St John's and Harley manuscripts. Foys suggests this map was added to a blank leaf *c.* 1090, showing that the original template for these maps was from pre-Conquest England.[18] This map's place in the Corpus manuscript is intriguing; CCCC, MS 265 is not in any way a *computus* manuscript: it is a copy of Wulfstan's Commonplace Book.[19] The unfinished map occurs apparently incongruously between *formulae* for excommunication and blessing; Teresi suggests its lack of relation to the other manuscript contents may be why it remained unfinished, but the fact it was begun in the first place is revealing.[20] The presence of the

---

15 These maps' puzzling layout is discussed by Teresi, 'Anglo-Saxon and Early Anglo-Norman "Mappaemundi"', pp. 353–54.

16 Edson, 'World Maps and Easter Tables', p. 37; Edson, *Mapping Time and Space*, pp. 86–93. For a discussion of Byrhtferth's diagram, and a reproduction, see the chapter by Kazutomo Karasawa in this volume.

17 Foys, 'An Unfinished *mappa mundi* from Late-Eleventh-Century Worcester'.

18 Foys, 'An Unfinished *mappa mundi* from Late-Eleventh-Century Worcester', p. 272. Only a small part of Asia Minor has been inked, but drypoint marks reveal that the map was planned to be more ornate in design than either of the surviving complete examples.

19 On its relation to the other manuscripts, see Sauer, 'The Transmission and Structure of Wulfstan's "Commonplace Book"'.

20 Teresi, 'Anglo-Saxon and Early Anglo-Norman "Mappaemundi"', p. 355.

map in a book primarily consisting, as Dorothy Bethurum notes, of 'entries relating to the affairs of a bishop', suggests that whoever began it thought it of utility to the book's users.[21] The map clearly does not have the practical quality of the principal texts, such as the penitentials, or other small contemporary additions such as *formulae*, but it does convey in an instant something about the nature of the world with, as Evelyn Edson notes, a strongly spiritual inflection.[22] CCCC, MS 265 seems to be using this map as a contemplative tool rather than for geographical information. The map, had it been complete, would have provided a valuable aid to reflection on the nature of the world for busy bishops; with a map, 'Rem magnam in parvo corpore nosse dabit' (it will allow you to know a great thing in a small body), as if receiving a vision, as Bishop Theodulf noted. The aborted copying of a world map into CCCC, MS 265 shows that in England in this period maps were thought of as carrying independent meaning and as contributing to the effect of a volume in their own right, rather than simply acting as aids to understanding other texts. This insight shapes how we should read the two maps in Cotton Tiberius B V which, although complementing several other geographical items in the volume, present a distinct way of interpreting the world.

The Maps of BL, MS Cotton Tiberius B V

The two Cotton Tiberius B V maps, like the Jerusalem T-O maps discussed above, reshape existing cartographic templates to create a new emphasis that shapes their viewers' understanding of the world. Rather than adding imagery that presents an explicitly spiritual interpretation, the Cotton Tiberius B V maps focus on empires and shifts in human power: their spiritual meaning is implied. The two maps connect physical geography with urban space to offer a narrative of transition, of the movement of empire from east to west, reflecting the manuscript's broader interest in human power and history alongside scientific information. Cotton Tiberius B V was produced around 1025–1050, during the reign of Cnut or his successors, possibly in Canterbury, although much of the material has an evident Glastonbury provenance.[23] Cotton Tiberius B V is a rather beautifully illuminated volume containing computistical, astronomical, genealogical, regnal, and geographical material in Latin and Old English.

---

21 Bethurum, 'Archbishop Wulfstan's Commonplace Book', p. 916.

22 Edson, 'World Maps and Easter Tables', pp. 35–37; Edson, *Mapping Time and Space*, pp. 87–90.

23 On the manuscript's origins, see Barber, 'Medieval Maps of the World', p. 4; Dumville, 'The Anglian Collection of Royal Genealogies and Regnal Lists', pp. 26–27; Gneuss and Lapidge, *Anglo-Saxon Manuscripts*, pp. 297–99; Ker, *Catalogue of Manuscripts Containing Anglo-Saxon*, pp. 255–56; McGurk, 'Conclusion'. On the Glastonbury connection, see McGurk, 'The Mappa Mundi', p. 79.

The principal surviving original contents in their current ordering are as follows:

Fols 2ʳ–19ʳ: A computistical miscellany including the labours of the months and a Metrical Calendar

Fols 19ᵛ–22ʳ: lists of popes, Roman emperors, and English bishops

Fols 22ʳ–23ᵛ: Anglo-Saxon royal genealogies

Fol. 23ᵛ: lists of Glastonbury abbots and tenth-century popes

Fols 23ᵛ–24ʳ: The *Itinerary of Archbishop Sigeric*

Fols 24ʳ–28ᵛ: Ælfric, *De temporibus anni*

Fol. 29ʳ: Macrobian zonal map (Fig. 11.1)

Fols 30ʳ–32ʳ: prayers and astronomical texts

Fols 32ᵛ–49ᵛ: Cicero, *Aratea*

Fols 49ᵛ–54ᵛ: astronomical excerpts

Fol. 56ᵛ: *mappa mundi* (Fig. 11.2)

Fols 57ʳ–73ʳ: Priscian, *Periegesis*

Fols 78ᵛ–87ᵛ: *Wonders of the East*, in Latin and Old English, including the account of Jannes and Mambres.[24]

A celestial map and a text of Hrabanus Maurus's *De laudibus sancte crucis* have been lost.[25] The manuscript became disordered prior to the twelfth century when material related to St Nicholas and Battle Abbey was added.[26] The manuscript's contents have broad thematic parallels, but the whole presents a somewhat eclectic assemblage of material related to earth and the heavens. There is *computus* material, but it cannot exactly be termed a *computus* manuscript. Cotton Tiberius B V has an interest in distant places — it contains a text of *Wonders of the East* — and pays much attention to Rome, as noted by Nicholas Howe and Kathy Lavezzo, but there is also a great deal of material relating to England, such as episcopal lists and genealogies.[27] In general, Cotton Tiberius B V takes a broad interest in the cosmos, the world, and mankind's place within them, as do its maps.[28]

---

24 A detailed list of contents is given by McGurk, 'Contents of the Manuscript'.

25 McGurk, 'The History of the Manuscript', pp. 25–27.

26 Fols 55ʳ–56ᵛ, 73ʳ⁻ᵛ, 77ʳ: *Vita metrica sancti Nicholai*; fol. 88ʳ⁻ᵛ: notes relating to Battle Abbey. Documents related to Ely and Exeter copied on parts of eighth-century gospel books have also been added.

27 Howe, *Writing the Map of Anglo-Saxon England*, p. 154; Lavezzo, *Angels on the Edge of the World*, p. 28.

28 A detailed study of the map in its manuscript context forms the basis of a recently completed

Figure 11.1. Macrobian zonal map. East is at the top. London, British Library, MS Cotton Tiberius B V, fol. 29ʳ. © British Library Board.

Cotton Tiberius B V is not an especially large manuscript; its folios measure 260 x 220 mm. Each of its two surviving maps occupies a single manuscript page: the zonal map on 29ʳ and the *mappa mundi* on 56ᵛ. The amount of detail that each map is able to reproduce within this relatively confined space is impressive. The zonal map (Fig. 11.1), which was originally paired with the

---

doctoral dissertation that I have been unable to consult: Tedford, 'The Anglo-Saxon Cotton Map in Context'.

now-lost celestial map, comes between Ælfric's *De temporibus anni* and Cicero's *Aratea*, but it is indebted to Macrobius's widely circulated fifth-century work, *Commentarii in somnium Scipionis*. The Cotton Tiberius B V zonal map is in many respects typical of the maps used to illustrate Macrobius's commentary, although it does not appear with that text in this manuscript.[29] *De temporibus anni* also offers information on the zones and tides, so in some respects the zonal map complements this text by offering a visual image of similar information, although in other ways its interests differ from those of Ælfric's work. The zonal map represents the globe; like the *mappa mundi* it is orientated with east to the top, whereas a north–south orientation might more commonly be expected for a macrobian map.[30] The globe is divided into five temperature zones: two frigid zones, one at each pole, then the temperate zones of the northern and southern hemispheres, with the torrid zone across the equator. The globe is surrounded by the *oceanus*, the world ocean, which is depicted in green, and this is in turn circled by a text, repeated for each quarter, which reads: 'hinc refluit oceanus ad septentrionem [for the northern hemisphere]/ austrum [for the southern hemisphere] per lxiii stadiorum' (from here the ocean flows back to the north/south through sixty-three stades). Across the equatorial zone is further information on the sea. The text derives, as Edson notes, from Macrobius II.4.2, but is unique to this map:

> aequinoctialis zona hic incipiens paene tota alluitur superius et inferius mari quod dum per medium taerrae circumlabitur in IIII quasi insulas totus orbis diuiditur quae inhabitentur est enim solstitialis superior et inferior habitabitabilis similiter superior et inferior hiemalis sicque fit ut per medium et in circuitu orbis mare currat quod calore uel frigore est intransmeabile est que deprehensus totius orbis ambitus in stadiis ducentis quinquaginta duobus milibus.

> (Here the equinoctial zone begins which is almost entirely washed, both above and below, by the sea, which flows through the middle of the earth as if the whole earth were divided into four islands, being inhabited above in the [summer] solstitial zone and below in the *hiemalis* [winter solstice] zone, Thus it is that the sea runs through the middle and around the edge of the earth and is impassable due to either heat or cold, and the circuit of the entire earth is 252,000 stades.)[31]

---

29 On Macrobian maps, see Hiatt, 'The Map of Macrobius before 1100'; Gautier Dalché, 'De la glose à la contemplation', pp. 713–14. As Edson notes, there are excerpts from Macrobius later in the manuscript on fols 51 and 54, but not the section on the zones. Edson, *Mapping Time and Space*, p. 78.

30 Teresi, 'Anglo-Saxon and Early Anglo-Norman "Mappaemundi"', p. 347. Other examples exist but they are the minority; see Hiatt, 'The Map of Macrobius before 1100', p. 175.

31 Translation from Edson, *Mapping Time and Space*, p. 78.

The map's focus on the behaviour of seas and tides is typical of the corpus of Macrobian maps.[32] Yet, in other ways the Cotton Tiberius B V zonal map is more unusual in the information it communicates. Whilst most zones are left blank, in the northern temperate zone the map depicts the three continents (labelled 'Africa', 'Asia Maior et Minor' and 'Aquitania'), two individuated turreted cities, and the pillars of Hercules which appear on the edge of the inhabited space. This level of detail for the *oikoumene* in a zonal map is unusual before 1100, although there are comparable examples, perhaps most notably the macrobian map associated with the *computus* of Abbo of Fleury and the more sophisticated Ripoll map.[33]

Alfred Hiatt tentatively connects the Cotton Tiberius B V zonal map to the map contained in Abbo of Fleury's *computus*, as exemplified by Berlin, Deutsche Staatsbibliothek, MS Phillipps 1833 (Rose 138), produced in Fleury during Abbo's time.[34] It features a zonal map on folio 39^v which gives similar details for the land masses and uses small icons to represent several cities. This model had a wide reach. A copy of this map is found on folio 76^r of the early eleventh-century computistical collection in Dijon, Bibliothèque municipal, MS 448, and a variant accompanies Macrobius's work on folio 74^r of Munich, Bayerische Staatsbibliothek, MS Clm. 6362, a scientific miscellany produced *c.* 1000 in southern Germany. Despite general similarities between this group and the Cotton Tiberius B V zonal map, closer examination reveals key differences. Members of the Abbo group are orientated with north at the top, and the cities are fairly accurately located (and in the case of MS Clm. 6362 labelled),[35] whereas the Cotton Tiberius B V map has east uppermost and shows only two large cities in the centre of the map. MSS Phillipps 1833 and Dijon 448 both depict Britannia, out in the world ocean together with Hibernia, and MS Clm. 6362 shows unlabelled islands off north-western Europe; but if the Cotton Tiberius B V zonal map shows Britain at all, it would be the very large landmass above the northernmost body of water within north-western Europe: as with this manuscript's *mappa mundi*, Britain is not depicted as peripheral. Gautier Dalché states of MS Phillipps 1833, 'Le rapport du texte et de l'image, par rapport à l'œvre d'origine, est ici inversé. C'est le texte qui glose la carte' (the relationship between the text and the image, compared to the original work, is here reversed. It is the text which glosses the map), a change he attributes to the use of Macrobius's work as a school text in Fleury under Abbo.[36] The Cotton Tiberius B V zonal map, as Gautier Dalché notes, takes a similar approach.[37] It seems likely that the

---

32   On these see Hiatt, 'The Map of Macrobius before 1100'.

33   Hiatt argues this is a post-1100 development generally ('The Map of Macrobius before 1100', p. 161).

34   Hiatt, 'The Map of Macrobius before 1100', p. 170 nn. 39 and 46. See also Chekin, *Northern Eurasia in Medieval Cartography*, pp. 104–06.

35   Rome, Corinth(?), Jerusalem, Syene (Aswan), and Meroë.

36   Gautier Dalché, 'De la glose à la contemplation', p. 732.

37   Gautier Dalché, 'De la glose à la contemplation', p. 732.

model for the Cotton Tiberius B V zonal map was found in a school book, but while Abbo's *computus* map may be the archetype, the orientation and the representation of urban space have been modified, as argued below, to serve a new purpose.

The Ripoll map is found across folios 143ᵛ–144ʳ in Città del Vaticano, Biblioteca Apostolica Vaticana, MS Reg. lat. 123, which is roughly contemporary with Cotton Tiberius B V.[38] This carefully assembled *computus* manuscript originated in the Benedictine monastery in Ripoll, Catalonia, and obviously depends on Carolingian material. The world map, which is zonal in design and orientated with east uppermost, logically follows the third section of the *computus* which deals with *De natura rerum*, but stands independently.[39] The Ripoll map offers an unusually detailed image of the *oikoumene*, depicting many cities of which Constantinople is the most significant.[40] The map claims to be derived from various sources and includes in the southern zones lines adapted from Theodulf's verse, including those about perceiving a great deal in a small space; it is accompanied by a short geographical text.[41] Although there are clear differences with the simpler Cotton Tiberius B V map, the independence of this map from the neighbouring material, yet evident commonality of purpose, suggests a similar utility. Gautier Dalché highlights that the encyclopaedia contained in the Ripoll manuscript has aims beyond the purely scientific — it is also spiritually edifying.[42] The same is true of the looser encyclopaedia that is Cotton Tiberius B V, which originally included the explicitly devotional *De laudibus sancte crucis* alongside more purely scientific material. If the Ripoll map, like the map evoked by Theodulf which it references, aims to offer spiritual as well as intellectual food and to serve a contemplative purpose, sharpening the effect of the manuscript's other contents, then the zonal map of Cotton Tiberius B V should be considered in the same way, as should the *mappa mundi* with which it is so evidently connected.

The Cotton Tiberius B V *mappa mundi* (Fig. 11.2) is much more obviously idiosyncratic than the zonal map. Although there are general commonalities with Y-O maps, it is notably independent of other cartographic traditions; this may be because of the very limited survival of detailed world maps from this period, but the distinctly insular perspective it offers suggest a significant element of local innovation in its design.[43] The *mappa mundi* was originally bound together with Priscian's Latin geographical text, the *Periegesis*, the incipit of which in this manuscript reads:

---

38 Gautier Dalché, 'De la glose à la contemplation', pp. 761–62.
39 See Edson, *Mapping Time and Space*, pp. 80–86.
40 On this map, see Chekin, *Northern Eurasia in Medieval Cartography*, pp. 181–83.
41 Gautier Dalché, 'Notes sur la "carte de Théodose II" et sur la "mappemonde de Théodulf d'Orléans"'.
42 Gautier Dalché, 'De la glose à la contemplation', p. 762.
43 Appleton, 'The Northern World of the Anglo-Saxon *mappa mundi*'.

Incipit liber Periegesis, id est de situ terrae Prisciani grammatici urbis Romae Caesariensis doctoris quem de priscorum dictis excerpsit ormistarum sed et huic operi de tribus partibus uidelicet Asia Africa Europa mappam depinxerat aptam in qua nationum promontoriorum fluminum insularumque situs atque monstrorum formatur honeste.

(Here begins the book, 'Periegesis', by Priscian, grammarian of the city of Rome, professor of Caesarea (Africa), that is about the situation of the earth, gathered by him from the writings in ancient world maps; and to this work of three arts, that is to say, Asia, Africa, and Europe, there is painted a suitable (*aptam*) map in which the location of nations, mountains, rivers, islands, and also wonders are accurately arranged.)[44]

The *mappa mundi* does serve to illustrate the inhabited world on which the *Periegesis* focuses, but as Konrad Miller noted, its geography is primarily derived from Paulus Orosius's *Historiarum adversum paganos libri VII*.[45] The immediate source was probably a larger wall-map which has not survived.[46] The *mappa mundi* is rectangular, allowing it to fill the manuscript page. It represents the three continents of the known inhabited world, Europe, Asia, and Africa, orientated with east at the top. The land, which has lovely crinkly edges, is surrounded by the *oceanus* shown in grey, and considerable space is given to other seas, especially the Mediterranean, on which the map centres. The seas are full of islands. A number of undulating mountain ranges are shown in green, and some inland seas, including the Red Sea, are red. Province boundaries and rivers are delineated in brown. Cities, in a similar plan and elevation design to those on the zonal map, albeit simplified, dot the landmasses, from Babylon in the east to Armagh in the west. In another echo of the zonal map the pillars of Hercules stand on the western boundary of the map. A fetching lion is drawn in Asia. The map's legend is fairly comprehensive, although not all features are labelled.[47] It is mostly in Latin, but the scribe was evidently accustomed to writing in Old English, as indicated by the use of the insular letterforms and the term 'suð Bryttas' applied to Brittany.[48] The map appears to draw on a number of sources; features such as the straight province boundary divisions in Africa and the Mediterranean-centric view show links

---

44 BL, MS Cotton Tiberius B V, fol. 57^r. Transcription and translation from Edson, *Mapping Time and Space*, pp. 75–76.

45 Miller, *Mappaemundi*, III, p. 35.

46 Edson, 'World Maps and Easter Tables', p. 32; Edson, *Mapping Time and Space*, p. 76. Large maps are far less likely to have survived, and most are known only from descriptions. Peter Barber has suggested that this putative exemplar may have been at Glastonbury. Barber, 'Medieval Maps of the World', p. 4; Barber, 'Updating the Roman World', p. 25. I have elsewhere suggested links to the royal court and tenth-centry West-Saxon expansionism: Appleton, 'The Northern World of the Anglo-Saxon *mappa mundi*'.

47 For a transcription of the legend, see McGurk, 'The Mappa Mundi', pp. 86–87.

48 Harvey, *Mappa Mundi*, p. 27; McGurk, 'The Mappa Mundi', p. 79; Hiatt, '"From Hulle to Cartage"', pp. 135–36.

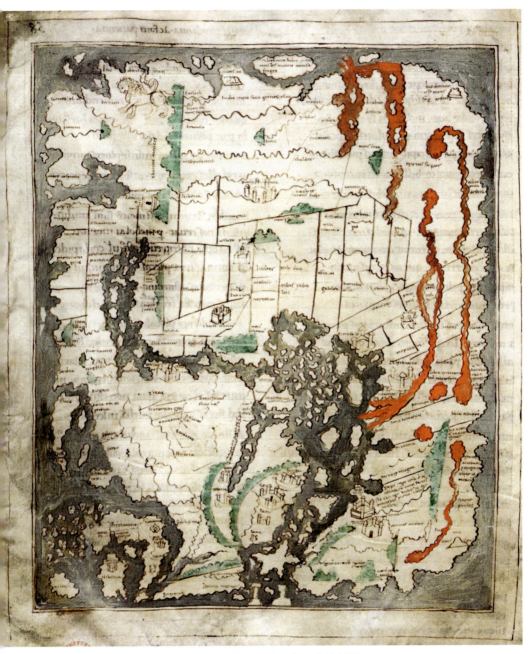

Figure 11.2. Mappa mundi. East is at the top. London, British Library, MS Cotton Tiberius B V, fol. 56ᵛ. © British Library Board.

to Roman imperial mapping and the world map of Marcus Vipsanius Agrippa, as P. D. A. Harvey suggests, while Carolingian influence is, as both Patrick McGurk and Peter Barber show, quite clear.[49] The map's legend derives from Orosius, but the Old Testament and the writings of Isidore are also used, and local knowledge supplies information for north-western Europe. The map offers an exceptionally exact depiction of Britain and Ireland, which are shown as containing a number of cities; the insular world, especially Wessex, appears quite urbanized.

There is something very concrete and very human about the world as represented on the *mappa mundi*. Although scripture is used as a source for the legend, which records the tribes of Israel and God's covenants with man on Sinai and Ararat (the latter with a drawing of the Ark), the map is otherwise comparatively secular, as is the zonal map. Jerusalem is not the centre of the world, no events from the life of Christ are depicted, and no location for the earthly paradise is given; the island in the far east is not Eden but Taprobane (Sri Lanka). There are no monstrous races depicted on the *mappa mundi*'s margins, despite the incipit to the *Periegesis* promising *monstra*. The lion, accurately represented in Asia, hardly counts as a monster and seems to be there to fill a space devoid of cities. A few potentially marvellous races appear in the legend, but either the copying is careless or their monstrosity downplayed. The manuscript as a whole contains a superabundance of strange creatures; they appear in the *Periegesis* and in the beautifully illustrated bilingual text of *Wonders of the East*, yet they are not emphasized by the map, which offers an image of the world complementary to yet distinct from those created elsewhere in the manuscript.

It is evident that the two Cotton Tiberius B V maps are designed to be connected. Their shared orientation, distinctive cities, and striking use of the pillars of Hercules create a commonality of perspective, inviting the viewer to imagine the *mappa mundi* as a close-up of the northern temperate zone represented on the zonal map. Both maps offer an image of the world primarily as a space occupied and organized by humans. The maps adapt cartographic tradition to create an increasing emphasis on *translatio imperii* from east to west, and in the case of the *mappa mundi* to highlight England as a part of this imperial project.[50] They do not explicitly emphasize the spiritual narrative behind the physical world, but that is not to say that the two maps are not shaped by Christian thought. Although they lack the explicit devotional intent evident with the Jerusalem T-O maps or Byrhtferthian diagrams, and later medieval English maps of comparable detail, such as the Hereford Cathedral Mappa Mundi and the Psalter map, they do still generate

---

49 Barber, 'Medieval Maps of the World', p. 5; Harvey, *Medieval Maps*, p. 21; McGurk, 'The Mappa Mundi', p. 86. Reused elements of Roman imperial mapping are relatively common in medieval cartography; see Gautier Dalché, 'L'héritage antique de la cartographie médiévale', p. 41.

50 Appleton, 'The Northern World of the Anglo-Saxon *mappa mundi*'.

an image to be contemplated. The synchronic image these two maps offer of imperial history simultaneously glorifies the West and highlights that all human power is fleeting.

Mapping Empires

Urban space draws the eye on both of the Cotton Tiberius B V maps. The zonal map depicts two cities, one in Europe, the other in Asia. The *mappa mundi*'s land masses are dotted with walled cities of various sizes. No single city appears to be the most prominent, but Alexandria, Babylon, Carthage, Constantinople, Jerusalem, Rome, Ravenna, Tarsus, and Tingis are on an impressive scale. The majority of the cities illustrated are clustered around the Mediterranean, but the urbanized area extends from Babylon in the east to Armagh in the west. This map's world view, centred on the Mediterranean, reproduces the perspective of the Roman Empire, creating a Western bias to the geography, yet there is also a real sense of breadth, and the large border of sea ensures that no place seems especially marginal. The numerous islands and scattered cities show a world with many regional centres, and the prominence of Britain with its concentration of urban spaces (Winchester, London, and another urban area in south-western England are depicted) serves to show a centre of significant power in the far west in contrast to the empty spaces of the east, where lions abound.

The cities on the *mappa mundi*, as on the smaller Macrobian map, are depicted as walled enclosures with varying numbers of turrets, although the drawing on the *mappa mundi* is less sophisticated, in part because they are smaller icons. On both maps cities are shown in semi-perspectival plan and elevation, a visual style that has obvious antecedents in Carolingian art, derived from Roman images, such as those of the *Agrimensores*.[51] The Utrecht Psalter (Utrecht, Universiteitsbibliotheek, MS Bibl. Rhenotraiectinae I Nr 32), which had significant influence on English art, shows similar polygonal cityscapes, for example Psalm 9 on folio 5[r].[52] This style of architectural representation can also be seen in the donation image of King Æthelstan in Cambridge,

---

51 For example, BAV, MS Pal. lat. 1564 (Aachen court, *c.* 830–900): Kaiser, 'Spätantike Rechtstexte in agrimensorischen Sammlungen', p. 282. See also Carder, *Art Historical Problems of a Roman Land Surveying Manuscript*, pp. 189–95; Deckers, 'Tradition und Adaptation', pp. 310–11; Dilke, 'Illustrations from Roman Surveyors' Manuals'; Mütherich, *Studies in Carolingian Manuscript Illumination*, pp. 118–46. I am grateful to Dr Tina Bawden (Freie Universität Berlin) for highlighting the similarities. Another eleventh-century Canterbury manuscript, the Missal of Robert of Jumièges (Rouen, Bibliothèque municipale, MS 274) shows the same style of city, for example in the image of the Magi on fol. 36[v].

52 This masterpiece of Carolingian art was in England by the end of the tenth century, and its cities are replicated in the Harley Psalter (BL, MS Harley 603, Canterbury, s.x/xi). Wormald, *English Drawings of the Tenth and Eleventh Centuries*, p. 21; Gneuss and Lapidge, *Anglo-Saxon Manuscripts*, pp. 680–81, 344–45.

Corpus Christi College, MS 183, folio 1ᵛ, which echoes the features of the unlabelled easternmost city on the Macrobian zonal map. Unlike the zonal map, the *mappa mundi*'s cities are labelled. As discussed above, much of the *mappa mundi*'s legend derives from Orosius, and the Orosian concept of the four empires is reflected in the cities it depicts. At the start of Book II of his *Historiarum adversum paganos*, Orosius describes the four empires of the world and the movement of power between them (II.1.4–5):

> si autem regna diuersa, quanto aequius regnum aliquod maximum, cui reliquorum regnorum potestas uniuersa subicitur, quale a principio Babylonium et deinde Macedonicum fuit, post etiam Africanum atque in fine Romanum quod usque ad nunc manet, eademque ineffabili ordinatione per quattuor mundi cardines quattuor regnorum principatus distinctis gradibus eminentes, ut Babylonium regnum ab oriente, a meridie Carthaginiense, a septentrione Macedonicum, ab occidente Romanum.[53]

> > (So, if there are a number of kingdoms, it is right that there is one supreme kingdom under which all the sovereignty of the rest is placed. In the beginning, this was the kingdom of Babylon, then the kingdom of Macedon, after that the African kingdom (i.e., Carthage), and finally Rome, which remains in place to this day. Through this same ineffable ordering of things, the four principal kingdoms which have been pre-eminent to differing degrees, have occurred at the four cardinal points of the world: the kingdom of Babylon to the east; that of Carthage to the south; that of Macedon to the north; and that of Rome to the west.)[54]

The scale of Babylon, Alexandria, Carthage, and Rome on the *mappa mundi* reflects this movement of imperial power from Babylonia through Macedon and Carthaginia to Rome.

The zonal map represents urban space even more symbolically, with two unlabelled cities, one in the east, the other in the west. It seems most probable that the European city is intended to represent Rome (although some suggest Constantinople), perhaps accounting for the two individuated heads, one blonde, the other brunette, represented within its walls — a possible nod to Romulus and Remus.[55] The eastern city is the larger of the two and is often assumed to be Jerusalem, but is arguably more likely to represent Babylon as it is depicted with one very tall tower, Babylon and Babel being conventionally equated.[56] If the two cities represent Rome and Babylon, then the zonal map

---

53 Orosius, *Historiarum adversum paganos libri VII*, ed. by Zangemeister, p. 35.

54 Orosius, *Seven Books of History against the Pagans*, trans. by Fear, pp. 73–74.

55 Edson, *Mapping Time and Space*, p. 77.

56 For a recent study of Babel in the period, see Major, *Undoing Babel*. Compare also the illustration of Babylon including the tower of Babel on the Hereford Mappa Mundi. On the tradition of equating the two, see further Scheil, 'Babylon and Anglo-Saxon England'.

also reflects the Orosian view of empire. After describing the four empires at the start of Book II, Orosius highlights the primacy of Rome and Babylon, stating (II.1.6):

> quorum inter primum ac nouissimum, id est inter Babylonium et Romanum, quasi inter patrem senem ac filium paruum, Africanum ac Macedonicum breuia et media, quasi tutor curatorque uenerunt potestate temporis non iure hereditatis admissi.[57]
>
> > (Between the first and last of them, that is to say Babylon and Rome, just as in the interval of time between an old father and his young son, come the short-lived and intermediate periods of the African and Macedonian kingdoms. These fulfilled roles like those of a teacher and guardian, and came into being though force of circumstance rather than from any right of succession.)[58]

Rome and Babylon are two clear symbols of imperial power, which moves between them. By depicting cities that evoke Rome and Babylon, the zonal map represents in a very contained image vast centuries of imperial history, offering an extreme example of the synchronous representation of diachronic history which characterized medieval mapping, especially that intended to prompt contemplation.

The zonal map adapts the traditional Macrobian scheme in order to reflect an interest in power and empire shared with the *mappa mundi*, on which Rome and Babylon receive the most complex drawings, and with other texts in Cotton Tiberius B V. On this map, between Babylon and Rome, east and west, we track down the manuscript page the transfer of power between the first Eastern empire of Babylon and the last Western empire of Rome. The orientation of the zonal map and the *mappa mundi* with east uppermost causes the viewer to move forwards through human history as they naturally read the image down the page, to where they themselves sit in the west. The eastern city is larger, perhaps as the shape of Asia affords more space, but also suggesting the overweening ambition that Babylon represents. The western city is shown as populated, creating an impression of activity, but the eastern contains no figures. By leaving the cities unlabelled, and locating them centrally, the zonal map creates a focus on *translatio imperii* that accommodates the drift of power westwards from Rome through Carolingia to England, so evident on the *mappa mundi*. The cities on the map are more representative of what Rome and Babylon symbolize than their literal geography. Power moves from east to west, from the worldly Babylonian empire to the Christian civilization of Rome.

The maps' perspective on human history, depicting great cities and extensive empires lost to time, connects with other texts in Cotton Tiberius B V which

---

57 Orosius, *Historiarum adversum paganos libri VII*, ed. by Zangemeister, pp. 35–36.
58 Orosius, *Seven Books of History against the Pagans*, trans. by Fear, p. 74.

show an interest in Rome and Babylon, and the transfer of power more generally. Cotton Tiberius B V's attention to Rome is evident; it includes lists of popes, and the itinerary of Sigeric lists churches to visit in Rome, followed by the rest stops on the journey back west to the channel coast. Babylon too is of interest, frequently occurring as a point of reference in *Wonders of the East*. The lists of bishops, kings, and popes and the genealogical material also display a focus on power and its historic transitions. The predominance of material related to England in these lists presents an assertive image of that country as part of the imperial project. Like the synchronic representation of urban space on both maps, these lists demonstrate both status and transience. The representation of time in Cotton Tiberius B V is often strange and synchronic. Sigeric cannot have visited all of the Roman sites in the time allotted. *Wonders of the East* presents Babylon as a present marker, rather than a ruin, switching the reader into a previous age; the reader travels backwards in time as the focus moves eastwards, as on the maps. In Cotton Tiberius B V *Wonders* uniquely ends with the apocryphon of Jannes and Mambres, Pharoah's magicians who contended with Moses. In this text the soul of Jannes, summoned by magic, warns the living Mambres of infernal punishment for the assumption of unnatural power and its misuse.[59] The reader is reminded that God cannot and should not be defied. In Cotton Tiberius B V the overweening ambitions of the past, of Jannes and Babylon, come back to warn us of God's power. In the Lumley Library catalogue of 1609 Cotton Tiberius B V is recognizable prior to its reordering by Robert Cotton. Intriguingly, in that catalogue *Wonders* appears first, then *De laudibus sancte crucis*, and finally the calendrical and geographical material which ends with the *Periegesis* and presumably the *mappa mundi*.[60] The manuscript in this form neatly echoes the general east to west flow of power and knowledge visible on its maps, but as it had already been disordered once by this point, this may not reflect the original scheme.

In using cartography to think about empires and the movement of human power the English are echoing the Carolingians. The Cotton Tiberius B V maps, like several of the manuscript's contents, must depend on material transmitted through Carolingian copyists, and it appears that alongside these materials came ways of reading and using them.[61] The Carolingians showed an intense interest in Roman geographical writing, using it, as Natalia Lozovsky highlights, to represent the transition of imperial power from the Romans to the Franks and selectively adapting and excerpting earlier material to

---

59 See Biggs and Hall, 'Traditions Concerning Jamnes and Mambres in Anglo-Saxon England'.

60 Johnson and Jayne, eds, *The Lumley Library*, p. 162; McGurk, 'The History of the Manuscript', p. 25.

61 For example, the *Aratea* depends on BL, MS Harley 647, a Carolingian book: McGurk, 'The Astronomical Section'. Lapidge makes the point that Carolingian knowledge of classical learning runs ahead of that of Anglo-Saxon England, making Francia the logical route of transmission for Roman mapping. Lapidge, *The Anglo-Saxon Library*, pp. 129–31.

serve new purposes.[62] As Gautier Dalché has shown, cartography was a key part of this programme of *renovatio imperii*; as noted above, Charlemagne understood the value of the statement made by maps, and by adjusting the image of the world inherited from earlier sources, contemporary interests could be served.[63] I have suggested elsewhere that if a wall map does indeed lie behind the Cotton Tiberius B V *mappa mundi* then it might have been the product of the imperial ambitions of the West Saxon court in the tenth century, designed to emulate Charlemagne and highlight the rising power of England.[64] By copying the *mappa mundi* into a manuscript context, rather than having it function as prestigious display item, the meaning shifts. Although the *mappa mundi*'s independence of the manuscript's other contents means that it retains the narrative function of its large ancestor, rather than serving as a gloss to the texts, the shift in scale foregrounds a reading more aligned with Theodulf's perspective on cartography than that of Charlemagne.

Conclusion: Politics, Piety, and Perspective

Cotton Tiberius B V is not a royal manuscript; it likely comes from Christ Church Canterbury, and the image of imperial power it presents is shaped by that context. Cotton Tiberius B V (as originally created) mixes geographical and historical information with spiritual material; as Edson states, its underlying theme 'concerns the measurement of time and space'.[65] Measurement by implication suggests limit, and this shared preoccupation with dimensions across the disparate items ensures that, even when an individual text offers a relatively secular perspective, the reader cannot forget that the world is God's creation — he is the *Metod*, the measurer. The Cotton Tiberius B V maps may not be as explicitly spiritual in intent as the Jerusalem T-O maps, but their reading context, in a Canterbury manuscript, provides a Christian interpretative frame for their image of imperial geography, and highlights the limits of human power by presenting a vast sweep of human history in a tiny space. The maps may be positive about the movement of imperial power in England's direction, working together with texts such as the regnal lists to present a confident assertion of English power and influence, but their synchronic perspective also allows the viewer, like Theodulf, to contemplate the inevitable transience of power, and ultimately the world, should they so choose.

---

62 Lozovsky, 'Roman Geography and Ethnography in the Carolingian Empire'.
63 Gautier Dalché, *La 'Descriptio mappae mundi' de Hughes de Saint-Victor*, pp. 122–23; Gautier Dalché, 'Les sens de mappa (mundi)', p. 188; Barber, 'Medieval Maps of the World', p. 5; Gautier Dalché, 'Tradition et renouvellement dans la représentation de l'espace géographique au IXe siècle'; Albu, *The Medieval Peutinger Map*, pp. 44–45; Albu, 'Imperial Geography and the Mediaeval Peutinger Map', pp. 136–38.
64 Appleton, 'The Northern World of the Anglo-Saxon *mappa mundi*'. On these ambitions, see also Leneghan, '*Translatio imperii*'.
65 Edson, 'World Maps and Easter Tables', p. 35.

Gautier Dalché makes the argument that the manuscript-bound world map came to have a particular value in the high medieval period for the way in which it echoed a divine vision, like those experienced by Columba and Benedict, of the world from the perspective of God. Manuscript maps cease merely to gloss texts and become contemplative objects in their own right. The independence of the Cotton Tiberius B V maps from the rest of the manuscript's contents and the level of detail they show suggest that they are early examples of this use of maps as aids to contemplation as well as knowledge. Gautier Dalché states:

> Toute *mappa mundi* rassemblant l'œcumène dans le bref espace de la page du codex met qui la contemple dans une situation analogue à celle du saint illuminé par la lumière divine, puisqu'elle permet d'embrasser ce que l'œil naturel, l'*oculus corporis*, ne peut voir: le petitesse du monde, rempli pourtant de si nombreuses cités, et formé de lieux témoins d'une si nombreuse histoire. De ce point de vue, le moindre schéma de l'œcumène peut servir à cette fonction contemplative [...]. Mais les cartes qui la remplissent au mieux sont celles qui offrent le plus de détails, traduisant la réalité du monde terrestre par des contours plus ou moins précis, et par des légendes abondantes. Car 'omnis mundis', comme dit Grégoire le Grand, c'est non seulement le monde physique, mais encore son histoire humaine, qui elle aussi est tout entière en Dieu, de son début à son accomplissement.[66]

>> (Any *mappa mundi* bringing together the *oikoumene* in the brief space of the page of the codex puts the one who contemplates it in a situation analogous to that of the saint illuminated by divine light, as it allows one to embrace what the natural eye, the *oculus corporis*, cannot see: the smallness of the world, yet filled with so many cities, and formed of places that bear witness to so much history. From this point of view, the slightest diagram of the *oikoumene* can serve this contemplative function [...]. But the maps which fill it best are those which offer the most details, translating the reality of the terrestrial world by more or less precise outlines, and by abundant legends. Because 'omnis mundis', as Gregory the Great says, it is not only the physical world, but also its human history, which too is entirely in God, from its beginning to its completion.)

As Cotton Tiberius B V is a relatively small book, its maps are especially effective at conveying 'le petitesse du monde'. A map, Gautier Dalché points out, shows time as well as place, like a universal chronicle.[67] In showing all times at once, it replicates the synchronic divine perspective and offers an echo of the view afforded the wise, enlightened soul, able to encompass the

---

66 Gautier Dalché, 'De la glose à la contemplation', p. 757.
67 Gautier Dalché, 'De la glose à la contemplation', p. 757.

world in the mind, as described in Gregory's *Dialogues* (II.35), Adomnán's *Life of Columba* (I.35), and *The Order of the World* (ll. 9–10a). In setting out this argument for the map as replica of enlightened vision, Gautier Dalché highlights the way in which Orosius, in Book I.1.15–16, talks about representing the world in his history as if seen from a watchtower, a *specula*, in order to contemplate a narrative of *cupiditas*.[68] The Tiberius maps replicate Orosius's imagined perspective on human history, viewing *translatio imperii* from Babylon to Rome from above. The viewer of the two Cotton Tiberius B V maps is therefore able, like Orosius, to overlay the passage of empires with a Christian interpretation and so contemplate the nature of the world. These maps are more than a complement to the manuscript's texts; they are an aid to enlightenment.

The two maps in Cotton Tiberius B V show that cartography in early medieval England served a similarly diverse range of roles to maps on the Continent, and that England participated fully in the development of new ideas and approaches. Early medieval English maps conveyed information and had an obviously didactic function, but they also communicated powerful political and spiritual messages by offering a synchronic view of human history and imagining the world as seen and ordered from above. The *mappa mundi* in Cotton Tiberius B V offers an image of a confident and prominent England participating in *translatio imperii* that reflects how large-scale world maps were used as statements of power, but this image is condensed onto a small page and beheld not from a distance by gazing upwards, as with a wall map, but close to and looking downwards into the manuscript. The explicit connection to the even more distanced view of the globe afforded by the zonal map highlights both human ambition and the insignificance of the world.[69] Working together the Cotton Tiberius B V maps articulate both the importance of the West, especially Rome and England, but also the transience of human endeavour. England is an important part of the world, but it is also a part of the world and so subject to the world's limits. To view a map is to perceive, as Theodulf says, a great deal in a small space; a map offers a replica of enlightenment and so allows its viewer to step outside the world and inhabit, momentarily, something akin to a divine perspective and assess England accordingly.

---

68 Gautier Dalché, 'De la glose à la contemplation', p. 755. Orosius, *Historiarum adversum paganos libri VII*, ed. by Zangemeister, p. 4. Orosius may have drafted his geography using maps, although no map appears to have originally accompanied the text. See Janvier, *La Géographie d'Orose*, pp. 165–69.

69 Nicole Discenza perceives a similar duality of perspective in Alfredian geographic texts: Discenza, 'A Map of the Universe'.

Works Cited

Manuscripts

Berlin, Deutsche Staatsbibliothek, MS Phillipps 1833 (Rose 138), <https://digital.staatsbibliothek-berlin.de/werkansicht?PPN=PPN83017379 X&PHYSID=PHYS_0084&DMDID=DMDLOG_0023> [accessed 1 March 2021]

Cambridge, Corpus Christi College, MS 183, <https://parker.stanford.edu/parker/ catalog/qv695jy8078> [accessed 1 March 2021]

Cambridge, Corpus Christi College, MS 265, <https://parker.stanford.edu/parker/ catalog/nh277tk2537> [accessed 1 March 2021]

Città del Vaticano, Biblioteca Apostolica Vaticana, MS Pal. lat. 1564

Città del Vaticano, Biblioteca Apostolica Vaticana, MS Reg. lat. 123, <https://digi.vatlib.it/view/MSS_Reg.lat.123> [accessed 1 March 2021]

Dijon, Bibliothèque municipal, MS 448, <http://patrimoine.bm-dijon.fr/pleade/img-viewer/MS00448/viewer.html?ns=FR212316101_MS00448_076_R.jpg> [accessed 1 March 2021]

Hereford, Hereford Cathedral, Mappa Mundi, <https://www.themappamundi.co.uk/ mappa-mundi/> [accessed 1 March 2021]

London, British Library, MS Cotton Tiberius B V, <http://www.bl.uk/manuscripts/ FullDisplay.aspx?ref=Cotton_MS_Tiberius_B_V/1> [accessed 1 March 2021]

London, British Library, MS Harley 603, <http://www.bl.uk/manuscripts/FullDisplay.aspx?ref=Harley_MS_603> [accessed 1 March 2021]

London, British Library, MS Harley 647, <http://www.bl.uk/manuscripts/FullDisplay.aspx?ref=Harley_MS_647> [accessed 1 March 2021]

London, British Library, MS Harley 3667, <http://www.bl.uk/manuscripts/Viewer.aspx?ref=harley_ms_3667_fs001r> [accessed 1 March 2021]

Munich, Bayerische Staatsbibliothek, MS Clm. 6362, <https://daten.digitale-sammlungen.de/~db/0006/bsb00065170/images/index.html?id=00065170&nativeno=74> [accessed 1 March 2021]

Oxford, St John's College, MS 17, <https://digital.library.mcgill.ca/ms-17/folio.php?p=6r> [accessed 1 March 2021]

Rouen, Bibliothèque municipale, MS 274, <https://portail.biblissima.fr/ark:/43093/mdata5fbcaea0b863279894164a1ad05c2570273bc91e> [accessed 1 March 2021]

Utrecht, Universiteitsbibliotheek, MS Bibl. Rhenotraiectinae I Nr 32, <https://psalter.library.uu.nl/?_ga=2.178285985.482096169.1590082356-1397587295.1590082356> [accessed 1 March 2021]

Primary Sources

Alexandrenko, N. A., 'The Poetry of Theodulf of Orleans: A Translation and Critical Study' (unpublished doctoral dissertation, Tulane University, 1970; *ProQuest Dissertations and Theses* 7108032)

Cassiodorus, *Cassiodori Senatoris Institutiones*, ed. by R. Mynors (Oxford: Clarendon Press, 1961)

——, *Institutions of Divine and Secular Learning; and, On the Soul*, trans. by James W. Halporn (Liverpool: Liverpool University Press, 2004)

Einhard, *Vita Karoli Magni*, ed. by O. Holder-Egger and G. H. Pertz, MGH: Scriptores rerum Germanicarum in usum scholarum separatim editi, 25 (Hanover: Hahn, 1911)

The Exeter Anthology of Old English Poetry: An Edition of Exeter Dean and Chapter MS 3501, ed. by Bernard J. Muir (Exeter: Exeter University Press, 1994)

Orosius, *Pauli Orosii Historiarum adversum paganos libri VII*, ed. by Karl F. W. Zangemeister, Corpus Scriptorum Ecclesiasticorum Latinorum, 5 (Leipzig: Teubner, 1889)

——, *Seven Books of History against the Pagans*, trans. by A. T. Fear, Translated Texts for Historians (Liverpool: Liverpool University Press, 2010)

Poetae Latini aevi Carolini, vol. I, ed. by E. Dümmler, MGH: Poetae Latini medii aevi, 1 (Berlin: Weidmann, 1881)

Secondary Sources

Albu, Emily, 'Imperial Geography and the Mediaeval Peutinger Map', *Imago Mundi*, 57 (2005), 136–48

——, *The Medieval Peutinger Map: Imperial Roman Revival in a German Empire* (Cambridge: Cambridge University Press, 2014)

Appleton, Helen, 'The Northern World of the Anglo-Saxon *mappa mundi*', *ASE*, 47 (2018), 275–305

Barber, Peter, 'Medieval Maps of the World', in *The Hereford World Map: Medieval World Maps and Their Context*, ed. by P. D. A. Harvey (London: British Library, 2006), pp. 1–43

——, 'Updating the Roman World', in *Mapping Our World: Terra Incognita to Australia* (Canberra: National Library of Australia, 2014), pp. 24–25

Bethurum, Dorothy, 'Archbishop Wulfstan's Commonplace Book', *PMLA*, 57 (1942), 916–29

Biggs, Frederick M., and Thomas N. Hall, 'Traditions Concerning Jamnes and Mambres in Anglo-Saxon England', *ASE*, 25 (1996), 69–89

Carder, James N., *Art Historical Problems of a Roman Land Surveying Manuscript: The Codex Arcerianus A, Wolfenbüttel* (New York: Garland, 1978)

Chekin, Leonid S., *Northern Eurasia in Medieval Cartography: Inventory, Text, Translation, and Commentary* (Turnhout: Brepols, 2006)

Deckers, Johannes G., 'Tradition und Adaptation: Bemerkungen zur Darstellung der christlichen Stadt', *Mitteilungen des deutschen archäologischen Instituts, Römische Abteilung*, 95 (1988), 303–82

Dilke, Oswald A. W., 'Illustrations from Roman Surveyors' Manuals', *Imago Mundi*, 21 (1967), 9–29

Discenza, Nicole Guenther, 'A Map of the Universe: Geography and Cosmology in the Program of Alfred the Great', in *Conversion and Colonization in Anglo-Saxon England*, ed. by Catherine E. Karkov and Nicholas Howe (Tempe: Arizona Centre for Medieval and Renaissance Studies, 2006), pp. 83–108

Dumville, David N., 'The Anglian Collection of Royal Genealogies and Regnal Lists', *ASE*, 5 (1976), 23–50

Edson, Evelyn, 'Isidore, Orosius, and the Medieval Image', in *Cartography in Antiquity and the Middle Ages: Fresh Perspectives, New Methods*, ed. by Richard J. A. Talbert and Richard W. Unger (Leiden: Brill, 2008), pp. 219–36

——, *Mapping Time and Space: How Medieval Mapmakers Viewed their World*, The British Library Studies in Map History, 1 (London: British Library, 1997)

——, 'World Maps and Easter Tables: Medieval Maps in Context', *Imago Mundi*, 48 (1996), 25–42

Foys, Marin K., 'An Unfinished *mappa mundi* from Late-Eleventh-Century Worcester', *ASE*, 35 (2006), 271–84

Gautier Dalché, Patrick, 'De la glose à la contemplation: Place et fonction de la carte dans les manuscrits du haut Moyen Âge', in *Testo e immagine nell'alto Medioevo*, 2 vols (Spoleto: Centro Italiano di Studi sull'Alto Medioevo, 1994), II, pp. 693–771; repr. in Patrick Gautier Dalché, *Géographie et culture: La représentation de l'espace du VIᵉ au XIIᵉ siècle* (Aldershot: Ashgate, 1997), pt. 8

——, *La 'Descriptio mappae mundi' de Hughes de Saint-Victor* (Paris: Etudes Augustiniennes, 1988)

——, 'L'héritage antique de la cartographie médiévale: Les problèmes et les acquis', in *Cartography in Antiquity and the Middle Ages: Fresh Perspectives, New Methods*, ed. by Richard J. A. Talbert and Richard W. Unger (Leiden: Brill, 2008), pp. 29–66

——, 'Notes sur la "carte de Théodose II" et sur la "mappemonde de Théodulf d'Orléans"', *Geographia antiqua*, 3/4 (1994/1995), 91–108; repr. in Patrick Gautier Dalché, *Géographie et culture: La représentation de l'espace du VIᵉ au XIIᵉ siècle* (Aldershot: Ashgate, 1997), pt. 9

——, 'Les sens de mappa (mundi): IVᵉ–XIVᵉ siècle', *Archivum latinitatis medii aevi*, 62 (2004), 187–202

——, 'Tradition et renouvellement dans la représentation de l'espace géographique au IXᵉ siècle', *Studi Medievali*, 3rd Ser., 24 (1983), 121–246

Gneuss, Helmut, and Michael Lapidge, *Anglo-Saxon Manuscripts: A Bibliographical Handlist of Manuscripts and Manuscript Fragments Written or Owned in England up to 1100*, Toronto Anglo-Saxon Series, 15 (Toronto: University of Toronto Press, 2014)

Harvey, Paul D. A., *Mappa Mundi: The Hereford World Map* (Toronto: University of Toronto Press, 1996)

——, *Medieval Maps* (London: British Library, 1991)

Hiatt, A., "'From Hulle to Cartage": Maps, England, and the Sea', in *The Sea and Englishness in the Middle Ages: Maritime Narratives, Identity, and Culture*, ed. by Sebastian I. Sobecki (Cambridge: D. S. Brewer, 2011), pp. 133–57

——, 'The Map of Macrobius before 1100', *Imago Mundi*, 59 (2007), 149–76

Howe, Nicholas, *Writing the Map of Anglo-Saxon England: Essays in Cultural Geography* (New Haven, CT: Yale University Press, 2008)

Janvier, Yves, *La Géographie d'Orose* (Paris: Société d'édition 'Les Belles Lettres', 1982)

Johnson, Francis R., and Sears Reynolds Jayne, eds, *The Lumley Library: The Catalogue of 1609* (London: Trustees of the British Museum, 1956)

Kaiser, Wolfgang, 'Spätantike Rechtstexte in agrimensorischen Sammlungen', *Zeitschrift der Savigny-Stiftung für Rechtsgeschichte: Romanistische Abteilung*, 130 (2013), 273–347

Ker, Neil R., *Catalogue of Manuscripts Containing Anglo-Saxon* (Oxford: Clarendon Press, 1957)

Kupfer, Marcia, 'Medieval World Maps: Embedded Images, Interpretive Frames', *Word & Image*, 10 (1994), 262–88

Lapidge, Michael, *The Anglo-Saxon Library* (Oxford: Oxford University Press, 2006)

Lavezzo, Kathy, *Angels on the Edge of the World: Geography, Literature, and English Community, 1000–1534* (Ithaca, NY: Cornell University Press, 2006)

Leneghan, Francis, '*Translatio imperii*: The Old English *Orosius* and the Rise of Wessex', *Anglia*, 133 (2015), 656–705

Lozovsky, Natalia, 'Roman Geography and Ethnography in the Carolingian Empire', *Speculum*, 81 (2006), 325–64

Major, Tristan, *Undoing Babel: The Tower of Babel in Anglo-Saxon Literature* (Toronto: University of Toronto Press, 2019)

McGurk, Patrick, 'The Astronomical Section', in *An Eleventh-Century Anglo-Saxon Illustrated Miscellany: British Library Cotton Tiberius B.V Part 1, Together with Leaves from British Library Cotton Nero D.II*, ed. by P. McGurk, D. N. Dumville, M. R. Godden, and Ann Knock, Early English Manuscripts in Facsimile, 21 (Copenhagen: Rosenkilde and Bagger, 1983), pp. 67–78

——, 'Conclusion', in *An Eleventh-Century Anglo-Saxon Illustrated Miscellany: British Library Cotton Tiberius B.V Part 1, Together with Leaves from British Library Cotton Nero D.II*, ed. by P. McGurk, D. N. Dumville, M. R. Godden, and Ann Knock, Early English Manuscripts in Facsimile, 21 (Copenhagen: Rosenkilde and Bagger, 1983), pp. 107–09

——, 'Contents of the Manuscript', in *An Eleventh-Century Anglo-Saxon Illustrated Miscellany: British Library Cotton Tiberius B.V Part 1, Together with Leaves from British Library Cotton Nero D.II*, ed. by P. McGurk, D. N. Dumville, M. R. Godden, and Ann Knock, Early English Manuscripts in Facsimile, 21 (Copenhagen: Rosenkilde and Bagger, 1983), pp. 15–24

——, 'The History of the Manuscript', in *An Eleventh-Century Anglo-Saxon Illustrated Miscellany: British Library Cotton Tiberius B.V Part 1, Together with Leaves from British Library Cotton Nero D.II*, ed. by P. McGurk, D. N. Dumville,

M. R. Godden, and Ann Knock, *Early English Manuscripts in Facsimile*, 21 (Copenhagen: Rosenkilde and Bagger, 1983), pp. 25–27

——, 'The Macrobian Zonal Map', *An Eleventh-Century Anglo-Saxon Illustrated Miscellany: British Library Cotton Tiberius B.V Part 1, Together with Leaves from British Library Cotton Nero D.II*, ed. by P. McGurk, D. N. Dumville, M. R. Godden, and Ann Knock, *Early English Manuscripts in Facsimile*, 21 (Copenhagen: Rosenkilde and Bagger, 1983), pp. 65–66

—— 'The Mappa Mundi', in *An Eleventh-Century Anglo-Saxon Illustrated Miscellany: British Library Cotton Tiberius B.V Part 1, Together with Leaves from British Library Cotton Nero D.II*, ed. by P. McGurk, D. N. Dumville, M. R. Godden, and Ann Knock, *Early English Manuscripts in Facsimile*, 21 (Copenhagen: Rosenkilde and Bagger, 1983), pp. 79–87

Miller, Konrad, *Mappaemundi: Die ältesten Weltkarten*, 6 vols (Stuttgart: J. Roth, 1895–1898)

Mütherich, Florentine, *Studies in Carolingian Manuscript Illumination* (London: Pindar, 2004)

Sauer, Hans, 'The Transmission and Structure of Wulfstan's "Commonplace Book"', in *Old English Prose: Basic Readings*, ed. by Paul E. Szarmach (New York: Garland, 2000), pp. 339–93

Scheil, Andrew P., 'Babylon and Anglo-Saxon England', *Studies in the Literary Imagination*, 36 (2003), 37–58

Tedford, Margaret, 'The Anglo-Saxon Cotton Map in Context' (unpublished doctoral dissertation, Queen's University Belfast, 2019)

Teresi, Loredana, 'Anglo-Saxon and Early Anglo-Norman "Mappaemundi"', in *Foundations of Learning: The Transfer of Encyclopaedic Knowledge in the Early Middle Ages*, ed. by Rolf H. Bremmer and Cornelis Dekker (Paris: Peeters, 2007), pp. 341–78

Vidier, Alexandre, 'La mappemonde de Théodulfe et la mappemonde de Ripoll (ixe–xie siècle)', *Bulletin de géographie historique et descriptive*, 3 (1911), 285–313

Wormald, Francis, *English Drawings of the Tenth and Eleventh Centuries* (London: Faber and Faber, 1952)

CAITLIN ELLIS

Good Neighbours?
Representations of the Britons, Welsh, Picts, and Scots in Pre-Conquest English Sources

This volume centres on ideas of the wider world in England before the Norman Conquest, with several chapters dealing with conceptions of geographically distant and unfamiliar places. In contrast, this chapter investigates how the early medieval English themselves perceived and depicted their nearest neighbours. It constitutes a thorough examination of how the non-English, Celtic-speaking peoples of Britain are portrayed and presented in Anglo-Latin and Old English texts from the sixth century to the time of the Norman Conquest. Scholars have discussed this issue in different contexts, usually by restricting themselves to a single people, time period, genre of text, or author; this chapter draws these different strands together for a more complete picture of how these representations developed and varied. To what extent did these attitudes change over time? Here, the focus is on English depictions of the Britons, Welsh, Picts, and Scots — that is, to the other inhabitants of the island of Britain — though not the Irish, a subject which deserves fuller treatment elsewhere.[1] Likewise, it does not deal in any great detail with English attitudes towards 'Vikings' or Scandinavians, since these interactions are explored in Ryan Lavelle's chapter in this volume. Of course, there are limitations in all such ethnonyms and cultural, linguistic, or political categories, which were no doubt changing in meaning and implications in the medieval period and are still contested today.[2] Wherever

---

[*] I am grateful to the editors, particularly Francis Leneghan, for their feedback and support, as well as to Katie Haworth, Lindy Brady, and the anonymous peer reviewer.

[1] See, with a linguistic focus, Milfull and Thier, 'Anglo-Saxon Perceptions of the Celtic Peoples', pp. 217–19. For Bede's views of the Irish in terms of Christianity and the Easter Controversy, see Stancliffe, *Bede, Wilfrid, and the Irish*; Thacker, 'Bede and the Irish'; Higham, *(Re-)Reading Bede*, pp. 134–42. For Bede's representations of the Irish in general, see McCann, *'Plures de Scottorum regione'*; Ahern, 'The Influence of Irish Learning', p. 56.

[2] This chapter's use of 'English' does not seek to imply that a coherent notion of 'Englishness' existed, nor a unified kingdom of England, until the end of the period under discussion.

Caitlin Ellis (caitlin@cantab.net) is an O'Donovan Scholar at the School of Celtic Studies, the Dublin Institute of Advanced Studies.

Ideas of the World in Early Medieval English Literature, ed. by Mark Atherton, Kazutomo Karasawa, and Francis Leneghan, SOEL 1 (Turnhout: Brepols, 2022)   pp. 335–364
BREPOLS ❧ PUBLISHERS   DOI 10.1484/M.SOEL.5.130567

possible, therefore, I will refer to peoples and places by the early medieval terms used in the sources discussed. While sources from the point of view of the Celtic speakers themselves are excluded to try to ascertain English attitudes, a complicating factor is revealed in the fact that several of these relevant sources were not fully or solely English — as discussed below in the cases of Gildas's influence on Bede and of Asser's *Life of King Alfred*. It should also be noted that most of the surviving texts from the ninth to eleventh centuries represent a West Saxon perspective, rather than that of the more immediate neighbours of the Welsh and of the Picts and Scots; that is, the Mercian or Northumbrian perspective is more difficult to discern. The focus of this chapter is textual reflexes rather than the reality of interactions between the early medieval English and their neighbours from the fifth to eleventh centuries, although some general trends will be referenced. A range of key textual sources, notably Bede's *Ecclesiastical History* and the Anglo-Saxon Chronicle entries up to 1066, will be examined in roughly chronological order within each section.[3] In bringing this material together in one place, this chapter will demonstrate how references to the Welsh, Britons, Picts, and Scots in English sources were manipulated for particular political contexts and vary with changing fortunes.

The Britons

'The Britons' is the label conventionally given to the Celtic-speaking peoples who inhabited Britain since the Iron Age at least. Early historians — Gildas and Bede in particular — related that they were pushed back by waves of invasion: first by the Roman conquests of the first century AD, then by attacks from

---

Nevertheless, many of the surviving sources — whether Bede's use of *Angli* or those from an Alfredian context — are aspirational in their treatment of this issue, attempting to promote unity and common feeling (cf. Foot, 'The Making of *Angelcynn*'). 'English' would not have been a monolithic identity given regional variation and the existence of different kingdoms; indeed, this regional perspective will be touched on where possible in this chapter. These different kingdoms at least shared a language, and linguistic division between English speakers and their Celtic-speaking neighbours is something highlighted in the sources: for instance, between the English and Britons or Welsh in Ine's law code, which is discussed below, though it cannot be ascertained if this reflects the seventh-century original or a ninth-century update (see Ward-Perkins, 'Why Did the Anglo-Saxons Not Become More British?', p. 524). Meanwhile, as Alaric Hall notes, Bede 'implicitly correlated language with ethnicity' ('Interlinguistic Communication', p. 61).

3 For ease and completeness all main recensions of the Chronicle will be examined, not just the tenth-century manuscripts A and B. MS C is dated to the mid-eleventh century, while D and E date to the mid-eleventh century at the earliest and to the early twelfth century, respectively (Stafford, *After Alfred*, p. 4). Stafford argues for a pre-Conquest date for most of the annals in D dated before 1066 (pp. 233–34) and, while E is the work of one late scribe, it does draw on earlier material and is still part of the chronicling tradition going back to Alfred (pp. 297, 300, 304, 305).

GOOD NEIGHBOURS? 337

the Picts and Gaels, and, finally and most significantly, by the fifth-century *adventus Saxonum* ('the arrival of the Saxons'), which involved the movement of various Germanic-speaking groups from the Continent, predominantly, according to Bede, the Angles, Saxons, and Jutes.[4] Our earliest witness is himself not an English source, but rather a Romano-British one — but Gildas is important because his account of the *adventus* influenced those of English authors such as Bede and the Anglo-Saxon Chronicle.[5] In the sixth century, Gildas writes that the Britons 'quin potius de ipsis montibus, speluncis ac saltibus, dumis consertis continue rebellabant' (kept fighting back, basing themselves on the mountains, caves, heaths and thorny thickets).[6] Drawing on Gildas, the Northumbrian Bede in the early eighth century likewise related that some Britons 'perstantes in patria trepidi pauperem uitam in montibus siluis uel rupibus arduis suspecta semper mente agebant' (remained in their own land and led a wretched existence, always in fear and dread, among the mountains and woods and precipitous rocks).[7] Thus, the Britons are presented as being driven to the margins of the landscape of the island of Britain, both literally and metaphorically.

Over the course of all the conflicts recorded in the *Ecclesiastical History*, in Bede's account the Britons are only successful in warfare when they benefit from chance occurrences, such as storms and shipwrecks, or when they are led by a non-Briton (St Germanus was from Gaul, and Bede identifies Ambrosius Aurelianus as a Roman).[8] Cadwallon, king of Gwynedd, is more notable than his counterparts but is depicted as a primitive brute. Namely, Bede records how he made the mistake of opposing Edwin of Northumbria, one of Bede's English heroes in the *Ecclesiastical History*, describing Cadwallon as 'animo ac moribus barbarus' (barbarous in temperament and behaviour).[9] Though Cadwallon was Christian, for Bede he was not the correct type of Christian and he had sided with the pagan Penda of Mercia; this explains his bestial portrayal.[10] Debby Banham suggests that Bede's claim that Cadwallon was 'totum genus Anglorum Brittaniae finibus erasurum se esse deliberans'

---

4 See Daniel Thomas's chapter in this volume. This traditional picture of the *adventus Saxonum* derived from these written sources has been problematized: see Harland, *Ethnic Identity and the Archaeology of the 'aduentus Saxonum'*, and Oosthuizen, *The Emergence of the English*. Additionally, Woolf suggests that Gildas may have overstated the level of attacks from the Picts and Scots on the northern frontier ('British Ethnogenesis', p. 29).

5 Scholars have debated whether Gildas would have identified himself as a Roman or a Briton or both: see Harland, 'Rethinking Ethnicity and "Otherness"', p. 116, and references therein; Higham, *The English Conquest*, pp. 90–97.

6 Gildas, *The Ruin of Britain and Other Works*, ed. and trans. by Winterbottom, p. 95. See Higham, *The English Conquest*, p. 26, for the parallel between the Britons' resistance to the Saxons in this episode and earlier to the persecutions of the Roman emperor Diocletian.

7 Bede, *HE*, 1.15, ed. and trans. by Colgrave and Mynors, pp. 52–53.

8 Banham, 'Anglo-Saxon Attitudes', p. 146.

9 Bede, *HE*, 11.20, ed. and trans. by Colgrave and Mynors, pp. 202–03.

10 Higham, *An English Empire*, pp. 133–35.

(set upon wiping out the whole English people in Britain) was 'more like a projection onto their victims of the English attitude to the Britons'.[11] The English did not wipe out all the Britons, but in Bede's account the Britons are if not airbrushed out, then portrayed in very broad brushstrokes. In contrast to the local detail about different English kingdoms, few Britons are named and even less often localized: they are generically 'British'.[12] Apart from his famous list of the languages of Britain, Bede never explicitly mentions Brittonic languages elsewhere in the text (unlike English and Irish), while his handling of Brittonic place-names suggests to Alaric Hall 'a desire to alienate Britons', not just a lack of knowledge.[13]

Three main reasons for Bede's interest in the Britons have been identified: their failure to try to convert the English to Christianity; their refusal to follow the Roman method of Easter calculation; their impact on the conflict between Mercia and Northumbria.[14] The latter factor makes the Britons purely incidental to an internal struggle for supremacy between different early English kingdoms. The first two factors connect to the disparaging portrayal of the Britons, which might more usually be reserved for pagans. For Gildas, the *adventus Saxonum* was a lesson to his own people for their immorality and perhaps a call to resistance. Bede was able to adapt this account, by making the English the instrument of divine vengeance.[15] The description of Cadwallon as 'pagano saeuior' (more savage than a pagan) reveals Bede's deep-seated antipathy towards the Britons who do not have the benefit of ignorance to excuse their conduct.[16]

Roughly contemporary to Bede, Felix's *Life of St Guthlac* contains a vivid depiction of the Britons. In a vision the saint is faced by 'Brittannica agmina' (British hosts).[17] This incident takes place in the fens of East Anglia, where the Mercian Guthlac is living as a hermit. While scholars have debated whether there was any genuine surviving British presence in this remote area in the seventh and eighth centuries, this demonic episode and other instances in the literary corpus suggest English misgivings about the region.[18] Gildas and Bede had described the Britons being pushed back to more inaccessible parts of the landscape. The fact that the Britons are a theological problem in Felix's

---

11 Banham, 'Anglo-Saxon Attitudes', p. 146.
12 Foley and Higham, 'Bede on the Britons', p. 172.
13 Hall, 'Interlinguistic Communication', pp. 42–43, 64.
14 Charles-Edwards, 'Wales and Mercia', p. 90.
15 It has been argued that Bede and other writers presented the English as 'God's chosen people' (Banham, 'Anglo-Saxon Attitudes', p. 145) in the manner of the Israelites, but this claim to special favour over other Christians has recently been critiqued (Molyneaux, 'Did the English Really Think They Were God's Elect?').
16 Bede, *HE*, ii.20, ed. and trans. by Colgrave and Mynors, pp. 202–03. See Charles-Edwards, 'Bede, the Irish and the Britons', pp. 46–47.
17 Felix, *Life of Guthlac*, ed. and trans. by Colgrave, pp. 110–11.
18 See Brady, 'Echoes of Britons on a Fenland Frontier', pp. 676–77; Banham, 'Anglo-Saxon Attitudes', p. 148; Higham, 'Guthlac's *Vita*', p. 88.

Life may stem from the English perception that the Britons did not adhere to the orthodoxy of Rome or to the authority of Canterbury.[19] The vision of the British hosts is often discussed alongside an equivalent episode in the *Life* involving a bestial horde and using similar vocabulary; both episodes have parallels in the *Life of Anthony*.[20] Heide Estes argues that the details of the demonic depictions in these episodes established Christian aristocratic English men 'in opposition to all others'.[21] Clearly, this presentation of Britons suggests inferiority and wickedness. Whether the demons are disguised as Britons, or the Britons as demons,[22] that the link is made is paramount here.

While Guthlac is able to identify the trickery — 'hostis pellacis millenis artibus millenas formas persentiens' (perceiving the thousand-fold forms of the insidious foe and his thousand-fold tricks) — as part of his trial, the associations of Britons and devils remains.[23] Guthlac recognizes the host as Britons due to their speech which he is familiar with from a period of exile in his youth.[24] The vision of the Britons is said to occur in the reign of Coenred of Mercia (r. 704–709) 'cum Brittones, infesti hostes Saxonici generis, bellis, praedis, publicisque vastationibus Anglorum gentem deturbarent' (while the Britons the implacable enemies of the Saxon race, were troubling the English with their attacks, their pillaging and their devastations of the people).[25] Colgrave took this as evidence of hostility, namely that a damaging Welsh attack on Mercia had taken place in Coenred's reign, unacknowledged in other sources.[26] Lindy Brady, who in general emphasizes interaction and co-existence between the English and their Celtic-speaking neighbours, suggests that the demonic aspect 'has overshadowed' Guthlac's earlier life and 'culturally mixed background' in terms of him knowing the British language.[27] This highlights that a single text can contain a multiplicity of portrayals of a given population group. Historical interactions between different cultures do not preclude

---

19 Capper, 'St Guthlac and the "Britons"', p. 213.

20 Brooks, *Restoring Creation*, pp. 198–201.

21 Estes, *Anglo-Saxon Literary Landscapes*, p. 111.

22 Brooks, Brady, and Bintley describe the host as devils disguised as Britons (Brooks, *Restoring Creation*, p. 200; Brady, *Writing the Welsh Borderland*, p. 57; Bintley, 'Romans, Britons, and the Construction of "Anglo-Saxon" Identity', p. 47), while O'Brien O'Keeffe allows for the reverse possibility ('Guthlac's Crossings', p. 21).

23 Felix, *Life of Guthlac*, ed. and trans. by Colgrave, pp. 110–11.

24 As Hall observes, the fact that Guthlac's comprehension of Brittonic 'requires explanation' in the text suggests that this ability was not common among early English monks and nobles ('Interlinguistic Communication', p. 65).

25 Felix, *Life of Guthlac*, ed. and trans. by Colgrave, pp. 108–09. According to Brady 'the Mercians are actually not the people whom the British are said to be attacking'; instead the Britons' enemies are the Saxons or English (*Writing the Welsh Borderlands*, p. 56). Capper interprets this differently, arguing that Felix aims to find fellow feeling between his Mercian subject and his East Anglian audience, also 'reflecting contemporary expectations that there should be common English hostility to the Britons' ('St Guthlac and the "Britons"', p. 187).

26 Felix, *Life of Guthlac*, ed. and trans. by Colgrave, p. 185.

27 Brady, *Writing the Welsh Borderland*, p. 57.

negative ideas and unfavourable literary depictions. Morn Capper has argued that the presence of the Britons in Guthlac's life contrasts with their presentation in Felix's demonic vision due to the text reflecting attitudes in the author's, rather than the saint's, lifetime: cross-border conflict and the growing power of Mercia in the late seventh and early eighth centuries, and under Æthelbald in particular, led to the 'hardening of attitudes' towards the Britons.[28] English representations of insular neighbours could shift depending on contemporary political circumstances and on narrative context: the Britons could be allies in the everyday, but they could also fulfil a more abstracted threatening role outside the ecclesiastical mainstream in a supernatural encounter.

Another, murkier depiction of the Britons may be present in the Old English poem *Andreas*, a reworking of Continental stories about St Andrew, specifically the Greek work *The Acts of Andrew and Matthew in the City of the Anthropophagi*. The poem is preserved in the late tenth-century Vercelli Book, but an Alfredian context for its composition has recently been put forward.[29] Brady argues that the cannibal nation of Mermedonia present in other versions of the original story can be connected to the Britons in the Old English poetic version. Other versions place Mermedonia in Scythia, but in *Andreas* no geographical location is given. Instead, Mermedonia is described simply as a *mearc* ('border, boundary') and an *igland* ('island' or 'water-land') in the poem (ll. 15, 28). Brady connects this depiction of Mermedonia to the East Anglian fens as wild watery landscape which might shelter remnants of the British population, as seen in the *Life of St Guthlac*.[30] The identification of the Britons with the cannibal nation cannot be proven, but the resonances between different texts and traditions suggest the overlapping of ninth- and tenth-century English attitudes towards the neighbouring peoples of the island of Britain and towards foreigners in general.

The multiple references to Britons in the Anglo-Saxon Chronicle are less allusive and curter. The common stock of the Anglo-Saxon Chronicle likely originates from the court of Alfred of Wessex in the late ninth century, with different continuations being made over the next 250 years.[31] One of the first entries in the Chronicle is the record of the Roman emperor Claudius's invasion of Britain. Manuscripts A, B, C simply state that he brought 'Bretene lond' (Britain) under his control,[32] while D and E add that he 'þæt egland geeode, 7 ealle Pihtas 7 Walas underþeodde Romana rice' (conquered the island and subjected all the Picts and Britons to the power of the Romans).[33]

---

28 Capper, 'St Guthlac and the "Britons"', pp. 181, 197.

29 For this argument, see *Andreas*, ed. by North and Bintley, pp. xiii, 47, 97–106. For the poem's use of Latin and Old English sources, see Orchard, 'The Originality of *Andreas*', and, on Cynewulf and *Beowulf* specifically, Leneghan, 'The Departure of the Hero in a Ship'.

30 Brady, 'Echoes of Britons on a Fenland Frontier', p. 669.

31 Stafford, *After Alfred*, pp. 1–2, 39–40.

32 ASC 47, MS A *s.a.* 46, ed. by Bately, p. 4.

33 ASC 47, MS D, ed. by Cubbin, p. 3; see also MS E, ed. by Irvine, p. 5; trans. in *EHD*, p. 150.

From the outset of this text, therefore, the much earlier conquest of the Britons is outlined, long before the *adventus Saxonum*. Likewise, the Britons are presented as desperate when faced with attacks by the Picts: 'sendon Brytwalas ofer \sæ/ to Rome 7 heom fultumes bædon wið Peohtas, ac hi þær nefdon nænne' (the Britons sent across the sea to Rome and begged for help against the Picts, but they got none there).[34] The helplessness of the Britons in this situation is also evident when it is related that the first English given land by Vortigern recruited more forces from their homeland by telling them of 'Brytwalana nahtscipe 7 þes landes cysta' (the cowardice of the Britons and the excellence of the land).[35] This detail is drawn from Bede's statement that the report of a Saxon victory and 'insulae fertilitas ac segnitia Brettonum' (of the fertility of the island and the slackness of the Britons) led to the arrival of a larger fleet.[36] Bede's Latin 'segnitia' (sloth, inactivity) is not only translated into Old English but heightened to the more insulting 'nahtscipe' (literally meaning 'nothingness' or 'worthlessness', but perhaps better translated as 'cowardice', 'pusillanimity');[37] likewise, the more specific fertility of the island has become more general quality and opportunity.

After this mid-fifth-century entry nearly every year in the next few decades and, in lower concentration, even until the Gregorian or Augustinian mission of 596 or 597 refers to battles with and defeat of the Britons. There are some similar references after this point, but the focus of the account has by now changed given the perception of the conversion to Christianity as pivotal. These reports of battles are quite terse. One more evocative image is that Hengest and Æsc 'gefuhton wiþ Walas 7 genamon unarimedlico hereaf, 7 þa Walas flugon þa Englan swa [þer] fyr' (fought against the Britons and captured countless spoils and the Britons fled from the English as from fire).[38] Often it is simply stated that an English leader 'fought against the British',[39] without any specificity of subgroups or kingdoms. The use of the term 'Walas' or 'Wealas' will be discussed below in the section on the Welsh. Unlike their legendary Germanic-speaking counterparts, British leaders are rarely even named.[40] Banham finds it 'hard to believe that the invaders were ignorant of

---

See Francis Leneghan's chapter in this volume for discussion of this narrative in light of West Saxon ideas of empire in the tenth and eleventh centuries.

34 ASC MS E (*s.a.* 443 recte 446), ed. by Irvine, p. 16; trans. in *EHD*, p. 153.

35 ASC 449, MS E, ed. by Irvine, p. 16; trans. in *EHD*, p. 153.

36 Bede, *HE*, 1.15, ed. and trans. by Colgrave and Mynors, pp. 50–51.

37 *A Thesaurus of Old English*, 06.02.07.07 (n.) Cowardice, pusillanimity. See also 'náwiht-ness', in *Bosworth Toller's Anglo-Saxon Dictionary Online*, ed. by Christ. The precise word *nahtscipe* seems to be unique in the extant corpus on Old English. An addition in MS A uses 'nahtness' instead (ed. by Bately, p. 17) which is perhaps more strongly associated with 'worthlessness'.

38 ASC 473, MS A, ed. by Bately, p. 18; trans. in *EHD*, p. 154.

39 For instance, MS A 485 'gefeaht wiþ Walas' (ed. by Bately, p. 19), 571 'feaht wiþ Bretwalas', 584 'fuhton wiþ Brettas' (p. 24). Banham, 'Anglo-Saxon Attitudes', p. 146.

40 The three kings named for the 577 (ABCE) entry is an exception, as is MS E's entry (*s.a.* 605, recte 604) naming 'Scromail' (ed. by Irvine, p. 23), which must be an error for 'Brocmail' in

the political entities they destroyed', despite the lack of references to them in the Chronicle.[41] A blank canvas was created onto which to project early English kingdoms; kingdoms which are of course described in considerably more detail than those they replaced.

The connection between Christianity and the English victory over the Britons continues in a lengthier Chronicle entry for the early seventh century. At the Battle of Chester, it is reported that Æthelfrith of Northumbria (d. c. 616) 'ofsloh unrim Walana' (killed a countless number of Britons), including two hundred priests who had come 'gebiddan for Walana here' (to pray for the army of the Britons).[42] Again, this annal is derived from Bede's account of the same event, in which, despite his Christian faith, he displays no sympathy for the monks, mostly from Bangor, who were cut down by swords.[43] Bede notes that this defeat of the Britons fulfilled the prophecy of Augustine that 'temporalis interitus ultione | sentirent perfidi, quod oblata sibi perpetuae salutis consilia spreuerant' (those heretics would also suffer the vengeance of temporal death because they had despised the offer of everlasting salvation).[44] While asserting Augustine's sanctity, Bede simultaneously criticizes the Britons for not submitting to the Roman Church. The Northumbrian king Æthelfrith is cast as an instrument of divine vengeance upon the Britons.[45] The version in the Chronicle is shorter and starker. It provides wording for Augustine's prophecy: 'Gif Wealas nellaþ sibbe wið us, hy sculon æt Seaxena handa forwurþan' (If the Britons do not wish to have peace with us, they shall perish at the hands of the Saxons).[46] The focus is therefore shifted from the ecclesiastical failings of the Britons to their military and political domination by the Saxons.

The Old English version of Bede's *Ecclesiastical History* dates to the late ninth or early tenth century, possibly as part of the Alfredian translation programme or a Mercian school of translation, but the translator/adaptor may have been operating separately.[47] Both Sharon Rowley and George Molyneaux have noted that this text does not include some of the sections of Bede which were most

---

Bede's account of the same incident. A killed British king is also specified in the 508 entry (ABCE) presumably due to toponymical interest, as 'Natanleod' gives his name to some 'lond' (land) named after him (MS A, ed. by Bately, p. 20).

41 Banham, 'Anglo-Saxon Attitudes', p. 147.

42 ASC MS E (*s.a.* 605 recte 604), ed. by Irvine, pp. 22–23; trans. in *EHD*, p. 159. A version of this is added to MS A by a later hand (Hand 8 who was the main scribe of MS F, see *The Anglo-Saxon Chronicle: MS A*, ed. by Bately, p. xl). From the *Annales Cambriae* and other evidence, the Battle of Chester is likely to have taken place *c.* 615 (see Charles-Edwards, *Wales and the Britons*, pp. 345, 388–89; Higham, *An English Empire*, p. 78).

43 Bede, *HE*, II.2, ed. and trans. by Colgrave and Mynors, pp. 140–41.

44 Bede, *HE*, II.2, ed. and trans. by Colgrave and Mynors, pp. 142–43.

45 Higham, *(Re-)Reading Bede*, pp. 135–36.

46 ASC MS E (*s.a.* 605 recte 604), ed. by Irvine pp. 22–23; trans. in *EHD*, p. 159.

47 Rowley, *Old English Version*, pp. 1, 5, 44–46, 54–56: the text is in the Anglian dialect which supports a Mercian origin for the translator/adaptor (pp. 27, 37).

critical of the Britons, including those on the Pelagian heresy, St Germanus, and the first criticism of the Britons for not proselytizing the Angles and Saxons, while the account of the Easter controversy is significantly abbreviated.[48] Rowley argues that the view of the Britons has significantly changed because the translator uses the same phrase — 'troiscan wæle' (Trojan slaughter) — to describe attacks by a British and an English king, Cadwallon of Gwynedd and Cædwalla of Wessex respectively.[49] She does, though, comment that at 'no point' is the Old English version 'entirely sympathetic to, or uncritical of, the Britons'.[50] Negative remarks about the Britons are reduced but are still present in the Old English version, which may simply reflect the fact that the text very rarely adds to but often subtracts from Bede.[51]

Overall, there are multiple layers to the presentation of the Britons in the English corpus, across different genres of text. While the precise nature of how the Britons were culturally subsumed by the 'Anglo-Saxons' is debated,[52] the fact that it occurred is most relevant here. The height of criticism and disparagement of the Britons seems to have been in Bede's day: the earliest surviving records are potentially more forceful in their views. It is possible that at this time, a couple of centuries after the *adventus Saxonum*, the early English did not yet feel fully 'secure' on the island.[53] It was also perhaps easier to try to create a sense of English identity in opposition to something else. I have identified two specific instances, however, where the Chronicle is harsher than Bede in its treatment of the Britons, or at least focused on political and military triumph rather than ecclesiastical. English literary depictions of the Britons decreased thereafter. Indeed, by the tenth century the Britons had essentially faded from historical record[54] — or at least the people who had been Britons identified themselves using different terminology. They were no longer a threat. It has also been argued that the ninth-century Viking attacks created common feeling between the English and British.[55] This still did not lead to any recognition of shared heritage in terms of the presumed contributions of Britons to early English genealogies, given the presence of

---

48 Rowley, *Old English Version*, esp. p. 79; Molyneaux, 'The *Old English Bede*', p. 1304.

49 *The Old English Version of Bede's Ecclesiastical History*, ed. by Miller, I, p. 154 ('traiscan wæles'), II, p. 306. Rowley, *Old English Version*, pp. 92–93.

50 Rowley, *Old English Version*, p. 83.

51 See Molyneaux, 'The *Old English Bede*', pp. 1291, 1304, who also notes that some criticisms of the Irish are omitted as well.

52 For different models, see Dark, *Civitas to Kingdom*; Halsall, *Barbarian Migrations and the Roman West*; Higham, *Rome, Britain and the Anglo-Saxons*; Ward-Perkins, 'Why Did the Anglo-Saxons Not Become More British?'. A historiographical overview is provided by Higham, 'Britons in Anglo-Saxon England', and briefly by Woolf, 'Apartheid and Economics in Anglo-Saxon England', pp. 115–16.

53 Banham, 'Anglo-Saxon Attitudes', p. 148.

54 Banham, 'Anglo-Saxon Attitudes', p. 143.

55 Banham, 'Anglo-Saxon Attitudes', p. 153.

Brittonic names, notably Cerdic, ancestor of the West Saxon dynasty.[56] Some echoes of English attitudes to the Britons remained as allusive references in literary works, or were transferred to their Welsh relatives.

The Welsh

The Welsh 'emerged slowly from the parent Britons',[57] so it is unsurprising that some similarities in English attitudes towards both related groups are evident. Originally referring to all inhabitants of the part of Britain which had been controlled by the Romans, the Old English term *Wealas* ('Welsh') was eventually restricted, as English control grew, to the western regions where Brittonic languages were still spoken.[58] By the ninth century, when the extant corpus of Old English commences in earnest, there was evidently some need to differentiate between now distinct groups of *Wealas* — those in the south-west of modern England, particularly the Cornish (*Westwealas* 'the West Welsh'), those in what is now Wales (*Norðwealas* 'the North Welsh', being north of Cornwall), and the Strathclyde Welsh (*Strædcledwealas*) in Cumbria.[59] Sometimes this was done purely geographically, but occasionally the terms reflected some knowledge of what they called themselves.[60] This section focuses on the Welsh of Wales, with some discussion of the Strathclyde Welsh in the context of the Chronicle poem *Battle of Brunanburh*.

Inge Milfull and Katrin Thier observe that ethnonyms in Old English for the Celtic-speaking peoples 'all reflect a view of them as "The Other"', while acknowledging their complicated interactions.[61] This is particularly true of *Wealas* ('Welsh'). Cognates to this term can be found in other Germanic languages referring to speakers of Romance languages, but it is usually interpreted more generally in the sense 'foreigners', particularly those whose language could not be easily understood.[62] This sense of 'foreigner' is perhaps maintained in the Old English usage. Initially in English *wealh* seems to have denoted 'Roman'.[63] One such notable instance is in the poem *Widsith*: this archaic usage aligns with a pre–*adventus Saxonum* context and, it has been recently argued by Leonard Neidorf, therefore supports an early date for that text.[64] The fact that

---

56 See Ward-Perkins, 'Why Did the Anglo-Saxons Not Become More British?', p. 515.
57 Charles-Edwards, *Wales and the Britons*, p. 2.
58 Charles-Edwards, *Wales and the Britons*, pp. 205–06.
59 Milfull and Thier, 'Anglo-Saxon Perceptions of the Celtic Peoples', pp. 204–05; Charles-Edwards, *Wales and the Britons*, p. 2, n. 8.
60 Milfull and Thier, 'Anglo-Saxon Perceptions of the Celtic Peoples', p. 206.
61 Milfull and Thier, 'Anglo-Saxon Perceptions of the Celtic Peoples', p. 198.
62 Milfull and Thier, 'Anglo-Saxon Perceptions of the Celtic Peoples', pp. 204–05.
63 Woolf, 'Reporting Scotland in the Anglo-Saxon Chronicle', p. 232, citing examples from the Chronicle referring to Gallo-Romans and France.
64 Neidorf, 'Caesar's Wine and the Dating of *Widsith*', pp. 124–25.

this usage is exceptional might simply reflect that the term evolved to refer to Brittonic-speaking peoples. Alex Woolf notes that *wealh* 'is always used of peoples who had at one time been within the Roman Empire' but not of 'Gaels, Picts, Finns, Slavs, or other more exotic peoples'.[65] He therefore argues that the English used it to refer to the Romanized Brittonic-speaking population. Presumably, though, the Romanized connotations decreased over time as a linguistic difference would have been much easier to detect than the perceived degree of fifth-century *Romanitas*, particularly for less Romanized areas such as north Wales and Strathclyde.[66] By the tenth century, *wealh* could simply mean 'slave' without specifically denoting a Brittonic-speaker, a semantic shift that is likely to stem from the overlap between the two categories: that many Britons had been slaves.[67] The exceptional use of *wealh* in *Widsith* may partially be explained by later English writers wishing to avoid applying the term's servile connotations to the Roman Empire, perhaps because the English had come to associate themselves, instead of the Brittonic speakers, with Rome. Although British and Welsh identity owed a great deal to its Roman inheritance,[68] the early English subsumed 'Roman identity *into* early English identity' at least from the time of Alfred.[69] Thus, the very terminology used by the English for the Welsh, with its connotations of foreignness and servility, is indicative of an underlying attitude of superiority and antagonism.

Several English legal texts suggest that in their area of jurisdiction the Welsh had lower status than the English. The ninth-century Laws of Alfred append the earlier law code of Ine of Wessex, apparently from the late seventh century. Ine's law code gives the *wergild* ('man-price', the compensation paid to the relatives of a killing victim) for *wealas* (Welsh or perhaps Britons in this early context), all of which are significantly lower than the *wergild* accorded to West Saxons of equivalent rank, who also seem to have more inherent value whereas the standing of the *wealas* seems more to do with landholding in this text.[70] Though noting that rank not just origin was important, Alex Woolf suggests that this clear delineation between the two groups suggests that they could not have easily assumed each other's identities and that it was economically

---

65 Woolf, 'Reporting Scotland in the Anglo-Saxon Chronicle', p. 232; see also Woolf, 'British Ethnogenesis', p. 25. Endorsed by Bintley, 'Romans, Britons, and the Construction of "Anglo-Saxon" Identity', p. 31.

66 Woolf himself notes that the boundary between Romanized and not Romanized areas of Britain 'may not have been clear-cut' at the time ('British Ethnogenesis', p. 28), while awareness of the precise bounds of the empire are likely to have been less relevant as the centuries wore on.

67 Banham, 'Anglo-Saxon Attitudes', p. 150.

68 See Woolf, 'British Ethnogenesis', p. 25.

69 Bintley, 'Romans, Britons, and the Construction of "Anglo-Saxon" Identity', p. 49.

70 See Grimmer, 'Britons in Early Wessex', pp. 103–07; Lambert, *Law and Order*, pp. 73–74. Ward-Perkins notes that a lower *wergild* also means that 'the burden of proof required to incriminate' *wealas* was much lower too ('Why Did the Anglo-Saxons Not Become More British?', p. 524).

beneficial to the West Saxons to preserve this 'segregation'.[71] The regulations of the Guild of Thanes in Cambridge, contained in an eleventh-century document, likewise places varying *wergild* values on different groups: 'gyf se ofstlagena ceorl si twegen oran, gif he Wylisc si, anne oran' (if the slain man is a *ceorl*, two ores; if he is servile (or Welsh?), one ore).[72] At this date it is unclear whether this is intended to refer to the Welsh, foreigners generally, or slaves,[73] but the negative associations remain.

A few of the Exeter Book Riddles refer to the *swearte Wealas* ('dark Welsh' or 'swarthy Welsh'). The manuscript dates to the tenth century, but the majority of the riddles are assumed to have an earlier date on the grounds of language and metre.[74] Drawing on critical race theory, Coral Lumbley argues that the motif of the 'dark Welsh', emphasizing dark hair and comparatively dark skin, suggests that the Welsh were racialized in Old English and Anglo-Latin tradition as part of a hierarchy of different peoples.[75] For example, Riddle 12 centres on an overtly sexualized image of a 'wonfeax wale' (dark-haired slave, l. 8), a phrasing which seems pejorative, like *swearte Wealas*.[76] This is suggestive of master-slave sexual relationships.[77] According to Lumbley 'the dark Welsh body is consumed by the reader as the fantasy of raced, Welsh sexual servility is offered up to the Anglo-Saxon reader or listener'.[78] Riddle 12's sexual theme may also be connected to the suggestive nature of quite a few riddles, although this one is more explicit than most. The Welsh slaves in Riddles 52 and 72 have usually been seen as herding cattle, since in daily life they would have performed such agricultural labour. Lindy Brady's reinterpretation of these riddles has the dark Welsh holding other humans captive, therefore 'illuminating the contradictory roles played by the Welsh as both victims and perpetrators of the slave trade in Anglo-Saxon England'.[79] While this is an important note of complexity, for current purposes it should

---

71   Woolf, 'Apartheid and Economics in Anglo-Saxon England', pp. 127–28.

72   *Diplomatarium Anglicum Ævi Saxonicum*, ed. by Thorpe, p. 612; trans. in *EHD*, p. 604.

73   *EHD*, p. 603; Lambert, *Law and Order*, pp. 228–29, follows Whitelock's translation and does not comment on this aspect. Brady, 'Echoes of Britons on a Fenland Frontier', pp. 680–81, maintains that this does refer to Brittonic speakers.

74   See Fulk, *A History of Old English Meter*, pp. 404–40; and Neidorf, 'Lexical Evidence for the Relative Chronology', p. 39, both of whom place most of the Exeter Book Riddles very early, in the eighth century. For a recent argument that they are roughly contemporary with the Exeter Book, see Niles, *God's Exiles and English Verse*. Exeter Riddles are numbered following *ASPR*.

75   Lumbley, 'The "Dark Welsh"', pp. 2–3, 10. This draws on arguments by Geraldine Heng (*The Invention of Race*, esp. p. 25).

76   Bintley, 'Romans, Britons, and the Construction of "Anglo-Saxon" Identity', pp. 46–47, and references therein.

77   Indeed, this dynamic within the riddle has even been interpreted in the context of voyeurism and leather fetishism (Rulon-Miller, 'Sexual Humor and Fettered Desire', pp. 124–25).

78   Lumbley, 'The "Dark Welsh"', p. 4.

79   Brady, 'The "Dark Welsh" as Slaves and Slave Traders', p. 251.

be noted that the depiction of the Welsh as selling their own people into slavery is not much more complimentary than a servile one.

Assessing English attitudes to the Welsh is hampered by the lack of material from the kingdom of Mercia and a lack of contemporary sources between Bede in the early eighth century, focusing on Kent and Northumbria, and the compilation of the Anglo-Saxon Chronicle, focusing on Wessex, in the late ninth century.[80] It has been noted in particular that the reign of Offa, king of Mercia (r. 757–796), is ill-served by historical sources.[81] Thus, the attitudes of the Mercians to their neighbours, the Welsh, cannot be reconstructed. Indeed, the very name 'Mercian' (Old English *Mierce*) means 'dwellers on the march', probably referring to the kingdom's position on the border with the Britons or the Welsh.[82] One assumes that sources from a Mercian perspective would have treated the Welsh and Anglo-Welsh relations in greater detail. While Offa's Dyke is well known, the earliest reference to it is in Asser's *Life of King Alfred* from the late ninth century: Offa 'universis circa se regibus & regionibus finitmus formidolosus [...] vallum magnum inter Britanniam atque Merciam [...] facere imperavit' (terrified all the neighbouring kings and provinces [...] had a great dyke built between Wales and Mercia).[83] It is only on the basis of Asser's account that the earthwork is associated with the powerful Mercian king.[84] There is therefore little context for its construction. Creating a less permeable boundary, its aim was presumably to defend Mercia against the Welsh.[85]

Alfred's more conciliatory policies towards the Welsh may have impacted their presentation in works from his reign. One of a number of scholars invited to Alfred's court was the Welshman Asser, who would write the king's biography, suggesting a more inclusive, welcoming attitude to the Welsh. Asser's *Life of King Alfred* records that one Welsh king visited Alfred's court where he was treated hospitably: Anarawd ap Rhodri, king of Gwynedd. He was 'in filium confirmationis acceptus' (accepted as a son in confirmation) by Alfred and 'regis dominio cum omnibus suis [...] subdidit' (subjected himself with all his people to King Alfred's lordship).[86] As is the case here, standing sponsor at a less powerful ally's baptism or confirmation put the sponsor or 'godfather' in the superior position over the subordinate: it symbolically

---

80 See Keynes, 'The Kingdom of the Mercians in the Eighth Century', pp. 1, 19. Charles-Edwards notes the difficulty in establishing a narrative for Welsh history between Penda and Mercia's absorption into the English polity ('Wales and Mercia', p. 89).

81 Keynes, 'Changing Faces', p. 14; Sisam, *Studies in the History of Old English Literature*, p. 133.

82 Brooks, 'The Formation of the Mercian Kingdom', pp. 160, 162.

83 *Annales Rerum Gestarum Ælfredi Magni, auctore Asserio Menevensi* (ch. 14), ed. by Wise, p. 10; *Alfred the Great*, trans. by Keynes and Lapidge, p. 71.

84 Williams, 'Offa's Dyke', p. 35.

85 Charles-Edwards, *Wales and the Britons*, p. 27, see also pp. 419–24.

86 *Annales Rerum Gestarum Ælfredi Magni, auctore Asserio Menevensi* (ch. 80), ed. by Wise, p. 50; *Alfred the Great*, trans. by Keynes and Lapidge, p. 96.

equated to taking political submission.[87] Of course, Asser's own Welsh origin must be remembered. It has also been argued that the intended audience for Asser's *Life of King Alfred* was the Welsh, to make them more amenable to West Saxon dominance.[88] Indeed, the growing power of Mercia and of the sons of Rhodri Mawr, king of Gwynedd, threatened the southern Welsh kings, driving them into the arms of Wessex.[89] One could also note that it is not so much Anarawd who is described positively, but Alfred's reception of him, in which he is shown bestowing 'maximis donis' (extravagant gifts) and offering rulers — Welsh or otherwise — 'amorem & tutelam ac defensionem' (support, protection and defense).[90]

With its strong West Saxon bias, the Anglo-Saxon Chronicle in its entirety does not have a great deal to say about Wales and its inhabitants, in contrast to the *Wealas* or *Brytwealas* (i.e. Britons in the more general sense) who are frequently mentioned in earlier sections of the Chronicle as opponents of the Saxons. Often, the Welsh are presented as the victims of Viking raids,[91] while on one occasion the West Welsh or Cornish collaborate with the Danes or Vikings.[92] Most other references attest to English military and political superiority over the Welsh. The earliest reference to the Welsh is that Egbert, king of the West Saxons, 'he hie to eaþmodre hersumnesse gedyde' (reduced them all to humble submission to him).[93] In 853 we are told that Burgred, king of the Mercians, asked for the help of Æthelwulf, king of the West Saxons, to subject the Welsh and 'hie him alle gehiersume dydon' (they made them all submissive to him).[94] In the political climate of Alfred's day this statement seems motivated to show a previous alliance between Wessex and Mercia,

---

87 *Alfred the Great*, trans. by Keynes and Lapidge, p. 249; Charles-Edwards, 'Alliances, Godfathers, Treaties and Boundaries', p. 56; for examples involving English kings and Scandinavians, see Ellis, 'Reassessing the Career of Óláfr Tryggvason', p. 63.

88 See *Alfred the Great*, trans. by Keynes and Lapidge, p. 56. Thomas and Callander argue that Asser may not have aimed his work at the Welsh alone, but that 'a Welsh audience was one of (possibly) several Asser may have envisaged' ('Reading Asser in Early Medieval Wales', p. 133).

89 Charles-Edwards, 'Wales and Mercia', p. 102.

90 *Annales Rerum Gestarum Ælfredi Magni, auctore Asserio Menevensi* (chs. 80, 81), ed. by Wise, p. 50; *Alfred the Great*, trans. by Keynes and Lapidge, p. 96. Keynes and Lapidge note that this tricolon (probably deliberately) reflects the technical terminology of alliances (*Alfred the Great*, pp. 263–64).

91 ASC 894 (895 C, D); 914 (917 A; 915 C, D); CDE 997.

92 The West Welsh or Cornish combine with the Vikings to fight against Egbert of Wessex in ASC ABCDE *s.a.* 835 (recte 838). In contrast, see ASC ABCD 893 (*s.a.* 894 in CD) when 'sum dæl þæs Norðweallcynnes' (MS C, ed. by O'Brien O'Keeffe; 'some portion of the Welsh people', trans. in *EHD*, p. 204) contribute to efforts coordinated by ealdormen and thegns to defeat a Danish army on the bank of the Severn.

93 ASC 830, MS A (*s.a.* 828), ed. by Bately, p. 42; trans. in *EHD*, p. 186.

94 ASC 853, MS A, ed. by Bately, p. 45; trans. in *EHD*, p. 189. The use of plural 'dydon' (they made) is important, as in MSS B and C the verb is singular, presumably referring to Burgred alone, whereas A (the pro-West-Saxon Winchester Chronicle) gives Æthelwulf a greater, or even equal, role. See also Anlezark, 'Wessex and the Welsh'.

especially as the rest of the entry concerns Alfred himself being sent to the pope in Rome. When Edward the Elder takes over Mercia on Æthelflæd's death it is related that 'þa cyningas on Norþwealum, Howel 7 Cledauc 7 Ieoþwel, 7 eall Norþwealcyn hine sohton him to hlaforde' (the kings in Wales, Hywel, Clydog and Idwal, and all the race of the Welsh, sought to have him as lord).[95] Again, the Welsh are perhaps incidental to the dynamics between Wessex and Mercia, as Wessex takes over Mercia's previous role as the dominant kingdom. In 927 when Æthelstan added the kingdom of Northumbria to his existing rule over the rest of England, 'ealle þa cyngas þe on þyssum iglande wæron he gewylde, ærest Huwal Westwala cyning, 7 Cosstantin Scotta cyning, 7 Uwen Wenta cyning, 7 Ealdred Eadulfing from Bebbanbyrig' (he brought under his rule all the kings who were in this island: first Hywel, king of the West Welsh, and Constantine, king of the Scots, and Owain, king of the people of Gwent, and Ealdred, son of Eadwulf from Bamburgh).[96] This established Æthelstan as the premier king of all Britain, at least in English (or perhaps West Saxon and Mercian) eyes.

The Battle of Brunanburh, discussed in detail in Paul Cavill's chapter in this volume, records Æthelstan's victory over his Scottish, Hiberno-Scandinavian, and Strathclyde Welsh opponents. This poem is recorded in the Anglo-Saxon Chronicle for the year 937 and is particularly striking as the first of a group of Chronicle poems.[97] The Mercians and West Saxons are presented as a united front in the poem, countering their enemies together.[98] This is reminiscent of the Chronicle's emphasis on Æthelwulf's assistance to Burgred in subjecting the Welsh. The Strathclyde Welsh barely feature in the poem in comparison to the other foes. At the poem's close, the comment that the Angles and Saxons 'begeatan' (won, l. 73b) Britain ties the victory at Brunanburh into a grander trajectory of territorial and ethnic domination.[99] The incoming Germanic-speaking groups 'Weealles ofercoman' (overcame the Welsh, l. 72b);[100] the use of this ethnonym, rather than 'Bryttas' (Britons), helps to suggest continuity of English superiority over the current inhabitants of Britain, not just over an already subsumed group within England. Michael Bintley describes the poem at this point as 'revelling in the scale of the slaughter'.[101] The lack of reference to the Strathclyde Welsh in the poem might be accounted for because they were deemed the junior partner in an alliance with the Scottish kingdom.

---

95 ASC 918 (at one point altered to 921 and 922), MS A, ed. by Bately p. 69; trans. in *EHD*, p. 216. Hywel Dda and Clydog were sons of Cadell ap Rhodri Mawr and ruled in south Wales, while Idwal Foel ab Anarawd ruled the northern kingdom of Gwynedd. This is not included in the 'Mercian register', which spends more time lamenting the death of Æthelflæd.

96 ASC 926, MS D, ed. by Cubbin p. 41; trans. in *EHD*, p. 218.

97 For further discussion of these poems, see the chapters by Daniel Thomas, Francis Leneghan, and Paul Cavill in this volume.

98 See Foot, 'Where English Becomes British', pp. 131, 134, 137.

99 ASC MS A, ed. by Bately, p. 72.

100 ASC MS A, ed. by Bately, p. 72.

101 Bintley, 'Romans, Britons, and the Construction of "Anglo-Saxon" Identity', p. 34.

It is possible that Owain, king of the Strathclyde Welsh, had also been omitted from the list of kings in the Anglo-Saxon Chronicle who were present at Eamont.[102] Yet, as Tyler comments, the poem's close implies that the Welsh had already been conquered centuries previously; thereby it 'insists on the subjugation of the Welsh' and, drawing on Bede's *Ecclesiastical History*, 'seeks to efface the earlier Britons from history'.[103]

While the tenth century saw the West Saxon dynasty's increased dominance over the island of Britain, the eleventh century saw alliances between different English factions and Welsh rulers, particularly in the 1040s and 1050s.[104] The different versions of the Anglo-Saxon Chronicle favour different groups, either the Godwinsons or the earls of Mercia, to various extents.[105] It could therefore be argued that the increasing interest in recording Welsh affairs only extended to their connection to internal English squabbles, namely between two powerful aristocratic houses. The alliance of the earls of Mercia, particularly Ælfgar, and Gruffudd ap Llywelyn formed a military and political force to be reckoned with.[106] The death in 1063 of Gruffudd, who was initially king of Gwynedd and Powys but could claim to be king of Wales from the mid-1050s, receives attention from the Chronicle. In MS E, which leans towards the Godwinsons, the defeated Welsh people 'brohton Harolde his heafod, 7 he sette oþerne cyng þærto' (brought Harold his head, and he appointed another king there).[107] MS D, which is more neutral in its recounting of English affairs, gives a greater role to the English king Edward the Confessor, who appoints Gruffudd's brothers to succeed to his lands and received Gruffudd's head and ship's figurehead from Harold.[108] As well as the English military victory and political control through hostages, the Welsh king's head being presented to the English by his own subjects is a powerful symbol of subjugation.[109] Nevertheless, there is nothing particular negative in the D Chronicler's depiction of Gruffudd himself.

The majority of English references to the Welsh appear in a political context, usually demonstrating the superiority of the West Saxon dynasty over Wales

---

102 It seems likely this is the same meeting as the one William of Malmesbury describes, where Owain of Strathclyde is present (William of Malmesbury, *Gesta Regum Anglorum*, II.134, ed. by Mynors, Thomson, and Winterbottom, I, pp. 214–15). This might be a replacement for the Owain the Chronicle assigned to Gwent (Edmonds, 'The Emergence and Transformation of Medieval Cumbria', p. 203). Charles-Edwards argues that both Owains were at Eamont (*Wales and the Britons*, pp. 511–12). The last reference in the Anglo-Saxon Chronicle to Strathclyde is 920 (just in A, *s.a.* 923) when Edward the Elder takes submissions of various kings, including of the Strathclyde Welsh, as discussed below. The next relevant reference, in 945, is to Cumberland.

103 Tyler, 'England between Empire and Nation', p. 175.

104 For the eleventh-century political context, see Thomas, 'The View from Wales'.

105 Brady, *Writing the Welsh Borderland*, p. 116.

106 Brady, *Writing the Welsh Borderland*, p. 120.

107 ASC 1063, MS E, ed. by Irvine, p. 86.

108 ASC 1063, MS D, ed. by Cubbin, p. 77.

109 Brady, *Writing the Welsh Borderland*, pp. 121–22.

as well as England. This does include diplomatic relations between Welsh and West Saxon kings. It is worth noting, though, that 'cooperation is not the same as equality', as Molyneaux puts it.[110] Likewise, interest in Wales in these sources extends little beyond these instances of cooperation and control. The depiction of the Welsh in the Riddles stands apart from the other references discussed here. The literary genre of the riddle naturally focusses on everyday life, on such activities as the herding of cattle, or on social relations and hierarchies, including sexual encounters, rather than on high-level political manoeuvrings and battles between nations. The Exeter Riddles certainly demonstrate some racial attitudes and stereotypes, but it is difficult to generalise from these literary texts or use them to reconstruct the actual attitudes of early medieval English people towards speakers of Welsh living among them.

The Picts and the Scots

There is less evidence of early English attitudes to the Scots than to the Welsh. Indeed, Lindy Brady notes that in comparison to her study area of the Anglo-Welsh border, there is not much material on the Anglo-Scottish border until the Norman period.[111] This is because of the general lack of sources from northern England, with the notable exception of the Northumbrian Bede. Clearly several seventh-century Northumbrian kings were quite involved with Dál Riata and Pictland, but Bede is relatively uninterested in the details.[112] The lack of northern English sources is particularly stark in comparison to the more distant Wessex. Alfred is particularly well represented in the surviving sources; a biography about Æthelstan or Edgar might have contained more material about the Scots.[113] The Anglo-Saxon Chronicle also has a bias towards southern and central England.[114] Events in this region are only patchily recorded, but furthermore, the attitudes towards the Scots held by their nearest neighbours are also somewhat lacking. The so-called 'Northern Recension' of the Anglo-Saxon Chronicle is lost, though recensions D and E (and in turn F) draw on it; but, even then, Pauline Stafford notes that it would

---

110 Molyneaux, 'Why Were Some Tenth-Century English Kings Presented as Rulers of Britain?', p. 69.

111 Brady, *Writing the Welsh Borderland*, p. 8.

112 The exile of the sons of Æthelfrith, notably Oswald and Oswiu, with the Picts and Scots is relevant to Bede in terms of their exposure to Christianity and the course of Northumbrian politics (*HE*, III.1, ed. and trans. by Colgrave and Mynors, pp. 212–15) and for the context of Aidan of Lindisfarne's invitation to Northumbria (*HE*, III.3, ed. and trans. by Colgrave and Mynors, pp. 218–21). Scholars are reliant on other sources to piece together a fuller picture of their exile: for the wider context of Northumbria's contacts, see Ziegler, 'The Politics of Exile in Early Northumbria', and references therein.

113 It is possible that William of Malmesbury had access to a now lost life of Æthelstan: see Wood, 'The Making of King Aethelstan's Empire', pp. 265–66; Firth, 'Constructing a King', pp. 71–72.

114 For example, Woolf notes that 'northern affairs are notably absent from the late tenth-century sections of the southern versions of the Chronicle' (Woolf, 'Reporting Scotland in the Anglo-Saxon Chronicle', p. 229).

have been 'ambiguously Northern', like the southern-approved archbishops of York, with whom it was linked.[115]

The Picts, the Brittonic-speaking inhabitants of modern Scotland, are famously ill-served by surviving written evidence, as they were subsumed into the new kingdom of Alba by 900.[116] The other major group in what is now Scotland were the Gaels of Scottish Dál Riata, but it can be difficult to differentiate them from the Irish of Ireland as they were initially considered the same people and in some earlier sources *Scotti* was usually used to mean Irish of Ireland rather than of Scotland.[117] The kingdom of the Scots, which gradually coalesced from Alba and surrounding regions, was thus a recent grouping or national identity for English sources to deal with.

Bede links the Britons and Picts, through the mouthpiece of Wilfrid, as being similar in character: with regards to the dating of Easter 'hos tantum et obstinationis oerum conplices, Pictos dico et Brettones, [...] contra totum orbem stulto labore pugnant' (these men and their accomplices in obstinacy, I mean the Picts and the Britons [...], foolishly attempt to fight against the whole world).[118] The Picts, along with the Irish, are arguably presented as being bolder or militarily superior to the Britons: the Britons 'subito duabus gentibus transmarainis uehementer saeuis [...] multos stupet' (were rapidly reduced to a state of terror and misery by two extremely fierce races from over the waters).[119] At a later stage, 'Saxones Pictique bellum aduersum Brettones iunctis uiribus susceperunt' (the Saxons and Picts had joined forces and were making war upon the Britons), suggesting at least temporary cooperation.[120] Bede also criticizes Ecgfrith of Northumbria for his attacks on the Picts and the Irish against the advice of leading churchmen, for example: 'cum temere exercitum ad uastandam Pictorum prouinciam duxisset, multum prohibentibus amicis et maxime beatae memoriae Cudbercto' (he rashly sent an army to ravage the kingdom of the Picts, against the urgent advice of his friends and particularly of Cuthbert of blessed memory).[121] This ill-conceived raid led to the death of the king and most of his forces when 'introductus est simulantibus fugam hostibus | in angustias inaccessorum montium' (the enemy feigned flight and lured [him] into some narrow passes in the midst of inaccessible

---

115 Stafford, *After Alfred*, pp. 106, 124–30, at p. 124. In MS D this northern voice does not emerge until the annals dated after 1066 (Stafford, *After Alfred*, pp. 264–65).

116 The first reference in the *Annals of Ulster* to a king of Alba, rather than king of the Picts (which last appears in 878), is in 900: 'Domnall m. Causantin, ri Alban, moritur' (Domnall son of Constantín, king of Alba, dies) (*The Annals of Ulster* 900.6, ed. by Mac Airt and Mac Niocaill, p. 350; my translation).

117 See Milfull and Thier, 'Anglo-Saxon Perceptions of the Celtic Peoples', p. 215. For example, the Anglo-Saxon Chronicle entry for 891 relates that 'þrie Scottas' (three Scots) came to Alfred's court 'of Hibernia' (from Ireland) (MS A, ed. by Bately, p. 54).

118 Bede, *HE*, III.25, ed. and trans. by Colgrave and Mynors, pp. 300–301.

119 Bede, *HE*, I.12, ed. and trans. by Colgrave and Mynors, pp. 40–41.

120 Bede, *HE*, I.20, ed. and trans. by Colgrave and Mynors, pp. 62–63.

121 Bede, *HE*, IV.26, ed. and trans. by Colgrave and Mynors, pp. 428–29.

mountains).[122] In Bede's account, the Pictish victory is due to sleight of hand and an ambush, rather than superior prowess. As with Bede's descriptions of the Britons, they operate in an inhospitable landscape. Bede's criticism of Ecgfrith, and indeed his account of this whole episode, is more concerned with good kingship, in particular the importance of not imperilling one's own kingdom, and with heeding the advice of churchmen, than it is with the Picts themselves.[123] The remaining references to the Picts in Bede's text are primarily ecclesiastical in nature, which is hardly surprising given the work's focus.[124] One of these references contains a positive depiction of Nechtan, king of the Picts, because 'admonitus ecclesiasticarum frequenti mediatione scripturarum' (having been convinced by his assiduous study of ecclesiastical writings), he met Bede's approval by switching to the Roman method of Easter calculation.[125]

Some similar patterns, and reasons for mentioning the Picts, can be detected in the Anglo-Saxon Chronicle. In some versions of the Chronicle the defeat of the Picts by the Romans is recorded alongside that of the Britons.[126] After the Roman withdrawal, the Picts are then described as attacking the Britons, but they also serve as a means for the Angles and Saxons to prove themselves as the superior fighting force.[127] Other than their conversion at the hands of Colum Cille/Columba, abbot of Iona, there are scattered references to the English fighting against the Picts.[128] As observed of the Britons previously, while the English leaders of these conflicts are named, the Pictish ones are not.

There are few references to the Scots in the Anglo-Saxon Chronicle. Most of these are in context of showing West Saxon or English domination of the island of Britain. For example, in 920 Edward the Elder travelled to Nottingham and the Peak District, adding manned fortifications there,[129] which might reveal a concern for northern affairs in terms of its control from the south and its defence from further north. This is the only context given for the significant statement that

> hine geces þa to fæder 7 to hlaforde Scotta cyning 7 eall Scotta þeod, 7 Rægnald 7 Eadulfes suna 7 ealle þa þe on Norþhymbrum bugeaþ, aegþer ge Englisce ge Denisce ge Norþmen ge oþre, 7 each Stræcledweala cyning 7 ealle Stræcledwealas.

---

122 Bede, *HE*, IV.26, ed. and trans. by Colgrave and Mynors, pp. 428–29.

123 See Leneghan, *The Dynastic Drama of 'Beowulf'*, pp. 225–27, comparing this with *Beowulf*.

124 For example, Bede, *HE*, III.3–4 (ed. and trans. by Colgrave and Mynors, pp. 220–23), IV.3 (ed. and trans. by Colgrave and Mynors, pp. 336–37).

125 Bede, *HE*, V.21, ed. and trans. by Colgrave and Mynors, pp. 532–33.

126 ASC 47 D and E but not ABC.

127 ASC 449 E.

128 It is recorded that in 565 that Columba converted the Picts and in 710 that Ealdorman Brihtferth battled the Picts, which is the penultimate reference to the Picts in the Chronicle, with the final being a mention in 875 alongside the Strathclyde Welsh.

129 ASC 920 (923 A).

(the king of the Scots and all the people of the Scots, and Ragnald, and the sons of Eadwulf and all who live in Northumbria, both English and Danish, Norsemen and others, and also the king of the Strathclyde Welsh and all the Strathclyde Welsh, chose him as father and lord.)[130]

Here, Edward's dominance over all northern Britain is claimed. This passage is only in recension A of the Chronicle, the Winchester (or Parker) chronicle which glorifies Wessex. Constantine, king of Scots, is included in the list of kings who submitted to Æthelstan at Eamont in 927, but just a few years later we are told that Æthelstan 'in on Scotland, aegþer ge mid landhere ge mid scyphere, 7 his micel oferhergade' (went into Scotland with both a land force and a naval force, and ravaged much of it).[131] On Eadred's succession it is related that he 'gerad eall Norðhymbra land him to gewealde, 7 Scottas him aþas sealdon þæt hi eall woldon þæt he wolde' (immediately reduced all Northumbria under his rule; and the Scots swore oaths to him that they would agree to all that he wanted).[132] The Scots apparently kowtowing to the English king's every whim seems more derogatory even than the pledges at Eamont. The core of the Anglo-Saxon Chronicles arose from the royal household, so it is no surprise that such entries would be complimentary to the West Saxon kings, while simultaneously downplaying the authority of rival insular rulers.[133] In both chronicle entries, influence over Scotland seems to go hand in hand with control over Northumbria, as elsewhere influence over Wales seems to go hand in hand with control over Mercia. Little interest is shown in Scottish affairs for their own sake.

The Battle of Brunanburh might seem the obvious place to look for evidence of how the English perceived their neighbours, as it exults Æthelstan and records a great defeat of his Scottish, Hiberno-Scandinavian, and Strathclyde Welsh opponents. The poem's very inclusion in the Chronicle shows how significant this event was perceived to be by Æthelstan's court. According to Elizabeth Tyler, Brunanburh 'reveals the imperial origins of the writing that has come to constitute "national" English literature'.[134] However, there is nothing overtly negative about the Scottish and Strathclyde Welsh forces in the poem. Brunanburh may simply focus on English military victory over their opponents rather than any cultural superiority. It is perhaps more disparaging about the Hiberno-Scandinavians returning to Dublin 'æwiscmode' (humiliated, l. 56b), as 'dreorig daraða laf' (sad left-overs of spears, l. 54a).[135] There is a parallel to the shameful flight of the sons of Odda in the later Battle of Maldon (ll. 185–97).[136]

---

130 ASC MS A (*s.a.* 920 recte 923), ed. by Bately, p. 69.
131 ASC MS A (*s.a.* 934 recte 933), ed. by Bately, p. 70.
132 ASC 946 ABCD (948 E), MS C, ed. by O'Brien O'Keeffe, p. 44.
133 Brooks, 'Why Is the *Anglo-Saxon Chronicle* about Kings?', esp. p. 62.
134 Tyler, 'England between Empire and Nation', p. 167.
135 ASC 973, MS A, ed. by Bately, p. 72.
136 See Atherton, *The Battle of Maldon*, pp. 38–39.

It might appear a standard battle description of the vanquished, but it is more reminiscent of — and perhaps derives from — Old Norse skaldic poetry, 'whose taste for violence and triumphalism is unparalleled', as Tyler observes, in Old English until *Brunanburh*.[137] The gory details of the vanquished thus mark it out. Further, Tyler notes the innovation in this being the earliest surviving heroic verse in Old English praising a contemporary, rather than legendary, leader and that it draws on Latin verse praising Carolingian emperors, as well as Norse skaldic verse.[138] The King of Scots, whose age is emphasized, survives the defeat but 'his sunu forlet [...] giungne' (left his young son, ll. 42b/44a) dead on the battlefield,[139] reflecting the idea of a new order being established by 'afaran Eadweardes' (the sons of Edward).[140] Constantine is described both as 'har hildering' (the hoary-haired warrior, l. 39a) and 'beorn blandenfeax [...] eald inwidda' (grey-haired warrior, the old, evil one, ll. 45a/46a),[141] with the repetition hammering this point home, rather than any grudging respect for his bravery or martial abilities. The vigour and vitality of the West Saxon dynasty is contrasted to the defeated Scots, whose decrepit king has been deprived of an heir.[142] Old age in Old English poetry, particularly *Beowulf*, is often associated with grief and loss, although ageing warriors, such as Ongentheow, king of the Swedes, may still be portrayed as active combatants.[143] Though the poem does not overtly insult the Scots, it perhaps hints that the English future is brighter than the Scottish one.

Overall, there is relatively little available material to appraise English attitudes to the Scots. There are, nevertheless, traces of negative depictions of the inhabitants of Scotland, including tapping into the generic tropes which can be seen before and after this period. Bede's description of the Picts in their inaccessible mountains has resonances with his account of the Britons. The only positive portrayal was Bede's of Nechtan for choosing the correct side in the Easter controversy. Other references to the Scots are designed to prove the dominance of the West Saxon dynasty. This contrasts to the Irish annals which records Scottish events, such as the deaths of kings, even when they do not touch directly on Ireland.[144] While in the early period the Picts are treated like the Britons, later English representations of the emergent kingdom of the Scots are somewhat less prevalent and less well developed than representations of the Welsh.

---

137 Tyler, 'England between Empire and Nation', p. 173. Tyler does not mention *Egils saga* in this context. Paul Cavill in this volume does compare *Brunanburh* to Egill's *Hǫfuðlausn*.

138 Tyler, 'England between Empire and Nation', p. 173.

139 ASC MS A, ed. by Bately, p. 71.

140 This is used on two occasions in the poem: MS A, ed. by Bately, pp. 70 and 72.

141 ASC MS A, ed. by Bately, p. 71. *Hildering* usually emended to *hilderinc*.

142 Constantine had one other son, Indulf, who would become king after Mael Coluim I.

143 Porck, *Old Age in Early Medieval England*, pp. 83, 164–66.

144 This remains true beyond the early Ionan phase of compilation. See Evans, *The Present and the Past*, pp. 1, 112–13, 208–13, 223.

Conclusions

This examination reveals that early medieval English attitudes to their immediate neighbours within the island of Britain changed considerably over the period, often serving a particular and contextually specific purpose within politically minded sources. Indeed, this variety of perspectives is suggestive of familiarity and the range of contacts that the English had with Celtic-speaking peoples: in contrast to exoticized portrayals of the East, those insular peoples whom the English encountered most regularly could not be reduced to literary tropes or singular depictions. Nevertheless, a few common threads emerge. The Britons, Welsh, Picts, and Scots are often presented in English sources as being cowardly or ineffective in warfare and as living on the margins, in inhospitable landscapes. The centrality of Christianity to these ideas is common across the period (particularly its first half), either in Bede's and the Chronicle's justification of the treatment of those who did not conform, or in having the Britons as demons battling the saintly Guthlac. Meanwhile the West Saxon kings used their apparent defence of Christianity and sponsoring of confirmations as means to demonstrate their own political superiority over their neighbours. It is also worth noting the lack of complimentary depictions of Celtic speakers in English sources. This investigation has not uncovered any truly positive references to the Britons, Welsh, or Scots with the exception of Bede's praise for one Pictish individual, King Nechtan, on the basis of his conforming to English ecclesiastical practice. The work of Asser, himself a Welshman, might be expected to be more positive about his own countrymen, but, even then, the real praise is reserved for the author's patron, Alfred.

In terms of chronology, some general fluctuations can be detected. The earliest major surviving text, that of Bede, is one of the most disparaging about the Britons. It seems that at the beginning of the period, from the seventh century, there was a more singular attitude to the *Bryttas* and *Wealas*: they were 'the foreigners', who spoke unintelligibly. Indeed, a cognate 'Kauderwelsch' is still used in modern German to mean 'nonsense talk'. The depiction of the Britons in Felix's *Life of St Guthlac*, another early text, highlights this very aspect. As Bintley notes, the British speech of the demons 'is a horror to be silenced' by Guthlac, which, in the long run, is also effectively what happened to the Brittonic language in England.[145] These findings support an early date for the Riddles (or at least for those discussed here), as the racialized, sexualized representation of the 'dark Welsh' fits this context better than the latter end of the period. When the Britons were no longer a threat — well before Alfred's day — there is a decline in references to them in English sources, with the exception of the Chronicle looking back to their defeat. There are fewer examples of negative portrayals of Celtic speakers from the ninth century

---

145 Bintley, 'Romans, Britons, and the Construction of "Anglo-Saxon" Identity', p. 48.

onwards perhaps due to the distracting presence of Scandinavians or Vikings who filled the role of the barbarian 'other'. Alfred had few English allies to turn to, which might partially explain his more conciliatory attitude to the Welsh. This wider situation created a relationship between the English and their Brittonic-speaking neighbours peculiar to the early 890s.[146] As the ambitions of English kings increased in the tenth and eleventh centuries, there is a greater emphasis on their political domination of insular neighbours. While relatively tolerant and dismissive attitudes towards Celtic-speakers coexisted, there were peaks and troughs: Bede's antipathy to the Britons was followed by Alfredian conciliation, rising to English self-confidence in Æthelstan's time, as notably seen in *Brunanburh*. The eleventh-century Chronicle entries deal with greater complexity in Anglo-Welsh relations with a tone of detachment.

This chapter has identified challenges in assessing how the early medieval English viewed their neighbours, notably due to the comparative lack of sources from Mercian and Northumbrian perspectives. Regardless, in the entire corpus of pre-Conquest English sources there are relatively few references to the Celtic-speaking peoples, and many of these are quite terse. There are glimpses of stereotyped English portrayals of neighbouring peoples that must have been well known enough to be referred to fairly obliquely, and presumably contributed to the overall entertainment of the Riddles. Though Celtic speakers play a role in the historical narrative of major sources, the extant depictions of them can be quite perfunctory. While the Britons are important in the story of the *adventus Saxonum*, little detail is given about them, their leaders, and their polities. While the record is not as stark for the Welsh and Scots, they are only mentioned in the Chronicle when connected to English affairs, usually submitting or being defeated; the Chronicle very rarely includes obits of kings of non-English kingdoms, thus comparing unfavourably with the Irish annals. In contrast, for example, the Chronicle frequently includes information on popes.[147] While on occasion this English neglect of their insular neighbours might be down to ignorance, it also displays a lack of interest. Woolf noted that the Chronicle's use of terminology for peoples and kingdoms broadly corresponded with the Irish annals, which would suggest a degree of knowledge, but that the West Saxon MS A of the Chronicle was only interested in northern affairs due to the presence of the Viking Great Army, which would suggest indifference.[148]

When this lack of interest leads to lack of detail and vagueness in English representations of their insular neighbours, it arguably extends to erasure and exclusion. Bede and the Chronicle in particular frequently reduce the Britons to faceless enemies. In later sections of the Chronicle Celtic speakers are still often nameless subordinates. For instance, the account of Edgar in

---

146 Anlezark, 'Wessex and the Welsh'.
147 See Stafford, *After Alfred*, pp. 41 n. 5, 150, 154, 289.
148 Woolf, 'Reporting Scotland in the Anglo-Saxon Chronicle', p. 225.

973 being met at Chester by other rulers from the island of Britain does not specify their names: 'þær him coman ongean .vi. cyningas, 7 ealle wið hine getreowsodon þæt hi woldon efenwyrhtan beon on sæ 7 on lande' (six kings came to meet him, and all gave him pledges that they would be his allies on sea and on land).[149] In this instance, it does not matter who the kings actually were, or even which kingdom they ruled, just that they submitted to the English king, and how many there were to heighten his achievement. It has been noted that the West-Saxon-leaning Chronicle downplays the importance of rival kingdoms, such as Mercia, but this is even more apparent for Celtic-speaking areas.

Perhaps one's immediate neighbours are simply not as interesting as the allure of more prestigious Continental connections or of more distant lands which need rationalizing or explaining within one's world view. The more quotidian interactions with near neighbours did not necessarily occasion mention in the extant texts. The Riddles offer a rare glimpse of an early medieval English depiction of the Welsh with no clear political goal, instead perhaps reflecting an undercurrent of an abstracted, stereotyped English view of a neighbouring people. In all these texts, the Britons, Welsh, Picts, and Scots simply enter the English stage at particular junctures as suits the narrative. References to Wales are often connected to a deeper interest in Mercia, and likewise references to Scotland are often connected to a deeper interest in Northumbria. While the Britons were convenient adversaries at the inception of Englishness, the Welsh and the Scots are incidental to the story of England in Old English and Anglo-Latin sources.

---

149 ASC 973 DE *s.a.* 972, MS D, ed. by Cubbin, p. 46. Ælfric presumably describes the same meeting (though of eight rather than six kings), but he does not name or locate the rulers either (Ælfric of Eynsham, *Lives of Saints*, ed. by Skeat, I, pp. 468–69). We are reliant on later sources, namely John of Worcester, to supply the names. For further discussion, see Williams, 'An Outing on the Dee', ultimately arguing that in reality this meeting was more a conference for various rulers to come to agreements, rather than a ceremonial gathering for an imperial overlord.

Works Cited

Primary Sources

Ælfric of Eynsham, *Ælfric's Lives of Saints*, ed. by W. W. Skeat, 2 vols (London: Kegan Paul, Trench, Trübner, 1881–1885)

Alfred the Great: Asser's 'Life of Alfred' and Other Contemporary Sources, ed. and trans. by Simon Keynes and Michael Lapidge (Harmondsworth: Penguin, 1983)

Andreas: An Edition, ed. by Richard North and Michael D. J. Bintley (Liverpool: Liverpool University Press, 2016)

The Anglo-Saxon Chronicle: A Collaborative Edition, III: *MS A*, ed. by Janet Bately (Cambridge: D. S. Brewer, 1986)

The Anglo-Saxon Chronicle: A Collaborative Edition, V: *MS C*, ed. by Katherine O'Brien O'Keeffe (Cambridge: D. S. Brewer, 2001)

The Anglo-Saxon Chronicle: A Collaborative Edition, VI: *MS D*, ed. by G. P. Cubbin (Cambridge: D. S. Brewer, 1996)

The Anglo-Saxon Chronicle: A Collaborative Edition, VII: *MS E*, ed. by Susan Irvine (Cambridge: D. S. Brewer, 2004)

Annales Rerum Gestarum Ælfredi Magni, auctore Asserio Menevensi, ed. by Francis Wise (Oxford: Oxford University Press, 1722)

The Annals of Ulster (to A.D. 1131), ed. and trans. by S. Mac Airt and G. Mac Niocaill (Dublin: Dublin Institute for Advanced Studies, 1983)

Bede, *Bede's Ecclesiastical History of the English People*, ed. and trans. by Bertram Colgrave and R. A. B. Mynors, 2 vols (Oxford: Clarendon Press, 1979)

Diplomatarium Anglicum Ævi Saxonicum: A Collection of English Charters from the Reign of King Æthelberht of Kent to That of William the Conqueror, ed. by Benjamin Thorpe (London: MacMillan, 1864)

Felix, *Felix's Life of Guthlac*, ed. and trans. by Bertram Colgrave (Cambridge: Cambridge University Press, 1985)

Gildas, *The Ruin of Britain and Other Works*, ed. and trans. by Michael Winterbottom (London: Phillimore, 1978)

The Old English Version of Bede's Ecclesiastical History of the English People, ed. by Thomas Miller, EETS OS, 95, 96, 110, 111, 4 vols (London: Oxford University Press, 1890–1898; repr. 1959–1963)

A Thesaurus of Old English (Glasgow: University of Glasgow, 2021), <http://oldenglishthesaurus.arts.gla.ac.uk> [accessed 15 April 2021]

William of Malmesbury, *Gesta Regum Anglorum: The History of the English Kings*, ed. and trans. by R. A. B. Mynors, R. H. Thomson, and Michael Winterbottom, Oxford Medieval Texts, 2 vols (Oxford: Clarendon Press, 1998–1999)

Secondary Sources

Ahern, Eoghan, 'The Influence of Irish Learning on Bede's Cosmological Outlook', *Quaestio Insularis*, 14 (2013), 56–87

Anlezark, Daniel, 'Wessex and the Welsh in the Alfredian *Chronicle*', in *Fír Fesso: A Festschrift for Neil McLeod*, ed. by Anders Ahlqvist and Pamela O'Neill (Sydney: Celtic Studies Foundation, University of Sydney, 2018), pp. 31–44

Atherton, Mark, *The Battle of Maldon: War and Peace in Tenth-Century England* (London: Bloomsbury, 2021)

Banham, Debby, 'Anglo-Saxon Attitudes: In Search of the Origins of English Racism', *European Review of History / Revue européenne d'histoire*, 1.2 (1994), 143–56

Bintley, Michael D. J., 'Romans, Britons, and the Construction of "Anglo-Saxon" Identity', in *Celts, Romans, Britons: Classical and Celtic Influence in the Construction of British Identities*, ed. by Francesca Kaminski-Jones and Rhys Kaminski-Jones (Oxford: Oxford University Press, 2020), pp. 31–49

Bosworth Toller's Anglo-Saxon Dictionary Online, ed. by Sean Christ (Prague: Faculty of Arts, Charles University, 2014), <https://bosworthtoller.com>

Brady, Lindy, 'The "Dark Welsh" as Slaves and Slave Traders in Exeter Book Riddles 52 and 72', *ES*, 95 (2014), 235–55

——, 'Echoes of Britons on a Fenland Frontier in the Old English "Andreas"', *RES*, 61 (2010), 669–89

——, *Writing the Welsh Borderland* (Manchester: Manchester University Press, 2017)

Brooks, Britton, *Restoring Creation: The Natural World in the Anglo-Saxon Saints' Lives of Cuthbert and Guthlac*, Nature and Environment in the Middle Ages, 3 (Cambridge: D. S. Brewer, 2019)

Brooks, Nicholas, 'The Formation of the Mercian Kingdom', in *The Origins of Anglo-Saxon Kingdoms*, ed. by Steven Bassett (Leicester: Leicester University Press, 1989), pp. 159–70

——, 'Why Is the *Anglo-Saxon Chronicle* about Kings?', *ASE*, 39 (2011), 43–70

Capper, Morn, 'St Guthlac and the "Britons": A Mercian Context', in *Guthlac of Crowland: Celebrating 1300 Years*, ed. by Jane Roberts and Alan Thacker (Stamford: Paul Watkins, 2020), pp. 180–213

Charles-Edwards, T. M., 'Alliances, Godfathers, Treaties and Boundaries', in *Kings, Currency, and Alliances: History and Coinage of Southern England in the Ninth Century*, ed. by Mark A. S. Blackburn and David N. Dumville, Studies in Anglo-Saxon History, 9 (Woodbridge: Boydell, 1998), pp. 47–62

——, 'Bede, the Irish and the Britons', *Celtica*, 15 (1983), 42–52

——, *Wales and the Britons, 350–1064* (Oxford: Oxford University Press, 2013)

——, 'Wales and Mercia, 613–918', in *Mercia: An Anglo-Saxon Kingdom in Europe*, ed. by Michelle P. Brown and Carol Ann Farr (Leicester: Leicester University Press, 2001), pp. 88–105

Dark, Ken, *Civitas to Kingdom: British Political Continuity, 300–800* (Leicester: Leicester University Press, 1994)

Edmonds, Fiona, 'The Emergence and Transformation of Medieval Cumbria', *Scottish Historical Review*, 93 (2014), 195–216

Ellis, Caitlin, 'Reassessing the Career of Óláfr Tryggvason in the Insular World', *Saga-Book of the Viking Society for Northern Research*, 43 (2019), 59–82

Estes, Heide, *Anglo-Saxon Literary Landscapes: Ecotheory and the Environmental Imagination*, Environmental Humanities in Pre-modern Cultures (Amsterdam: Amsterdam University Press, 2017)

Evans, Nicholas, *The Present and the Past in Medieval Irish Chronicles*, Studies in Celtic History, 27 (Woodbridge: Boydell, 2010)

Firth, Matthew, 'Constructing a King: William of Malmesbury and the Life of Athelstan', *Journal of the Australian Early Medieval Association*, 13 (2017), 67–90

Foley, W. Trent, and Nicholas J. Higham, 'Bede on the Britons', *Early Medieval Europe*, 17 (2009), 154–85

Foot, Sarah, 'The Making of *Angelcynn*: English Identity before the Norman Conquest', *Transactions of the Royal Historical Society*, 6th Ser., 6 (1996), 25–49; repr. in *Old English Literature: Critical Essays*, ed. by Roy M. Liuzza (New Haven, CT: Yale University Press, 2002), pp. 51–78

——, 'Where English Becomes British: Rethinking Contexts for Brunanburh', in *Myth, Rulership, Church and Charters: Essays in Honour of Nicholas Brooks*, ed. by Julia Barrow and Andrew Wareham (Aldershot: Ashgate, 2008), pp. 127–44

Fulk, R. D., *A History of Old English Meter* (Philadelphia: University of Pennsylvania Press, 1992)

Grimmer, Martin, 'Britons in Early Wessex: The Evidence of the Law Code of Ine', in *Britons in Anglo-Saxon England*, ed. by Nicholas J. Higham, Publications of the Manchester Centre for Anglo-Saxon Studies, 7 (Woodbridge: Boydell, 2007), pp. 102–14

Hall, Alaric, 'Interlinguistic Communication in Bede's *Historia ecclesiastica gentis Anglorum*', in *Interfaces between Language and Culture in Medieval England: A Festschrift for Matti Kilpiö*, ed. by Alaric Hall, Agnes Kiricsi, and Olga Timofeeva with Bethany Fox, The Northern World, 48 (Leiden: Brill, 2010), pp. 37–80

Halsall, Guy, *Barbarian Migrations and the Roman West, 376–568* (Cambridge: Cambridge University Press, 2007)

Harland, James M., *Ethnic Identity and the Archaeology of the 'aduentus Saxonum': A Modern Framework and its Problems* (Amsterdam: Amsterdam University Press, 2021)

——, 'Rethinking Ethnicity and "Otherness" in Early Anglo-Saxon England', *Medieval Worlds*, 5 (2017), 113–42

Heng, Geraldine, *The Invention of Race in the European Middle Ages* (Cambridge: University of Cambridge Press, 2018)

Higham, Nicholas J., 'Britons in Anglo-Saxon England: An Introduction', in *Britons in Anglo-Saxon England*, ed. by Nicholas J. Higham, Publications of the Manchester Centre for Anglo-Saxon Studies, 7 (Woodbridge: Boydell, 2007), pp. 1–15

——, *The English Conquest: Gildas and Britain in the Fifth Century* (Manchester: Manchester University Press, 1994)

——, *An English Empire: Bede and the Early Anglo-Saxon Kings* (Manchester: Manchester University Press, 1995)

——, 'Guthlac's *Vita*, Mercia and East Anglia in the First Half of the Eighth Century', in *Æthelbald and Offa: Two Eighth-Century Kings of Mercia. Papers from a Conference held in Manchester in 2000, Manchester Centre for Anglo-Saxon Studies*, ed. by David Hill and Margaret Worthington (Oxford: BAR Publishing, 2005), pp. 85–90

——, *(Re-)Reading Bede: The 'Ecclesiastical History' in Context* (London: Routledge, 2006)

——, *Rome, Britain and the Anglo-Saxons* (London: Seaby, 1992)

Keynes, Simon, 'Changing Faces: Offa, King of Mercia', *History Today*, 40.11 (1990), 14–19

——, 'The Kingdom of the Mercians in the Eighth Century', in *Æthelbald and Offa: Two Eighth-Century Kings of Mercia. Papers from a Conference held in Manchester in 2000, Manchester Centre for Anglo-Saxon Studies*, ed. by David Hill and Margaret Worthington (Oxford: BAR Publishing, 2005), pp. 1–26

Lambert, Tom, *Law and Order in Anglo-Saxon England* (Oxford: Oxford University Press, 2017)

Leneghan, Francis, 'The Departure of the Hero in a Ship: The Intertextuality of *Beowulf*, Cynewulf and *Andreas*', *SELIM: Journal of the Spanish Society for Medieval English Language and Literature*, 24 (2019), 105–32

——, *The Dynastic Drama of 'Beowulf'*, Anglo-Saxon Studies, 39 (Cambridge: D. S. Brewer, 2020)

Lumbley, Coral, 'The "Dark Welsh": Color, Race, and Alterity in the Matter of Medieval Wales', *Literature Compass*, 16 (2019), 1–19

McCann, Sarah, '*Plures de Scottorum regione*: Bede, Ireland, and the Irish', *Eolas: The Journal of the American Society of Irish Medieval Studies*, 8 (2015), 20–38

Milfull, Inge, and Katrin Thier, 'Anglo-Saxon Perceptions of the Celtic Peoples', in *England, Ireland, and the Insular World: Textual and Material Connections in the Early Middle Ages*, ed. by Mary Clayton, Alice Jorgensen, and Juliet Mullins (Tempe: Arizona Center for Medieval and Renaissance Studies, 2017), pp. 197–221

Molyneaux, George, 'Did the English Really Think They Were God's Elect in the Anglo-Saxon Period?', *Journal of Ecclesiastical History*, 65 (2014), 721–37

——, 'The *Old English Bede*: English Ideology or Christian Instruction?', *English Historical Review*, 124 (2009), 1289–1323

——, 'Why Were Some Tenth-Century English Kings Presented as Rulers of Britain?', *Transactions of the Royal Historical Society*, 21 (2011), 59–91

Neidorf, Leonard, 'Caesar's Wine and the Dating of *Widsith*', *MÆ*, 88 (2019), 124–28

——, 'Lexical Evidence for the Relative Chronology of Old English Poetry', *SELIM: Journal of the Spanish Society for Medieval English Language and Literature*, 20 (2013–2014), 7–48

Niles, John D., *God's Exiles and English Verse: On the Exeter Anthology of Old English Poetry* (Exeter: University of Exeter Press, 2019)

O'Brien O'Keeffe, Katherine, 'Guthlac's Crossings', *Quaestio Insularis*, 2 (2001), 1–26

Oosthuizen, Susan, *The Emergence of the English* (Leeds: ARC Humanities Press, 2019)

Orchard, Andy, 'The Originality of *Andreas*', in *Old English Philology Studies in Honour of R. D. Fulk*, ed. by Leonard Neidorf, Rafael J. Pascual, and Tom Shippey, Anglo-Saxon Studies, 31 (Cambridge: D. S. Brewer, 2016), pp. 331–70

Porck, Thijs, *Old Age in Early Medieval England: A Cultural History*, Anglo-Saxon Studies, 33 (Cambridge: D. S. Brewer, 2019)

Rowley, Sharon M., *The Old English Version of Bede's Historia Ecclesiastica*, Anglo-Saxon Studies, 16 (Cambridge: D. S. Brewer, 2011)

Rulon-Miller, Nina, 'Sexual Humor and Fettered Desire in Exeter Book Riddle 12', in *Humour in Anglo-Saxon Literature*, ed. by Jonathan Wilcox (Cambridge: D. S. Brewer, 2000), pp. 99–126

Sisam, Kenneth, *Studies in the History of Old English Literature* (Oxford: Clarendon Press, 1953; repr. 1967)

Stafford, Pauline, *After Alfred: Anglo-Saxon Chronicles and Chroniclers, 900–1150* (Oxford: Oxford University Press, 2020)

Stancliffe, Clare, *Bede, Wilfrid, and the Irish*, Jarrow Lecture (Jarrow: St Paul's Church Council, 2003)

Thacker, Alan, 'Bede and the Irish', in *Beda Venerabilis: Historian, Monk and Northumbrian*, ed. by L. A. J. R. Houwen and A. A. MacDonald (Groningen: E. Forsten, 1996), pp. 31–59

Thomas, Rebecca, 'The View from Wales: Anglo-Welsh Relations in the Time of England's Conquests', in *Conquests in Eleventh-Century England: 1016, 1066*, ed. by Laura Ashe and Emily Joan Ward (Woodbridge: Boydell, 2020), pp. 287–306

Thomas, Rebecca, and David Callander, 'Reading Asser in Early Medieval Wales: The Evidence of *Armes Prydein Vawr*', *ASE*, 46 (2017), 115–45

Tyler, Elizabeth M., 'England between Empire and Nation in *The Battle of Brunanburh*', in *Whose Middle Ages? Teachable Moments for an Ill-Used Past*, ed. by Andrew Albin, Mary C. Erler, Thomas O'Donnell, Nicholas L. Paul, and Nina Rowe (New York: Fordham University Press, 2019), pp. 166–80

Ward-Perkins, Bryan, 'Why Did the Anglo-Saxons Not Become More British?', *English Historical Review*, 115 (2000), 513–33

Williams, Ann, 'Offa's Dyke: "The Stuff that Dreams Are Made Of"', *Offa's Dyke Journal*, 1 (2019), 32–57

——, 'An Outing on the Dee: King Edgar at Chester, A.D. 973', *Mediaeval Scandinavia*, 14 (2004), 229–43

Wood, Michael, 'The Making of King Aethelstan's Empire: An English Charlemagne?', in *Ideal and Reality in Frankish and Anglo-Saxon Society: Studies Presented to J. M. Wallace-Hadrill*, ed. by Patrick Wormald, with Donald Bullough and Roger Collins (Oxford: Blackwell, 1983), pp. 250–72

Woolf, Alex, 'Apartheid and Economics in Anglo-Saxon England', in *Britons in Anglo-Saxon England*, ed. by Nicholas J. Higham, Publications of the Manchester Centre for Anglo-Saxon Studies, 7 (Woodbridge: Boydell, 2007), pp. 115–29

——, 'British Ethnogenesis: A Late Antique Story', in *Celts, Romans, Britons: Classical and Celtic Influence in the Construction of British Identities*, ed. by Francesca Kaminski-Jones and Rhys Kaminski-Jones (Oxford: Oxford University Press, 2020), pp. 19–30

——, 'Reporting Scotland in the Anglo-Saxon Chronicle', in *Reading the Anglo-Saxon Chronicle: Language, Literature, History*, ed. by Alice Jorgensen, SEM, 23 (Turnhout: Brepols, 2010), pp. 221–39

Ziegler, Michelle, 'The Politics of Exile in Early Northumbria', *The Heroic Age*, no. 2 (Autumn/Winter 1999), <http://www.heroicage.org/issues/2/ha2pen.htm>

RYAN LAVELLE

From (North-)East to West: Geographical Identities and Political Communities in the Ninth- to Eleventh-Century Anglo-Scandinavian World

The political and social developments which took place in ninth- and early tenth-century Wessex and England saw a situation in which the othering of Scandinavian invaders and settlers was followed by the Scandinavianization of the 'Jutish' identity used as part of the English ethnogenesis during this period. The effect of this was, essentially, to bring Scandinavians into a West Saxon court from a North Sea zone to the north and north-east of Britain, with profound effects on the ways in which the inhabitants of emergent kingdoms — of 'the Anglo-Saxons', 'the English' and, by the eleventh century, 'of England' — could perceive themselves, including through to the reign of Cnut the Great (1016/17–1035).

The sense of the 'shape' of the northern world relative to the space occupied by early medieval audiences is at the heart of this chapter. While the identity of groups of people could not have relied on any geospatial precision with regard to cardinal points, the sense of the geographical identity of groups relative to each other does seem to be apparent. In that sense the perception of the world by the inhabitants of early medieval England can be seen to have played out across the North Sea. In what follows, I wish first to discuss the process of localizing groups of people in early medieval English sources, initially through addressing the manner in which this takes place with regard to Scandinavians and 'Anglo-Scandinavians' in the ninth century. This is followed by consideration of the eleventh-century localization of Anglo-Danish interests in Scandinavia. The representation of Scandinavian identity in the heart of Wessex is important here, but I also wish to reflect on the bringing together for an English audience in 1027 of groups of people hitherto seen in the late ninth-/ early tenth-century report of northern regions in the Old English *Orosius*,[1] an activity which makes use of a toponymic ambiguity which could have been helpful for an English-speaking audience whose interests lay both within and without the English kingdom.

---

[1] OE *Orosius*, I.1.16–27, in *The Old English History of the World*, ed. and trans. by Godden, pp. 36–49.

Ryan Lavelle (ryan.lavelle@winchester.ac.uk) is Professor of Early Medieval History at the University of Winchester.

Ideas of the World in Early Medieval English Literature, ed. by Mark Atherton, Kazutomo Karasawa, and Francis Leneghan, SOEL 1 (Turnhout: Brepols, 2022)   pp. 365–384
BREPOLS ❧ PUBLISHERS   DOI 10.1484/M.SOEL.5.130568

RYAN LAVELLE

This discussion builds on points made with regard to the ninth century in my contribution to a 2016 piece jointly authored with Simon Roffey, published in our volume *Danes in Wessex*.[2] A certain amount of retreading of existing ground is necessary here, but some of these ideas are developed here both in terms of the discussion of the ninth century and in particular through consideration of the implications for the study of Anglo-Scandinavian identity in the eleventh century.

Ninth-Century Scandinavians

There are some potential issues regarding the identification of Scandinavians in England which should move us away from simplistic notions of distinguishing the 'Northmen' and 'Danes' as distinct ethnic groups. Just as the notion of distinguishing 'Black Foreigners' from 'White Foreigners' as ethnically distinct groups in early medieval Ireland has been proven to be an untrustworthy reading of the Gaelic sources, we should not assume that 'Northmen' (sometimes translated as 'Norse' or 'Norsemen') were Norwegians while 'Danes' were from Denmark.[3]

The apparent interchangeability of 'Danes' and 'Northmen' is comparable with Continental European sources, where *Northmanni* and *Dani* appear to be used with some flexibility.[4] However, notwithstanding the references to the actions of *pagani* in Insular Latin sources, the early Viking Age references to 'Northmen' are worth noting here, in the light of which the emergence of references to 'Danes' in sources relating to the late ninth century is noteworthy. Why Danes? In the ninth century this seems to relate to an increasing awareness of the geographical links of the Vikings, which reflects interest in the Vikings in the Frankish court and indeed connections with the area seen as Denmark. What we see in Francia is the ethnogenesis of 'Danes' as a group of people with whom Christian rulers could do business, enhancing their prestige in the process, culminating in the 826 conversion of the Danish ruler, Harald Klak.[5]

The consideration of ethnogenesis here relates to two important works published in French in the early 2000s, works which, to my knowledge, are given less recognition than they ought to be in anglophone historiography. One, by Magali Coumert from 2007, is considered below; the other is a 2009

---

2 Roffey and Lavelle, 'West Saxons and Danes', pp. 8–13.

3 Downham, '"Hiberno-Norwegians" and "Anglo-Danes"'. See also Bibire, 'North Sea Language Contacts', pp. 89–90.

4 See Roffey and Lavelle, 'West Saxons and Danes', p. 11, citing the reference to 'Northmen' who had 'come from Denmark', noted by Regino of Prüm: Regino of Prüm, *Chronicon*, ed. by Kurze, p. 122; trans. from *History and Politics in Late Carolingian and Ottonian Europe*, ed. and trans. by MacLean, p. 191.

5 Roffey and Lavelle, 'West Saxons and Danes', pp. 9–10, and Bauduin, *Le monde franc et les Vikings*, pp. 123–49.

monograph by Pierre Bauduin, *Le monde franc et les Vikings*, a book whose central thesis considers the significance of the royal and indeed imperial status of Frankish rulers in the light of their links with Vikings.[6] Bauduin's study has implications for consideration of the reference to 'Danes' in an English context.

Thus it is notable that the earliest references to 'Danish men' in Wessex render them as 'Northmen'. In the Anglo-Saxon Chronicle's entry for the year 789, when Vikings arrived in Portland, the group are described in some of the manuscripts as 'Northmen' (in reference to 'iii. scipu Norðmanna' (three ships of the Northmen)). Perhaps retrospectively recognizing the momentousness in the descriptions of ships arriving on the shores of Britain in the context of tales of the *adventus Saxonum*, the reference to the ships is glossed in all the manuscripts of the Chronicle as 'þa ærestan scipu deniscra monna þe Angelcynnes lond gesohton' (the first ships of Danish men which sought out the land of the *Angelcynn*).[7] It is as if every subsequent reference to 'Danish' activity, perhaps including those to come *after* the time at which the author wrote, led from this eighth-century moment in the reign of Beorhtric.

David Dumville has suggested that additions to the D text (and, with that, the B, C, and E texts) which link the Vikings to Hordaland ('Hæreðelande') in southern Norway are somewhat later, written in a tenth-century northern English context.[8] While Dumville's suggestion is plausible, it does not detract from the ways in which 'Northmen' were becoming 'Danes' — in this case that their ships were seen as those of 'Danish men', as if to explain that the *Dena* of later Anglo-Saxon Chronicle entries should be linked to this 787 entry (for the year 789). Indeed, the A version of the Chronicle, which of all the manuscripts is perhaps closest to a Winchester court's view of affairs, does not refer to them as 'Northmen' at all, but the *Annals of St Neots* (a text which translates into Latin another, perhaps earlier, version of the Chronicle) refers to 'Northmen' and does not include the other manuscripts' reference to the 'first ships of Danish men'.[9] This suggests that this 'first ships' element, expressly referring to 'Danish men', had been edited into the text of the so-called Common Stock of the Chronicle to reflect the concerns of its late ninth-century audience, whose reading of the Danish *adventus* would match with the arrivals of ships of Anglo-Saxons in the fifth- and sixth-century annals of the Chronicle — a narrative which was itself creating a particular view of

---

6 Bauduin, *Le monde franc et les Vikings*.

7 ASC MS A *s.a.* 787 (for 789), translated in *The Anglo-Saxon Chronicles*, ed. and trans. by Swanton, p. 55 (here cited with minor modification); references to the ASC text are according to manuscript, edited in the *Collaborative Edition* by Bately (MS A), O'Brien O'Keefe (MS C), Cubbin (MS D), and Irvine (MS E). For the theme of migration and landing, see Daniel Thomas in this volume, pp. 167–201.

8 Dumville, 'Vikings in Insular Chronicling', p. 356. ASC MS D, *s.a.* 787 (for 789).

9 *The Anglo-Saxon Chronicle: The Annals of St Neots*, ed. by Dumville and Lapidge, *s.a.* 787 (for 789). See Roffey and Lavelle, 'West Saxons and Danes', pp. 10–11.

West Saxon history for the Chronicle's late ninth-century audience.[10] Thus, if 'Northmen' and 'Danes' were interchangeable, by the late ninth century it may have been important to indicate this.

It is also relevant to mention the insertion of the accounts of Scandinavia and the Baltic, apparently drawn from otherwise unknown seafarers, Ohthere and Wulfstan, in the vernacular world history the Old English *Orosius*, a version of the fifth-century *History against the Pagans* by the late Roman author Paulus Orosius.[11] In these accounts we see the geographical determinism of placing the origins of the 'Jutes' (here rendered in Old English as the inhabitants of 'Gotland') in a manner which made sense to the West Saxons and probably also King Alfred. This linguistic confusion of 'Jutes' and 'Goths' may have been particularly pertinent to the king, as his mother is described as a daughter of Oslac, who was 'Gothus' by 'natione'; presumably *natione* here was a reference to ethnic descent rather than birth, given that Asser explains that Oslac 'ortus [...] erat de Gothis et Iutis' (was descended from the Goths and Jutes).[12]

Notwithstanding whether the Jutes of the Old English *Orosius* could ever be equated with the Geats of *Beowulf* (or indeed the equation of the Swedish island of Gotland with the description of Jutland with Old English *Gotland*),[13] it is appropriate here to consider where the Jutes can be placed in early medieval ethnography. Magali Coumert observed that the notion of the English as 'Angles' originally had nothing to do with a German province of 'Angeln' but is linked to a non-specific geographical placement by Pope Gregory the Great.[14] The *Angli* were people in an *angulus*, an 'angle', a little place which was essentially in the middle of nowhere. If the *angulus* of the English is left floating in a space beyond geographical anchor points, then there was originally no easy way to link the *Iutae* of Bede to Jutland because the geographical link relies on the context of identifying 'Angeln'.

Philip Bartholemew addressed the issue from a different angle, so to speak, considering the nature of the Jutes and pointing out that the material culture of what are now referred to as 'Jutes' has more in common with the Merovingian Franks.[15] This is a significant issue for debate, and there is much discussion of whether there is a Jutlandic material provenance for Kent and the Isle of Wight. No matter whether the evidence is considered to be conclusive,[16]

---

10 ASC MS A, *s.a.* 477, 495, 501, 514, ed. by Bately, pp. 19–20. For the West Saxon narrative, see Yorke, 'Fact or Fiction?', and for the 'Common Stock', see Bately, 'The Compilation of the Anglo-Saxon Chronicle'.

11 OE *Orosius*, 1.1.16–27, in *The Old English History of the World*, ed. and trans. by Godden, pp. 36–49. See Allport, 'Home Thoughts of Abroad'.

12 Asser, *Vita Ælfredi*, ch. 2, in *Asser's Life of King Alfred*, ed. by Stevenson, p. 4; *Alfred the Great*, trans. by Keynes and Lapidge, p. 68.

13 For a review of the issues here, see Roffey and Lavelle, 'West Saxons and Danes', pp. 12–13.

14 Coumert, *Origines des peuples*, pp. 416–30; see also Coumert, 'Les Angles dans les coins'.

15 Bartholemew, 'Continental Connections', pp. 22–24.

16 Stoodley, 'Costume Groups in Hampshire', pp. 88–89.

FROM (NORTH-)EAST TO WEST   369

Bartholemew's point — and, later, independently, that of Coumert — that *Iutae* is a term which was not originally connected to geographical meaning, or at least not a Scandinavian geography, is a powerful one. In the later ninth century, then, if the interpretations from Bede are put to one side, it is possible to see the 'Scandinavianization' of the Jutes. Moreover, there is a geographical reference to the *Angle* homeland of the *Angli*, in references in the Old English *Orosius*.[17] That does not mean to say that we need suggest that 'Jutland' (*Jylland*) itself is so-named because of an extrapolation from Bedan geography, as Coumert has suggested for 'Angeln', though it is hardly inappropriate to entertain such a notion.[18] What is significant to the above discussion is that in the ninth century there was a confluence of interests, of the northern record of geographical identity and the West Saxon reading of it at a time when it was politically advantageous to do so.

There is a further dynamic related to geographical space which also needs to be acknowledged: that of the way in which the groups of people associated with Scandinavian settlers in different areas in England began to be associated with the areas themselves. At times the 'Danes' are often referred to in more amorphous terms by way of their raiding identity, as the *here*, but the interests of the precision of annal entries (which *here* was doing what and where in Britain was it operating from?) seems to lead to links between raiding armies and their geographical spaces, in terms of the east and the north. The notion of 'the *here* in the [land of] the East Angles/Northumbrians' is shortened in three crucial references in the Anglo-Saxon Chronicle, by way of referring to them as 'Northumbrians' and 'East Angles'.[19] West Saxon rulers may have aspired to control these zones of influence (although of course our perception of this may be determined by what happened in the tenth century), but they were tacitly recognizing the control of those areas by the Scandinavians and those affiliated with them. Even if it was only for a short period, essentially a generation, in the late ninth and early tenth centuries, these were areas which were politically within a Scandinavian sphere of political influence.

Nonetheless, 'Danes' still lurk in the pages of the Anglo-Saxon Chronicle in its entries for the last years of the ninth century and the early tenth century. That this is the case has implications for how we might consider that late Alfredian account of nefarious Viking activity in 896, when six 'Danish' ships wrought havoc on the south coast of England. Those ships were pursued by West Saxon vessels, which had serious difficulties in catching them. While the 896 annal is well known for the account of a new type of West Saxon ship,

---

17 We might note here also the suggestion of the *Beowulf* poem's potential links to a ninth-century context: Davis, 'An Ethnic Dating of *Beowulf*'.

18 Coumert, 'Les Angles dans les coins', pp. 45–46, discussing her *Origines des peuples*, pp. 416–30.

19 ASC MS A, *s.a.* 894 (for 893), 906 (for 905); *here* in East Anglia/Northumbria in ASC MS A, *s.a.* 901 (for 899/900), 905 (for 904); see also 'those who dwelt in Northumbria and East Anglia' ('þe in Norþhymbrum bugeað 7 on Eastenglum') in ASC MS A, *s.a.* 893 (*The Anglo-Saxon Chronicles*, ed. and trans. by Swanton, p. 86).

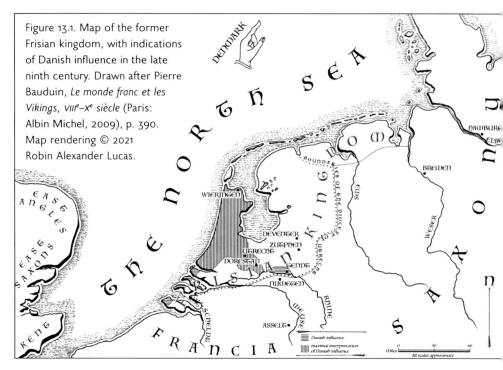

Figure 13.1. Map of the former Frisian kingdom, with indications of Danish influence in the late ninth century. Drawn after Pierre Bauduin, *Le monde franc et les Vikings, VIIIᵉ–Xᵉ siècle* (Paris: Albin Michel, 2009), p. 390. Map rendering © 2021 Robin Alexander Lucas.

'næron nawðer ne on fresisc gescæpene ne on denisc, bute swa him selfum ðuhte þæt hie nytwyrðoste beon meahten' (neither of Frisian design nor of Danish, but as it seemed to [Alfred] himself that they might be most useful),[20] there is something to be said about the portrayal of the participants in the action. The antagonists in that account are referred to as 'Danes', but the Anglo-Saxon Chronicle is emphatic about the fact that they had travelled from East Anglia, again suggesting the Chronicle's geographical concerns. Those Danes ended up hanged in Winchester at the king's orders, but naming the good conduct of those who died fighting for the king is revealing. It is possible that the 'Frisians' among the crews of Alfred's ships may be indicative of the ninth-century interest in geographical identities in an entry which emphasizes not 'Saxons' but 'English' fighting and dying alongside the 'Frisians':

> Þær wearð ofslægen Lucumon cynges gerefa 7 Wulfheard Friesa 7 Æbbe Friesa, 7 Æðelhere Friesa, 7 Æðelferð cynges geneat, 7 ealra monna fresiscra 7 engliscra .lxii. 7 þara deniscena .cxx.
>
> > (There were killed Lucumon, the king's reeve, and Wulfheard the Frisian, and Æbbe the Frisian, and Æthelhere the Frisian, and Æthelfrith the king's *geneat*, and of all men Frisian and English, 62, and of the Danish, 120.)

---

20 ASC MS A, *s.a.* 896; *The Anglo-Saxon Chronicles*, ed. and trans. by Swanton, pp. 90–91.

Much has justifiably been made of well-established links between English and Frisians, as the recent collection on the subject edited by John Hines and Nelleke IJssennagger has shown, and it is not my wish to downplay the significance of these links.[21] It is, instead, important to emphasize the fact that different groups could be associated with a single area. What if those 'Frisians' were Frisian Vikings, either Scandinavian settlers or Frisians linked with Viking warbands, or both? At first sight, the evidence may suggest not. In the Chronicle's account for 896, the Frisians had Old English name forms, and Old Norse names are constructed differently from those in Old English; of the three names distinguished as 'Frisian', Æbbe may be commensurate with the name of a certain Abba. There is an obvious punchline here, but Abba was not a Scandinavian name in sources linked with Anglo-Saxons. A certain Abba is recorded in Willibald's *Vita Bonifatii* as erecting a mound and church, establishing a monastic community at the spot in Frisia where Boniface was martyred.[22] Nonetheless, the name elements *Wulf-* and *-here* are not without meaning in a 'Viking' context for an English audience, and the account of the 'furthest north of all the Northmen', Ohthere, attests to the Anglicization of an Old Norse name, Ottárr, not only for Old English orthography but also arguably for English pronunciation. Likewise, although the name of Ohthere's fellow sea-captain, Wulfstan, was 'typically Anglo-Saxon', it did not mean, as Judith Jesch admits, that he had been born in England.[23] Could the names in the Chronicle's 896 annal have provided 'Anglo-Saxon' identities for people with Scandinavian names?

There were more significant 'facts on the ground', however, which indicated that Alfred and his contemporaries would have had to think of 'Frisia' in terms of its links with 'Danes'. As can be seen from Figure 13.1, there is evidence for Scandinavian settlement and the receipt of benefices in Frisia in the later ninth century. In the Frankish zones west of Dorestad, islands on the River Scheldt provided Scandinavian warlords and their men with the perfect opportunity to establish themselves in important political zones.[24] The year 885 had marked the end of Danish influence in Frisia, and the apparent expulsion of Danes

---

21 See here Hines and IJssennagger, eds, *Frisians and their North Sea Neighbours*, in particular, Pestell, 'The Kingdom of East Anglia, Frisia and Continental Connections'. For the wide range of 'Frisian' interpretations, see Lebecq, 'On the Use of the Word "Frisian" in the 6th–10th Centuries Written Sources'.

22 *Vita Bonifatii auctore Willibaldo*, ch. 9, p. 57. Search of Prosopography of Anglo-Saxon England, <http://www.pase.ac.uk> s.v. 'Abba' (12 examples) undertaken 9 February 2021. Of the six examples of 'Æbbe', four cases are identifiably the names of women.

23 Jesch, 'Who Was Wulfstan?', p. 30.

24 Bauduin, *Le monde franc et les Vikings*, pp. 89–90. The Frankish policies towards Scandinavian benefices are considered in Coupland, 'From Poachers to Gamekeepers', and recently in Coupland, 'The Blinkers of Militarisation', pp. 171–72; Lebecq, 'Les Vikings en Frise'. An important perspective on the manner in which Frisia can be seen as much a part of the Scandinavian world as the Frankish is IJssennagger, 'Between Frankish and Viking'. (I am grateful to the Rev. Dr Coupland for correspondence on this issue.).

saw the growth of an aristocratic elite there, as Jan Besteman noted in 2004.[25] But while the re-emergence of Viking activities in England in the 890s may be associated with the 880s victories over Vikings in Continental Europe, it is appropriate to question whether some of those *Vikings* from Frisia, in the service of the Danish chieftain Godfrid until 885, had found service in Wessex, retaining some adopted 'Frisian' identity in order to make their presence more palatable in what was emerging once again as an Anglo-Danish conflict.

Of course, Ockham's razor hangs over such a suggestion, demanding that we ought to take the written sources at face value. Asser is a useful source for the various groups of people, including *pagani* at Alfred's court and at the royal minster of Athelney; 'Frisians' were included among those rewarded through Alfred's lordship.[26] Those in 896 are normally read simply as Frisians, without specifically referring to the Danish settlements in Frisia.[27] But given the ways in which Vikings based in provinces were beginning to be referred to with names which linked them *with* those provinces, there is something to be said for a look at the 'Frisians' of the Chronicle's 896 account in that respect. The building of Alfred's new longships according to a design that was 'neither Danish nor Frisian' might be a reference to the building of ships in a fashion which did not reflect known 'Danish' shipbuilding traditions — or, for that matter, 'Frisian'.[28] Although attributions to a particular area or group of people are not necessarily indications of ultimate origin, the references to 'Frisians' and 'Frisian' ships nonetheless mean that we should be attuned once again to the notion that there is not a single homogeneous 'Viking' culture, a matter which relates just as easily to an understanding of shipbuilding — a 'Friso-Danish' culture which may have developed from contacts between maritime cultures, perhaps, just as heterogeneous maritime cultures emerged in Normandy after 911.[29] Viking settlers from Frisia would have been well placed to aid with the development of ships of the 896 episode, which were neither Danish nor Frisian but had the potential to 'be most useful'. Importantly, in the late ninth-century West Saxon court, the authors and audience of the Anglo-Saxon Chronicle were evidently attuned to the meanings of such descriptions of people.

As Pauline Stafford noted in 1985, Danishness was something which could be manipulated according to political circumstances,[30] and shifts may

---

25 Besteman, 'Two Viking Hoards from the Former Island of Wieringen'.

26 Asser, ch. 76 (on the court, with references to Frisians) and chs 92–97 (on Athelney), in *Asser's Life of King Alfred*, ed. by Stevenson, pp. 59–60 and 79–85; *Alfred the Great*, trans. by Keynes and Lapidge, pp. 91 and 102–05. See Nelson, 'England and the Continent II'.

27 This is the perspective taken by Hines, 'The Anglo-Frisian Question', pp. 37–38.

28 See here Swanton, 'King Alfred's Ships'.

29 See e.g. Ridel, 'Bateaux de type scandinave en Normandie'. However, see Lebecq, 'On the Use of the Word "Frisian" in the 6th–10th Centuries Written Sources', pp. 88–89, who notes the significance of established Frisian shipbuilding traditions in this period.

30 Stafford, *The East Midlands in the Early Middle Ages*, pp. 124–25.

FROM (NORTH-)EAST TO WEST 373

be perceived in an Anglo-Danish dynamic in the second half of the tenth century, when the legal distinctions of Danes may be seen within England.[31] This may have been a way of rationalizing the political shift which had taken place when the political independence of East Anglia and Northumbria was no longer guaranteed, and thus the actions taken by 'Danes' in an enlarged English kingdom were depicted in negative terms.[32] The discussion in this chapter closes by returning briefly to the mid-tenth century, but the spotlight needs first to move to the other part of the 'late Anglo-Saxon period', and the Danish conquest of England by Cnut.

Cnut's English Kingship: From East to West

The second part of this chapter provides a reflection on the reading of England from Scandinavia (or from a Scandinavian perspective) with the reflection *back* on the English kingdom at a point when the Anglo-Danish link became significant once more as a way of determining geographical connections. The first Anglo-Saxon Chronicle reference to a Danish link with Denmark itself comes in Æthelred's reign, in the CDE Chronicle's entry for 1005, when the 'fleet' (not specifically 'Danes') returned to Denmark in the wake of famine in England.[33] However, a statement of royal legitimacy makes a more auspicious statement of geographical identity. Cnut famously wrote, probably from Denmark around late 1019 or 1020, where he had just come to the throne, the first of two letters that survive from an English ruler to his subjects. This letter was a communication of royal policy, which may have been intended to be declared within the localities, to free men subject to the English king.[34]

While it is not impossible that the whole letter was written on Cnut's return from Denmark, the likelihood that Thorkell — a figure later outlawed by Cnut — was regent in Cnut's absence may explain the fact that the letter is directed to, amongst others, 'Þurcyl eorl · 7 ealle his eorlas' (Earl Thorkell · And all his earls'), emphasizing that Thorkell was responsible for dealing with those who defied the law.[35] An important element in the letter is its address to the people 'in England', a detail which, like the record of Cnut as a king of England in charters, may indicate a shift towards a polity which was a kingdom in terms of geographical area rather than a people 'of the English'

---

31 See Hadley, 'Ethnicity and Acculturation', p. 238, for the suggestion that for much of the period between 920 and 990, very few references were made to 'Danes' in anything but a hostile fashion.

32 Lavelle, 'Representing Authority in an Early Medieval Chronicle', pp. 73–84.

33 ASC 1005 (MSS C, D, and E).

34 *Die Gesetze der Angelsachsen*, ed. by Liebermann, I, p. 273; see Lavelle, 'Cnut, King of the English, 1017–19', and Lavelle, *Cnut*, pp. 43–44.

35 Dorothy Whitelock notes, in her translation of the letter, in *EHD*, p. 452, that otherwise Cnut would simply have directed it at 'all the earls' or 'all his earls.'

(i.e. of 'English descent').[36] What is evident here is the geographical identity of 'England'; the detail in the Chronicle of the king's departure for Denmark in 1019 is significant. Here Dorothy Whitelock's translation of the Old English *gewenden* as Cnut having 'returned' to Denmark is misleading — this is better translated by Swanton as 'turned to Denmark', as the 1020 annal reference that 'com Cnut cyng to Englalande' ('com eft', 'came back', in the C and D MSS) indicates where the Chronicler's interests, understandably, lay.[37]

The letter may be seen as evidence of the strength of the king's authority: a king who was absent from the kingdom could still rule, perhaps because the systems of law and government still functioned effectively — an issue which Patrick Wormald termed 'informal channels of communication'.[38] Cnut declared how he was protecting his subjects from threats, with his ('my') money. I have commented elsewhere on the audacity of this claim in view of the fact that the dangers to the kingdom had been from armies led — at least in part — by Cnut and by Thorkell.[39] That Cnut had taken English money to pay Viking mercenaries associated with Cnut's bid for power was audacious, but if the letter shows, as Pauline Stafford argued in 1981, the relationship between king and people, then the notion of support given *rihtlice* (clause 5) shows the continuity of relationships that built on the kingship of Æthelred and his father Edgar as Cnut's predecessors.[40]

Intriguingly, and perhaps emphasizing the manner in which the letter's primary purpose was associated with the legitimation of Cnut as an English ruler, neither the Chronicle nor the letter makes clear mention of Cnut assuming the throne of the Danish kingdom. It was the declarations of English legitimacy which presumably mattered to an English audience, but what is interesting here is the legitimacy operated in a wider political sphere than it had been just a generation before, when 'Danes' were associated with activities *in* England more often than in the North Sea. It was probably relevant to contemporaries that Cnut was the first king of an Anglo-Saxon polity to go overseas as a ruler, remaining as such on his return, since the days of Æthelwulf, father of Alfred — a figure who lost part of his kingdom to his rebellious son on his return.[41]

Cnut's sense of English identity expressed from abroad is also apparent in a Latin translation of a letter dispatched (or thus said to have been) by

---

36 Gates, '*Ealles Englalandes Cyningc*'. See also Hobson, 'National-Ethnic Narratives in Eleventh-Century Literary Representations of Cnut'.

37 ASC 1019, 1020 (MSS C, D, and E); *The Anglo-Saxon Chronicles*, ed. and trans. by Swanton, pp. 154–55. Cf. *The Anglo-Saxon Chronicle: A Revised Translation*, ed. and trans. by Whitelock, Tucker, and Douglas, p. 97.

38 Wormald, *The Making of English Law*, p. 348.

39 Lavelle, *Cnut*, pp. 43–44. See also Lavelle, 'Cnut, King of the English, 1017–19'.

40 Stafford, 'The Laws of Cnut and the History of Anglo-Saxon Royal Promises'.

41 Asser, chs 11–13, in *Asser's Life of King Alfred*, ed. by Stevenson, pp. 8–12; *Alfred the Great*, trans. by Keynes and Lapidge, pp. 69–71. Lavelle, *Cnut*, p. 45.

Cnut in 1027 while en route back to England after attending the imperial coronation of Conrad II in Rome. This letter is known because it was recorded by William of Malmesbury in his twelfth-century *Gesta Regum*. Cnut there claimed to be 'rex totius Anglię et Denemarcię et Norreganorum et partis Suanorum' (King of All England and Denmark and of the Norwegians and of part of the Swedes).[42] Although William of Malmesbury wrote in Latin and could just as easily have written this letter from a Latin original (an issue which is particularly pertinent if we consider the Latin linguistic world of the early eleventh century noted by Elizabeth Tyler),[43] there is much to be said that the letter can be considered in terms of the vernacular of Cnut's letter of 1020/21.[44] We might also note that the 1020×21 law code of Cnut, *I Cnut*, prefaces the king's legal declaration with a version of a grandiose title in Old English, referring to his status as king of 'all England and king of the Danes', with a later recension including his rule over the Norwegians.[45]

There is also something to be said about Cnut's claim in 1027 being in the tradition of the larger Jelling Runestone, erected in a royal complex in central Jutland, on which the mid-tenth-century Danish ruler Harald Bluetooth claimed to be bringing together a realm of Danes and Norwegians.[46] The fourth part of his grandson Cnut's title is, at first glance, perhaps the most remarkable. As the furthest east-reaching of any pre-Conquest rulers of England, did his control of 'Swedes', or *pars Suanorum* cast his authority even further east?

Although much has been done over the last two decades to show the significance of a North Sea empire for Cnut, any authority that Cnut's control of the territory in eastern Sweden granted was very limited.[47] Those Swedes over whom the kings of Denmark had claimed sovereignty had rejected Cnut's brother, Harald Sweinsson, perhaps after hearing of the death of Swein Forkbeard, and the setbacks at the battle of 'Holy River' (1026) made the dashed hopes painfully obvious.[48] Still, Cnut does seem to have been nothing

---

42 William of Malmesbury, *Gesta Regum Anglorum*, ch. 183. *Die Gesetze der Angelsachsen*, ed. by Liebermann, I, p. 276.

43 Tyler, *England in Europe*, esp. pp. 101–34. See Treharne, 'The Performance of Piety', p. 347, for the suggestion that the letter had been written in both Latin and Old English.

44 *Die Gesetze der Angelsachsen*, ed. by Liebermann, I, pp. 273–75.

45 'Cnut cyning, ealles Englalandes cyningc, 7 Dena cyningc 7 Norþrigena cyningc'; *I Cnut*, preface, in *Die Gesetze der Angelsachsen*, ed. by Liebermann, I, p. 278. See P. Sawyer, 'Cnut's Scandinavian Empire', p. 19, who notes this as an early claim. However, the text is from BL, MS Harley 55, fol. 5ʳ; in the BL, MS Cotton Nero A I version, fol. 3ʳ, the reference to Norwegians is absent.

46 Danish National Museum, 'The Jelling Stone', <https://en.natmus.dk/historical-knowledge/denmark/prehistoric-period-until-1050-ad/the-viking-age/the-monuments-at-jelling/the-jelling-stone/> [accessed 23 February 2021].

47 On the 'North Sea Empire', see in particular Bolton, *The Empire of Cnut the Great*; the Swedish limits of Cnut's territorial control were considered by P. Sawyer, 'Cnut's Scandinavian Empire', pp. 18–20.

48 ASC MS E, *s.a.* 1025 (for 1026).

Figure 13.2. Runestone U344, from Yttergårde, Sweden, now in Orkesta churchyard. The inscription, with 'Knutr' not in view, reads: 'And Ulf has taken three payments in England. That was the first that Tostig paid. Then Thorkell paid. Then Cnut paid.' By I. Berig, CC BY 2.5, <https://commons.wikimedia.org/w/index.php?curid=2260607>.

if not tenacious and evidently did not let the matter of a lack of territorial authority get in the way of a projection of power. Birgit Sawyer and Peter Sawyer provide a logical interpretation of the claim to Swedish power in the context of the many Swedish runestones which remember the *lithsmen* who died in Cnut's service or received a share of geld in the service of Cnut (see Fig. 13.2).[49] Perhaps such stones recorded the names of men who gave service to Cnut in his northern adventures, and so the claim in his letter to have been king of 'part' of the Swedes is elucidated by a contextual reading of the term *pars* from the titular 'Pars Suanorum'. The Old English noun *dæl*, closely related to the Old Norse *deild*,[50] may have been the term used in Cnut's original letter, which William of Malmesbury rendered as *pars*.

The Anglo-Saxon Chronicle had referred to the division of the English kingdom using the word *dæl* in both 1016 (under Edmund and Cnut) and in 1017 (under Cnut and his earls), so this was a term with some real currency.[51] Cnut's Swede-encompassing realm of 1027 was divided into four, a division which, even if assigning the groups to the cardinal points defies any conventional sense of geography, could perhaps have provided a manifestation on a wider stage of the four-part division of English territory recorded in the Anglo-Saxon Chronicle at the start of Cnut's reign in 1017. Referring to the *Pars Suanorum* in Cnut's title may have evoked a sense of the military group which owed

---

49 P. Sawyer, 'Cnut's Scandinavian Empire', pp. 19–20, as well as B. Sawyer, 'Appendix: The Evidence of Scandinavian Runic Inscriptions'.
50 Cleasby and Vigfusson, eds, *An Icelandic-English Dictionary*, p. 98.
51 ASC MS D, *s.a.* 1016 ('to þam norðdæle'; NB, the C and E MSS mention Mercia rather than the north 'part'); D, *s.a.* 1017 ('todælde hit on feower'; variant also in MS E). On the context of the Chronicle's record of the 1016 peace agreement, see now Townend, *The Road to Deerhurst*.

FROM (NORTH-)EAST TO WEST   377

allegiance to Cnut. In Old English, *dæl* could refer to part of an army, and it may be this military context which was important to a militaristic kingship identified by right of conquest.[52] Cnut's Swedes, however few they may have been by 1027, were thus brought into a political sphere which made sense to both English *and* Danes.

If this title had to acknowledge the limits of Cnut's empire, for an English audience to be brought together with the groups of people hitherto only seen in the report of northern regions provided to King Alfred in the Old English *Orosius* must have had special meaning. There may be a significance to the eleventh-century date of the version of the Old English *Orosius* in London, British Library, MS Cotton Tiberius B I.[53] The fact that the English kingdom and the Danish kingdom were referred to in terms of being *lands* in regnal title used in Cnut's 1027 letter while the Norwegians and Swedes were referred to as *peoples* may have had particular resonance. In the Old English *Orosius*, Alfred's interrogatee Ohthere had referred to himself as having 'ealra norðmanna norðmest bude' (lived the furthest north of all the northmen).[54] In the ninth century, Wessex had thus been placed within a wider northern geography for a receptive audience that could imagine 'northmen' living on the edge of territory that, paradoxically, stretched yet further north. In Cnut's address of 1027 the fourfold division placed England and Denmark into a northern context ripe for a revival of such an Orosian world view.

Pertinent to my contribution to this volume, however, is also an eastern dimension. A final issue related to this is Cnut's departure in 1022 to a place recorded in the Anglo-Saxon Chronicle as 'Wiht' or 'Wihtland', depending on the manuscript.[55] Although 'Wiht' could refer to the Isle of Wight in the context of the Chronicle's place names (as in its 998 entry), as far back as the 1870s the Danish historian Johannes Steenstrup noted that the Chronicler's 'Wihtland' was recorded in a way which linked it to the *Witland* in the Baltic in the Old English *Orosius*.[56] It is fair to say that, although the Baltic ultimately seems more likely, the matter has never been fully resolved. Whether 'Wiht' referred to the Isle of Wight or somewhere further afield in the Baltic beyond the eastern reaches of Cnut's empire remains a point of contention for an understanding of Cnut's reign — why would the Chronicler be concerned

---

52 On the depiction of Cnut's forceful legitimacy on the frontispiece of the New Minster *Liber Vitae*, BL, MS Stowe 944, fol. 6ʳ, see Karkov, *The Ruler Portraits of Anglo-Saxon England*, p. 134.

53 BL, MS Cotton Tiberius B I, fols 1–111. On the place of the description of the world in a wider Tiberius manuscript which itself 'reflects and shapes the history and the geography of its land of origin', see Gilles, 'Territorial Interpolations in the Old English *Orosius*', pp. 94–95 (quotation at p. 95). See also Helen Appleton above, pp. 310–29, and Francis Leneghan below, pp. 406–09.

54 OE *Orosius* I.1.16, in *The Old English History of the World*, ed. and trans. by Godden, p. 37.

55 ASC *s.a.* 1022 (MSS D ('to Wihtlande'), C, and E ('to Wiht')).

56 Steenstrup, *Normannerne*, IV, pp. 324–25.

about Cnut going to the Isle of Wight, which is 'Wihtland' in the 998 entry of the Chronicle?[57]

That there are differing interpretations of 'Wiht' may not be entirely problematic, however. While, given the context of Cnut's activities in the 1020s, his presence in the Baltic seems more likely than the Isle of Wight, perhaps the fact that different members of the Chronicle's audience could *read* Cnut as being in the Baltic while also reading him on a little island off the Solent may have been a useful ambiguity for an Anglo-Scandinavian court audience, whose opportunities and world view were being widened by the spread of Cnut's ambitions in the 1020s.[58]

Conclusion: Localizing Danish England

What might have been the purposes of this shift and re-energized interest in 'Scandinavian Danes' — what we might term 'Danes proper' — in the eleventh century? For a period from the end of Alfred's reign to the early years of that of Æthelred, the English may have been in contact with 'Danes' and called people thus, but these were links with Danes who were primarily from places other than Denmark. In that respect, it is noteworthy that reference to 'Danes' in locations outside Denmark, particularly Norway, are frequent in English sources, perhaps more than those in Denmark itself.[59] In relation to Danes in England, for example, that marker of the emergent respectability of Vikings, the reference to Archbishop Oda's descent in the *Vita S. Oswaldi*, links Oda to 'the Army', a group alluded to in English law, rather than to Denmark itself.[60]

Given that 'Dane' was a term which effectively made reference to Scandinavians more generally rather than inhabitants of Denmark specifically, this may not be surprising. However, in the tenth century, we may witness a manipulation of the Danes into an Insular world that was not specifically linked with Denmark or even the North Sea world, in a kind of geographical dissolution that had brought 'Danes' into an English kingdom in a manner that may contrast with the 'lack of interest' in Celtic neighbours, observed elsewhere in this volume by Caitlin Ellis.[61] Æthelstan's claim in a New Minster

---

57 See the chronology in Rumble, ed., *The Reign of Cnut*, p. 4, which is ambiguous; while Lund, 'Cnut's Danish Kingdom', p. 36, reads it as Wendland. Keynes, 'The Æthelings in Normandy', makes a case for Cnut being in the Isle of Wight.

58 The English Earl Godwine's overseas service with Cnut is a useful example: see Barlow, *The Godwins*, p. 28.

59 The first reference in terms of Denmark is in ASC *s.a.* 1005 (MSS C, D, and E; see Ellis above, p. 357). For 'Danes' from Norway during the 990s, see Lavelle, 'Law, Death and Peacemaking in the "Second Viking Age"', and on earlier tenth-century English links with Norway, Sawyer, 'English Influence on the Development of the Norwegian Kingdom', esp. p. 226.

60 Byrhtferth of Ramsey, *Vita S. Oswaldi*, 1.4, in Byrhtferth, *The Lives of St Oswald and St Ecgwine*, pp. 16–17.

61 Caitlin Ellis in this volume, p. 357.

Winchester charter of the 920s or early 930s to be king of the Anglo-Saxons and Danes ('Angelsaxonum Denorumque gloriosissimus rex') is perhaps telling here. At the same time, the English court was linked with a wider diaspora, as we see with other Scandinavians — Icelanders and Norwegians — who were at Æthelstan's court.[62]

If the 'Danes' of the mid- to late tenth-century English kingdom became subsumed by a wider sense of a *gens Anglorum*, in the early eleventh century, it is significant that the identification of Danes became focused once again on the 'Jutish' homelands of the Anglo-Saxons: thus, we see Cnut referred to as 'Lord of the Jutes' in Skaldic poetry, and the Sigmund legend is used to evidence shared ancestry in the 'Winchester Frieze' excavated from the site of Old Minster Winchester.[63]

Thus, while the concepts of specific geolocalization, of the actual identification of particular groups at cardinal points in an 'Anglo-Saxon' or 'Anglo-Danish' world view may have proved elusive in the above discussion, I wonder if such identification might not ultimately be necessary. The geographical identifiers attributed to 'Vikings' in early medieval England, and the changing relations that they indicate, have proved less elusive and are a useful way to chart the changing concepts of identity and its political meaning. They reflect processes of both othering and inclusion in the early Middle Ages, allowing us to consider how the identity of groups could be linked to particular locales and ultimately placed in the early medieval conceptualization of the world.

---

62 S 1417 (AD 924×33). See Roffey and Lavelle, 'West Saxons and Danes', p. 12. The international nature of the court leads Michael Wood to refer to a 'kind of intellectual *Comitatus*': Wood, 'The Making of King Aethelstan's Empire', p. 258. For discussion of Æthelstan's imperial aspirations, see above, Introduction, p. 30, and, on their representation in the *Brunanburh* poem, Paul Cavill below, pp. 395–98.

63 Óttarr Svarti, *Knútsdrápa*, 3, l. 5, in *Den Norsk-Islandske Skjaldedigtning*, ed. by Jónsson, vol. BI, p. 273, cited by Townend, 'Contextualizing the Knútsdrápur', p. 173. Biddle and Kjølbye-Biddle, 'Danish Royal Burials in Winchester', pp. 215–17.

Works Cited

Manuscripts

London, British Library, MS Cotton Nero A I
London, British Library, MS Cotton Tiberius B I
London, British Library, MS Harley 55
London, British Library, MS Stowe 944

Primary Sources

Alfred the Great: Asser's 'Life of King Alfred' and Other Contemporary Sources, ed. and trans. by Simon Keynes and Michael Lapidge (Harmondsworth: Penguin, 1983)

The Anglo-Saxon Chronicle: A Collaborative Edition, III: *MS A*, ed. by Janet Bately (Cambridge: D. S. Brewer, 1986)

The Anglo-Saxon Chronicle: A Collaborative Edition, V: *MS C*, ed. by Katherine O'Brien O'Keeffe (Cambridge: D. S. Brewer, 2001)

The Anglo-Saxon Chronicle: A Collaborative Edition, VI: *MS D*, ed. by G. P. Cubbin (Cambridge: D. S. Brewer, 1996)

The Anglo-Saxon Chronicle: A Collaborative Edition, VII: *MS E*, ed. by Susan Irvine (Cambridge: D. S. Brewer, 2004)

The Anglo-Saxon Chronicle: A Collaborative Edition, XVII: *The Annals of St Neots with Vita Prima Sancti Neoti*, ed. by David N. Dumville and Michael Lapidge (Cambridge: D. S. Brewer, 1985)

The Anglo-Saxon Chronicle: A Revised Translation, ed. and trans. by Dorothy Whitelock, S. I. Tucker, and David C. Douglas (London: Eyre and Spottiswoode, 1965)

The Anglo-Saxon Chronicles, ed. and trans. by Michael Swanton, rev. edn (London: Phoenix, 2000)

Asser's Life of King Alfred, together with the Annals of Saint Neots Erroneously Ascribed to Asser, ed. by W. H. Stevenson (Oxford: Oxford University Press, 1904)

Byrhtferth of Ramsey, *The Lives of St Oswald and St Ecgwine*, ed. and trans. by Michael Lapidge (Oxford: Oxford University Press, 2009)

Die Gesetze der Angelsachsen, ed. by Felix Liebermann, 3 vols (Halle: Max Niemeyer, 1903–1916)

History and Politics in Late Carolingian and Ottonian Europe: The Chronicle of Regino of Prüm and Adalbert of Magdeburg, ed. and trans. by Simon MacLean (Manchester: Manchester University Press, 2009)

Den Norsk-Islandske Skjaldedigtning, ed. by Finnur Jónsson, 4 vols (Copenhagen: Arnamagnæanske Stiftelse, 1912–1915)

The Old English History of the World: An Anglo-Saxon Rewriting of Orosius, ed. and trans. by Malcolm R. Godden, DOML, 44 (Cambridge, MA: Harvard University Press, 2016)

Regino of Prüm, *Regionis abbatis Prumiensis Chronicon cum continuatione Treverensi*, ed. by F. Kurze, MGH: Scriptores rerum Germanicarum in usum scholarum separatim editi, 50 (Hanover: Hahn, 1890)

Vita Bonifatii auctore Willibaldo, in *Vitae sancti Bonifatii archepiscopo Moguntini*, ed. by W. Levison, MGH: Scriptores rerum Germanicarum in usum scholarum separatim editi, 57 (Hanover: Hahn, 1905), pp. 1–58

William of Malmesbury, *Gesta Regum Anglorum: The History of the English Kings*, I, ed. by R. A. B. Mynors, R. M. Thomson, and M. Winterbottom, Oxford Medieval Texts (Oxford: Oxford University Press, 1998)

Secondary Sources

Allport, Ben, 'Home Thoughts of Abroad: Ohthere's Voyage in its Anglo-Saxon Context', *Early Medieval Europe*, 28 (2020), 256–88

Barlow, Frank, *The Godwins: The Rise and Fall of a Noble Dynasty* (London: Longman, 2002)

Bartholemew, Philip, 'Continental Connections: Angles, Saxons and Others in Bede and in Procopius', *Anglo-Saxon Studies in Archaeology and History*, 13 (2006), 19–30

Bately, Janet, 'The Compilation of the Anglo-Saxon Chronicle, 60 BC to AD 890: Vocabulary as Evidence', *Proceedings of the British Academy*, 64 (1978), 93–129

Bauduin, Pierre, *Le monde franc et les Vikings, VIIIe–Xe siècle* (Paris: Albin Michel, 2009)

Besteman, Jan, 'Two Viking Hoards from the Former Island of Wieringen (The Netherlands): Viking Relations with Frisia in an Archaeological Perspective', in *Land, Sea and Home: Proceedings of a Conference on Viking-Period Settlement, at Cardiff, July 2001*, ed. by John Hines, Alan Lane, and Mark Redknap (Leeds: Maney, 2004), pp. 93–108

Bibire, Paul, 'North Sea Language Contacts in the Early Middle Ages: English and Norse', in *The North Sea World in the Middle Ages*, ed. by Thomas R. Liska and Lorna E. M. Walker (Dublin: Four Courts Press, 2001), pp. 88–107

Biddle, Martin, and Birthe Kjølbye-Biddle, 'Danish Royal Burials in Winchester: Cnut and his Family', in *Danes in Wessex: The Scandinavian Impact on Southern England, c. 800–c. 1100*, ed. by Ryan Lavelle and Simon Roffey (Oxford: Oxbow, 2016), pp. 212–49

Bolton, Timothy, *The Empire of Cnut the Great: Conquest and the Consolidation of Power in Northern Europe in the Early Eleventh Century* (Leiden: Brill, 2009)

Cleasby, Richard, and Gudbrand Vigfusson, eds, *An Icelandic-English Dictionary* (Oxford: Clarendon Press, 1874)

Coumert, Magali, 'Les Angles dans les coins: L'identité ethnique angle en Angleterre du Ve au VIIIe siècle', in *De la mer du Nord à la mer Baltique: Identités, contacts et communications au Moyen Âge*, ed. by Alban Gautier and Sébastien Rossignol (Lille: Publications de l'Institut de recherches historiques du Septentrion, 2012), pp. 45–59

——, *Origines des peuples: Les récits du Haut Moyen Âge occidental (550–850)* (Paris: Institut d'Etudes Augustiniennes, 2007)

Coupland, Simon, 'The Blinkers of Militarisation: Charles the Bald, Lothar I and the Vikings', in *Early Medieval Militarisation*, ed. by Ellora Bennett, Guido M. Berndt, Stefan Esders, and Laury Sarti (Manchester: Manchester University Press, 2021), pp. 164–78

——, 'From Poachers to Gamekeepers: Scandinavian Warlords and Carolingian Kings', *Early Medieval Europe*, 7 (1998), 85–114

Davis, Craig R., 'An Ethnic Dating of *Beowulf*', *ASE*, 35 (2006), 111–29

Downham, Clare, '"Hiberno-Norwegians" and "Anglo-Danes": Anachronistic Ethnicities in Viking Age England', *Mediaeval Scandinavia*, 19 (2009), 139–69

Dumville, David N., 'Vikings in Insular Chronicling', in *The Viking World*, ed. by Stefan Brink and Neil Price (London: Routledge, 2008), pp. 350–67

Gates, J. P., '*Ealles Englalandes Cyningc*: Cnut's Territorial Kingship and Wulfstan's Paronomastic Play', *The Heroic Age: A Journal of Early Medieval Northwestern Europe*, no. 14 (November 2010), <http://www.heroicage.org/issues/14/gates. php>

Gilles, Sealy, 'Territorial Interpolations in the Old English *Orosius*', in *Text and Territory: Geographical Imagination in the European Middle Ages*, ed. by Sylvia Tomasch and Sealy Gilles (Philadelphia: University of Pennsylvania Press, 1998), pp. 79–96

Hadley, D. M., 'Ethnicity and Acculturation', in *A Social History of England, 900–1200*, ed. by Julia Crick and Elisabeth van Houts (Cambridge: Cambridge University Press, 2012), pp. 235–46

Hines, John, 'The Anglo-Frisian Question', in *Frisians and their North Sea Neighbours: From the Fifth Century to the Viking Age*, ed. by John Hines and Nelleke IJssennagger (Woodbridge: Boydell, 2017), pp. 25–42

Hines, John, and Nelleke IJssennagger, eds, *Frisians and their North Sea Neighbours: From the Fifth Century to the Viking Age* (Woodbridge: Boydell, 2017)

Hobson, Jacob, 'National-Ethnic Narratives in Eleventh-Century Literary Representations of Cnut', *ASE*, 43 (2014), 267–95

IJssennagger, Nelleke L., 'Between Frankish and Viking: Frisia and Frisians in the Viking Age', *Viking and Medieval Scandinavia*, 9 (2013), 69–98

Jesch, Judith, 'Who Was Wulfstan?', in *Wulfstan's Voyage: The Baltic Region in the Early Viking Age as Seen from Shipboard*, ed. by Anton Englert and Athena Trakadas (Roskilde: Viking Ship Museum, 2009), pp. 29–36

Karkov, Catherine, *The Ruler Portraits of Anglo-Saxon England* (Woodbridge: Boydell, 2004)

Keynes, S. D., 'The Æthelings in Normandy', *Anglo-Norman Studies*, 13 (1990), 173–206

Lavelle, Ryan, 'Cnut, King of the English, 1017–19', in *Anglo-Danish Empire: A Companion to the Reign of Cnut the Great*, ed. by Richard North, Erin Goeres, and Alison Finlay (Kalamazoo: Medieval Institute Publications, 2022), pp. 169–89

——, *Cnut: The North Sea King* (London: Allen Lane, 2017)

——, 'Law, Death and Peacemaking in the "Second Viking Age": An Ealdorman, his King, and Some Danes in Wessex', in *Danes in Wessex: The Scandinavian Impact on Southern England, c. 800–c. 1100*, ed. by Ryan Lavelle and Simon Roffey (Oxford: Oxbow, 2016), pp. 122–43

——, 'Representing Authority in an Early Medieval Chronicle: Submission, Rebellion and the Limits of the *Anglo-Saxon Chronicle, c. 899–1065*', in *Authority and Gender in Medieval and Renaissance Chronicles*, ed. by Juliana Dresvina and Nicholas Sparks (Newcastle-upon-Tyne: Cambridge Scholars Publishing, 2012), pp. 62–102

Lebecq, Stéphane, 'On the Use of the Word "Frisian" in the 6th–10th Centuries Written Sources: Some Interpretations', in *Maritime Celts, Frisians and Saxons*, ed. by Seán McGrail (London: Council for British Archaeology, 1990), pp. 85–90

——, 'Les Vikings en Frise: Chronique d'un échec relatif', in *Les fondations scandinaves en Occident et les débuts du duché de Normandie: Actes du colloque de Cerisy-la-Salle (25–29 septembre 2002)*, ed. by Pierre Bauduin (Caen: Publications du CRAHM, 2005), pp. 97–112

Lund, Niels, 'Cnut's Danish Kingdom', in *The Reign of Cnut: King of England, Denmark and Norway*, ed. by Alexander Rumble (London: Leicester University Press, 1994), pp. 27–42

Nelson, Janet L., 'England and the Continent in the Ninth Century: II, The Vikings and Others', *Transactions of the Royal Historical Society*, 6th Ser., 13 (2003), 1–28

Pestell, Tim, 'The Kingdom of East Anglia, Frisia and Continental Connections, c. AD 600–900', in *Frisians and their North Sea Neighbours: From the Fifth Century to the Viking Age*, ed. by John Hines and Nelleke IJssennagger (Woodbridge: Boydell, 2017), pp. 193–222

Ridel, Élisabeth, 'Bateaux de type scandinave en Normandie', in *L'héritage maritime des Vikings en Europe de l'Ouest: Colloque international de la Hague (Flottemanville-Hague, 30 septembre–3 octobre 1999)*, ed. by Élisabeth Ridel (Caen: Presses universitaires de Caen, 2001), pp. 287–319

Roffey, Simon, and Ryan Lavelle, 'West Saxons and Danes: Negotiating Early Medieval Identities', in *Danes in Wessex: The Scandinavian Impact on Southern England, c. 800–c. 1100*, ed. by Ryan Lavelle and Simon Roffey (Oxford: Oxbow, 2016), pp. 7–34

Rumble, Alexander, ed., *The Reign of Cnut: King of England, Denmark and Norway* (London: Leicester University Press, 1994)

Sawyer, Birgit, 'Appendix: The Evidence of Scandinavian Runic Inscriptions', in *The Reign of Cnut: King of England, Denmark and Norway*, ed. by Alexander Rumble (London: Leicester University Press, 1994), pp. 22–26

Sawyer, Peter, 'Cnut's Scandinavian Empire', in *The Reign of Cnut: King of England, Denmark and Norway*, ed. by Alexander Rumble (London: Leicester University Press, 1994), pp. 10–21

——, 'English Influence on the Development of the Norwegian Kingdom', in *Anglo-Saxons: Studies Presented to Cyril Roy Hart*, ed. by Simon Keynes and Alfred P. Smyth (Dublin: Four Courts Press, 2006), pp. 224–29

Stafford, Pauline, *The East Midlands in the Early Middle Ages* (Leicester: Leicester University Press, 1985)

——, 'The Laws of Cnut and the History of Anglo-Saxon Royal Promises', *ASE*, 47 (1981), 173–90

Steenstrup, Johannes C. H. R., *Normannerne*, 4 vols (Copenhagen: Rudolph Klein, 1876–1882)

Stoodley, Nick, 'Costume Groups in Hampshire and their Bearing on the Question of Jutish Settlement in the Later 5th and 6th Centuries AD', in *The Land of the English Kin: Studies in Wessex and Anglo-Saxon England in Honour of Professor Barbara Yorke*, ed. by Alexander Langlands and Ryan Lavelle, Brill's Series on the Early Middle Ages, 26 (Leiden: Brill, 2020), pp. 70–94

Swanton, M. J., 'King Alfred's Ships: Text and Context', *ASE*, 28 (1999), 1–22

Townend, Matthew, 'Contextualizing the Knútsdrápur: Skaldic Praise-Poetry at the Court of Cnut', *ASE*, 30 (2001), 145–79

——, *The Road to Deerhurst: 1016 in English and Norse Sources*, Deerhurst Lecture 2016 (Deerhurst: The Friends of Deerhurst Church, 2017)

Treharne, Elaine, 'The Performance of Piety: Cnut, Rome, and England', in *England and Rome in the Early Middle Ages: Pilgrimage, Art, and Politics*, ed. by Francesca Tinti, SEM, 40 (Turnhout: Brepols, 2014), pp. 343–64

Tyler, Elizabeth M., *England in Europe: English Royal Women and Literary Patronage, c. 1000–c. 1150* (Toronto: Toronto University Press, 2017)

Wood, Michael, 'The Making of King Aethelstan's Empire: An English Charlemagne?', in *Ideal and Reality in Frankish and Anglo-Saxon Society: Studies Presented to J. M. Wallace-Hadrill*, ed. by Patrick Wormald, with Donald Bullough, and Roger Collins (Oxford: Blackwell, 1983), pp. 250–72

Wormald, Patrick, *The Making of English Law: King Alfred to the Twelfth Century*, I: *Legislation and its Limits* (Oxford: Blackwell, 1999)

Yorke, Barbara, 'Fact or Fiction? The Written Evidence for the Fifth and Sixth Centuries AD', *Anglo-Saxon Studies in Archaeology and History*, 6 (1993), 45–50

PAUL CAVILL

Kings, People, and Lands:
The Rhetoric of *The Battle of Brunanburh*

Scholars have seen the poem *The Battle of Brunanburh* as a panegyric, propagandist piece.[1] It has given rise to numerous differences of opinion about such things as whether it is hackneyed and clichéd or poetically sharp and effective; whether it was composed soon after the battle or much later; whether it was composed for the Chronicle or was independent; whether, or how, it shares features with Scandinavian skaldic poetry; why it omits details that we know from elsewhere in the historical record; and whether the poem can tell us anything about where the battle took place, among others.[2] It is generally agreed that the poem has a relentless rhetoric glorifying the English victory, though some see glimmers of sympathy for the defeated. Among the latter, Dolores Warwick Frese writes that the poem's 'radical poetic centre [...] inducts us into sympathy for the invaders'; Frances Randall Lipp argues that 'it is hardly possible to remain unmoved by the account of Constantine or by the image of the slain left to the mercy of the raven, the eagle, and the wolf'; and Alice Jorgensen, with rather more nuance, argues that the poem is not 'a subtle expression of pity, tender towards the feelings of the defeated, but it is not entirely cold and detached either.'[3]

Rhetoric can be understood in several ways. What we might call formal rhetoric uses the diction and style of the poem to identify tropes and schemes. Ann Johnson analysed the poem in terms of Latin rhetorical patterns described by Bede and found a number of parallelisms and repetitions that could be identified as schemata or tropes. She concluded that 'there is a deliberateness about the craftsmanship as the poet intentionally establishes a formal pattern

---

1 All quotations from the poem are from *The Battle of Brunanburh*, ed. by Campbell; quotations from other Old English poems are from *ASPR*; Latin and Middle English sources are quoted from *Brunanburh: A Casebook*, ed. by Livingston, except where otherwise indicated. Translations of the vernacular are my own.
2 See below for discussion of some of these, and for further references.
3 Frese, 'Poetic Prowess', p. 84; Lipp, 'Contrast and Point of View', p. 176; Jorgensen, 'Reading Emotion', p. 673.

> **Paul Cavill** (paul.cavill1@nottingham.ac.uk) is Honorary Senior Lecturer in Early English at the University of Nottingham. He has worked for many years on Old English poetry.

Ideas of the World in Early Medieval English Literature, ed. by Mark Atherton, Kazutomo Karasawa, and Francis Leneghan, SOEL 1 (Turnhout: Brepols, 2022)   pp. 385–402
BREPOLS ❧ PUBLISHERS   DOI 10.1484/M.SOEL.5.130569

of parallel sequences. [...] Thus rhetoric becomes the instrument of conscious artistry'.[4] She acknowledged, however, that classical types were inadequate to describe many of the figures native to Old English poetry. W. F. Bolton gave direct attention to one of these, the variation in the poem, and showed that the artefact has a remarkable series of patterns and symmetrical structuring using this native technique.[5] Most studies of the poem as poetry highlight these kinds of features. But more recently, scholars have shifted the focus from formal rhetoric to the purpose of the poem, the propagandistic aim, the panegyric nature of the verse, identifying and using both internal features and its context. This is the 'rhetoric' which will be the focus of the first part of this chapter.

This chapter will discuss some aspects of the poem's rhetorical strategy, and indeed will argue that understanding the rhetorical force of the poem, focusing particularly on names and places, is crucial to its interpretation.

Æthelstan and Edmund

The poem *The Battle of Brunanburh* is overwhelmingly likely to be the earliest extant source of information about the battle.[6] It was distributed in a tranche of annals to various monastic centres to be copied into the locally kept manuscripts of the national history, the Anglo-Saxon Chronicle.[7] The section of annals containing the poem was distributed sometime around 955, and it is sometimes proposed that the poem was composed not long before that date, partly because the run of annals, and the poem on the *Capture of the Five Boroughs*, have the conventional *Her* (Here, In this year) opening and some similarities of diction;[8] partly because the poem mentions Edmund as

---

4 Johnson, 'The Rhetoric of *Brunanburh*', p. 493.

5 Bolton, '"Variation" in *The Battle of Brunanburh*'.

6 Wood, 'Searching for Brunanburh', p. 155, argues for the name *Wendun* in the *Historia regum* (*Brunanburh: A Casebook*, ed. by Livingston, pp. 64–65) to have been 'written in Chester-le-Street in the second quarter of the tenth century', thus antedating the extant A Chronicle version, but the argument is confused and does not engage with the manuscript evidence or modern scholarship. The section of the *Historia regum* where the name occurs is in a compilation which borrows often inaccurately from several sources including the Anglo-Saxon Chronicle and the *Annales Cambriae*. The entries in the compilation relate to the years 888–957, but the reference to Edward the Confessor as the descendant of Edgar at the end indicates that the compilation was made in or after the middle of the eleventh century. A copy of this compilation was known at Durham in the twelfth century, where it was entered into the only extant manuscript, CCCC, MS 139, but there is no indication where the 'Chronicle from 888 to 957' was originally written. See further Blair, 'Some Observations on the *Historia Regum*', especially pp. 104–06, and Cavill, 'The Battle of Brunanburh'.

7 ASC, MSS A, B, C, and D; E and F do not have the poem, but a brief prose notice of the battle.

8 Scragg, 'A Reading of *Brunanburh*', p. 113, argues that the annals 924–955, written by a single scribe, were 'composed by the same chronicler-cum-poet, someone necessarily working at the end of Edmund's reign'. Bredehoft, 'The Battle of Brunanburh in Old English Studies',

Æthelstan's co-belligerent and co-honorand;[9] and partly because it is supposed that the propagandist nature of the poem might have been more necessary in the rather difficult years of Edmund's early reign.[10] What has not been registered fully is the fact that whether or not the poem was composed for the Chronicle has no specific bearing on its date of composition beyond the two termini of the battle and the promulgation of the set of annals.[11] And while the emphasis in the block of annals from the death of Edward the Elder to the death of Edmund, Æthelstan's half-brother (924–946), is on Edmund, and relatively little is said in this block about Æthelstan overall, the Brunanburh poem does in fact focus mostly on Æthelstan and his concerns. The poem's rhetoric, I suggest, is that of Æthelstan and his court.[12]

The first lines signal Æthelstan's nature and achievement, and the last lines refer to Æthelstan's well-known interest in books, the 'bec | ealde uðwitan' (books, ancient authorities, ll. 68b–69a) which contextualize both the significance of the battle in relation to the past, but also record the king's deeds in the present.[13]

---

p. 287, remarks, 'nothing in the poem, I think, marks it as especially close in time to the events described, and it may well take a retrospective viewpoint'. The long-running debate about *Her* and its significance as a possible indicator that the poem was composed for the Chronicle is hard to summarize: on the side of *Her* and other features indicating a possible independent poem, see Townend, 'Pre-Cnut Praise Poetry', p. 352; on the side of *Her* as indicating possible composition for the Chronicle, see Bredehoft's books and articles, and the argument that in the B text of *Brunanburh*, where monosyllabic 'cing' occurs in l. 1, *Her* is metrically necessary, '*The Battle of Brunanburh* in Old English Studies', p. 286. The views of Isaacs, 'Battlefield Tour', p. 237, that it also draws attention to the place, and Trilling, *The Aesthetics of Nostalgia*, p. 201, that the word 'functions to bridge the distance between a number on a manuscript page and its referent in a past event' are of particular interest in the present chapter.

9   See discussion below.

10 Walker, 'A Context for *Brunanburh*', p. 33, observes, 'The crisis of political control that created a need for such propaganda [as the *Brunanburh* poem] was at its most acute early in Edmund's reign and continued to exist, in a less threatening manner, until 955.' It was also, of course, acute at the time of the battle of Brunanburh: 'Exaggerating the importance of this victory is difficult, for had Æthelstan's opponents won, the West Saxon hegemony over the whole of mainland Britain would have disintegrated', as Foot, *Æthelstan*, p. 171, puts it.

11 Note, however, Walker's contention, 'A Context for *Brunanburh*', pp. 34–35, that the layout of the 937–946 annals in A, and the identity of the material with that in B and C for these years, might suggest that those annals were 'a single unit', and that the poem 'had been composed by 946'; see *The Anglo-Saxon Chronicle: MS A*, ed. by Bately, p. xlix.

12 See further Francis Leneghan's chapter in this volume for a discussion of the rhetorical purpose of the Chronicle poems and the argument that 'it is in the six Old English poems embedded in tenth- and eleventh-century annals that the Chronicle's underlying imperial theme is given its fullest expression', p. 417. Leneghan argues that *The Death of Edward* was similarly produced by the West Saxon court, possibly by supporters of Godwin.

13 See Keynes, 'King Athelstan's Books'. The phrase '(þæs þe) us secgað bec' (as the books tell us) is a poetic commonplace, appearing in *Genesis*, ll. 227, 1723, *Christ*, l. 785, *Guthlac*, l. 878, *The Lord's Prayer* II 20, and numerous times in Ælfric; also frequent are variants such as 'us cyðað bec' (as books tell us). While the *bec* (books) may be 'the Chronicle itself', as Trilling, *The Aesthetics of Nostalgia*, p. 198, puts it, or as Scragg implies, 'A Reading of *Brunanburh*',

The wordplay on *æþel-* in the opening lines foregrounds a wish to display the king's name and attributes in a similar way to other extant poems. Zacher analyses the contemporary Latin *Adalstan* acrostic *Archalis clamare triumuir* and the poem *Carta dirige gressus*, and notes extensive wordplay on the 'noble stone' etymology of the king's name, 'forming a multilingual aggregate of puns that run between Old English, Latin, and Greek'.[14] Gallagher suggests that the 'nomina' (names) of the last line of the acrostic, in a poem 'crammed full of onomastic puns playing on Æthelstan's name [...] could perhaps, therefore, be nothing more than a nod to this wordplay, acknowledging that the verses contain numerous implicit references to the name of the king',[15] that is, that the poet was not only playing on the name, but was also self-consciously referring to the technique of naming wordplay. Another Latin poem of Æthelstan's reign, *Rex pius Æðelstan*, begins almost echoing *Brunanburh* with emphatic reference to the king and his nature, *pius* (devout, holy), and similarly goes on both to mention his defeat of enemies, 'Scilicet ut ualeat reges rex ipse feroces | Vincere bellipotens, colla superba terens' (plainly so that this king himself, mighty in war, might be able to conquer other fierce kings, treading down their proud necks, ll. 5–6), and to dwell on the book in which the poem was written.[16]

Æthelstan as king is noble in name and nature, his brother shares a similar but lesser nobility as 'æþeling' (prince, l. 3), their valour is natural to them, 'geæþele' (l. 7), and the very creation smiles on them as the sun, the 'æþele gesceaft' (noble creation, l. 16), presides over their victory.[17] The fact that they were brothers and sons of Edward is also mentioned more than once and is further discussed below. But it seems doubtful to me that the poem therefore 'ascribes to Edmund, a boy of sixteen at the time of the battle [...] a degree of responsibility that is entirely lacking in those accounts of the *Brunanburh*

---

p. 118, 'a self-referential passage by a poet composing for the ASC itself', the phrase is plural, and in the vast majority of cases in Old English applies to books more generally, such as the Bible and Christian authors. The term *uðwita* (authority) often refers to secular writers such as Plato, Cato, and Epicurus, that is, writers available in Latin. Scragg, 'A Reading of *Brunanburh*', p. 118, rules out reference to Bede since he is 'normally described as a *bocere*', but this probably underemphasizes the connection between *boc/bec* (book, books) and *bocere* (scribe), and the fact that Bede is also and more frequently called other things such as *lareow* and *leornere* (teacher), and *trahtere* (commentator): see the *DOE Corpus* for examples.

14 Zacher, 'Multilingualism', pp. 88–89, 94. The *Adalstan* acrostic *Archalis clamare triumuir* and *Carta dirige gressus* are both ed. by Lapidge, 'Some Latin Poems as Evidence', the latter also in *Brunanburh: A Casebook*, ed. by Livingston, pp. 36–39.

15 Gallagher, 'Latin Acrostic Poetry in Anglo-Saxon England', re-edits the *Adalstan* acrostic, pp. 257–58.

16 *Rex pius Æðelstan* is also edited by Lapidge, 'Some Latin Poems as Evidence' and in *Brunanburh: A Casebook*, ed. by Livingston, pp. 38–39.

17 This play on the element *æþel-* has been very frequently noted; see e.g. Addison, 'Aural Interlace', p. 270; Bolton, '"Variation" in *The Battle of Brunanburh*', p. 371; Lipp, 'Contrast and Point of View', p. 172; Lawler, '*Brunanburh*: Craft and Art', pp. 56–57; Taylor, 'Onomastics and Propaganda', pp. 67–68; Zacher, 'Multilingualism', pp. 97–98.

KINGS, PEOPLE, AND LANDS   389

campaign that are independent of the poem'.[18] Or that this constitutes a focus on Edmund that might lead to the conclusion that 'it makes most sense to see the stress on Edmund as reflecting a late date'.[19] Essentially, the poem may reflect historical reality in two particular regards: the position and importance of Edmund as subordinate to Æthelstan; and Æthelstan's own regard for his brother.

This focus on the *æþel-* element in the first few lines of the poem not only foregrounds the king's name but is also a marked usage in relation to the Chronicle.[20] David Dumville surveys the usage of the term *æþeling* in prose and concludes 'from the mid-ninth century to the end of the eleventh, the word *æþeling* seems [...] to carry no more specific meaning than that of "prince"'.[21] When the A version of the Chronicle records the deeds of the other famous West Saxon royal brothers, Æthelred and Alfred, with a view to exalting Alfred in retrospect, it never refers to Alfred as *æþeling*, but consistently refers to the pair as 'King Æthelred and Alfred his brother' (e.g. 868, 871 (x 5), and compare 860). The *Brunanburh* poem refers to Edmund as *æþeling* twice (ll. 3, 58), making clear Edmund's status as 'a prince of the royal family', but not at this stage the king he was to be: he is subordinate to Æthelstan while sharing his noble lineage. The use of the *æþeling* status title suggests that when the poem was composed, the king was still alive, and was expected to remain so for some time.

When the scribe of the F version of the Chronicle was writing, he knew that Edmund had been king after Æthelstan. The entries for 938 read as follows:

Her Æðestan cing \and [Ead]mund his broðer/ lædde fyrde to Brun(an) byri [and] þar gefeht wið Anelaf [and] Criste fultumegende sige hæfde \ [and] þar ofslogon .v. cingas [and] .vii. eor[las]./

(In this year King Æthelstan \and his brother Edmund/ led an army to Brunanburh and fought there against Anlaf; with Christ helping him, he had the victory \and there they killed five kings and seven noblemen./)

---

18   Walker, 'A Context for *Brunanburh*', p. 31. In one sense this is true: accounts independent of the poem tend to mention Æthelstan alone, e.g. Æthelweard, *Chronicon*, in *Brunanburh: A Casebook*, ed. by Livingston, pp. 48–49, Wulfstan of Winchester, *Vita sancti Ethelwoldi*, in *Brunanburh: A Casebook*, ed. by Livingston, pp. 50–51, and the E Chronicle, in *Brunanburh: A Casebook*, ed. by Livingston, pp. 54–55; or Æthelstan and Anlaf, e.g. Ælfric, *Epilogue to Judges*, in *Brunanburh: A Casebook*, ed. by Livingston, pp. 50–51. These texts have their own rhetoric, to be sure, but they do not share the poem's characteristic balancing and contrast.

19   Jorgensen, 'Reading Emotion', p. 671.

20   See Francis Leneghan in this volume for similar expressions and collocations in *The Death of Edward*.

21   Dumville, 'The Ætheling', p. 6. Dumville is wary of much discussion of the term in Old English verse, 'We may pass by the uses of *æþeling* in poetry, where it is employed generally of men, in a good and noble sense' (p. 3). Clearly *Brunanburh* uses the term in a technical sense, though undoubtedly with some heroic gloss.

Hic factum est illud magnum et famosum bellum in Brunanbyri cum rex Æðestanus \et frater eius Eadmundus/ pugna(uerunt) contra Anelaf et auxiliante Christo uictoriam ce(perunt) \et occiderunt .v. reges et .vii. comites de sociis Anelafi./

(Here happened that great and famous battle at Brunanburh when King Æthelstan \and his brother Edmund/ fought against Anlaf; and with Christ helping them, they took the victory \and killed five kings and seven noblemen among Anlaf's allies./)[22]

The additions in the manuscript show that the writer knew the tradition of the poem, or at least came across it later, by reference to the added information about the number of enemy notables killed. But the writer did not copy the *æþeling* title given in the poem, and rather inserted the 'king and his brother' formula.

The brotherly relationship is important in the poem. These modes of reference to the brothers are part of the rhetoric of English unity in the poem. It begins with Æthelstan, but immediately names 'his broþor […] Eadmund' (Edmund his brother, ll. 2b–3a); the brothers together return home in victory, 'þa gebroþor begen ætsamne' (l. 57). Both are sons of Edward the Elder, their notably warlike and effective father, 'afaran Eadweardes' (l. 7), 'Eadweardes afaran' (l. 52). This contrasts with the disunited forces opposing, with Anlaf's unseemly departure in a single ship (ll. 32–36) 'litle weorode' (with a small band, l. 34) before the main body of the Norse survivors (ll. 53–56); and Constantine's abandonment of responsibility for avenging his dead son, left on the battlefield (ll. 37–46).

There is no particular reason why the poem should mention that the brothers were in fact half-brothers with the same father but different mothers; but this relationship was one that was at the root of several dynastic quarrels in the Old English period.[23] Dumville notes the tradition of Æthelstan's treatment of his brother Edwin, who drowned at sea, 'Her adranc Ædwine æðeling on sæ', as the E version of the Chronicle diplomatically puts it, *s.a.* 933.[24] William of Malmesbury tells a sorrowful story of how Æthelstan, deceived by false tales, put the delicate youth into a worm-eaten boat and set him adrift; in despair he drowned himself, and his squire survived to reveal the deceit.[25] Peter Langtoft has Æthelstan order him to be bound and drowned in the Thames.[26] Æthelstan had to share rule with his older brother Ælfweard, before the latter died. Æthelstan's early position as king was somewhat precarious,

---

22 *The Anglo-Saxon Chronicle: MS F*, ed. by Baker, pp. 79–80.
23 Dumville, 'The Ætheling', p. 30.
24 *The Anglo-Saxon Chronicle: MS E*, ed. by Irvine, p. 55.
25 William of Malmesbury, *Gesta Regum Anglorum*, ed. by Mynors, Thomson, and Winterbottom, II. 139–40, pp. 226–29.
26 Langtoft, in *Brunanburh: A Casebook*, ed. by Livingston, pp. 92–93.

and it is possible that Ætheling Edwin was a threat: even if Edwin was not murdered or executed, he was exiled.[27]

Young princes are notoriously disposable, and if Edmund had been a threat to Æthelstan, he, too, might have disappeared. In this light, it is far from improbable that a degree of warmth and regard existed between the royal brothers. William of Malmesbury is very fulsome about Æthelstan's regard for his brothers: 'suae pietatis diligentiam in reliquos fratres intenderit, quos, cum pater puerulos admotum reliquisset, ille paruos magna dulcedine fouit et adultos regni consortes fecit' (he gave practical proof of remarkable affection towards his other brothers: mere infants at his father's death, he brought them up lovingly in childhood, and when they grew up gave them a share in his kingdom).[28] Malmesbury was held in particular affection by Æthelstan, as the place where he buried his cousins and was himself interred; while William's account of Æthelstan's fraternal love might in part have had the purpose of exculpating Æthelstan from the charge of fratricide, it might equally have been founded on local tradition. An unrelated text, the Lindisfarne monks' *Historia de Sancto Cuthberto*, records that in 934 the thirteen-year-old Edmund was with Æthelstan on his northern expedition at Chester-le-Street and 'fratrem uero suum Eadmundum […] ut si quid sinistri sibi in hac expeditione euenerit, corpus suum sancto Cuthberto referret' (then he fraternally instructed his brother Edmund […] that if anything sinister should befall him on this expedition to return his body to St Cuthbert).[29] The apparent implication of this is that Æthelstan regarded Edmund as his successor; certainly the latter was already engaged with Æthelstan, and with a measure of responsibility, on arduous and dangerous military expeditions.

One of the details not given in the poem is the losses on the English side. From William of Malmesbury and others we learn that two of Æthelstan's cousins, Ælfwine and Æthelwine, were killed in the battle.[30] This kind of omission is to be expected in a panegyric poem. One of the reasons for the emphasis on Edmund and Æthelstan as *afaran Eadweardes* (sons of Edward, twice) could well be that the two dead cousins were athelings, sons of Æthelweard, grandsons of King Alfred, and thus potential contenders for the throne.

---

27 Keynes, 'King Athelstan's Books', p. 187; Walker, 'A Context for *Brunanburh*', p. 32, suggests that the kingship was initially shared between Æthelstan and Edwin after Ælfweard's death.

28 William of Malmesbury, *Gesta Regum Anglorum*, ed. by Mynors, Thomson, and Winterbottom, II. 140, pp. 228–29.

29 *Historia de Sancto Cuthberto*, ed. by South, 27, pp. 64–67; South's translation.

30 William of Malmesbury, *Gesta Regum Anglorum*, ed. by Mynors, Thomson, and Winterbottom, II. 135, pp. 220–21. The *Eulogium Historiarum*, a fourteenth-century text, notes 'ceciderunt autem ibi duo nepotes regis Athelstani, scilicet, Elwyn et Athelwyn' (two nephews of King Æthelstan also died there, namely Ælfwine and Æthelwine), so also Walter Bower in his fifteenth-century *Scotichronicon*, in *Brunanburh: A Casebook*, ed. by Livingston, pp. 132–33 and 142–43, respectively. The *Annals of Ulster* mention 'multitudo Saxonum cecidit' (a great number of Saxons died), *Brunanburh: A Casebook*, ed. by Livingston, pp. 144–45.

The elision of this detail conceals the threat to the Cerdicing dynasty in the loss of two scions, while at the same time stressing the close unity of the royal brothers. The fact that one of those not mentioned was called Æthelwine points to the potential for confusion and disruption of that name in the scheme of the poem, and also possibly for another element to the panegyric wordplay using *æþel-* if Æthelwine had not died.[31]

The Enemies

It has often been observed that the poem is a panegyric, a praise-poem similar to Norse skaldic poetry, or propaganda, and Lapidge's, Zacher's, and Gallagher's work on the Latin poems of Æthelstan's reign has added another linguistic dimension to the propaganda. Some assume that this means *Brunanburh* is less than historical in its details, but this is to misunderstand the nature and purpose of such poetry. While there is a good deal of formulaic tradition and motif — the beasts of battle, the eagle, raven, and wolf as scavengers attending to the dead after the battle, is a good example of a traditional theme — much of the detail such as the battle's day-long duration and the large number of dead is confirmed by independent sources. In living memory of the battle and among those who participated in it, it would be counterproductive for the poem to claim more or give a significantly different account of the conflict than that widely known and accepted. Panegyric relies on selected and telling detail, not on fiction or gross exaggeration for its effect.[32]

Rhetorical embellishment is particularly evident in the passage at lines 44b–52, with its kennings and *hapax legomena* alongside the scornful litotes. The personal shame and discomfiture of the two enemy leaders is emphasized by this rhetorical device: Constantine had no need to rejoice (l. 39b), no need to boast (l. 44b), and together with Anlaf and the other survivors, had no need to laugh (l. 47b), at the outcome of the battle. Jorgensen reads this 'boasting sequence', by its very negation in the case of Constantine and Anlaf, to focus on the victors: 'By implication, the whole performance of boasting, laughter and noise is evoked in relation to Æthelstan and Edmund.'[33] This is plausible, but the litotes and the syntactic repetition imply a unity among the enemies which is in contrast to that of Æthelstan and Edmund: Anlaf and Constantine are only united in not being able to celebrate.

It is implied that the carrion left behind for the beasts to gorge on is the bodies of enemies, including those of five young kings and seven men

---

31 Trilling, *The Aesthetics of Nostalgia*, p. 219, remarks that the omission of the names 'shows how carefully *Brunanburh* guards its ideological investments'.

32 We might contrast the numbers of the enemy dead in another source: thirty thousand Scots, the eight hundred captives around Anlaf, and the four thousand Danish men mentioned in the *Annals of Clonmacnoise*, in *Brunanburh: A Casebook*, ed. by Livingston, pp. 152–53.

33 Jorgensen, 'Reading Emotion', p. 669.

KINGS, PEOPLE, AND LANDS   393

of the highest noble status below the king, possibly that of *jarl* (ll. 28–32), rendered in Old English here as 'eorl'.[34] English losses are not mentioned, as has already been noted. A further detail used for effect is the way the poem divides the forces: so far as the poet is concerned, the enemies were Scots under Constantine and Norsemen under Anlaf. The West Saxons and Mercians (ll. 20b, 24b) are given equal metrical and syntactic weight at the head of a main clause and the head-stave of a b-verse, and thereby the poem creates rhetorical unity between the English, whatever may have been the historical actuality.[35]

We know from other sources that a substantial body of Cumbrians was involved,[36] and that Northumbrians in England also joined forces with the coalition.[37] The poem omits reference to these other forces.[38] There are likely to be two reasons for this. The first is that the West Saxons and Mercians neatly balance the opposing Scots and Norsemen, just as Æthelstan and Edmund balance Constantine and Anlaf; the overall concern of the poem is to foreground the achievements of Wessex and Mercia against two powerful and recognizable enemies. This concern for rhetorical balance, which shows up the utter inadequacy of the opponents, is also seen in the account of the departures from the battlefield: the Norse left for Dublin ashamed, the English left for home rejoicing (ll. 53–59). The second reason is related: the English, West Saxons and Mercians, are united, and to mention the fact that some

---

34 In *The Battle of Brunanburh*, ed. by Campbell, p. 108, the note on *eorl* is as follows: 'The word *eorl* may be taken here in its new sense "Scandinavian chief"'. Page, 'A Tale of Two Cities', pp. 337–39, objects to Smyth's assumption, *Scandinavian York and Dublin*, II, pp. 38–39, that 'eorl' (l. 31a) means the same as *jarl*, and suggests an alternative gloss 'Anlaf's (leading) retainers' on the basis of the normal meaning of *eorl* in Old English poetry, '(noble) warrior, hero'. The term is undoubtedly ambiguous, but the numbering of those dead, seven, leads us to expect that these men were of especial status, marked out by some degree of significance. Moreover, the *Annals of Clonmacnoise*, in *Brunanburh: A Casebook*, ed. by Livingston, pp. 152–53, gives the names of seven *captaines* of Anlaf's company killed in the battle. See the discussion of this difficult text and the names, in *Brunanburh: A Casebook*, ed. by Livingston, pp. 237–40.

35 Page, 'A Tale of Two Cities', p. 340, argues, correctly, but possibly over-literally, that 'there is no mention at all of the Mercians fighting all day', suggesting the possibility that 'Athelstan's army at *Brunanburh* was the West Saxon *fyrd* only', and that the retreating Northmen were harassed on their flight through English Mercia by the Mercians.

36 Texts in *Brunanburh: A Casebook*, ed. by Livingston, which mention the Cumbrians include Symeon of Durham, *Libellus de exordio*, pp. 54–55; the *Historia regum*, pp. 64–65; Gaimar, *Estoire des Engleis*, pp. 64–65; Pseudo-Ingulf, *Ingulfi Croylandensis historia*, pp. 136–37; the *Prose Brut*, pp. 138–39; and Bower, *Scotichronicon*, pp. 142–43.

37 Texts in *Brunanburh: A Casebook*, ed. by Livingston, which mention the Northumbrians include William of Malmesbury, *Gesta Regum Anglorum*, pp. 58–59; Henry of Huntingdon, *Historia Anglorum*, pp. 60–61; Bartholomew of Cotton, *Historia Anglicana*, pp. 82–83; Bower, *Scotichronicon*, pp. 142–43; and *Annals of Clonmacnoise*, pp. 152–53.

38 Jorgensen, 'Reading Emotion', pp. 670–71, proposes that this might mean that the poem was composed long after the battle as other forces would be 'harder to omit closer in time to the actual event', but this perhaps misreads the rhetoric.

living within the bounds of former English dominions such as Northumbria or East Mercia were part of the enemy coalition would be to diminish the effectiveness of Æthelstan's power over the peoples in England and undermine his imperial ambition.[39] The rhetoric of the poem overrides insignificant detail.

Linguistic detail is perhaps rhetorically used in the loanword *cnear*. Matthew Townend has perceptively summarized earlier discussion of the possible influence of Norse on the poem. Roberta Frank, he notes, demonstrates possible lexical and syntactic parallels between some Old English expressions and those frequent in skaldic poetry;[40] John Niles focuses on vocabulary in the *Brunanburh* poem.[41] While he acknowledges the force and subtlety of these arguments, Townend prefers a wider interpretation that sees heroic praise poetry as a product of the 'Heroic Age' conditions produced by the Viking Age.[42] This is an argument well made and readily demonstrable, but Townend's example of 'mere linguistic influence from speakers of Old Norse', the use of *cnear* (ship), is mistaken. He writes,

> *cnear* is only evidence of [...] a Norse-derived loan having entered West Saxon [...] and its significance is especially minimal since it is a loanword of the most common type [...]. Its supposed extension in *Brunanburh* may well be simply due to the need for a 'ship' word alliterating on *c-*: Old English poetic diction possessed no such word, and thus the Norse-derived loan fills a perceived gap.[43]

The usual word for a ship in Old English is *ceol*, alliterating on *c-*, and it occurs some thirty times as a simplex in Old English verse, and frequently as a compound. The loanword *cnear*, derived from Old Norse *knǫrr* (ship), however, only occurs twice in poetry, once as a simplex, line 35a, once as a compound, 'nægledcnear' (studded ship, l. 53b), in *Brunanburh*; and once more as a gloss.[44] Clearly the usage here is not in default of an English 'ship' word, and while it may not reflect skaldic usage, it is at least intriguing that the word is used by Egill Skallagrímsson in his *Hǫfuðlausn*, a (slightly later) skaldic poem recited in York: 'mundknarrar skut' (cabin of the ship of the mind), a kenning for memory.[45] The word in *Brunanburh* is precise and technical, certainly unusual;[46] and while it may not reflect the semantic development

---

39 See further the chapters by Caitlin Ellis, Helen Appleton, and Francis Leneghan in this volume for discussion of West Saxon imperialism.

40 Frank, 'Did Anglo-Saxon Audiences Have a Skaldic Tooth?'; Townend, 'Pre-Cnut Praise Poetry', pp. 357–58.

41 Niles, 'Skaldic Technique in *Brunanburh*'; Townend, 'Pre-Cnut Praise Poetry', especially pp. 358–59.

42 Townend, 'Pre-Cnut Praise Poetry', pp. 359–70.

43 Townend, 'Pre-Cnut Praise Poetry', p. 359.

44 For fuller discussion of the term, see Cavill, 'Ships and *Brunanburh*'.

45 *Hǫfuðlausn*, in *Egils saga Skalla-Grímssonar*, ed. by Nordal, Chapter 60, st. 1, l. 4.

46 The scribe of the D text of the Chronicle made no sense of it, garbling 'nægledcnearrum' to 'dæg gled on garum' at l. 53; see *The Anglo-Saxon Chronicle: MS D*, ed. by Cubbin, p. 42.

suggested by Niles, from 'cargo ship' to 'war ship', it may reflect some scorn at the vaunted ships of the Vikings.[47] Use of the word can hardly have been accidental: it unequivocally shows Scandinavian influence on the language of the poem, but it might also show a rhetorical and metaphorical curling of the lip at those whose workmanship in making studded sea-going vessels was not matched by their prowess in 'beaduweorc' (works of war, l. 48a) and in contrast to that of the 'wigsmiþas' (battle-craftsmen, l. 73a) who first came to the shores of Britain.[48]

Lands

Much is made of the fact that the poem is modest in its claims about Æthelstan, who is not said to be King of Mercia:[49] but then, there is no mention that Æthelstan was King of Wessex, that Anlaf was King of Dublin or Constantine King of Scotland. The people are differentiated as West Saxons, Mercians, Scots, Northmen, Irish, Welsh, and the various protagonists are associated with the people-names. It is customary in Old English to define territory by the people occupying it, and the people by the ruler they acknowledged. Compare the other Chronicle poems: 'Eadmund cyning Engla þeoden' (King Edmund, lord of the English, *Capture of the Five Boroughs*, l. 1); 'Eadgar [...] Engla waldend' (Edgar, ruler of the English, *The Coronation of Edgar*, l. 1); 'Eadgar, Engla cyning' (Edgar, king of the English, *The Death of Edgar*, l. 2); 'Eadward kingc, Engla hlaford' (King Edward, lord of the English, *The Death of Edward*, l. 1).[50] By comparison, *Brunanburh* perhaps gives Æthelstan greater, more generalized, power as 'eorla dryhten' (lord of warriors, l. 1): an *imperium* of valour rather than tribe. In this context, less is very probably more.

The land itself is nevertheless a potent symbol of possession and power in the poem. Æthelstan and his brother Edmund 'land ealgodon' (defended the land, l. 9) against enemies. The other references to *land* are collocated with the verb *secan* and offer contrasting styles of 'seeking land'. The Mercians attacked the Dublin Vikings, those who 'on lides bosme land gesohton' (sought the land in the bosom of a ship, l. 27); and then the latter went back 'Difelin secan | eft Ira land' (to seek Dublin, back to the land of the Irish, ll. 55b–56a). Here they are rootless adventurers, seeking a land, failing, and having to return to a land that is not theirs: metrical stress in the D-type

---

47 Cavill, 'Ships and *Brunanburh*', discusses the semantic issue, pp. 553–55.
48 See Lawler, '*Brunanburh*: Craft and Art', for more on the emphasis on physical craftsmanship in the poem.
49 Jorgensen, 'Reading Emotion', p. 671, notes this observation from Jayne Carroll, and quotes her statement, '*Brunanburh* is positively modest in its claims about Athelstan's power'.
50 See Francis Leneghan's chapter in this volume, pp. 422-23, for discussion of the line in *The Death of Edward*.

verse 56a falls on *eft* (back). The garbled version in the A manuscript, '\and/ eft hira land' (\and/ thereafter their own land),[51] works nearly as well: they came to invade 'our' land and left to go back to 'their own', humiliated. This is all reinforced by the contrasting return journeys from battle of Æthelstan and Edmund, 'cyþþe sohton | Westseaxna land' (sought home, the land of the West Saxons, ll. 58b–59a), and Constantine who runs away home to the north ('on his cyþþe norð', l. 38a).

There is, though, one land that is given a simplex name in the Latin fashion, and this makes it emphatic: 'Brytene' (Britain, l. 71). This was the land taken by Æthelstan's ancestors, who made it their 'eard' (country, l. 74). The echoes in the poem make the significance of the land clear: on the larger scale, the whole poem is what Bartlett calls an 'envelope pattern' in which Æthelstan's prowess echoes that of his illustrious predecessors.[52] He is 'eorla dryhten' (lord of warriors, l. 1) as his forebears were 'eorlas arhwate' (glorious warriors, l. 74); he gains glory in war 'sweorda ecgum' (with the edges of swords, l. 4) as they cut down armies 'sweordes ecgum' (with the sword's edges, l. 68). There can be no doubt about the claim of the English, and specifically Æthelstan, at the end of the poem: the land obtained in the *adventus Saxonum* was the land Æthelstan and Edmund defended (l. 9): Smith concurs, 'This ancestral *eard* historically prefigures the *land* placed under the protection of Æthelstan and Edmund in the poem's first lines.'[53] The name *Brytene* itself echoes Æthelstan's imperial ambition which appeared in his charters and on his coins where he styled himself 'rex totius Britanniae' (king of all Britain).[54] Constantine could have a 'cyþþe' (home, l. 32a) in this island ('on þis eiglande', l. 66a), this land of *Brytene*, under its overlord, Æthelstan, except that he persisted in breaking the treaties as an inveterate deceiver ('eald inwidda', l. 46a).

The propagandist rhetoric of the poem is sometimes explicit, and sometimes less obvious. The poet develops threads of reference such as seeing the battle as an elaborate game: the survivors 'hlehhan ne þorfton' (had no need to laugh, l. 47) when they 'wiþ Eadweardes afaran plegodan' (played with the sons of Edward, l. 52);[55] rather they left 'dreorig' (sad, l. 54) and 'æwiscmode' (humiliated, l. 56), by contrast with the brothers who were 'wiges hremig' (exulting in war, l. 59). In line 19, the poet indulges in a little word-game at the expense of the enemies. The Scots are twice given that name *Sceottas* (ll. 11a, 32a). In line 19, Scots are shot: 'ofer scild scoten, swilce Scittisc eac'

---

51 The Tironian *and* is superscript in CCCC, MS 173, fol. 26ᵛ, and was presumably inserted later to improve the metre.

52 Bartlett, *The Larger Rhetorical Patterns*. The patterns mentioned below are frequently noted.

53 Smith, *Land and Book*, p. 184.

54 Foot, 'Where English Becomes British', pp. 140–41, discusses the terms Æthelstan used of himself in charters, and lists the charters, p. 141 n. 64. Walker, 'A Context for *Brunanburh*', pp. 24–26, argues that Æthelstan regarded himself as *Bretwalda* and similarly lists the charters, p. 25 n. 18. The coins are discussed by Blunt, 'The Coinage of Athelstan', p. 56.

55 Lipp, 'Contrast and Point of View', p. 170.

(shot over the shield, likewise [many a] Scottish [man]).[56] Once again, the poet uses onomastic wordplay to elaborate his point.[57]

Traugott Lawler broached the idea of play on the names Anlaf and Constantine, for the former, mentioning the various terms using the word *laf* (what remains) in the poem, and for the latter, remarking that Constantine 'exhibits neither stability [...] nor constancy', playing on Latin *constans* 'firm, persistent'.[58] This play on Anlaf, whose name 'in Old English probably means "solitary remainder"', is taken up by Samantha Zacher,[59] who sees it as an aspect of the multilingual learning in Æthelstan's court. She notes the poem's usage of 'hamora laf-' (remnant of the hammers, l. 6b), 'herelaf-' (remnant of the army, l. 47), and 'daroða laf' (remnant of spears, l. 54), thereby linking weapons of destruction with those destroyed, and playing on the second element of Anlaf's name.[60] Zacher subtly traces the resonances of Æthelstan's name in the Latin poems dedicated to him, but she does not pursue the play on Anlaf's name in *Brunanburh* beyond the *laf* element.[61] The central passage of the poem focuses on Anlaf's escape from the battle, and this is where the play on the name is most explicit, despite the fact (or, perhaps, more so because of the fact) that the poem does not name him here:

> Þær geflemed wearð
> Norðmanna bregu,   nede gebeded,
> to lides stefne   litle weorode;
> cread cnear on flot,   cyning ut gewat
> on fealene flod,   feorh generede.   (ll. 32b–36)

> (There the chief of the Northmen was put to flight, forced by necessity to the stem (or prow) of a ship with little company; he pushed the ship afloat, the king went out on the fallow sea and saved his life.)[62]

---

56 For other echoic and punning terms, see Zacher, 'Multilingualism', pp. 100–101.

57 See above for the play and punning on Æthelstan's name; for more on literary onomastic play in Old English, see Robinson, 'The Significance of Names', Taylor, 'Onomastics and Propaganda', and Cavill, 'Language-Based Approaches to Names'.

58 Lawler, '*Brunanburh*: Craft and Art', p. 58, nn. 6 and 7. See also Zacher, 'Multilingualism', p. 94, who notes 'the predictable pairing of *Constantinus* with *fidelis* [in *Carta dirige gressus*, stanza 5] (an equivalent to *constans*)'.

59 Zacher, 'Multilingualism', p. 99.

60 Zacher, 'Multilingualism', pp. 98–99. She also notes the possible play on the name Edmund, for which she suggests '*Eadmund* ("blessed hand") and *heard handplega* (hard handplay) of the Mercians [...] in l. 25a' (p. 98). But the sense of *mund* here may be 'protector, security', and the play may thus be with 'land ealgodon' (protected the land, l. 9).

61 Scragg, 'A Reading of *Brunanburh*', p. 118, points out that the word *herelaf* is 'not found elsewhere is verse but [is] commonplace in prose, especially in the ASC'. In fact, the word is frequent in Ælfric, but does not occur in the Chronicle at all apart from in *Brunanburh*.

62 See Cavill, 'Ships and *Brunanburh*', for translation and discussion, especially the notion that Anlaf is the subject of the transitive verb *cread* (pushed).

The poem makes Anlaf a sole survivor, 'a solitary remainder' as Zacher puts it, with singular verbs: he is literally the one that got away.

Land and *leode* are deeply significant in this poem. This raises some questions about the particular names *Brunanburh* and *Dingesmere* (ll. 5a, 54b). The latter appears in no other source dealing with the battle than the Chronicle poem. Henry of Huntingdon's translation of the poem simply omits it,[63] and the general disregard for this name suggests that it had no significance for those who were otherwise interested in the battle in later times. The *mere* element of *Dingesmere* refers in place names to marginal, water-logged land;[64] this might suggest that the place was of only local importance. The name *Brunanburh* suffers a rather different fate from that of *Dingesmere*. In over a millennium of discussion and reporting, the name has gone through many variations, with dozens of identifications of the site. The consensus spelling of the name across the tradition remains <brunanburh> or predictable grammatical cases and later medieval spellings such as <brun(n)anbyri(g)>,[65] but early authorities give different forms, mostly (as it appears) in order to locate the battle in an area known to the writers or their audiences.[66] In more recent years a similar impulse has inspired writers to identify numerous places beginning with *B-* and usually having *r* and *u* in the first syllable as Brunanburh.[67]

The corollary of this ancient and modern 'searching for Brunanburh' is that the name had meaning as a signifier of place mainly in the immediate temporal and geographical context. Even the poem makes the reference to the place vague: 'ymbe Brunanburh' (around Brunanburh, l. 5a). As Janet Thormann puts it, 'Brunanburh is not situated by descriptive, physical features or within a geographical context.'[68] 'Bruna's fortification' was a specific place to those who had fought there and to the local community. Beyond that locale, and afterwards, it quickly became a signifier of English victory and Æthelstan's glory, and any sense of the place was lost. This neatly illustrates another of the points that Thormann makes, that 'the site [...] is an effect of the language of the poem' and 'writing produces Brunanburh as a site of memory.'[69] The poem becomes less about a place than about the making of history. This too is a function of the poet's rhetoric.

---

63 Henry of Huntingdon, *Historia Anglorum*, in *Brunanburh: A Casebook*, ed. by Livingston, pp. 62–63.

64 Cavill, Harding, and Jesch, 'Revisiting *Dingesmere*', pp. 32–36.

65 Cavill, 'The Place-Name Debate'; the main forms are listed pp. 329–30.

66 Not only early authorities, though: Wood, *In Search of England*, pp. 213–21, details his bus rides around the area of south Yorkshire where he suggests the battle was fought.

67 Hill, *The Age of Athelstan*, pp. 141–42; Cockburn, *The Battle of Brunanburh and its Period*. Page, 'A Tale of Two Cities', p. 344, observes drily, 'It is hardly enough to look round for the nearest modern name beginning *Br-* and identify that as *Brunanburh*.'

68 Thormann, 'The Battle of Brunanburh and the Matter of History', p. 9.

69 Thormann, 'The Battle of Brunanburh and the Matter of History', pp. 5 and 9.

Conclusion

The poem on *Brunanburh* focuses sharply on kings, peoples, and lands. While it is true that the poem constructs an idea, a locus rather than a place, it does that by employing a relentless, detailed rhetoric which exalts Æthelstan particularly in his achievements and his aspirations: his brother and his men, co-belligerents and united in supporting Æthelstan's royal claims over peoples and lands, contrast with his enemies. Onomastic wordplay is used to glorify the English and diminish the enemies, as is balance and contrast of protagonists and their fates. Linguistic details in technical terms and kennings, litotes and game-references, numbers and even verbal echo, are repeatedly employed. Large-scale structure and careful selection of detail are also clearly deployed rhetorically in the poem. These rhetorical devices point to the poem being West Saxon propaganda.

The focus on West Saxon imperial claims is not a peculiarity of this poem or the Anglo-Saxon Chronicle, but is a preoccupation of texts and artefacts of the period more generally as other chapters in this volume demonstrate.[70] This chapter has argued that the details of the poem, while propagandistic, are nevertheless historically located, and the poem can be read as being driven by knowledge of the reality of the battle and the people involved. But the battle is made iconic, elevated to literary history, through rhetoric.

---

70 See particularly the chapters in this volume in Part III.

Works Cited

Manuscripts and Archival Sources

Cambridge, Corpus Christi College, MS 139, *Historia Regum*, attributed to Symeon of Durham

Cambridge, Corpus Christi College, MS 173, the Parker Chronicle, MS A

Primary Sources

The Anglo-Saxon Chronicle: A Collaborative Edition, III: *MS A*, ed. by Janet Bately (Cambridge: D. S. Brewer, 1986)

The Anglo-Saxon Chronicle: A Collaborative Edition, VI: *MS D*, ed. by G. P. Cubbin (Cambridge: D. S. Brewer, 1996)

The Anglo-Saxon Chronicle: A Collaborative Edition, VII: *MS. E*, ed. by Susan Irvine (Cambridge: D. S. Brewer, 2004)

The Anglo-Saxon Chronicle: A Collaborative Edition, VIII: *MS F*, ed. by Peter S. Baker (Cambridge: D. S. Brewer, 2000)

The Battle of Brunanburh, ed. by Alistair Campbell (London: Heinemann, 1938)

The Battle of Brunanburh: A Casebook, ed. by Michael Livingston, Exeter Medieval Texts and Studies (Exeter: University of Exeter Press, 2011)

Egils saga Skalla-Grímssonar, ed. by Sigurður Nordal, Íslenzk Fornrit, 2 (Reykjavik: Hið íslenzka fornritafélag, 1933)

Historia de Sancto Cuthberto, ed. by Ted Johnson South (Cambridge: D. S. Brewer, 2002)

William of Malmesbury, *Gesta Regum Anglorum: The History of the English Kings*, ed. and trans. by R. A. B. Mynors, R. H. Thomson, and Michael Winterbottom, Oxford Medieval Texts, 2 vols (Oxford: Clarendon Press, 1998–1999)

Secondary Sources

Addison, James, C., Jr, 'Aural Interlace in *The Battle of Brunanburh*', *Language and Style*, 15 (1982), 261–76

Bartlett, Adeline Courtney, *The Larger Rhetorical Patterns in Anglo-Saxon Poetry*, Columbia University Studies in English and Comparative Literature, 112 (New York: Columbia University Press, 1935)

Blair, Peter Hunter, 'Some Observations on the *Historia Regum* Attributed to Symeon of Durham', in *Celt and Saxon: Studies in the Early British Border*, by Kenneth Jackson and others (Cambridge: Cambridge University Press, 1963), pp. 63–118

Blunt, C. E., 'The Coinage of Athelstan, 924–939: A Survey', *British Numismatic Journal*, 42 (1974), 36–160

Bolton, W. F., '"Variation" in *The Battle of Brunanburh*', *RES*, n.s. 19 (1968), 363–72

Bredehoft, Thomas A., '*The Battle of Brunanburh* in Old English Studies', in *The Battle of Brunanburh: A Casebook*, ed. by Michael Livingston, Exeter Medieval Texts and Studies (Exeter: University of Exeter Press, 2011), pp. 285–94

——, *Textual Histories: Readings in the 'Anglo-Saxon Chronicle'* (Toronto: University of Toronto Press, 2001)

Cavill, Paul, 'The Battle of Brunanburh: The Yorkshire Hypothesis', forthcoming

——, 'Language-Based Approaches to Names in Literature', in *The Oxford Handbook of Names and Naming*, ed. by Carole Hough with the assistance of Daria Izdebska (Oxford: Oxford University Press, 2016), pp. 355–67

——, 'The Place-Name Debate', in *The Battle of Brunanburh: A Casebook*, ed. by Michael Livingston, Exeter Medieval Texts and Studies (Exeter: University of Exeter Press, 2011), pp. 327–49

——, 'Ships and *Brunanburh*', *ES*, 98 (2017), 549–61

Cavill, Paul, Stephen Harding, and Judith Jesch, 'Revisiting *Dingesmere*', *Journal of the English Place-Name Society*, 36 (2004), 25–38

Cockburn, John Henry, *The Battle of Brunanburh and its Period Elucidated by Place-Names* (London: Sir W. C. Leng, 1931)

Dumville, David N., 'The Ætheling: A Study in Anglo-Saxon Constitutional History', *ASE*, 8 (1979), 1–33

Foot, Sarah, *Æthelstan: The First King of England* (New Haven, CT: Yale University Press, 2011)

——, 'Where English Becomes British: Rethinking Contexts for Brunanburh', in *Myth, Rulership, Church and Charters: Essays in Honour of Nicholas Brooks*, ed. by Julia Barrow and Andrew Wareham (Aldershot: Ashgate, 2008), pp. 127–44

Frank, Roberta, 'Did Anglo-Saxon Audiences Have a Skaldic Tooth?', *Scandinavian Studies*, 59 (1987), 338–55

Frese, Dolores Warwick, 'Poetic Prowess in *Brunanburh* and *Maldon*: Winning, Losing, and Literary Outcome', in *Modes of Interpretation in Old English Literature: Essays in Honour of Stanley B. Greenfield*, ed. by Phyllis Rugg Brown, Georgia Ronan Crampton, and Fred C. Robinson (Toronto: University of Toronto Press, 1986), pp. 83–99

Gallagher, Robert, 'Latin Acrostic Poetry in Anglo-Saxon England: Reassessing the Contribution of John the Old Saxon', *MÆ*, 86 (2017), 249–74

Hill, Paul, *The Age of Athelstan: Britain's Forgotten History* (Stroud: Tempus, 2004)

Isaacs, Neil D., 'Battlefield Tour: *Brunanburg*', *Neuphilologische Mitteilungen*, 64 (1962), 236–44

Johnson, Ann S., 'The Rhetoric of *Brunanburh*', *PQ*, 47 (1968), 487–93

Jorgensen, Alice, 'Reading Emotion in *The Battle of Brunanburh*', *Neophilologus*, 100 (2016), 663–76

Keynes, Simon, 'King Athelstan's Books', in *Learning and Literature in Anglo-Saxon England: Studies Presented to Peter Clemoes on the Occasion of his Sixty-Fifth Birthday*, ed. by Michael Lapidge and Helmut Gneuss (Cambridge: Cambridge University Press, 1985), pp. 143–201

Lapidge, Michael, 'Some Latin Poems as Evidence for the Reign of Athelstan', *ASE*, 9 (1980), 61–98

Lawler, Traugott, '*Brunanburh*: Craft and Art', in *Literary Studies: Essays in Memory of Francis A. Drumm*, ed. by John H. Dorenkam (Wetteren: Cultura Press, 1973), pp. 52–67

Lipp, Frances Randall, 'Contrast and Point of View in *The Battle of Brunanburh*', *PQ*, 48 (1969), 166–77

Niles, John D., 'Skaldic Technique in *Brunanburh*', *Scandinavian Studies*, 59 (1987), 356–66

Page, R. I., 'A Tale of Two Cities', *Peritia*, 1 (1982), 335–51

Robinson, Fred C., 'The Significance of Names in Old English Literature', *Anglia*, 86 (1968), 14–58

Scragg, Donald, 'A Reading of *Brunanburh*', in *Unlocking the Wordhord: Anglo-Saxon Studies in Memory of Edward B. Irving, Jr.*, ed. by Mark C. Amodio and Katherine O'Brien O'Keeffe (Toronto: University of Toronto Press, 2003), pp. 109–22

Smith, Scott T., *Land and Book: Literature and Land Tenure in Anglo-Saxon England* (Toronto: University of Toronto Press, 2012)

Smyth, Alfred P., *Scandinavian York and Dublin: The History and Archaeology of Two Related Viking Kingdoms*, 2 vols repr. as 1 (Dublin: Irish Academic Press, 1987)

Taylor, Paul Beekman, 'Onomastics and Propaganda in *Brunanburh*', *American Notes & Queries*, n.s. 7 (1994), 67–68

Thormann, Janet, '*The Battle of Brunanburh* and the Matter of History', *Mediaevalia*, 17 (1994), 5–13

Townend, Matthew, 'Pre-Cnut Praise Poetry in Viking Age England', *RES*, 51 (2000), 349–70

Trilling, Renée R., *The Aesthetics of Nostalgia: Historical Representation in Old English Verse* (Toronto: University of Toronto Press, 2009)

Walker, Simon, 'A Context for *Brunanburh*', in *Warriors and Churchmen in the High Middle Ages: Essays Presented to Karl Leyser*, ed. by Timothy Reuter (London: Hambledon Press, 1992), pp. 21–39

Wood, Michael, *In Search of England: Journeys into the English Past* (London: Penguin, 2000)

——, 'Searching for Brunanburh: The Yorkshire Context of the "Great War" of 937', *Yorkshire Archaeological Journal*, 85 (2013), 138–59

Zacher, Samantha, 'Multilingualism at the Court of King Æthelstan', in *Conceptualizing Multilingualism in Medieval England, c. 800–c. 1250*, ed. by Elizabeth M. Tyler (Turnhout: Brepols, 2012), pp. 77–103

FRANCIS LENEGHAN

End of Empire?
Reading *The Death of Edward*
in MS Cotton Tiberius B I

Embedded within the prose annals of the Anglo-Saxon Chronicle are six Old English poems commemorating major events in tenth- and eleventh-century English political history. Concentrating on the last, and least studied, of the six Chronicle poems, *The Death of Edward*, this chapter reassesses this poem's problematic place in English literary history within the context of the emergence of West Saxon imperialism in the tenth and eleventh centuries. Seemingly out of step with developments in English poetic style as well as contemporary politics, this thirty-four-line panegyric for Edward the Confessor is often overlooked in histories of Old English literature. Previous studies have tended to approach the poem as a nostalgic throwback to the heroic style of a bygone era, the last gasp of a dying poetic tradition, or a poignant tribute to a doomed political regime.[1] In what remains the most detailed study, Katherine O'Brien O'Keeffe contrasts this work's deeply conservative metre and diction with the more experimental style of the other eleventh-century Chronicle poem, *The Death of Alfred* (ASC 1036).[2] While noting that both of these poems strike the modern reader as 'a journeyman's performance — perfunctory, gestural, and dull', O'Brien O'Keeffe stresses that they nevertheless serve to illustrate the contrasting work that traditional verse forms could do in the eleventh century: while *The Death of Alfred* hints at 'something emergent', namely the looser alliterative style of Early Middle English verse, *The Death of Edward* 'puts the past to work in the service of contemporary politics'.[3] This chapter asks just what sort of political work *The Death of Edward* might have done around the time of its composition by resituating it within its original manu-

---

* I am grateful to Daniel Anlezark, Mark Atherton, Paul Cavill, Caitlin Ellis, Rafael J. Pascual, and Harriet Soper for their helpful comments on this chapter.
1 Trilling, *The Aesthetics of Nostalgia*, pp. 208–11; Bredehoft, *Textual Histories*, pp. 110–12.
2 O'Brien O'Keeffe, 'Deaths and Transformations'.
3 O'Brien O'Keeffe, 'Deaths and Transformations', pp. 150, 171–72.

> **Francis Leneghan** (francis.leneghan@ell.ox.ac.uk) is Professor of Old English at the University of Oxford and a Fellow of St Cross College.

Ideas of the World in Early Medieval English Literature, ed. by Mark Atherton, Kazutomo Karasawa, and Francis Leneghan, SOEL 1 (Turnhout: Brepols, 2022)   pp. 403–434
BREPOLS ❧ PUBLISHERS   DOI 10.1484/M.SOEL.5.130570

script context, as part of London, British Library, MS Cotton Tiberius B I.[4] This eleventh-century codex reflects the imperialist world-view of the West Saxon royal house during a period of political crisis.[5] Reading *The Death of Edward* against the backdrop of the preceding prose and verse texts in this manuscript encourages us to to view it not as a lament for the end of empire but rather as a celebration of an ongoing process of *translatio imperii* set within the broader narrative of salvation history.

The Imperialist World-View of British Library, MS Cotton Tiberius B I

Cotton Tiberius B I is a composite codex that was compiled at several stages in the eleventh century. The first part of Cotton Tiberius B I (fols 3^r–111^v) comprises an early eleventh-century version of the Old English *Orosius*, a vernacular adaptation of Orosius's *Historiae adversus paganos* composed c. 900 and closely related to the programme of translations associated with King Alfred.[6] The text was copied out by four scribes. Part Two contains two short Old English poems copied in the mid-eleventh century—a calendar poem now misleadingly known as the *Menologium* (fols 112^r–114^v) and *Maxims II* (fol. 115$^{r–v}$)—and finally the C text of the Anglo-Saxon Chronicle (fols 115^v–164^r), written in stages by several hands.[7] The short verse texts and the Chronicle entries up to 490 are all the work of a single mid-eleventh-century scribe (Scribe 5). Scribe 6 then continued the annals from 491 to 1044 (possibly 1045). Palaeographical analysis places the compilation of the C text of the Chronicle c. 1045, which also marks the point at which the two parts of the manuscript were first joined. This point seems to mark the end of the second

---

4 For descriptions of the manuscript, see Ker, *Catalogue of Manuscripts Containing Anglo-Saxon*, § 191 (pp. 251–53); and Gneuss and Lapidge, *Anglo-Saxon Manuscripts*, §§ 370, 370.2 (pp. 294–95). The codex was probably produced at Abingdon.

5 For an influential statement of the value of reading Old English texts in their manuscript contexts more generally, see Robinson, 'Old English Literature in its Most Immediate Context'. *The Death of Edward* is also preserved in MS D of the ASC, BL, MS Cotton Tiberius B IV. MS D is largely derived from C, though the eleventh-century section also contains writs dating from Cnut's reign. On the compilation of D, see Stafford, *After Alfred*, pp. 233–67.

6 Bately's edition for EETS uses the early tenth-century Lauderdale/Tollemach text (BL, MS Additional 47967) as its base text, but Godden's recent edition for Dumbarton Oaks, *The Old English History of the World*, uses BL, MS Cotton Tiberius B I; I therefore cite from his text and translation. Latin text is from Orosius, *Historiarum adversum paganos libri VII*, ed. by Zangemeister, translation from Orosius, *Seven Books of History against the Pagans*, trans. by Fear.

7 *Maxims II* is sometimes referred to as the 'Cotton Gnomes', to distinguish it from *Maxims I*, a similar poem preserved in the Exeter Book. All quotations from the ASC are taken from *The Anglo-Saxon Chronicle: MS C*, ed. by O'Brien O'Keeffe, though I have silently emended all Tironian signs to 'ond'; translations are my own, with reference to *The Anglo-Saxon Chronicles*, ed. and trans. by Swanton.

phase of the book's production. After this, several scribes continued to update the Chronicle up to 1066, probably writing very close in time to the events described.[8] Scribe 6 added the annals up to 1048 on two or three separate occasions. Three further scribes copied the annals up to 1056, after which there is a gap in the Chronicle entries for a decade, before Scribe 10 wrote the annal for 1065, including *The Death of Edward*, and the first part of the entry for 1066 describing the appearance of Haley's comet, up to Earl Tostig's arrival at Sandwich.[9] The 1066 annal was taken up by Scribe 11, whose work breaks off midway through an account of Harold Godwinson's victory over Harald Hardrada at the Battle of Stamford Bridge. It appears that these last two scribes were working shortly after 1066.[10] The remainder of the account of the Battle of Stamford Bridge was completed by a twelfth-century scribe, and at this point the C text, and Cotton Tiberius B I itself, comes to an end. There is no mention of the Battle of Hastings.

Despite this protracted compilation, with multiple scribes working over several decades, the overall impression is nevertheless of a coherent, carefully planned book.[11] Although the original plan for the codex may not have extended beyond the initial copying of the *Orosius*, the expansion of the project *c.* 1045 with the addition of Part Two links the Orosian world history with the Chronicle's account of the fortunes of the *Angelcynn* and, in particular, their West Saxon rulers.[12] Indeed, the scribes who wrote out Part Two modelled the layout of *Menologium, Maxims II*, and ASC MS C on that of the *Orosius*, despite its unsuitability for the annalistic format of the Chronicle.[13] *The Death of Edward* was among the last of the items to be added to the codex, yet as we shall see, the poem makes a significant contribution to this ambitious project of vernacular historiography.

The rationale behind the selection and arrangement of prose and verse texts in Cotton Tiberius B I has attracted occasional interest over the years, though notably less than the other so-called 'poetic codices'. In 1947, Leslie Whitbread suggested that the *Menologium* might have struck the compiler as a suitable preface to the ASC because of its concern with the measuring of time, while also noting that *Maxims II*, lines 5–9, shares with *Menologium*

---

8   See Ker, *Catalogue of Manuscripts Containing Anglo-Saxon*, pp. 251–53.

9   Stafford, *After Alfred*, pp. 192–93.

10 See Stafford, *After Alfred*, pp. 228–32.

11 As noted by Stafford, *After Alfred*, p. 191.

12 As O'Brien O'Keeffe notes, the last quire of the manuscript is a singleton, suggesting 'that the final copyist of the *Orosius* did not envision adding other texts to his book' (*The Anglo-Saxon Chronicle: MS C*, ed. by O'Brien O'Keeffe, p. xxii).

13 O'Brien O'Keeffe comments that the decision to follow the layout of the *Orosius*, in a single block of text with narrow margins, posed no problems for the copying of *Menologium* and *Maxims II* but was not well suited for the copying of the ASC (*The Anglo-Saxon Chronicle: MS C*, ed. by O'Brien O'Keeffe, p. xxiii). Other ASC manuscripts are laid out in parallel columns, with dates to the left. See further O'Brien O'Keeffe, 'Reading the C-Text', pp. 140–41.

an interest in the seasons.[14] In 1980, Fred C. Robinson pointed out that as well as being copied by the same scribal hand (at least up to the annal for 490) these three items share certain themes, such as the measuring of time and kingship, as well as the structural device of listing.[15] Developing this approach, in 2015 Kazutomo Karasawa demonstrated how the positioning of *Menologium* and *Maxims II* between the two prose texts prepares the reader of Cotton Tiberius B I for the shift from the preceding Orosian dating system, in which time is measured in relation to the date of the foundation of Rome, to the BC/AD system used in the text of the Chronicle that follows.[16] In the same year, Eric G. Stanley noted that the presence of several political gnomes in *Maxims II* made this poem a fitting preface to the ASC.[17] Most recently, Elizabeth Tyler has argued that the addition of all three texts — *Menologium*, *Maxims II*, and ASC MS C — to the copy of the *Orosius c.* 1045 transforms national history into universal history.[18] In the discussion that follows, I will highlight how poetry plays a key role in the manuscript, inviting reflection on the processes of history and giving voice to the imperial ambitions of the royal house of Wessex. *The Death of Edward* draws together several themes from the preceding poetry and prose in order to present a confident vision of the stability of the West Saxon house at a time of national and dynastic crisis.

Reading the Old English *Orosius* in Eleventh-Century England

In order to convince his readers that Rome had not in fact fallen in 410, Orosius downplayed the impact of the Gothic invasions (VII.40.1), explaining that she was spared the miserable fates of the three great world empires that preceded her, Babylon, Macedon, and Carthage, on account of the Christian morality of her leaders (II.3.6–7).[19] In Orosius's narrative, Rome outlasted the Gothic invasions by assimilating its would-be conquerors into the Christian faith; instead of destroying the Roman Empire, the Goths became its protectors and are now responsible for its renewal (VII.43.6).[20] The Old English adaptor of Orosius's *Historiae*, working during King Alfred's reign or shortly thereafter, seems to have been particularly interested in the imperial theme of his source.[21]

---

14 Whitbread, 'Two Notes on Minor Old English Poems', pp. 192–93.
15 Robinson, 'Old English Literature in its Most Immediate Context', pp. 26–29. See further Bollard, 'The Cotton Maxims'.
16 Karasawa, 'The *Menologium* and *Maxims II* in the Manuscript Context'.
17 Stanley, 'The *Gnomes* of Cotton Tiberius B.i', p. 199.
18 Tyler, 'Writing Universal History in Eleventh-Century England'; Tyler, 'Cross-Channel Networks of History Writing'.
19 Orosius, *Seven Books of History against the Pagans*, trans. by Fear, p. 77.
20 Orosius, *Seven Books of History against the Pagans*, trans. by Fear, p. 412.
21 On the dating of the translation and its sources, see Godden, 'The Old English *Orosius* and its Sources'; Godden, 'The Old English *Orosius* and its Context'; and Bately, 'The Old

Notably, where the opening sections to most of the seven books are abridged or omitted entirely, the introduction to Book II, on the succession of the four great world empires and their distribution in the four cardinal points of the world, is translated in full:[22]

> II.i. An wæs Babylonicum, þær Ninus ricsade. Þæt oþer wæs Cræca, þær Alexander ricsade. Ðridda wæs Affricanum, þær Phtolome ricsedon. *Se feorða is Romane, þa gyt ricsiende sindon.* Þas feower heafodlicu ricu sindon feower endas þyses middangeardes, mid unasegendlicre Godes tacnunge. Þæt Babylonicum wæs þat forme, and on eastewerdum. Þæt æftere wæs þæt Crecisce, and on norðewerdum. Þæt þridde wæs þæt Affricanum, and on suðeweardum. Þæt feorðe *is* Romane, and on westeweardum. (Emphasis added).
>
> > (One was the Babylonian Empire, where Ninus reigned. The second was the Greek Empire, where Alexander reigned. The third was the African Empire, where the Ptolemies reigned. *The fourth is the empire of the Romans, who still rule.* These four major empires are the four corners of the world, with a divine significance that cannot be expressed. The Babylonian Empire was the first, in the east. The second was the Greek one, in the north. The third was the African Empire, in the south. The fourth *is* the Roman Empire, in the west.)[23]

The English translator's use of the present tense to describe the Roman Empire might seem surprising to the modern reader familiar with the narrative of 'the fall of Rome' in the early fifth century. However, the appropriation of Roman imperial titles first by the Carolingians and subsequently by other Western rules, including the West Saxons, gave Orosius's *Historiae* new meaning in the early Middle Ages. This vernacular rendering of a Latin classic invites its English readers to compare the present-day rulers of Wessex with the Roman emperors of old, whom the text presents as defenders of *cristendom.*[24]

English *Orosius'.* On the translator's interest in the history of empires, see Kretzschmar, 'Adaptation and *anweald* in the Old English *Orosius'*; Leneghan, '*Translatio imperii'.*

22 See Khalaf, 'A Study on the Translator's Omissions and Instances of Adaptation'.

23 *The Old English History of the World*, ed. and trans. by Godden, pp. 98–99. Cf. Orosius, *Historia* II.1.4–5: 'quale a principio Babylonium et deinde Macedonicum fuit, post etiam Africanum atque in fine Romanum quod usque ad nunc manet, eademque ineffabili ordinatione per quattuor mundi cardines quattuor regnorum principatus distinctis gradibus eminentes, ut Babylonium regnum ab oriente, a meridie Carthaginiense, a septentrione Macedonicum, ab occidente Romanum' (In the beginning was the kingdom of Babylon, then the kingdom of Macedon, after that the African kingdom, and finally that of Rome, which remains in place to this day. Through this same ineffable ordering of things, the four principal kingdoms which have been pre-eminent to differing degrees, have occurred at the four cardinal points of the world: the kingdom of Babylon to the east; that of Carthage to the south; that of Macedon to the north; and that of Rome to the west) (Orosius, *Seven Books of History against the Pagans*, trans. by Fear, pp. 73–74).

24 See further Godden, 'The Old English *Orosius* and its Context'; Pezzarossa, 'Reading

I have argued elsewhere that the Old English *Orosius* maps onto the political ambitions of the West Saxon royal house in the early tenth century, bolstering West Saxon claims to hegemony over Britain.[25] Indeed, the author may have had contemporary West Saxon rulers in mind when, in a rare expansion to the Latin source, he attributes the survival of Rome after the Gothic invasions of the early fifth century to the Christian faith and morality of its *caseras*:

> II.1.7. And swa eac sylce wearð Romeburh ymb m wintra and hund and syxtig and fulneah feower, þæt Eallrica hire ealldorman and Gotona cyning hyre anwaldes hi beniman woldan, and hio hwæþere onwealh on hire onwealde æfter ðæm þurhwanade. [...] þa hi hire agen ealdorman and Gotona cyning hyre anwaldes beniman woldon, hit þeah God for hiora cristendome [...] naðer ne for hiora caseras ne for hyra sylfra — ac hi nu gyt synd ricsiende ægþer ge mid hiora cristendome ge mid hiora anwalde ge mid hiora caseran.

>> (So also the city of Rome lasted almost one thousand one hundred and sixty-four years until Alaric, its count and the king of the Goths, tried to take its power away, but it remained undiminished in power after that. [...] when both its own governor and the king of the Goths wanted to take its power away, God would not allow this because of their Christian faith [...] both that of their emperors and the Romans' own — and the Romans are still ruling with their Christian faith and their empire and their emperors.)[26]

If anything, however, the imperial theme of the *Orosius* would only have increased in its relevance to the West Saxon royal house during the later part of the tenth and early eleventh centuries, when its kings became ever more confident in their claims to overlordship of Britain. Around the time when the *Orosius* was copied into Cotton Tiberius B I, in the early eleventh century, Æthelred was issuing charters as 'rex nationum totius gentis Brittanie' (King of all the nations and people of Britain) and 'industrius Anglorum basileos' (Diligent Emperor of the Angles).[27] By *c.* 1044, when the second part of Cotton Tiberius B I was copied, Edward the Confessor was using imperial titles that emphasized the geographical reach of his power over all the peoples of Britain and its surrounding isles, such as 'rex totius Britanniae' (King of all the Britons) and 'rex Anglorum omniumque insularum in circuitu persistentium' (King of the Angles and of all of the islands in the surrounding area).[28]

Orosius in the Viking Age'. On the theme of *cristendom* in the OE *Orosius*, see Harris, 'The Alfredian World History and Anglo-Saxon Identity'.

25 Leneghan, '*Translatio imperii*'. For discussion of the Orosian history and its significance in early medieval England, see above, Introduction.

26 *The Old English History of the World*, ed. and trans. by Godden, pp. 102–05.

27 S 926, charter issued by King Æthelred to Bishop Godwine in 1002; S 93, charter issued by King Æthelred to Bishop Brihtwold in 1015.

28 S 1009, charter issued by Edward to Godwine in 1045; S 1012, charter issued by Edward to

Coins and seals issued during the 1050s depict Edward crowned and enthroned in the style of the Byzantine and German emperors,[29] while the *Vita Edwardi Regis* (*c.* 1065–1067) praises him as a new Solomon whose succession in 1042 ushered in 'a golden age […] for his English race'.[30] The copying of the Old English *Orosius* into this eleventh-century codex similarly promotes the cause of West Saxon imperialism, inviting readers to compare the current political situation facing the house of Wessex with the tribulations of the ancient Christian kings of Rome. Read in an eleventh-century context, the *Orosius* implies that the preservation of West Saxon *anwald* will rest on the faith of its people and their rulers, just as the survival of Rome had centuries before. The duty of West Saxon kings to ensure the correct observance of Christian feasts throughout Britain is the central theme of the next item in the codex.

The Positioning of *Menologium* and *Maxims II* in the Manuscript

The early eleventh-century copy of the *Orosius* ends towards the bottom of folio 111ᵛ, at the end of a quire (Fig. 15.1), with the description of the bloodless conquest of Rome by the mild Christian king, Alaric, and the subsequent settlement of the Goths within the Empire, in Italy, Spain, and Africa (VI.38).[31] The remainder of the page is left blank. The text of the *Menologium* begins in a mid-eleventh-century hand (Scribe 5) at the top of a new page (folio 112ʳ) with an ornate capital 'C' (Fig. 15.2).

The *Menologium*, a 231-line calendar poem composed during the tenth-century English Benedictine Reform, is the first in a series of poems in Cotton Tiberius B I, culminating in *The Death of Edward*, that employ envelope patterning, repetition, and variation to link important events in ecclesiastical and royal history with the cyclical turning of the seasons. Cementing the link between the Christian rulers of Rome and Wessex implied by the *Orosius*, the poem contains several references to the central role of 'folc mycel' (the great people, i.e. the Romans, l. 9b) in the history of the English Church, first through the Augustinian mission (ll. 95b–106a) and then in bequeathing the names of the months around which the Christian calendar revolves 'in foldan her' (here in the land, i.e. in Britain, l. 15a). As Karasawa notes, the extra detail which the

---

Old Minster, Winchester in 1045. Other Edwardian titles found in charters include 'Engla landes cyngc' (King of England) (S 1032), 'tocius Albionis basileos' (Emperor of all of Albion) (S 1017), and 'Christo conferente rex et primicerius Anglorum atque Danorum' (King Conferred by Christ and Leader of the Angles and Danes) (S 1025).

29 See further Licence, *Edward the Confessor*, pp. 167–69.
30 *The Life of King Edward Who Rests at Westminster*, Proem, ed. and trans. by Barlow, pp. 6–7.
31 The scribe who added the rubricated section numbers has incorrectly numbered this section XXXVI where it should read XXXVIII.

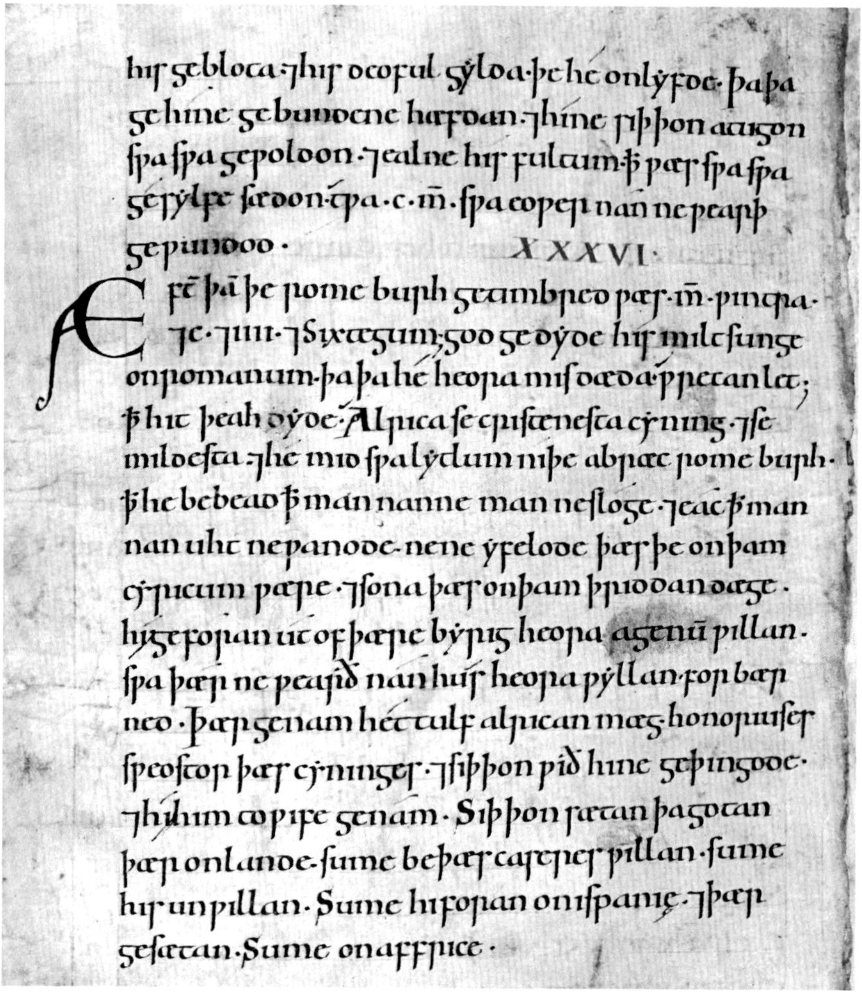

Figure 15.1. End of Old English *Orosius* (conquest of Rome by Alaric), London, British Library, MS Cotton Tiberius B I, fol. 111ᵛ. Early eleventh century. © British Library Board.

poet devotes to describing the feast of St Augustine, combined with the five references to *Bryten-* scattered throughout the text (ll. 14, 98, 104, 155, 230), are indicative of 'the domestic perspective of the poem'.[32] I would go further in arguing that although the poem's main goal is to facilitate memorization of the key feasts of the liturgical year, the *Menologium* also advances the cause

---

32 *The Old English Metrical Calendar*, ed. by Karasawa, pp. 89, 104. Karasawa notes that the term *Bryten* never occurs more than once in any other Old English poem. On the use of the similarly ambiguous term *Bretwalda/Bretenwalda* in ASC 827, see below.

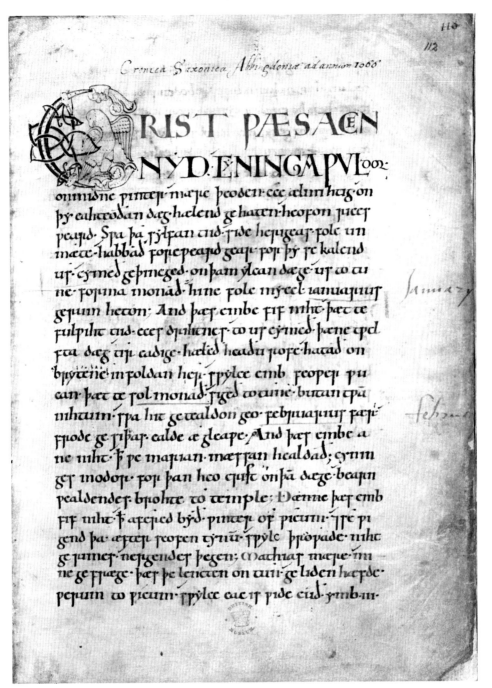

Figure 15.2. Opening of *Menologium* (the feast of Christ the King), London, British Library, MS Cotton Tiberius B I, fol. 112ʳ. Mid-eleventh century. © British Library Board.

of West Saxon Christian imperialism. Hence, the opening and closing lines place the heavenly kingdom of Christ (ll. 1–15a, 226–28a) in apposition with the broad kingdom of Britain ruled by the King of Wessex:[33]

> Crist wæs acennyd,   *cyninga wuldor,*
> on midne winter,   mære þeoden,
> ece ælmihtig;   on þy eahteoðan dæg
> Hælend gehaten,   *heofonrices* weard.   (ll. 1–4)
> [...]
> Þænne emb feower niht   þætte fæder engla
> his sunu sende   on þas *sidan gesceaft*
> folcum to frofre.   Nu ge findan magon,
> haligra tiida   þe man healdan sceal,
> swa bebugeð gebod   *geond Brytenricu*
> *Sexna kyninges*   on þas sylfan tiid.[34]   (ll. 226–31, emphasis added)

> (Christ, *the glory of kings*, was born in midwinter, the great Lord, the eternal Almighty, and on the eighth day, the guardian of the *heavenly kingdom* was called Saviour. [...] Then it is after four nights that the Father of angels sent his son into this *broad creation* as a comfort to the people. Now you can find the feasts of the saints that should be observed as far as the command of *the king of the Saxons* extends over *the spacious kingdoms of Britain* at the very same time.)

As well as helping the reader of Cotton Tiberius B I to navigate the transition from the Orosian dating system to the BC/AD system employed in Chronicle, as argued by Karasawa,[35] the *Menologium* also positions *Sexna kyninges* (the King of the Saxons) as the protector of the Roman faith throughout the island of Britain. As discussed below, the imperial might of Wessex and the Christian faith of its rulers is a recurring theme in the Chronicle poems, culminating in *The Death of Edward*.

In between the *Menologium* and the C text of the Anglo-Saxon Chronicle, on folio 115[r–v], stands another short poem, *Maxims II*. Although this collection of wise sayings might appear removed from the codex's imperial theme,[36] on closer inspection *Maxims II* universalizes certain themes implicit in the surrounding historical material, while also consolidating links between present-day English rulers and their Roman predecessors. Echoing both the *Orosius* and *Menologium*, the poem opens with a series of short, gnomic

---

33 Cf. Tyler, 'Writing Universal History in Eleventh-Century England', p. 82. As Karasawa notes, the term *Brytenricu* here may mean both 'kingdoms of Britain' and 'spacious kingdoms' (*The Old English Metrical Calendar*, ed. by Karasawa, p. 129).

34 Text and translation from *The Old English Metrical Calendar*, ed. by Karasawa, with modifications.

35 Karasawa, 'The *Menologium* and *Maxims II* in the Manuscript Context'.

36 For a study of the poem's structure and theme, see Bollard, 'The Cotton Maxims'.

END OF EMPIRE? 413

statements highlighting the duties of earthly kings and the material legacy of Rome in the English landscape:

> Cyning sceal rice healdan.   Ceastra beoð feorran gesyne
> orðanc enta geweorc,   þa þe on þysse eorðan syndon,
> wrætlic weallstana geweorc.[37]   (*Maxims II*, ll. 1–3a)

> > (A king must rule a kingdom. Cities are visible from afar, the ingenious work of giants, those that are on this earth, the wondrous work of wall-stones.)

As Elizabeth Tyler notes, these lines present 'a figure of continuity or *translatio imperii* rather than of destruction, hiatus and a new order'.[38] In other words, the opening of *Maxims II* emphasizes links between present-day English rulers and their Roman forebears who built great cities (*ceastra*) in the same land.[39] In the lines that follow, however, these images of royal and imperial continuity give way to a series of contrasts between changes in the natural world, such as the swift movement of the wind and the passing of the seasons, and the permanence of humanity's suffering and the eternal power of God (ll. 3b–14). In the closing lines, the poem foregrounds the theme of God's determination of the fates of men's souls:

> Meotod ana wat
> hwyder seo sawul sceal   syððan hweorfan,
> ond ealle þa gastas   þe for gode hweorfað
> æfter deaððæge   domes bidað
> on fæder fæðme.   (*Maxims II*, ll. 57b–61a)

> > (The Measurer alone knows where the soul must turn afterwards, and all the spirits that turn towards God after death-day, dwelling in glory in the father's embrace.)

By emphasizing the secret and hidden ('digol ond dyrne', l. 62a) nature of the mind of God and the uncertainty of salvation, *Maxims II* establishes the limits of human knowledge — a striking conclusion to a wisdom poem primarily concerned with what is known about the created world. As we shall see, the fate of the souls of Christian rulers is also a recurring theme in several of the Chronicle poems, not least *The Death of Edward*.

Together, these two short poems serve as a bridge between the world history of the *Orosius* and the national history of the Chronicle, consolidating links between the Christian emperors of old and the kings of Wessex who

---

37   Text of *Maxims II* is cited from *The Anglo-Saxon Chronicle: MS C*, ed. by O'Brien O'Keeffe.

38   Tyler, 'Writing Universal History in Eleventh-Century England', p. 82.

39   On King Alfred's rebuilding of Roman *castra* as 'burhs', see Bintley, *Settlements and Strongholds*, pp. 119–56.

styled themselves as protectors of the faith throughout Britain in the eleventh century. The poems also invite the reader of Cotton Tiberius B I to reflect on the passage of time, linking the process of *translatio imperii* to the broader narrative of salvation history.

The Imperial Theme of Anglo-Saxon Chronicle MS C

Immediately following *Maxims II* at the bottom of folio 115ᵛ in Cotton Tiberius B I is the opening of the C text of the ASC, announced by a large capital 'Æ' (Fig. 15.3). Nicholas Brooks has recently commented that the Anglo-Saxon Chronicle's main themes are Englishness and the deeds of English kings, pointing to the origin of each of its various versions at royal courts rather than local centres:

> The *Chronicle* is indeed about kings from the time of arrival of the first boat-loads of Anglo-Saxons in the fifth century through until the final entry (for 1154) in the manuscript that continued this annalistic record the longest [i.e. MS F].[40]

Qualifying Brooks's statement, we might add that the Chronicle's history of kings in fact begins several centuries before the arrival of Hengest and Horsa, with the Roman Conquest of Britain. Dovetailing with the *Orosius*'s account of Caesar's conquest of Britain earlier in the manuscript, the first Chronicle entry describes the earliest encounter between a Roman *casere* and the people of Britain:[41]

> Ær Cristes geflæscnesse lx wintra Gaius Iulius se casere ærest Romana Brytenland gesohte ond Bryttas mid gefeohte cnysede ond hy oferswiðde and swa þeah ne mihte þær rice gewinnan.
>
> > (60 years before Christ's incarnation, the emperor Julius Caesar was the first of the Romans who sought out Britain and beat the Britons in battle and overcame them, although he was unable to establish a kingdom there.)

---

40 Brooks, 'Why Is the *Anglo-Saxon Chronicle* about Kings?', p. 43.

41 The Chronicle is probably following Bede here, who similarly uses Julius Caesar's conquest of Britain as the beginning of his historical narrative in his *HE* (1.2). The account of the same event in OE *Orosius* v.12 (*The Old English History of the World*, ed. and trans. by Godden, pp. 332–35) is a truncated rendering of *Historiae* VI.9.28 (Orosius, *Seven Books of History against the Pagans*, trans. by Fear, pp. 280–81), omitting details such as the number of ships in Caesar's fleet and the names of the tribune Labienus and the British leader 'Cassovellaunus'. However, the OE author adds certain British geographical details and an account of the submission of the British *cyning* and all the inhabitants of the island. The ASC uses similar language to describe the submission of the various Welsh/British, Anglo-Saxon, and Scottish kings to the rulers of Wessex during the ninth and tenth centuries: see ASC (all MSS) *s.a.* 872, 828, 853, 878, 886, 894, 900, 918, 921, 922, 924. See further Leneghan, '*Translatio imperii*', pp. 669–71.

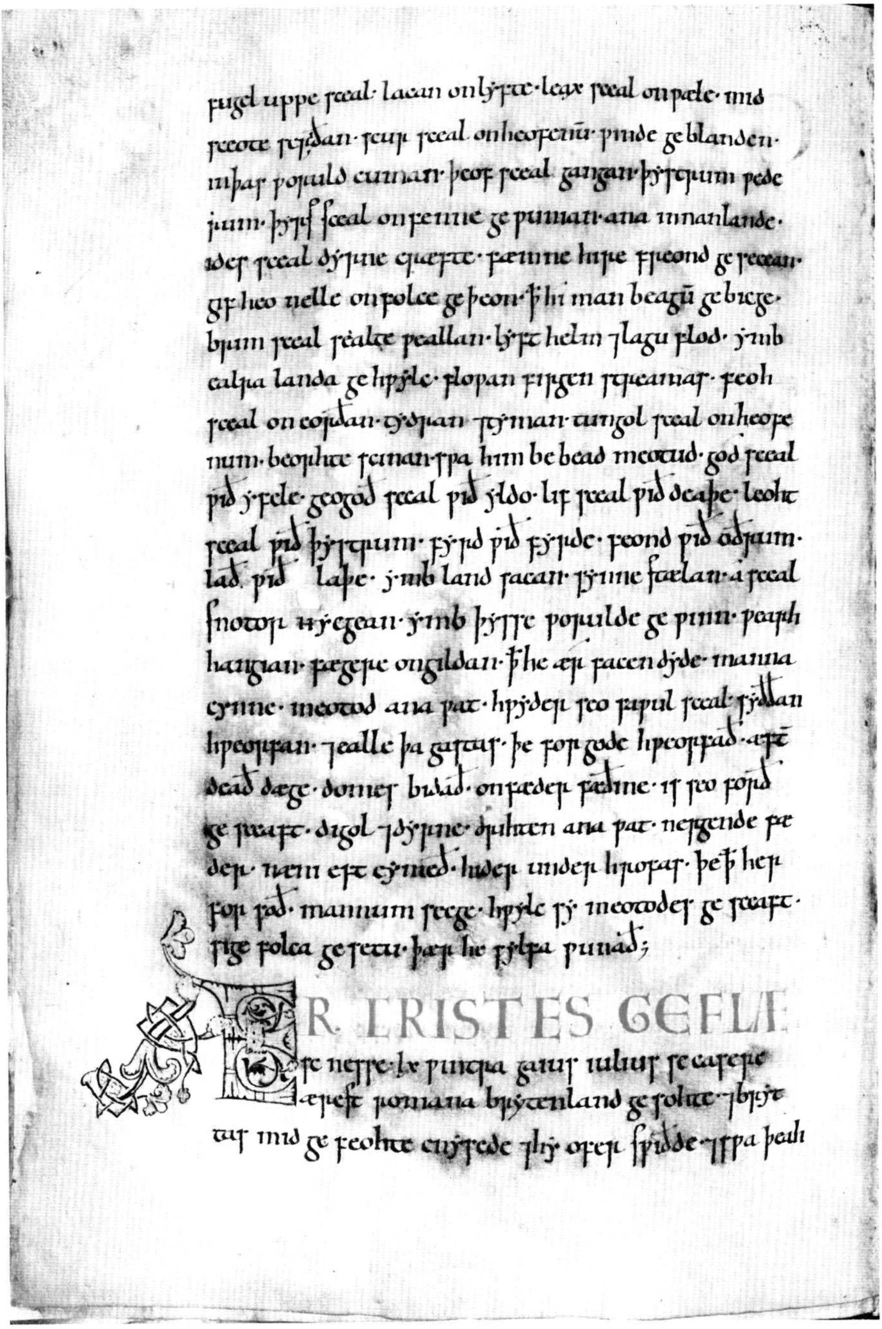

Figure 15.3. End of *Maxims II*, opening of Anglo-Saxon Chronicle MS C
(Julius Caesar's partial conquest of Britain), London, British Library,
MS Cotton Tiberius B I, fol. 115ᵛ. Mid-eleventh century. © British Library Board.

As we have seen, the term *casere* is used in the *Orosius* to refer to those Christian rulers of Rome who ensured her survival beyond the crisis of 410, as well as earlier, pagan rulers.[42] Although *casere* was occasionally used to refer to Anglo-Saxon kings in other sources, such as a charter for Eadred of Wessex (r. 946–955; S 566), the compilers of the Chronicle reserve this term for Holy Roman Emperors such as Otto II (ASC MS C 982), Henry II (ASC MS D 1067), and Henry III (ASC MS C 1049). Nevertheless, the wide distribution of this Latin loanword in Old English, and its association with the traditional vernacular term for a ruler, provides further evidence for the enduring appeal of Roman models of royal power in Anglo-Saxon England more generally.[43]

The use of the BC/AD dating system throughout the Chronicle, as opposed to the Orosian system of measuring events by their distance from the foundation of Rome, anchors these early events in the history of Britain in the narrative of salvation history. Strengthening these connections, the few annals that are included for the centuries following Caesar's invasion are mostly devoted to the key events of Christ's life, the early growth of the Church, and the more succesful conquest of Britain by Claudius, 'oþer Romana kyninga' (another king of the Romans), in 47 AD.

After describing the Roman withdrawal from Britain in 410, the Chronicle's focus shifts to the arrival of a new wave of conquerors in Britain, led this time not by Roman *caseras* but by the war-leaders of Germanic-speaking peoples, Hengest and Horsa, Cerdic and Cynric, and Ælle.[44] In the Chronicle's account, these newcomers conquered the land from the British kings like the Romans before them. Subsequent annals chart the conversion of the earliest English kingdoms to Roman Christianity in the wake of the Augustinian mission. This preliminary stage of the Chronicle thus sets the tone for the more detailed later annals that take as their main subject the wars of the West Saxon kings against the Danes in the ninth and tenth centuries. As with the account of the Roman conquest, the Viking wars are described primarily in territorial terms, as a struggle for dominion over the island of Britain. Yet even in ninth-century

---

42 On connections between Orosian *caseras* and West Saxon kingship, see Khalaf, '*Ælfred se casere*'.

43 OE *casere* appears in prose and verse as an alliterative doublet with *cyning*, as in *The Seafarer*, ll. 82–83: 'næron nu cyningas ne caseras | ne goldgiefan swylce iu wæron' (there are no kings or emperors of gold-givers now as there once were). On the Anglo-Saxons' close identification with Rome more generally, see Howe, 'Rome: Capital of Anglo-Saxon England'; Tinti, ed., *England and Rome in the Early Middle Ages*; Leneghan, '*Translatio imperii*', pp. 663–65. A rare exception is the Exeter Book poem *Widsith*, in which the Roman Empire is referred to as *Wala ric* (l. 78b: 'wala rices') and the Romans as *Rumwealh* (l. 69b: 'mid rumwalum'), both rare and probably very early terms. Neidorf, 'Caesar's Wine and the Dating of *Widsith*', argues that these terms, together with the reference to Caesar's 'winburga' (wine halls, l. 77a), reflect pre-migratory perceptions of the Romans and are therefore suggestive of this poem's great antiquity.

44 Hengest and Horsa and Ælle are not given titles in the ASC, though Bede describes the former as *duces* (*HE*, I.15); Cerdic and Cynric are referred to as *ealdormen* (ASC MS C 495). For discussion of the English 'migration myth', see the chapter by Daniel Thomas in this volume.

entries, describing events centuries after the conversion, the link between the English and Rome is sustained through references to the regular sending of alms and the exhange of gifts between West Saxon kings and the papacy.[45]

The increasingly imperial self-image of the West Saxon kings from the ninth century onwards is clearly expressed in the annal for 827 (= 829), which extends Bede's list of seven rulers who had enjoyed *imperium* over Southumbrian Britain (*HE*, II.5) with the statement that the West Saxon king, Egbert, 'eahtaþa cing se ðe Bretenanwealda wæs' (was the eighth king who was Wide Ruler/Ruler of Britain).[46] However, it is in the six Old English poems embedded in tenth- and eleventh-century annals that the Chronicle's underlying imperial theme is given its fullest expression.[47] As Pauline Stafford has recently commented, these Chronicle poems 'act as explicit commentary and judgement' on the historical events described in the otherwise terse style of the surrounding prose annals.[48] Yet despite their obvious value as historical documents reflecting the attitudes of the West Saxon court, and their relatively wide manuscript circulation, aside from *The Battle of Brunanburh* the Chronicle poems have rarely attracted the attention of either literary scholars or historians.[49]

As discussed by Paul Cavill elsewhere in this volume, the first of the Chronicle poems, *The Battle of Brunanburh* (*s.a.* 937), presents a highly stylized account of the decisive victory won by Æthelstan, king of Wessex, and his brother Edmund over 'flotan ond Scotan' (Vikings and Scots, l. 32a) and 'Wealas' (i.e. Strathclyde Welsh).[50] Wedding the high style of Old English heroic verse to the rhetoric employed in the prose annals to describe the Roman conquest

---

45 See Irvine, 'The Anglo-Saxon Chronicle and the Idea of Rome in Alfredian Literature'.

46 On the idea of *imperium* in early Anglo-Saxon kingship, see Higham, *An English Empire*. For debate as to the meaning of the title *Bretwalda*, see, for example, Wormald, 'Bede, the *Bretwaldas* and the Origins of the *Gens Anglorum*'; Fanning, 'Bede, *Imperium*, and the Bretwaldas'; Atherton, *The Making of England*, pp. 101–04, 119–21.

47 The poems appear in the following Chronicle manuscripts: *The Battle of Brunanburh* (MSS A, B, C, and D for 937); *The Capture of the Five Boroughs* (MSS A, B, C, and D for 942); *The Coronation of Edgar* (MSS A, B, and C for 973); *The Death of Edgar* (MSS A, B, C, and E for 975); *The Death of Alfred* (MSS C and D for 1036); and finally, *The Death of Edward* (MSS C and D for 1065). Bredehoft, *Textual Histories*, pp. 91–94, has identified a further short poem, *The Second Death of Edgar* in MSS D and E 975, composed in a looser style with intermittent alliteration and off-rhyme. A final Chronicle poem, *The Rime of King William*, included in the annal for 1086 in MS E, is closer to Early Middle English verse than Old English. For a recent discussion of developments in English verse style in the eleventh century, see Weiskott, *English Alliterative Verse*, pp. 23–52.

48 Stafford, *After Alfred*, p. 326. On the style of the Anglo-Saxon Chronicle more generally, see Foot, 'Finding the Meaning of Form'.

49 The most comprehensive analyses of the Chronicle poems are Bredehoft, *Textual Histories*, pp. 72–118; and Trilling, *The Aesthetics of Nostalgia*, pp. 175–252. See also Clarke, *Writing Power*, pp. 44–79. For discussion of the four tenth-century poems as a group, see Thormann, 'The *Anglo-Saxon Chronicle* Poems'; and Atherton, *The Making of England*, pp. 166–71.

50 See further Foot, 'Where English Becomes British'; Scragg, 'A Reading of *Brunanburh*'; Tyler, 'England between Empire and Nation'.

of Britain, the poet presents the battle as the greatest slaughter to have taken place on the island since the 'Engle ond Sexe' (Angles and Saxons) first 'Bretene sohton [...] Wealas ofercomon [...] eard begeaton' (sought out Britain [...] overcame the Welsh [...] won the land, ll. 70–73). As Cavill argues, this is the rhetoric of Æthelstan's own royal court, promoting the cause of West Saxon imperialism.[51]

The second Chronicle poem, *The Capture of the Five Boroughs* (*s.a.* 942), uses equally traditional, heroic diction in order to celebrate the liberation of Danes living in Mercia from Norse rule by the same Edmund, now king of Wessex and 'Engla þeoden' (lord of the English/Angles, l. 1b).[52] Here as in *Brunanburh*, a major West Saxon military victory is praised in terms that are simultaneously territorial, religious, and dynastic:

> Dene wæron æror
> under Norðmannum   nyde gebæded
> on hæþenra   hæftclommum
> lange þrage,   oþ hi alysde eft
> for his weorðscype   wiggendra hleo
> afora Eadweardes,   Eadmund cing.

(*Capture of the Five Boroughs*, ll. 8b–13)

(Previously the Danes were under the Northmen, subjugated by force, in the wicked grips of heathens, for a long time, until they were saved again, to the honour of Edward's heir, protector of warriors, King Edmund.)

The Chronicle's promotion of West Saxon imperialism is raised to new heights in the two Edgar poems copied into the annals for 973 and 975. The first celebrates Edgar's royal consecration in the former Roman city of Bath, surrounded by 'preosta heap' (a multitude of priests, l. 8b), while the second commemorates his death and confirms that his soul now rests with the elect. Both Edgar poems employ a calendrical style similar to that of the *Menologium*, linking important moments in the history of the West Saxon royal house with the cyclical passage of the seasons and the liturgical year. Hence the first poem records that Edgar's coronation took place on 'Pentecostenes dæg' (l. 8a), 973 years 'fram gebyrdtide bremes cinges, | leohta hirdes' (from the birth of the Famous King, Shepherd of Lights, ll. 12–13a), while *The Death of Edgar* describes how, after the decline of English monastic life during the brief reign of Edgar's son, Edward, and resultant famine, God restored the joys of the earth to the English:

---

51 Paul Cavill in this volume.

52 See Foot, 'Where English Becomes British', p. 131; Matyushina, 'Skaldic Panegyric and the Anglo-Saxon Chronicle Poem on the Redemption of the Five Boroughs'.

> þæt eft heofona weard,
> gebette brego engla, geaf eft blisse gehwæm
> egbuendra þurh eorðan wæstm. (*Death of Edgar*, ll. 35b–37)

> (Afterwards the Guardian of the Heavens, Lord of Angels, remedied that, gave bliss to each of the island dwellers through the fruits of the earth.)[53]

In a further echo of the cyclical structure of the *Menologium*, the Bedan pun on 'Angla/engla' (ll. 2a, 36a) and the variation of 'eorþan dreamas' (l. 1a) with 'eorðan wæstm' (l. 37b) participate in an envelope pattern linking Edgar's earthly kingship to that of Christ the king of heaven.

The *Death of Alfred* (*s.a.* 1036) is exceptional among the Chronicle poems in that it does not expressly promote the cause of West Saxon imperialism; instead, it laments the cruel blinding of King Æthelred's son, and Edward the Confessor's brother, by Earl Godwin. The *Death of Alfred* also marks a departure from the traditional alliterative patterns of Old English verse, even featuring intermittent end-rhyme; nevertheless, it echoes some of the other Chronicle poems in its imagery.[54] For example, the poet's statement that no greater evil had been done in the land since the arrival of the Danes (ll. 6–7) directly parallels the ending of *Brunanburh*, while two references to Alfred's soul being now 'mid Criste' (with Christ, ll. 10b, 20b) are reminiscent of *The Death of Edgar* (and, indeed, *Maxims II*). The absence of imperial rhetoric in *The Death of Alfred* matches the generally terse style of the annals in the C text from Cnut's reign, no doubt reflecting the poet's sensitivity to the new Anglo-Danish political regime. With the surviving members of the West Saxon house now exiled to Normandy, it would not be politically expedient to champion what might have seemed at the time a lost cause. As we shall see, however, the West Saxon imperial theme returns to the C text of the Chronicle with the restoration of the Cerdicing line by Edward in 1042, to be given its fullest expression in the last of the six Old English poems, *The Death of Edward*.

The Death of Edward in its Manuscript Context

The annal for 1065 containing *The Death of Edward* opens on folio 160[r] with a lengthy prose account of the conflict between Harold Godwinson and the Welsh prince Caradog, the deposition and exile of Earl Tostig and his replacement by Morcar, and finally King Edward's arrival at Westminster and subsequent

---

53 See Salvador Bello, 'The Edgar Panegyrics'; Smith, 'The Edgar Poems and the Poetics of Failure'; and Atherton, *The Making of England*, pp. 277–83.

54 See O'Brien O'Keeffe, 'Deaths and Transformations', pp. 150–64; Bredehoft, *Textual Histories*, pp. 110–11.

death. All of these events are dated not only according to the standard BC/AD temporal scheme employed throughout the Chronicle but also in relation to the feasts of the liturgical year, as set out in the *Menologium* and referred to in *The Coronation of Edgar*. Hence, we read that the 'mannsliht' committed by Caradog 'wæs on Sancte Bartolomeus mæssedæig', while the killing of Tostig's thegns took place 'æfter Michaheles mæssan'; a great meeting then took place at Northampton and Oxford 'on þon dæig Simonis and Iude', before Edward himself arrived at Westminster 'to þam Middanwintre':

> And seo circhalgung wæs on Cilda mæssedæig. And he forðferde on Twelftan Æfen, and hyne man bebyrigde on Twelftan Dæig on þam ylcan mynstre swa hyt her æfter seigð.

> (And the consecration of the church was on Holy Innocents' Day. And he passed away on the eve of Twelfth Night, and he was buried on Twelfth Night in the same minster, as it says hereafter.)

The use of feast days as temporal markers is not in itself remarkable in the wider context of the Chronicle, though the authors of the C text tend to use days of the month.[55] Nevertheless, feast days are mentioned far more frequently in the 1065 annal than elsewhere in the Edwardian annals. The effect is to anchor the momentous events of this year — in particular Edward's death at the time of Christ's birth — in the cycle of the Christian liturgical year, with its promise of salvation and renewal.[56]

The poem on Edward's death begins at the top of a new page (fol. 160ᵛ, Fig. 15.4). As has often been noted, *The Death of Edward* is decidedly conservative in diction and metre, closer in style to 'classical' Old English verse than more contemporary works such as *The Metres of Boethius* or the *Metrical Psalms* or, indeed, the other eleventh-century Chronicle poem, *The Death of Alfred*.[57] With the benefit of hindsight, modern commentators have tended to

---

55 For example, the annal for 1042 simply records that Harthacnut 'forðferde on .vi. Id .Iun.' (died on 8 June).

56 Feast days are used intermittently in the C-text annals from 1043 to 1055: Edward's consecration took place on the first day of Easter (1043); the severe weather of 1046 arrived after Candlemas; the 1050 annal records that Edward held a council at mid-Lent in 1051; the annal for 1052 states that Swein died on Michaelmas Day, and that Godwin came to Southward on the Monday after the Feast of St Mary, before a strong wind did great damage on the eve of the Feast of St Thomas; and the 1053 entry describes how Earl Godwin was taken ill on the second day of Easter.

57 Fulk, *A History of Old English Meter*, § 300 (p. 258), describes the metre of *The Death of Edward* as 'surprisingly regular', noting the presence of only three verses disallowed in earlier Old English verse (l. 29b: 'befæste ðæt rice'; l. 34a: 'þæs þe þearf wæs'; l. 34b: 'ðæs ðeodkyninges'). For full scansion of all the Chronicle poems, following Bliss's system, see Townsend, 'The Metre of the *Chronicle*-Poems'. Townsend finds the poet of *The Death of Edward* 'the least skilful' of the Chronicle poets, noting an over-reliance on A- and D-types, and a high proportion of problematic lines (158). Like *The Death of Alfred*, the recently identified poem, *The Second Death of Edgar*, embedded in the Chronicle entry

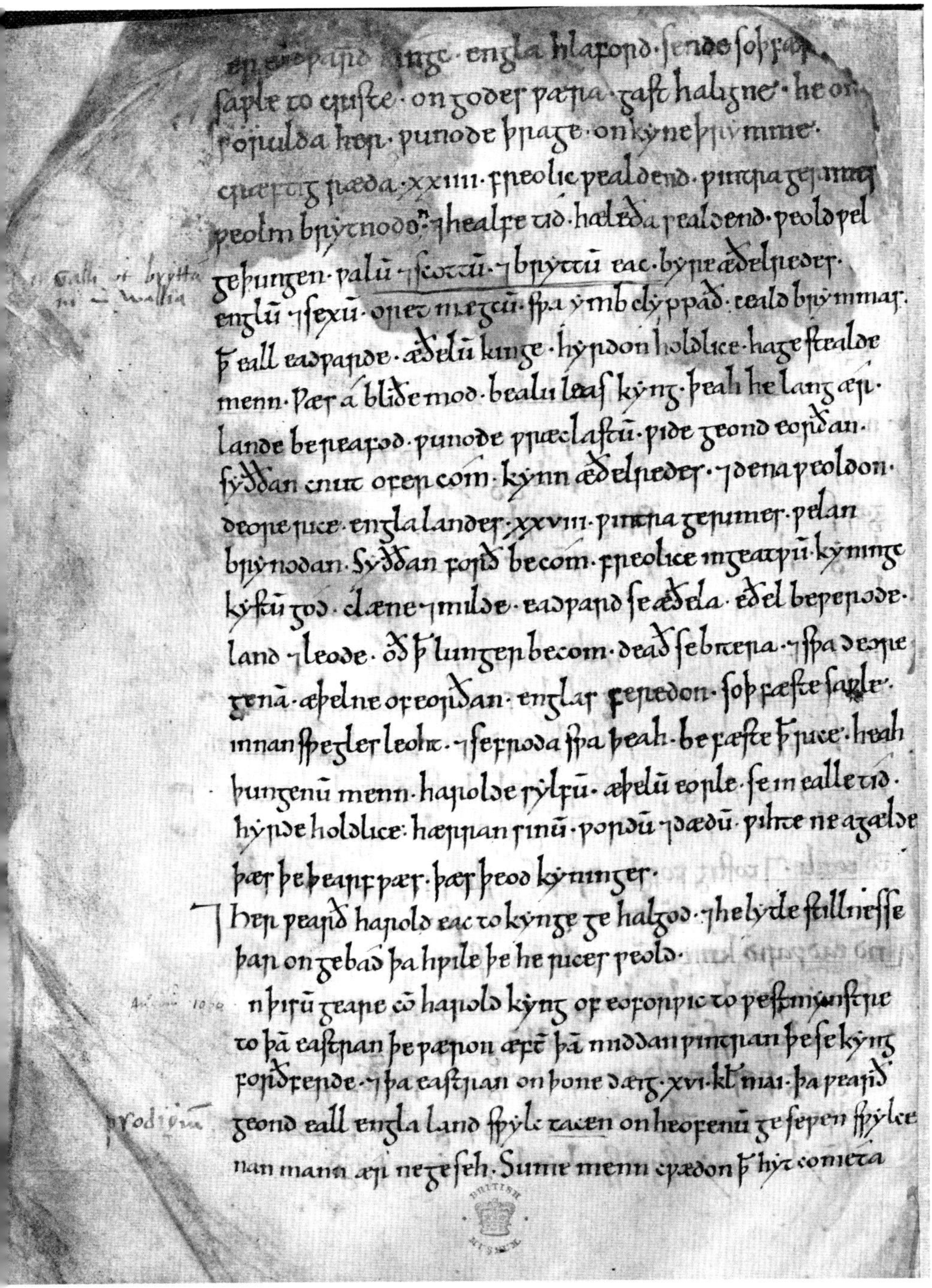

Figure 15.4. *The Death of Edward* (ASC MS C 1065), London, British Library, MS Cotton Tiberius B I, fol. 160ᵛ. Mid-eleventh century. © British Library Board.

categorize the poem's traditional style as nostalgic or outmoded.[58] Catherine Clarke, on the other hand, proposes that the poem's traditional style sends 'political signals about English identity and continuity even at this moment of rupture and crisis',[59] a view recently echoed by Erin Goeres, who argues that the poet 'uses the tropes of exile and lordship not to mark the end of the Anglo-Saxon period, but to celebrate — however briefly — its continuation'.[60] In the discussion that follows, I argue that the poem's traditional style is a fitting vehicle to convey the imperial world-view that links the prose and verse items in Cotton Tiberius B I.

The poem begins in the style of a royal eulogy or epitaph, celebrating Edward's lordly status and connecting the purity of his soul with his fitness to rule:[61]

> Her Eadward kingc,   Engla hlaford,
> sende soþfæste   sawle to Criste
> on Godes wæra,   gast haligne.
> He on worulda her   wunode þrage
> on kyneþrymme,   cræftig ræda.   (*The Death of Edward*, ll. 1–5)

> (Here King Edward, Lord of the English, sent his righteous soul to Christ, into God's protection, (his) holy spirit. He dwelt for a time here in the world, in lordly splendour, skilful in counsel.)

These lines closely echo the openings of several previous Chronicle poems, aligning Edward with his illustrious West Saxon predecessors.[62] A number of themes introduced here are subsequently developed over the course of this short poem, including the Bedan association of Angles and angels (recalling *The Death of Edgar*), the heavenly destination of Edward's soul, and his exemplary piety and skill as a ruler. The half-line 'on Godes wæra' (into God's protection) at line 3a presents a direct verbal parallel to *Menologium* lines 39b and 217b, as O'Brien O'Keeffe notes, but also recalls more generally the meditations on individual salvation that run through *Maxims II*, *The Death of Edgar*, and *The Death of Alfred*.

---

for 975 in MSS D and E, also displays little respect for the traditional rules of alliteration and metre. O'Brien O'Keeffe provides a useful list of the various 'traditional formulas' (i.e. parallel words, phrases, and half-lines) shared with other Old English poems ('Deaths and Transformations', pp. 173–78).

58 O'Brien O'Keeffe, 'Deaths and Transformations', pp. 164–72; Trilling, *The Aesthetics of Nostalgia*, p. 209; Bredehoft, *Textual Histories*, pp. 111–13.

59 Clarke, *Writing Power*, p. 63.

60 Goeres, 'Exile and Migration', p. 59.

61 Trilling, *The Aesthetics of Nostalgia*, p. 208, treats the poem as a eulogy; Clarke, *Writing Power*, pp. 63–64, reads it as epitaph.

62 Cf. *Brunanburh*, l. 1: 'Her Æþelstan cing, eorla dryhten'; *Capture of the Five Boroughs*, l. 1: 'Her Edmund cing, Engla þeoden'.

Echoing the imperial language of Edward's charters, as well as the close of *Menologium*, the next section focuses on the geographical reach of the West Saxon king's power, as both 'Engla hlaford' and ruler of all the peoples of Britain:

.xxiiii.   freolic wealdend
wintra gerimes   weolan brytnode
ond healfe tid,   hæleða wealdend,
weold wel geþungen   Walum ond Scottum
ond Bryttum eac,   byre Æðelredes   10
Englum ond Sexum   oretmægcum,
swa ymbclyppað   ceald brymmas,
þæt eall Eadwarde,   æðelum kinge,
hyrdon holdlice   hagestealde menn. (*The Death of Edward*, ll. 6–14)

(For twenty-four-and-a-half years, generous ruler, he distributed wealth, ruler of warriors, greatly distinguished he ruled over the Welsh and Scots, and the Britons too, Æthelred's son, over the Angles and Saxons, over the champions — whatever the icy waters encircle, all that (land) — the young warriors loyally obeyed Edward, the noble king.)

While O'Brien O'Keeffe sees this poem as mourning 'the end of the Cerdicing dynasty', I would argue that it confidently presents Edward and, by implication, his chosen successor Harold as links in the Chronicle's long chain of rulers of Britain, stretching through Cerdic and Cynric (ASC 495) and Hengest and Horsa (ASC 455), back to the emperors Claudius (ASC AD 47) and Julius Caesar (ASC 60 BC).[63] As we have seen, the *Orosius* extends Cotton Tiberius B I's history of earthly rulers back even further into the past, to the reign of the world's first king, Ninus.

The middle section of the poem contrasts Edward's happy reign with his long period of exile in Normandy during the reign of Cnut (1016–1036):[64]

Wæs a bliðemod   bealuleas kyng   15
þeah he lang ær   lange bereafod,
wunode wræclastum   wide geond eorðan,
syððan Cnut ofercom   kynn Æðelredes
ond Dena weoldon   deore rice
Engla landes   .xxviii.   20
wintra gerimes   welan brytnodan.   (*Death of Edward*, ll. 15–21)

---

63 O'Brien O'Keeffe, 'Deaths and Transformations', p. 150. The presentation of Britain as encircled by icy waters also recalls the opening to the *Orosius*, which follows its source in describing the world as a series of islands (OE *Orosius* I.1; *Historiae* II.1). On the Anglo-Saxon insular imagination, see Appleton, 'The Northern World of the Anglo-Saxon *mappa mundi*', and Appleton's chapter in this volume.

64 On Edward's exile in Normandy, see Baxter, 'Edward the Confessor and the Succession Question', pp. 96–98; and Licence, *Edward the Confessor*, pp. 38–79.

(The blameless king was always happy in spirit, although he was previously deprived of land for a long time, remained in exile-tracks far across the earth, after Cnut conquered Æthelred's kin, and the Danes ruled the beloved kingdom of England for twenty-eight years, dispensed (its) wealth.)

As several scholars have noted, the poet draws here on the common Old English poetic trope of exile, as displayed, for example, in the Exeter Book 'elegies'.[65] There are also striking parallels with two famous literary accounts of exiled kings: Scyld Scefing, the *god cyning* (good king) abandoned as an infant but who later came to rule a great kingdom (*Beowulf*, ll. 4–52) and was himself regarded as an ancestor of the West Saxon kings (ASC *s.a.* 855);[66] and Aeneas, 'fato profugus' (exiled by fate) from Troy before building the city of Latium, whence emerged Rome (*Aeneid* I, ll. 1–7).[67]

Bredehoft has criticized the *Death of Edward*-poet for his over-reliance on recycled words and formulas, citing this feature of the text as further evidence of the decline of the Old English verse tradition in the eleventh century.[68] Yet, within the context of Cotton Tiberius B I — and the poem's immediate political moment — the repetition of the formula 'weolan brytnode' / 'welan brytnodan' serves an immediate political purpose, to emphasize the succession of rulers in Britain, as first Edward (l. 7b) and then Cnut (l. 21b) distribute the wealth of 'deore rice | Engla landes' (the beloved kingdom of England). Wordplay on the adjective 'deor' (beloved/valuable), the forms of the verb *brytnian* (to distribute), and the noun *Bryttas* (Britons) implies that Britain itself is a prize to be fought over by successive rulers.[69]

The poet's treatment of Cnut's rule over 'deore rice Engla landes' has important implications for reading of *The Death of Edward* as a response to the 'second conquest' of 1066. As Bredehoft notes, 'the reference here would seem to look both backward (with a historical perspective of the other

---

65 O'Brien O'Keeffe, 'Deaths and Transformations', p. 170; Trilling, *The Aesthetics of Nostalgia*, p. 210; Goeres, 'Exile and Migration', pp. 55–58.

66 *Beowulf* was copied into the Nowell Codex *c.* 1000 and was evidently still being read well into the eleventh century; see Thomson, *Communal Creativity in the Making of the 'Beowulf' Manuscript*, esp. pp. 232–39. ASC 855 (MS C) traces the genealogy of King Æthelwulf of Wessex back to Beaw, son of Sceaf, son of Noah. In the version of the West Saxon genealogy preserved in the *Chronicon* of the West Saxon ealdorman Æthelweard, this same royal progenitor 'Scef' is said to have arrived among the Danes as an infant in a boat before being taken in by them and becoming their king. On the incorporation of Scyld Scefing (as Scef, son of Scyld/Sceldwa) into the West Saxon royal genealogy, and links with the opening section of *Beowulf*, see Anlezark, 'Sceaf, Japheth and the Origins of the Anglo-Saxons'; and Leneghan, *The Dynastic Drama of 'Beowulf'*, pp. 143–52.

67 On the importance of the *Aeneid* in Anglo-Saxon England, and its possible influence on contemporary accounts of Edward's exile, see Licence, *Edward the Confessor*, p. 39.

68 Bredehoft, *Textual Histories*, pp. 112–13.

69 Cf. *Maxims II*, ll. 28b–29a: 'Cyning sceal on healle | beagas dælan' (a king must share out rings in the hall). The term *deor* is used in l. 26b to refer to Edward.

Chronicle poems) and forward, to the possible end of a (hopefully temporary) Norman rule'.[70] Consideration of the poem's manuscript context lends support to this reading. As we have seen, the *Orosius* provided English readers with a narrative of Roman history characterized by a series of invasions, from the Carthaginians to the Goths. Although on occasion Rome had nearly succumbed to its enemies, eventually it prevailed, firstly due to the exceptional bravery of certain consuls, but ultimately thanks to the Christian faith of her rulers. The ASC entries for the first half of the eleventh century leading up to *The Death of Edward* tell a similar story, describing the disasters that befell the English, a litany of invasions and betrayals, the ignominy of subjugation to a foreign king, and the near loss of 'onweald', but for the heroic leadership of pious West Saxon kings.[71]

Edward's glorious restoration of the West Saxon line in 1042 forms the narrative climax of the central section of the poem:

> Syððan forð *becom*   freolice in geatwum
> kyningc kystum god,   clæne ond milde,
> Eadward se *æðela*   *eðel* bewerode,
> *land ond leode*   oð þæt lunger *becom*   25
> deað se bitera   ond swa deore genam
> *æþelne of eorðan.*   (ll. 22–27a, emphasis added)

> (Afterwards the king, gracious in customs, chaste and mild, *came forth*, noble in array, the *noble* Edward defended *the homeland, land and people*, until the bitter death *came forth* and took so beloved a *noble* from the *earth*.)

Wordplay on *æðel-/eðel/eorðan* (nobility/homeland/earth, ll. 24, 27a), as well as the formulaic half-line 'land ond leode', ties Edward's nobility to the land itself and anticipates the final section of the poem in which, as we shall see, the nobility of his successor, Harold, is similarly stressed.[72] The description of Edward's glorious return from exile and subsequent death, framed by the structural repetition of the verb *becom*, closely parallels the accounts of the passage of the seasons in both *Maxims II* (ll. 5–9) and the *Menologium*: just

---

70 Bredehoft, *Textual Histories*, p. 112. Bredehoft does not discuss connections with the surrounding material in BL, MS Cotton Tiberius B I.

71 For the Mercian bias of these annals, and their antipathy towards the house of Godwin (the annal for 1065 aside), see Baxter, 'MS C of the Anglo-Saxon Chronicle'.

72 In his chapter in this volume, Paul Cavill detects similar wordplay in the earlier Chronicle poem, *Brunanburh* (ASC 937). The formula *land ond leode* also appears in *Andreas*, l. 1321a, and twice in the context of the succession of the patriarchs after the Flood in *Genesis A*: 'eaforan læfde | land and leodweard' (he [i.e. Mahalaleel] left to his heir land and guardianship of the people, ll. 1179b–1180a); 'gleawum læfde | land and leodweard leofum rince' (he [i.e. Jared] wisely left land and guardianship of the people to the beloved man [i.e. Enoch], ll. 1195b–1196). Cf. *Maldon*, l. 54a: 'folc ond foldan'. OE *leod* also means 'prince'. For example, *Beowulf*, l. 24a: 'leode gelæseten' (support the prince).

as Edward 'forð becom freolice in geatwum', so in springtime 'smicere on gearwum, | wudum and wyrtum cymeð wæitig scriðan | Þrymilce on tun' (beautiful Þrymilce [i.e. May] comes gliding into the citadel, into town, elegantly clad in adornments, woods and plants, ll. 76b–78a).[73] This passage also recalls the reversals of the earlier Chronicle poems *The Capture of the Five Boroughs*, in which the Danes of Mercia suffered for a time under Norse rule until their liberation by King Edmund (ll. 8b–13), and *The Death of Edgar*, which concludes with a plea that God will revive the fortunes of the English after a famine that took place during the reign of Edward the Martyr (ll. 33b–37).

As the work nears its conclusion, the poet returns to the subject of the destination of the king's soul, another theme that, as we have seen, recurs in several of the Chronicle poems in this manuscript as well as *Maxims II*. While the wisdom poem stresses how God alone knows 'hwyder seo sawul sceal syððan hweorfan' (where the soul must turn afterwards, *Maxims II*, l. 58), *The Death of Edward* recalls the verse encomiums on Edgar and Alfred in confidently proclaiming that the West Saxon ruler is already among the elect: 'Englas feredon | soþfæste sawle innan swegles leoht' (Angels carried his righteous soul into the light of heaven, ll. 27b–28). The pun on *Englas* (l. 27b) / *Engla hlaford* (l. 1b) and the repetition of 'soþfæste sawle' (ll. 2/28a) again underlines the poem's central theme, and a key theme in the Chronicle as a whole: the Christian virtue of English kings.

Having assured the reader of Edward's salvation, the poet turns in the final lines to the matter of succession:

ond se froda swa þeah	befæste þæt rice	
heahþungenum menn,	Harolde sylfum,	30
æþelum eorle,	se in ealle tid	
hyrde holdlice	hærran sinum	
wordum ond dædum,	wihte ne agælde	
þæs þe þearf wæs	þæs *þeodkyninges.*	(ll. 29–34, emphasis added)

> (And the wise man committed that kingdom to a distinguished man, Harold himself, *noble* Earl, who at all times loyally obeyed his elder in words and deeds, in no way did he neglect anything that was needful to the *people-king*.)

Noting that Harold was not of the line of Æthelred and Edward, Bredehoft argues that 'the poem implies that the end of the West Saxon dynasty will, in fact, coincide with the end of Anglo-Saxon history'.[74] However, far from drawing attention to the weakness of Harold's claim, the poem in fact presents him as Edward's chosen heir, highlighting his distinction ('heahþungenum

---

73   For an overview of this topic, see Anderson, 'The Seasons of the Year in Old English'. For links between the seasonal theme of *Menologium* and *Maxims II*, see Whitbread, 'Two Notes on Minor Old English Poems', pp. 192–93.

74   Bredehoft, *Textual Histories*, p. 112.

men', l. 30a) and nobility ('æþelum', l. 31a) in terms which bind him closely to his predecessor, Edward (ll. 24a, 27a). Indeed, Harold's throne-worthiness is further exemplified by his loyalty to 'hærran sinum' (his elder, l. 32b), Edward, and his attentiveness to the needs of the 'people-king' ('þearf [...] þeodkyninges', l. 34).[75] Harold may not be Edward's son or direct heir, but in the eyes of our poet, he is certainly the next best thing. The placement of this poetic compound, *þeodkyning* (people-king), as the poem's last word affirms Harold's place in an illustrious line of West Saxon *kyningas* stretching back to Cerdic, all of whom fought for and ruled over 'land and people'. In its treatment of the succession of 1065, *The Death of Edward* can therefore be read as a vernacular parallel to the conclusion of the contemporary *Vita Edwardi*, in which Edward commends the queen and kingdom to Harold with his dying words.[76] The poem can also be compared with panels 27–31 of the Bayeux Tapestry, which seem to depict Edward conferring the throne on Harold (Fig. 15.5).

Indeed, Stephen Baxter has described *The Death of Edward* as 'a sudden and uncharacteristic burst of enthusiasm for Harold', given the clear bias in MS C annals between 1035 and 1065 towards the cause of Earl Leofric and Mercia and general antipathy towards the house of Godwin and Wessex.[77] Perhaps the poem was commissioned to celebrate Harold's accession, which took place on 6 January 1065, just a day after Edward's death — the fact that the poem does not mention Harold's death may indicate that he was indeed still alive at the time of the poem's composition. Alternatively, like the conclusion to the 1065 annal, *The Death of Edward* may have been composed shortly after Harold's death in 1066 by members of a court faction who remained loyal to the Godwinson cause.[78] Certainly, by presenting Harold Godwinson as Edward's legitimate and worthy heir, *The Death of Edward* glosses over the rival claims of both Edward's great nephew, Edgar Ætheling, and his distant cousin, Duke William of Normandy, to say nothing of Harald Hardrada of Norway and Sweyn Estridsen of Denmark.[79] Reading this poem in its manuscript context brings into focus its emphasis on dynastic stability and imperial

---

75 See O'Brien O'Keeffe, 'Deaths and Transformations', pp. 170–71. See further Baxter, 'Edward the Confessor and the Succession Question'.

76 *The Life of King Edward Who Rests at Westminster*, II.ix, ed. and trans. by Barlow, pp. 122–23. Queen Edith was Harold's own sister. Harold was also related to Cnut. On Harold's claim, see Howard, 'Harold II'. On the political agenda of the *Vita Edwardi*, see Sykes, 'The Sense of an Ending'.

77 Baxter, 'MS C of the Anglo-Saxon Chronicle', p. 1213. Baxter suggests that Harold's recent marriage to Ealdgyth, daughter of Ælfgar, earl of Mercia, and sister of Eadwine, earl of Mercia, and Morcar, earl of Northumbria, may account for the softening of the Chronicle's attitude to the house of Godwin at this point.

78 The remainder of the annal states: 'Her wearð Harold eac to kynge gehalgod, ond he lytle stillnesse þar on gebad þa hwile þe he rices weold' (Here Harold was also consecrated as king, and he had little peace while he ruled the kingdom).

79 See Licence, *Edward the Confessor*, pp. 242–43.

continuity (possibly to the point of defiance), even as the foundations of the West Saxon *anwald* were crumbling.

Conclusion

Although late Old English verse has enjoyed something of a critical rehabilitation in recent years, as scholars have begun to challenge the traditional narrative of the decline of the vernacular poetic tradition in the tenth and eleventh centuries, the Chronicle poems remain a neglected corpus.[80] Traditional in style and loyal to a doomed political cause, *The Death of Edward* in particular has for too long been treated as an anomaly. In order to make sense of this puzzling work, scholars have sought to associate it with various endings — of Old English poetry, of the West Saxon royal line, of 'Anglo-Saxon England'

---

80 See esp. Thornbury, *Becoming a Poet*, pp. 223–38. Thornbury identifies several tenth- and eleventh-century poems, including *The Metres of Boethius*, *Metrical Psalms*, *Kentish Hymn*, and *Menologium*, as representative of a distinctive 'southern mode' of composition that was developed in this period to provide vernacular 'simulacra' of Latin sources. Rejecting the narrative that these works are indicative of the decay of the Old English poetic tradition, Thornbury categorizes this style as 'the apotheosis of Old English verse, not its downfall' (p. 224).

Figure 15.5. Details of the Bayeux Tapestry, Panels 27–31: *Hic Edwardus rex in lecto alloquitur fideles. Et hic defunctus est. Hic dederunt Haroldo corona[m] regis.* (Here Edward speaks in bed to his followers. And here he is dead. Here they gave the king's crown to Harold.) Eleventh Century, City of Bayeux.

itself.[81] Approaching *The Death of Edward* in the light of the complex overlapping historiographical narratives of Cotton Tiberius B I, as this chapter has done, allows us to see it in a very different light, as a poem that gives voice to the imperialist world-view of the house of Wessex in the mid-eleventh century. Like the codex as a whole, this poem encourages its readers to believe that the royal house of Wessex will continue to prevail against foreign challengers, just as centuries before the *folc mycel* (great people) of Rome had succeeded in preserving their *anwald* on account of the Christian virtue of their rulers. Of course, with the benefit of hindsight, we know that the poet's optimism

---

81 Bredehoft, for example, comments that 'the apparent failure of the West Saxon line (as presented in this poem) leaves post-Conquest readers (such as we are) with a powerful sense of an Anglo-Saxon ending' (*Textual Histories*, p. 112), while Trilling states: 'The self-conscious archaizing of poetic form in the twilight of Anglo-Saxon England is itself enough to provoke a powerful sense of nostalgia, especially in modern readers' (*The Aesthetics of Nostalgia*, p. 209).

would prove misplaced — there would be no glorious restoration of the West Saxon line after 1066, as there had been in 1042.[82] Working in the midst of these tumultuous events, however, our poet could not have envisaged that Edward would prove to be the last member of 'kynn Æðelredes' to rule over Britain, any more than he might have known that his short encomium would one day come to acquire its dubious modern reputation as the last Old English poem.[83]

---

82 The Plantagenets would in fact go on to adopt Edward as a symbol of continuity with the Anglo-Saxon past, while Anglo-Norman chroniclers would propagate the myth that Edward had nominated William, not Harold, as his heir. See Garnett, *Conquered England*; Ashe, 'The Anomalous King of Conquered England'; Clifton Brown, 'Sacral Kingship and Resistance to Authority'.

83 The last Old English poem in the 'classical' style is in fact the similarly neglected *Durham*, which probably dates to *c.* 1100. Concern with the West Saxon dynasty persists in the accounts of Edgar Ætheling and Matilda, daughter of Malcolm, king of Scotland, and great-niece of Edward the Confessor, in the continuations of the ASC in MSS D and E. Matilda married Henry I on his accession in 1100 after the death of William Rufus. Had Matilda and Henry I's son, William Adelin (i.e. ætheling), not died in the sinking of the White Ship in 1120, Edward might not have been the last member of the West Saxon line to rule. According to ASC MS E 1100, Matilda was 'of than rihtan Aenglalandes kynekynne' (of that true English noble family).

Works Cited

Manuscripts and Archival Sources

London, British Library, MS Additional 47967
London, British Library, MS Cotton Tiberius B I
London, British Library, MS Cotton Tiberius B IV

Primary Sources

The Anglo-Saxon Chronicle: A Collaborative Edition, v: *MS C*, ed. by Katherine
   O'Brien O'Keeffe (Cambridge: D. S. Brewer, 2001)
The Anglo-Saxon Chronicles, ed. and trans. by Michael Swanton (London: J. M.
   Dent, 1996)
Bede, *Bede's Ecclesiastical History of the English People*, ed. and trans. by Bertram
   Colgrave and R. A. B. Mynors, 2 vols (Oxford: Clarendon Press, 1969)
The Life of King Edward Who Rests at Westminster, Attributed to a Monk of Saint Bertin,
   2nd edn, ed. and trans. by Frank Barlow (Oxford: Clarendon Press, 1992)
The Old English History of the World: An Anglo-Saxon Rewriting of Orosius, ed.
   and trans. by Malcolm R. Godden, DOML, 44 (Cambridge, MA: Harvard
   University Press, 2016)
The Old English Metrical Calendar (Menologium), ed. by Kazutomo Karasawa,
   Anglo-Saxon Texts, 12 (Cambridge: D. S. Brewer, 2015)
The Old English Orosius, ed. by Janet Bately, EETS SS, 6 (London: Oxford
   University Press, 1980)
Orosius, *Pauli Orosii Historiarum adversum paganos libri VII*, ed. by Karl F. W.
   Zangemeister, Corpus Scriptorum Ecclesiasticorum Latinorum, 5 (Leipzig:
   Teubner, 1889)
——, *Seven Books of History against the Pagans*, trans. by A. T. Fear, Translated
   Texts for Historians (Liverpool: Liverpool University Press, 2010)

Secondary Sources

Anderson, Earl A., 'The Seasons of the Year in Old English', *ASE*, 26 (1997), 231–63
Anlezark, Daniel, 'The Northern World of the Anglo-Saxon *mappa mundi*', *ASE*, 47
   (2018), 275–305
——, 'Sceaf, Japheth and the Origin of the Anglo-Saxons', *ASE*, 31 (2002), 13–46
Ashe, Laura, 'The Anomalous King of Conquered England', in *Every Inch a King:
   Comparative Studies on Kings and Kingship in the Ancient and Medieval Worlds*,
   ed. by Lynette Mitchell and Charles Melville (Boston: Brill, 2013), pp. 173–93
Atherton, Mark, *The Making of England: A New History of the Anglo-Saxon World*
   (London: I. B. Tauris, 2017)
Bately, Janet, 'The Old English *Orosius*', in *A Companion to Alfred the Great*, ed. by
   Nicole Guenther Discenza and Paul E. Szarmach, Brill's Companions to the
   Christian Tradition, 58 (Leiden: Brill, 2014), pp. 313–43

Baxter, Stephen, 'Edward the Confessor and the Succession Question', in *Edward the Confessor: The Man and the Legend*, ed. by Richard Mortimer (Woodbridge: Boydell and Brewer, 2009), pp. 77–118

——, 'MS C of the Anglo-Saxon Chronicle and the Politics of Mid-Eleventh-Century England', *English Historical Review*, 122 (2007), 1189–1227

Bintley, Michael D. J., *Settlements and Strongholds in Early Medieval England: Texts, Landscapes, and Material Culture*, SEM, 45 (Turnhout: Brepols, 2020)

Bollard, J. K., 'The Cotton Maxims', *Neophilologus*, 57 (1973), 179–87

Bredehoft, Thomas A., *Textual Histories: Readings in the 'Anglo-Saxon Chronicle'* (Toronto: University of Toronto Press, 2001)

Brooks, Nicholas, 'Why Is the *Anglo-Saxon Chronicle* about Kings?', *ASE*, 39 (2011), 43–70

Clarke, Catherine A. M. *Writing Power in Anglo-Saxon England: Economies, Texts, Hierarchies*, Anglo-Saxon Studies, 17 (Cambridge: D. S. Brewer, 2012)

Clifton Brown, Matthew, 'Sacral Kingship and Resistance to Authority in the Middle English Life of Edward the Confessor', *Royal Studies Journal*, 6 (2019), 16–37

Fanning, Steven, 'Bede, *Imperium*, and the Bretwaldas', *Speculum*, 66 (1991), 1–26

Foot, Sarah, 'Finding the Meaning of Form: Narrative in Annals in Chronicles', in *Writing Medieval History*, ed. by Nancy F. Partner (London: Hodder Arnold, 2005), pp. 88–108

——, 'Where English Becomes British: Rethinking Contexts for Brunanburh', in *Myth, Rulership, Church and Charters: Essays in Honour of Nicholas Brooks*, ed. by Julia Barrow and Andrew Wareham (Aldershot: Ashgate, 2008), pp. 127–44

Fulk, Robert D., *A History of Old English Meter* (Philadelphia: University of Pennsylvania Press, 1992)

Garnett, George, *Conquered England: Kingship, Succession, and Tenure, 1066–1166* (Oxford: Oxford University Press, 2008)

Gneuss, Helmut, and Michael Lapidge, *Anglo-Saxon Manuscripts: A Bibliographical Handlist of Manuscripts and Manuscript Fragments Written or Owned in England up to 1100*, Toronto Anglo-Saxon Series, 15 (Toronto: University of Toronto Press, 2014)

Godden, Malcolm R., 'The Old English *Orosius* and its Context: Who Wrote It, for Whom, and Why?', *Quaestio Insularis*, 12 (2011), 1–30

——, 'The Old English *Orosius* and its Sources', *Anglia*, 129 (2011), 297–320

Goeres, Erin Michelle, 'Exile and Migration in the Vernacular Lives of Edward the Confessor', in *Remembering the Past: Generative Uses of England's Pre-Conquest Past, 10th to 15th Centuries*, ed. by Jay Paul Gates and Brian Thomas O'Camb, Explorations in Medieval Culture, 2 (Leiden: Brill, 2019), pp. 51–86

Harris, Stephen J., 'The Alfredian World History and Anglo-Saxon Identity', *JEGP*, 100 (2001), 482–510; repr. in his *Race and Ethnicity in Anglo-Saxon Literature* (New York: Taylor & Francis, 2003), pp. 83–106

Higham, N. J., *An English Empire: Bede and the Early Anglo-Saxon Kings* (Manchester: University of Manchester Press, 1995)

Howard, Ian, 'Harold II: A Throne-Worthy King', in *King Harold II and the Bayeux Tapestry*, ed. by Gale Owen-Crocker, Publications of the Manchester Centre for Anglo-Saxon Studies (Woodbridge: Boydell and Brewer, 2005), pp. 35–52

Howe, Nicholas, 'Rome: Capital of Anglo-Saxon England', *Journal of Medieval and Early Modern Studies*, 34 (2001), 147–72; repr. in his *Writing the Map of Anglo-Saxon England: Essays in Cultural Geography* (New Haven, CT: Yale University Press, 2008), pp. 101–24

Irvine, Susan, 'The Anglo-Saxon Chronicle and the Idea of Rome in Alfredian Literature', in *Alfred the Great: Papers from the Eleventh-Centenary Conferences*, ed. by Timothy Reuter (Aldershot: Ashgate, 2003), pp. 63–78

Karasawa, Kazutomo, 'The *Menologium* and *Maxims II* in the Manuscript Context', *N&Q*, 62 (2015), 353–56

Ker, Neil R., *Catalogue of Manuscripts Containing Anglo-Saxon* (Oxford: Clarendon Press, 1957)

Khalaf, Omar, '*Ælfred se casere*: Kingship and Imperial Legitimation in the Old English *Orosius*', in *The Age of Alfred: Translation, Adaptation, Innovation*, ed. by Amy Faulkner and Francis Leneghan, Studies in Old English Literature (Turnhout: Brepols, forthcoming)

——, 'A Study on the Translator's Omissions and Instances of Adaptation in *The Old English Orosius*: The Case of Alexander the Great', *Filologia Germanica*, 5 (2013), 195–221

Kretzschmar, William A., Jr., 'Adaptation and *anweald* in the Old English *Orosius*', *ASE*, 16 (1987), 127–45

Leneghan, Francis, *The Dynastic Drama of 'Beowulf'*, Anglo-Saxon Studies, 39 (Cambridge: D. S. Brewer, 2020)

——, '*Translatio imperii*: The Old English *Orosius* and the Rise of Wessex', *Anglia*, 133 (2015), 656–705

Licence, Tom, *Edward the Confessor: Last of the Royal Blood* (Yale: Yale University Press, 2020)

Matyushina, Inna, 'Skaldic Panegyric and the Anglo-Saxon Chronicle Poem on the Redemption of the Five Boroughs', *International Journal of Language and Linguistics*, 7 (2020), 13–23

Neidorf, Leonard, 'Caesar's Wine and the Dating of *Widsith*', *MÆ*, 88 (2019), 124–28

O'Brien O'Keeffe, Katherine, 'Deaths and Transformations: Thinking through the "End" of Old English Verse', in *New Directions in Oral Theory*, ed. by Mark C. Amodio, Medieval and Renaissance Texts and Studies, 287 (Tempe: Arizona Center for Medieval and Renaissance Studies, 2005), pp. 149–78

——, 'Reading the C-Text: The After-Lives of London, British Library, Cotton Tiberius B. i', in *Anglo-Saxon Manuscripts and their Heritage*, ed. by Philip Pulsiano and Elaine M. Treharne (London: Routledge, 1998), pp. 136–60

Pezzarossa, Lucrezia, 'Reading Orosius in the Viking Age: An Influential Yet Problematic Model', *Filologia Germanica*, 5 (2013), 223–40

Robinson, Fred C., 'Old English Literature in its Most Immediate Context', in *Old English Literature in Context*, ed. by John D. Niles (Cambridge: D. S. Brewer, 1980), pp. 11–29

Salvador Bello, Mercedes, 'The Edgar Panegyrics in the Anglo-Saxon Chronicle', in *Edgar, King of the English*, ed. by Donald G. Scragg (Woodbridge: Boydell and Brewer, 2008), pp. 252–72

Scragg, Donald G., 'A Reading of *Brunanburh*', in *Unlocking the Wordhord: Anglo-Saxon Studies in Memory of Edward B. Irving, Jr.*, ed. by Mark C. Amodio and Katherine O'Brien O'Keeffe (Toronto: University of Toronto Press, 2001), pp. 109–22

Smith, Scott Thompson, 'The Edgar Poems and the Poetics of Failure in the *Anglo-Saxon Chronicle*', *ASE*, 39 (2011), 105–37

Stafford, Pauline, *After Alfred: Anglo-Saxon Chronicles and Chroniclers, 900–1150* (Oxford: Oxford University Press, 2020)

Stanley, E. G., 'The *Gnomes* of Cotton Tiberius B.i', *N&Q*, 62 (2015), 190–99

Sykes, Katharine, 'The Sense of an Ending: Time and Temporality in the *Vita Ædwardi regis*', in *Medieval Temporalities: The Experience of Time in Medieval Europe*, ed. by Almut Suerbaum and Annie Sutherland (Cambridge: D. S. Brewer, 2021), pp. 17–32

Thomson, S. C., *Communal Creativity in the Making of the 'Beowulf' Manuscript: Towards a History of Reception for the Nowell Codex*, Library of the Written Word, 67, The Manuscript World, 10 (Leiden: Brill, 2018)

Thormann, Janet, 'The *Anglo-Saxon Chronicle* Poems and the Making of the English Nation', in *Anglo-Saxonism and the Construction of Social Identity*, ed. by Allen J. Frantzen and John D. Niles (Gainesville: University Press of Florida, 1997), pp. 60–85

Thornbury, Emily V., *Becoming a Poet in Anglo-Saxon England* (Cambridge: Cambridge University Press, 2014)

Tinti, Francesca, ed., *England and Rome in the Early Middle Ages: Pilgrimage, Art, and Politics*, SEM, 40 (Turnhout: Brepols, 2014)

Townsend, Julie, 'The Metre of the *Chronicle*-Poems', *Studia Neophilologica*, 68 (1996), 143–76

Trilling, Renée, *The Aesthetics of Nostalgia: Historical Representation in Old English Verse* (Toronto: University of Toronto Press, 2009)

Tyler, Elizabeth M., 'Cross-Channel Networks of History Writing: The *Anglo-Saxon Chronicle*', in *Medieval Historical Writing: Britain and Ireland, 500–1500*, ed. by Jennifer Jahner, Emily Steiner, and Elizabeth M. Tyler (Cambridge: Cambridge University Press, 2019), pp. 172–91

——, 'England between Empire and Nation in *The Battle of Brunanburh*', in *Whose Middle Ages? Teachable Moments for an Ill-Used Past*, ed. by Andrew Albin, Mary C. Erler, Thomas O'Donnell, Nicholas L. Paul, and Nina Rowe (New York: Fordham University Press, 2019), pp. 166–80

——, 'Writing Universal History in Eleventh-Century England: Cotton Tiberius B.i, German Imperial History-writing and Vernacular Lay Literacy', in *Universal Chronicles in the High Middle Ages*, ed. by Michele Campopiano and Henry Bainton (York: York Medieval Press, 2017), pp. 65–95

Weiskott, Eric, *English Alliterative Verse: Poetic Tradition and Literary History* (Cambridge: Cambridge University Press, 2016)

Whitbread, Leslie George, 'Two Notes on Minor Old English Poems', *Studia Neophilologica*, 20 (1947), 192–98

Wormald, Patrick, 'Bede, the *Bretwaldas* and the Origins of the *Gens Anglorum*', in *The Times of Bede, 625–865: Studies in Early English Christian Society and its Historian*, ed. by Stephen Baxter (Oxford: Blackwell, 2006), pp. 106–34

Index

Abbo of Fleury: 278, 288, 318
Acedia: 74, 78, 82–84, 90, 223, 228
Adomnán of Iona: 18, 329
Adventus Saxonum: 167, 337, 338,
    341, 343, 344, 357, 367, 396
Ælfflæd (wife of Byrhtnoth): 277,
    287, 288–91, 295–96, 300
Ælfric of Eynsham: 20, 21, 26, 83,
    114, 127–43, 149, 150, 154–56,
    158–61, 223, 228, 244, 290, 315,
    317, 358, 387, 389, 397
  Catholic Homilies: 21, 133–35, 149,
    150, 155, 160, 244
      De Passione Domini: 21, 149
  De falsis diis: 135, 143
  De temporibus anni: 128, 315, 317
  Letter to Sigeweard: 158, 159
  Lives of Saints: 26, 128–37, 139,
    140–43
      Life of St Thomas: 20, 114,
      127–35, 138–43
Æthelflæd of Damerham
    (Byrhtnoth's sister-in-law):
    288–91, 296, 298
Æthelred (II, the Unready), King:
    31, 273, 275, 278, 373, 374, 378,
    408, 419, 423, 424, 426
Æthelstan, King: 19, 30, 32, 87,
    191–94, 273, 323, 349, 351, 354,
    357, 378, 379, 386–99, 417, 418
Æthelweard: 47, 48, 130, 131, 139,
    389, 391, 424
  Chronicon: 47, 389, 424
Africa: 17, 19, 21, 25, 142, 154,
    157–59, 161, 225, 318, 320, 409
Alcuin: 158, 159, 169
Aldhelm: 17, 19, 55, 159, 204, 205,
    209, 212–14, 216, 217, 228
  Carmen rhythmicum: 204, 205,
    212, 216, 217

De virginitate: 55, 213, 214, 228
Enigmata: 17
Alexander's Letter to Aristotle: 20,
    43, 44, 104, 129, 132, 218
  see also Epistola Alexandri ad
    Aristotelem
Alexandria: 45, 59, 60, 72, 323, 324
Alfred the Great, King: 19, 27,
    29–31, 43–50, 53, 59, 60, 61–63,
    106, 136, 185, 223, 298, 336, 340,
    345, 347, 349, 351, 356, 357,
    368, 370, 371, 374, 377, 389, 391,
    404, 426
  see also under Asser,
    Life of King Alfred
Andreas: 19, 43, 56, 176, 206, 210,
    212, 215, 340, 425
Angelcynn: 13–16, 18, 26, 29–31, 48,
    367, 405
Angli: 12, 28, 29, 336, 368, 369
Apatheia: 25, 228, 229, 233–36,
    242–45
Anglo-Saxon Chronicle: 12, 15, 18,
    27, 29, 30, 44, 48, 49, 53, 58,
    60, 61, 127, 168, 187, 190, 191,
    193, 194, 298, 336, 337, 340,
    342, 343, 344, 347–53, 356, 358,
    367, 369, 370, 372, 373, 374,
    376–78, 385–87, 389, 395, 397,
    398, 399, 403–06, 410, 413,
    414, 416–20, 422–26, 428
  MS A: 28, 30, 48, 298, 336,
    340–42, 348–50, 352–55, 357,
    367–70, 386, 387, 389, 417
  MS B: 30, 48, 53, 336, 340, 348,
    353, 354, 386, 387, 417
  MS C: 30, 48, 49, 53, 336, 340,
    348, 349, 353, 354, 367, 373, 374,
    377, 378, 386, 387, 404–06, 410,
    412–17, 419–25, 427

436 INDEX

MS D: 44, 48, 49, 336, 340, 348–54, 358, 367, 373, 374, 376–78, 386, 394, 404, 416, 417, 422, 430

MS E: 12–14, 48, 49, 336, 340–42, 348, 350, 351, 353, 354, 357, 358, 367, 373–78, 386, 389, 390, 417, 422, 430

MS F: 48, 342, 352, 386, 390, 414

Poems

Battle of Brunanburh, The: 123, 191–94, 196, 344, 349, 354, 355, 357, 379, 385–99, 417–19, 422, 425

Capture of the Five Boroughs, The: 29, 123, 386, 395, 417, 418, 422, 426

Coronation of Edgar, The: 395, 417, 420

Death of Alfred, The: 403, 417, 419, 420, 422

Death of Edgar, The: 395, 417, 418, 419, 420, 422, 426

Death of Edward, The: 15, 193, 387, 389, 395, 403–06, 409, 412, 413, 417, 419–29

Asia: 18, 19, 21, 43, 44, 46, 48, 50, 52, 55, 57–59, 63, 71, 104, 154, 157–59, 161, 226, 313, 318, 320, 322, 323, 325

Asser: 30, 45–49, 61, 136, 336, 347, 348, 356, 368, 372, 374

Life of King Alfred: 30, 45, 136, 336, 347, 348, 368, 372, 374

Athelstan

pilgrimage of: 19, 44, 48, 49, 50, 58, 59, 60, 63, 64

see also Sigehelm

Augustine of Hippo: 31, 80, 95, 108, 130, 131, 132, 157, 160, 240

De civitate Dei: 108, 157

Babel, Tower of: 22, 73, 171, 172, 174, 175, 177, 179, 184, 185, 188, 324

Babylon: 31, 32, 51, 52, 53, 59, 135, 320, 323–26, 329, 406, 407

Bald's Leechbook: 17, 46

Battle of Brunanburh, The

see under Anglo-Saxon Chronicle, Poems

Battle of Maldon, The: 23, 176, 210, 237, 273, 276, 277, 278, 283, 285, 286, 288, 291, 294, 296, 297, 298, 299, 354, 425

Bartholomew, St: 19, 44, 48–50, 53, 55, 56–58, 63

Bede: 11–13, 17–19, 21, 26–29, 56, 137, 150–52, 154, 157, 159, 168–70, 190, 206, 207, 209, 212–16, 218, 224, 225, 254, 278, 287, 335–38, 341–43, 347, 350–53, 355–57, 368, 369, 385, 388, 414, 416, 417

Commentarius in Lucam: 150

De natura rerum: 152, 157, 207, 215, 216

De temporum ratione: 21

Ecclesiastical History: 11, 17, 18, 26–29, 159, 168–70, 212, 214, 224, 225, 336–38, 341, 342, 350–53, 414, 416, 417

Historia ecclesiastica: see under Ecclesiastical History

In Genesim: 207, 213, 214

Beowulf: 19, 20, 28, 29, 76, 78, 80, 104, 106, 111, 112, 169, 170, 176, 193, 194, 208, 210, 211, 215, 294, 340, 353, 355, 368, 369, 424, 425

Benedict, St: 31, 88–91, 240, 245, 311, 328,

Rule of: 31, 141, 231, 240, 245

Blair, John: 24, 135, 136, 249, 250, 255, 257–59, 265, 267–69, 285, 286, 295, 297

Boethius: 88

De consolatione philosophiae: 88

see also under Old English Boethius

Boethius, Old English: 207, 420, 428

see also under Boethius, *De consolatione philosophiae*

Britons: 13, 26, 27, 28, 30, 335–58, 409, 414, 423, 424
English perceptions of: 339
see also under Welsh

Bury St Edmunds: 282, 287, 288, 290, 297

Byrhtferth of Ramsey: 153, 154, 275, 278, 279, 289, 297, 313, 322, 378
Enchiridion: 153–55
Vita S. Oswaldi: 275, 278, 279, 297, 378

Byrhtnoth: 23, 24, 257, 273–78, 281–84, 286–92, 294–301
see also *Battle of Maldon, The*
see also Ælfflæd (wife of Byrhtnoth)
see also Æthelflæd of Damerham (Byrhtnoth's sister-in-law)

Cambridge: 70, 275, 276, 281, 282, 285–87, 289, 296, 301, 313, 323, 346

Carthage: 31, 323, 324, 406, 407

Cassian, John: 83, 89, 91, 225, 227, 228, 232, 245

Cassiodorus: 84, 85, 312

Chester: 342, 357, 391

Christ II (Ascension)
see under Cynewulf

Cnut the Great, King: 206, 288, 314, 365, 373–79, 404, 419, 423, 424, 427

Computus: 313, 315, 318, 319

Constable, John: 274, 294, 295

Coronation of Edgar, The
see under Anglo-Saxon Chronicle, Poems

Cornwall: 344

Cynewulf: 25, 223, 225–27, 229, 230, 232–45, 340
Christ II (Ascension): 225
Elene: 19, 43, 176, 209, 215, 225, 233
Fates of the Apostles, The: 43, 56, 225, 226

Juliana: 19, 25, 176, 223, 225, 226, 229, 230, 232, 233, 236, 237, 240–45

Cynocephali: 106–08, 129

Dalché, Gautier: 309, 311, 312, 317–19, 322, 327–29

Danes: 29, 32, 49, 58, 61, 348, 366–71, 373–75, 377–79, 409, 416, 418, 419, 424, 426
see also under Vikings, Northmen

Death of Alfred, The
see under Anglo-Saxon Chronicle, Poems

Death of Edgar, The
see under Anglo-Saxon Chronicle, Poems

Death of Edward, The
see under Anglo-Saxon Chronicle, Poems

Dialogues, Old English: 311
see also under Gregory the Great, *Dialogi*

Dicuil: 60
Liber de mensura orbis terrae: 60

Dream of the Rood, The: 229, 230

East Anglia, Kingdom of: 15, 27, 273–75, 278, 282, 284, 287, 288, 294, 298, 301, 338–40, 369–71, 373

Edmund, King: 191, 193, 288, 291, 296, 376, 386–93, 395–97, 417, 418, 422, 426

Edward the Elder, King: 30, 49, 62, 193, 349, 350, 353–55, 387, 388, 390, 391, 396, 418, 426, 427

Edgar, King: 31, 275, 289, 291, 296, 351, 357, 374, 386, 395, 417–20, 422, 426, 427, 430

Epistola Alexandri ad Aristotelem: 19
see also under *Letter of Alexander to Aristotle, The*

Elene
see under Cynewulf

INDEX

Ely: 275, 276, 282–84, 287, 289, 290, 297
Ely, The Book of
see under *Liber Eliensis*
England, Kingdom of: 336, 424
Essex, County of: 12, 273–305
Kingdom of: 24, 27
Ealdordom of: 23–24, 273–305
Europe: 11, 19, 21, 26, 47, 71, 73, 104–06, 154, 157–59, 161, 185, 227, 310, 311, 318, 320, 322, 323, 372
Evagrius Ponticus: 25, 83, 88, 91, 223–45
Exeter Book Riddles
see under Riddles, Exeter Book
Exodus: 19, 169, 170, 191

Fates of the Apostles, The
see under Cynewulf
Felix of Crowland
see under Guthlac
Foot, Sarah: 29, 30, 32, 193, 273, 336, 349, 387, 396, 417, 418
Frisia: 370, 371, 372

Gelling, Margaret: 24, 78, 263, 276, 278, 285, 297
Genesis A: 19, 22, 167, 170–73, 175–79, 183–90, 206, 212, 425
Genesis B: 212
Gildas: 167–69, 190, 336, 337, 338
De excidio Britanniae: 167, 168
Gregory of Tours: 55, 57, 155
Libri Miraculorum: 55, 57, 155
Gregory the Great: 83, 88, 89, 223, 311, 328, 329, 368
Dialogi (Dialogues): 88, 311, 329
see also under *Dialogues*, Old English
Moralia in Iob (Morals on Job): 83, 88, 89
Regula Pastoralis/ Cura Pastoralis (Pastoral Care): 223
see also under *Pastoral Care*, Old English

Guthlac, St: 338, 339, 356
Felix of Crowland's *Life of St Guthlac*: 49, 338–40, 356
Guthlac A: 83
Guthlac B: 215, 387

Harold Godwinson: 350, 405, 419, 423, 425–27, 429, 430
Hesychasm: 91, 229, 236, 237, 240, 241, 243, 245
Hoskins, W. G.: 23, 274
Howe, Nicholas: 18–22, 104, 127, 169, 172, 185, 186, 190, 191, 194–96, 315, 416

India: 16, 17, 19–21, 44, 45, 48–58, 60, 63, 64, 70–73, 127, 129, 130, 132–34, 138–40, 142, 143, 226
Instructions for Christians: 91
Isidore of Seville: 108, 136, 151, 157, 207, 215, 279, 312, 322
De natura rerum: 151, 157, 207, 312, 319
Etymologiae: 108, 136, 151, 157
Italy: 32, 46, 58–61, 63, 128, 224, 409
see also under Rome

Jerome, St: 31, 72, 73, 84, 94, 227, 228, 279
Epistula: 72, 94
Jelling Runestone: 375
Jerusalem: 18, 19, 22, 43, 44–47, 50, 53, 59, 60, 69, 70, 71, 73, 85, 86, 90, 92, 93, 123, 152, 160, 195, 226, 228, 313, 314, 318, 322–24, 327
Judith: 19, 104, 110, 123, 210
Juliana
see under Cynewulf
Julius Caesar: 13, 414, 415, 416, 423
Jutes: 26, 337, 368, 369, 379
association with Geats and Goths: 368, 369, 379

Kenelm, St: 250–53
Kent
County of: 27, 300, 368
Kingdom of: 27, 49, 347
Origin myth of royal house
of: 168 n. 4, 195
English settlement of: 27, 265 n. 64
Kings Sutton: 254–59, 261–69

Letter of Alexander to Aristotle, The
see under *Alexander's Letter to Aristotle*
Liber Eliensis (The Book of Ely):
275, 276, 282–84, 286–88
Liber monstrorum: 19, 20, 132
London: 14, 15, 44, 48, 49, 50, 53,
58, 60–62, 76, 77, 250, 263,
297, 323

Manuscripts
BL, MS Cotton Tiberius B I: 377,
403–06, 408–15, 421–25, 429
BL, MS Cotton Tiberius B V:
20, 21, 106–08, 112, 115, 140, 152,
310, 311, 312, 314–23, 325–29
BL, MS Cotton Vitellius A XV
(The Nowell Codex): 20, 104,
107
Oxford, Bodleian Library, MS
Ashmole 328: 153
Maps
Anglo-Saxon *mappa mundi*: 21,
73, 128, 140, 152, 316, 318–27, 329
Macrobian zonal map: 21, 315,
316, 324
Ripoll map: 318, 319
T-O maps: 21, 151, 152, 157,
312–14, 322, 327
Marinus, Pope: 48, 49, 60–63
Martyrology, The Old English: 43,
44, 53–56, 58, 105, 122
Maxims I (*Exeter Maxims*): 87
Maxims II: 404–06, 409, 412–15,
419, 422, 424–26
Menologium, The: 404–06, 409,
411, 412, 418–20, 422, 423, 425,
426, 428

Mercia, Kingdom of: 27–30, 49,
250, 252–54, 256, 259, 264,
286, 337–40, 347–49
Mirabilia Orientis: 19, 20
see also under *Wonders of the East, The*

Noah's Ark: 22, 179–83, 185–88,
212, 322
Northmen: 366–68, 371, 377, 393,
395, 397, 418
see also Vikings, Danes
Northumbria, Kingdom of: 18, 27,
28, 30, 253, 256, 268, 282, 298,
337, 338, 342, 347, 349, 351, 352,
354, 358, 369, 373, 394, 427

Ocean: 11, 21, 51, 56, 113, 157, 206,
207, 211–13, 312, 317, 318
Offa of Mercia, King: 17, 18, 29, 347
Oikoumene: 21, 157, 310, 318, 319, 328
Olaf Tryggvason: 49
Order of the World, The: 309, 329
Orosius: 31, 157, 158, 322, 324, 325,
329, 368, 406
Historiae adversus paganos: 19,
31, 43, 50, 110, 112, 157, 320, 324,
325, 329, 404, 406, 407, 414
Orosius, Old English: 32, 43, 44,
50–53, 62, 110, 141, 157, 158, 365,
368, 369, 377, 404–10, 412–14,
416, 423, 425
Voyages of Ohthere and
Wulfstan: 32, 62, 368,
371, 377

Passion of St Christopher, The: 20,
45, 103–05, 108, 110, 117–19,
122, 123
Pastoral Care, Old English: 223
Prose Preface: 223
see also under Gregory the
Great, *Regula pastoralis*
Pater Noster: 79, 85, 93, 94
Paulinus of Nola: 150, 151
Penda, King: 253–55, 268, 337, 347

Picts: 11, 13, 28, 335–37, 340, 341, 345, 351–53, 355, 356, 358
  English perceptions of: 335–37, 340, 341, 345, 351–53, 355, 356, 358
Priscian: 315, 320,
  Periegesis: 315, 319, 320, 322, 326

Rackham, Oliver: 23, 24
Riddles, Exeter Book: 24, 204, 207, 346, 351, 356–58
  Riddle 1: 24, 204, 205, 207, 209, 210, 212–19
  Riddle 12: 346
  Riddle 20: 210
  Riddle 35: 210
  Riddle 43: 209
  Riddle 52: 346
  Riddle 72: 346,
Rome: 13, 17, 18, 20, 22, 30–32, 47–49, 58, 59, 61–63, 123, 127, 128, 130, 133, 134, 135, 137, 138, 140–43, 224–26, 251, 310, 315, 318, 320, 323–26, 329, 339, 341, 345, 349, 375, 406–10, 413, 416, 417, 424, 425, 429
Rumwold, St: 23, 249, 250, 252–58, 263, 264, 266–68

Scots: 13, 335–37, 349, 351–58, 392, 393, 395, 396, 417, 423
  English perceptions of: 335–37, 349, 351–58
Seafarer, The: 78, 210, 211, 416
Sedulius, Caelius: 21, 150, 151, 154–56, 160
  Carmen paschale: 150, 155
Sigehelm
  pilgrimage of: 19, 44, 48–50, 58–60, 63, 64
  see also Athelstan
Solomon and Saturn I: 70, 73, 74, 78–81, 83–89, 93, 94
Solomon and Saturn II: 19, 43, 44, 50, 52, 69, 70–75, 78, 80–83, 85–88, 92–94, 223, 274

Soul and Body I: 79
Soul and Body II: 79
Swein Forkbeard: 49, 290, 375, 420

Thomas, St: 19, 44, 48, 50, 53–55, 58, 59, 60, 63, 64, 131, 136
Thorkell, Earl: 373, 374, 376
Tower of Babel
  see under Babel, Tower of
Translatio imperii: 32, 127, 322, 325, 329, 404, 413, 414

Vercelli Book: 79, 340
Vikings: 29, 50, 169, 282, 288, 298, 343, 348, 357, 366, 369, 371, 372, 374, 394, 416
  see also Danes, Northmen
Vita sancti Rumwoldi: 249

Wanderer, The: 75, 78, 91, 94, 245
Welsh: 26–28, 45, 191, 192, 266, 335, 336, 339, 341, 344, 345–51, 353–58, 395, 414, 417, 418, 419, 423
  English perceptions of: 335, 336, 339, 341, 344, 345–51, 353–58
Wessex, Kingdom of: 27, 29, 30, 32, 47, 168, 175, 250, 254, 264, 296, 322, 340, 343, 345, 347–49, 351, 354, 365–67, 372, 377, 393, 395, 406, 408, 409, 412, 414, 416, 417, 418, 424, 427, 429
Wight, Isle of: 168, 368, 377, 378
William of Malmesbury: 63, 350, 351, 375, 376, 390, 391, 393,
  Gesta Pontificum Anglorum: 63
Willibald: 18, 59, 371
  Hodoeporicon: 18, 59
  Vita Bonifatii: 371
Wonders of the East, The: 20, 43, 44, 50, 52, 63, 104–08, 112–18, 121, 122, 129, 132, 140, 142, 315, 322, 326
  see also *Mirabilia Orientis*
Wulfstan of York, Archbishop: 169

Studies in Old English Literature

All volumes in this series are evaluated by an Editorial Board, strictly on academic grounds, based on reports prepared by referees who have been commissioned by virtue of their specialism in the appropriate field. The Board ensures that the screening is done independently and without conflicts of interest. The definitive texts supplied by authors are also subject to review by the Board before being approved for publication. Further, the volumes are copyedited to conform to the publisher's stylebook and to the best international academic standards in the field.

In Preparation

Sources of Knowledge: Studies in Old English and Latin Literature in Honour of Charles D. Wright, ed. by Stephanie Clark, Janet Schrunk Ericksen, and Shannon Godlove